KU-450-745

Residential Possession Proceedings

4th Edition

Gary Webber
Barrister

DISPOSED OF BY LIBRARY HOUSE OF LORDS

LAW & TAX

© Longman Group Ltd 1994

© Pearson Professional Limited 1995

ISBN 0 85121 0465

First edition 1984
Second edition 1987
Third edition 1990
Reprinted 1991
Reprinted 1992
Fourth edition 1994
Reprinted 1995

Published by
F.T Law & Tax
21–27 Lamb's Conduit Street
London WC1N 3NJ

Associated offices:
Australia, Hong Kong, Malaysia, Singapore, USA

All rights reserved. No part of this publication may be reproduced, stored in a retrieval system, or transmitted in any form or by any means, electronic, mechanical, photocopying, recording or otherwise, without the prior written permission of the publishers, or a licence permitting restricted copying issued by the Copyright Licensing Agency Ltd, 90 Tottenham Court Road, London W1P 9HE

No responsibility for loss occasioned to any person acting or refraining from action as a result of the material in this publication can be accepted by the author or publishers.

A CIP catalogue record for this book is available
from the British Library

Printed by Bell & Bain of Glasgow

Contents

Part 2: Termination and the Right to Possession—Particular Cases

List of Forms

Preface

This edition contains some changes to the structure, including a new chapter devoted entirely to forfeiture and a reorganised and expanded chapter on mortgage possession. Throughout the book a number of statutory extracts and case citations have been added close to the relevant parts of the text.

Important changes in procedure dealt with include the new rules and prescribed forms in rent and mortgage possession cases and the accelerated possession procedure available since 1 November 1993 in relation to assured and assured shorthold tenancies. New cases include the House of Lords decisions in *Billson v Residential Apartments Ltd* (peaceable reentry and relief from forfeiture), *Hammersmith and Fulham London BC v Monk* (determination of periodic tenancy by joint tenants), *Westminster CC v Clarke* (homeless persons and licences), *Waltham Forest LBC v Thomas* (succession to secure tenancy on death), *Hughes v Greenwich LBC* (requirement of employee to occupy for better performance of duties) and *Barclays Bank plc v O'Brien* (spouses rights to set aside mortgages for undue influence and misrepresentation).

I would like to thank readers who have written to me suggesting improvements. In particular, I have reconsidered some points in the assured tenancy chapters as a result of comments received. I would also like to thank my pupil, Tim Pullen, and the members of the Property Practice Group in Chambers for their help and suggestions.

The law is stated as at the end of April 1994.

Gary Webber   33 Bedford Row
June 1994   London, WC1

Table of Cases

Table of Statutes

(References in bold type refer to a section or subsection that is reprinted in the text)

Table of Statutory Instruments

Part 1

Termination and the Right to Possession

Chapter 1

Has a Tenancy Been Created?

This chapter is concerned with preliminary matters that sometimes arise in possession proceedings relating to the existence or otherwise of a tenancy. The distinction between a tenancy and a licence is dealt with in Chapter 5. The basic rules as to termination of tenancies and recovery of possession are dealt with in Chapters 2 and 3.

The requirement of certainty

A fundamental requirement of all leases and tenancy agreements is that the commencement date and the duration of the term must be certain. The parties must be able to ascertain the maximum duration of the term at the outset of the tenancy. If it is not possible to do so the lease is void. However, if the tenant takes possession and pays rent on a periodic basis in accordance with the terms of the agreement a periodic tenancy is created, on the terms of the agreement so far as they are consistent with a periodic tenancy. Such a tenancy is certain because each party has the power to determine it by service of an appropriate notice to quit *(Prudential Assurance Co Ltd v London Residuary Body* [1992] 3 All ER 504, HL).

Fixed terms: when is a deed required?

Where the tenancy is for a fixed term of more than three years it must be created by deed. If it is not created by deed it will be void (unless a periodic tenancy can be implied or it operates as an equitable lease, see *below* (p7)). A fixed term of three years or less may be granted either orally or in writing if it takes effect in possession (ie if it takes effect from the time it is created) at the best rent which can be reasonably obtained without taking a fine (see ss52 and 54(2) of the Law of Property Act 1925). A lease is regarded as being for a term of more than three years even if it contains a term permitting termination within that period (*Kushner v Law Society* [1952] 1 All ER 404).

Formalities for creation of leases: Law of Property Act 1925
      52.—(1) All conveyances of land or of any interest therein are void for the purpose of conveying or creating a legal estate unless made by deed.
      (2) This section does not apply to . . .

(*d*) leases or tenancies . . . not required by law to be made in writing
. . .

(*g*) conveyances taking effect by operation of law.

53.—(1) Subject to the provisions hereinafter contained with respect to the creation of interests in land by parol—

(*a*) no interest in land can be created or disposed of except by writing signed by the person creating or conveying the same, or by his agent thereunto lawfully authorised in writing, or by will, or by operation of law; . . .

54.—(1) All interests in land created by parol and not put in writing and signed by the persons so creating the same, or by their agents thereunto lawfully authorised in writing, have, notwithstanding any consideration having been given for the same, the force and effect of interest at will only.

(2) Nothing in the foregoing provisions of this Part of this Act shall affect the creation by parol of leases taking effect in possession for a term not exceeding three years (whether or not the lessee is given power to extend the term) at the best rent which can be reasonably obtained without taking a fine.

55. Nothing in the last two foregoing sections shall . . . affect the right to acquire an interest in land by virtue of taking possession;

Executing the deed   Since 31 July 1990 it has no longer been necessary for an individual to seal a deed. The deed is validly executed if it is duly signed and delivered. The procedure is governed by s 1 of the Law of Property (Miscellaneous Provisions) Act 1989. Where a party is a company, regard should be had to s36A of the Companies Act 1985.

Deeds and their execution: Law of Property (Miscellaneous Provisions) Act 1989, s1

1.—(1) Any rule of law which—

(*a*) restricts the substances on which a deed may be written;

(*b*) requires a seal for the valid execution of an instrument as a deed by an individual; or

(*c*) requires authority by one person to another to deliver an instrument as a deed on his behalf to be given by deed, is abolished.

(2) An instrument shall not be a deed unless—

(*a*) it makes it clear on its face that it is intended to be a deed by the person making it or, as the case may be, by the parties to it (whether by describing itself as a deed or expressing itself to be executed or signed as a deed or otherwise); and

(*b*) it is validly executed as a deed by that person or, as the case may be, one or more of those parties.

(3) An instrument is validly executed as a deed by an individual if, and only if—

(*a*) it is signed—

(i) by him in the presence of a witness who attests the signature; or

(ii) at his direction and in his presence and the presence of two witnesses who each attest the signature; and (*b*) it is delivered as a deed by him or a person authorised to do so on his behalf.

(4) In subsections (2) and (3) above 'sign', in relation to an instrument, includes making one's mark on the instrument and 'signature' is to be construed accordingly.

(5) Where a solicitor or licensed conveyancer, or an agent or employee of a solicitor or licensed conveyancer, in the course of or in connection with a transaction involving the disposition or creation of an interest in land, purports to deliver an instrument as a deed on behalf of a party to the instrument, it shall be conclusively presumed in favour of a purchaser that he is authorised so to deliver the instrument.

(6) In subsection (5) above—
'disposition' and 'purchaser' have the same meanings as in the Law of Property Act 1925; and
'interest in land' means any estate, interest or charge in or over land or in or over the proceeds of sale of land.

(10) The references in this section to the execution of a deed by an individual do not include execution by a corporation sole . . .

(11) Nothing in this section applies in relation to instruments delivered as deeds before this section comes into force.

Execution of documents by companies: Companies Act 1985, s36A

(1) Under the law of England and Wales the following provisions have effect with respect to the execution of documents by a company.

(2) A document is executed by a company by the affixing of its common seal.

(3) A company need not have a common seal, however, and the following subsections apply whether it does or not.

(4) A document signed by a director and the secretary of a company, or by two directors of a company, and expressed (in whatever form of words) to be executed by the company has the same effect as if executed under the common seal of the company.

(5) A document executed by a company which makes it clear on its face that it is intended by the person or persons making it to be a deed has effect, upon delivery, as a deed; and it shall be presumed, unless a contrary intention is proved, to be delivered upon its being so executed.

(6) In favour of a purchaser a document shall be deemed to have been duly executed by a company if it purports to be signed by a director and the secretary of the company, or by two directors of the company, and, where it makes it clear on its face that it is intended by the person or persons making it to be a deed, to have been delivered upon its being executed.

A 'purchaser' means a purchaser in good faith for valuable consideration and includes a lessee, mortgagee or other person who for valuable consideration acquires an interest in property.

Delivery of deeds In *Longman v Viscount Chelsea* [1989] 2 EGLR 242 Nourse LJ at 245E explained that there are three ways in which a deed may be 'delivered':

First, it may be delivered as an unconditional deed, being irrevocable and taking immediate effect. Second, it may be delivered as an escrow, being irrevocable but not taking effect unless and until the condition or conditions of the escrow are fulfilled. Third, it may be handed to an agent of the maker with instructions to deal with it in a certain way in a certain event, being revocable and of no effect unless and until it is so dealt with, whereupon it is delivered and takes effect.

Registration of leases

Certain leases are required to be registered at the Land Registry. The position in respect of grants since 1 January 1987 has been as follows: where the land is in a compulsory registration area and the lease is for a term of more than 21 years from the date of delivery of the grant it must be registered within two months (or any authorised extension) of that date (s123(1) of the Land Registration Act 1925; s2(1) of the Land Registration Act 1986). Registration became compulsory in all areas of England and Wales on 1 December 1990 (SI 1989 No 1347).

Where the lease was granted on or before 1 January 1987 the lease had to be registered (*a*) if the land was in a compulsory registration area and the lease was granted for a term of 40 years or more from the date of the delivery of the grant, or (*b*) the freehold or leasehold out of which the lease was granted was registered and the term granted was for more than 21 years (see ss8, 22, 123 of the Land Registration Act 1925, prior to amendment by the 1986 Act).

If a lease which is required to be registered is not registered within the two-month period (or within any extended period that is authorised) it is ineffective to transfer a legal estate to the tenant (s123 of the Land Registration Act 1925). However, in situations where the tenant is in occupation under the void lease the parties will generally be regarded in equity as being landlord and tenant and the landlord will be unable to recover possession.

Periodic terms and tenancies at will

Periodic tenancies are tenancies that are granted on a yearly, monthly, weekly or indeed any other periodic basis. They are not tenancies just for the period specified, but are tenancies which continue from period to period indefinitely until determined by notice to quit (*Leek and Moorlands Building Society v Clark* [1952] 2 QB 788 at 793). A periodic tenancy may be created by oral agreement (*Hammond v Farrow* [1904] 2 KB 332, 335).

A 'tenancy at will exists where the tenancy is on terms that either party may determine it at any time' as opposed to a periodic tenancy which is one that 'continues from period to period indefinitely until determined by proper notice' (*Javad v Aqil* [1991] 1 All ER 243, CA, per Nicholls LJ at 244). A tenancy at will may, therefore, be determined by simply asking the tenant to leave, or by the service of proceedings for possession (*Martinali v Ramuz* [1953] 2 All ER 892). No special form of notice is required. See further p71 (Chapter 3) and p244 (Chapter 18) for an example of a tenancy at will.

Estoppel between landlord and tenant

Where a person has been granted a tenancy both he and the landlord are estopped from denying its existence. The landlord cannot derogate from the tenant's grant and the tenant cannot dispute the landlord's title, even though the landlord has no interest in the land. Thus, if the landlord sues the tenant for possession the tenant cannot defend himself by saying 'the property does not belong to you but to another' (*Industrial Properties (Barton Hill) Ltd v Associated Electrical Industries Ltd* [1977] QB 580 at 596; *Stratford v Syrett* [1958] 1 QB 107). The principle applies whether the tenancy was created by deed, other writing or orally and whatever the length or period of the term (see generally 16 Halsbury (4th edn, reissue para 1074). The estoppel applies to successors in title (*Mackley v Nutting* [1949] 2 KB 55; but see 16 Halsbury (4th edn, reissue) para 1078 in relation to the landlord's assignee).

As to whether the tenant can rely upon proof of termination of the landlord's title as a defence to a claim for possession brought by the landlord see 16 Halsbury (4th edn, reissue) para 1076.

An estoppel between a landlord and a tenant does not prevent the true owner of the property with a better claim to possession from denying the tenancy. Where a tenant has been removed by such a person the tenant will only be able to sue his landlord for breach of the covenant for quiet enjoyment if the covenant is an unqualified one (27(1) Halsbury (4th edn) paras 406, 410).

Possession pursuant to agreement for lease or void lease

Introduction

Where a finally concluded agreement for a lease has been entered into (see p8 *below*) but no lease has actually been granted, or where a lease is void because it was granted for a term of more than three years and was not made by deed (see *above*, p3), the parties will nevertheless be regarded as landlord and tenant if the latter has actually entered into possession. However, the precise status of the occupant is different depending upon whether the common law applies or the rules of equity apply.

Difference between common law and equity

If the agreement provides for rent to be calculated on a yearly basis the tenant is regarded by the common law as being a tenant from year-to-year upon the terms of the intended lease but only so far as they are consistent with a yearly tenancy (*D'Silva v Lister House Development Ltd* [1970] 1 All ER 858). Thus, whatever the terms of the proposed lease the tenancy is determinable by six months' notice to quit, although note that at the end of the intended term the tenancy comes to an end without the necessity of a notice. If the rent is calculated on a monthly or weekly basis the tenant has only a monthly or weekly tenancy (*Adler v Blackman* [1953] 1 QB 146).

The rules of equity take the matter further. If the agreement is such that it is capable of being specifically enforced the tenant will be treated in equity as holding the property under the same terms as if the lease had been granted (*Walsh v Lonsdale* (1882) 21 ChD 9). A void lease (ie a lease in respect of which the formal requirements have not been complied with (see p3) is treated for this purpose as being an agreement for a lease on the terms contained therein (*Parker v Taswell* (1858) 2 De G&J 559).

Where the *Walsh v Lonsdale* doctrine applies the tenant may rely upon it as a defence to a claim for possession whether the landlord commences proceedings in the county court or the High Court (*Kingswood Estate Co Ltd v Anderson* [1963] 2 QB 169). However, an action for specific performance of the agreement may only be commenced in the county court if the value of the property (ie of the freehold interest) does not exceed the county court limit, presently £30,000 (s23(*d*) of the County Courts Act 1984; *Foster v Reeves* [1892] 2 QB 255; *Angel v Jay* [1911] 1 KB 666); *Amec Properties Ltd v Planning Research & Systems* [1992] 2 EGLR 70.

The difference between the position at common law and in equity is unlikely to be of importance where the tenant has some statutory protection but may be crucial where he has no such protection. If, for example, the landlord serves a six-month notice to quit so as to terminate the tenancy at the end of the first year he will not be entitled to possession at its expiry if the tenant can show that he has an equitable lease of more than one year.

Finally concluded agreement

It cannot be stressed too highly that there must be a finally concluded agreement. The court will not order specific performance if there are any terms still being negotiated. For a recent case in which there was no finally concluded agreement see *Brent London Borough Council v O'Bryan* [1993] 1 EGLR 59, CA—agreement to let a scout hut on a monthly basis on terms to be laid down by valuers.

However, for the *Walsh v Lonsdale* doctrine to apply it is not necessary that all the terms should have been agreed. What is required is agreement as to the 'essential terms', that is, agreement as to the parties to the lease, the property to be let, the commencement and duration of the term and the rent or other consideration to be paid. If those terms have been agreed and no other terms have been offered but left unaccepted the court will, subject to any equitable reasons for not doing so, make an order for specific performance of a lease, such lease to contain 'usual covenants' (see generally 27(1) Halsbury (4th edn, reissue), paras 59–62; and see further note (4) *below*, p10).

Agreement to be in writing

By virtue of s2 of the Law of Property (Miscellaneous Provisions) Act 1989 a contract for the grant of a lease of more than three years (s2(5)(*a*)), entered into on or after 27 September 1989 (the date upon which the Act came into force), can only be made in writing and all the terms *which the parties have expressly agreed* must be contained in one document which must be signed by or on behalf of each party to the contract. Where contracts are exchanged, all the express terms must be contained in each contract and one of the documents, but not necessarily the same one, must be signed by or on behalf of each party.

Law of Property (Miscellaneous Provisions) Act 1989, s2

    2.—(1) A contract for the sale or other disposition of an interest in land can only be made in writing and only by incorporating all the terms which the parties have expressly agreed in one document or, where contracts are exchanged, in each.

    (2) The terms may be incorporated in a document either by being set out in it or by reference to some other document.

    (3) The document incorporating the terms or, where contracts are exchanged, one of the documents incorporating them (but not necessarily the same one) must be signed by or on behalf of each party to the contract.

    (4) Where a contract for the sale or other disposition of an interest in land satisfies the conditions of this section by reason only of the rectification of one or more documents in pursuance of an order of a court, the contract shall come into being, or be deemed to have come into being, at such time as may be specified in the order.

    (5) This section does not apply in relation to—

        (*a*) a contract to grant such a lease as is mentioned in section 54(2) of the Law of Property Act 1925 (short leases);

        (*b*) a contract made in the course of a public auction; or

        (*c*) a contract regulated under the Financial Services Act 1986;

and nothing in this section affects the creation or operation of resulting, implied or constructive trusts.

    (6) In this section—

'disposition' has the same meaning as in the Law of Property Act 1925;

'interest in land' means any estate, interest or charge in or over land or in or over the proceeds of sale of land.

    (7) Nothing in this section shall apply in relation to contracts made before this section came into force.

    (8) Section 40 of the Law of Property Act 1925 (which is superseded by this section) shall cease to have effect.

Note:

(1) Section 2 is only relevant to executory contracts. It has no relevance to contracts that have been completed. If parties choose to complete a contract that does not comply with the section they are free to do so (*Tootal Clothing Ltd v Guinea Properties Management Ltd* [1992] 2 EGLR 80).

(2) An agreement for the *grant* of an option falls within s2 and must therefore be signed by, or on behalf of, all parties to the contract, but a letter *exercising* the option is not a 'sale or other disposition of an interest in land' and so need only be signed by the purchaser (*Spiro v Glencrown Properties Ltd* [1991] 1 All ER 600).

(3) The section does not apply where the lease is to be for a term of three years or less. Nor does it apply to auction sales or contracts regulated by the Financial Services Act 1986. Furthermore, the section does not affect the creation or operation of resulting, implied or constructive trusts (s2(5)).

(4) Section 2(1) of the 1989 Act requires all terms 'which the parties have expressly agreed' to be in one document or, where contracts are exchanged, in each. The author's understanding of this section is that it does not affect the old rule that it is only necessary expressly to agree the essential terms (see *above*, p8) and that the court will still make an order for specific performance so long as the requirements of the section have been complied with in relation to those terms.

(5) Where the agreement was entered into before 27 September 1989 the provisions of s40 of the Law of Property Act 1925 apply to the contract (as to which, see 42 Halsbury (4th edn) para 27.

Chapter 2

Forfeiture

A written tenancy agreement will usually contain a clause enabling the landlord to forfeit the term if the tenant is in breach of one of the covenants in the lease; for example, for the payment of rent, the carrying-out of repairs or the prohibition of subletting. This chapter deals with the common law and statutory rules that generally apply in all forfeiture cases. However, it should be noted that the rules relating to forfeiture are modified in certain cases. The special rules that apply in any particular case are dealt with in the appropriate chapter.

Forfeiture clauses

Introduction

The usual name for the clause in a lease entitling the landlord to bring the tenancy to an end prior to its originally intended expiry date is the 'proviso for reentry'. The proviso operates by entitling the landlord to reenter the property if one of a number of stated events occurs and goes on to declare that upon reentry the lease comes to an end; hence, the other title used: 'forfeiture clause'. By reentry the landlord forfeits the lease.

Where there is no express forfeiture clause in a lease, no such clause will be implied. The landlord may, however, be able to forfeit without a forfeiture clause if an event occurs which is specified as being a condition of the term (see s 146(7) of the Law of Property Act 1925 on p 14, and see generally 27(1) Halsbury (4th edn, reissue) para 503; Woodfall, *Landlord and Tenant*, Sweet & Maxwell, 17.058). Impugning the landlord's title amounts to breach of an implied condition entitling the landlord to forfeit (*WG Clark (Properties) Ltd v Dupre Properties Ltd* [1992] 1 All ER 596, Ch D).

Where the tenant holds over after the expiry of a fixed term so that he becomes a periodic tenant (p 71), the forfeiture clause in the fixed term is carried over into the periodic term (*Thomas v Packer* (1857) 1 H&N 699).

11

Disguising the forfeiture clause so as to avoid relief provisions

The purpose of the forfeiture clause is to provide the landlord with security for performance of the terms of the lease. The courts 'lean against forfeiture' and if the tenant remedies the breach he will invariably be able to obtain relief from forfeiture. Any attempt, therefore, to exclude the court's equitable and statutory jurisdiction to grant relief by dressing up a forfeiture clause as something else will fail (*Richard Clarke & Co Ltd v Widnall* [1976] 1 WLR 845, CA—a clause providing for termination of the lease on non-payment of rent which required the landlord to serve a termination notice in that event did not deprive the clause of its status as a forfeiture clause and the tenant did not lose his right to claim relief). But a clause requiring notice of termination upon default will only operate as a forfeiture clause if it brings the lease to an end before its natural termination date (*Clays Lane Housing Co-operative v Patrick* (1984) 49 P&CR 72).

Furthermore, s 146(12) of the Law of Property Act 1925 expressly provides that the relief provisions of that section will have effect notwithstanding any stipulation to the contrary (p 14). A forfeiture in the guise of a surrender remains a forfeiture for the purposes of the section (*Plymouth Corporation v Harvey* [1971] 1 All ER 623).

The effect of forfeiture

Forfeiture brings the tenancy, and all interests derived from the tenancy (ie sub-tenancies, mortgages and other charges), to an end so that the landlord is immediately entitled to possession (*Official Custodian for Charities v Mackey* [1984] 3 All ER 689). If the tenant wishes to retain possession he will have to apply for relief from forfeiture which will invariably require payment of any arrears and the remedying of any breach of covenant. As forfeiture brings the tenancy to an end the landlord ceases to be entitled to rent that would otherwise become payable and may no longer rely upon the tenant's covenants in the lease (see p 40), although he may sue in respect of past arrears and breaches.

If the landlord elects to pursue an alternative remedy and to waive the right to forfeit in respect of a particular breach he will not subsequently be allowed to forfeit in respect of that breach. 'Waiver' is dealt with in detail below, p 30.

Forfeiture for non-payment of rent; two preliminary points

Various matters that are relevant to claims for non-payment of rent are dealt with in Chapter 23. Two particular points that relate specifically to forfeiture are dealt with here.

Deemed rent payments: service charges, insurance etc

Many leases contain covenants requiring the tenant to contribute to the cost of insuring the building of which the demised premises forms part, and to pay service charges etc and these payments are deemed by the lease to be payable as rent. They are normally called 'insurance rent', 'additional rent', 'maintenance rent' or some other similar term. Each covenant of this type and its relationship to the forfeiture clause must be construed according to the terms of the lease. However, the effect is often that the landlord will not have to serve a notice under s146 of the Law of Property Act 1925 in respect of the failure to pay these sums and that the relief provisions relating to non-payment of rent will apply (p43), rather than s146(2) of the 1925 Act which deals with relief in other cases (p49). A s146 notice for use where these sums are not payable as rent is to be found on p15 (Form 1).

Formal demands for rent

The common law requires a formal demand to be made for the rent before the landlord can forfeit in respect of non-payment unless the lease dispenses with the requirement. The modern forfeiture clause in dealing with non-payment of rent does dispense with the requirement for a formal demand. It provides for reentry if the rent is more than, say, 21 days in arrears, whether or not the landlord has made a formal demand for overdue rent.

If the forfeiture clause does not dispense with the requirement for a formal demand, the common law provides that such a demand must be made at the place specified in the lease or, if none is specified, at the demised premises. It must be made before sunset on the last day for payment and should only relate to the sum due in respect of the last rental period. However, the strict common law position is ameliorated by statute. In the county court, service of the summons in the action will count as a demand where there is *one half year's rent in arrear* and no sufficient distress is found on the premises (s139(1) of the County Courts Act 1984; see p44). Where proceedings are commenced in the High Court see s210 of the Common Law Procedure Act.

Forfeiture for other breaches; section 146 notices

Introduction

If a tenant is in breach of covenant (other than a covenant to pay rent: see s146(11) of the Law of Property Act 1925) the landlord cannot (subject to certain limited exceptions set out in s146(9) of the 1925 Act, see p29) exercise any right of reentry in the lease in respect of that breach unless he has first served a notice under s146(1) of the 1925 Act. The notice must be in writing (s196(1) of the Act; p19).

Law of Property Act 1925, s146
    (1) A right of reentry or forfeiture under any proviso or stipulation in a lease for a breach of any covenant or condition in the lease shall not be

enforceable, by action or otherwise, unless and until the lessor serves on the lessee a notice—

(a) specifying the particular breach complained of; and

(b) if the breach is capable of remedy, requiring the lessee to remedy the breach; and

(c) in any case, requiring the lessee to make compensation in money for the breach;

and the lessee fails, within a reasonable time thereafter, to remedy the breach, if it is capable of remedy, and to make reasonable compensation in money, to the satisfaction of the lessor, for the breach.

(5) For the purposes of this section—

(a) 'Lease' includes an original or derivative underlease; also an agreement for a lease where the lessee has become entitled to have his lease granted; also a grant at a fee farm rent, or securing a rent by condition;

(b) 'Lessee' includes an original or derivative underlessee, and the persons deriving title under a lessee; also a grantee under any such grant as aforesaid and the persons deriving title under him;

(c) 'Lessor' includes an original or derivative underlessor, and the persons deriving title under a lessor; also a person making such grant as aforesaid and the persons deriving title under him;

(d) 'Underlease' includes an agreement for an underlease where the underlessee has become entitled to have his underlease granted;

(e) 'Underlessee' includes any person deriving title under an underlessee.

(7) For the purposes of this section a lease limited to continue as long only as the lessee abstains from committing a breach of covenant shall be and take effect as a lease to continue for any longer term for which it could subsist, but determinable by a proviso for reentry on such a breach.

(11) This section does not, save as otherwise mentioned, affect the law relating to reentry or forfeiture or relief in case of non-payment of rent.

(12) This section has effect notwithstanding any stipulation to the contrary.

As the purpose and effect of a s 146 notice is to operate as a preliminary to forfeiture, service of such a notice cannot be an unequivocal affirmation of the existence of the lease and, therefore, does not operate to waive a right to forfeit (*Church Commissioners for England v Nodjoumi* (1986) 51 P&CR 155; see p35); but a notice served under s 146 should not contain a demand for arrears of rent accruing since the breach complained of in the notice. This is because the demand may possibly waive that breach, it not being necessary to serve a s 146 notice in respect of arrears of rent.

Where the breach of covenant is a continuing one (see p31), eg where the tenant is failing to keep the premises in good repair, and the landlord has waived the right to forfeit in respect of the earlier stages of the breach but is seeking to forfeit in respect of the stages that have occurred since

Form 1: Section 146 notice—service charges

NOTICE PURSUANT TO S146 OF THE LAW OF PROPERTY ACT 1925

Re: [address of property]

I, [state name and address of the landlord], hereby give you notice that:

To: [name of tenant]

1.   The above-mentioned premises were let to you by me under a lease dated the [insert date] for a term of [state number] years commencing on the [state date].

2.   By clause [state number of clause] of the said lease you covenanted to pay service charges calculated in accordance with schedule [state number of schedule] to the said lease on the usual quarter days.

3.   In breach of the said clause you failed to pay the sum of £ [state amount] due in respect of service charges on [insert date].

4.   I require you to remedy the breach by paying the said sum within 7 days of service of this notice. If you fail to do so I shall take proceedings to forfeit your lease.

DATED   [signed by the landlord]

---

the waiver, he does not need to serve a fresh s 146 notice if such a notice was served prior to the waiver and if there has been no change in the condition of the premises (*Greenwich London Borough Council v Discreet Selling Estates Ltd* [1990] 2 EGLR 65).

It seems to me that a notice under section 146 asserts not only that the tenant is presently in breach but also that he will continue to be in breach unless and until he carries out the repairs required. It must necessarily assert that, if the landlord is to be able to rely at the trial on further delay which will have occurred up to the commencement of proceedings. In those circumstances I see no practical need for any fresh notice if a landlord wishes to rely on that continuing breach as a ground of forfeiture in the future and no legal reason why a fresh notice should be required in respect of the same defects. (*Greenwich LBC v Discreet Selling Estates Ltd*, per Staughton LJ at 68).

Contents of the notice

Section 146(1) of the Law of Property Act 1925 requires that the notice should:
  (1) specify the breach complained of; and
  (2) if the breach is capable of remedy, require the tenant to remedy it; and
  (3) in any case, require the tenant to make compensation in money for the breach.

The notice does not need to refer to the statute (*Van Haarlam v Kasner* [1992] 2 EGLR 59 ChD).

Form 2: Section 146 notice—assignment

NOTICE SERVED PURSUANT TO S146 OF THE LAW OF PROPERTY ACT 1925

Re: [address of property]

To: [name of the assignee]

I, [name and address of the landlord] hereby give you notice that:

1. The above-mentioned premises were let under a lease dated the [insert date] and made between [state names] for a term of [insert number] years commencing on the [insert date].

2. The lease contains a covenant not to assign, sublet or part with possession of the said premises without the written permission of the landlord.

3. The said covenant has been broken that on or about [insert date] [name the original tenant] assigned the said lease to you without my previous consent.

4. I require you to remedy the breach if the same is capable of remedy.

DATED   [signed by the landlord]

A s146 notice must be served even if the breach is not capable of remedy. The notice has a two-fold purpose; firstly, to give the tenant the opportunity to remedy the breach (if it is capable of remedy) before the landlord forfeits and secondly, to give the tenant the opportunity to apply to the court for relief (*Expert Clothing and Sales Ltd v Hillgate House Ltd* [1985] 2 All ER 998).

> In a case where the breach is 'capable of remedy' . . . the principal object of the notice procedure . . . is to afford the lessee two opportunities before the lessor actually proceeds to enforce his right of re-entry, namely (1) the opportunity to remedy the breach within a reasonable time after service of the notice and (2) the opportunity to apply to the court for relief from forfeiture. In a case where the breach is not 'capable of remedy', there is clearly no point in affording the first of these two opportunities; the object of the notice procedure is thus simply to give the lessee the opportunity to apply for relief. (Expert Clothing, per Slade LJ at 1005c)

Each of the three requirements will be looked at in turn. Examples of s146 notices are to be found on pp15 and *above*, Forms 1 and 2.

Specify the breach   The breach complained of should clearly be set out in the notice. The usual practice is to set out the terms of the lease that have allegedly been breached and then to give details of the breach by reference to those terms. The notice will be invalid if it refers to the wrong covenant (*Jacob v Down* [1900] 2 Ch 156).

Remedy the breach: If a breach can be remedied, remedial action must be required of the tenant in the notice but, notwithstanding the wording of s 146, it is not necessary to require the tenant to remedy the breach if it is not capable of remedy within a reasonable time after service of the notice (*Expert Clothing* at 1009f).

Whether a breach of covenant is 'capable of remedy' for the purposes of s 146(1)(*b*) depends on whether the harm suffered by the landlord by the relevant breach is capable of being remedied in practical terms. The breach of a positive covenant, whether continuous or once and for all, is ordinarily remediable provided the remedy is carried out within a reasonable time. The amount of time that is to be regarded as reasonable will depend upon the particular circumstances of the case (*Expert Clothing* at 1008c).

The position, so far as negative covenants are concerned, is not quite so clear. Although there may be negative covenants that are capable of being remedied (*Scala House and District Property Co Ltd v Forbes* [1974] QB 575 at 585), they are less likely to be remediable than positive ones. Fortunately, there are authorities in respect of some negative covenants. For example, if the tenant assigns, sublets or parts with possession in breach of covenant he commits an act which is incapable of remedy (*Scala House v Forbes*). Breach of a covenant not to use the premises for illegal or immoral purposes is a breach that is incapable of remedy if a stigma is thereby attached to the premises (*Rugby School (Governors) v Tannahill* [1935] 1 KB 87; *British Petroleum Pension Trust Ltd v Behrendt* (1985) 2 EGLR 97, CA); but for the position where the sub-tenant has used the premises in an immoral or illegal way without the knowledge of the tenant, see *Glass v Kencakes Ltd* [1966] 1 QB 611.

If the landlord is not sure whether the breach is one that is capable of remedy his notice should require the tenant to remedy it 'if it is capable of remedy' (*Glass v Kencakes Ltd* and see Form 2, p 16).

Although not required by s 146(1) it is common practice to state the time in which the breach is to be remedied, which must be a reasonable one. Three months will be sufficient in most cases (see *Gulliver Investments v Abbott* [1966] EGD 299—a repairs case, and p 20) but obviously every case will depend upon its own facts and in many cases a much shorter period will be all that is required. Where the breach is incapable of remedy and the only purpose of the notice is to give the tenant the opportunity to apply for relief an extended period will not be necessary.

Compensation   Notwithstanding the terms of s 146(1)(*c*), the landlord need not include a provision in the notice requiring compensation if he does not in fact desire to be compensated (*Rugby School (Governors) v Tannahill*); but if he does not ask for it in the notice he will not be entitled to recover compensation in the proceedings (*Lock v Pearce* [1893] 2 Ch 271).

Surveyors' and solicitors' costs

Many leases contain specific provision for payment of professional fees incurred in the preparation and service of a s146 notice even if forfeiture of a lease is avoided without a court order. However, even if there is no such clause in the lease s146(3) provides for recovery of such costs.

Section 146(3) of the Law of Property Act 1925
> (3) A lessor shall be entitled to recover as a debt due to him from a lessee, and in addition to damages (if any), all reasonable costs and expenses properly incurred by the lessor in the employment of a solicitor and surveyor or valuer, or otherwise, in reference to any breach giving rise to a right of reentry or forfeiture which, at the request of the lessee, is waived by the lessor, or from which the lessee is relieved, under the provisions of this Act.

Service of the notice: upon whom

The notice should be served upon the tenant. If there is more than one tenant all the tenants must be served (*Blewett v Blewett* [1936] 2 All ER 188). Where the lease has been assigned, the notice should be served on the assignee and not the assignor, even if the assignment is unlawful. This is because the assignment, although unlawful, is effective to transfer the tenancy to the assignee. He is now the tenant and the person who is interested in avoiding the forfeiture (*Old Grovebury Manor Farm Ltd v W Seymour Plant Sales and Hire Ltd (No 2)* [1979] 1 WLR 1397). It is not necessary to serve the notice on sub-tenants or mortgagees (*Egerton v Jones* [1939] 2 KB 702; *Church Commissioners for England v Ve-Ri-Best Manufacturing Co Ltd* [1957] 1 QB 238).

Mode of service

Having said that the landlord must serve the notice on the tenant, it is not actually necessary to search out the tenant and place the notice in his hand. The provisions of s196 of the Law of Property Act 1925 (see p19), as extended by s1 of the Recorded Delivery Act 1962, apply. The effect of these sections is as follows:
  (1) A s146 notice is sufficiently served if it is sent by registered post or recorded delivery addressed to the tenant by name at the tenant's last known place of abode or business in the United Kingdom. If the letter is not returned through the post office undelivered, service is deemed to be made at the time at which the letter would in the ordinary course of post be delivered (s196(4)). To prove service the landlord need only show that the letter was prepaid, properly addressed and actually posted.
  (2) The landlord may also serve the s146 notice by leaving it at the tenant's last known place of abode or business in the United

Kingdom or affixing it or leaving it for him on the land or on any house or building comprised in the lease (s196(3)). If this method is used it is sufficient if it is addressed to 'the lessee' (s196(2)).

In either of the above two cases the landlord will not need to show that the tenant actually received the s146 notice (*Re 88 Berkeley Road, London NW9* [1971] Ch 648). In *Van Haarlam v Kasner* [1992] 2 EGLR 59, a notice which was served at the property pursuant to s196(3) was held to be good service even though at the date of service the landlord knew that the tenant was in prison and unlikely to receive it.

The notice may also be left at the tenant's property with some person provided that it is reasonable to suppose that it will be passed on to the tenant (*Cannon Brewery Co Ltd v Signal Press Ltd* (1928) 139 LT 384).

The landlord should plead service of the notice as a matter of good pleading but he will not be prejudiced if he fails to do so (*Gates v WA and RJ Jacobs Ltd* [1920] 1 Ch 567).

Law of Property Act 1925, s196; service of notices
  (1) Any notice required or authorised to be served or given by this Act shall be in writing.
  (2) Any notice required or authorised by this Act to be served on a lessee or mortgagor shall be sufficient, although only addressed to the lessee or mortgagor by that designation, without his name, or generally to the persons interested, without any name, and notwithstanding that any person to be affected by the notice is absent, under disability, unborn, or unascertained.
  (3) Any notice required or authorised by this Act to be served shall be sufficiently served if it is left at the last-known place of abode or business in the United Kingdom of the lessee, lessor, mortgagee, mortgagor, or other person to be served, or, in case of a notice required or authorised to be served on a lessee or mortgagor, is affixed or left for him on the land or any house or building comprised in the lease or mortgage, or, in case of a mining lease, is left for the lessee at the office or counting-house of the mine.
  (4) Any notice required or authorised by this Act to be served shall also be sufficiently served, if it is sent by post in a registered letter addressed to the lessee, lessor, mortgagee, mortgagor, or other person to be served, by name, at the aforesaid place of abode or business, office, or counting-house, and if that letter is not returned through the post-office undelivered; and that service shall be deemed to be made at the time at which the registered letter would in the ordinary course be delivered.
  (5) The provisions of this section shall extend to notices required to be served by an instrument affecting property executed or coming into operation after commencement of this Act unless a contrary intention appears.
  (6) This section does not apply to notices served in proceedings in the court.

Tenant's action on receipt of notice

A tenant in receipt of a s146 notice (who wishes to retain his lease) has three choices:

(1) He may remedy the breach complained of within the time stated, if the breach is capable of remedy.

(2) If he suspects that the landlord will reenter without taking proceedings for possession, he may apply to the court for an injunction to prevent the landlord from so doing (see Chapter 27). He may wish to apply for an injunction where he denies that he is in breach of covenant at all or where the landlord specifies a time in which to remedy the breach which the tenant considers to be unreasonably short.

(3) He may apply for relief from forfeiture. He is entitled to make the application immediately on receipt of the notice and does not need to wait for the landlord to commence proceedings for possession (see p49).

Depending upon the circumstances of the case, the tenant may wish to combine two or more of these courses of action, but where it is clear that the landlord will only forfeit by taking proceedings it will not be necessary to seek an injunction or to apply for relief prior to service of those proceedings.

Tenant's failure to comply with notice

If the tenant fails, within a reasonable time of service of the notice, to remedy the breach (if it is capable of remedy) and to make reasonable compensation in money to the landlord's satisfaction (if the landlord has required compensation), the landlord may reenter the property and thereby forfeit the lease. If there is a person lawfully residing in the premises he may only do so by the issue *and* service of proceedings (see p38). The landlord must not commence proceedings until a reasonable time has elapsed. This is the position even where the breach is incapable of remedy for even in these circumstances the tenant needs time to consider his position and to decide whether to apply for relief, and to take such action as will assist his claim (*Scala House*—14 days held sufficient in the circumstances of the case; and see *Expert Clothing*, *above*, p16).

Repairing covenants

Particular rules apply where the landlord is seeking to forfeit for breach of the covenant to repair. In certain cases the landlord's right to recover possession is limited by the provisions of the Leasehold Property (Repairs) Act 1938 (see p25 for the provisions of the Act). In all cases special rules apply in relation to service of s146 notices.

Section 146 notices in repair cases

All s146 notices in repair cases must, in accordance with the usual requirement to specify the breach complained of, give details of the

Form 3: Particulars of claim—Breach of covenant

IN THE   COUNTY COURT   Case No

BETWEEN

Plaintiff

—AND—

Defendant

PARTICULARS OF CLAIM

1.   The Plaintiff is the leasehold owner and is entitled to possession of the property known as [*state address*].

2.   By a Lease made on the [*state date*] between the Plaintiff's predecessor in title, [*state name*] ('the Lessor') and the Defendant, the Lessor demised the property to the Defendant for the term of [*state number*] years from [*state date*]. The Plaintiff will refer to the said Lease at the trial hereof of its full terms, true meaning and effect.

3.   By virtue of Clause [*state number of Clause*] of the said Lease, the Defendant agreed and covenanted, inter alia, not to [*set out details of covenant broken*].

4.   The Lease contained a proviso for reentry entitling the Lessor to forfeit the term and reenter the property in the event of the Defendant failing or neglecting to observe or perform any of the covenants and agreements contained in the said Lease.

5.   By a transfer dated [*state date*] the reversion immediately expectant upon the determination of the term became and is now vested in the Plaintiff.

6.   In breach of the said Lease, the Defendant has [*set out breaches of covenants alleged*].

7.   On the [*state date*], the Plaintiff served on the Defendant a notice in writing specifying the said breach in accordance with Section 146(1) of the Law of Property Act 1925. The Defendant failed within a reasonable time or at all to remedy the said breach [or to pay compensation to the plaintiff therefor].

8.   By reason of the matters aforesaid the Lease has become liable to be forfeited to the plaintiff and by service of these proceedings is forfeited so that the Plaintiff is entitled to possession of the demised property.

9.   The property is a dwelling house but the rent payable is less than two-thirds of the rateable value on the appropriate day, namely £ [*state amount*]. In the premises, the property is not one to which the Rent Act 1977 applies. [*Adapt in accordance with the provisions of the Housing Act 1988 where that Act is applicable*]. The Plaintiff does not know of any person entitled to claim relief against forfeiture under lessee [*see CCR Ord 6, r3(2); See p40*].

10.   The daily rate of rent is £ [*state amount*].

AND the Plaintiff claims:
(1)   Possession of the said property.

(2)   Mesne profits at the rate of £ [*state amount*] per annum from service of these proceedings until possession be delivered up (£ [*state amount*] per day).

DATED

repairs that have not been carried out. The usual and most sensible practice is to attach a schedule of dilapidations prepared by a surveyor to the notice. However, it is not necessary to specify in the minutest detail the items that need repairing so long as the tenant clearly knows what he has to do to avoid forfeiture. The schedule of dilapidations will normally set out the work that is required to put the property into good repair, but it is not in fact necessary to specify the acts required to remedy the breach (*Fox v Jolly* [1916] 1 AC 1 at p11). The notice is not invalid if it alleges some breaches which were not in fact committed (*Blewett v Blewett* [1936] 2 All ER 188).

Where the lease was originally granted for a term of seven years or more, and more than three years or more remain unexpired at the date of service of the notice, the provisions of the Leasehold Property (Repairs) Act 1938 apply (see p25). In those circumstances the landlord must serve the s146 notice at least one month before he intends to reenter and must inform the tenant in the notice of his right to serve a counternotice. If the tenant does serve a counternotice the landlord may not forfeit without the leave of the court (s1 of the 1928 Act). As to the application for leave see p23.

Service of the notice

Landlord and Tenant Act 1927, s18

   18.—(2) A right of reentry or forfeiture for a breach of any such covenant or agreement as aforesaid [ie any covenant or agreement to keep or put premises in repair during the currency of a lease, or to leave or put premises in repair at the termination of a lease: see s18(1) below] shall not be enforceable, by action or otherwise, unless the lessor proves that the fact that such a notice as is required by section 146 of the Law of Property Act 1925 had been served on the lessee was known either—

   (*a*) to the lessee; or

   (*b*) to an underlessee holding under an underlease which reserved a nominal reversion only to the lessee; or

   (*c*) to the person who last paid the rent due under the lease either on his own behalf or as agent for the lessee or underlessee,

and that a time reasonably sufficient to enable the repairs to be executed had elapsed since the time when the fact of the service of the notice came to the knowledge of any such person.

   Where a notice has been sent by registered post addressed to a person at his last known place of abode in the United Kingdom, then, for the purposes of this subsection, that person shall be deemed, unless the contrary is proved, to have had knowledge of the fact that the notice had been served as from the time at which the letter would have been delivered in the ordinary course of post.

   This subsection shall be construed as one with s146 of the Law of Property Act 1925.

Service of s146 notices was dealt with in general terms on p18. However, where one is concerned with breach of a repairing covenant there are further requirements imposed on the landlord in relation to

service of the notice (s18 of the Landlord and Tenant Act 1927). He may
not exercise his right to reenter unless he proves that service of the notice
was known either:

(1) to his tenant,

(2) to a sub-tenant holding under a sub-lease which reserved only a nominal reversion to the tenant, or

(3) to the person who last paid the rent,

and that a reasonable time has elapsed since the time when the fact of
service was known to such a person.

However, the landlord's position is ameliorated by the fact that where
the notice is sent by registered post or recorded delivery to a person at his
last known place of abode in the United Kingdom, proof of posting
means that the notice is deemed to have come to his knowledge in the
ordinary course of post unless the contrary is proved (s18(2) of the 1927
Act; s1(1) of the Recorded Delivery Service Act 1962).

Tenant's action on receipt of the notice; counternotice

The tenant has 28 days in which to serve a counternotice. If he serves the
counternotice within this period the landlord will have to apply to the
court for leave to reenter the property, which the court will only grant in
limited circumstances (see *below*). *If the tenant fails to serve a counter-
notice within this period he will lose his rights under the Act.* The
counternotice should inform the landlord that he claims the benefit of the
1938 Act. There is no prescribed form and a simple letter will suffice.

Section 23(2) of the Landlord and Tenant Act 1927, which authorises a
tenant to serve documents on the person to whom he has been paying
rent, applies in relation to service of the counternotice (s51 of the
Landlord and Tenant Act 1954).

Landlord's application for leave to enforce right of reentry

The landlord will only be granted leave to reenter the property (whether
by proceedings or otherwise: s1(1)(3)) if the landlord proves one of the
five grounds set out in s1(5) of the 1938 Act. The full subsection is on
p25. The grounds may be summarised as follows:

(a) immediate remedying of the breach is required to prevent substantial diminution in value of reversion, or substantial diminution has occurred;

(b) immediate remedying of the breach is required to comply with statute, bye-law, court order etc;

(c) immediate remedying of the breach is required in interests of occupiers other than the tenant;

(d) immediate remedying of the breach is cheap compared to result of delay;

Form 4: Application for leave under 1938 Act

IN THE   **COUNTY COURT**

In the matter of the Leasehold Property (Repairs) Act 1938

BETWEEN:

[*Name of the landlord*]   *Applicant*

—AND—

[*Name of the tenant*]   *Respondent*

[*Name of the landlord*] of [*address*] applies to the Court for an order in the following terms:

1. Leave under section 1 of the Leasehold Property (Repairs) Act 1938 to take proceedings for the enforcement of its right of reentry by reason of breaches of the repairing covenants contained in a Lease granted by the Applicant to the Respondent on _____ whereby the dwelling known as [*address of dwelling*] was demised to the Respondent for a term of _____ years from _____ ;

2. Leave under section 1 of the 1938 Act to take proceedings for damages for breaches of the said repairing covenants;

3. A direction under section 2 of the 1938 Act that the Applicant do have the benefit of section 146(3) of the Law of Property Act 1925 in relation to the costs and expenses incurred in reference to the said breaches; and

4. An order that the Respondent do pay the cost of this application.

The grounds upon which the Applicant claims to be entitled to the order are that the property is in a state of disrepair and that subs [*(a) and (d)*] of section 1(5) of the 1938 Act apply. Full particulars of the said grounds are set out in the affidavit of _____ dated _____ and filed with this application.

The Applicant's address for service is:

DATED

(*e*) special circumstances.

The application is made by originating application in the county court (CCR Ord3, r4; see precedent *above*, Form 4) and by originating summons in the High Court (RSC Ord 7; see Ord 28 for the procedure to be adopted) in each case supported by affidavit evidence. Where the proceedings are brought in the High Court, the jurisdiction may be exercised in chambers by a Master (RSC Ord 32, r9). The proceedings may only be issued in a district registry if the premises to which the application relates are situated in the district of that registry (RSC Ord 32, r9(2)). The originating summons is in Form No 10 of Appendix A.

The affidavit will usually be sworn by the landlord's surveyor who will exhibit his original schedule of dilapidations that was served with the s146 notice. The affidavit will state the grounds in s1(5) of the 1938 Act relied upon and the facts and matters relied upon to establish those grounds. See Form 5, p28 for a precedent.

It is not good enough for the landlord to show that he has an arguable or *prima facie* case. He must prove on a balance of probabilities that one or more of the grounds set out in s1(5) of the 1938 Act applies (*Associated British Ports v CH Bailey plc* [1990] 1 All ER 929, HL). Thus, if a dispute arises as to whether or not any of the grounds apply it will be necessary to have a full trial of the issue with oral evidence given.

The court may, in granting or refusing leave, impose on the landlord or the tenant such terms and conditions as it thinks fit (s1(6)).

An application under the 1938 Act for leave to commence proceedings for forfeiture of a lease is a 'pending land action' within the meaning of s17(1) of the Land Charges Act 1972 and is, therefore, registerable as a 'pending action' under s5 of the 1972 Act (*Selim Ltd v Bickenhall Engineering Ltd* [1981] 3 All ER 210). Where the land is registered the action is protected by entry of a caution against dealings (s59(1)(5) of the Land Registration Act 1925).

Recovery of landlord's costs

Section 146(3) of the Law of Property Act 1925 gives the landlord the right to recover as a debt due to him all reasonable costs and expenses properly incurred in the employment of a solicitor and surveyor or valuer in reference to any breach giving rise to a right of reentry which, at the request of the tenant, is waived by the landlord or for which the tenant is relieved under the provisions of s146(4) of the 1925 Act (see p18). However, a landlord on whom a counternotice has been served under s1 of the 1938 Act may not rely on s146(3) unless he makes an application for leave under that section (s2 of the 1938 Act).

Leasehold Property (Repairs) Act 1938

1.—(1) Where a lessor serves on a lessee, under subsection (1) of section 146 of the Law of Property Act 1925, a notice that relates to a breach of a covenant or agreement to keep or put in repair during the currency of the lease all or any of the property comprised in the lease, and at the date of the service of the notice three years or more of the term of the lease remain unexpired, the lessee may within 28 days from that date serve on the lessor a counter-notice to the effect that he claims the benefit of this Act.

(2) A right to damages for a breach of such a covenant as aforesaid shall not be enforceable by action commenced at any time at which three years or more of the term of the lease remain unexpired unless the lessor has served such a notice as is specified in subsection (1) of section 146 of the Law of Property Act 1925, and where a notice is served under this subsection, the lessee may, within 28 days from the date of the service thereof, serve on the lessor a counter-notice to the effect that he claims the benefit of this Act.

(3) Where a counter-notice is served by a lessee under this section, then, notwithstanding anything in any enactment or rule of law, no proceedings, by action or otherwise, shall be taken by the lessor for the enforcement of any right of reentry or forfeiture under any proviso or stipulation in the lease

for breach of the covenant or agreement in question, or for damages for breach thereof, otherwise than with the leave of the court.

(4) A notice served under subsection (1) of s 146 of the Law of Property Act 1925 in the circumstances specified in subsection (1) of this section, and a notice served under subsection (2) of this section shall not be valid unless it contains a statement, in characters not less conspicuous than those used in any other part of the notice, to the effect that the lessee is entitled under this Act to serve on the lessor a counter-notice claiming the benefit of this Act, and a statement in the like characters specifying the time within which, and the manner in which, under this Act a counter-notice may be served specifying the name and address for service of the lessor.

(5) Leave for the purposes of this section shall not be given unless the lessor proves—

    (a) that the immediate remedying of the breach in question is requisite for preventing substantial diminution in the value of his reversion, or that the value thereof has been substantially diminished by the breach;

    (b) that the immediate remedying of the breach is required for giving effect in relation to the premises to the purposes of any enactment, or of any byelaw or other provision having effect under any enactment or for giving effect to any order of a court or requirement of any authority under any enactment or any such byelaw or other provision as aforesaid;

    (c) in a case in which the lessee is not in occupation of the whole of the premises as respects which the covenant or agreement is proposed to be enforced, that the immediate remedying of the breach is required in the interests of the occupier of those premises or of part thereof;

    (d) that the breach can be immediately remedied at an expense that is relatively small in comparison with the much greater expense that would probably be occasioned by postponement of the necessary work; or

    (e) special circumstances which, in the opinion of the court, render it just and equitable that leave should be given.

(6) The court may, in granting or in refusing leave for the purposes of this section, impose such terms and conditions on the lessor or on the lessee as it may think fit.

2. A lessor on whom a counter-notice is served under the preceding section shall not be entitled to the benefit of subsection (3) of section 146 of the Law of Property Act 1925 (which relates to costs and expenses incurred by a lessor in reference to breaches of covenant), so far as regards any costs or expenses incurred in reference to the breach in question, unless he makes an application for leave for the purposes of the preceding section, and on such an application the court shall have power to direct whether and to what extent the lessor is to be entitled to the benefit thereof.

3. This Act shall not apply to a breach of a covenant or agreement in so far as it imposes on the lessee an obligation to put premises in repair that is to be performed upon the lessee taking possession of the premises or with n a reasonable time thereafter.

7.—(1) In this Act the expressions 'lessor', 'lessee' and 'lease' have the same meanings assigned to them respectively by sections 146 [see p 14] and 154 of the Law of Property Act 1925, except that they do not include any reference to such a grant as is mentioned in the said section 146, or to the person making, or to the grantee under such a grant, or to persons deriving title under such a person; and 'lease' means a lease for a term of seven years or more, not being a lease of an agricultural holding within the meaning of the Agricultural Holdings Act 1986.

(2) The provisions of section 196 of the said Act [ie Law of Property Act 1925] (which relate to the service of notices) shall extend to notices and counter-notices required or authorised by this Act.

Landlord and Tenant Act 1954, s51

(3) The said Act of 1938 shall apply where there is an interest belonging to Her Majesty in right of the Crown or to a Government department, or held on behalf of Her Majesty for the purposes of a Government department, in like manner as if that interest were an interest not so belonging or held.

Form 5: Affidavit in support of application under 1938 Act

[Name of Deponent] (1)

Sworn _____

Filed on behalf of the Applicant

IN THE   COUNTY COURT

In the matter of the Leasehold Property (Repairs) Act 1938

BETWEEN:

[Name of the Applicant]   *Applicant*

—AND—

[Name of The Respondent]   *Respondent*

I, *[Name of the Applicant's surveyor]* FRICS, Chartered Surveyor, of *[address]* hereby MAKE OATH and say as follows:

1. I make this affidavit with the authority of the Applicant and in support of its application for leave to take the proceedings referred to in the Originating Application dated _____ and for the other relief sought in that application. I have been a qualified surveyor for _____ years and am a partner in the firm of _____, Chartered Surveyors, of _____ The facts stated herein are within my own knowledge and belief.

2. The counter-part of the Lease dated _____ between _____ and _____ referred to in the Originating Application is now produced and shown to me marked '_____ I'. Under the terms of the Lease the Applicant granted the Respondent a tenancy of the property known as _____ for a term of _____ years from _____.

3. By Clause _____ of the Lease, the Respondent covenanted with the Applicant to keep the Property in good and proper repair. By Clause _____ of the Lease the Respondent covenanted to pay to the Applicant the legal costs and surveyor's fees incurred by the Applicant in preparing a notice under section 146 of the Law of Property Act 1925.

contd

---

contd

4. On _____ I visited the Property and subsequently prepared a Schedule of Dilapidation. I confirm that it is necessary to carry out the remedial works listed in the Schedule. I served a copy of my Schedule together with a notice under section 146 of the Law of Property Act 1925 and section 1 of the Leasehold Property (Repairs) Act 1938 upon the Respondent by recorded delivery on _____. A copy of the notice and attached Schedule are now produced and shown to me marked ' _____ 2'. A counter notice was served by the Respondent on _____. A copy of that notice is now produced and shown to me marked ' _____ 3'.

5. There are a large number of items in the Schedule. The items upon which the Applicant relies for the purpose of this application are marked with an asterisk on the copy exhibited to this affidavit. *All the items so marked relate to dampness. The Property is being severely damaged by the ingress of water through the roof, and by rising damp around the foundations. If the remedial works are not carried out immediately there is a grave risk that the structural timbers could be affected by the damp penetration. It is, therefore, most urgent that steps are taken to eliminate damp penetration. The cost of the works listed in the Schedule connected with remedying the problem of damp is approximately* _____. *If the works are left for any period and the structural timbers are affected the cost of remedying the defects will be greatly increased.*

6. Having regard to the above, I consider that subsections (*a*) and (*d*) of section 1(5) of the Leasehold Property (Repairs) Act 1938 apply, namely:
   (*a*) That the breaches must be remedied immediately in order to prevent substantial diminution in the value of the Plaintiff's reversion; and
   (*b*) That the breach can be immediately remedied at an expense that is relatively small in comparison with a much greater expense that would probably be occasioned by postponement of the necessary work.

7. On _____ I returned to the property. Notwithstanding service of the notice, the necessary repairs have not been carried out.

SWORN etc

Damages for failure to repair

Where the landlord forfeits for breach of the repairing covenant it is also likely that he will wish to recover damages for breach of that covenant. A full discussion of the subject is beyond the scope of this book, but the following points are particularly worth noting.

Limitation on amount of damages   The sum that the landlord may recover for damages for breach of covenant to repair is limited by s18(1) of the Landlord and Tenant Act 1927 to the amount by which the value of the landlord's interest in the property is damaged by the breach. The section also precludes the landlord from recovering damages if the landlord intended to pull down the premises or make structural alterations which would render the repairs valueless.

Landlord and Tenant Act 1927, s18
   (1) Damages for breach of a covenant or agreement to keep or put premises in repair during the currency of a lease, or to leave or put premises

in repair at the termination of a lease, whether such covenant or agreement is expressed or implied, and whether general or specific, shall in no case exceed the amount (if any) by which the value of the reversion (whether immediate or not) in the premises is diminished owing to the breach of such covenant or agreement as aforesaid; and in particular no damage shall be recovered for a breach of any such covenant or agreement to leave or put premises in repair at the termination of a lease, if it is shown that the premises, in whatever state of repair they might be, would at or shortly after the termination of the tenancy have been or be pulled down, or such structural alterations made therein as would render valueless the repairs covered by the covenant or agreement.

If appropriate, the cost of repairs may be used as a guide to the amount of the diminution in value of the property (*Jones v Herxheimer* [1950] 2 KB 106), but if the repairs are not actually going to be carried out the cost of them is unlikely to be a good guide (*Smiley v Townshend* [1950] 2 KB 311). However, it does not necessarily follow that where repairs are not going to be done the damages will be nominal (*Culworth Estates Ltd v Society of Licensed Victuallers* [1991] 2 EGLR 54).

Date at which damages are assessed   Where the landlord has forfeited the lease by proceedings and is claiming damages for failure to deliver up the property in good repair, the date at which damages are assessed is the date upon which proceedings in the forfeiture action were served. This is because the lease (and the covenants contained therein) came to an end on that date and thereafter the ex-tenant remained in occupation as a trespasser. If the ex-tenant has caused further damage after service of the writ or summons the landlord should seek to recover his loss by claiming damages in tort (*Associated Deliveries Ltd v Harrison* (1984) 50 P&CR 91 CA; see also p40).

Insolvency

Subsections (9) and (10) of s146 are relevant on the bankruptcy of the tenant. Where the tenant is a corporation the term 'bankruptcy' means the winding up of the company (s205(1) of the Law of Property Act 1925).

Law of Property Act 1925, s146(9)(10); Bankruptcy of the lessee
    (9) This section does not apply to a condition for forfeiture on the bankruptcy of the lessee or on taking in execution of the lessee's interest if contained in a lease of—
    (*a*) agricultural or pastoral land;
    (*b*) mines or minerals;
    (*c*) a house used or intended to be used as a public-house or beershop;
    (*d*) a house let as a dwelling-house, with the use of any furniture, books, works of art, or other chattels not being in the nature of fixtures;

(*e*) any property with respect to which the personal qualifications of the tenant are of importance for the preservation of the value or character of the property, or on the ground of neighbourhood to the lessor, or to any person holding under him.

(10) Where a condition of forfeiture on the bankruptcy of the lessee or on taking in execution of the lessee's interest is contained in any lease, other than a lease of any of the classes mentioned in the last subsection then—

(*a*) if the lessee's interest is sold within one year from the bankruptcy or taking in execution, this section applies to the forfeiture condition as aforesaid;

(*b*) if the lessee's interest is not sold before the expiration of that year, this section only applies to the forfeiture condition aforesaid during the first year from the date of the bankruptcy or taking in execution.

The effect of those subsections is that, save in the limited circumstances set out in subs (9), s 146 applies:

(1) forever, if the lease is sold within one year from the bankruptcy or winding-up;

(2) for a period of one year only, if the lease is not sold within that year.

Nothing in subss (9) or (10) affects the right of sub-tenants to apply for an order under s 146(4) (s 1 of the Law of Property (Amendment) Act 1929), as to which see p 54.

Waiver

Introduction

The landlord waives the right to forfeit if, after becoming aware of the breach, he does any act which unequivocally recognises the continued existence of the tenancy:

> The basic principle is that the court leans against forfeitures. Therefore, if a landlord, after he knows of a breach of covenant entitling him to forfeit a lease, either communicates to the tenant his election to treat the tenancy as continuing, or does any act which recognises the existence of the tenancy or is inconsistent with its determination, he is deemed to have waived the forfeiture. It is for the lessee to establish the facts which in law constitute the waiver. (*David Blackstone Ltd v Burnetts (West End) Ltd* [1973] 3 All ER 782, per Swanwick J at 790f).

There is no waiver if at the time of the landlord's act he has no actual or implied knowledge of the breach (see *Official Custodian for Charities v Parway Estates Development Ltd* [1984] 3 All ER 679). The landlord must have knowledge of the breach before he can be said to have waived his right to forfeit. The knowledge required to put the landlord to his election is the knowledge of the basic facts which in law constitute the breach of covenant entitling him to forfeit the lease. Where the landlord suspects the breach but feels unable to prove it, see *Van Haarlam v*

Kasner [1992] 2 EGLR 59 at 63. If he wishes to forfeit he will usually be best advised not to demand rent or take any other steps that may be construed as a waiver whilst he investigates the position.

Once the landlord or his agent, such as an employee working at the premises, has the requisite knowledge any appropriate act by the landlord or his agent will in law effect a waiver or a forfeiture (*David Blackstone Ltd v Burnetts (West End) Ltd* [1973] 3 All ER 782; *Metropolitan Properties Co Ltd v Cordery* (1979) 39 P&CR 10):

> It is also clear . . . that a principal is affected by the knowledge of his agent and that he cannot escape the consequences of an act done by one agent by saying that it was not that agent but another that had the actual knowledge. . . . the knowledge required to put a landlord to his election is knowledge of the basic facts that in law constitute a breach of covenant entitling him to forfeit the lease. Once he or his agent knows these facts, an appropriate act by himself or any agent will in law effect a waiver or a forfeiture. His knowledge or ignorance of the law is . . . irrelevant. (*David Blackstone Ltd v Burnetts (West End) Ltd* [1973] 3 All ER 782, per Swanick J at p789h, 795c).

However, simply allowing the tenant to commit the breach without doing anything to prevent it is not sufficient to amount to a waiver (*Perry v Davies* (1858) CB(NS) 769).

To constitute a waiver the election must be communicated to the tenant:

> The landlord has an election whether to waive or to forfeit, and it seems to me as at present advised that a statement or act by the landlord which is neither communicated to the tenant nor can have any impact on the tenant should not be taken to be an election to waive the forfeiture (*London & County (A&D) Ltd v Wilfred Sportsman Ltd* [1971] Ch 764, per Russell LJ at 782A; see also Swanwick J at 793c in *David Blackstone Ltd v Burnetts (West End) Ltd* [1973] 3 All ER 782).

'Continuing' and 'once and for all' breaches

In considering whether or not a breach has been waived it is necessary to distinguish between 'continuing' and 'once and for all' breaches. Where the breach is a continuing one (eg where the tenant is failing to keep the premises in good repair), the landlord will not be able to forfeit in respect of the earlier stage of the breach that he has waived, but he may forfeit for any continuation of the breach that has occurred since the waiver. Thus, if the tenant continues to fail to repair the premises after the waiver the landlord may forfeit. If a notice under s146 of the Law of Property Act 1925 has previously been served in respect of the breach there is no need to serve a further notice if there has been no change in the condition of the premises (*Greenwich London Borough Council v Discreet Selling Estates Ltd* [1990] 2 EGLR 65; see p15).

In most cases there is no difficulty in distinguishing between 'continuing' and 'once and for all' breaches. For example, failure to pay rent is a 'once and for all' breach that can be waived by subsequent action (*Church Commissioners for England v Nodjoumi* (1986) 51 P&CR 155). Breach of the covenant to repair is a 'continuing' breach (*Penton v Barnett* [1898] 1 QB 276; *Greenwich London Borough Council v Discreet Selling Estates Ltd* [1990] 2 EGLR 65); as is breach of the covenant to use the premises as a private residence (*Segal Securities v Thoseby* [1963] 1 QB 887) or only for business use (*Cooper v Henderson* (1982) 263 EG 592 at 594).

The landlord may, of course, forfeit in respect of any breach that has occurred since the waiver whether the new breach is a 'continuing' or 'once and for all' breach. Waiver of the breach does not waive the existence of the covenant (see *below*, p37).

Waiver by acceptance etc of rent

Acceptance of rent   Acceptance of rent payable in arrears, as a matter of law, waives the right to forfeit. The landlord may not protect his position by accepting the rent 'without prejudice' to that right. He must make an election: forfeiture or acceptance of the rent. He cannot have both (*Segal Securities v Thoseby* [1963] 1 QB 887 at 898).

Acceptance of future rent payable in advance waives a 'once and for all' breach which has occurred in the past (*Segal Securities* at 901) and apparently a breach which occurs in the period covered by the rent (*Segal Securities* at 901; but is this correct?). So far as 'continuing' breaches are concerned the acceptance of rent in advance can only waive those breaches that are at the time of the demand known to be 'continuing' and will only waive them for such periods as it is definitely known they will continue:

> . . . I now turn to the important and decisive question as to the circumstances in which a demand for or acceptance of rent payable in advance constitutes a waiver of breaches during the period covered by the rent demanded. Clearly it cannot be a waiver of future breaches of which the landlord has no advance knowledge . . . Equally clearly, an acceptance of rent in advance does waive a once and for all—that is to say, a non-continuing—breach in the past: such a waiver applies both to the past and to the period covered by the rent.
>
> As regards continuing breaches, it seems to me that, in the absence of express agreement, the acceptance of rent in advance can at highest only waive those breaches that are at the time of demand known to be continuing, and to waive them for such period as it is definitely known they will continue. (*Segal Securities Ltd v Thoseby* [1963] 1 QB 887 per Sachs J at 901).

It is important to note that acceptance *after* the event giving the landlord the right to forfeiture of the *rent that accrued prior* to that date does not waive the right to forfeit in respect of that breach (*Stephens v Junior Army and Navy Stores Ltd* [1914] 2 Ch 516 at 523).

Where, in order to avoid waiver of the breach, the landlord refuses to accept rent he will subsequently be able to claim mesne profits (damages for use and occupation) in proceedings for possession and may seek an order for an interim payment in those proceedings (RSC Ord 29, r18; CCR Ord 13, r12).

Where the landlord delays in returning rental payments he may be held to have accepted the rent and waived the right to forfeit. However, if the rent is returned within a reasonable time of receipt he will not be regarded as having done so. Some delay will be acceptable particularly if the landlord has written stating that he will not accept rent. Every case will turn upon its own facts, the issue in each case being whether or not the landlord can be said to have accepted the rent (*John Lewis Properties plc v Viscount Chelsea* [1993] 2 EGLR 77 ChD).

Demand for rent An unambiguous demand for rent that has accrued since the right to forfeit has arisen is no different from acceptance of rent. It amounts in law to an election to treat the tenancy as continuing and waives the right to forfeit if at the time it is made the landlord has sufficient knowledge (see *above*) of the facts to put him to his election. It does not matter that the demand was sent by mistake by a person employed by the landlord or his agent who has no personal knowledge of the breach. Likewise, the mere fact that the landlord did not intend to waive the breach is irrelevant (*David Blackstone v Burnetts (West End) Ltd* [1973] 3 All ER 782; *Central Estates (Belgravia) Ltd v Woolgar (No2)* [1972] 3 All ER 610).

Distress for rent The general rule is that a distraint for rent does waive a prior breach (*Doe d David v Williams* (1835) 7 C&P 322). However, where the lease provides that a landlord may not forfeit for non-payment of rent until he has attempted to distrain for the rent, any such act of distraint does not operate as a waiver (*Shepherd v Berger* [1891] 1 QB 597). In that case, part of the arrears were recovered by the distraint but that did not prevent the landlord from being able to forfeit in respect of the balance (see also s139(1) of the County Courts Act 1984 (p44) and s210 of the Common Law Procedure Act 1952 where the proceedings are in the High Court). Note that it is not possible to distrain in respect of various statutorily protected tenancies without leave of the county court (s147 of the Rent Act 1977; s8 of the Rent (Agriculture) Act 1976; s19 of the Housing Act 1988).

Proceedings for rent To bring a straightforward claim for rent is clearly no different from a demand for rent and thus waives the right to forfeit (*Dendy v Nicholl* (1858) 4 CB(NS) 376).

However, it often occurs that the tenant is in breach of covenant. The landlord serves a notice under s146 of the Law of Property Act 1925, but before he commences proceedings a further quarter's rent falls due. If the rent is tendered and accepted the landlord waives the right to forfeit. If no rent is tendered may the landlord seek to forfeit in respect of both the earlier breach and the non-payment of rent and may he claim the arrears in the proceedings? The arguments each way are as follows.

On the one hand, the service of proceedings for possession is an unequivocal election to forfeit and anything else done or claimed in the proceedings cannot amount to a waiver. On the other hand, a claim based upon non-payment of rent implies that the landlord considers the lease to be in existence on the date upon which the rent falls due. Such a claim is therefore inconsistent with an election to treat the lease as forfeited.

The decision in *Dendy v Nicholl* is sometimes cited as authority for the proposition that one may not make a claim for possession based upon forfeiture and claim arrears of rent. However, in *Penton v Barnett* [1898] 1 QB 276 it was stated that *Dendy v Nicholl* is simply authority for the proposition that an action for rent is as good as a waiver of forfeiture as an action of possession is a forfeiture of the tenancy. In *Penton v Barnett* the lease contained a covenant to repair and the landlord served a s 146 notice requiring the tenant to repair within three months. Three days after the expiration of the notice a quarter's rent became due. No repairs having been carried out the landlord brought an action for possession based on the breach of covenant and non-payment of rent and in the proceedings claimed the quarter's rent (the defendant paid the rent into court). The Court of Appeal held that as the breach of covenant was a continuing one the claim for rent did not affect the right to possession in respect of non-repair after the date when the rent fell due. The implication is that the claim for rent in the proceedings did waive the failure to repair up to the date upon which the rent fell due and that if the breach had been a 'once and for all' breach the claim for rent would have waived the breach.

> The position on January 14, 1897 would be that as nothing had been done since the notice as to repairs, the plaintiff had the right to determine the tenancy by the issue of the writ, and to sue in respect of such rights as had accrued to him during the tenancy. . . . Then he brought his action for possession, and in it he claimed for a quarter's rent due on the previous December 25. In my opinion, this claim does not constitute a waiver of the forfeiture. All that was laid down in *Dendy v Nicholl* was that an action for rent was as good as a waiver of forfeiture as an action of ejectment was as a determination of the tenancy. If there had not been a recurring breach, but something which had happened once and for all, the state of things might have been different; but in this case, in my opinion, there is nothing in the statement of claim inconsistent with an election to determine the lease from December 25. (*Penton v Barnett* [1898] 1 QB 276 per Rigby LJ at 280–1.)

In conclusion, therefore, it would seem that a claim for arrears of rent that is included in proceedings for possession based upon forfeiture for breach of covenant will waive the breach if it is a 'once and for all' breach but not if it is a 'continuing' breach (see also the discussion of *Penton v Barnett* in *Greenwich LBC v Discreet Selling Estates Ltd* [1990] 2 EGLR 65 at 67).

After reentry has occurred the landlord is entitled to bring a claim for the rent that accrued prior to the reentry (*Hartshorne v Watson* (1838) 4 Bing NC 178). Perhaps, therefore, the solution is to commence proceedings for possession based upon forfeiture for the breach of covenant with an *alternative* claim based upon forfeiture for non-payment of rent but not to include a claim for those arrears. Once those proceedings have been served (ie once the reentry is deemed to have taken place; see p39) a claim for rent up to the date of service of the proceedings (ie the date of reentry) and for mesne profits thereafter can be issued and served. The two actions can then be consolidated.

Waiver by other means

Where no demand for rent is involved different considerations apply. The general principle was set out in *Expert Clothing Service and Sales Ltd v Hillgate House Ltd* [1985] 2 All ER 998.

> In the present case where no acceptance of rent (or demand for rent) is involved, the court is, I think, free to look at *all* the circumstances of the case to consider whether [the landlord's act] was so unequivocal that, when considered objectively, it could only be regarded as having been done consistently with the continued existence of a tenancy. (per Slade LJ at 1012c).

This general principle should always be borne in mind but there are also authorities dealing with particular circumstances.

Service of a notice to quit   Service of a valid notice to quit recognises the continuing existence of the lease and thus waives the right to forfeit (*Marche v Christodoulakis* (1948) 64 TLR 466).

Service of a s146 notice   As the purpose and effect of a s146 notice is to operate as a preliminary to actual forfeiture (see p14), service of such a notice cannot be an unequivocal affirmation of the existence of the lease and therefore does not operate to waive a right to forfeit (*Church Commissioners for England v Nodjoumi* (1986) 51 P&CR 155); but a notice served under s146 should not contain a demand for arrears of rent accruing since the breach complained of in the notice because the demand may possibly waive that breach, it not being necessary to serve a s146 notice in respect of arrears of rent.

Negotiations that recognise the continued existence of the tenancy   In *Expert Clothing* the sending of a letter enclosing a proposed deed of variation was not, on the facts, regarded as a waiver but it was recognised that in certain circumstances the proffering of a mere negotiating document might amount to an unequivocal recognition of the existence of a presently subsisting tenancy (at p1012). But it seems that it will be necessary to know the terms of the negotiations before it will be held that the right to forfeit has been waived. The mere fact that negotiations have taken place will be insufficient and the court will not have regard to the contents of 'without prejudice' negotiations (*Re National Jazz Centre Ltd* [1988] 2 EGLR 57).

> The test that was adopted by Slade LJ in *Expert Clothing* . . . was whether the sending of a letter in the course of negotiations could be reasonably understood as unequivocally indicating the landlord's intention to treat the lease as subsisting on the date of the letter.
>
> The facts of that case were much stronger than the present case in favour of the tenant's submission of the existence of the lease, in that a draft had been proffered which referred to the continuation of a lease. Nevertheless, the Court of Appeal held that there had been no such waiver. That case in itself demonstrates that the mere existence of negotiations is not sufficient to show that the landlord participating in the negotiations is accepting that the tenancy does not exist and that there has been no forfeiture. It is true that if rent is proffered and accepted without prejudice, the court will look at the fact of acceptance of the rent and will hold that is sufficient to constitute an admission of the existence of the lease and a waiver of any forfeiture said to have occurred prior to that date. But I cannot see that there is any similarity between the acceptance of a rent without prejudice and the mere entering into of negotiations. It is impossible, in my judgment, to reach a conclusion that there has been an unequivocal acceptance of the existence of a lease by the entering into of negotiations, without looking at what occurred in the [without prejudice] negotiations themselves, and that, it is quite clear . . . is something which the court cannot do. (per Gibson J at 58H).

Grant of a reversionary lease   The grant of a reversionary lease 'subject to and with the benefit' of the tenant's lease does not waive the right to forfeit. It is not an unequivocal act of recognition of the pre-existing lease and as a statement or act which is neither communicated to nor could have any impact on the tenant is not an election to waive a right to forfeit (*London & County (A&D) Ltd v Wilfred Sportsman Ltd* [1971] 1 ChD 764).

Court proceedings; injunction claim   A claim in forfeiture proceedings for possession and an injunction restraining the tenant from continuing with the breaches will waive the right to forfeit. However, the landlord may seek an injunction in the alternative without waiving the right to forfeit (*Calabar Properties Ltd v Seagull Autos Ltd* [1969] 1 Ch 451). For an example of a recent case where the landlord waived his right to forfeit by seeking an injunction (as well as demanding rent) see *Iperion Investments Corporation v Broadwalk House Residents Ltd* [1992] 2 EGLR 235).

Waiver of breach does not waive the covenant

It is sometimes thought that a waiver of a breach amounts to a waiver of the covenant, for example, that a waiver by the landlord of a particular subletting in breach of covenant prevents the landlord from complaining about sublettings that may occur in the future. This view is incorrect. Section 148 of the Law of Property Act 1925 expressly provides that this is not so 'unless a contrary intention appears'.

Section 148 of the Law of Property Act 1925
    148.—(1) Where any actual waiver by a lessor or the persons deriving title under him of the benefit of any covenant or condition in any lease is proved to have taken place in any particular instance, such waiver shall not be deemed to extend to any instance, or to any breach of covenant or condition save that to which such waiver specially relates, nor operate as a general waiver of the benefit of any such covenant or condition.
    (2) This section applies unless a contrary intention appears . . .

However, circumstances may arise where the landlord is estopped from relying on a term of the lease (*Central London Property Trust Ltd v High Trees House Ltd* [1947] KB 130; *Brikom Investments Ltd v Carr* [1979] 2 All ER 753).

Clauses that attempt to avoid waiver

Some leases contain a proviso to the effect that the right to forfeit will continue notwithstanding the acceptance of or demand for rent by the landlord with knowledge of the breach. However, the consequences of an act, relied on by a tenant as a wavier, are a matter of law and not of intention (*David Blackstone v Burnetts (West End) Ltd* [1973] 3 All ER 782 at 789h). It is, therefore, submitted that any clause in a lease which seeks to permit the landlord to forfeit notwithstanding an act waiving the breach is of no effect.

No waiver after service of proceedings

Once the landlord has unequivocally elected to reenter, whether by service of proceedings for possession or otherwise, no subsequent act will be treated as waiving the right to forfeit (*Civil Service Co-operative Society v McGrigor's Trustee* [1923] 2 Ch 347 at 358). Further receipt of 'rent' may, however, give rise to an inference that a new tenancy has been created (*Evans v Wyatt* (1880) 43 LT 176).

The landlord should not, therefore, accept any monies until after he has served his writ/summons and if he does so he is best advised to do so expressly on the basis that the payments are being accepted as mesne profits (damages for occupation) and that there is no intention to create a new tenancy. (For a specimen letter see Form 6, p38.) Receipt of monies in such circumstances does not create a new tenancy because

Form 6: Letter accepting mesne profits

Dear

RE: _____

Please find enclosed a county court summons claiming possession of the property which you occupy at _____ .

All further payments in respect of your occupation of the property should be sent to _____ at _____. These payments will be accepted by your landlord as damages for your use and occupation of the property whilst the proceedings continue, it being clearly understood that acceptance by the landlord of such sums does not give rise to the creation of a new tenancy.

Yours etc

---

there is no intention to create legal relations (see discussion of *Street v Mountford,* p93). See also the ability to apply for interim payments in respect of mesne profits (p270).

The act of reentry

Where an event has occurred permitting the landlord to forfeit, he must do some act evidencing his intention to reenter. Service of proceedings for possession is equivalent to an act of reentry and this is the normal method by which a landlord of residential premises forfeits a lease (see p39). Two other methods of reentry are as follows.

Peaceable reentry

At common law peaceable reentry brings the lease to an end, but a landlord is not permitted to enforce a right of reentry where the premises were 'let as a dwelling' otherwise than by proceedings in court while any person is lawfully residing in them or part of them (s2 of the Protection from Eviction Act 1977).

Protection from Eviction Act 1977
> **2.** Where any premises are let as a dwelling on a lease which is subject to a right of reentry or forfeiture it shall not be lawful to enforce that right otherwise than by proceedings in the court while any person is lawfully residing in the premises or part of them.

Where the property is let for mixed residential and business purposes, for example where it consists of a shop with a flat above, the property is probably not to be regarded as having been 'let as a dwelling' and if not the landlord will be entitled to forfeit by peaceably reentering the shop (see p211 for Rent Act cases in relation to mixed business and residential user of property). However, the point is not beyond doubt and it is at least arguable that the Rent Act cases referred to do not assist when one is interpreting the Protection from Eviction Act 1977, the clear purpose of which is generally to prevent a landlord from taking possession otherwise than by court proceedings where persons are living in them (except where one of the exceptions applies; see p225). In any event, any reentry must be peaceful. The landlord may not use force to enter the property where there is someone in occupation (s6 of the Criminal Law Act 1977; see p259). Furthermore, although forfeiture of the head lease by reentry to the shop may possibly be lawful, that forfeiture of the head lease will not destroy a sub-tenancy which is assured (s18(1) of the Housing Act (1988, p117), and any eviction of the assured tenant is prohibited by s1 of the Protection from Eviction Act 1977. Self-help is, therefore, only a practical proposition where the premises are clearly abandoned and any landlord who reenters otherwise than by court proceedings where persons are in residence is to be regarded as foolhardy.

For a reentry to be effective the landlord must actually reenter the property with the intention of terminating the tenancy but he does not need to be in possession for any substantial period of time (*Billson v Residential Apartments Ltd* [1992] 1 All ER 141, HL).

If the circumstances are such that the tenant appears to have disappeared from the property and the landlord has merely reentered for the purpose of securing the premises the lease will not have been brought to an end (*Relvock Properties Ltd v Dixon* (1972) 25 P&CR 1, CA).

Dealing with sub-tenants and other persons in actual occupation

In principle, it is possible to effect a reentry of premises, where the person in occupation is a sub-tenant or trespasser as against the tenant, by coming to an arrangement with the occupier whereby that person remains in occupation as the immediate tenant of the landlord on the terms of a new tenancy (*London & County (A&D) Ltd v Wilfred Sportsman Ltd* [1970] 2 All ER 600; *Ashton v Sobelman* [1987] 1 All ER 755 at 763f and 764h; *Hammersmith and Fulham London Borough Council v Top Shop* [1989] 2 All ER 655 at 669e). However, where any such person is lawfully residing in the dwelling any such arrangement would, it is submitted, amount to a breach of s2 of the Protection from Eviction Act 1977 and is not permitted.

Forfeiture proceedings

Introduction

In nearly all cases a landlord of residential premises will forfeit the lease by taking proceedings for possession (see *above*). Where he does so it is the service of the summons or writ (not its issue) which operates as the decisive election to forfeit and which is equivalent to reentry. The lease is determined from the date of service. Thereafter, the former tenant remains in occupation as a trespasser and the landlord's claim is a claim for possession. Forfeiture as such is not claimed in the prayer to the proceedings. Rather, it is the basis upon which the claim for possession is made (see Form 3, p21).

The following consequences result from the rule that it is the service of the proceedings that brings the lease to an end. Firstly, rent is payable by the tenant up until the date of service of the proceedings. From that date the landlord is entitled to recover payments for the occupation of the land from the ex-tenant as trespasser, as mesne profits (damages for use and occupation), see *Canas Property Co Ltd v K L Television Services Ltd* [1970] 2 All ER 795, CA. See further Chapter 23, Rent Cases (p329). Secondly, from the date of service of the proceedings the tenant is no longer bound by any of the other covenants in the lease, such as the covenant to repair. If after that date the ex-tenant damages the property the landlord's remedy will be in tort (*Associated Deliveries Ltd v Harrison* (1984) 50 P&CR 91, CA).

> . . . in appropriate proceedings it seems to me that the landlord could well have a very adequate remedy in a claim for damages for wrongful occupation of the land . . . the authorities seem to indicate that in appropriately constituted proceedings the damages recoverable could extend beyond mere payment for the use and occupation of land, to include any loss within the ordinary rules of remoteness of damage which the plaintiff has suffered from being denied possession of the property and so unable to secure and occupy the property for his own purposes. (per Dillon LJ at 103).

Between service of the proceedings and the final conclusion of the action there is a 'twilight period' during which it is not clear whether the forfeiture is going to be effective. It may be that the landlord will not establish his allegations or that the tenant will succeed in an application for relief from forfeiture. As will be seen below, if relief from forfeiture is granted the tenant is restored to his original position as if the lease had never been forfeited. The tenant can enforce the landlord's covenants during this period if he is claiming relief (*Peninsula Maritime Ltd v Padseal Ltd* (1981) 259 EG 860).

The Particulars of Claim/Writ

Where the proceedings are brought in the county court the Particulars of Claim must be endorsed with the name and address of any person entitled to claim relief against forfeiture as undertenant, including a mortgagee, and where such particulars are stated an extra copy of the Particulars of Claim should be filed with the court for service on that person (CCR Ord 6, r3(2); see further p265 in respect of proceedings generally and p319 where the proceedings include a claim for rent *in* prescribed form to be used).

Form 7: Defence and counterclaim for relief from forfeiture

IN THE   **COUNTY COURT**   **Case No**

BETWEEN

Plaintiff

—AND—

Defendant

DEFENCE

1. to 5.   [*admit and deny the allegations in the Particulars of Claim as appropriate*]

COUNTERCLAIM

6.   If, which is denied, the said lease has become liable to be forfeited the Defendant seeks to be relieved from the forfeiture on such terms as the court shall think fit.

AND the Defendant counterclaims for relief from forfeiture upon such terms as the court shall think fit.

DATED   [*signed*]

To the Plaintiff and
the District Judge

Where the proceedings are brought in the High Court the Writ must state the name and address of any person the plaintiff knows is entitled to claim relief against forfeiture as undertenant (including a mortgagee) under s146(4) of the Law of Property Act 1925 or in accordance with s38 of the Supreme Court Act 1981 (RSC Ord 6, r2(1)(c)(iii)). Where such particulars are given the plaintiff must send a copy of the writ to the person named (RSC Ord 6, r2(2). See p300 as to the further particulars required to be endorsed on a writ in a claim for possession).

Where the person concerned is a sub-tenant in occupation the landlord may well wish to join him as a party to the proceedings in any event.

The Particulars of Claim or Writ should not include a claim for an injunction in addition to the claim for possession as this may be construed as a waiver of the right to forfeit, although a claim in the alternative may be added (see *above*, p262).

Where the tenant was a protected tenant under the Rent Act 1977 it is necessary for the landlord to obtain an order for possession based upon one of the Rent Act grounds, in addition to the forfeiture, but both the forfeiture and the Rent Act claims should be dealt with together (see p328. For the relationship between forfeiture and assured tenancies see p108, and for the position in relation to secure tenancies see p167).

Registration of the action

A claim for the forfeiture of a lease is a 'pending land action' within the meaning of s17(1) of the Land Charges Act 1972 and is, therefore, registerable as a 'pending action' under s5 of the 1972 Act (*Selim Ltd v Bickenhall Engineering Ltd* [1981] 3 All ER 210). Where the land is registered the action may be protected by entry of a caution against dealings (s59(1)(5) of the Land Registration Act 1925).

Summary judgment

It is not possible to obtain summary judgment in the county court (CCR Ord 9, r14(1)(*b*)—the fact that there is an early hearing date in a fixed date action renders it unnecessary; see p269).

It is highly unlikely that any claim for possession of residential premises will be brought in the High Court (see p259), but if proceedings are brought in the High Court and summary judgment is sought under RSC Ord 14 those acting for the tenant should bear in mind the case of *Liverpool Properties Ltd v Oldbridge Investments Ltd* [1985] 2 EGLR 111. It was held that a claim for relief is inextricably linked to the landlord's claim for possession and that if genuine and arguable it amounts to an arguable defence precluding the making of an order for possession on an application for summary judgment. There will be few cases where the court comes to the conclusion that the tenant's application for relief is bound to fail (*Sambrin Investments Ltd v Taborn* [1990] 1 EGLR 61 per Gibson J at 63A).

If a practitioner is presented with a case (perhaps initially dealt with by the client in person) where judgment has been given for possession and the claim for relief adjourned, the first step to take is to see whether a stay of execution has been granted. If not it should be applied for immediately, if necessary in the first instance by *ex parte* application. If no application for relief has been issued, such an application should be issued immediately. The tenant may apply for relief pursuant to RSC Ord 14, r10 (see further p302).

Company in liquidation; the 'Blue Jeans' order

If the letting was a 'company let' and the tenant is a company in liquidation under a winding-up order which has no defence to a claim for possession based upon forfeiture the landlord may, instead of issuing a writ (which would require leave from the companies court) and making an application for summary judgment, seek an order for possession in the winding-up (*Re Blue Jeans Sales Ltd* [1979] 1 All ER 641—possession was sought on the ground that the lease was forfeit by reason of non-payment of rent. It was not disputed that there were substantial arrears).

In *Re Blue Jeans Sales Ltd* the company had sublet and there were sub-tenants in occupation. The question arose as to their protection as they were obviously not a party to the proceedings. The court held that the parties in actual occupation were protected by RSC Ord 45, r3 (see p304) which precludes the Companies Registrar from giving leave to issue a writ of possession until notice to the occupiers has been given enabling them to apply for relief from forfeiture.

Relief from forfeiture; non-payment of rent

County court

Sections 138 to 140 of the County Courts Act 1984 (as amended) contain the rules relating to relief from forfeiture where proceedings are brought in the county court. Section 138 applies where the landlord has commenced proceedings for possession. Section 139(2) applies where the landlord has reentered the property without taking proceedings.

County Courts Act 1984, ss138—140

    138.—(1) This section has effect where a lessor is proceeding by action in a county court (being an action in which the county court has jurisdiction) to enforce against a lessee a right of reentry or forfeiture in respect of any land for non-payment of rent.

    (2) If the lessee pays into court or to the lessor not less than 5 clear days before the return day all the rent in arrear and the costs of the action, the action shall cease, and the lessee shall hold the land according to the lease without any new lease.

    (3) If—
        (*a*) the action does not cease under subsection (2); and
        (*b*) the court at the trial is satisfied that the lessor is entitled to enforce the right of reentry or forfeiture,
the court shall order possession of the land to be given to the lessor at the expiration of such period, not being less than 4 weeks from the date of the order, as the court thinks fit, unless within that period the lessee pays into court or to the lessor all the rent in arrear and the costs of the action.

    (3A) . . .

    (4) The court may extend the period specified under subsection (3) at any time before possession of the land is recovered in pursuance of the order under that subsection.

    (5) If—
        (*a*) within the period specified in the order; or
        (*b*) within that period as extended under subsection (4), the lessee pays into court or to the lessor—
          (i) all the rent in arrear; and
          (ii) the costs of the action,
he shall hold the land according to the lease without any new lease.

    (6) Subsection (2) shall not apply where the lessor is proceeding in the same action to enforce a right of reentry or forfeiture on any other ground as well as for non-payment of rent, or to enforce any other claim as well as the right of reentry or forfeiture and the claim for arrears of rent.

    (7) If the lessee does not—
        (*a*) within the period specified in the order; or

(b) within that period as extended under subsection (4), pay into court or to the lessor—
    (i) all the rent in arrear; and
    (ii) the costs of the action,

the order shall be enforceable in the prescribed manner and so long as the order remains unreversed the lessee shall, subject to subsections (8) and (9A), be barred from all relief.

(8) The extension under subsection (4) of a period fixed by a court shall not be treated as relief from which the lessee is barred by subsection (7) if he fails to pay into court or to the lessor all the rent in arrear and the costs of the action within that period.

(9) Where the court extends a period under subsection (4) at a time when—
    (a) that period has expired; and
    (b) a warrant has been issued for the possession of the land,

the court shall suspend the warrant for the extended period; and, if, before the expiration period, the lessee pays into court or to the lessor all the rent in arrear and all the costs of the action, the court shall cancel the warrant.

(9A) Where the lessor recovers possession of the land at any time after the making of the order under subsection (3) (whether as a result of the enforcement of the order or otherwise) the lessee may, at any time within 6 months from the date on which the lessor recovers possession, apply to the court for relief; and on any such application the court may, if it thinks fit, grant to the lessee such relief, subject to such terms and conditions, as it thinks fit.

(9B) Where the lessee is granted relief on an application under subsection (9A) he shall hold the land according to the lease without any new lease.

(9C) An application under subsection (9A) may be made by a person with an interest under a lease of the land derived (whether immediately or otherwise) from the lessee's interest therein in like manner as if he were the lessee; and on any such application the court may make an order which (subject to such terms and conditions as the court thinks fit) vests the land in such a person, as lessee of the lessor, for the remainder of the term of the lease under which he has any such interest as aforesaid, or for any lesser term.

In this subsection any reference to the land includes a reference to part of the land.

(10) Nothing in this section or section 139 shall be taken to affect—
    (a) the power of the court to make any order which it would otherwise have power to make as respects a right of reentry or forfeiture on any ground other than non-payment of rent; or
    (b) section 146(4) of the Law of Property Act 1925 (relief against forfeiture).

139.—(1) In a case where section 138 has effect, if—
    (a) one-half-year's rent is in arrear at the time of the commencement of the action; and
    (b) the lessor has a right to reenter for non-payment of that rent; and
    (c) no sufficient distress is to be found on the premises countervailing the arrears then due,

the service of the summons in the action in the prescribed manner shall stand in lieu of a demand and reentry.

(2) Where a lessor has enforced against a lessee, by reentry without action, a right of reentry or forfeiture as respects any land for non-payment of rent, the lessee may, at any time within six months from the date on which the lessor reentered, apply to the county court for relief, and on any such application the court may, if it thinks fit, grant to the lessee such relief as the High Court could have granted.

(3) Subsections (9B) and (9C) of section 138 shall have effect in relation to an application under subsection (2) of this section as they have effect in relation to an application under subsection (9A) of that section.

140.—For the purposes of sections 138 and 139—

'lease' includes—

    (*a*) an original or derivative under-lease;

    (*b*) an agreement for a lease where the lessee has become entitled to have his lease granted; and

    (*c*) a grant at a fee farm rent, or under a grant securing a rent by condition;

'lessee' includes—

    (*a*) an original or derivative under-lessee;

    (*b*) the persons deriving title under a lessee;

    (*c*) a grantee under a grant at a fee farm rent, or under a grant securing a rent by condition; and

    (*d*) the persons deriving title under such a grantee;

'lessor' includes—

    (*a*) an original or derivative under-lessor;

    (*b*) the persons deriving title under a lessor;

    (*c*) a person making a grant at a fee farm rent, or a grant securing a rent by condition; and

    (*d*) the persons deriving title under such a grantor;

'under-lease' includes an agreement for an under-lease where the under-lessee has become entitled to have his under-lease granted; and 'under-lessee' includes any person deriving title under an under-lessee.

Particular points to note are as follows:

(1) There is an automatic grant of relief if all the arrears and costs are paid into court not less than five clear days before the return date (s 138(2)). The 'return date' is the date stated on the summons for the hearing of the claim for possession. Thus, if the hearing does not go ahead on that date the tenant may not take advantage of this provision by paying the arrears and fixed court fee and fixed solicitor's costs not less than five clear days prior to the actual hearing (*Swordheath Properties Ltd v Bolt* [1992] 2 EGLR 68, CA). He will have to rely upon the other relief provisions in the section and pay any further costs that have been incurred in the meantime and that he may be ordered to pay.

(2) Where the money is not paid into court more than five clear days prior to the return date so that the case proceeds the court must give the tenant at least four weeks to pay the arrears and costs (s 138(3)).

(3) The order for possession is in County Court Form N27 (Appendix 3; see further Chapter 23, Rent Cases, p 328).

(4) An application for an extension under s 138(4) should be made on notice (CCR Ord 13, r1).

(5) The words 'the lessee shall be barred from all relief' in subs (7) mean barred from relief in all courts. The tenant may not, therefore, attempt to obtain relief in the High Court relying upon that court's inherent jurisdiction (*Di Palma v Victoria Square Property Co Ltd* [1985] 2 All ER 676), but by virtue of subs (9A) the tenant may apply for relief in the county court at any time within six months from the date on which the landlord recovers possession.

(6) For the exercise of the discretion in cases where an application for relief is made under s 138(9A) or s 139(2) after reentry see the cases mentioned *below* in relation to High Court applications for relief (p41). See Form 8, 47 for an order granting relief.

(7) Sub-tenants and mortgagees may apply for relief under s 138(9C)—see further p54.

(8) Where the tenancy is in joint names it is probably necessary for any application under s 138(9C) or by a tenant pursuant to s 139(2) to be made by all the joint tenants (cf *TM Fairclough & Sons Ltd v Berliner* [1931] 1 Ch 60; *Jacobs v Chaudhuri* [1968] 2 QB 470).

Relief: High Court

Supreme Court Act 1981, s38

(1) In any action in the High Court for the forfeiture of a lease for non-payment of rent, the court shall have power to grant relief against forfeiture in a summary manner, and may do so subject to the same terms and conditions as to the payment of rent, costs or otherwise as could have been imposed by it in such an action immediately before the commencement of this Act.

(2) Where the lessee or a person deriving title under him is granted relief under this section, he shall hold the demised premises in accordance with the terms of the lease without the necessity for a new lease.

Time limits for applications   Where there are at least six months' rent in arrears, if at any time before the trial of the landlord's claim for possession the tenant pays or tenders to the landlord or pays into court all the rent and arrears due, together with the costs, the proceedings are automatically discontinued, and the tenant holds the property without any need for a new lease (s212 of the Common Law Procedure Act 1852; *Standard Pattern Co Ltd v Ivey* [1962] Ch 432).

If the tenant fails to pay this sum before the trial he may apply for relief thereafter (s38 of the Supreme Court Act 1981). The application must, however, be made within six months of the order for possession being

Form 8: Order granting relief from forfeiture

IN THE   COUNTY COURT

BETWEEN:

[Name of landlord]   *Plaintiff*

—AND—

[Name of tenant]   *Defendant*

Upon the application of the Defendant[1] for relief from forfeiture dated _____

And upon hearing Counsel for the Plaintiff and for the Defendant

It is ordered that

1. Upon payment by the Defendant to the Plaintiff of the sums referred to below within _____ days of the date hereof the Defendant be granted relief from forfeiture of the lease dated _____ 19 _____ of the premises known as _____ and that the Defendant thereafter do hold the premises according to the lease without the grant of a new lease. The sums referred to are as follows:

    (1) £_____ in respect of rent, mesne profits and service charges for the whole of the period up to the date hereof; and

    (2) £_____ on account[2] of the Plaintiff's costs of the action including the costs occasioned by the Defendant's application for relief from forfeiture.

2. The Defendant do pay the Plaintiff's costs of the application for relief to be taxed if not agreed.[3]

3. If the Defendant fails to pay the sums referred to in paragraph 1 to the Plaintiff within the said period of _____ days (or within such further period or periods as the parties may agree or the Court may allow) the Defendant's application for relief from forfeiture shall stand dismissed and the Defendant shall pay the Plaintiff's costs of and occasioned by the said application to be taxed on Scale _____ if not agreed.

DATED

Notes:

[1] This form assumes that the application is made in the landlord's proceedings for possession. If made by way of separate proceedings it will need to be adapted accordingly.

[2] This provision allows for relief to take effect without waiting for a taxation of the landlord's costs.

[3] As the landlord will have obtained an order for costs in the possession action it is not necessary to make an order for such costs here.

executed. After six months have elapsed he is barred from applying for relief (s210 of the Common Law Procedure Act 1852).

Where the tenant owes less than six months' rent or the landlord has reentered without the benefit of a court order the tenant may apply for relief at any time after the order has been made. There is no six-month time limit but the court will take into account any delay when deciding whether or not relief should be granted (*Thatcher v Pearce & Sons* [1968] 1 WLR 748).

Method of application   Where the landlord has brought proceedings for possession the application for relief may be made by way of counterclaim or summons in the landlord's proceedings or informally during the course of the hearing of the landlord's claim (*Lam Kee Ying Sdn Bhd v Lam Shes Tong* [1974] 3 All ER 137). Alternatively, the tenant may commence his own proceedings by way of writ or originating summons (RSC Ord 5 r4(1), Ord7; Form No 8 in Appendix A). The procedure to be adopted where an application is made by originating summons is contained in RSC Ord 28. There are automatic time limits for service of affidavit evidence and setting down for hearing etc. Application for relief by writ or originating summons is the procedure to adopt if the landlord reenters otherwise than by court proceedings.

Where the tenancy is in joint names it is probably necessary for all the joint tenants to join in the application for relief together (see *T M Fairclough & Sons Ltd v Berliner* [1931] 1 Ch 60; *Jacobs v Chaudhuri* [1968] 2 QB 470).

Exercise of discretion to grant relief   The court may grant relief on such terms and conditions as to the payment of rent, costs or otherwise as the court thinks fit (s38 of the Supreme Court Act 1981). It is well settled law that the purpose of including in a lease a right of reentry for non-payment of rent is to secure payment of rent and that:

> . . . save in exceptional circumstances, the functions of the court in exercising this equitable jurisdiction is to grant relief when all that is due for rent and costs has been paid up, and (in general) to disregard any other causes of complaint that the landlord may have against the tenant (*Gill v Lewis* [1956] 2 QB 1 at 13).

The fact that the tenant has been a bad payer in the past is not even a good reason for refusing relief; nor is the fact that the tenant is insolvent (*Re Brompton Securities Ltd (No 2)* [1988] 3 All ER 677, ChD):

> The case for Langham House [the landlord], in substance, is that it is unfair and unjust that Langham House should have to continue to look for payment of rent and performance of the other covenants in the lease to a company which is admittedly insolvent and which is, in effect, a trustee of the benefit of the lease for another. I do not think that that is a ground for refusing relief. Once arrears are brought up to date Langham House will be in no different position from any other lessor with an impecunious tenant. It would be an entirely new departure for the court to decline to grant relief on the ground that a tenant has been a bad payer in the past and is likely to continue to be a bad payer in the future. (per Vinelott at 680j)

However, where the parties have altered their position prior to the application for relief the court may well refuse relief, particularly where third parties have acquired rights and the effect of the order would be to defeat those rights or would be unfairly prejudicial to the landlord (*Gill v Lewis* [1956] 2 QB 1; *Silverman v AFCO (UK) Ltd* [1988] 1 EGLR 51, CA).

. . . where parties have altered their position in the meantime, and in particular where the rights of third parties have intervened, relief ought not to be granted where the effect of it would be to defeat the new rights of third parties or be unfair to the landlord having regard to the way in which he has altered his position. (*Gill v Lewis*, per Jenkins LJ at p10).

Effect of relief   Where the tenant is relieved from the forfeiture, either by payment made before trial or pursuant to a court order, the tenant holds the demised premises in accordance with the terms of the lease and without the necessity for a new lease (s212 of the Common Law Procedure Act 1852; s38 of the Supreme Court Act 1981).

Where the court considers it appropriate to grant relief, notwithstanding a grant of a new tenancy by the landlord to a third party, it would seem that the tenant (who has applied for relief) will be put into the position of immediate reversioner of the new tenant's lease and entitled to payment of rent from the new tenant (*Fuller v Judy Properties Ltd* [1992] 1 EGLR 75 at p78, CA).

Relief from forfeiture; other covenants

Where the landlord brings proceedings, whether in the county court or the High Court, for forfeiture of a lease or forfeits by actual reentry in respect of a breach of covenant other than by non-payment of rent, the tenant may apply for relief pursuant to s146(2) of the Law of Property Act 1925. Where relief is granted to the tenant the relief reinstates the lease as if there had never been a forfeiture (*Official Custodian for Charities v Mackey* [1984] 3 All ER 689 at 694f).

Relief from forfeiture; section 146(2) of the Law of Property Act 1925
    (2) Where a lessor is proceeding, by action or otherwise, to enforce such a right of reentry or forfeiture, the lessee may, in the lessor's action, if any, or in any action brought by himself, apply to the court for relief; and the court may grant or refuse relief, as the court, having regard to the proceedings and conduct of the parties under the foregoing provisions of this section, and to all the other circumstances, thinks fit; and in case of relief may grant it on such terms, if any, as to costs, expenses, damages, compensation, penalty, or otherwise, including the granting of an injunction to restrain any like breach in the future, as the court, in the circumstances of each case, thinks fit.
    . . .
    (13) The county court has jurisdiction under this section.

Time for applying

The wording of subs(2) of s146 states that the tenant may apply for relief where the landlord '*is proceeding* by action or otherwise to enforce' his right of reentry. The landlord is proceeding the moment he serves his s146 notice (*Pakwood Transport Ltd v 15 Beauchamp Place Ltd* (1977)

245 EG 309). The tenant may therefore apply for relief upon receipt of the notice.

In *Rogers v Rice* [1892] 2 Ch 170 the landlord had forfeited by bringing proceedings. It was held that the words 'is proceeding' mean that the tenant may apply for relief at any time up until the time the landlord has actually reentered pursuant to the order for possession. After that date it is no longer possible to make an application under s146(2). If the landlord has obtained a judgment for possession but has not actually reentered the landlord is still 'proceeding' and the tenant may still apply for relief (*Egerton v Jones* [1939] 2 KB 702).

The decision in *Rogers v Rice* does not apply where the landlord has forfeited by peaceable reentry, in which case the tenant may apply for relief after actual reentry (*Billson v Residential Apartments Ltd* [1992] 1 All ER 141, HL).

Joint tenants

Where the lease is in joint names all the tenants must join in the application for relief (*TM Fairclough & Sons Ltd v Berliner* [1931] 1 Ch 60).

Method of application

In the county court the tenant may apply for relief by the following methods:

(1) By application in the landlord's proceedings (CCR Ord 13, r1).
(2) By counterclaim in the landlord's claim for possession.
(3) By application at the hearing of the landlord's claim for possession (*Lam Kee Ying Sdn Bhd v Lam Shes Tong* [1974] 3 All ER 137).
(4) By originating application (CCR Ord 3, r4; s146(13) of the Law of Property Act 1925, as amended by the High Court and County Court Jurisdiction Order 1991.

In the High Court the tenant may apply for relief by the following methods:

(1) By summons in the landlord's proceedings.
(2) By counterclaim in the landlord's action for possession.
(3) By making application at the hearing of the landlord's claim for possession (*Lam Kee Ying Sdn Bhd v Lam Shes Tong* [1974] 3 All ER 137).
(4) If the landlord is proceeding by way of summary judgment, the tenant may apply for relief on the landlord's summons. If the tenant can show that he has an arguable case for relief he has a defence to the landlord's claim for possession and he should be given unconditional leave to defend.

(5) By writ or originating summons, in the Queen's Bench Division or Chancery Division (RSC Ord 5, r4(1); Ord 7, r2; Form 8, Appendix A). The originating summons procedure is set out in RSC Ord 28.

Exercise of discretion to grant relief to the tenant

The first point to bear in mind when considering whether or not a tenant is likely to be granted relief is the width of the discretion granted to the court by s146(2). The position was clearly stated by the Lord Chancellor, Lord Loreborn, in the leading case of *Hyman v Rose* [1912] AC 623 (in relation to the statutory predecessor to s146):

> . . . the discretion given by the section is very wide. The court is to consider all the circumstances and the conduct of the parties. Now it seems to me that when the Act is so express to provide a wide discretion, meaning, no doubt, to prevent one man from forfeiting what in fair dealing belongs to some one else, by taking advantage of a breach from which he is not commensurately and irreparably damaged, it is not advisable to lay down any rigid rules for guiding that discretion . . . It is not safe I think to say that the court must and always will insist upon certain things when the Act does not require them, and the facts of some unforeseen case may make the court wish it had kept a free hand. (*Hyman v Rose* [1912] AC 623; per Lord Loreborn at p631).

Some of the reported cases (including some referred to *below*) come close to losing sight of this general principle and this needs to be borne in mind when looking at the authorities. For a recent case in which the above statement of Lord Loreborn was considered and applied, see *Southern Depot Co Ltd v British Railways Board* [1990] 2 EGLR 39—referred to *below*, p32.

Remedying the breach as a condition of relief 'In the ordinary way relief is almost always granted to a person who makes good the breach of covenant and is able and willing to fulfil his obligations in the future' (*Bathurst (Earl) v Fine* [1974] 2 All ER 1160, per Lord Denning at 1162h). In accordance with the principle that the court's discretion under s146(2) is unfettered, there is no rule of law that the breach must be remedied prior to the hearing of the application for relief. However, unless there is some good reason why the breach has not been remedied by that date or, at least, that all reasonable steps have been taken to remedy the breach, the court will usually take a dim view of the tenant's case and may exercise its discretion in refusing to grant relief. It will almost invariably require the breach to be remedied as a condition precedent to relief. See *Cremin v Barjack Properties Ltd* [1985] 1 EGLR 30 at 32 CA where the tenant makes good the breach and is able and willing to fulfil his obligations in the future he will usually be granted relief.

'Wilful' breaches It is sometimes argued that the court will not grant relief against forfeiture to a tenant who is in 'wilful breach', except in exceptional circumstances (see *Ropemaker Properties Ltd v Noonhaven*

Ltd [1989] 2 EGLR 50). The following passage of Lord Wilberforce in *Shiloh Spinners v Harding* [1973] AC 691 at 725 is usually relied upon.

> Established and, in my opinion, sound principle requires that wilful breaches should not, or at least should only in exceptional cases, be relieved against, if only for the reason that the assignor should not be compelled to remain in a relation of neighbourhood with a person in deliberate breach of his obligations.

However, *Shiloh Spinners v Harding* was not a case concerned with relief from forfeiture of a lease and in *Southern Depot Co Ltd v British Railways Board* [1990] 2 EGLR 39 Morritt J refused to hold that relief was confined to exceptional cases where the tenant had been in wilful breach. The court granted relief on stringent terms which included payment of the landlord's costs of the action on an indemnity basis:

> There can be no doubt that the wilfulness of the breach is a relevant consideration and that the court should not in exercising its discretion encourage a belief that parties to a lease can ignore their obligations and buy their way out of any consequential forfeiture. But to impose a requirement that relief under section 146(2) should be granted only in an exceptional case seems to me to be seeking to lay down a rule for the exercise of the court's discretion which the decision of the House of Lords in *Hyman v Rose* [1912] AC 623 said should not be done. Certainly Lord Wilberforce in *Shiloh Spinners v Harding* did not purport to do so in cases under the statute.
> Accordingly, in my judgment, although I should give considerable weight to the fact that two out of the three breaches were wilful, I am not required to find an exceptional case before granting relief from forfeiture. (*Southern Depot Co Ltd v British Railways Board* [1990] 2 EGLR 39; per Morritt J at 43M to 44A).

Serious breaches   Relief may be granted where a serious breach is involved, such as using the premises as a brothel in breach of a covenant against immoral user (*Central Estates (Belgravia) Ltd v Woolgar (No 2)* [1972] 1 WLR 1048). It has been stated that it is the established practice of the court not to grant relief in cases where the breach involves immoral user 'save in very exceptional circumstances' (*GMS Syndicate Ltd v Gary Elliott Ltd* [1982] Ch 1), although to be quite so definite may be to lay down a 'rigid rule' that fetters the court's discretion (see dicta of Lord Loreborn in *Hyman v Rose*, p51 *above*).

Personal qualifications of the tenant   Where the personal qualifications of the tenant are of importance for the preservation of the value or character of the property, those qualifications may be taken into account by the court in determining whether to exercise its discretion to grant relief against forfeiture (*Earl Bathurst v Fine* [1974] 2 All ER 1160).

Relief in respect of part of the premises   The court has power to grant relief in respect of only part of the premises (*GMS Syndicate Ltd—the* tenant was not granted relief in respect of the other part used by sub-tenants for immoral purposes).

Tenant altering position and third parties affected   Where the landlord has altered his position before the application for relief, or where a third party has acquired an interest in the property prior to that date, relief will invariably not be granted if the landlord or the third party would be unfairly prejudiced by the order (*Gill v Lewis* [1956] 2 QB 1—a rent case; see further p48 *above*, where this point is more fully discussed).

Where a landlord has recovered possession pursuant to a court order and the tenant subsequently has the order set aside or successfully appeals and makes an application for relief in the continuing proceedings the court, in deciding whether or not to grant relief, will take into account any consequences of the original order and repossession and any delay on the part of the tenant (*Billson v Residential Apartments Ltd* [1992] 1 All ER 141, HL).

Terms and conditions of relief

The court may (and usually does) grant relief on such terms as to costs, expenses, damages, compensation, penalty or otherwise, including the grant of an injunction to restrain any like breach in the future, as the court thinks fit (s146(2) of the Law of Property Act 1925). See Form 8, p47 for a specimen order. Different parties may be granted relief on different terms (*Duke of Westminster v Swinton* [1948] 1 KB 524).

Where relief is granted subject to a condition as to the doing of something within a certain time the court may extend the time for compliance (*Starside Properties Ltd v Mustapha* [1974] 1 WLR 816). Where the landlord alleges that the tenant has failed to comply with the condition he may not apply for leave to enforce the order for possession without notifying the tenant of the application (see p305).

Exercise of discretion on an appeal

On an appeal from a Master to a judge against an order refusing or granting an application for relief the court must consider the case on the facts as they appear at the date of the appeal (*Cremin v Barjack Properties Ltd* [1985] 1 EGLR 30). But on an appeal to the Court of Appeal the court will only exercise its discretion if there has been a change in circumstances (*Darlington BC v Denmark Chemists Ltd* [1993] 1 EGLR 62, CA).

Costs

The tenant is usually ordered to pay the costs of the application for relief, even where successful, but the order should not be made on an indemnity basis. There is no reason why an unsuccessful applicant for relief should be in any worse position than any other unsuccessful litigant (*Billson v Residential Apartments Ltd* [1992] 1 All ER 141, HL). In *Billson*, Lord Templeman also expressed the view that the practice of ordering indemnity costs as a condition of granting relief was ripe for consideration: 'indemnity costs to a landlord encourage lawyers and surveyors and other advisers to charge large fees'.

In order to minimise the costs payable the tenant should make a 'Calderbank offer', preferably no later than the date upon which he serves his application, setting out his proposed terms which should include an offer to pay the costs to date. If the offer is rejected but the court subsequently makes an order for relief in the proposed terms (or better) the court may well order the landlord to pay the tenant's costs from the date of the offer.

Relief to sub-tenants and mortgagees; rent and other covenants

Introduction

Forfeiture of a lease brings any sublease or other derivative interest to an end. Where an order is made granting the tenant relief from forfeiture all derivative interests are automatically reinstated (*Dendy v Evans* [1910] 1 KB 263). Where, however, the tenant has not been granted or has not applied for relief the sub-tenant may wish to make his own application. If the lease was subject to a mortgage the mortgagee may also wish to make an application for relief.

Depending on the circumstances, relief may be obtained under s 138 of the County Courts Act 1984 (rent cases only), s 38 of the Supreme Court Act 1981 (rent cases only, High Court) or s 146 of the Law of Property Act 1925 (rent and other covenants, either court).

County court rent cases

Where proceedings have been commenced in the county court, based upon non-payment of rent, a sub-tenant may obtain automatic relief by the payment of arrears of rent and costs pursuant to s 138(2) or (5) (see p 43) even though the landlord has brought the action against the tenant, and the sub-tenant is not itself a party to the proceedings (*United Dominions Trust Ltd v Shellpoint Trustees Ltd* [1993] 4 All ER 310, CA—because the term 'lessee' in s 138(2)(5), by virtue of s 140, includes an underlessee). If automatic relief is granted by reason of payment by the sub-tenant *all* the leasehold interests in the property, including the tenant's, are restored unconditionally (*United Dominions Trust Ltd* at p 316f and 318j).

If automatic relief has not been obtained by the tenant or a sub-tenant pursuant to s 138(2) or (5) and the landlord obtains possession an

Form 9: Sub-tenant's application for relief from forfeiture

IN THE   **COUNTY COURT**   Case No

IN THE MATTER OF the Law of Property Act 1925

BETWEEN

Plaintiff

—AND—

Defendant

NOTICE OF APPLICATION

I, [*state name of Applicant*], of [*state address*] wish to apply for an order vesting the property comprised in the lease referred to in the Particulars of Claim in myself for the remainder of the said term upon such conditions as to the execution of any deed or other document and the payment of rent and costs, or such other conditions as the court may think fit.

The grounds upon which I make this application are that:

(1) By an agreement dated the [*insert date*] the Defendant sublet the whole of the said property to me for a term of years.

(2) I am prepared to pay to the Plaintiff all the sums claimed in the Particulars of Claim.

(3) I am prepared to pay the rent and service charges payable under the terms of the said lease and to perform all the other covenants contained therein.

(4) I am entitled to make this application under section 146(4) of the Law of Property Act 1925.

DATED

[*signed*]

---

application for a *vesting order* may be made pursuant to s138(9C) at any time within six months from the date on which the landlord recovers possession (p44; see Form 9 *above*). The court's power to make an order under this section is discretionary. If made, a vesting order does not reinstate the interests derived from the original underlease or mortgage but gives rise to a new interest (see further *below* in relation to vesting orders made under s146(4)). If the sub-tenant fails to make an application within the six-month time limit he will thereafter be barred from all relief in both the county court and High Court (s138(7); *United Dominions Trust Ltd v Shellpoint Trustees Ltd*).

High Court rent cases

Relief may be sought in the High Court, in a rent case, pursuant to s38 of the Supreme Court Act 1981 (p46). The application may be made after the landlord has enforced the order, but if the rent is six months or more in arrears s210 of the Common Law Procedure Act 1852 applies so that the application must be made within six months of the date of execution.

County court or High Court; rent or other covenants

A vesting order may also be sought pursuant to s 146(4) of the Law of Property Act 1925 both in the county court and High Court. This subsection applies to rent cases as well as to breaches of other covenants.

Section 146(4) of the Law of Property Act 1925
> (4) Where a lessor is proceeding by action or otherwise to enforce a right of reentry or forfeiture under any covenant, proviso, or stipulation in a lease, or for non-payment of rent, the court may, on application by any person claiming as underlessee any estate or interest in the property comprised in the lease or any part thereof, either in the lessor's action (if any) or in any action brought by such person for that purpose, make an order vesting, for the whole term of the lease or any less term, the property comprised in the lease or any part thereof in any person entitled as underlessee to any estate or interest in such property upon such conditions as to execution of any deed or other document, payment of rent, costs, expenses, damages, compensation, giving security, or otherwise, as the court in the circumstances of each case may think fit, but in no case shall any such underlessee be entitled to require a lease to be granted to him for any longer term than he had under his original sublease.

An order made pursuant to s 146(4) does not restore the original underlease. A new lease is created and vested in the sub-tenant (see *Cadogan v Dimovic* [1984] 2 All ER 168 at 172). The position is the same where a mortgagee is granted a new lease under s 146(4) save that the new lease is held subject to the equity of redemption in the mortgagor (*Chelsea Estates Investment Trust Co Ltd v Marche* [1955] 1 All ER 195).

The court's power under s 146(4) is discretionary. When making an order under s 146(4) the court's discretion is very wide and the new lease may be different from that which he originally held. The position is explained by Warner J in *Hammersmith and Fulham LBC v Top Shop Centres Ltd* [1989] 2 All ER 655, at 664–5:

> The court may not under that subsection vest in the applicant a new lease beginning before the date of its order or ending later than the original underlease would have done; but the discretion is otherwise unfettered. . . . Thus the court may, under s 146(4), order that the new lease should be at a rent different from that reserved by the original underlease. . . . It may order that the new lease should be for a term ending sooner than the term granted by the original underlease. It may order that the new lease should contain different covenants and it may, on my reading of the subsection, order that the new lease should comprise a lesser part of the property demised by the forfeited lease than was comprised in the original underlease.

However, the court is unlikely to grant a lease containing terms less stringent than those in the head-lease (*Hill v Griffin* [1987] 1 EGLR 81—vesting order refused because the sub-tenant was not prepared to accept a lease containing a repairing covenant which was as onerous as in the head-lease). It is an invariable condition that the sub-tenant pay the landlord's costs of the proceedings (on a standard basis: see p53). The

Form 10: Mortgagee's application for relief

```
IN THE                  COUNTY COURT

BETWEEN:

                              [Name of landlord]              Plaintiff

                              —AND—

                              [Name of tenant]               Defendant


                       NOTICE OF APPLICATION

MONASTERY BUILDING SOCIETY ('the Society') of _____ wishes to apply for:

1.   An order that it be joined in these proceedings pursuant to CCR Ord 15, r3; and
2.   An order that [the property referred to in the Particulars of Claim] be vested in the Society
pursuant to s146(4) of the Law of Property Act 1925.

The grounds upon which the Society makes the application are that it is a mortgagee of the said
property under a first charged dated _____, that it is entitled to make this application
under the said statutory provision and that it is willing to comply with such conditions as the court
may think fit.

SIGNED   etc.
```

fact that the sub-tenant is legally aided does not prevent the court from imposing such a condition (*Factors (Sundries) Ltd v Miller* [1952] 2 All ER 630, CA).

The decision of the House of Lords in *Billson v Residential Apartments Ltd* [1992] 1 All ER 141 (see p50) that a tenant may apply for relief after peaceable reentry but not after a landlord has recovered possession pursuant to a court order (unless that order is set aside), probably applies to applications made by 'any person claiming as underlessee'. Thus, if a sub-tenant or mortgagee is served with proceedings (see p40) or otherwise discovers that the landlord has served a s146 notice on the tenant, he will usually be best advised to make an immediate application under s146(4) (see further under 'Procedure', p59).

Persons who may apply: sub-tenants and mortgagees

Sub-tenants may clearly apply for relief under the various provisions, including unlawful sub-tenants (*Southern Depot Co Ltd v British Railways Board* [1990] 2 EGLR 39 at 42M–43A).

As the vesting of a new lease in an sub-tenant or mortgagee, pursuant to s146(4) of the 1925 Act or s138(9C) of the 1984 Act, does not reinstate the interests derived from the sublease or mortgage any sub-undertenant must make his own application for a vesting order even if the sub-tenant

Form 11: Affidavit in support of application for relief

IN THE   COUNTY COURT

BETWEEN:

[Name of landlord]   Plaintiff

—AND—

[Name of tenant]   Defendant

AFFIDAVIT

I, [name], Solicitor, of [address] hereby MAKE OATH and say as follows:

1. I am the solicitor acting on behalf of Monastery Building Society. I make this affidavit, with due authority from my client, in support of the Society's application to be joined in these proceedings and for a vesting order. Save where otherwise appears the facts stated herein are within my own knowledge and belief.

2. The Plaintiff's claim is for possession of the dwelling known as [address]. The dwelling is held by the Defendant under a lease for a term of 99 years granted to him by the Plaintiff on _____. A copy of the lease is now produced and shown to me marked '_____ 1'. This lease is subject to a legal mortgage in favour of the Society. A copy of the Charge Certificate is now produced and shown to me marked '_____ 2'.

3. The Defendant fell into arrears with his mortgage and the Society took possession on _____ 1994 pursuant to an order for possession in this court dated _____ 1994. The amount outstanding to the Society on the mortgage at today's date is £_____. The Society is in the process of selling the dwelling although a buyer has not yet been found.

4. The Society has been served with these proceedings pursuant to CCR Ord 6, r3(2). It is in these circumstances that the Society applies to be joined in the proceedings and seeks a vesting order pursuant to the statutory provisions referred to in the application. The Society is ready, able and willing to comply with such conditions as the court may consider it proper to impose.

SWORN

---

has made an application (*Hammersmith and Fulham LBC v Top Shop Centres Ltd* [1989] 2 All ER 655).

Mortgagees, whether legal or equitable, of the tenant's interest are persons who derive title under a tenant and so may apply for relief (s 40 of the 1984 Act; s38 of the 1981 Act; s146(4) of the 1925 Act; see *Belgravia Insurance Co Ltd v Meah* [1963] 3 All ER 828—general principles and legal mortgages; *Good v Wood* [1954] 1 All ER 275—equitable mortgages). Mere equitable chargees, such as a person who has obtained a charging order against the tenant's interest under the Charging Orders Act 1979 may apply (*Ladup Ltd v Williams & Glyn's Bank plc* [1985] 1 WLR 851). See Forms 10 and 11 (p57 and *above*) for an application for relief and affidavit in support to be used by a mortgagee, and Form 12 on p60 for Vesting Order.

Where the landlord has forfeited for non-payment of rent and the sub-tenant or mortgagee applies for relief under the Supreme Court Act 1981 he should join the original tenant in the proceedings (or, if the lease was assigned, the assignee), or if it is not possible to do so the absence of that party should be explained (*Hare v Elms* [1893] 1 QB 604; *Humphreys v Morten* [1905] 1 Ch 739). Lord Denning has stated, obiter, that it is not necessary to join the tenant (or his assignee) where the sub-tenant claims relief under s146(4) of the Law of Property Act 1925 (*Belgravia Insurance Co Ltd* at 832H), but it is advisable to do so (or at least to notify him of the application) unless it is not possible, in which case his absence should be explained.

County court procedure

A sub-tenant or mortgagee who has been joined by the landlord as a party to the action for possession may make an application for a vesting order by way of counterclaim, or by application in the landlord's action (CCR Ord 13, r1; County Court Form N244—see Form 9, p57). If he is not an original defendant he may apply to be joined as a party (CCR Ord 15, r3) and then apply by counterclaim or application. Alternatively, he may issue his own originating application pursuant to CCR Ord 3, r4 (County Court Form N393). This is the way to proceed if the sub-tenant or mortgagee discovers that the landlord has served a s146 notice on the tenant but proceedings have not yet been commenced.

The applicant should support his application by an affidavit setting out his case which should be served with the application (see Form 11, p58).

As stated *above*, if the landlord reenters the property pursuant to an order for possession made after service of a s146 notice (ie for breach of covenant other than payment of rent), any such sub-tenant or mortgagee (probably) has no right to apply for relief until he has had that order set aside (*Billson v Residential Apartments Ltd*). Nor may he apply under s138(9C) in a rent case outside the six-month time limit (p55). If the landlord does manage to obtain and enforce an order for possession in the county court without the knowledge of the sub-tenant or a mortgagee, any such person should apply to have the order for possession set aside (see p299), to be joined in the action (p269) and for an order pursuant to s146(4) in the continuing proceedings.

Form 12: Vesting Order in favour of mortgagee

IN THE   COUNTY COURT

BETWEEN:

[*Name of landlord*]   *Plaintiff*

—AND—

(1) [*Name of tenant*]
(2) MONASTERY BUILDING SOCIETY   *Defendants*

ORDER

UPON the application of Monastery Building Society

AND UPON HEARING solicitors for the Plaintiff and for Monastery Building Society

IT IS ORDERED THAT:

1. The Monastery Building Society be joined as a Second Defendant to these proceedings.

2. The dwelling known as [*address*] be vested in the Second Defendant pursuant to section 146(4) of the Law of Property Act 1925 upon the terms of the draft lease attached to this Order provided that the Second Defendant do within 28 days hereof:

    (1) Pay to the Plaintiff the sum of £_____ in respect of rent, mesne profits and service charges outstanding;

    (2) Pay the Plaintiff £_____ in respect of the costs of its action against the First Defendant and the costs of and occasioned by the Second Defendant's application dated _____;

    (3) Execute a lease in the terms of the draft annexed hereto.

3. If the Second Defendant fails to comply with the said conditions within the said period of 28 days or within such further period or periods as the parties may agree or the Court may allow the Second Defendant's application for a vesting order shall stand dismissed and the Second Defendant shall pay the Plaintiff's costs of and occasioned by the Second Defendant's application to be taxed on Scale 1 if not agreed.

4. Liberty to apply.

DATED

High Court procedure

An application to be joined as a party to existing proceedings is made pursuant to RSC Ord 15, r10. If the sub-tenant or mortgagee is a party to the possession proceedings his application may be made by counterclaim or summons. If there are no proceedings or he is not a party he may make an application by writ or originating summons (RSC Ord 5, r4(1) and Ord 7). The originating summons procedure, which includes automatic directions for affidavits and setting down, is set out in RSC Ord 28.

Where the landlord has proceeded by action in the High Court and has obtained an order for possession he may not enforce the order without leave, and leave will not be given unless it is shown that every person in actual possession has sufficient notice of the proceedings to enable him to apply for relief (RSC Ord 45, r3(3); see further p304). The sub-tenant will, therefore, have an opportunity to make an application for relief (there is no equivalent provision in the county court). As stated *above*, if the landlord reenters the property pursuant to an order for possession made after service of a s146 notice (ie for breach of covenant other than payment of rent), any such sub-tenant or mortgagee (probably) has no right to apply for relief unless the order is set aside (*Billson v Residential Apartments Ltd*; p50). Thus, if the sub-tenant or mortgagee is notified of the order pursuant to RSC Ord 45, r3(3) he should immediately make an application for relief.

Chapter 3

Other Methods of Termination

At common law a tenancy may be brought to an end in a number of ways. The most important are by forfeiture, notice to quit, effluxion of time and surrender. Forfeiture was dealt with in the last chapter. This chapter deals with the other methods. However, it should be noted that many modern tenancies are governed by specific statutory provisions and require specific notices to be served. For example, an assured tenancy under the Housing Act 1988 requires a 'notice of intention to commence proceedings for possession' to be served. The special rules that apply to the termination of specific tenancies are dealt with in the appropriate chapter.

Notice to quit by landlord

Service of a notice to quit is appropriate where the tenancy the landlord wishes to determine is a periodic one (oral or written). A notice to quit may not be used to determine a fixed term tenancy unless the lease contains an express clause (commonly known as a 'break clause') permitting the landlord to bring it to an end in this way.

The notice

As a general rule a notice to quit premises let as a dwelling will only be valid if it is in writing and contains such information as may be prescribed by statutory instrument, presently the Notice to Quit (Prescribed Information) Regulations 1988 (SI No 2201); s5(1)(a) of the Protection from Eviction Act 1977. However, the notice need not be in writing and need not contain the prescribed information if the premises are let on an 'excluded tenancy' (see Chapter 19, p255) which was entered on or after the date on which the Housing Act 1988 came into force (15 January 1989) unless it was entered into pursuant to a contract made before that date (s5(1B) of the 1977 Act).

Protection from Eviction Act 1977, s5
    (1) Subject to subsection (1B) *below* no notice by a landlord or a tenant to quit any premises let (whether before or after the commencement of this Act) as a dwelling shall be valid unless—

    (*a*) it is in writing and contains such information as may be prescribed, and

    (*b*) it is given not less than 4 weeks before the date on which it is to take effect.

(1A) _____

(1B) Nothing in subsection (1) . . . above applies to—

    (*a*) premises let on an excluded tenancy (see p255) which is entered into on or after the date on which the Housing Act 1988 came into force unless it is entered into pursuant to a contract made before that date;

Where the notice is required to contain the prescribed information it will not be invalid merely because the exact words used in the regulations are not used in the notice. So long as the words used clearly impart the information that is prescribed the notice will be valid. (See *Wilsher v Foster* [1981] CLY 1546; compare *Meretane Investments v Martin* [1984] CLY 1917—county court cases coming to opposite conclusions on the use of out of date standard forms).

See Form 13 (p66) for a specimen notice to quit containing the prescribed information.

Every notice to quit must relate to the whole of the premises let and must be served the proper period before its expiry.

Appropriate notice periods   The appropriate period of notice and the date upon which a notice to quit is to expire may be provided for in the tenancy agreement. If so the notice to quit should be served in accordance with the tenancy (but subject to the minimum requirement of four weeks' notice where s5(1)(*b*) of the Protection from Eviction Act 1977 applies (see *below*)). Where there are no such terms the following rules apply.

Where by virtue of s5(1)(*a*) of the Protection from Eviction Act 1977 a notice to quit is required to be in writing and to contain prescribed information (see *above*) the notice to quit must be given not less than four weeks before the date on which it is to take effect (s5(1)(*b*)). Thus, in the usual case a weekly tenant must be given at least four weeks' notice. However, if s5(1) does not apply he may be given only a week's notice.

Section 5(1) of the 1977 Act only provides for a minimum period of notice. If the tenancy is of a type that requires longer notice such longer notice must be given. Thus, a monthly tenancy requires at least a calendar month's notice and a quarterly tenancy requires at least one quarter's notice.

A yearly tenancy requires at least six months' notice. Usually this means 183 days but if the tenancy is to end on one of the quarter days (25 March, 24 June, 29 September and 25 December) then at least two quarters' notice must be given.

In calculating the minimum notice period required include the day of service and exclude the day of expiry (*Schnabel v Allard* [1967] 1 QB 627). The date of expiry must be at the end of a complete period of the tenancy or the first day of a new period (*Sidebotham v Holland* [1895] 1 QB 378; *Crate v Miller* [1947] KB 946). Unless there is an indication in the lease to the contrary a tenancy stated to be 'from' a particular date commences immediately after midnight the following day (*Ladyman v Wirral Estates* [1968] 2 All ER 197). If the tenancy is a monthly tenancy and the notice is given on the last day of the month it should be dated to expire on the last day of the next month even where that month is a shorter month. The notice should not give a particular time in the day before which the tenant must leave.

Examples

(a) If a weekly tenancy commences on a Monday the notice to quit must expire on a Sunday (or a Monday) and must be given by the Sunday (or, if it is to expire on a Monday, by the Monday) four weeks beforehand (unless s5(1)(b) of the Protection from Eviction Act 1977 does not apply in which case it may be given one week beforehand).

(b) If a monthly tenancy commences on the 20th of a month, the notice to quit must be given by the 19th (or 20th) of any particular month to expire on the 19th (or 20th) of the next month. If a monthly tenancy commences on 31 January, the notice to quit can be given to expire on 28 February (or 29 February in a leap year). Where the landlord served a notice on 30 September 1978 under the business tenancy provisions of the Landlord and Tenant Act 1954 and the tenant had four months from the date of service to apply for a new tenancy and did so on 31 January 1979 it was held that as the term 'month' meant a calendar month the notice ended on 30 January 1979 and the tenant's application was dismissed (*Dodds v Walker* [1980] 1 WLR 1061).

(c) If a yearly tenancy is granted on 1 May 1982 the notice to quit must be given by 29 October 1982 to determine on 30 April 1983 or 1 May 1983 (ie 183 days).

In order to ensure that the notice expires on the proper day the landlord may insert the following clause in the notice to quit: 'I hereby give you notice to quit on the   day of   19   or at the expiration of the period of your tenancy which shall expire next after the expiration of four weeks from the service upon you of this notice.'

Unless the above requirements are strictly complied with the notice will generally be ineffective. Only minor clerical errors will not invalidate a notice to quit, if the meaning would be clear to a reasonable tenant (*Carradine Properties Ltd v Aslam* [1976] 1 WLR 442). For example a notice to quit dated in error 1894 when the landlord clearly meant 1994 will not invalidate the notice. If proceedings for possession have been commenced on the basis of a defective notice to quit, they will be dismissed and the landlord will have to serve a valid notice before fresh proceedings can be commenced.

It should be noted that the landlord must never commence proceedings until the notice to quit has expired. If he does so the proceedings are premature and will be dismissed.

Who may give a notice

The notice must be given by or on behalf of the tenant's immediate landlord at the time of the notice. Thus a prospective purchaser cannot serve a notice to quit, but once a landlord has given the tenant notice his successors in title may rely upon it (*Doe d Earl of Egremont v Forwood* (1842) 3 QB 627). A notice to quit given by one of two or more joint landlords is valid if the tenancy is a periodic one (*Parsons v Parsons* [1983] 1 WLR 1390; see also *Hammersmith and Fulham LBC v Monk* [1992] 1 All ER 1, HL—a decision relating to the termination by one of two joint tenants without the consent of the other). However, if the tenancy is for a fixed term with a clause providing for termination by a notice to quit, all of the joint owners must agree to service of the notice to quit unless the lease otherwise provides (cf *Hounslow LBC v Pilling* [1994] 1 All ER 432 CA—a decision relating to termination by joint tenants).

Notice given by agents

It is worth bearing in mind that the purpose of the rules contained in this paragraph is to ensure that the tenant can rely upon the notice to quit; that he can be sure that it comes from the landlord. The first rule is that a person such as a managing agent, who has been given a general authority to deal with a property on behalf of a landlord, may give a tenant a notice to quit in his own name without having to show a specific authority to determine the tenancy. The notice is even valid if it is given by the agent as if he were the landlord and fails to disclose his own agency (*Doe d Earl Manvers v Mizem* (1837) 2 Mood & R56); *Harmond Properties Ltd v Gajdzis* [1968] 3 All ER 263; *Townsend Carriers Ltd v Pfizer Ltd* (1977) 33 P & CR 361).

The second rule is that all other persons (eg rent collectors, solicitors, the landlord's husband or wife) may only give a notice to quit on behalf of the landlord if they have the landlord's actual authority to do so at the time the notice is given (*Jones v Phipps* (1868) LR 3 QB 567). A landlord may not subsequently ratify the notice and thereby validate it. The fact of the agency should be expressed on the notice which should be expressly given on behalf of the landlord, who should be named or otherwise identified (*Lemon v Lardeur* [1946] 2 All ER 329; *Divall v Harrison* [1992] 2 EGLR 64, CA. There is, of course, nothing to prevent a solicitor

Form 13: Notice to quit by landlord

NOTICE TO QUIT

(BY LANDLORD OF PREMISES LET AS A DWELLING)

Name and
Address
of Tenant

To ....

of...

....

Name and
Address of
Landlord

[I][We] [as] [on behalf of] your landlord[s], ...

of...

....

*Me/them or
as appropriate

†Address of premises

give you NOTICE TO QUIT and deliver up possession to* ....

of†...

....

‡Date for
possession

on‡ ....19..........., or the day on which a complete period of your tenancy

expires next after the end of four weeks from the service of this notice.

Date of notice

Dated................................... 19 ....

Signed..

Name and
Address of
Agent if Agent
serves notice

....

....

....

INFORMATION FOR TENANT
(See Note 2 below)

1.   If the tenant or licensee does not leave the dwelling, the landlord or licensor must get an order for possession from the court before the tenant or licensee can lawfully be evicted. The landlord or licensor cannot apply for such an order before the notice to quit or notice to determine has run out.

2.   A tenant or licensee who does not know if he has any right to remain in possession after a notice to quit or a notice to determine runs out can obtain advice from a solicitor. Help with all or part of the cost of legal advice and assistance may be available under the Legal Aid Scheme. He should also be able to obtain information from a Citizens' Advice Bureau, a Housing Aid Centre or a Rent Officer.

NOTES

1.   Notice to quit premises let as a dwelling must be given at least four weeks before it takes effect, and it must be in writing (Protection from Eviction Act 1977, s 5 as amended).

2.   Where a notice to quit is given by a landlord to determine a tenancy of any premises let as a dwelling, the notice must contain this information (the Notices to Quit etc (Prescribed Information) Regulations 1988).

3.   Some tenancies are excluded from this protection: see Protection from Eviction Act 1977, ss 3A and 5(1B).

Reproduced by kind permission of The Solicitors' Law Stationery Society Ltd or a wife having a general authority to manage the property in which case the first rule set out above will apply.

Service upon whom?

The landlord must serve notice on the existing tenant; his immediate tenant. He may not serve an assignor of the tenancy nor a sub-tenant. An assignment in breach of covenant although unlawful is effective, and so even in these circumstances the notice to quit should be served on the assignee (*Old Grovebury Manor Farm Ltd v W Seymour Plant Sales and Hire Ltd (No 2)* [1979] 1 WLR 1397). If the tenancy is held by joint tenants but only one tenant lives upon the premises, service on that tenant is sufficient unless the lease provides that all must be served (*Doe d Bradford (Lord) v Watkins* (1806) 7 East 551); although address it to both.

Landlords are often faced with a situation where the person in occupation is not the original tenant. If the tenancy was in writing service of a notice to quit should present no real problems because the provisions of s 196 of the Law of Property Act will be available (see *below* 'Mode of service for written tenancies'). However, where the tenancy was an oral one, service of the notice to quit can often be a problem. If those in occupation are sub-tenants service of a notice addressed to the tenant but given to the sub-tenant or simply left at the premises will not be sufficient, although if they are truly sub-tenants it should usually be possible to find out to whom they pay their rent and thus to find the tenant. Where there has been no subletting the persons who are left in occupation of the premises will, in the absence of any evidence to the contrary, be assumed to be the tenant's assigns and notice to quit may be given to them (*Doe d Morris v Williams* (1826) 6 B & C 41; see also *Egerton v Rutter* [1951] 1 TLR 58). Compare *Chamberlain v Scalley* (1992) 26 HLR 26 where the tenant had left her 'common law husband' in occupation upon whom the notice to quit was served. No notice to quit was served as the tenant. The tenancy was not therefore brought to an end and the court refused to find there has been a surrender (see further p71).

If the tenant has died the notice to quit may be served upon the premises pursuant to s196(3) of the Law of Property Act 1925 *if* that provision applies (see *below*, 'Mode of service for written tenancies'). If s196 does not apply the notice to quit should be served on the executors of the tenant's estate who should be named in the notice. If no executors exist or the tenant died intestate and no administrators have yet been appointed, the notice should be addressed to the President of the Family Division (in whom the estate vests during this period: see s9 of the Administration of Estates Act 1925; see p86) and served upon the Treasury Solicitor at Queen Anne's Chambers, 28 Broadway, London, SW1H 9JS (Practice Direction [1985] 1 All ER 832). In *Wirral Borough*

Council v Smith (1982) 43 P & CR 312 the periodic tenant died intestate but because he did not serve notice on the President the landlord could not maintain an action for possession even though the defendants were trespassers. Once personal representatives have been appointed any notice to quit should be served on them. If the landlord is unable to ascertain the names of the personal representatives from the tenant's relatives or friends he may lodge an application for a standing search at the Probate Registry. The applicant will be sent an office copy entry of any grant issued not more than 12 months before nor more than six months after the date of the application. The application may be renewed after six months.

For the position where the landlord has granted a new tenancy to a person who has remained in occupation after the death of the original tenant see *Mackely v Nutting* [1949] 2 KB 55; *Epping Forest DC v Pomphrett* [1990] 2 EGLR 46).

Mode of service for oral tenancies

The notice to quit must come to the tenant's attention before the notice period begins to run. Personal service is not required, although this is clearly the best method of service. If the notice is served by post the landlord should send it by recorded delivery or registered post. Where service is by post there is a presumption that the notice was delivered in the ordinary course of post, but this presumption may be rebutted by evidence from the tenant that the notice was not in fact received. Simply leaving the notice to quit at the premises will not be sufficient unless the landlord can show (whether by the tenant's admission or otherwise) that it came to the tenant's attention prior to the commencement of the notice period.

Whatever the method of service the landlord should also serve the tenant with a copy of the notice with a memorandum of service upon it. The tenant should be asked to sign, date and return the copy on the date of receipt. He may not always do so but if he does it should prevent arguments about service at a later stage.

Mode of service for written tenancies

If the tenancy is in writing the provisions of s196 of the Law of Property Act 1925 and s1 of the Recorded Delivery Act 1962 will apply 'unless a contrary intention appears' (Law of Property Act 1925, s196(5); see p19). The effect of these sections is that the notice to quit is sufficiently served if it is sent by registered post or recorded delivery addressed to the tenant by name at the tenant's last known place of abode or business in the United Kingdom. If the letter is not returned through the post office undelivered, service is deemed to be made at the time at which the letter would in the ordinary course of the post be delivered (Law of Property

Act 1925, s 196(4)). To prove service the landlord need only show that the letter was prepaid, properly addressed and actually posted.

If the tenancy is in writing the landlord may also serve the notice by leaving it at the tenant's last known place of abode or business in the United Kingdom or by affixing it or leaving it for him on the land or on any house or building comprised in the lease (Law of Property Act 1925, s 196(3)). If this method is used it is sufficient if it is addressed to 'the lessee' (Law of Property Act 1925, s 196(2)).

In either case it will not be necessary for the landlord to show that the tenant actually received the notice (*Re 88 Berkeley Road London NW9* [1971] Ch 648).

Proof of service

See Chapter 22, p308.

Payment of rent after notice to quit

If the landlord accepts rent after expiry of the notice to quit a new tenancy will not necessarily be implied and all the circumstances must be looked at to show the parties' true intentions (*Clarke v Grant* [1950] 1 KB 104; *Marcroft Wagons Ltd v Smith* [1951] 2 KB 496). In order to ensure that no intention to create a new tenancy is found a landlord requiring rent after service of a notice to quit should demand payment of mesne profits (equal to the rental sum) without prejudice to the effect of the notice to quit. In the circumstances the court will probably hold that there has been no tenancy created on the basis that there was no intention to create legal relations (see *Street v Mountford* [1985] 2 All ER 289 and p93 *below*). Receipt of rent by the landlord of a tenant who has held over after the expiry of the notice to quit, as a statutory tenant under the Rent Act 1977, does not raise any implied agreement to a renewal of the contractual tenancy; the landlord has no option but to accept the rent (*Davies v Bristow* [1920] 3 KB 428—see further p136).

Withdrawal of notice to quit

Withdrawal will only be effective if both parties consent to it and it will result in a new tenancy commencing from the expiry of the notice; the old tenancy does not continue (see generally Woodfall, *Landlord and Tenant*, 17.264).

Notice to quit by tenant

Periodic tenancies

Except where the premises are let on an 'excluded tenancy' (see Chapter 19, p255) which was entered into on or after the date on which the

Housing Act 1988 came into force (15 January 1989) (and which was not entered into pursuant to a contract made before that date), a tenant of a contractual periodic tenancy must give his landlord notice to quit in writing. The notice need not be in any particular form (because no information has been prescribed by statutory instrument) but it must state the date on which the tenancy is to be determined and the notice must be given at least four weeks before that date (s5 of the Protection from Eviction Act 1977). However, as with notices given by landlords a monthly tenancy requires one month's notice, a quarterly tenancy requires a quarter's notice and a yearly tenancy requires six months' notice. The notice should be made to expire on the last day of the tenancy or the anniversary of the tenancy (cf p64).

A periodic joint tenancy held by two or more joint tenants may be determined by a notice to quit given by one of the joint tenants without the concurrence of the others unless the terms of the tenancy provide otherwise (*Hammersmith and Fulham LBC v Monk* [1992] 1 All ER 1, HL). If the tenancy was a protected tenancy a statutory tenancy will arise (*Lloyd v Sadler* [1978] 2 All ER 529; see p138 *below*).

However, a notice served pursuant to a break clause in a lease must be served by all the joint tenants unless the lease expressly provides for it to be determined by one of them (*Re Violas Indenture of Lease* [1909] 1 Ch 244; *Hounslow London BC v Pilling* [1994] 1 All ER 432, CA). If all the tenants must give notice but the notice is signed by one only, it may still be effective if that tenant has the other tenants' authority to give notice as their agent. Thus a landlord before acting on a notice signed by one joint tenant should enquire directly of the other joint tenants to learn whether the signing tenant had their authority so to do. If the tenancy is regulated the landlord may seek to recover possession under Case 5 of Sched 15 to the Rent Act 1977 if the tenant refuses to leave at the end of the notice period.

A tenant's notice may be served in accordance with the provisions of s196 of the Law of Property Act 1925 (if the tenancy was in writing and s196 is not excluded; see s196(5); p19) by service at an address furnished by the landlord in accordance with s48 of the Landlord and Tenant Act 1987 or, if no such address has been furnished, at the last address furnished in accordance with s47 of that Act (s49 of the 1987 Act; as to ss47 and 48, see p318).

Landlord and Tenant Act 1987, s49

49.—In Section 196 of the Law of Property Act 1925 (regulations respecting notices), any reference in subsection (3) or (4) to the last known place of abode or business of the person to be served shall have effect, in its application to a notice to be served by a tenant on a landlord of premises to which this Part applies, as if that reference included a reference to—

(*a*) the address last furnished to the tenant by the landlord in accordance with section 48, or (*b*) if no address has been so furnished in accordance with section 48, the address last furnished to the tenant by the landlord in accordance with section 47.

Fixed term tenancies

The tenant cannot terminate before the end of a fixed term unless there is a specific clause in the lease allowing him to do so. The tenant need not give notice to the landlord that he is leaving on the last day of a fixed term.

Expiration of fixed term

Unless the lease provides otherwise, it is not necessary for the landlord or the tenant to serve the other party with a notice to quit at the end of the fixed term (cf assured and secure tenancies). The tenant has until midnight on the last day before he need leave (*Re Crowhurst Park* [1974] 1 WLR 583 at 588).

At common law a tenant who remains in occupation without the landlord's consent does so as a tenant at sufferance, and is liable to the landlord for damages for use and occupation (*Bayley v Bradley* (1848) 5 CB 396 at 406; see further p329). It is not necessary to serve a notice to terminate a tenancy at sufferance. The landlord may simply commence proceedings for possession. A tenant who remains in possession with the landlord's consent, however, is a tenant at will. The landlord must demand possession from a tenant at will before he commences proceedings for possession although it is not necessary to give four weeks' notice under s5 of the Protection from Eviction Act 1977 (*Crane v Morris* [1965] 1 WLR 1104). A tenant who remains in possession paying rent on a periodic basis becomes a periodic tenant. Unless there is an agreement to the contrary the terms of the periodic tenancy will be the same as the terms that applied to the fixed term so far as they are consistent with a periodic tenancy. In particular this means that any forfeiture clause in the fixed term carries over into the periodic term (*Thomas v Packer* (1857) 1 H & N 669) but that the tenancy may also be determined by giving notice appropriate to the period of the tenancy.

The above rules are the general common law rules that apply in the absence of agreement to the contrary. The parties may agree, however, that after the tenancy has come to an end the tenant should become a licensee under either a revocable or irrevocable licence (see *Foster v Robinson* [1951] 1 KB 149).

Surrender and abandonment

A tenancy is brought to an end by surrender when the landlord and tenant both agree that the tenant should yield up the term to the landlord. If the tenancy is a joint tenancy all the joint tenants must agree to the surrender for it to be effective (*Leek and Moorlands Building Society v Clark* [1952] 2 QB 788). Where the tenants owe a substantial amount of rent and one of the joint tenants has been absent for a long period it *may* be possible to infer that he has given an authority to the others to surrender on behalf of them all (*Preston Borough Council v Fairclough* (1982) *The Times*, 15 December; cf *Cooper v Varzdari* (1986) 18 HLR 299. The surrender may be express or by operation of law.

Express surrender

An express surrender must be made by deed unless the lease is granted for a term of three years or less at the best rent that could reasonably be obtained without taking a fine in which case the lease may be surrendered in writing (ss52(1), 52(2)(*d*) and 54(2) of the Law of Property Act 1925). When presented with a document that is expressed to be a surrender it is necessary to ensure that that is exactly what it is. A forfeiture that is disguised as a surrender in order to prevent the tenant from being able to take advantage of the provisions relating to relief against forfeiture will nonetheless be treated as a forfeiture (*Plymouth Corporation v Harvey* [1971] 1 WLR 549).

Surrender by operation of law

It is much more common, when one is dealing with possession of residential premises, to find surrenders operating as a matter of law. The essence of a surrender by operation of law is the consensual giving up of possession of the premises to the landlord by the tenant; the landlord must do some act accepting the surrender. Thus where the tenant returns the keys to the landlord with the intention of giving up possession of the premises and the landlord accepts them with the intention of accepting possession there is a surrender by operation of law. Simply leaving the keys at the landlord's office or abandoning the premises will not, however, operate as a surrender. The landlord's act accepting the surrender must also be unequivocal. Thus, there is no surrender where the landlord accepts the key 'without prejudice' to see if he can re-let the premises (*Re Panther Lead Co* [1896] 1 Ch 978); or where after the tenant has absconded he changes the locks of the premises merely for security reasons and not to shut out the tenant (*Relvock Properties Ltd v Dixon* (1973) 25 P & CR 1). If the landlord does re-let the premises without telling the tenant that he is doing it on his behalf there is then a surrender (*Walls v Atchenson* (1826) 3 Bing 462); but an attempt to re-let is not of itself an unequivocal act accepting the surrender (*Oastler v Henderson* (1877) 2 QBD 575).

If the tenant has abandoned the premises the landlord may accept the surrender by changing the locks and re-letting the premises (*R v London*

Borough of Croydon, ex parte Toth (1988) 20 HLR 576), but any landlord that does so is taking quite a risk. He may be mistaken. The tenant may not have absconded the premises at all. He may just be on an extended holiday. The landlord may find himself being accused of committing the offence of unlawful eviction, although he does have a defence if he can prove that he believed, and had reasonable cause to believe, that the tenant had ceased to reside in the premises (s1(2) of the Protection from Eviction Act 1977). By far the safest solution is to terminate by some other method, such as a notice to quit (if possible), and then to commence proceedings for possession. As to service of the proceedings in these circumstances see p294. See also *below* for the procedure under s54 of the Landlord and Tenant Act 1954 where the tenant has been missing for over six months and for the procedure in the magistrates' court.

A surrender also comes about when the landlord grants the tenant a new tenancy of the premises on different terms from those of his former tenancy whether or not they realise that the law would analyse their agreement as having the effect of the grant of a new tenancy and a surrender of the former tenancy (*Take Harvest Ltd v Liu* [1993] 2 All ER 459, PC at 468c). However, an agreement between the landlord and tenant for an increase in rent will not necessarily be sufficient to give rise to a new tenancy and a surrender of the old.

> Viewing the matter apart from authority it is difficult to see why the fiction of a new lease and a surrender by operation of law should be necessary in this case; for by simply increasing the amount of rent and providing that the additional rent shall be annexed to the reversion, one is not altering the nature of the pre-existing item of property (*Jenkin R Lewis & Son v Kerman* [1970] 3 All ER 414 (CA) per Russell LJ at 420b).

An agreement adding a new person as a joint tenant constitutes an agreement to vary the existing contract and does not operate as a surrender and regrant (*Frances Perceval Saunders Dec'sd Trustees v Ralph*, [1993] 2 EGLR 1 QBD). There is also a surrender where the landlord and tenant agree that the tenant is to occupy the premises in the future as a licensee (*Foster v Robinson* [1951] 1 KB 149). See also *Dibbs v Campbell* (1988) 20 HLR 374—surrender of a protected tenancy intended to be a protected shorthold followed by grant of a valid protected shorthold tenancy.

Evidence of abandonment

It is not uncommon for the landlord to seek an immediate order for possession at the trial on the basis that the tenant has not turned up at the hearing and that he has abandoned the premises. He will try to rely upon evidence of conversations that he has had with neighbours, the milkman etc who have told him that the tenant has disappeared. This evidence is hearsay and if the landlord wishes to rely upon it he will have to call these people or adduce their evidence in the form of an affidavit, or statement under the provisions of the Civil Evidence Act 1968. However, if no defence has been filed no notice of intention to give a statement in evidence need be served; CCR Ord 20, r15(2) (see Chapter 22).

Effect of surrender

Where the tenant surrenders by actually giving up possession to the landlord it is obviously not necessary to obtain an order for possession. But if the surrender was an express one and the tenant refuses to give up possession it will be necessary to obtain a court order before the landlord can recover possession unless the tenancy is an 'excluded tenancy' (see p255) entered into on or after commencement of the Housing Act 1988 (15 January 1989) otherwise than pursuant to a contract entered into before that date (s3 of the Protection from Eviction Act 1977).

For the effect on sub-tenants, see p82. Other occupiers who remain on the premises are trespassers who may be evicted in proceedings under CCR Ord 24 (or RSC Ord 113).

Rent

If the tenant abandons the premises his liability for rent continues until the landlord accepts the surrender. The onus is on the tenant to show that the landlord's act amounts to an unequivocal acceptance of the surrender if he wishes to avoid paying rent for the period after he left (*Relvock Properties Ltd v Dixon* (1973) 25 P & CR 1); *Boyer v Warbey* [1953] 1 QB 234—a statutory tenant who did not give notice as required by s3 of the Rent Act 1977).

Landlord and Tenant Act 1954, s54

Where a landlord has power to determine a tenancy by notice to quit he may apply to the court for an order determining the tenancy if he can show that he has taken all reasonable steps to contact the tenant and has been unable to do so; that during the six-month period ending with the date of the application neither the tenant nor any person claiming under him has been in occupation of the premises; and that during that period no rent has been paid by the tenant. The procedure is by originating application (CCR Ord 43, r2). See 24 *Atkin's Court Forms*, Forms 212 and 213 and Practice para 64.

Determination by the magistrates' court where the premises are deserted

Under s16 of the Distress for Rent Act 1737 possession may be recovered where there is a tenancy at a rack rent, or the rent is three-quarters of the yearly value of the premises and there is half a year's rent in arrear and the tenant has deserted the premises and left them uncultivated or unoccupied and there is no sufficient distress to meet the arrears. See 24 *Atkin's Court Forms*, Forms 204–211 and Practice para 63.

On the request of the landlord, two or more justices may view the premises and affix a notice to the premises informing of a second view to take place after 14 days. In London a police constable visits the premises. If on the second view the tenant does not appear or pay the rent arrears, the justices will put the landlord into possession. Proceedings are commenced by complaint. Appeal lies to the High Court in London and the crown court elsewhere (s 17 of the Distress for Rent Act 1737).

Recovery of possession

Once the tenancy has come to an end the landlord may recover possession, but only by way of court proceedings unless the tenancy is an 'excluded tenancy' (see p255) entered into on or after the commencement of the Housing Act 1988 (15 January 1989) otherwise than pursuant to a contract made before that date (s3 of the Protection from Eviction Act 1977). Where the tenant has no statutory security of tenure, the court has power at common law to suspend the order for possession. This power has, however, been severely limited by the Housing Act 1980 where the proceedings are in the county court. The effect of the order may now only be postponed for a maximum of 14 days unless such a short order would cause exceptional hardship in which case the court may postpone the date for possession for up to six weeks (s89 of the Housing Act 1980). The only exception to this rule is where the lease has been brought to an end by forfeiture in which case the tenant may be able to obtain relief against the forfeiture (s89(2) of the Housing Act 1980). The limitations imposed on the court's discretion by s89 do not apply when proceedings are in the High Court (*Bain & Co v Church Commissioners for England* [1989] 1 WLR 24).

Housing Act 1980, s89
    (1) Where a court makes an order for the possession of any land in a case not falling within the exceptions mentioned in subsection (2) *below*, the giving up of possession shall not be postponed (whether by the order or any variation, suspension or stay of execution) to a date later than fourteen days after the making of the order, unless it appears to the court that exceptional hardship would be caused by requiring possession to be given up by that date; and shall not in any event be postponed to a date later than six weeks after the making of the order.
    (2) The restrictions in subsection (1) *above* do not apply if—
        (a) the order for possession is made in an action by a mortgagee for possession; or
        (b) the order is made in an action for forfeiture of a lease; or
        (c) the court had power to make the order only if it considered it reasonable to make it; or

(*d*) the order relates to a dwelling-house which is the subject of a restricted contract (within the meaning of section 19 of the 1977 Act); or

(*e*) the order is made in proceedings brought as mentioned in section 88(1) *above* (rental purchase agreements).

Chapter 4

Leases: Assignment, Subletting, Bankruptcy and Death

Assignment by landlord

In this section, we are concerned with the sale of the landlord's interest in the property, ie the assignment of the reversion.

Binding nature of tenancy on new landlord

Where a lease is registered under the Land Registration Act 1925, any purchaser of the landlord's interest will obviously be subject to the lease. Where the lease is for a term of 21 years or less it will constitute an overriding interest under s70(1)(*k*) of the Land Registration Act 1925 (as amended) and thus bind purchasers of the landlord's estate whether or not the tenant is in occupation (*City Permanent Building Society v Miller* [1952] Ch 840 at 848). Furthermore, a lease of any length (including an equitable lease) where the tenant is in occupation will bind any purchaser of the landlord's estate as an overriding interest under s70(1)(*g*), unless enquiry made of such person fails to disclose the right (*Mornington Permanent Building Society v Kenway* [1953] Ch 382). Where the tenant's interest is not an overriding one (perhaps because he is not in actual occupation), it may be protected as a minor interest by an entry on the register of a notice or caution (s59(2) of the Land Registration Act 1925).

If the land is unregistered the purchaser takes subject to any tenant with a legal estate. If the tenant has only an equitable interest, ie an agreement for a lease operating in equity as a lease (see p7), the purchaser is bound by it if it is registered under the Land Charges Act 1972.

If the new landlord is bound by the tenant's interest he will not be able to obtain possession of the premises unless the old landlord has been able to.

Rights of new landlord against tenant

On assignment of the reversion, the right to sue the tenant in respect of all future and any outstanding breaches committed prior to the date of the assignment passes to the new landlord (s141 of the Law of Property Act 1925). The provision applies to all tenancies, including oral ones (see definition of lease in s205(xxii) of the Law of Property Act 1925; *Re King, Robinson v Gray* [1963] 1 All ER 781, per Upjohn LJ at p792, CA) and to a specifically enforceable agreement for lease (p336.*Rickett v Green* [1910] 1 KB 253; see further p336 in relation to claims for rent which have accrued prior to the assignment.

Law of Property Act 1925, s141

(1) Rent reserved by a lease, and the benefit of every covenant or provision therein contained, having reference to the subject matter thereof, and on the lessee's part to be observed or performed, and every condition of reentry and other condition therein contained, shall be annexed and incident to and shall go with the reversionary estate in the land, or in any part thereof, immediately expectant on the term granted by the lease, notwithstanding severance of that reversionary estate, and without prejudice to any liability affecting a covenantor or his estate.

(2) Any such rent, covenant or provision shall be capable of being recovered, received, enforced, and taken advantage of, by the person from time to time entitled, subject to the term, to the income of the whole or any part, as the case may require, of the land leased.

(3) Where that person becomes entitled by conveyance or otherwise, such rent, covenant or provision may be recovered, received, enforced or taken advantage of by him notwithstanding that he becomes so entitled after the condition of reentry or forfeiture has become enforceable, but this subsection does not render enforceable any condition of reentry or other condition waived or released before such person becomes entitled as aforesaid.

Liabilities of old and new landlord after assignment

By virtue of s142 of the Law of Property Act 1925, the new landlord becomes liable to comply with the obligations under the lease on the assignment of the reversion; but he is not liable in damages for breaches that occurred prior to the date of the assignment of the landlord's interest (*Duncliffe v Caerfelin Properties Ltd* [1989] 2 EGLR 38, QBD). The tenant will, therefore, have to sue the old landlord in respect of any such breaches.

Law of Property Act 1925, s142

(1) The obligation under a condition or of a covenant entered into by a lessor with reference to the subject-matter of the lease shall, if and as far as the lessor has power to bind the reversionary estate immediately expectant on the term granted by the lease, be annexed and incident to and shall go with that reversionary estate, or the several parts thereof, notwithstanding severance of that reversionary estate, and may be taken advantage of and enforced by the person in whom the term is from time to time vested by conveyance, devolution, in law or otherwise; and, if and as far as the lessor has power to bind that person from time to time entitled to that reversionary

estate, the obligation aforesaid may be taken advantage of and entered against any person so entitled.

This section takes effect without prejudice to any liability affecting a covenantor or his estate.

By virtue of the contract between them an *original* landlord continues to be liable to an original tenant on his covenant after assignment of the reversion (see final sentence of s142). Where the landlord is an asignee of the reversion, in principle, he ceases to be liable after a further assignment of the reversion because there is no longer any privity of estate between that landlord and the tenant. However, the liability does not actually cease until the tenant has been notified of the new landlord's name and address in accordance with s3 of the Landlord and Tenant Act 1985 (see s3(3A)).

Landlord and Tenant Act 1985, s3
    (1) If the interest of the landlord under a tenancy of premises which consist of or include a dwelling is assigned, the new landlord shall give notice in writing of the assignment, and of his name and address, to the tenant not later than the next day on which rent is payable under the tenancy or, if that is within two months of the assignment, the end of that period of two months.
    (2) If trustees constitute the new landlord, a collective description of the trustees of the trust in question may be given as the name of the landlord, and where such a collective description is given—
        (*a*) the address of the new landlord may be given as the address from which the affairs of the trust are conducted, and
        (*b*) a change in the persons who are for the time being the trustees of the trust shall not be treated as an assignment of the interest of the landlord.
    (3) A person who is the new landlord under a tenancy falling within subsection (1) and who fails, without reasonable excuse, to give the notice required by that subsection, commits a summary offence and is liable on conviction to a fine not exceeding level 4 on the standard scale.
    (3A) The person who was the landlord under the tenancy immediately before the assignment ('the old landlord') shall be liable to the tenant in respect of any breach of any covenant, condition or agreement under the tenancy occurring before the end of the relevant period in like manner as if the interest assigned were still vested in him; and where the new landlord is also liable to the tenant in respect of any such breach occurring within that period, he and the old landlord shall be jointly and severally liable in respect of it.
    (3B) In subsection (3A) 'the relevant period' means the period beginning with the date of the assignment and ending with the date when—
        (*a*) notice in writing of the assignment, and of the new landlord's name and address, is given to the tenant by the new landlord (whether in accordance with subsection (1) or not), or
        (*b*) notice in writing of the assignment, and of the new landlord's name and last-known address, is given to the tenant by the old landlord
    whichever happens first.

(4) In this section—
  (a) 'tenancy' includes a statutory tenancy, and
  (b) references to the assignment of the landlord's interest include ary conveyance other than a mortgage or charge.

Date upon which assignment takes effect

Where the landlord's interest is a freehold or a lease of more than three years the assignment of the interest must be made by deed (ss52 and 54 of the Law of Property Act 1925). Section 141 of the Law of Property Act 1925 does not, therefore, come into operation, and the new landlord may not enforce the covenants or forfeit, until the legal estate is conveyed ro him by the deed.

Where the landlord's estate is registered it is the registration which confers on the new landlord the interest transferred together with all rights, including the rights and interest which would, under the Law of Property Act 1925, have been transferred if the land had not been registered (s20 of the Land Registration Act 1925 in the case of freeholds, and ss22 and 23 of that Act in the case of leaseholds). Thus, n the case of registered land the landlord may not take steps to enforce the covenants or forfeit until the disposition of the estate has been registered.

If proceedings are commenced by the old landlord the new landlord can be substituted as plaintiff once the legal interest has been vested in the new landlord.

Assignment by tenant

Has there been an effective assignment?

An assignment is ineffective to pass the tenant's legal estate to the proposed assignee unless it is made by deed (s52(1) of the Law of Property Act 1925). This is the position even where the tenancy is a yearly or other periodic tenancy (*Crago v Julian* [1992] 1 All ER 744). However, a deed is not necessary where the landlord expressly or impliedly agrees to the assignee becoming the tenant and accepts him in the place of the former tenant. There is, strictly speaking, no assignment but a new tenancy which can be created orally (*Crago v Julian* at 749b), but note that the old tenant must also expressly or impliedly agree to the new arrangement (see further Surrender, p72).

An assignment of a registered leasehold interest is not effective to pass the legal estate until it is registered (ss22 and 23 of the Land Registration Act 1925).

A contract for the assignment of a lease will, as between the contracting parties, vest an equitable interest in the assignee if it is capable of being specifically enforced (see the doctrine of *Walsh v Lonsdale*, p8). An assignee in possession will, therefore, invariably have an effective interest in the property as against the assignor, whether the assignment was made by deed or not. However, the agreement to assign is not binding on the landlord (*Cox v Bishop* (1857) 8 De GM & G 815). Furthermore, the fact that the intended assignee has paid the rent does not of itself mean that the landlord is estopped from denying the assignment, for the rent could be paid by him as agent for the real tenant (*Official Trustee of Charity Lands v Ferriman Trust* [1937] 3 All ER 85).

Although the landlord may not be bound to accept an equitable assignee as the assignee of the lease he may wish to do so, particularly if he wishes to serve a notice to quit. In the absence of evidence to the contrary there is a presumption that the occupier is an assignee, thus permitting the landlord to serve a notice to quit upon him (see cases cited on p67). Furthermore, where a licence to assign is granted at the request of the tenant and the assignee enters into possession pursuant to the licence he may be estopped from denying that a valid assignment has been made (*Rodenhurst Estates v Barnes* [1936] 2 All ER 3).

Assignment in breach of covenant

An assignment is effective and transfers the tenancy to the assignee, even if it is made in breach of an absolute or qualified covenant prohibiting assignments (*Old Grovebury Manor Farm v W Seymour Plant Sales and Hire Ltd (No 2)* [1979] 3 All ER 504, CA; *Governors of Peabody Donation Fund v Higgins* [1983] 3 All ER 122). However, if the covenant has taken place in breach of any such covenant and there is a right of reentry provided for in the lease the landlord may forfeit. An assignment is not unlawful unless it is committed in breach of a term of the tenancy agreement (*Allcock v Moorehouse* (1882) 9 QBD 366—a periodic tenancy), but it may still give rise to a ground for possession (Case 6, Rent Act 1977; see p448). See further *RC Glaze Properties Ltd* in relation to sublettings (p82).

Effect of assignment

Once the lease has been assigned the assignee is liable to the landlord on the covenants that touch and concern the land pursuant to the principle of 'privity of estate', ie he is liable so long as he holds the estate. However, he will cease to be liable after he has himself assigned the lease to someone else unless he previously entered into an agreement with the landlord (usually pursuant to a licence to assign permitting him to take the lease) to remain liable throughout the remainder of the term.

The new tenant is not liable in damages for breaches committed by his predecessor (*Parry v Robinson-Wyllie* [1987] 2 EGLR 133) unless the breach is a continuing one, in which case he will be liable for that continuing breach. However, the landlord will be entitled to forfeit in respect of any breaches that have not been remedied or waived and the new tenant will have to apply for relief from forfeiture (see Chapter 2).

A tenant who assigns his lease retains the right to sue the landlord for breaches of covenant that occurred before the assignment. The right to sue in respect of past breaches does not pass to the assignee, but if the breach is a continuing one the new tenant may sue in respect of that continuing breach (*City & Metropolitan Properties v Greycroft* [1987] 3 All ER 839, QBD).

Subletting

Unless there is a covenant against subletting the tenant may sublet all or part of the premises without the risk of prejudicing his tenancy. In the absence of a written tenancy agreement it is often difficult to determine whether or not the tenant is prohibited from subletting. In *RC Glaze Properties Ltd v Alabdingoni* [1992] EGCS 141, the Court of Appeal held that the county court judge was entitled to infer the presence of a term prohibiting subletting where a rent book used consistently by the landlord stated in bold type that subletting was prohibited. It is a question of fact in every case whether such a term can be inferred.

However, once the landlord lawfully determines the tenancy by service of a valid notice to quit the sub-tenancy disappears along with the head lease whether or not it was lawfully granted. Or, as it is often graphically expressed 'the branch falls with the tree' (see *Moore Properties (Ilford) Ltd v McKeon* [1976] 1 WLR 1278 where the tenants were in fact unlawful). The position is the same at the end of a fixed term tenancy. Where the tenancy is unlawful, ie created in breach of covenant, the landlord may bring the tenancy to an end by forfeiting it provided that the lease contains a forfeiture clause. If the landlord does forfeit the lease the sub-tenancy will once again also disappear. The tenant and the sub-tenant will, however, have the right to claim relief against forfeiture under s146 of the Law of Property Act 1925 (see p54).

The position is rather different where the tenant surrenders his term. In that case the 'branch does not fall with the tree' because a tenant by voluntarily surrendering his term will not be permitted to destroy the sub-tenancy that he has created (*Parker v Jones* [1910] 2 KB 32; *Cow v Casey* [1949] 1 KB 474 at 478). Instead the tenant in effect becomes the tenant of the landlord (s139 of the Law of Property Act 1925). This situation continues until the landlord grants a new lease to the person who surrendered the original tenancy or to some other third party. The sub-tenant once again becomes a sub-tenant and his rights and obligations continue as if nothing had occurred (s150 of the Law of Property Act 1925). If the landlord was aware of the sub-tenancy at the time that he accepted the surrender he may not even forfeit if the subletting was in breach of covenant (*Parker v Jones*—query whether he may forfeit if he was not aware of the breach at the time that he accepted the surrender). A similar position prevails where the tenant terminates his tenancy by serving a notice to quit upon the landlord. Service of the notice will not destroy the sub-tenancy (see article at (1950) EG 45 per Hilbury J).

A subletting of the whole term operates as an assignment, so that the tenant loses his interest in the property and will not be able to claim possession from the sub-tenant (*Milmo v Carreras* [1946] KB 306). But in a case where the tenant held under a periodic tenancy and sublet for a fixed term that was greater than the period an assignment was not deemed to have taken effect (*Curteis v Corcoran* (1947) 150 EG 44).

Bankruptcy

Bankruptcy of the landlord

Where the landlord is the freehold owner of the premises the tenant's position is unaffected if the landlord goes bankrupt. The reversion simply becomes vested in the landlord's trustee in bankruptcy/liquidator unless and until he assigns the property to someone else. If the landlord was himself a tenant the sub-tenant's position is slightly different and is dealt with *below*.

Bankruptcy of the tenant (Insolvency Act 1986, ss283, 306, 308A, 315–321)

The general position is that upon the bankruptcy of a tenant the tenant's interest in the dwelling house vests, as part of his estate (s283), in the trustee in bankruptcy immediately on the trustee's appointment taking effect (s306 of the Insolvency Act 1986). However, it should be noted that certain assured, protected, agricultural and secure tenancies and occupancies do not form part of the estate unless a specific notice is served upon the bankrupt by the trustee (ss283(3A) and 308A as introduced by s117 of the Housing Act 1988—see the relevant chapter in relation to each type of tenancy).

Where the tenant's interest in the dwelling house does vest in the trustee in bankruptcy s315 of the 1986 Act provides that the trustee may, by the giving of a prescribed notice (ie prescribed by rules made under ss384 and 412), disclaim the tenancy. He may do so notwithstanding that he has taken possession of the property, endeavoured to sell it or otherwise exercised rights of ownership in relation to it. (See s315(1), (2)(*b*).) In addition to serving a notice upon the landlord, the trustee must also (so far as he is aware of their addresses) serve a copy of the disclaimer on every person claiming under the bankrupt as sub-tenant or mortgagee and upon every person in occupation or claiming a right to occupy the dwelling house. In these circumstances the disclaimer will take effect if there is no application made for a vesting order under s 320 (see *below*) within a period of 14 days beginning with the day on which the last notice was served or, if there is such an application, the court directs that the disclaimer is to take effect. (See ss317 and 318.)

The trustee may not disclaim where a 'person interested in the property' has applied in writing to the trustee to ask him whether he will disclaim or not and the trustee has not served a notice of disclaimer within the period of 28 days beginning with the date of that application (s316).

Where the trustee does disclaim the disclaimer operates 'so as to determine, as from the date of the disclaimer, the rights, interests and liabilities of the bankrupt and his estate in or in respect of the property disclaimed' but does not affect third party rights 'except so far as is necessary for the purpose of releasing the bankrupt, the bankrupt's estate and the trustee from any liability' (s315(3)).

Any person who claims an interest in the disclaimed dwelling-house, any person who is under any liability in respect of it, and any person in occupation or claiming a right to be in occupation may seek a vesting order pursuant to s320. The terms upon which a vesting order may be made are set out in s321.

If the trustee is entitled to and does disclaim, the original tenant has no right to remain on the premises and if he continues to do so without the consent of the landlord summary proceedings for possession may be taken under CCR Ord 24 or RSC Ord 113 (*Smalley v Quarrier* [1975] 1 WLR 938; see Form 14, p85). The landlord may not, however, recover possession from the bankrupt tenant's sub-tenant (*Smalley v Hardinge* (1881) 7 QBD 524). The sub-tenants are released from their obligations to the tenant but they must perform the obligations which the tenant originally owed to his landlord. If they do not do so and there is a proviso for reentry the landlord may forfeit (*Re Finley, ex parte Clothworkers' Co* (1888) 21 QBD 475 at 486; *Re Levy, ex parte Walton* (1881) 17 ChD 746). If any sub-tenant wishes to regularise the position he may apply for an order vesting the tenant's interest in himself, pursuant to s320 of the 1986 Act.

If the bankrupt is an assignee of the term the lease continues in existence after disclaimer and the landlord can claim the rent from the original tenant who may apply for an order vesting the estate in himself (*Warnford Investments Ltd v Duckworth* [1979] Ch 127). Thereafter the original tenant will once again be able to occupy the premises.

Some leases contain a clause permitting the landlord to forfeit the lease on the tenant's bankruptcy and if the trustee does not disclaim the lease the landlord may seek to recover possession by commencing forfeiture proceedings (s146(9) and (10) of the Law of Property Act 1925; see further p29).

Form 14: Order 24 affidavit—bankruptcy

IN THE   **COUNTY COURT**   Case No

IN THE MATTER OF [address of property]
BETWEEN

Applicant

—AND—

Respondent

I, [state name of Applicant and occupation], of [state address] MAKE OATH and say as follows:

1. I am the freehold owner of the property known as [state address of property] which consists of four self-contained flats. I purchased the property in 1992 subject to a number of tenancies, one of which was held by the Respondent who occupied Flat 3 under a weekly tenancy which was not an [assured] tenancy because [state the reason].

2. On a date prior to the [insert date] the Respondent was adjudicated bankrupt and because it was not [assured] his tenancy of the said flat formed part of his estate under s283 of the Insolvency Act 1986 and vested in his trustee in bankruptcy. The Respondent remained in occupation as a licensee of the trustee. On the [insert date] the Respondent's trustee in bankruptcy disclaimed the tenancy. There is now produced and shown to me and marked ['. . . 1'] a copy of the notice of disclaimer.

3. On the [insert date] I wrote to the Respondent demanding possession of the said flat. A copy of the said letter is now produced and shown to me and marked ['. . . 2']. Despite the demand for possession the Respondent has failed to vacate the flat and thus remains in occupation without my licence or consent.

4. I do not know the name of any person occupying the land who is not named in the originating application.

SWORN

Death

Death of landlord

The tenant's position is unaffected by the death of the landlord. During the administration of his estate the landlord's interest will vest in his personal representatives and eventually the beneficiary of the original landlord's estate will become the lessor. These changes do not, however, give any of these persons the right to claim possession of the premises in circumstances other than those which would have given the deceased landlord the right to claim possession. See p261 for the rights of personal representatives to sue for possession.

Death of tenant

The death of the tenant does not terminate the tenancy. As with the landlord's interest on death the tenant's interest, whether it be for a fixed or periodic term, becomes vested in personal representatives who are liable to pay the rent from the estate (*Youngmin v Heath* [1974] 1 All ER 461). Where the tenant has left a will and the named executors are alive and prepared to administer the estate the tenancy will vest in them from the date of death if they have obtained a grant of probate (*Re Crowhurst Park* [1974] 1 WLR 583). Where the tenant has died intestate the estate becomes vested in the President of the Family Division until administrators are appointed (s9 of the Administration of Estates Act 1925; *Wirral Borough Council v Smith* (1982) 43 P & CR 312). As to service of a notice to quit during this period see p67. Thereafter the estate vests in the administrators but only from the grant of letters of administration. Their title to the property does not date back to the date of death as with executors (*Long (Fred) and Sons Ltd v Burgess* [1950] KB 115).

The beneficiaries become entitled to hold the tenancy when it has been vested in them by an assent (s36 of the Administration of Estates Act 1925). If the title is registered the beneficiary should register as proprietor (s41(4) of the Land Registration Act 1925).

Although the death of the tenant does not automatically terminate the tenancy it may give the landlord the right to forfeit the lease if there is a forfeiture clause in the agreement allowing him to do so.

Chapter 5

Licence Agreements

It is usually important to know whether an agreement is a tenancy or a licence. A licensee cannot be an assured tenant (under the Housing Act 1988) or a regulated tenant (under the Rent Act 1977) and his rights in relation to the property which he occupies are likely to be very limited. This chapter considers the circumstances in which a person is a licensee, the termination of licences and recovery of possession from licensees.

In recent years there has been much litigation on this subject culminating in three decisions of the House of Lords. In *Street v Mountford* [1985] 2 All ER 289 the traditional view that, save for certain limited exceptions, an occupier of land for a term at a rent is a tenant provided that the occupier is granted exclusive possession was reaffirmed. The position where two or more persons occupy one property under separate agreements which purport to be 'licences' was considered by the House of Lords in *AG Securities v Vaughan* and *Antoniades v Villiers* [1988] 3 All ER 1058.

In each of these cases the leading judgment was given by Lord Templeman. The quotations in this chapter are taken from his judgments.

Distinction between leases and licences

Generally

The traditional view that the grant of exclusive possession for a term creates a tenancy is consistent with the elevation of a tenancy into an estate in land. The tenant possessing exclusive possession is able to exercise the rights of an owner of land, which is in the real sense his land albeit temporarily and subject to certain restrictions. A tenant armed with exclusive possession can keep out strangers and keep out the landlord unless the landlord is exercising limited rights reserved to him by the tenancy agreement to enter and view and repair. A licensee lacking exclusive possession can in no sense call the land his own and cannot be said to own any estate in the land. The licence does not create an estate in the land to which it relates but only makes an act lawful which would otherwise be unlawful (*Street* 292d to e).

. . . the traditional distinction between a tenancy and a licence of land lay in the grant of land for a term at a rent with exclusive possession (*Street* 292g).

87

After the decision of the Court of Appeal in *Somma v Hazlehurst* [1978] 1 WLR 1014 the courts, when dealing with written agreements for the occupation of land, had adopted the practice of analysing their provisions for the purpose of assigning some of them to the category of terms which are usually thought to be found in tenancy agreements and of assigning others to the category of terms which are usually thought to be found in licences. In *Street v Mountford* Lord Templeman stated that this was the wrong way to assess such agreements. The proper approach is to analyse each agreement in order to decide whether exclusive possession has been granted (299h).

Furthermore, the label that the parties attach to an agreement is not conclusive. The mere fact that they call it a licence does not necessarily mean that it is a licence. If upon its true construction the agreement is a tenancy, ie it gives a right to exclusive possession for a fixed or periodic term at a rent, the court will hold that it is a tenancy whatever the parties might say about their intentions.

> The consequences in law of the agreement, once concluded, can only be determined by consideration of the effect of the agreement. If the agreement satisfied all the requirements of a tenancy, then the agreement produced a tenancy and the parties cannot alter the effect of the agreement by insisting that they only created a licence. The manufacture of a five-pronged implement for manual digging results in a fork even if the manufacturer, unfamiliar with the English language, insists that he intended to make and has made a spade (*Street* 294j) . . . the only intention which is relevant is the intention demonstrated by the agreement to grant exclusive possession for a term at a rent (*Street* p 300b; see further *below*, section (*d*), 'Shams' and 'Pretences').

Application of the rule to residential premises

> In the case of residential accommodation there is no difficulty in deciding whether the grant confers exclusive possession. An occupier of residential accommodation at a rent for a term is either a lodger or a tenant. The occupier is a lodger if the landlord provides attendance or services which require the landlord or his servants to exercise unrestricted access to and use of the premises. A lodger is entitled to live in the premises but cannot call the place his own . . . If on the other hand residential accommodation is granted for a term at a rent with exclusive possession, the landlord providing neither attendance nor services, the grant is a tenancy; any express reservation to the landlord of limited rights to enter and view the state of the premises and to repair and maintain the premises only serve to emphasise the fact that the grantee is entitled to exclusive possession and is a tenant (*Street* 293g to j).
> . . . in my opinion, in order to ascertain the nature and quality of the occupancy and to see whether the occupier has or has not a stake in the room or only permission for himself personally to occupy, the court must decide whether on its true construction the agreement confers on the occupier exclusive possession (*Street* 299a).

A lodger will very often be a person who lives in a house with a family using one bedroom and sharing the other accommodation. Meals may be provided and perhaps his room will be cleaned for him. However, there are other cases where occupiers of single rooms will be held to be licensees rather than tenants. In *Marchant v Charters* [1977] 3 All ER 918 a bed-sitting room was occupied on terms that the landlord cleaned the rooms daily and provided clean linen each week. Lord Templeman stated that the court's decision that the occupier was a licensee and not a tenant was sustainable on the grounds that the occupier was a lodger and did not enjoy exclusive possession (*Street* 298g). In *Abbeyfield (Harpenden) Society Ltd v Woods* [1968] 1 All ER 352 the occupier of a room in an old people's home was held to be a licensee and not a tenant. Besides occupying one room, the occupier was provided with services, meals and a resident housekeeper. Lord Templeman stated that as far as he understood the decision 'the court came to the conclusion that the occupier was a lodger and was therefore a licensee and not a tenant' (*Street* 298a to c).

The retention of a key, by itself, is not decisive in determining whether or not the landlord retains exclusive possession (*Aslan v Murphy (Nos 1 and 2)* [1989] 3 All ER 130; *Family Housing Association v Jones* [1990] 1 All ER 385).

Written licence agreements: genuine cases

The question of whether or not the agreement confers upon the occupier exclusive possession has caused most difficulty in cases where there have been two or more occupiers who are in occupation pursuant to written agreements which are expressed to be licence agreements.

In *Crancour Ltd v Da Silvaesa* [1986] 1 EGLR 80 the accommodation concerned was bed-sit type accommodation in a large house. The owners sought possession under the summary procedure contained in RSC Ord 113 (see Chapter 25). The occupiers had entered into written agreements that were called 'licences'. Clause 1 licensed the occupiers to use the furnished room provided

> on each day between the hours of midnight and 10.30 am and between noon and midnight but at no other time for a period of 26 weeks . . . for the purpose of temporary accommodation for the licensee's personal use only . . .

The agreement also contained the following clauses:

> 2. The possession, management and control of the flat remains vested in the licensor, who is the occupier for all purposes including taxation and rating. The licensor will retain the keys to the flat and has an absolute right of entry at all times for the purpose of exercising such management and control and . . . for the purpose of effecting any repairs or cleaning to the flat or building or for the purpose of providing the attendance mentioned in clause 9 hereof or for the purpose of removing or substituting such articles of furniture from the flat as the licensor may see fit.

3. The licensee shall pay the licensor a fee of £110 per fortnight for his use of the flat . . .

4. The licensor may for any reason and at any time require the licensee forthwith to vacate the flat and move into any other flat of comparable size in the building which the licensor may offer the licensee . . .

5. This licence agreement confers upon the licensee merely a personal privilege to use the flat.

. . .

9. The licensor will provide the following attendance for the licensee: (i) Housekeeper; (ii) Lighting of common parts; (iii) Cleaning of common parts; (iv) Window cleaning; (v) Service to front door; (vi) Telephone; (vii) Cleaning of flat; (viii) Collection of rubbish; (ix) Provision and laundering of bed linen; (x) Hot water.

The Court of Appeal held that the provision relating to the times at which the room could be used (in Clause 1) and as to the right to remove furniture were arguably 'sham' provisions and that the case was not therefore sufficiently clear to justify a summary order for possession. However, it also held that *if* the written agreements represented the true agreement of the parties the occupants were lodgers and not tenants. (In relation to Clause 4 of the agreement compare *Dresden Estates v Collinson* [1987] 1 EGLR 45—a case concerned with business premises.)

Genuine non-possession agreements are not confined to bed-sitter/ hostel type accommodation. They may also exist, for example, in flat-sharing cases. In *AG Securities v Vaughan* [1988] 3 All ER 1058 the property consisted of six living rooms, a kitchen and bathroom. Four rooms were furnished as bedrooms, a fifth as a lounge and a sixth as a sitting room. The owner entered into separate agreements with each occupant. Each agreement was in the same form and described the occupier as a licensee who had 'the right to use in common with others who have or may from time to time be granted the like right the flat known as (Flat 25) but without the right to exclusive possession of any part of the said flat'. The flat was kept fully occupied; whenever one agreement was terminated the *owner of the property* invited applications to fill the vacancy. The monthly sum payable by each applicant was not necessarily the same as the monthly sum payable by any of the continuing occupiers of the flat. The four occupiers at the time of the proceedings were all in occupation under agreements of different dates and were each paying different sums. The House of Lords held that each occupier was a licensee of the whole flat. There was no unity of interest, no unity of title, no unity of time and no unity of possession (see Lord Oliver at 1074j). It was impossible to hold that they were joint tenants. For similar cases, where the occupiers were held to be licensees, see *Stribling v Wickham* (1989) 21 HLR 318 and *Mikeover Ltd v Brady* [1989] 3 All ER 618

(Note that in *AG Securities v Vaughan* it was not contended that any individual occupier had a tenancy of a particular room in the flat with a right to use the remainder in common with the tenants of other rooms: see Lord Oliver at 1074b. In other circumstances this may be the situation in which case the occupiers will be entitled to the protection afforded by s22 of the Rent Act 1977 or, as the case may be, s10 of the Housing Act 1988 (see p180).)

In *Westminster City Council v Clarke* [1992] 1 All ER 695 the local authority provided homeless persons with temporary accommodation in a hostel whilst dealing with their applications for permanent accommodation under the Housing Act 1985. Those persons occupied bed-sitting rooms under agreements which negatived exclusive possession. The grant of exclusive possession would have been inconsistent with the purposes for which the council provided the accommodation and the House of Lords held that the agreements were genuine licences. However, Lord Templeman pointed out that the case was a very special one which was unlikely to have more than limited application (at p703f).

Written 'licence' agreements: 'shams' and 'pretences'

The House of Lords considered this type of agreement in *Antoniades v Villiers* [1988] 3 All ER 1058. In that case the accommodation comprised a bedroom, a bed-sitting room, kitchen and bathroom. The occupiers, a man and a woman, had spent three months looking for a flat where they could live together. When they were shown the flat by the owner the bedroom lacked a bed. They expressed a preference for a double bed and this was provided. The occupiers entered into separate 'licence agreements' in standard form whereby 'the licensor licences the licensee to use (but not exclusively) all those rooms etc'. In particular, Clause 16 of the agreement was in the following terms:

> 16. The licensor shall be entitled at any time to use the rooms together with the licensee and permit other persons to use all of the rooms together with the licensee.

The two agreements were clearly interdependent. Both would have been signed or neither. In those circumstances the court held that the two agreements should be read together:

> Mr Villiers and Miss Bridger applied to rent the flat jointly and sought and enjoyed an exclusive occupation of the whole of the flat. They shared the rights and the obligations imposed by the terms of their occupation. They acquired joint and exclusive occupation of the flat in consideration of periodical payments and they therefore acquired a tenancy jointly. Mr Antoniades required each of them, Mr Villiers and Miss Bridger, to agree to pay one-half of each aggregate periodical payment, but this circumstance cannot convert a tenancy into a licence. A tenancy remains a tenancy even though the landlord may choose to require each of two joint tenants to agree expressly to pay one-half of the rent. The tenancy conferred on Mr Villiers and Miss Bridger the right to occupy the whole flat as their dwelling. Clause 16 reserved to Mr Antoniades the power at any time to go into occupation of the flat jointly with Mr Villiers and Miss Bridger. The exercise of that power would at common law put an end to the exclusive occupation of the flat by Mr Villiers and Miss Bridger, terminate the tenancy of Mr Villiers and Miss

Bridger and convert Mr Villiers and Miss Bridger into licensees. But the powers reserved to Mr Antoniades by cl. 16 cannot be lawfully exercised because they are inconsistent with the provisions of the Rent Acts (1066e). . . . Where a landlord creates a tenancy of a flat and reserves the right to go into exclusive occupation at any time of the whole or part of the flat with or without notice, that reservation is inconsistent with the provisions of the Rent Acts and cannot be enforced without an order of the court under s98. Where a landlord creates a tenancy of a flat and reserves the right to go into occupation of the whole or part of the flat with or without notice, jointly with the existing tenants, that reservation also is inconsistent with the provisions of the Acts. Were it otherwise every tenancy agreement would be labelled a licence and would contract out of the Rent Acts by reserving power to the landlord to share possession with the tenant at any time after the commencement of the term (1067c).

Earlier in his judgment Lord Templeman had said:

Parties to an agreement cannot contract out of the Rent Acts; if they were able to do so the Acts would be a dead letter because in a state of housing shortage a person seeking residential accommodation may agree to anything to obtain shelter. The Rent Acts protect a tenant but they do not protect a licensee. Since parties to an agreement cannot contract out of the Rent Acts, a document which expresses the intention, genuine or bogus, of both parties or of one party to create a licence will nevertheless create a tenancy if the rights and obligations enjoyed and imposed satisfy the legal requirements of a tenancy. A person seeking residential accommodation may concur in any expression of intention in order to obtain shelter. Since parties to an agreement cannot contract out of the Rent Acts, a document expressed in the language of a licence must nevertheless be examined and construed by the court in order to decide whether the rights and obligations enjoyed and imposed create a licence or a tenancy. A person seeking residential accommodation may sign a document couched in any language in order to obtain shelter. Since parties to an agreement cannot contract out of the Rent Acts, the grant of a tenancy to two persons jointly cannot be concealed, accidentally, or by design, by the creation of two documents in the form of licences. Two persons seeking residential accommodation may sign any number of documents in order to obtain joint shelter. In considering one or more documents for the purpose of deciding whether a tenancy has been created, the court must consider the surrounding circumstances, including any relationship between the prospective occupiers, the course of negotiations and the nature and extent of the accommodation and the intended and actual mode of occupation of the accommodation (1064f).

In deciding whether or not the terms of a so-called 'licence agreement' in fact create a tenancy the court does not simply ask itself whether the agreement is a sham. It also considers whether in the light of all the circumstances its provisions truly represent the agreement between the parties or whether they are a 'pretence' (*AG Securities v Vaughan* per Lord Templeman at 1067h; *Aslan v Murphy (Nos 1 and 2)* [1989] 3 All ER 130). And see *Family Housing Association v Jones* [1990] 1 All ER 385 where a term in the agreement which expressly stated that exclusive possession was not granted was held to be a 'pretence'.

Cases where occupier with exclusive possession is not a tenant

There can be no tenancy unless the occupier enjoys exclusive possession but there are exceptional cases where an occupier with exclusive possession is not a tenant; exceptional circumstances may exist which negative the prima facie intention to create a tenancy:

> There can be no tenancy unless the occupier enjoys exclusive possession; but an occupier who enjoys exclusive possession is not necessarily a tenant. He may be the owner in fee simple, a trespasser, a mortgagee in possession, an object of charity or a service occupier. To constitute a tenancy the occupier must be granted exclusive possession for a fixed or periodic term certain in consideration of a premium or periodical payments. The grant may be express, or may be inferred where the owner accepts weekly or other periodic payments from the occupier (*Street* 294a).
>
> The intention to create a tenancy was negatived if the parties did not intend to enter into legal relationships at all, or where the relationship between the parties was that of vendor and purchaser, master and service occupier, or where the owner, a requisitioning authority, had no power to grant a tenancy (*Street* 295j to 296a).

Thus, one can see from the judgment of Lord Templeman in *Street v Mountford* that the following cases are examples where notwithstanding an agreement granting the occupant the right to exclusive possession for a term at a rent no tenancy has been granted:

(*a*) Where there has been no intention to create legal relations, for example where there has been in the circumstances such as a family arrangement, an act of friendship or generosity (see Lord Templeman at 294e; 295b, j; 296c; 298f); but note that the mere fact of family relationship or act of friendship, etc will not necessarily prevent the creation of legal relations. There are many cases where one member of a family grants to another a tenancy of premises.

(*b*) Service occupancies (see Chapter 14).

(*c*) Occupancy by reference to the holding of an office (see Lord Templeman at 300d).

(*d*) Body conferring right to exclusive possession having no power to grant a tenancy (Lord Templeman at 295j).

(*e*) Contract between vendor and purchaser for the sale of land (see Chapter 18, p243).

In *Sharp v McArthur* (1987) 19 HLR 364 (Court of Appeal), the owner of a flat which was for sale let the occupier, who was in urgent need of accommodation, into possession as a favour pending the sale. Rent was paid. It was held that there were exceptional circumstances that rebutted the presumption of a tenancy.

In *Westminster CC v Basson* [1991] 1 EGLR 277, CA, an unlawful occupier was told that proceedings had been commenced and that until they were determined she would be expected to pay damages for use and occupation. The letter concluded: In making the payments as Use and

Occupation Charges this arrangement is not intended as the creation of a tenancy or a licence akin to a tenancy in any way whatsoever'. It was held that the intention to create a tenancy was negatived by that sentence At p278B Mustill LJ said:

> The sense of the letter is perfectly clear . . . The council were saying 'We desire you to vacate the premises. We trust that you will do so voluntarily. If not we shall take steps to remove you. Meanwhile we are not going to let you remain in there free of charge and to make sure that we are paid we shall expect to receive payment at the stated rate in the stated manner until we succeed in regaining possession'.

Irrevocable licences

Most licences may be determined in accordance with the terms of the agreement or upon the giving of reasonable notice (see *below*). This section is concerned with those licences that may not be so revoked by the licensor.

In *DHN Food Distributors v London Borough of Tower Hamlets* [1976] 3 All ER 462 at 467a Lord Denning stated that 'a contractual licence under which a person has the right to occupy premises indefinitely gives rise to a constructive trust under which the legal owner is not allowed to turn out the licensee'. Whether or not a licence is revocable depends upon the terms of the agreement (*Millenium Productions Ltd v Winter Garden Theatre (London) Ltd* [1946] 1 All ER 680 per Lord Greene MR; *Hounslow London Borough Council v Twickenham Garden Developments Ltd* [1971] Ch 233).

A licensee does not necessarily have to show that there is a contract before he can argue that he has an irrevocable licence. He may instead be able to rely upon the equitable doctrine of estoppel. Where the licensor has made a promise that the licensee may live on the premises for a certain period of time and the licensee has acted in reliance upon the promise and thereby suffered a detriment, the licensor is estopped from revoking the licence before that period has passed. (See *Errington v Errington and Woods* [1952] 1 KB 290.) It is important to remember where the burden of proof lies in these cases. The licensee must show that the licensor made a representation intending that the licensee should act upon it. There is then a presumption that the licensee relied upon it. If the licensor is to succeed *he* must show that there was no reliance (see *Greasley v Cooke* [1980] 3 All ER 710). The licensee must show that he has suffered a detriment as a result of the reliance (*Stevens & Cutting v Anderson* [1990] 1 EGLR 95). The licensor may be able to resist the licensee's claim for an estoppel by showing that the licensee has not come to court with 'clean hands' (*Williams v Staite* [1979] Ch 291; *Willis & Son v Willis* (1985) 277 EG 1133).

If the court comes to the conclusion that the property owner is estopped from turning out the licensee 'an equity arises' and the court will then consider how to satisfy that equity. The licensee is usually given a right to remain in the property for the period promised but in extreme cases outright ownership might be transferred (see eg *Greasley v Cooke*; *Inwards v Baker* [1965] 2 QB 29; *Dillwyn v Llewellyn* (1862) 4 De GF & J 517). Each case will depend upon its own facts and will turn upon the nature of the promise, the way in which the licensee acted in reliance upon it and the detriment that was sustained. For the problems that arise when deciding how to satisfy the equity see *Dodsworth v Dodsworth* (1973) 228 EG 1115; *Griffiths v Williams* (1977) 248 EG 947; *Burrows & Burrows v Sharp* (1989) 23 HLR 82 CA).

For constructive trust cases where the defendant in a possession action claims to be the sole or joint beneficial owner of the property, see *Grant v Edwards* [1986] 2 All ER 426 and *Lloyds Bank plc v Rossett* [1990] 1 All ER 1111—requirement to show common intention of the parties to share the property beneficially and defilement or significant alteration of position in reliance on the agreement. See also *Springette v Defoe* (1992) *The Independent*, 10 March, CA, where the legal title to the property was held in joint names. However, it was held that the court could not infer a common intention that they were to share the beneficial interest in the property equally as the parties had not communicated such an intention to each other. Where there has been no discussion between the parties about their respective beneficial interests, their shares are presumed to be in proportion to their contributions.

Termination and recovery of possession

Termination

Subject to the requirement to give not less than four weeks' notice in the case of periodic licences (see *below*), a licensor wishing to revoke a revocable licence should give such notice as is required by the terms of the agreement. Where there are no such terms the licensor should give the licensee a reasonable amount of time to leave (*Minister of Health v Bellotti* [1944] KB 298; *Vaughan v Vaughan* [1953] 1 QB 762). Whether the amount of time given is sufficient is a question of fact in each case. The periods in respect of which the licence fees are paid will be relevant, as will the length of time the licensee has been in occupation.

However, no notice by a licensor (or licensee) to determine a *periodic* licence to occupy premises as a dwelling is valid, unless it is in writing and contains such information as may be prescribed by statutory instrument (presently the Notices to Quit etc (Prescribed Information) Regulations 1988, SI No 2201) and is given not less than four weeks before the date on which it is to take effect (s5(1A) of the Protection from Eviction Act 1977). As emphasised, this provision only applies to periodic licences (*Norris v Checksfield* [1991] 4 All ER 327—as the right of an employee/licensee to remain in occupation comes to an end on termination of the employment (see p208), the licence is not a periodic licence and it is not necessary to serve a notice to quit in accordance with s5(1A)). Furthermore, s5(1A) need not be complied with where the premises are occupied under an 'excluded licence' (s5(1B), see p255 for definition of excluded licence).

Protection from Eviction Act 1977, s5
    (1A) Subject to subsection (1B) below, no notice by a licensor or a licensee to determine a periodic licence to occupy premises as a dwelling (whether the licence was granted before or after the passing of this Act) shall be valid unless—
        (*a*) it is in writing and contains such information as may be prescribed, and
        (*b*) it is given not less than four weeks before the date on which it is to take effect.
    (1B) Nothing in . . . subsection (1A) above applies to—
        (*a*) [ ]
        (*b*) premises occupied under an excluded licence (see p255).

For a form of notice to be served by a licensor, containing the prescribed information, see Form 15, p97. No information has been prescribed in relation to notices to be given by licensees.

Where a valid notice has been served in accordance with s5 of the Protection from Eviction Act 1977 (if applicable) but a reasonable amount of time has not been given the court will nevertheless make an order for possession if a reasonable amount of time had elapsed by the date proceedings were commenced. It is submitted that as the licence is revoked immediately the notice is given the court also has power to make an order for possession if a reasonable amount of time has elapsed at the date of the hearing even if it had not done so on the date the proceedings were commenced (*Minister of Health v Bellotti*).

One of two joint licensors may revoke the licence without the consent of the other (see *Annen v Rattee* [1986] 1 EGLR 136).

For a discussion as to whether an irrevocable licence may be revoked by the licensor where it would be inequitable to permit the licensee to continue to rely upon it see *Williams v Staite* [1979] Ch 291 and *Willis & Son v Willis* (1985) 277 EG 113.

Proceedings for possession

Unless the licence is an 'excluded licence' the licensor may only recover possession by way of court proceedings (s3(2B) and s3A of the Protection from Eviction Act 1977; see pp254–6).

The proceedings for possession may usually be commenced by originating application under CCR Ord 24 (RSC Ord 113 in the High Court); see Chapter 25. Alternatively, the proceedings may be commenced by summons; see Chapter 18. The former procedure will normally result in a quicker hearing date but the licensor will not be able

Form 15: Form of notice to determine licence to be served by licensor

NOTICE TO DETERMINE LICENCE

(BY LICENSOR OF PREMISES OCCUPIED AS A DWELLING)

Name and
Address of
Licensee

To ....

of ....

....

Name and
Address of
Licensor

[I] [We] [as] [on behalf of] your licensor[s] ....

of ....

give you notice to determine your licence to occupy and to deliver up possession to

Address of
Premises

[me] [them] of ....

....

on ....19........., or the day on which a complete period of
your licence expires next after the end of four weeks from the service of this notice.

Dated ....19......

Signed ....

Name and
Address of Agent
if Agent serves
notice

....

....

....

INFORMATION FOR LICENSEE

1. If the tenant or licensee does not leave the dwelling, the landlord or licensor must get an order for possession from the court before the tenant or licensee can lawfully be evicted. The landlord or licensor cannot apply for such an order before the notice to quit or notice to determine has run out.
2. A tenant or licensee who does not know if he has any right to remain in possession after a notice to quit or notice to determine runs out can obtain advice from a solicitor. Help with all or part of the cost of legal advice and assistance may be available under the Legal Aid Scheme. He should also be able to obtain information from a Citizens' Advice Bureau, a Housing Aid Centre or a Rent Officer.

NOTES

1. Notice to determine a periodic licence to occupy premises as a dwelling must be given at least four weeks before it takes effect and it must be in writing (Protection from Eviction Act 1977, s 5 as amended).
2. Where a notice to determine a licence is given by a licensor the notice must contain the above information (the Notices to Quit etc (Prescribed Information) Regulations 1988).
3. Some licences are excluded from this protection: see Protection from Eviction Act 1977, ss 3A and 5 (1B)

Reproduced by kind permission of The Solicitors' Law Stationery Society Ltd

to claim any outstanding licence fees or mesne profits in those proceedings, which are confined to the question of possession.

Licensees, like tenants, may not dispute the title of their 'landlords' (*Government of Penang v Oon* [1972] AC 425 at 433E). Thus, a licensee will not be able to avoid an order for possession by arguing that the licensor has no interest in the property.

Most contractual licensees in the private sector given the right to occupy prior to the commencement of the Housing Act 1988 will have been in occupation under restricted contracts. In these cases the court has power to suspend the order for possession for up to three months upon certain conditions as to the payment of sums for use and occupation etc (see Chapter 9). In all other cases the county court will only be able to postpone the date for possession for up to 14 days, unless such a short order would cause exceptional hardship in which case the court will have the power to suspend the order for up to six weeks (s89 of the Housing Act 1980; see p75). The High Court's discretion is unfettered by s89 of the 1980 Act (*Bain and Co v Church Commissioners for England* [1989] 1 WLR 24).

For licensees who are protected under the Rent (Agriculture) Act 1976, see Chapter 15, and for licensees in the public sector, see Chapter 10.

Assignment, subletting, bankruptcy and death

Revocable licences

As an ordinary contractual licence creates no interest in land it is automatically determined by the bankruptcy or death of the licensor or by the licensor voluntarily assigning the land over which the licence is exercised (see *Terunnanse v Terunnanse* [1968] AC 1086, per Lord Devlin at 1095G).

A licensee may not assign the benefit of the agreement unless there is a term in the agreement, express or implied, permitting him to assign (*Dorling v Honnor Marine Ltd* [1964] Ch 560 and see s136 of the Law of Property Act 1925). A licensee may not sublet as such (ie so as to bind the licensor in any way) but as between the licensee and the 'sub-tenant' a tenancy by estoppel will have been created (see p7). Where a licensee goes bankrupt or dies the licence automatically comes to an end (*Coleman v Foster* (1856) 1 H & N 37—compare secure tenancies (Chapter 10) and agricultural accommodation (Chapter 15)).

Irrevocable licences

Irrevocable licences have been held to bind a purchaser of the licensor's interest in the land who had notice of the licence (*Binions v Evans* [1972] Ch 359), a licensor's trustee in bankruptcy (*Re Sharpe (a bankrupt)*

[1980] 1 WLR 219), and the personal representatives and beneficiaries of a licensor's estate (*Errington v Errington and Woods* [1952] 1 KB 290; *Inwards v Baker* [1965] 2 QB 29). But all these cases should now be read in the light of *Ashburn Anstalt v Arnold* [1988] 2 All ER 147, CA (overruled on another point in *Prudential Assurance Co v London Residuary Body* [1992] 3 All ER 504, HL) where it was held that a contractual licence was not an interest in land capable of binding a purchaser even where that purchaser had notice; and that the only circumstances in which the licence may be binding upon third parties is where a constructive trust is imposed and that the court will not impose such a trust unless it is satisfied that the conscience of the purchaser is affected.

Where the licensor has died those acting for the licensee should consider whether the client has any rights under the Inheritance (Provision for Family and Dependants) Act 1975. Under that Act it may be possible to obtain an interest in the property giving the licensee a right to live there (see s2(1)(*c*), (*d*)). The application under the Act should be made within six months from the date on which representation with respect to the estate of the deceased is first taken out (s4). If the personal representatives are seeking to obtain an order for possession the licensee should apply for the possession proceedings to be adjourned until after the application under the 1975 Act has been determined.

Part 2

Termination and the Right to
Possession—Particular Cases

Chapter 6

Assured Tenancies

The assured tenancy and the assured shorthold tenancy (see Chapter 7) were created by the Housing Act 1988 with the intention of encouraging private owners of dwelling houses to let their properties. Parliament has not repealed the Rent Act 1977; regulated tenancies in existence at the date of the commencement of the 1988 Act (15 January 1989) continue to exist. However, all private sector tenancies (save for a few transitional exceptions) created after that date are governed by the new regime.

An assured tenancy is similar to a regulated tenancy in that the landlord may not recover possession unless he can prove a ground for possession. However, the grounds are more favourable to the landlord than those that apply in Rent Act cases. The termination procedure is similar to that which applies to secure tenancies under the Housing Act 1980 in that a periodic assured tenancy may only be determined by an order of the court after a notice of intention to commence proceedings has been served (unless the notice requirement is dispensed with). Notices to quit are irrelevant and of no effect.

Fixed term assured tenancies do come to an end at the expiry of the term but thereupon a 'statutory periodic tenancy' automatically arises. This periodic tenancy like other assured periodic tenancies may not be determined by the landlord without service of a notice of intention to commence proceedings (unless dispensed with) and an order of the court. Unlike the statutory tenancy that follows a protected tenancy under the Rent Act 1977, which merely confers a status of irremovability, a statutory periodic tenancy under the 1988 Act is a true interest in land capable of assignment (s5(3); s15(3) of the 1988 Act).

Definition of assured tenancies

The basic rule: s1 of the Housing Act 1988

Section 1 of the Housing Act 1988 provides that:

> A tenancy under which a dwelling-house is let as a separate dwelling is for the purposes of this Act an assured tenancy *if and so long as*—

(a) the tenant or, as the case may be, each of the joint tenants is an individual; and

(b) the tenant or, as the case may be, at least one of the joint tenants occupies the dwelling-house as his only or principal home; and

(c) the tenancy is not one which, by virtue of subsection (2) or subsection (6) below, cannot be an assured tenancy.

Note the words in italics. If one of the conditions ceases to apply the tenancy will cease to be assured. The exceptions referred to in subs (c) are dealt with below.

A 'dwelling house' may be a house properly so called or part of a house: s45. Where a dwelling house is let together with other land the land is treated as part of the dwelling house and therefore assured if and so long as the main purpose of the letting is the provision of a home for the tenant or, where there are joint tenants, at least one of them: s2(1)(a) (unless the land is agricultural land exceeding two acres in which case the letting cannot be assured: Sched 1, para 6). However, the tenancy will not be assured if and so long as the main purpose of the letting is not the provision of a home for the tenant or, where there are joint tenants, at least one of them (s2(1)(b)).

The requirement that the tenant be an individual means that a letting to a company cannot be an assured tenancy (see further p214). Note the requirement that the dwelling be occupied by the tenant 'as his only or principal home'.

For further assistance with the definition of the assured tenancy compare p131 in relation to protected tenancies. See Chapter 11 for the position where the tenant shares some of his accommodation.

The exceptions (s2(2), (6) of and Sched 1 to the 1988 Act)

The main exceptions are to be found in Part 1 of Sched 1 to the Housing Act 1988, the full text of which is set out in Appendix 2. They are as follows:

1 Tenancies entered into before the commencement of the Housing Act 1988 or pursuant to contracts made before that date.

2 Tenancies of dwelling houses with high rateable values/high rents (see Appendix 1—see also para 2A).

3 Tenancies at a low rent (see Appendix 2—see also paras 3A, 3B and 3C).

4 Business tenancies (see Chapter 14).

5 Licensed premises (see Chapter 14).

6 Tenancies of agricultural land.

7 Tenancies of agricultural holdings (see Chapter 15).

8 Lettings to students (see Chapter 16).

9 Holiday lettings (see Chapter 16).

10 Resident landlords (see Chapter 11).

11 Landlord's interest belonging to the Crown, save where the property is under the management of the Crown Estate Commissioners.

12 Landlord a local authority etc (see Chapter 10).

13 Transitional cases (see *below*).

Temporary housing of homeless persons   There is a further exception which is dealt with in s 1(6), (7) of the 1988 Act. It relates to the situation where a local authority makes an arrangement with another person to provide accommodation for a homeless person:

> (6) If, in pursuance of its duty under—
>> (a) section 63 of the Housing Act 1985 (duty to house pending enquiries in case of apparent priority need),
>> (b) section 65(3) of that Act (duty to house temporarily person found to have priority need but to have become homeless intentionally), or
>> (c) section 68(1) of that Act (duty to house pending determination whether conditions for referral of application are satisfied),
>
> a local housing authority have made arrangements with another person to provide accommodation, a tenancy granted by that person in pursuance of the arrangements to a person specified by the authority cannot be an assured tenancy before the expiry of the period of twelve months beginning with the date specified in subsection (7) below unless, before the expiry of that period, the tenant is notified by the landlord (or in the case of joint landlords, at least one of them) that the tenancy is to be regarded as an assured tenancy.
>
> (7) The date referred to in subsection (6) above is the date on which the tenant received the notification required by section 64(1) of the Housing Act 1985 (notification of decision on question of homelessness or threatened homelessness) or, if he received a notification under section 68(3) of that Act (notification of which authority has duty to house), the date on which he received that notification.

where the tenancy is not assured and no other statutory protection applies (eg in resident landlord cases), the common rules set out in Chapters 2 and 3 as to termination will apply. Thus, in the case of a periodic tenancy a standard note to quit should be served (p62).

Assured tenancies under the Housing Act 1980

Sections 56–58 of the Housing Act 1980 created a form of tenancy called an 'assured tenancy' which could only be granted by certain approved bodies. These tenancies were subject to the provisions of the Landlord and Tenant Act 1954, Parts II and IV (the business tenancy code) as modified by the Housing Act 1980 so as to be applicable to residential premises. This form of assured tenancy came to an end with the enactment of the Housing Act 1988.

By virtue of s37 of the 1988 Act any tenancy entered into on or after the commencement of the 1988 Act cannot be an assured tenancy for the purposes of ss56–58 of the Housing Act 1980. Furthermore, by virtue of s1(3) of the 1988 Act at the commencement of the 1988 Act all 1980 Act assured tenancies became assured tenancies under the 1988 Act.

There is a limited exception. Where before the commencement of the 1988 Act a tenant under a 1980 Act assured tenancy had made an application to the court for the grant of a new tenancy and at the commencement the tenancy was continuing by virtue of s24 or any provisions of Part IV of the 1954 Act it continues to be a 1980 Act assured tenancy. However, any new tenancy granted will be a 1988 Act assured tenancy: see s37(2), (3), (6)—see also subss (4) and (5) for further transitional provisions.

In the case of 1980 Act assured tenancies that have become 1988 Act assured tenancies Part I of Sched 1 to the 1988 Act (the list of exceptions) has effect as if it consisted only of para 11 (Crown) and 12 (other public bodies). In the case where the landlord is and was prior to commencement a fully mutual housing association (see Housing Associations Act 1985, Part I) para 12 of Sched 1 is also amended so as to delete the reference to such associations (sub-para 1(h): s4(5)).

Transitional provisions

There are four types of tenancy created after the commencement of the Housing Act 1988 that may be protected (under the Rent Act 1977) rather than assured:

- (a) a tenancy entered into in pursuance of a contract made before the commencement of the 1988 Act;
- (b) a tenancy granted to a person who, immediately before the tenancy was granted, was a protected or statutory tenant (except for shorthold cases) of the landlord;
- (c) certain tenancies granted after an order for possession made pursuant to s98 of the Rent Act 1977 on the ground that suitable alternative accommodation is available to the tenant;
- (d) cases where the tenancy has been transferred from a new town corporation to the private sector pursuant to s38 of the Act.

See further p132 in relation to protected and statutory tenancies and p190 in relation to protected shorthold tenancies. See also s35 of the 1988 Act in relation to 'housing association tenancies'.

Termination by landlord

Housing Act 1988, s5(1)(2) and s45(4)

    5.—(1) An assured tenancy cannot be brought to an end by the landlord except by obtaining an order of the court in accordance with the following provisions of this Chapter or Chapter II below or, in the case of a fixed term tenancy which contains power for the landlord to determine the tenancy in certain circumstances, by the exercise of that power and, accordingly the service by the landlord of a notice to quit shall be of no effect in relation to a periodic assured tenancy.

(2) If an assured tenancy which is a fixed term tenancy comes to an end otherwise than by virtue of—

(*a*) an order of the court, or

(*b*) a surrender or other action on the part of the tenant,

then, subject to section 7 and Chapter II below, the tenant shall be entitled to remain in possession of the dwelling-house let under that tenancy and, subject to subsection (4) below, his right to possession shall depend upon a periodic tenancy arising by virtue of this section.

. . .

45.—(4) For the avoidance of doubt, it is hereby declared that any reference in this Part of this Act (however expressed) to a power for a landlord to determine a tenancy does not include a reference to a power of reentry or forfeiture for breach of any term or condition of the tenancy.

Introduction

The rules set out in this section only apply to termination by landlords. (For termination by the tenant, see p116.)

Furthermore, they do not apply where the proceedings for possession are brought by a mortgagee who has lent money on the security of the assured tenancy: s7(1).

Nor do these rules apply where the tenancy was originally assured but has ceased to be so, perhaps because the dwelling house ceased to be the tenant's principal home. In these circumstances, it becomes an ordinary common law tenancy. If the tenancy is a periodic tenancy it may be determined in the normal way, ie by notice to quit. If it is a fixed term it will expire at the end of the term, or it may be possible to determine it during the fixed term by forfeiture.

Periodic tenancies   A landlord may not bring an assured tenancy which is a periodic tenancy to an end by service of a notice to quit (s5(1)). It may only be determined by an order of the court and the court may not 'entertain the proceedings for possession' unless the landlord has served a 'notice of intention to commence proceedings for possession' (or the court considers it just and equitable to dispense with the requirement of such a notice (s8(1)(*b*): see pp109 and 112).

Expiry of fixed terms and statutory periodic tenancies   A fixed term assured tenancy will come to an end at the expiry of the term. However, on the coming to an end of such a tenancy, otherwise than by virtue of (*a*) an order of the court, or (*b*) surrender or other action on the part of the tenant, a statutory periodic tenancy arises (s5(2)(3)(7)) unless, on the coming to an end of the fixed term, the tenant is entitled, by virtue of the grant of another tenancy, to possession of the same or substantially the same dwelling house as was let to him under the fixed term tenancy (s5(4)).

A statutory periodic tenancy, like any other assured periodic tenancy, may not be brought to an end by notice to quit but only by court proceedings initiated by a notice of intention to commence proceedings (unless the requirement for such a notice is dispensed with; see pp 109 and 119).

(The landlord cannot prevent a periodic tenancy from arising by requiring the tenant, on or before the date the fixed term tenancy is entered into or the periodic tenancy arises, (*a*) to enter into an obligation to do any act which will cause the tenancy to come to an end, or (*b*) to execute, sign or give any surrender, notice to quit or other document which has the effect of bringing the tenancy to an end, at a time when it is an assured tenancy: s5(5).)

Terms of statutory periodic tenancies: s5(3), s6 Where a statutory periodic tenancy arises the periods of the tenancy are the same as those for which rent was last payable under the fixed term and the terms are (subject to certain other provisions eg ss 15 and 16) the same as those of the fixed term except that any term which makes provision for determination by the landlord or the tenant has no effect while the tenancy remains an assured tenancy (s5(3)(*d*), (*e*)), unless the terms are varied in accordance with the procedure set out in s6.

Termination during fixed term; break clauses The landlord may exercise a break clause in a lease so as to bring the fixed term to an end (s5(1)), but if he does so a statutory periodic tenancy automatically arises (s5(2)), unless a new tenancy is granted (s5(4)). If the landlord wishes to obtain an order for possession by reliance upon a break clause see s7(6) on p 115.

Termination during fixed term; 'forfeiture' The landlord will not be able to obtain an order for possession during the fixed term (by reliance upon a forfeiture clause or other term entitling the landlord to determine) unless (*a*) the ground relied upon by the landlord is one of a number of specified grounds and (*b*) the terms of the tenancy make provision for it to be brought to an end on the ground in question (s7(6)—see further *below* p 115).

Whether or not a court order terminating the tenancy is in fact a true 'forfeiture', so that the usual statutory provisions relating to forfeiture apply where the term relied upon is expressed as a forfeiture clause, is not clear (see Hill and Redman's *Law of Landlord and Tenant*, vol 2, p 641; Woodfall, *Landlord and Tenant*, vol 3, 24.048, note 16a; and R E Megarry, *The Rent Acts*, vol 3, p 136 where it is considered that they do not).

The arguments to the effect that termination of a fixed term assured tenancy in reliance upon a forfeiture clause is not a forfeiture are as follows:

(1) Section 5(1) provides that an assured tenancy cannot be brought to an end by the landlord except by obtaining an order of the court in accordance with the 1988 Act 'or, in the case of a fixed term

tenancy which contains power for the landlord to determine the tenancy in certain circumstances by the exercise of that power'. The words quoted suggest that a fixed term may be forfeited. However, s45(4) provides that any reference in the Act 'to a power for a landlord to determine a tenancy does not include a reference to a power of reentry or forfeiture'. Section 5(1), therefore, precludes the landlord from terminating the fixed term otherwise than by an order of the court obtained in accordance with the Act.

(2) Where there is a forfeiture the lease is brought to an end by service of the proceedings (see p39), but in the case of an assured tenancy the introductory words of s7(6) (p115) imply that the fixed term is still in existence at the date of the order.

(3) Section 7(6) states that the court may not make an order for possession unless two conditions are satisfied. The converse must be that the court may make an order for possession if those conditions are satisfied. The first condition is that one of a number of specified grounds applies (subs (a)). The second is, simply, that there be a term in the tenancy making provision for the tenancy to be brought to an end on the ground in question 'whether that provision takes the form of a provision for reentry, for forfeiture, for determination by notice or otherwise' (subs (b)). Thus, all that is required is that the tenancy contain such a provision. The section does not state that the forfeiture procedure must be followed. Hence, it is not necessary, for example, to serve a s146 notice.

(4) The mandatory ground for possession in relation to non-payment of rent (Ground 8) is inconsistent with the automatic relief provisions contained in s138 of the 1984 Act (see p43).

However, as the point is not free from doubt it is suggested that the safest course to adopt where the landlord is relying upon a forfeiture clause in a lease is to serve a s146 notice prior to serving the s8 notice seeking possession.

If it is necessary to comply with s146 of the Law of Property Act 1925, it has been pointed out that a s8 notice will not, in most cases, be sufficient to operate as a s146 notice because although it specifies the breach it does not require the tenant to remedy the breach (Woodfall, *Landlord and Tenant*, vol 3, 24.048; however, it is not necessary to require the breach to be remedied where it is incapable of remedy, see p17).

Notice of intention to commence proceedings for possession; s8

Where there are joint landlords not all of them need serve the notice. It is validly served so long as it is served by at least one of them (s8(1)(a)). The notice must comply with the following requirements:

(1) It must be in the prescribed form or in a form substantially to the same effect (see reg 2 and Form No 3 of the Assured Tenancies and Agricultural Occupancies (Forms) Regulations 1988 (SI No 2203): Form 16 of this book, p 111).

(2) The notice must specify the landlord's ground for possession (see p 113) and particulars of that ground; but the grounds specified in the notice may be altered or added to with the leave of the court (s 8(2)—see p 113). When setting out the ground relied upon, t is not necessary to state the full text of the relevant ground, but the landlord must set out the substance of the ground so that the notice gives 'the tenant the information which the provision requires to be given in the notice to enable the tenant to consider what she should do and, with or without advice, to do that which is in her power and which will best protect her against the loss of her home' (*Mountain v Hastings* [1993] 2 EGLR 53, per Ralph Gibson at 55H; notice stating—'Ground 8. At least three months rer t is unpaid'—not good enough). 'It is difficult to think of any good reason why a person, given the task of settling a form of not ce, should choose to use words different from those in' the statute (per Ralph Gibson at 55M).

(3) The particulars should be properly stated so that the tenant knows what he has to do to put matters right. For example, if the ground for possession is based upon arrears of rent, the amount of the arrears should be stated (cf the similar provisions in the Housing Act 1985; see p 166).

(4) The notice must inform the tenant that the landlord intends to begin proceedings for possession of the dwelling house on one or more of the grounds specified in the notice.

(5) It must inform the tenant that the proceedings will not begin earlier than the date specified in the notice which in the majcrity of the cases must not be earlier than the expiry of the period of two weeks from the date of service of the notice. However, if the notice specifies any of the Grounds 1, 2, 5, 6, 7, 9 or 16 (whether with or without other grounds) the date specified in the notice must not be earlier than (*a*) two months from the date of service of the notice; and (*b*) if the tenancy is a periodic tenancy, the earliest date on which if it were an ordinary common law tenancy it could be brought to an end by a notice to quit given by the landlord on the same date as the date of service of the notice.

(6) It must inform the tenant that the proceedings will not begin *later* than 12 months from the date of service of the notice.

Fixed terms: statutory periodic tenancies The landlord may serve a notice of intention to commence proceedings for possession at a time when the dwellinghouse is let on a fixed term, or after a fixed term tenancy has come to an end but in relation (in whole or in part) to events

Form 16: Notice by landlord of intention to commence proceedings for possession

HOUSING ACT 1988
Section 8

**Notice of Seeking Possession of a Property
Let on an Assured Tenancy**

- Please write clearly in black ink.
- Do not use this form if possession is sought from an assured shorthold tenant under section 21 of the Housing Act 1988 or if the property is occupied under an assured agricultural occupancy.
- **This notice is the first step towards requiring you to give up possession of your home. You should read it very carefully.**
- If you need advice about this notice, and what you should do about it, take it as quickly as possible to any of the following—
- a Citizens' Advice Bureau,
- a Housing Aid Centre,
- a Law Centre,
- or a Solicitor.

You may be able to get Legal Aid but this will depend on your personal circumstances.

(1) Name(s) of tenant(s).

1. To([1]):

(2) Address of premises

2. Your landlord intends to apply to the court for an order requiring you to give up possession of([2]):

- If you have an assured tenancy under the Housing Act 1988, which is not an assured shorthold tenancy, you can only be required to leave your home if your landlord gets an order for possession from the court on one of the grounds which are set out in Schedule 2 to the Act.
- If you are willing to give up possession of your home without a court order, you should tell the person who signed this notice as soon as possible and say when you can leave.

(3) Give the full text of each ground which is being relied on. (Continue on a separate sheet if necessary).

3. The landlord intends to seek possession on ground(s) [   ] in Schedule 2 of the Housing Act 1988, which reads([3]):

- Whichever grounds are set out in paragraph 3 the court may allow any of the other grounds to be added at a later date. If this is done, you will be told about it so you can discuss the additional grounds at the court hearing as well as the grounds set out in paragraph 3.

(4) Give a full explanation of why each ground is being relied on. (Continue on a separate sheet if necessary).

4. Particulars of each ground are as follows([4]):

- If the court is satisfied that any of grounds 1 to 8 is established it must make an order (but see below in respect of fixed term tenancies).
- Before the court will grant an order on any of grounds 9 to 16, it must be satisfied that it is reasonable to require you to leave. This means that, if one of these grounds is set out in paragraph 3, you will be able to suggest to the court that it is not reasonable that you should have to leave, even if you accept that the ground applies.
- The court will not make an order under grounds 1, 3 to 7, 9 or 16, to take effect during the fixed term of the tenancy; and it will only make an order during the fixed term on grounds 2, 8 or 10 to 15 if the terms of the tenancy make provision for it to be brought to an end on any of these grounds.
- Where the court makes an order for possession solely on grounds 6 to 9, your landlord must pay your reasonable moving expenses.

(5) Give the date after which court proceedings can be brought.

5. The court proceedings will not begin until after (5):

- Where the landlord or licensor is seeking possession under grounds 1, 2, 5 to 7, 9 or 16 in Schedule 2, court proceedings cannot begin earlier than 2 months from the date this notice is served on you and not before the date on which the tenancy (had it not been assured) could have been brought to an end by a notice to quit served at the same time as this notice.   *contd*

contd

- Where the landlord is seeking possession on grounds 3, 4, 8 or 10 to 15, cour t proceedings cannot begin until 2 weeks after the date this notice is served.
- After the date shown in paragraph 5, court proceedings may be begun at once but not later than 12 months from the date this notice is served. After this time the notice wi l lapse and a new notice must be served before possession can be sought.

To be signed by the landlord or his or her agent (someone acting for him/her).

Signed:

Name(s) of landlord(s):

Address of landlord(s):

If signed by agent, name and address of agent

Telephone: Date: 19

Reproduced by kind permission of The Solicitors' Law Stationery Society Ltd

occurring during that tenancy. If he does so the notice has effect notwithstanding that the tenant becomes or has become a tenant under a statutory periodic tenancy arising on the coming to an end of the fixed term. It is not necessary to serve another notice to determine the periodic tenancy (s8(6)).

Proceedings for possession

Commencing proceedings

The landlord must commence proceedings after the date specified in the notice of intention to commence proceedings for possession but before 12 months from the date specified have elapsed. If he does not do so, the court may not entertain proceedings for possession (s8(1)(a)).

Note:

(1) Where the landlord is relying upon Grounds 1, 3, 4 or 5 he may use the accelerated possession procedure (see p272).

(2) Where the landlord's claim for possession is based upon or includes an allegation of non-payment of rent the particulars of claim must be in prescribed form (see p319).

Dispensing with requirement of a notice: s8(1)(b)

Section 8 of the 1988 Act provides that the court shall not entertain proceedings for possession of a dwelling house let on an assured tenancy unless the landlord serves a notice of proceedings for possession or the court considers it just and equitable to dispense with the requirement of such a notice (subs (b)).

The court may not dispense with the requirement where the ground for possession is Ground 8 (13 weeks' rent arrears etc); s8(5).

The grounds for possession

The court is not permitted to make an order for possession of a dwelling house let under an assured tenancy except on one or more of the 16 grounds for possession set out in Sched 2 to the 1988 Act. There are two categories of ground: those where the court must make an order for possession (Grounds 1 to 8) and those where the court possesses a discretion as to whether or not to make an order (Grounds 9 to 16). As shown above the ground relied upon must be specified in the notice of intention to commence proceedings. If it is not, the court may not make an order for possession on that ground. The grounds specified in the notice may be altered or added to with the leave of the court (s8(2)) but the court is unlikely to give leave where extensive amendments to the notice are required (for example, where it is necessary in effect to add a schedule of dilapidations: *South Buckinghamshire County Council v Francis* [1985] CLY 1900—a secure tenancy case, see p171).

(None of these provisions relate to proceedings brought by a mortgagee who has lent money on the security of the assured tenancy: s7(1).)

The mandatory grounds: Grounds 1 to 8 If the court is satisfied that any of these grounds is established the court *must* make an order for possession (s7(3)). The grounds, which are set out in Part 1 of Sched 2 to the 1988 Act (see Appendix 2), are as follows:

(1) Owner has lived in or wishes to live in the property (see Chapter 24, p352).
(2) Mortgagee requiring possession in order to exercise power of sale (see Chapter 24, p402).
(3) Holiday homes let out of season (see Chapter 16).
(4) Student accommodation let during vacation (see Chapter 16).
(5) Ministers of religion (see Chapter 18).
(6) Demolition, reconstruction or substantial works.
(7) Death of the tenant—periodic tenancy (see p119).
(8) Substantial arrears of rent (see generally Chapter 23).

Grounds 1 to 5 require a notice to have been served not later than the beginning of the tenancy (unless, in the case of Grounds 1 and 2, the court is of the opinion that it is just and equitable to dispense with the requirement of notice: cf cases under the Rent Acts—see p352). Where such a notice is required Part IV of Sched 2 applies to those notices. Where there are joint landlords the notice is sufficiently served, so long as it is served by at least one of the joint landlords. Further, notice served

Form 17: Assured tenancy: particulars of claim (not to be used in rent cases; see p 112)

IN THE   COUNTY COURT   Case No

BETWEEN:

Plaintiff

—AND—

Defendant

PARTICULARS OF CLAIM

1. The Plaintiff is the freehold owner and is entitled to possession of the dwelling house known as [*state address*].

2. By a tenancy agreement dated [*insert date*] and made between the Plaintiff and the Defendant, the Plaintiff agreed to let the dwelling house to the Defendant on a monthly tenancy commencing on [*insert date*] at a rent of £_____ per month payable in advance on the _____ day of each month. The said tenancy is an assured tenancy and is subject to the provisions of the Housing Act 1988.

3. Prior to the grant of the said tenancy the Plaintiff gave notice in writing to the Defendant that possession might be recovered on Ground 1 of Schedule 2 to the Housing Act 1988.

4. Prior to the beginning of the tenancy the Plaintiff occupied the dwelling house as his only home [*or, The Plaintiff requires possession of the dwelling house so that he can occupy it as his only home*].

5. On [*insert date*] the Plaintiff, pursuant to section 8 of the Housing Act 1988, served on the Defendant a notice of his intention to commence proceedings for possession on Ground 1 of Schedule to the said Act. The notice stated that proceedings would not be commenced until after [*insert date*].

6. The Plaintiff is therefore entitled to possession of the dwelling house pursuant to the said Ground.

AND the Plaintiff claims:

(1) Possession of the dwelling house.

(2) Rent and/or mesne profits at the rate of £_____ per month from the date hereof until possession be delivered up.

DATED

in relation to initial tenancies will usually be effective in relation to later tenancies of the same kind.

The discretionary grounds: Grounds 9 to 16   If the court is satisfied that any of these grounds is established then the court *may* make an order for possession if it considers it reasonable to do so. The grounds, which are set out in Part II of Sched 2 to the 1988 Act, are as follows:

(9) Suitable alternative accommodation (see Chapter 24).

(10) Some arrears of rent (see Chapter 23).

(11) Persistent delay in paying rent (see Chapter 23).
(12) Breach of obligation of tenancy.
(13) Deterioration of dwelling house or common parts.
(14) Nuisance, annoyance, immoral or illegal user.
(15) Deterioration of furniture.
(16) Tenancy resulting from employment by landlord—employment has ceased.

Fixed terms (s7(6), (7))

The court may not make an order for possession of a dwelling house to take effect at a time when it is let on an assured fixed term tenancy unless:
   (a) the ground for possession is Ground 2, 8, 10, 11, 12, 13, 14 or 15; and
   (b) the terms of the tenancy make provision for it to be brought to an end on the ground in question (whether that provision takes the form of a provision for reentry, for forfeiture, for determination by notice or otherwise): s7(6).

As to whether the usual provisions for relief will apply where the landlord has relied upon a forfeiture clause, see p108.

Where the court makes an order for possession on grounds relating to a fixed term tenancy which has come to an end any statutory periodic tenancy which has arisen on the ending of the fixed term automatically comes to an end (without any notice and regardless of the period) on the day on which the order takes effect (s7(7)).

Housing Act 1988, s7(6), (7)
   (6) The court shall not make an order for possession of a dwelling-house to take effect at a time when it is let on an assured fixed term tenancy unless—
         (a) the ground for possession is Ground 2 or Ground 8 in Part I of Schedule 2 to this Act or any of the grounds in Part II of that Schedule, other than Ground 9 or Ground 16; and
         (b) the terms of the tenancy make provision for it to be brought to an end on the ground in question (whether that provision takes the form of a provision for reentry, for forfeiture, for determination by notice or otherwise).
   (7) Subject to the preceding provisions of this section, the court may make an order for possession of a dwelling-house on grounds relating to a fixed term tenancy which has come to an end; and where an order is made in such circumstances, any statutory periodic tenancy which has arisen on the ending of the fixed term tenancy shall end (without any notice and regardless of the period) on the day on which the order takes effect.

The order for possession

Where the landlord is relying upon any of the discretionary grounds for possession (ie Grounds 9 to 16 of Sched 2) the court may, on the making of an order for possession or at any time before execution of such an order, stay or suspend the execution of the order or postpone the date for possession for such period or periods as the court thinks just (s9). If any such stay, suspension or postponement is ordered the court must, unless it considers that to do so would cause exceptional hardship or would otherwise be unreasonable, impose conditions with regard to payment by the tenant of arrears of rent (if any) and rent or payments in respect of occupation after the termination of the tenancy (mesne profits) and may impose such other conditions as it thinks fit. If any of these conditions are imposed and then complied with the court may, if it thinks fit, discharge or rescind the order for possession.

The court has no such discretion where the ground for possession is one of the mandatory grounds contained in Part I of Sched 2 to the 1988 Act. In these cases the court may not suspend the order for possession for more than 14 days (six weeks in cases of exceptional hardship) (s89 of the Housing Act 1980) (see p75).

Where an order for possession is made on Ground 6 (demolition, reconstruction or substantial works) or Ground 9 (suitable alternative accommodation) the landlord is required to pay to the tenant a sum equal to the reasonable removal expenses likely to be incurred by the tenant in removing from the dwelling house (s11(1)). Any question as to the amount to be paid is determined by agreement between the landlord and the tenant or, in default of agreement, by the court (s11(2)). Any sum so payable to the tenant is recoverable as a civil debt from the landlord (s11(3)).

Termination by tenant

There are no special provisions in the Housing Act 1988 governing termination by the tenant. An assured tenant may therefore determine the tenancy in the usual way, ie by surrender and, in the case of a periodic tenancy, by service of a notice to quit (see Chapter 3).

Where a tenant freely surrenders his tenancy or gives the landlord a notice to quit (presumably a valid one) the fixed term comes to an end and is not replaced by a statutory periodic tenancy (s5(2); p107).

Assignment, subletting, bankruptcy and death

Assignment, subletting and parting with possession: Housing Act 1988, s15

Subject to what is written in the next paragraph, it is an implied term of every assured tenancy which is a *periodic tenancy* that, except with the consent of the landlord, the tenant shall not (*a*) assign the tenancy (in whole or in part), or (*b*) sublet or part with possession of the whole or any part of the dwelling house let on the tenancy (s15(1)). Section 19 of the Landlord and Tenant Act 1927 does not apply to this implied term. The landlord therefore has an absolute right to refuse such an assignment, subletting or parting with possession. He does not have to show that his refusal was reasonable (s15(2)).

However, there is no such implied term in the case of a periodic tenancy which is *not* a statutory periodic tenancy (ie not a periodic tenancy that has arisen after the end of a fixed term: see p107) *if*:

(*a*) there is a provision (whether contained in the tenancy or not) under which the tenant is prohibited (whether absolutely or conditionally) from assigning or subletting or parting with possession or is permitted (whether absolutely or conditionally) to assign, sublet or part with possession; or

(*b*) a premium is required to be paid on the grant or renewal of the tenancy: s15(3).

The term 'premium' includes (*a*) any fine or other like sum; (*b*) any other pecuniary consideration in addition to rent; and any sum paid by way of deposit, other than one which does not exceed one-sixth of the annual rent payable under the tenancy immediately after the grant or renewal in question (s15(4)).

There are no provisions in the 1988 Act relating to *fixed* term tenancies. Thus, the right of the tenant to assign, sublet or part with possession will depend upon the terms of the agreement and s19 of the 1927 Act will apply. After expiry of the fixed term the tenant will become a statutory periodic tenant and the provisions of s15(1) of the 1988 Act will apply (see *above*) (ie the implied covenant against assigning, etc without consent).

If the tenant does assign, sublet or part with possession in breach of a term of the tenancy the landlord may rely upon that fact as a ground for possession (Ground 12, which is a discretionary ground). But note that in the case of an assignment the assignment is effective to transfer the tenancy (Chapter 4, p81) and that the notice of intention to commence proceedings for possession should therefore be served upon the assignee.

Termination of head tenancy: effect on assured tenancy The common law provides that where a tenancy is determined all sub-tenancies automatically come to an end unless the superior tenancy has been determined by surrender or tenant's notice to quit (see Chapter 4, p82). Section 18 of the 1988 Act nullifies this rule in relation to assured sub-tenancies *lawfully* granted by providing that where the superior tenancy is determined any such assured sub-tenancy shall continue in existence. The person who would but for the assured tenancy be entitled to possession of the dwelling house becomes the new landlord: s18(1). This rule will not apply if the person who would be the new landlord is entitled to rely upon one of the exclusions contained in Sched 1 to the 1988 Act (s18(2)).

Bankruptcy of the tenant

Section 283(3A) of the Insolvency Act 1986 (as introduced by s117 of the Housing Act 1988) provides that an assured tenancy the terms of which inhibit an assignment as mentioned in s127(5) of the Rent Act 1977 does not form part of a bankrupt tenant's estate. Thus, the assured tenancy does not automatically vest in the trustee in bankruptcy under s306 of the Insolvency Act 1986 on the bankruptcy of the tenant (see generally Chapter 4, p83). However, s308A of the Insolvency Act 1986 (as introduced by s117 of the 1988 Act) provides that where the trustee serves a notice in writing upon the bankrupt under s308A the assured tenancy 'vests in the trustee as part of the bankrupt's estate; and except against a purchaser in good faith, for value and without notice of the bankruptcy, the trustee's title to that tenancy has relation back to the commencement of the bankruptcy'.

If the trustee in bankruptcy does serve a notice under s308A so that the tenancy becomes vested in him the former tenant, who remains in occupation of the dwelling house, does so as a licensee of the trustee. If the trustee disclaims the tenancy the original tenant will have no right to remain in occupation and if he continues to do so without consent the 'landlord' may take summary proceedings for possession (*Smalley v Quarrier*; see p84).

Death of the tenant

Fixed term tenancies   The general law applies. Where a fixed term is held by joint tenants the survivors become the tenants. If a sole tenant dies the tenancy devolves according to his will or on intestacy. (See generally p86.)

Periodic tenancies: joint tenancies   In the case of an assured tenancy which is a periodic tenancy (including a statutory periodic tenancy) held by joint tenants where one of the joint tenants dies the general law applies and the survivors become the tenants.

Periodic tenancies: spouse living with sole tenant   Where the tenant was a sole tenant and immediately before the tenant's death the tenant's spouse was occupying the dwelling house as his or her only or principal home the tenancy vests in the spouse and not according to the tenant's will or intestacy. However, the tenancy will not vest in the spouse if the deceased tenant was 'himself a successor' as defined in subs (2) or subs (3) of s17. The effect of these subsections is that the tenancy will not vest in the spouse by virtue of s17 where:

(1) the tenancy becomes vested in the original tenant by virtue of s17(1) (ie as a spouse on the death of his or her former spouse) under the will or intestacy of a previous tenant;

(2) at some time before his death the original tenant was a joint tenant and prior to his death he became the sole tenant by survivorship;

(3) the original tenant became entitled to an assured periodic tenancy after the death of a regulated tenant under the Rent Act 1977 pursuant to s39(5) of the Housing Act 1988 (see p155).

Subsection 3 deals with the situation where the deceased tenant was a successor by virtue of subs (2) in relation to one tenancy and he has subsequently entered into a tenancy agreement of the same or substantially the same premises. In order to ensure that there is a transfer to the spouse under s17 in these circumstances subs (3) provides that a tenant (ie the deceased tenant) is also a successor in relation to a tenancy ('the new tenancy') which was granted to him (alone or jointly with others) if—

(a) at some time before the grant of the new tenancy, he was, by virtue of subs (2), a successor in relation to an earlier tenancy of the same or substantially the same dwelling house as is let under the new tenancy; and

(b) at all times since he became such a successor he has been a tenant (alone or jointly with others) of the dwelling house which is let under the new tenancy or of a dwelling house which is substantially the same as that dwelling house.

A person who was living with the tenant as his or her wife or husband is treated as the tenant's spouse (s17(4)). Where there is more than one person who was a 'spouse' of the tenant occupying the dwelling house immediately before the death of the tenant the person who is entitled to succeed is the person who is decided upon by agreement or in default by decision of the county court (s17(5))!

Periodic tenancy: sole tenant—no spouse entitled to succeed Where there is no succession of the tenancy to a spouse pursuant to s17 the tenancy will devolve under the will or on intestacy but the landlord will be entitled to recover possession under Ground 7 if he begins proceedings not later than 12 months after the death of the former tenant or, if the court so directs, after the date on which, in the opinion of the court, the landlord or, in the case of joint landlords, any one of them became aware of the former tenant's death.

Ground 7 is a mandatory ground for possession and so the court must make an order without considering the reasonableness of the landlord's request for possession.

Ground 7 expressly states that for the purposes of that ground the acceptance by the landlord of rent from a new tenant after the death of the former tenant shall not be regarded as creating a new periodic tenancy, unless the landlord agrees in writing to a change (as compared with the tenancy before the death) in the amount of the rent, the period of the tenancy, the premises which are let or any other term of the tenancy.

Chapter 7

Assured Shorthold Tenancies

An assured shorthold tenancy is a type of assured tenancy. The rules relating to assured tenancies therefore apply to shortholds unless they conflict with the provisions explained in this chapter. The purpose of the assured shorthold tenancy is to enable the landlord to let his property with the knowledge that he will be able to recover possession at the end of the contractual term or thereafter without having to rely upon the usual assured tenancy grounds.

Rent control in respect of assured shorthold tenancies is dealt with in ss 22 and 23 of the 1988 Act. In certain circumstances the tenant may refer the rent to a rent assessment committee.

Definition of assured shorthold tenancy

The basic rule: s 20 of the 1988 Act

An 'assured shorthold tenancy' is an 'assured tenancy' (see p 103):

- (a) which is a fixed term tenancy granted for a term certain of not less than six months; and
- (b) in respect of which there is no power for the landlord to determine the tenancy at any time earlier than six months from the beginning of the tenancy (other than by a power of reentry or forfeiture for breach of the tenancy (s45(4))); and
- (c) in respect of which an assured shorthold notice in prescribed form (or in a form 'substantially to the same effect') was served by the landlord (or, in the case of joint landlords, at least one of them: s20(6)(a)) upon the tenant (or, in the case of joint tenants, upon *all* of them: s45(3) *before* the tenancy was entered into stating that the assured tenancy to which it related was to be an assured shorthold (reg 2 and Form 7 of the Assured Tenancies and Agricultural Occupancies (Forms) Regulations 1988 (as amended): see Form 18 on p123). A notice containing an incorrect termination date is invalid unless the mistake is an obvious one (*Panayi v Roberts* [1993] 2 EGLR 51, CA; a notice which stated that the tenancy would be for a term of six months to 6 May 1991

was held to be invalid when the tenancy was in fact for a year to 4 November 1991).

An exception: grant to existing assured tenant (s20(3))

Notwithstanding that the above conditions apply a new tenancy will not be an assured shorthold tenancy where:

(a) immediately before the grant of the new tenancy the person to whom it is granted (or, if there are joint tenants, at least one of them) was a tenant under an assured tenancy which was not a shorthold tenancy; and

(b) the new tenancy is granted by the person who, immediately before the beginning of the tenancy, was the landlord under the previous assured tenancy.

Persons who were protected shorthold tenants under the Rent Act 1977 (s34(2), (3))

Where a new tenancy is granted on or after the commencement of the Housing Act 1988 (15 January 1989) to a person who immediately before the grant was:

(a) a tenant under a protected shorthold tenancy (ie pursuant to s52 of the Housing Act 1980; see Chapter 12, p190); or

(b) a protected or statutory tenant of a dwelling house which was let under a protected shorthold tenancy which ended before 15 January 1989 and in respect of which at that date either there had been no grant of a further tenancy or any grant of a further tenancy had been made to the person who immediately before that grant was in possession of the dwelling house as a protected or statutory tenant and who fulfils all the requirements of an assured tenancy (p103),

the new tenancy is an assured shorthold tenancy even if the usual conditions for assured shorthold tenancies do not apply (see *above*) (s34(3)).

However, if the landlord (or, in the case of joint landlords, all of them: s45(3)) serve notice on the tenant that the new tenancy is not to be a shorthold tenancy (ie an assured shorthold) before the tenancy is entered into the tenancy will be an ordinary assured tenancy (s34(3)).

Termination by landlord before fixed term has expired

Section 21(1) of the 1988 Act expressly preserves the landlord's right to recover possession pursuant to Chapter I of the 1988 Act. An assured shorthold tenancy, like any other assured tenancy, may therefore be brought to an end during the fixed term if:

Form 18: Notice of an assured shorthold tenancy

©1993 **OYEZ** Form No. 7 of the Assured
Tenancies and Agricultural Occupancies
(Forms) Regulations 1988 (as amended)

HOUSING ACT 1988
Section 20
Notice of an Assured Shorthold Tenancy

- Please write clearly in black ink.
- If there is anything you do not understand you should get advice from a solicitor or a Citizens' Advice Bureau, before you agree to the tenancy.
- The landlord must give this notice to the tenant before an assured shorthold tenancy is granted. It does not commit the tenant to take the tenancy.
- **THIS DOCUMENT IS IMPORTANT, KEEP IT IN A SAFE PLACE.**

(1) Name of proposed tenant. If a joint tenancy is being offered enter the names of the joint tenant(s).

To(¹):

1. You are proposing to take a tenancy of the dwelling known as:

(2) The tenancy **must** be for a term certain of at least six months.

(²) from the   day of   19
to the   day of   19

2. This notice is to tell you that your tenancy is to be an *assured shorthold tenancy*. Provided you keep to the terms of the tenancy, you are entitled to remain in the dwelling for at least the first six months of the fixed period agreed at the start of the tenancy. At the end of this period, depending on the terms of the tenancy, the landlord may have the right to repossession if he/she wants.

3. The rent for this tenancy is the rent we have agreed. However, you have the right to apply to a rent assessment committee for a determinaton of the rent which the committee considers might reasonably be obtained under the tenancy. If the committee considers (i) that there is a sufficient number of similar properties in the locality let on assured tenancies and that (ii) the rent we have agreed is significantly higher than the rent which might reasonably be obtained having regard to the level of rents for other assured tenancies in the locality, it will determine a rent for the tenancy. That rent will be the legal maximum you can be required to pay from the date the committee directs. If the rent includes a payment for council tax, the rent determined by the committee will be inclusive of council tax.

To be signed by the landlord or his/her agent (someone acting for him/her). If there are joint landlords each must sign, unless one signs on behalf of the rest with their agreement.

Signed:

Name(s) of landlord(s):

Address of landlord(s):

Telephone:

If signed by agent, name and address of agent

Telephone: Date: 19

SPECIAL NOTE FOR EXISTING TENANTS
- Generally, if you already have a protected or statutory tenancy and you give it up to take a new tenancy in the same or other accommodation owned by the same landlord, that tenancy cannot be an assured tenancy. It can still be a protected tenancy.
- But if you currently occupy a dwelling which was let to you as a protected shorthold tenant, special rules apply.
- If you have an assured tenancy which is not a shorthold under the Housing Act 1988, you cannot be offered an assured shorthold tenancy of the same or other accommodation by the same landlord.

Reproduced by kind permission of The Solicitors' Law Stationery Society Ltd

(a) the ground for possession is any of the following grounds: 2 (mortgagee requiring possession), 8 (substantial arrears of rent), 10 (some rent due), 11 (persistent delay in paying rent), 12 (breach of the tenancy), 13 (deterioration of the dwelling house or common parts), 14 (nuisance, annoyance, immoral or illegal user) or 15 (deterioration in condition of furniture); and

(b) the terms of the tenancy make provision for it to be brought to an end on the ground in question, whether that provision takes the form of a provision for reentry, for forfeiture, for determination by notice or otherwise (s7(6)).

In order to terminate the tenancy during the currency of the fixed term the landlord must carry out the procedure applicable to all assured tenancies. As to whether the statutory provisions relating to forfeiture apply where the landlord is relying upon a forfeiture clause, see p108.

But note that if the tenancy contains a clause permitting the landlord to terminate the tenancy within the first six months on any of the above grounds the tenancy will not be an assured shorthold tenancy unless that clause is 'a power of reentry or forfeiture [clause] for breach of any term or condition of the tenancy' (s20(1)(b) and s45(4); see p121). This issue is most likely to arise where the tenancy permits the landlord to terminate the tenancy on Ground 2 (see p402).

Status of tenant after expiry of fixed term: subsequent tenancies

Where the tenant remains in occupation of the dwelling house at the end of the fixed term he will usually do so as a statutory periodic tenant pursuant to s5(2) of the 1988 Act, but as will be seen *below*, the landlord will be able to regain possession from such a tenant by service of a notice under s21 of the 1988 Act.

In some cases the fixed term is followed by a contractual periodic tenancy pursuant to the terms of the original tenancy or the landlord grants the tenant a new tenancy. If, on the coming to an end of an assured shorthold tenancy (including a tenancy which was an assured shorthold but ceased to be assured before it came to an end), a new tenancy of the same or substantially the same premises comes into being under which the landlord and the tenant are the same as at the coming to an end of the earlier tenancy, then if and so long as the new tenancy is an assured tenancy, it is an assured shorthold tenancy whether or not the three conditions set out in s20(1) (p121) are satisfied (s20(4)).

However, it will not be an assured shorthold if before the new tenancy is entered into (or, in the case of a statutory periodic tenancy (p107), takes effect in possession) the landlord (or, in the case of joint landlords, at least one of them: s20(6)(b)) serves notice on the tenant that the new tenancy is not to be a shorthold tenancy. In the unlikely event that he does so, the tenancy will be an ordinary assured tenancy (s20(5)).

Termination after expiry of fixed term

Housing Act 1988, s21

21.—(1) Without prejudice to any right of the landlord under an assured shorthold tenancy to recover possession of the dwelling house let on the tenancy in accordance with Chapter I above, on or after the coming to an end of an assured shorthold tenancy which was a fixed term tenancy, a court shall make an order for possession of the dwelling house if it is satisfied—

    (*a*) that the assured shorthold tenancy has come to an end and no further assured tenancy (whether shorthold or not) is for the time being in existence, other than an assured shorthold periodic tenancy (whether statutory or not); and

    (*b*) the landlord or, in the case of joint landlords, at least one of them has given to the tenant not less than two months' notice stating that he requires possession of the dwelling house.

(2) A notice under paragraph (*b*) of subsection (1) above may be given before or on the day on which the tenancy comes to an end; and that subsection shall have effect notwithstanding that on the coming to an end of the fixed term tenancy a statutory periodic tenancy arises.

(3) Where a court makes an order for possession of a dwelling house by virtue of subsection (1) above, any statutory periodic tenancy which has arisen on the coming to an end of the assured shorthold tenancy shall end (without further notice and regardless of the period) on the day on which the order takes effect.

(4) Without prejudice to any such right as is referred to in subsection (1) above, a court shall make an order for possession of a dwelling house let on an assured shorthold tenancy which is a periodic tenancy if the court is satisfied—

    (*a*) that the landlord or, in the case of joint landlords, at least one of them has given to the tenant a notice stating that, after a date specified in the notice, being the last day of a period of the tenancy and not earlier than two months after the date the notice was given, possession of the dwelling house is required by virtue of this section; and

    (*b*) that the date specified in the notice under paragraph (*a*) above is not earlier than the earliest day on which, apart from section 5(1) above, the tenancy could be brought to an end by a notice to quit given by the landlord on the same date as the notice under paragraph (*a*) above.

If the landlord wishes to regain possession after the fixed term he must serve a notice under s21(1)(*b*) or s21(4) of the 1988 Act stating that he requires possession. There are no prescribed forms. Law stationers do provide forms (see Form 19, p 127 and Form 20, p 129) but so long as the notice complies with the terms of the relevant provision it may be in any form. In the case of joint landlords the notice must be given by at least one of them (s21); and where there are joint tenants the notice must be given to all of them (s45(3)).

It is not necessary to serve a notice of intention to commence proceedings under s8 of the 1988 Act (see p 109) in addition to the s21 notice; section 8 notices 'have no apparent relevance to the termination of an assured shorthold' (*Panayi v Roberts* [1993] 2 EGLR 51, CA, per Mann LJ at p53A—*obiter*, but surely correct?). It should also be noted that s5(1) and s5(2) (see p106) indicate that the court can make an order under Chapter I (which includes s8) or Chapter II (which includes s21).

The general consensus is that:

(*a*) a notice in accordance with s21(1)(*b*) is required where the notice is served on or before the last day of the fixed term (Form 19); and

(*b*) a notice in accordance with s21(4), which relates to periodic tenancies, is required where the notice is served thereafter (Form 20).

The reasoning is that s21 (2) states that a notice may be given under s21(1)(*b*) before or on the day on which the tenancy comes to an end; and that after the fixed term has expired a statutory periodic tenancy comes into being (s5(2); see p107) unless a new tenancy is granted. (See *Hill & Redman*, vol 21, C665, para 2155; RE Megarry, *The Rent Acts*, vol 3, p 163.)

However, it is submitted that a notice served in accordance with s21(1)(*b*) after the fixed term has expired is valid in relation to a statutory periodic tenancy (and possibly a new contractual periodic tenancy which would itself be an assured shorthold; s20(4); see p124). The reasoning is as follows:

(1) There is nothing in s21(1) to prevent such a notice being served after that date. It merely states that the court shall make an order if the notice has been given.

(2) Subsection (2) of s21 does not state that the notice may *only* be served before or on the day on which the tenancy comes to an end. Rather, it makes it clear that a notice can be served before or on that date even though it will take effect after that date.

(3) The opening words of s21(4) are 'Without prejudice to any such right as is referred to in subsection (1) . . . '. Thus, it may well be that there are situations covered by both s21(1) and s21(4) and the landlord may choose between them.

(4) Subsection (4) (as originally drafted) was probably introduced to ensure that a contractual periodic shorthold tenancy could be brought to an end on the shorthold ground. It is possible that this position is in fact now covered by the words 'an assured shorthold periodic tenancy (whether statutory or not)' in s21(1)(*a*), which were introduced by s194, Sched 11, para 103 of the Local Government Act 1989. (Section 21(1)(*a*) as originally drafted only referred to statutory periodic tenancies.) However, the existence of subs (4) does ensure that all periodic tenancies can be brought to an end.

(5) In particular, it may be that a contractual periodic tenancy that arises by virtue of a clause in the fixed term can only be brought to an end by a notice under s21(4) (eg a demise of a dwelling for a period of one year and thereafter from month to month).

Form 19: Assured shorthold tenancy: notice requiring possession—expiry of fixed term tenancy

© 1988 *OYEZ*

HOUSING ACT 1988
Section 21(1)(b)

Assured Shorthold Tenancy : Notice Requiring Possession:

Fixed Term Tenancy
(Notes)

(1) Name and address of tenant.

To(¹)

of

(2) Name and address of landlord (Note 2 overleaf)

From(²)

of

(3) Address of dwelling.

I give you notice that I require possession of the dwelling house known as(·)

(4) Date of expiry (Note 3 overleaf)

after(⁴)

(5) Note 3 overleaf.

Dated(⁵)   19

Landlord

(6) Name and address

[Landlord's agent](⁶)

NOTES

1. On or after the coming to an end of a fixed term assured shorthold tenancy, a court must make an order for possession if the landlord has given a notice in this form.

2. Where there are joint landlords, at least one of them must give this notice.

3. The length of the notice must be at least two months and the notice may be given before or on the day on which the fixed term comes to an end.

© 1988 *OYEZ*   The Solicitors' Law Stationery Society Ltd, Oyez House, 7 Spa Road, London SE16 3QQ   7 93 F25333
HA 21   5045201
• • •

Reproduced by kind permission of The Solicitors' Law Stationery Society Ltd

Perhaps, in these circumstances, s21(1) does not apply as there has been no 'coming to an end of an assured shorthold tenancy which was a fixed term tenancy'. It has continued in existence as a contractual periodic term.

Recovery of possession

The accelerated possession procedure (see Chapter 20, p272) is available in respect of assured shorthold tenancies determined in accordance with s21 of the 1988 Act, ie where proceedings are being commenced after expiry of the fixed term. If the necessary conditions are satisfied the landlord will be able to obtain possession without a court hearing. Note that the procedure is commenced by prescribed form (p273).

Where the necessary conditions are not satisfied or where the landlord is seeking to obtain possession prior to expiry of the fixed term (see p122), it will be necessary to utilise the fixed date action (Chapter 20, p255).

(*Quaere* whether proceedings may be commenced before the date specified in the notice requiring possession. The usual rule that a plaintiff may not bring proceedings before he has a cause of action would not seem to apply because strictly speaking his cause of action, ie his right to possession, does not arise until the court makes the order for possession. Compare s8(3)(*b*) in relation to assured tenancies that are not assured shortholds.)

If the court is satisfied that the notice complies with s21(4) it must make an order for possession. The court may not postpone or suspend the order for possession for more than 14 days (or six weeks in the case of exceptional hardship: s89 of the Housing Act 1980 (see p75)).

Form 20: Assured shorthold tenancy: notice requiring possession—periodic tenancy

© 1989 *OYEZ*

HOUSING ACT 1988
Section 21(4)(a)

Assured Shorthold Tenancy : Notice Requiring Possession: Periodic Tenancy
(Notes)

(1) Name and address of tenant.

To(')

of

(2) Name and address of landlord (Note 2 overleaf).

From(')

of

(3) Address of dwelling.

I give you notice that I require possession of the dwelling house known as(')

(4) Date of expiry (Note 3 overleaf).

after(')

(5) Note 3 overleaf.

Dated(')   19

Landlord

(6) Name and address.

[Landlord's agent](')

NOTES

1. Where an assured shorthold tenancy has become a periodic tenancy, a court must make an order for possession if the landlord has given proper notice in this form.

2. Where there are joint landlords, at least one of them must give this notice.

3. This notice must expire:
   (a) on the last day of a period of the tenancy.
   (b) at least two months after this notice is given.
   (c) no sooner than the earliest day on which the tenancy could ordinarily be brought to an end by a notice to quit given by the landlord on the same day.

© 1989 *OYEZ* The Solicitors' Law Stationery Society Ltd. Oyez House, 7 Spa Road, London SE16 3QQ   12 92 F2.8819
5045332

HA 21A

Reproduced by kind permission of The Solicitors' Law Stationery Society Ltd

Chapter 8

Regulated Tenancies

The Rent Act 1977 is concerned with two principal forms of tenancy: the 'protected tenancy' and the 'statutory tenancy'. Collectively they are referred to as 'regulated tenancies' (s18). As long as it is in existence a protected tenancy is contractual in nature and is determined according to contractual principles. Immediately upon termination, however, contractual principles cease to be of importance in relation to the landlord's right to recover possession and a so-called 'statutory tenancy' arises. A statutory tenancy is not a tenancy in the strict sense. It is a personal right to occupy a dwelling house until a court orders that the tenant should give up possession which the court will only do if it is satisfied that one of a number of specified grounds has been made out. As the terms 'protected tenancy' and 'statutory tenancy' are differently defined the tenant may be a protected tenant before the tenancy's determination but not a statutory tenant thereafter (eg if he does not actually live on the premises or if the tenant is a company). The consequences of such an outcome are that as a protected tenant he is able to take advantage of some of the rights that are available to regulated tenants (eg the ability to apply for a fair rent to be registered) but after termination he will not be able to take advantage of the provisions relating to security of tenure.

Where the occupier of the premises is not a regulated tenant he may nevertheless have some protection under s19 of the Rent Act 1977 if his tenancy or licence is a restricted contract (see Chapter 9).

Effect of the Housing Act 1988

Since the Housing Act 1988 came into force on 15 January 1989 it has not been possible (save in a few limited cases: see below 'Transitional provisions') to create a protected tenancy. The Act has not abolished existing regulated tenancies. A person who was a protected or statutory tenant prior to commencement of the 1988 Act will continue to be entitled to remain in occupation pursuant to the Rent Act 1977. The major effect of the 1988 Act on existing regulated tenancies relates to the right to succeed to the tenancy on the death of the tenant (see p151).

The protected tenancy

Rent Act 1977, s1

    1.—Subject to this Part of this Act, a tenancy under which a dwelling house (which may be a house or part of a house) is let as a separate dwelling is a protected tenancy for the purposes of this Act.

    Any reference in this Act to a protected tenant shall be construed accordingly.

'House' is not defined in the Act but the words 'which may be a house or part of a house' indicate that the section does not only apply to houses properly so called. A flat is a house for the purposes of the section. A single room within a house or a hostel can be 'a house' (*Luganda v Service Hotels Ltd* [1969] 2 Ch 209). Two separate properties may be a dwelling house where the two are let together as one unit to be used as a single dwelling (*Langford Property Co Ltd v Goldrich* [1949] 1 KB 511; *Whitty v Scott-Russell* [1950] 2 KB 32). A caravan may be a 'house' within the meaning of the section if there is a sufficient degree of permanence (*R v Rent Officer of Nottingham Registration Area, ex p Allen* [1985] 2 EGLR 153). A caravan which can be towed away, however, cannot be a dwelling house within the meaning of the Act (*Morgan v Taylor* (1949) 153 EG 3). Occupiers of mobile homes have a separate code of protection (see Chapter 17).

For the house to be 'a dwelling house . . . let as a . . . dwelling' the premises to which the tenancy applies must be suitable for living in and the purpose of the tenancy must be that someone is to live there. Whether the premises are suitable for living in is a question of fact but the tenant must be able to at least sleep and cook on the premises. The fact that the tenant is unable to wash or use a toilet on the premises does not mean that the tenancy is thereby precluded from protection (*Cole v Harris* [1945] KB 474; *Goodrich v Paisner* [1957] AC 65). (See also 'Shared accommodation' in Chapter 11.)

An express term as to the purpose of the tenancy is conclusive evidence of the purpose (*Wolfe v Hogan* [1949] 2 KB 194). Where there is no such express term the court will look to the actual use to which the tenant puts the premises to ascertain the intention of the parties. The tenancy will not be protected unless the use of the premises concerned extends to all those activities which are essential to enable them to exhibit the characteristics of a complete home (*Kavanagh v Lyroudias* [1985] 1 All ER 560 at 562g to be read in the light of *Hampstead Way Investments Ltd v Lewis-Weare* [1985] 1 All ER 564). Thus, unless the tenant sleeps and eats at the premises on a regular basis the tenancy will not be protected. Simply carrying on one of these activities is insufficient:

> Where a person is a tenant of two different parts of the same house under different lettings by the same landlord, and carries on some of his living activities in one part of the house and the rest of them in the other part, neither tenancy will normally be protected. If, however, the true view of the facts is that there is, in substance, a single combined or composite letting of

the two parts of the house as a whole, then the tenancies of both parts together will, or anyhow may, be protected (*Hampstead Way per* Lord Brandon at 568h).

Note that it is not necessary for the tenant to live on the premises himself for the tenancy to be protected but once the contractual tenancy has been determined it will be necessary for him to live there if the tenancy is to be a statutory one (see *below* 'The statutory tenancy').

The effect of the word 'separate' is dealt with in Chapter 11 (see 'Shared accommodation').

Where *land*, such as a garden, is let together with the dwelling house, that land is also treated as part of the house and therefore protected under s1 unless it is agricultural land exceeding two acres (s26). Distinguish cases where the *house* is incidentally let with the land in which case the dwelling house will not be protected (s6).

The exceptions The words 'subject to this Part of this Act' in the definition of a protected tenancy refer to those tenancies that are not protected even though they fall within the definition contained in s1 of the Rent Act. The exceptions are set out in ss4–16 of the Rent Act:

(1) Dwelling houses above certain rateable values/rents (ss4 and 25—see Appendix 1).
(2) Tenancies where no rent or a low rent is payable (s5—see Appendix 1).
(3) Dwelling houses let with land (s6).
(4) Payments for board or attendance (s7—see Chapter 16).
(5) Lettings to students by specified institutions (s8—see Chapter 16).
(6) Holiday lettings (s9—see Chapter 16).
(7) Agricultural holdings (s10—see Chapter 15).
(8) Licensed premises (s11—see Chapter 14, p209).
(9) Resident landlords (s12—see Chapter 11).
(10) Landlord's interest belonging to the Crown, save where the property is under the management of the Crown Estate Commissioners (s13 as amended by s73 of the Housing Act 1980).
(11) Landlord a local authority or housing association etc (ss14, 15 and 16—see Chapter 10).

A protected tenancy obtained by fraud can be rescinded even after it has expired by effluxion of time thus preventing the tenant from obtaining a statutory tenancy (*Killick v Roberts* [1991] 4 All ER 289, CA).

Housing Act 1988: transitional provisions

The basic rule is that it has not been possible to create a protected tenancy since the commencement of the Housing Act 1988 (15 January 1989). There are, however, exceptions. In certain circumstances a tenancy of residential premises created on or after 15 January 1989 may be protected.

In order to fully understand the position it is necessary to remember that s 1 of the Rent Act 1977 has not been repealed. Thus, if there were no other provisions in the 1988 Act dealing with the situation a tenancy would be both assured and protected. To avoid such an absurdity para 13(1) of Sched 1 to the 1988 Act provides that if a tenancy is protected within the meaning of the Rent Act 1977 it cannot be assured. The exceptions are as follows:

Pre-commencement contracts

A tenancy which is entered into on or after the commencement of the 1988 Act pursuant to a contract made before the commencement of the 1988 Act, cannot be assured (Sched 1, para 1).

If it satisfies the requirements of a protected tenancy it will be protected under the 1977 Act (s34(1)(*a*); Sched 1, para 13(1)).

Existing protected or statutory tenants

Section 34(1)(*b*) of the Housing Act 1988 provides that:

34.—(1) A tenancy which is entered into on or after the commencement of this Act cannot be a protected tenancy, unless—

. . .

(b) it is granted to a person (alone or jointly with others) who, immediately before the tenancy was granted, was a protected or statutory tenant and is so granted by the person who at that time was the landlord (or one of the joint landlords) under the protected or statutory tenancy.

This subsection clearly applies where the tenant is being granted a new tenancy of the same dwelling house. The new tenancy is protected rather than assured.

It is possible that the subsection also applies where the landlord grants, to his existing protected or statutory tenant, a tenancy of *different* premises. However, if Parliament intended this result, it is surprising that the subsection does not say so explicitly. Furthermore, the existence of subs (1)(*c*) (relating to the provision of suitable alternative accommodation: see *below*) perhaps implies that subs (1)(*b*) does not apply where the landlord grants a tenancy of different premises to an existing protected or statutory tenant. Presumably, subs (1)(*c*) would not have been considered necessary if subs (1)(*b*) had the effect of making that tenancy a protected tenancy.

Pre-existing shorthold tenancies   The exception contained in s34(1)(*b*) does not apply to a person who entered into occupation prior to 15 January 1989 under a protected shorthold tenancy and who has entered into a new agreement after that date. His tenancy will be an assured tenancy (in fact an assured shorthold—for a full explanation see p 122).

Suitable alternative accommodation cases

Section 34(1)(*c*) (when read with s1 of the Rent Act 1977 and para 13(1) of Sched 1 to the 1988 Act) provides that a tenancy will be protected (rather than assured) if it was granted on or after 15 January 1989 to a person in the following circumstances:

(*a*) prior to the grant of the tenancy an order for possession was made against the tenant on the court being satisfied that suitable alternative accommodation was to be made available to him (either under the 1977 Act or the Rent (Agriculture) Act 1976); and

(*b*) the tenancy is of the suitable alternative accommodation as to which the court was satisfied; and

(*c*) in the proceedings for possession the court considered that, in the circumstances, the grant of an assured tenancy would not afford the required security and, accordingly, directed that the tenancy would be a protected tenancy.

Tenancies transferred from public to private sector

This is a special exception relating to the transfer of tenancies from new town corporations to the private sector: see s34(1)(*d*) and s38(4) of the 1988 Act.

The statutory tenancy

Section 2(1)(*a*) of the Rent Act 1977 provides that 'after termination of a protected tenancy of the dwelling house the person who, *immediately* before that termination, was the protected tenant of the dwelling house shall, if and *so long* as he occupies the dwelling house as his residence, be the statutory tenant of it'.

As explained in the introduction to this chapter the protected tenancy is a contractual tenancy and is brought to an end by the ordinary contractual methods dealt with in Chapters 2 and 3, ie notice to quit, forfeiture, expiration of fixed term or surrender. If the surrender is an express one (ie as opposed to a surrender by operation of law; see p 71) and, notwithstanding the surrender, the tenant remains in occupation, he becomes a statutory tenant. A protected tenancy can also be converted into a statutory tenancy by service of a notice of increase in rent under s49 of the Rent Act 1977 (see *below*).

Notice of increase (s49 of the Rent Act 1977)

A protected tenancy is converted into a statutory tenancy where the landlord serves a notice of increase under s45(2) or s46 of the Rent Act

1977 (see p324) in circumstances where the tenancy could, by a notice to quit served by the landlord at the same time, be brought to an end before the date specified in the notice of increase (s49(4)).

Rent Act 1977, s49
    49.—(1) Any reference in this section to a notice of increase is a reference to a notice of increase under section 45(2) or 46 of this Act.
    (2) A notice of increase must be in prescribed form.
    (3) Notwithstanding that a notice of increase relates to statutory periods, it may be served during a contractual period.
    (4) Where a notice of increase is served during a contractual period and the protected tenancy could, by a notice to quit served by the landlord at the same time, be brought to an end before the date specified in the notice of increase, the notice of increase shall operate to convert the protected tenancy into a statutory tenancy as from that date.
    (5) If the county court is satisfied that any error or omission in a notice of increase is due to a *bona fide* mistake on the part of the landlord, the court may by order amend the notice by correcting any errors or supplying any omission therein which, if not corrected or supplied, would render the notice invalid and, if the court so directs, the notice as so amended shall have effect and be deemed to have had effect as a valid notice.
    (6) Any amendment of a notice of increase under subsection (5) above may be made on such terms and conditions with respect to arrears of rent or otherwise as appear to the court to be just and reasonable.
    (7) No increase of rent which becomes payable by reason of an amendment of a notice of increase under subsection (5) above shall be recoverable in respect of any statutory period which ended more than 6 months before the date of the order making the amendment.

The court will not infer that a notice of increase in rent of sufficient length to convert the contractual tenancy into a statutory tenancy has been served merely by reason of the fact that there has been an increase in rent (*Trustees of Thomas Pocklington v Hill* [1989] 2 EGLR 97 at 99D–H). However, where a notice was served during the period prior to the revocation of the phasing provisions (see p324), which was of insufficient length to convert the periodic tenancy into the statutory tenancy at the time of the first increase in rent, it will have been sufficient to operate the conversion at the time of the second increase (*Thomas Pocklington* at 99K–M).

Note that it is also possible to apply to the court to amend the notice under s49(5) in certain limited circumstances.

A statement on a certified copy of the rent register that the tenancy is a statutory tenancy may be admitted in evidence of that fact (s66(3) of the Rent Act 1977). See also *White v Wareing* [1992] 1 EGLR 272, where the tenancy was pleaded as a statutory tenancy and there was no defence filed (by the unrepresented tenant). In the Court of Appeal the defendant was represented by counsel who argued that there was no evidence that the contractual tenancy had been converted into a statutory tenancy. The court held that:

It is reasonable to assume, in the case of a tenancy lasting for a long time, as this had lasted, where there had been a number of references to the rent tribunal, among other things, that this was a tenancy that had converted to a statutory tenancy . . . The majority of cases in the county court these days are statutory tenancies. It is, I would have thought, rare to have a contractual tenancy. When it is pleaded as a statutory tenancy it is perfectly reasonable for the judge so to assume it unless it is raised that it is not. Indeed, in this particular case, any other conclusion than a statutory tenancy would have been an absurd one (*per* Butler-Sloss LJ at 272G–H).

Payment of rent after termination of protected tenancy

If the landlord continues to accept rent after termination of the protected tenancy whether by expiry of a fixed term or service of a notice to quit, a new contractual tenancy is not inferred even if the rent is an increased rent (*Morrison v Jacobs* [1945] KB 577; *Davies v Bristow* [1920] 3 KB 428). This is because the statutory tenant is entitled to remain in occupation until the court orders otherwise and the landlord is therefore entitled to the rent. There is no reason why a statutory tenancy should not continue for many years. A new contractual tenancy will, however, come into being if the parties genuinely intend to create one.

Where the landlord accepts rent after termination of the protected tenancy in circumstances where he is not sure whether the person in occupation is entitled to the protection afforded by the Rent Act and while he is considering his position the monies received will be considered as mesne profits if he subsequently goes on to take possession proceedings. Acceptance of the monies will not be treated as creating a new tenancy (*Marcroft Wagons Ltd v Smith* [1951] 2 KB 496, discussed by Lord Templeman in *Street v Mountford* [1985] 2 All ER 289 at 295).

Terms of the statutory tenancy

So long as he retains possession of the dwelling house the statutory tenant must observe, and is entitled to the benefit of, all the terms and conditions of the original contractual tenancy so far as they are consistent with the provisions of the Rent Act 1977 (s3(1); eg in *Henry Smith's Charity v Willson* [1983] QB 316 a covenant against subletting in the contractual tenancy was held to be a term of the statutory tenancy).

Termination of statutory tenancy by tenant

Where a protected tenancy has come to an end and the tenant has held over as a statutory tenant he must give the landlord notice to quit in writing (s5 of the Protection from Eviction Act 1977) if he wishes to give up possession of the dwelling house. The notice period is the same as may have been required by the protected tenancy (subject to s5 of the Protection from Eviction Act 1977 which provides that the tenant must give at least four weeks' notice). Where the protected tenancy did not require any such notice the tenant must give three months' notice to determine the statutory tenancy (see s3(3) of the Rent Act 1977). There is no prescribed form.

Where the tenant fails to leave at the end of the notice period the landlord may be able to recover possession under Case 5 of Sched 15 to the Rent Act 1977 if in reliance on the notice the landlord has contracted to sell or let the premises or has taken other steps as a result of which he would in the court's opinion be seriously prejudiced if he could not obtain possession. The landlord will only be able to rely on this case if the notice given by the tenant was a valid one (*De Vries v Sparks* (1927) 137 LT 411). A conditional contract to sell is not sufficient for there to be 'serious prejudice' (*Hunt v Bliss* (1919) 89 LJ KB 174).

Where a statutory tenant gives up possession without giving the requisite notice or properly surrendering, ie with the agreement of the landlord (see p72), he will cease to be a statutory tenant because he will no longer be occupying the dwelling house as his residence (s2 of the Rent Act 1977) *but* he will still be liable for the rent due in the notice period unless the landlord unequivocally accepts the tenant's abandonment as a surrender (*Boyer v Warbey* [1953] 1 QB 234 – see also p74).

For surrender of statutory tenancies see *Hulme v Langford* (1985) 50 P&CR 199.

Occupation as a residence

It is not always easy to determine whether the tenant is continuing to occupy the premises as his residence within s2 of the Rent Act 1977. Two problems in particular arise.

Abandonment and temporary absence   If a person abandons a dwelling house he clearly ceases to occupy it as his residence and he will therefore cease to be a statutory tenant. A person may, however, leave the dwelling house on a temporary basis with the intention of returning. The position was considered in the leading case of *Brown v Brash and Ambrose* [1948] 2 KB 247, where it was held that:

(a) it is a matter of fact and degree as to whether the absence is sufficiently long or continuous so as to raise the inference that the occupation as a residence has ceased; if the period of absence is relatively brief the burden of proof that occupation as a residence has ceased lies on the landlord;

(b) if that inference is raised on the facts the onus is then on the tenant to show that his residence has not ceased—the tenant may show this by establishing a *de facto* intention to return after his absence (the *animus revertendi* or *possidendi*); the tenant must also show a formal, visible and outward sign of his intention to return (the *corpus possessionis*) eg by leaving his belongings or a caretaker on the premises;

(c) if the *corpus possessionis* ceases, eg by the tenant removing his belongings, the tenant ceases to occupy as his residence.

The tenant may thus be able to be absent for a long time but nevertheless remain a statutory tenant. (As to the onus of proof see also *Roland House Gardens v Cravitz* (1975) 29 P&CR 432 at 438.)

Thus, a person who is ill in hospital for a temporary period, even a lengthy one, remains a statutory tenant (*Tickner v Hearn* [1961] 1 All ER 65), so does a sailor who is at sea for months on end (*Skinner v Geary* [1931] 2 KB 546 at 558) or a person who often goes away for the weekend. In *Richards v Green* (1983) 268 EG 443 the tenant left his home to nurse his sick parents but left his furniture, books, records and some clothing there. He spent over two years nursing his parents and when they died he stayed on at their home to arrange the sale of it. He always intended to return to his flat but in the meantime allowed two friends to live there from time to time. It was held that the tenant still treated the flat as his home and was still a statutory tenant. A 'temporary' period may be many years (*Gofor Investments v Roberts* (1975) 29 P&CR 366; *Brickfield Properties Ltd v Hughes* (1988) HLR 108).

A husband tenant of a 'deserted wife', though absent, is deemed to be in occupation of the dwelling house through the presence of his wife (*Griffiths v Renfree* (1989) 21 HLR 338). See also Chapter 18 for the rights of one spouse to remain where the other is the statutory tenant and the right to have the tenancy transferred into his or her name under Sched 1 to the Matrimonial Homes Act 1983. But if the tenancy is not transferred under that Act the husband will cease to be a statutory tenant and the wife will lose her right to remain in possession upon divorce (*Metropolitan Properties Co Ltd v Cronan* (1982) 44 P&CR 1).

A statutory tenant who departs forever leaving behind a mistress does not, through her occupation, continue as a statutory tenant even if she has borne him children. She will therefore have to leave if required to do so (*Colin Smith Music v Ridge* [1975] 1 All ER 290).

It is possible for a person to be a statutory tenant of only part of premises of which he had previously been the protected tenant of the whole (*Regalian Securities Ltd v Ramsden* [1981] 1 WLR 611).

If one of two joint tenants leaves the other will be the statutory tenant (*Lloyd v Sadler* [1978] QB 774).

Two homes   A person may have two dwelling houses, each of which he occupies as his home, so that, if either of them is let to him, his tenancy of it is protected by the Rent Act 1977; and where a person owns one dwelling house which he occupies as his home for most of his time and is at the same time the tenant of another dwelling house which he only occupies rarely or for limited purposes it is a question of fact and degree whether he occupies the latter dwelling house as his second home (*Hampstead Way Investments Ltd v Lewis-Weare* [1985] 1 All ER 564 HL at 568).

For examples of where the occupier was held to be a statutory tenant of the second property see *Langford Property Co Ltd v Athanassoglou* [1948] 2 All ER 722 (a home in the country and a property in London used during the week) and *Bevington v Crawford* (1974) 232 EG 191 (a home in France where the tenant spent most of his time and a home in England). For examples of where the occupier was held not to be a statutory tenant of the second property see *Regalian Securities Ltd v Scheuer* (1982) 263 EG 973 (tenant occupied the flat in question two months a year as a residence and spent some time there during the daytime for the rest of the year) and *Hampstead Way* (tenant owned a house half a mile away from the flat concerned and used the flat to sleep in when he worked late at night in a local club, so as not to disturb the family by arriving home in the early hours of the morning).

The question in every case will really be whether the dwelling house can be said to be a *home* to the tenant (eg see *Hampstead Way* at 568d and 570f).

Termination by the landlord and recovery of possession

The landlord will not be entitled to an order for possession unless he can show that the contractual tenancy has come to an end and that there is a ground for possession. The methods of determination, ie notice to quit, forfeiture, expiration and surrender are dealt with in Chapters 2 and 3 (and see further p134 *above*). Except in the case of forfeiture proceedings where it is the service of the proceedings that operates as the forfeiture, the landlord must show that the contractual tenancy has come to an end prior to commencement of the action. This follows from the rule that the plaintiff must have a cause of action at the time of commencement. Thus, where the tenancy has been determined by a notice to quit the landlord should be very careful to ensure that the notice has expired before any further steps are taken. Service of a notice to increase rent pursuant to s49(4) of the Rent Act 1977 also converts a periodic contractual tenancy into a statutory tenancy (see p134). The landlord need take no steps to determine a statutory tenancy other than commence proceedings for possession (s3(4) of the Rent Act 1977). However, 'the lack of a letter before action or similar warning may affect the issue of reasonableness under s98(1) and costs' (*White v Wareing* [1992] 1 EGLR 271 at 272J). Prior to commencing proceedings the landlord should therefore send the tenant a letter before action requiring the tenant to leave. A notice to quit, although not technically required, would be a 'similar warning'.

Where a landlord wishes to obtain possession of a dwelling house that has been let on a protected tenancy the steps to be taken will therefore depend on whether the contractual tenancy was for a periodic or fixed term, whether forfeiture is appropriate and whether the contractual tenancy has already been determined.

(1) *Fixed term contractual tenancy that has expired*: send a letter before action requiring the tenant to leave and then commence proceedings for possession.

(2) *Fixed term tenancy, containing forfeiture clause, that has not expired*: if the tenant is in breach of covenant commence proceedings for possession based upon forfeiture, preceded if necessary by s 146 notice.

(3) *Periodic contractual tenancy without forfeiture clause*: serve appropriate notice to quit and when it has expired commence proceedings for possession.

(4) *Periodic contractual tenancy with forfeiture clause*: if tenant is in breach of covenant either commence proceedings for possession based upon the forfeiture, preceded if necessary by s 146 notice or serve appropriate notice to quit and then commence proceedings for possession (see further p 319).

(5) *Periodic tenancy that was determined by a notice to quit at some earlier time thus giving rise to a statutory tenancy*: if the landlord is able to prove service of the notice to quit send a letter before action and then commence proceedings for possession. If not, serve a fresh notice to quit and, after expiry, commence proceedings.

(6) *Periodic contractual tenancy that has been converted into a statutory tenancy by service of a notice of increase in rent under s 49 of the Rent Act 1977*: make sure that the notice complies with s 49(4) (see p 135) and if the landlord is able to prove service of the notice, send a letter before action and then commence proceedings for possession. If he is not able to do so, serve a notice to quit and after it has expired commence proceedings for possession.

The grounds

The grounds for possession are referred to in s 98 of the Rent Act 1977. They consist of two types: the discretionary grounds and the mandatory grounds. Section 98(1) which deals with the discretionary grounds provides that the court *shall not* make an order for possession unless it considers it reasonable to make the order and either suitable alternative accommodation is or will be available or one of the Cases set out in Part I of Sched 15 applies (Cases 1–10). Section 98(2) which deals with the mandatory grounds provides that the court *shall* make an order for possession if one of the Cases in Part II of Sched 15 applies (Cases 11–20).

The discretionary grounds   Where the landlord is relying upon one of the discretionary grounds the onus is on him to show that the court should make an order for possession (*Nevile v Hardy* [1921] 1 Ch 404).

He must show that it is reasonable to make the order having regard to the circumstances that exist at the date of the hearing (*Smith v McGoldrick* (1976) 242 EG 1047).

In deciding whether it is reasonable to make the order for possession the judge may not take into account the fact that the tenant has relied upon his statutory rights under s 11 of the Landlord and Tenant Act 1985 (implied repairing obligations), the Matrimonial Homes Act 1983, the Rent Act 1977, or indeed any other statute (*Sopwith v Sturchbury* (1983) 17 HLR 50).

The court must consider the question of overall reasonableness even where the case itself refers to this question (eg Case 9). Any failure to do so makes the decision appealable (*Peachey Property Corporation Ltd v Robinson* [1967] 2 QB 543). But the issue of reasonableness is a matter of discretion for the county court and the Court of Appeal will not interfere if it has been properly considered, even though the latter court might have come to a different conclusion on the facts (*Fuggle (RF) Ltd v Gadsden* [1948] 2 KB 236 at 243). However, if the Court of Appeal considers that an appeal should be allowed on some other ground it can consider circumstances that have occurred since the date of the hearing (*King v Taylor* [1955] 1 QB 150; *Alexander v Mohamedzadeh* [1985] 2 EGLR 161). As to appeals generally see p292.

The mandatory grounds   Where the landlord seeks to rely upon one or more of the mandatory grounds it is not necessary for the landlord to show that it is reasonable for the court to make the order although he must show that he gave notice in writing that possession might be recovered under the relevant case not later than the 'relevant date' (usually the date the tenancy commenced) unless it is 'just and equitable' to grant the order for possession notwithstanding that no such notice was given (eg, see p352). Such a notice should be in writing.

The grounds   The full text of Sched 15 to the Rent Act is set out in Appendix 2. The grounds for possession set out in that schedule are as follows:

The discretionary grounds (Cases 1–10):
  (1) Arrears of rent and breach of obligation (see Chapter 23)
  (2) Nuisance, annoyance, immoral or illegal user (see Chapter 24)
  (3) Deterioration of the dwelling house (see Chapter 24)
  (4) Deterioration of furniture (see Chapter 24)
  (5) Tenant's notice to quit (see p70)
  (6) Assigning or subletting without consent (see p143)
  (7) *repealed*
  (8) Dwelling house required for employee (see p209)
  (9) Dwelling house required by landlord (see p345)
  (10) Overcharging sub-tenants

The mandatory grounds (Cases 11–20):
   (11) Owner-occupiers
   (12) Retirement homes
   (13) Holiday homes let out of season (see Chapter 16)
   (14) Student accommodation let during the vacations (see Chapter 16)
   (15) Ministers of religion (see Chapter 18)
   (16) Required for agricultural employee (see Chapter 15)
   (17) Farmhouse after amalgamation (see Chapter 15)
   (18) Other farmhouses required for farmers (see Chapter 15)
   (19) Shortholds (see Chapter 12)
   (20) Serviceman's accommodation

Proceedings

Almost invariably the proceedings should be commenced in the county court (see p259). In the county court all proceedings may be commenced by action; but if the landlord is relying upon one of the mandatory grounds he will usually be able to use the sometimes quicker originating application procedure (see Chapter 20).

The order

Where the court makes an order for possession under one of the discretionary grounds the court may stay or suspend execution of the order, or postpone the date for possession, for such period or periods as it thinks fit, at the time the order is made or at any time before the order is executed (s100(2) of the Rent Act 1977). On any such stay, suspension or postponement the court *must*, unless it considers that to do so would cause exceptional hardship to the tenant or would otherwise be unreasonable, impose conditions with regard to the payment of arrears of rent (if any) and rent or mesne profits and *may* impose such other conditions as it thinks fit (s100(3)). If any such conditions are complied with the court may, if it thinks fit, discharge or rescind the order for possession (s100(4)). See further p298.

   Where the order for possession is made under one of the mandatory grounds the court may only postpone the date for possession for up to 14 days unless exceptional hardship would be caused by such a short order in which case the court may postpone the effect of the order for up to six weeks (s100(5) of the Rent Act 1977; s89 of the Housing Act 1980; see p75).

Enforcing the order

A statutory tenant remains a statutory tenant (so long as he occupies the dwelling house as his residence) between the time the order for possession is made and eviction pursuant to a warrant for possession. The landlord may not, therefore, resort to self-help to enforce the order for possession and if he does so will be liable to pay the tenant damages for unlawful eviction (*Haniff v Robinson* [1993] 1 All ER 185).

Assignment, subletting, bankruptcy and death

Assignment of landlord's interest

Where the tenancy is protected, ie a contractual tenancy, the provisions dealt with in Chapter 4 at p77 will apply.

It never seems to be doubted that a purchaser of land acquires his interest subject to the rights of *statutory* tenants but surprisingly enough the precise basis upon which statutory tenancies are binding has never been clearly established. As an interest under a statutory tenancy is purely a personal right it is probably not an overriding interest within s70(1)(*g*) of the Land Registration Act 1925 (cf Lord Denning in *National Provincial Bank Ltd v Hastings Car Mart Ltd (No 2)* [1964] Ch 665 at 689—a decision reversed on other grounds in the House of Lords [1965] AC 1175). However, it does seem that a statutory tenant's status of irremovability is effective against 'all the world' by reason of the clear words of s98 of the Rent Act 1977 which states that an order for possession shall not be made against the tenant unless the conditions referred to in the section are satisfied (see *Jessamine Investment Co v Schwartz* [1978] 1 QB 264 and the discussion at para 2.15, note 71 of Law Commission Report No 158, *Property Law: Third Report on Land Registration* upon which this paragraph is based). But note that a statutory tenancy that arises following upon the termination of a protected tenancy granted after the execution of a mortgage, in breach of the terms of the mortgage, is not binding on the mortgagee (*Britannia Building Society v Earl* [1990] 2 All ER 469, where the tenant unsuccessfully argued that the mortgagee was bound by the statutory tenancy on the basis that it was effective against 'all the world'; see further p400).

Assignment of protected tenancies

The ordinary rules relating to the assignment of contractual tenancies dealt with in Chapter 4 apply to protected tenancies (see p50). The assignment will therefore be effective whether lawful or unlawful but in either case, if the tenant did not obtain the landlord's consent to the assignment and the landlord is not prepared to accept the assignee as his tenant, he may be able to recover possession. If the assignment was unlawful he should serve a notice under s146 of the Law of Property Act 1925 upon the assignee (see p18) and commence proceedings based on forfeiture and Case 1 or 6 of Sched 15 to the Rent Act 1977. If there was no covenant against assigning in the tenancy agreement the landlord should (if the tenancy is for a periodic term) serve a notice to quit and then commence proceedings based upon Case 6. Both Cases 1 and 6 are discretionary grounds and the landlord will have to show that it is reasonable to make the order for possession. In deciding whether it is reasonable to make an order for possession the court is entitled to take into account the fact that by assigning the tenancy in *breach of covenant* a person has been put into possession who is able to qualify for a statutory tenancy at the end of the term. The fact of assignment in breach of covenant is a significant factor (*Pazgate Ltd v McGrath* (1984) 272 EG 1069).

The proper defendant will be the assignee as he is the person in possession (see p262) although it is often worth making the original tenant a defendant as well, as the fact of the assignment may be disputed.

For transfer of the tenancy by order of the court in matrimonial cases see p242.

Assignment of statutory tenancies

A statutory tenancy cannot be assigned except pursuant to Sched 1, para 13 of the Rent Act 1977, which provides for the transfer of statutory tenancies by agreement. The agreement must be in writing and must be made between the outgoing tenant, the ingoing tenant and the landlord. If under the previous contractual tenancy the consent of a superior landlord was required for an assignment he must also be a party to the agreement (para 13(1) and (2)).

Any purported assignment of a statutory tenancy other than a transfer under para 13 of Sched 1 is wholly ineffective (see *Oak Property Co v Chapman* [1947] KB 886; *Roe v Russel* [1928] 2 KB 117 at 126; *Atyeo v Fardoe* (1978) 37 P&CR 494). If the statutory tenant, without any intention of returning, ceases to occupy the dwelling house he loses his statutory tenancy and the purported assignees will be trespassers who can be removed in summary possession proceedings under CCR Ord 24 (RSC Ord 113). If the tenant intends to return he may well continue to be the statutory tenant and the landlord will not be able to regain possession from either the tenant or those in occupation (see *Atyeo v Fardoe*, and further at p137).

For transfer of the tenancy by order of the court in matrimonial cases see p242.

Subletting

Position of tenant   There is nothing to prevent a protected or statutory tenant from subletting the whole or part of the dwelling house and creating a valid sub-tenancy as between himself and the sub-tenant. If, however, the tenant has sublet without the landlord's permission the landlord may be able to obtain an order for possession, at least as against the tenant.

Where the tenancy agreement contains a covenant forbidding subletting (see p82) and a right of reentry, the landlord may forfeit. He will first have to serve a notice under s146 of the Law of Property Act 1925 and then commence proceedings for possession based upon the forfeiture (see Chapter 2). If the tenancy is a periodic tenancy the landlord may bring the term to an end by serving the appropriate notice to quit.

There are two cases in Sched 15 to the Rent Act 1977 upon which the landlord may then rely in order to try to obtain possession. These are Cases 1 and 6. Case 1 may be relied upon if the subletting was in breach of a term in the lease. Case 6 may be relied upon whenever a tenant sublets the *whole* of the dwelling house, or first part and then the remainder, without the landlord's consent whether or not the subletting was forbidden by the terms of the tenancy. Both cases are, however, discretionary grounds for possession and the court will not make an order unless it also considers it reasonable to do so (s98(1) of the Rent Act 1977). If, for example, the covenant was 'not to sublet without the landlord's consent' the court will not make an order for possession if the tenant sublet after the landlord had been asked for but unreasonably withheld his consent.

Where a tenant who has sublet the *whole* of the dwelling house has ceased to occupy the premises as his residence the landlord will also be entitled to possession as against him on the ground that the tenant has ceased to be a statutory tenant (*Haskins v Lewis* [1931] 2 KB 1). In these circumstances, of course, the landlord will not have to show that it is reasonable to make the order. However, this rule is not absolute. If the tenant has only sublet for a certain period and has done so with the intention of returning he remains the statutory tenant of the whole. As the landlord is invariably unaware of the full facts of these situations until the evidence actually comes out in court it is always worth pleading his case in the alternative, ie on the basis that the tenant is not a statutory tenant but that if he is the landlord is entitled to possession under Case 1 or 6 (see Form 21 on p146).

If the tenant sublets a part of the premises which he has never occupied and never intends to occupy the tenant loses his right to be a statutory tenant of that part (*Crowhurst v Maidment* [1953] 1 QB 23). If the tenant is not sure whether he wishes to re-occupy that part at the termination of the sub-tenancy he remains a statutory tenant of the whole. It is only when he makes a final decision never to re-occupy the part that he has sublet that he loses his right to be a statutory tenant of it (*Berkeley v Papadoyannis* [1954] 2 QB 149). If the tenant does cease to be a statutory tenant of a part of the premises he nevertheless continues to be a statutory tenant of the rest (*Regalian Securities Ltd v Ramsden* [1981] 1 WLR 611). See Form 22, p150.

Position of sub-tenant The sub-tenant, who at common law would lose his right to remain in possession as against the landlord at the

Form 21: Particulars of claim—assignment/subletting the whole

IN THE   COUNTY COURT   Case No

BETWEEN:

                                                                        Plaintiff

                                    —AND—

                                                                        Defendants

PARTICULARS OF CLAIM

1. The Plaintiff is the freehold owner and is entitled to possession of the premises comprising a dwelling house known as [*state address*].

2. By an agreement in writing made on the [*insert date*] the Plaintiff let the said premises to the First Defendant on a tenancy at a rent of £ [*State amount*] per [*state how frequent*] payable on the [*state number*] day of each [*state how frequent*] in [*advance/arrears*].

3. The said tenancy was duly determined by a notice to quit addressed to 'the lessee' and left at the said premises pursuant to the provisions of section 196 of the Law of Property Act 1925 on the [*insert date*]. The said notice expired on the [*insert date*]. The First Defendant did not, upon the said expiration, and/or does not now occupy the said premises as his residence.

4. Further or in the alternative on a date prior to the commencement of these proceedings the First Defendant, without the consent of the Plaintiff, assigned or sublet the whole of the said premises to the Second Defendant.

5. By reason of the First Defendant's cesser of occupation of the said premises as his residence he is not entitled to the protection of the Rent Act 1977.

6. In the alternative the said premises are premises to which the Rent Act 1977 applies and possession is claimed pursuant to Case 6 of Schedule 15 of the said Act.

AND the Plaintiff claims:
(1) Possession of the said premises.

(2) Mesne profits at the rate of £_____ from the date hereof until possession be delivered up.

DATED

determination of the tenant's interest, is not, if he is a lawful sub-tenant, affected by any order for possession made against the tenant upon one of the discretionary grounds pursuant to s98(1) (s137(1) of the Rent Act 1977). Furthermore, s137(2) of the Rent Act 1977 provides that the sub-tenant is deemed to become the tenant of the landlord on the same terms as if the head tenant's protected or statutory tenancy had continued *if* the following conditions are satisfied:
  (a) the sub-tenancy must be lawful at the date of termination of the *head* tenancy (or, if the head tenant is a statutory tenant, at the date proceedings were issued: *Oak Property Co Ltd v Chapman* [1947] KB 886); and

(*b*) the *head* tenancy must be protected or statutory at the determination of the head tenant's tenancy; and

(*c*) the *sub-tenancy* must be protected or statutory at the determination of the head tenant's tenancy.

The sub-tenancy will be unlawful if it was granted contrary to the terms of the headlease (see p82); and will also be unlawful if the sub-tenancy was created after the protected tenancy has been determined, as statutory tenants are bound by s3(1) of the Rent Act 1977 to observe all the terms and conditions of the original contractual tenancy. A demand for rent from a statutory tenant after knowledge of the unlawful act does not amount to an election to treat the sub-tenant as lawful. This is because the landlord is entitled to demand rent so long as the statutory tenancy continues. However, a demand for rent from a contractual tenant will usually waive the unlawfulness (*Henry Smith's Charity v Willson* [1983] 1 All ER 73).

Requirements (*a*) and (*b*) above appear from the wording of s137(2); although see example (3) *below*. Requirement (*c*) is not so clear from the wording of s137 but appears to be generally agreed upon by the leading authors. Any other interpretation of s137 would mean that the sub-tenant would be in a better position as against the head landlord than he is in as against his own landlord, ie the tenant. (For authority for the proposition that it is the date of the determination of the head tenant's tenancy that is relevant when considering requirements (*b*) and (*c*) see *Jessamine Investment Co v Schwartz* [1978] QB 264 at 273e.)

Listed below are a number of situations that may arise and the consequences that flow from an application of the three requirements referred to above.

(1) The head tenant is a protected or statutory tenant. If he sublets *part* of the dwelling house he is a resident or sharing landlord (see Chapter 11) as against the sub-tenant and condition (*c*) is not satisfied (*Stanley v Compton* [1951] 1 All ER 859; *Solomon v Orwell* [1954] 1 WLR 629).

(2) The head tenant is a protected tenant. If the tenant sublets the whole conditions (*b*) and (*c*) are satisfied, and if the sub-tenancy is lawful s137(2) will apply. But if the tenant created the sub-tenancy without the landlord's consent the court may order that the sub-tenant deliver up possession where it considers that it would be reasonable to make the order (see Case 6 and *Leith Properties Ltd v Springer* [1983] QB 433).

(3) The head tenant is a statutory tenant. If he sublets the *whole* he will cease to be a statutory tenant because of his failure to occupy the dwelling house as his residence as required by s2 of the Rent Act 1977 and so condition (*b*) will not be satisfied. (See, however, the case of *Henry Smith's Charity v Willson*, particularly Ormrod LJ, which suggests that the sub-tenant *does* become the tenant even if condition (*b*) is not satisfied.)

(4) The head tenant is a statutory tenant. If he dies and is not survived by any person entitled to become a statutory tenant by succession pursuant to Sched 1 to the Rent Act 1977 the tenancy will determine immediately on death. If at that time he is a resident or sharing landlord (see Chapter 11) condition (c) is not satisfied.

(5) The head tenant is a protected tenant as against the landlord and a resident landlord as against the sub-tenant. The tenancy will not determine at his death but will vest in his personal representatives (see p86). If the sub-tenancy then ceases to be a resident landlord tenancy for one of the reasons set out at p189, the sub-tenant becomes protected, and if the sub-tenancy is lawful, s137(2) will apply. But if the person entitled to the head tenancy becomes a 'resident landlord' again within two years from the date of the original head tenant's death the sub-tenant once again becomes unprotected and s137(2) will no longer apply.

Prima facie subss (1) and (2) of s137 afford no protection to the sub-tenant where the head tenant was not protected, perhaps because the rateable value of the premises which are subject to the head tenancy exceeds the rateable values set out in s4 of the 1977 Act (*Cow v Casey* [1949] 1 KB 474) or because the head tenancy was a tenancy at a low rent (*Knightsbridge Estates Trust Ltd v Deeley* [1950] 2 KB 228). However, s137(3) may provide assistance in such circumstances. The subsection applies where a dwelling house:

(a) forms part of premises which have been let as a whole on a superior tenancy but do not constitute a dwelling house let on a statutorily protected tenancy (defined in subss (4) and (5)); and

(b) is itself subject to a protected or statutory tenancy.

The 'premises' (of which the dwelling house forms part) must itself be 'a dwelling house' (or in certain circumstances an agricultural holding: see the final paragraph of subs (3)) within the meaning of the 1977 Act. Thus, if the property is a shop with a flat above it will not be a dwelling house within the meaning of the Act but business premises to which Part II of the 1954 Act applies (see p211), and s137(3) will not apply so as to protect the flat (*Pittalis v Grant* [1989] 2 All ER 622; *Bromley Park Garden Estates Ltd v George* [1991] 2 EGLR 95, CA).

If subs (3) does apply, the Rent Act 1977 (including, of course, subss (1) and (2) of s137) applies, from the coming to an end of the superior tenancy, 'in relation to the dwelling house as if, in lieu of the superior tenancy, there had been separate tenancies of the dwelling house and of the remainder of the premises, for the like purposes as under the superior tenancy and at rents equal to the just proportion of the rent under the superior tenancy'. The notional 'separate tenancies' referred to in the subsection are notional separate tenancies to the *head tenant*, not the sub-tenant (*Cadogan v Henthorne* [1956] 3 All ER 851). This means that in order to decide whether s137(2) affords the sub-tenant any protection where the head tenancy is not statutorily protected it is necessary to look at the head tenancy and its terms. The part occupied by the sub-tenant must be taken and a proportion of the rent payable by the head tenant must be attributed to the part occupied by the sub-tenant. For example if the sub-tenant occupies one quarter of the premises let on the superior tenancy it is necessary to divide the rent payable by the *head tenant* by four. If the effect of this is that rent payable in respect of the quarter is, as thus calculated, a low rent within s5 of the 1977 Act the head tenancy will still not be regarded as being protected and the sub-tenancy will not be protected; but if the rent as calculated in this way is not a low rent the sub-tenancy will be protected. A similar calculation can be applied to the rateable value on the appropriate day in respect of the premises that are subject to the superior tenancy and s4 of the 1977 Act (see Appendix 1). Thus the rateable value on the appropriate day in respect of the whole of the premises may be too high to afford protection to the head tenant but once the figure is divided in four it may be within the limits. If so the head tenant will be regarded as protected for these purposes and the sub-tenant will be able to rely upon s137(2).

The fact that the sub-tenant is entitled to the protection of s137(3) does not prevent him from applying for a vesting order under s146(4) of the Law of Property Act 1925 (*Factor) Sundries Ltd v Miller* [1952] 2 All ER 630, CA).

Note that s137 is not comprehensive. There may be circumstances where it does not apply but where (by reason of s98 of the 1977 Act) the head landlord is precluded from recovering possession from a sub-tenant (see *Jessamine Investment Co v Schwartz* [1978] 1 QB 264 at 273F—statutory sub-tenancy ceasing to exist as against immediate landlord by operation of the Limitation Act, thus making s137(2) inapplicable, but nevertheless binding on the head landlord upon expiry of head lease).

If the head tenancy is a protected tenancy and is brought to an end by the tenant surrendering his lease the sub-tenant will become the tenant of the landlord even if the sub-tenancy was unlawful (see p82); but where a statutory tenant has granted a sub-tenancy this rule will not apply (*Solomon v Orwell* [1954] 1 WLR 629).

Bankruptcy: protected tenants

Section 283(3A) of the Insolvency Act 1986 (as introduced by s117 of the Housing Act 1988) provides that a protected tenancy within the meaning of the Rent Act 1977, in respect of which, by virtue of Part IX of that Act, no premium can lawfully be required as a condition of assignment, does not form part of a bankrupt tenant's estate. Thus, the protected tenancy does not automatically vest in the trustee in bankruptcy under s306 of the Insolvency Act 1986 on the bankruptcy of the tenant (see generally Chapter 4, p83). However, s308A of the Insolvency Act 1986 (as introduced by s117 of the 1988 Act) provides that where the trustee serves a notice in writing upon the bankrupt under s308A the protected

Form 22: Particulars of claim—subletting part

IN THE   **COUNTY COURT**   Case No

BETWEEN:

Plaintiff

—AND—

Defendant

PARTICULARS OF CLAIM

1. The Plaintiff is the [*freehold/leasehold*] owner and is entitled to possession of the premises comprising a dwelling house known as [*state address*].

2. By a Lease dated the [*insert date*] and made between the Plaintiff and the Defendant, the Plaintiff agreed to let the said premises to the Defendant for a period of [*state number of years*] from the [*insert date*].

3. By Clause [2] of the said Lease the Defendant, inter alia, covenanted:

    (1) Not to part with possession of the whole or part of the said premises and not to assign or underlet part of the said premises (Clause 2(7)).

    (2) To use the said premises for the purposes of a private residence of the Defendant only (Clause 2(10)).

4. The said Lease expired on the [*insert date of expiry*] and by virtue of Section 2 of the Rent Act 1977 the Defendant became a statutory tenant of the said premises immediately after the said expiry.

5. By virtue of Section 3(1) of the Rent Act 1977 the Defendant is bound to observe the terms and conditions of the original Lease including subclauses 2(7) and (10).

6. The rent payable by the Defendant in respect of the said premises is £[*state amount*] per month payable in advance on the [*state number*] day of each [month].

7. In breach of subclauses 2(7) and 2(10), the Defendant has parted with possession of, and/or assigned, and/or underlet, part of the said premises to persons whose names are not known to the Plaintiff.

8. The said premises are premises to which the Rent Act 1977 applies and possession is claimed pursuant to Case 1 of Schedule 15 to the said Act.

AND the Plaintiff claims:

(1) Possession of the said premises.

(2) Rent and/or mesne profits at the rate of [*state amount*] per month from the date hereof until possession be delivered up.

DATED

tenancy 'vests in the trustee as part of the bankrupt's estate; and except against a purchaser in good faith, for value and without notice of the bankruptcy, the trustee's title to that tenancy has relation back to the commencement of the bankruptcy'.

It is unlikely that a trustee in bankruptcy will ever serve a notice under s308A but where he does serve such a notice so that the tenancy becomes vested in him a former tenant who remains in occupation of the dwelling house does so as a licensee of the trustee (see p84).

If the trustee disclaims the tenancy the former tenant then being a licensee does not become a statutory tenant. He therefore has no right to remain in occupation and if after a request from the landlord he refuses to leave the landlord may recover possession in summary proceedings (*Smalley v Quarrier* [1975] 1 WLR 938) (see Chapter 25 for summary possession procedure and Form 14; p85). The landlord will not be able to recover any arrears of rent in summary proceedings and if he wishes to obtain a money judgment in respect of arrears he should commence the proceedings by action. The best course to adopt, however, is probably to obtain possession under CCR Ord 24 which will be quicker than by action and to prove the arrears in the bankruptcy proceedings. If the trustee does not disclaim the landlord can regain possession at the end of the contractual term (*Stafford v Lay* [1948] 2 All ER 256).

Bankruptcy: statutory tenants

A statutory tenancy not being property within the meaning of s283 of the Insolvency Act 1986 cannot vest in the trustee in bankruptcy (*Sutton v Dorf* [1932] 2 KB 304). If therefore the tenant is made bankrupt after the contractual tenancy has been determined and a statutory tenancy has come into existence the landlord may not use the summary procedure to recover possession. If as a result of his state of impecuniosity the tenant fails to pay his rent the landlord should commence normal possession proceedings based on Case 1.

Where the statutory tenant is a sub-tenant and the tenant is a company that has gone into liquidation, the statutory tenant may apply for a vesting order under s181 of the Insolvency Act 1986 if the liquidator serves a notice of disclaimer under s178, but if he subsequently discontinues the application he does not lose his statutory tenancy (*Re Vedmay Ltd* [1993] EGCS 167).

Death of the tenant

Whether or not the landlord will be able to obtain possession of the dwelling house on the death of the tenant will depend upon whether there is a person who is entitled to succeed to the tenancy. The position is governed by Sched 1 to the Rent Act 1977 (as amended by s76 of the Housing Act 1980 and s39 of and Sched 4 to the Housing Act 1988).

The amendments made by the Housing Act 1988 have substantially altered the position in relation to deaths occurring on or after 15 January 1989 (the date upon which the Housing Act 1988 came into force). The paragraphs of Sched 1 to the Rent Act 1977 referred to here are as amended.

Death of original tenant: spouse to succeed (Sched 1, paras 1 and 2)   If on his death the original tenant leaves a spouse he or she is the person who is entitled to succeed to the tenancy, *if* he or she was residing in the dwelling house immediately before the death of the tenant. He or she will be the 'statutory tenant by succession' (ie under the Rent Act 1977) if and so long as he or she occupies the dwelling house as his or her residence.

A person who was living with the original tenant as his or her wife or husband is treated as the spouse of the original tenant. Under the law prior to amendment by the Housing Act 1988 a 'common law wife' was entitled to succeed because she was regarded as a member of the deceased tenant's family. In deciding whether the person hoping to succeed was so entitled the court looked to see whether the relationship had sufficient stability and permanence for an ordinary person to say that the parties were members of one another's family (eg see *Watson v Lucas* [1980] 1 WLR 1493 and *Chios Property Investment Co Ltd v Lopez* [1988] 1 EGLR 98). The courts are likely to adopt a similar approach when deciding whether or not a man and woman are living together as man and wife.

If, because the tenant was living with someone as his or her husband or wife, there is more than one person who would be entitled to succeed to the tenancy as the tenant's 'spouse' (an unlikely occurrence) the person who is in fact to succeed is decided by agreement or, in default of agreement, by decision of the county court.

Where the original tenant was a protected (but not a statutory) tenant the position at the end of the statutory tenancy by succession can be somewhat confused. This is because on the death of the protected tenant the contractual tenancy devolves according to the ordinary law on his successor in title, who may be a different person to the person who is to become the statutory tenant by succession. In *Moodie v Hosegood* [1952] AC 61 it was held that during the currency of the statutory tenancy by succession the contractual tenancy goes into abeyance and does not arise again until the statutory tenancy by succession has come to an end. It may be that by that time the holder of the contractual tenancy, which may have passed through several hands, is almost impossible to trace. Yet if the landlord is to regain possession he must have an immediate right to possession which he will not have until the contractual tenancy has been determined (see *Wirral Borough Council v Smith* (1982) 43 P&CR 312). If the contractual tenancy was for a fixed term it will probably have come to an end by the time the statutory tenancy by succession has ended, but if it was a periodic tenancy it will be necessary to serve a notice to quit upon the current contractual tenant. To find out who is the contractual tenant the landlord should make a search at the probate registry for the names of the personal representatives of the estate of the original tenant. It should then be possible to trace the contractual tenancy to its present holder. It will usually be held by the personal representatives because they are unlikely to have vested the interest in the beneficiaries. If they have also died it will be necessary to repeat the process. For the argument that after a number of years the contractual tenancy 'dies a natural death' thus relieving the confusion see RE Megarry, *The Rent Acts*, 11th ed (Sweet & Maxwell 1988), vol 1, 284. It should also be noted that if a notice of increase in rent was ever served on the original tenant during the contractual period under s49(4) of the Rent Act 1977, that notice would have terminated the contractual tenancy and brought about a statutory tenancy. Thus, when the tenant died there would have been no contractual tenancy left to go into abeyance. Also note s196(3) of the Law of Property Act 1925 when the contractual tenancy agreement was in writing (see p67). See also *Egerton v Rutter* [1951] 1 TLR 58 where a notice to quit addressed to 'the executors of the late . . . ' and served upon the person in possession was held sufficient to determine the tenancy. It was not necessary to find the personal representatives. But *quaere* whether this case can apply to the circumstances discussed here, ie where the person last in possession was not the original deceased tenant but the statutory tenant.

Death of original tenant: member of tenant's family to succeed (Sched 1, para 3)   Where there is no surviving spouse entitled to succeed but a member of the original tenant's family was residing with him *in the dwelling house* at the time of and for the period of two years immediately before his death then, after his death, that person is entitled to an *assured tenancy* of the dwelling house by succession, ie an assured tenancy under the Housing Act 1988 (see *below* and Chapter 6). A person may be 'residing with' the tenant even though the tenant is temporarily absent from the premises (*Hedgedale Ltd v Hards* [1991] 1 EGLR 118, CA: tenant living elsewhere while recovering from the effects of an accident).

(If the original tenant died within the period of 18 months beginning on 15 January 1989 then a person who was residing in the dwelling house with the original tenant at the time of his death and for the period which began six months before 15 January 1989 is taken to have been residing with the original tenant for the period of two years immediately before his death.)

If there is more than one family member entitled to succeed the persons entitled may agree amongst themselves as to who is to succeed. If they cannot agree the county court may decide between them. The court must look at all the factors including the wishes of the deceased but these are not conclusive (*Williams v Williams* [1970] 1 WLR 1530). The landlord has no say in determining who should be chosen (*General Management v Locke* (1980) 255 EG 155).

As to meaning of 'family' see *below*.

Death of statutory tenant by succession: member of original tenant's family and successor's family entitled to succeed (Sched 1, paras 4, 5 and 6)   Where the tenant who has died ('the first successor') was a statutory tenant by succession who succeeded as a spouse of the original tenant pursuant to para 2 of Sched 1 and there is a person who was:

(*a*) a member of the *original tenant's* family immediately before the tenant's death; *and*

(*b*) was a member of the first successor's family immediately before the first successor's death; *and*

(*c*) was residing in the dwelling house with the first successor at the time of and for the period of two years immediately before the first successor's death,

then that person (or, if there is more than one person, such one of them as may be decided by agreement or, in default of agreement, by the county court) is entitled to an *assured tenancy* of the dwelling house by succession (see *below*).

(If the first successor died within the period of 18 months beginning on 15 January 1989 then a person who was residing in the dwelling house with the first successor at the time of his death and for the period which began six months before 15 January 1989 and ended at the time of his death is taken to have been residing with the first successor for the period of two years immediately before his death.)

A situation can occur whereby a person ('the new tenant') remains in occupation after the death of the original tenant in circumstances which give rise to a new tenancy as between the landlord and the new tenant (by estoppel; see p7) so that on the death of the new tenant the person then in occupation will be treated as the first successor to the *new tenant's* tenancy, even though the original tenant's tenancy was never determined (*Epping Forest District Council v Pomphrett* [1990] 2 EGLR 46, CA).

'Family'   The word 'family' is not used in any technical sense. It is the popular meaning of the word that applies (*Langdon v Horton* [1951] 1 KB 667 at 666). Brothers, sisters, mothers, fathers, children (adopted, illegitimate or stepchildren), grandchildren, brothers and sisters-in-law, aunts and uncles, nephews and nieces have all been held to be members of the same family. However, the cases should not be seen as binding authorities: the more distant relatives such as grandchildren, nephews and nieces and certainly cousins may not always be held to be members of the same family (see eg *Jones v Whitehill* [1950] 2 KB 204 and *Langdon v Horton*).

It is necessary to draw a distinction between being a member of a family and living as a member of a family (*Sefton Holdings Ltd v Cairns*

(1988) 20 HLR 124). Thus, a young man and an elderly lady who assumed a nephew and aunt relationship were held not to be members of the same family (*Carega Properties SA (formerly Joram Developments Ltd) v Fox* [1979] 1 WLR 13) and in *Sefton Holdings Ltd v Cairns* a girl taken in and treated as a daughter was held not to be a member of the family. *Quaere* whether the courts are prepared to regard partners in a permanent homosexual relationship as members of each other's family (cf *Harrogate Borough Council v Simpson* (1984) 17 HLR 205—a case concerning secure tenancies: see p177). Presumably not in the light of the distinction drawn in *Sefton Holdings Ltd v Cairns*.

The 'assured tenancy by succession' (s39(5), (6), (7), (9)) Where a person becomes entitled to an assured tenancy by succession 'that tenancy shall be a periodic tenancy arising by virtue of' s39(5) of the 1988 Act. It takes effect in possession immediately after the death of the tenant. The periods of the tenancy are the same as those for which rent was last payable by the predecessor. (See further s39(6).) If before the death of the predecessor the tenancy was one to which the landlord would be entitled to possession pursuant to Case 19 of Sched 15 to the Rent Act 1977 (shortholds) the tenancy is an assured shorthold tenancy (s39(7)). See s39(9) in relation to variation of terms under s6 of the 1988 Act. The terms of the assured tenancy by succession may be varied pursuant to s13 of the 1988 Act (see s39(6)(*e*), (*f*)).

In addition to the usual assured tenancy grounds (see p113) the landlord under an assured tenancy by succession may seek to recover possession pursuant to Cases 11, 12, 16, 17, 18 and 20 of Sched 15 to the Rent Act 1977 (Housing Act 1988, s39(10), Sched 4, Part III, para 13—and see para 15 in relation to notices). Note that Ground 6 of Sched 2 (demolition or construction of the dwelling house) does not apply where the tenancy is an assured tenancy by succession (see para (*c*) of that ground).

Quaere whether the *Moodie v Hosegood* problem (see p152) arises where the tenancy succeeded to is an assured tenancy (cf s17(1) of the Housing Act 1988).

Chapter 9

Restricted Contracts

A tenancy or other contract entered into after the commencement of the Housing Act 1988 (15 January 1989) cannot be a restricted contract for the purposes of the Rent Act 1977 unless it was entered into in pursuance of a contract made before the commencement of the Act (s36(1) of the 1988 Act). The rest of this chapter must be read with that fact in mind. (See s36(2) and (3) of the 1988 Act where the terms of a restricted contract are varied for the purpose of deciding whether there has been a new letting granted after the commencement of the 1988 Act.)

Where an occupier of a house or part of a house is neither a protected nor a statutory tenant he may nevertheless have some protection, albeit very limited, where the rent 'includes payment for the use of furniture or for services' (s19 of the Rent Act 1977). In these circumstances the agreement under which he occupies the premises is termed a restricted contract. (See also Chapter 11, 'Resident landlords'.) If the tenant is a protected or statutory tenant the fact that his rent includes payment for the use of furniture or services does not convert his tenancy from a protected tenancy into a restricted contract (s19(5)(a) of the Rent Act 1977 and *Baldock v Murray* (1980) 257 EG 281). Thus such a payment does not lessen a fully protected tenant's protection. Rather, it gives some protection to a lessee or a licensee who may otherwise not have any. The contract will not be a restricted contract unless the tenant has 'exclusive occupation' of some part of the premises. The term 'exclusive occupation' does not have the same meaning as 'exclusive possession'. Thus, the fact that the landlord is entitled to enter the room for the purpose of providing services etc does not of itself mean that the occupant does not have exclusive occupation. (See *Luganda v Service Hotels Ltd* [1969] 2 Ch 209.) But, subject to a limited exception referred to in s19(6) of the Rent Act 1977, the fact that he has to share any other part of the premises does not of itself prevent the contract from being a restricted contract (s19(6)). A contract is not prevented from being a restricted contract by reason of the fact that it was created in breach of a covenant not to sublet (*R v Islington Rent Tribunal, ex p Haines* (1962) 181 EG 339).

The protection that is afforded is set out in s 106A of the Rent Act 1977 which was introduced by s 69(2) of the Housing Act 1980 and amounts to a power in the court to defer the date upon which possession must be given up for up to three months. (Note, however, that s 106A of the Rent Act 1977 only applies to tenancies and licences created after 28 November 1980. Residential occupiers who entered into restricted contracts before that date may apply to a rent tribunal for a deferment of the requirement to leave: see ss 102A–106 of the Rent Act 1977.)

Definition of restricted contracts

Section 19(2) of the Rent Act 1977 provides as follows:

> . . . this section applies to a contract, whether entered into before or after the commencement of this Act [but note the introduction to this chapter in relation to tenancies entered into after 15 January 1989], whereby one person grants to another person, in consideration of a rent which includes payment for the use of *furniture* or for *services*, the right to occupy a dwelling as a residence.

A tenant or a licensee may be an occupier of a dwelling house under a restricted contract, but the terms 'landlord' and 'tenant' are used throughout this chapter for the sake of convenience (see *Luganda v Service Hotels Ltd* [1969] 2 Ch 209). The term 'dwelling' means a house or part of a house (s 19(8)). The meaning of the term 'house' is discussed at p 131. (Where the tenant occupies part as a residence and the rest for business purposes the contract can still be restricted: *R v York, Harrogate, Ripon and Northallerton Areas Rent Tribunal, ex p Ingle* [1954] 1 QB 456.)

A tenant who seeks to rely on the provision of furniture in order to establish that the contract is a restricted contract must show that under the agreement the landlord has provided furniture in addition to the fixtures and fittings that would normally be present in a house. There must therefore be more than such items as a bath, cooker or fitted wardrobes. (For a full discussion of the type of furniture that will turn an agreement into a restricted contract see *Property Holding Co Ltd v Mischeff* [1948] AC 291.)

If the tenant is relying upon the provision of services the definition of 'services' set out in s 19(8) of the Rent Act 1977 applies:

> 'services' includes attendance, the provision of heating or lighting, the supply of hot water and any other privilege or facility connected with the occupancy of a dwelling, other than a privilege or facility requisite for the purposes of access, cold water supply or sanitary accommodation.

The landlord must be obliged by the *agreement* to provide the furniture or services before they can be taken into account (*R v Hampstead and St Pancras Rent Tribunal, ex p Ascot Lodge* [1947] KB 973). But, so long as more than a minimal amount of furniture or services is provided under the agreement the contract will be a restricted contract (*R v Blackpool Rent Tribunal, ex p Ashton* [1948] 2 KB 277).

Exceptions

There are exceptions where the tenant will not even have the limited protection afforded by s106A of the Rent Act 1977 (or ss103–6 in case of agreements entered into before 28 November 1980), even though the agreement falls within the definition set out in s19. The exceptions are as follows.

High rateable values (s19(3) and (4) of the Rent Act 1977)

As with the protected tenancy it is first necessary to ascertain the rateable value of the premises on the appropriate day. The method for doing this is set out in Appendix 1. The contract will not be a restricted contract if the appropriate day in relation to the dwelling falls or fell *on or after 1 April 1973* and the dwelling on the appropriate day has or had a rateable value exceeding £1,500 if the dwelling is in Greater London, or £750 if elsewhere. If the appropriate day in relation to the dwelling fell *before 1 April 1973* the contract will not be a restricted contract if on the appropriate day the dwelling had a rateable value exceeding £400 in Greater London (£200 elsewhere) *and* on 1 April 1973 the dwelling had a rateable value exceeding £1,500 in Greater London (£750 elsewhere).

Regulated tenancies (s19(5)(*a*) of the Rent Act 1977)

A contract is not a restricted contract if it creates a protected or statutory tenancy; see introduction *above*.

Local authorities and housing associations etc (s19(5)(*aa*), (*e*) of the Rent Act 1977)

A contract is not a restricted contract if under the contract the interest of the lessor belongs to a body mentioned in s14 of the Rent Act 1977 or the tenancy is a 'housing association' tenancy as defined in s86 of the 1977 Act. These agreements are dealt with in Chapter 10. If, however, the tenant of one of these bodies sublets, the agreement between the tenant and the sub-tenant is not precluded from being a restricted contract by this exception. (See further p175.)

The Crown (s19(5)(*b*) of the Rent Act 1977)

A contract is not a restricted contract if the landlord is the Crown or a government department, or is held by the Crown for the purposes of a government department, except that it may be so if the property is under the management of the Crown Estate Commissioners. The position of the sub-tenants is the same as where the landlord is the local authority (see *above*).

Board (s 19(5)(c) of the Rent Act 1977)

If the rent includes payment in respect of board and the value of the board to the tenant forms a substantial proportion of the whole rent the contract is not a restricted contract (see Chapter 16).

Agricultural premises (s 19(5)(d) of the Rent Act 1977)

A contract is not a restricted contract if it is a protected occupancy as defined in the Rent (Agriculture) Act 1976 (see Chapter 15).

Holiday lets (s 19(7) of the Rent Act 1977)

No contract under which a person is entitled to occupy a dwelling for the purpose of a holiday can be a restricted contract (see Chapter 16). But although a temporary occupation in a hotel cannot be occupation 'as a residence', a permanent stay where the tenant actually lives in the hotel can be (*Luganda v Service Hotels Ltd* [1969] 2 Ch 209).

Overcrowded dwelling houses (s 101 of the Rent Act 1977)

Section 106A cannot operate to prevent the landlord from obtaining possession of the dwelling house at any time when it is overcrowded (see further Chapter 18).

Termination and recovery of possession

If the restricted contract is a tenancy it is brought to an end in the normal way, ie by notice to quit, effluxion of time, forfeiture or surrender (see Chapters 2 and 3). If it is a licence it will be brought to an end according to the terms of the agreement, subject to the provisions of s5 of the Protection from Eviction Act 1977 if applicable (see p95). Once validly determined, proceedings for possession may be commenced. If it is a forfeiture case the lease is forfeited by service of the proceedings. The court must make an order for possession but if the contract was entered into after 28 November 1980 the court may on the making of the order, or at any time before its execution, stay or suspend execution of the order, or postpone the date of possession, but the giving up of possession cannot be postponed for longer than three months (s 106A(1), (2) and (3) of the Rent Act 1977). Where the court does stay, suspend or postpone the operation of the order the court must, unless it considers that to do so would cause exceptional hardship to the tenant or would otherwise be unreasonable, impose conditions with regard to payment by the tenant of arrears of rent (if any) and rent or payments in respect of occupation after termination of the tenancy and may impose such other conditions as it thinks fit (s 106(4)). The tenant's spouse or former spouse who remains in occupation has the same rights to postponement of the order under s 106A of the Rent Act 1977 as the tenant himself (s 106A(5), (6)).

If the contract was entered into before 28 November 1980 the tenant's security of tenure is governed by ss 103–106 of the Rent Act 1977, ie the tenant may apply to the rent tribunal to extend a notice to quit (see s 102A). If the notice to quit has expired no such application may be made (*R v City of London Rent Tribunal, ex p Honig* [1951] 1 KB 641) and the court will only be able to delay possession for up to 14 days, or six weeks in cases of exceptional hardship (s 89 of the Housing Act 1980; see p 75).

Chapter 10

Local Authority Housing and Housing Associations etc

Tenants of dwelling houses owned by local authorities and a number of other public bodies are excluded from protection under the Rent Act 1977 by ss 14, 15 and 16 thereof. Public sector tenants do, however, have a code of protection of their own if they fall within the definition of 'secure tenants'. The code was introduced by the Housing Act 1980 and is now set out in ss 79 to 117 of the Housing Act 1985 ('the 1985 Act'). It came into force on 3 October 1980 and applies to tenancies granted before as well as after that date (s 47 of the Housing Act 1980).

Tenancies granted by housing associations, the Housing Corporation and charitable housing trusts prior to the commencement of the Housing Act 1988 are also governed by this code. However, the position has changed in relation to most tenancies granted on or after that date. Such tenancies will no longer be secure but will usually be assured. See note (3) on p 163.

The 1985 Act specifically treats most licensees of these bodies as tenants (s 79(3), (4)) although whether it needs to do so in the light of the decision in *Street v Mountford* [1985] 2 WLR 877 (see Chapter 5) is doubtful (see further: 'Tenant Condition', *below*). Unless the context otherwise requires, the person in occupation of the dwelling house is referred to as the tenant throughout this chapter whether he is a licensee or a tenant strictly so called.

Quite apart from any rights he may have under the Housing Act 1985 a tenant of a public authority may defend a claim for possession by claiming that his *private law* rights have been infringed by a decision of that body (see *Wandsworth London Borough Council v Winder* [1984] 3 All ER 976; *Wandsworth LBC v Winder (No 2)* (1987) 19 HLR 204 (council tenant defended the possession action by challenging the validity of the local authority's rent increases)).

However, a failure by a housing authority to offer a homeless person suitable permanent accommodation in accordance with Part III of the Housing Act 1985 is an infringement of a *public* law right and is no defence to a claim for possession brought against that person in respect of the temporary accommodation in which he has been living pending the authority's determination of his application. His only remedy is by way of judicial review and any defence raising the issue in the possession action is an abuse of process which will be struck out (*Tower Hamlets LBC v Abdi* [1993] 1 EGLR 69, CA). The homeless person cannot circumvent the decision in *Abdi* by arguing that the notice to quit served in respect of the temporary accommodation is unlawful and void because the authority has failed to offer suitable alternative accommodation (*Hackney LBC v Lambourne* [1992] EGCS 151, CA). (Once the authority has performed its duty by allocating accommodation the homeless person does have a private right to that particular accommodation which may be enforced by specific performance: *Abdi* at 70M.)

Definition of secure tenancies

A secure tenancy is defined by s79(1) of the 1985 Act in the following terms:

> A tenancy under which a dwelling house is let as a separate dwelling is a secure tenancy at any time when the conditions described in sections 80 and 81 as the landlord condition and the tenant condition are satisfied.

Section 79(1) is subject to the exceptions set out in Sched 1 to the 1985 Act (see below: s79(2)(*a*)).

A dwelling house is defined in the 1985 Act as a house or part of a house, and land let together with a dwelling house is treated as part of the dwelling house unless the land is agricultural land exceeding two acres (s112). See also Chapter 8, p131. The effect of the word 'separate' is dealt with in Chapter 11.

The landlord condition (s80)

As stated in the introduction to this chapter the position was changed by the Housing Act 1988 and is now somewhat complicated:
(1) The landlord condition is satisfied when the interest of the landlord belongs to one of the following bodies:
    (*a*) a local authority;
    (*b*) a new town corporation;
    (*c*) an urban development corporation;
    (*d*) a housing action trust (s83 of the 1988 Act);
    (*e*) the Development Board for Rural Wales;
    (*f*) a housing co-operative within the meaning of s27B of the Housing Act 1985 (agreements between local housing authorities and housing co-operatives for the exercise of the authorities' housing management functions) and the tenancy or licence is of a dwelling house comprised in a housing co-operative.
(See s80 of the 1985 Act and s35(4)(*a*) and (*b*) of the 1988 Act.)

Where the interest of the landlord belongs to two bodies the landlord condition will not be satisfied unless they are both one of the above bodies (*R v Plymouth City Council etc, ex p Freeman* (1987) 19 HLR 328).

   (2) The landlord condition is also satisfied where the tenancy was entered into *before 15 January 1989* and the interest of the landlord belongs to:

   (*a*) the Housing Corporation;

   (*b*) a housing trust which is a charity;

   (*c*) a housing association to which s80 applies (see s80(2));

and did so immediately prior to that date (Sched 18, para 4 to the 1988 Act).

Section 80 applies to:

   (*a*) a registered housing association (ie registered with the Housing Corporation under the Housing Associations Act 1985: s5(4)) *other than* a co-operative housing association (ie a 'fully mutual' housing association which is a society registered under the Industrial and Provident Societies Act 1965: see s5(2)); and to

   (*b*) an unregistered housing association which is a co-operative housing association.

Where the interest of the landlord belongs to a body which is registered with the Housing Corporation *and* with the Registrar of Friendly Societies under the 1965 Act, or with neither, the landlord condition is not satisfied and the tenants will not be secure (although they may be regulated tenants or occupiers under restricted contracts—see Chapters 8 and 9). See s80(3) in relation to co-operative housing associations which cease to be registered under the Housing Associations Act 1985.

(See *ex p Freeman* (1987) *above*, where the interest of the landlord belongs to more than one body.)

   (3) Tenancies and licences granted by the Housing Corporation, housing associations and charitable housing trusts *on or after 15 January 1989* will not be secure (unless one of the exceptions contained in s35(4)(*c*)–(*f*) and s35(5) applies). If the necessary conditions are satisfied tenancies (but not licences) granted by such bodies (except fully mutual housing associations other than where the tenancy was assured under the Housing Act 1980: Sched 1, para 12(1) (*h*) and s1(5) of the Housing Act 1988) will be assured.

   (4) See also s38 of the Housing Act 1988 in relation to secure tenancies *granted* before 15 January 1989 (or pursuant to contracts entered into before that date) *where after that date* the landlord condition ceases to apply, perhaps because the property is sold to a private sector landlord pursuant to Part IV of the Housing Act 1988. In most cases the tenancy will become assured and cannot become secure again unless the landlord is one of the public

bodies listed in s38(5). Tenancies transferred to the private sector that were granted on or after 15 January 1989 become assured tenancies pursuant to the provisions of s1 of the 1988 Act, unless one of the exceptions in Sched 1 to that Act applies (see Chapter 6). Note s100 of the 1988 Act in relation to tenants who wish to retain their public sector landlord.

The tenant condition (s81)

The tenant condition is that the tenant is an individual and occupies the dwelling house as his only or principal home; or, where the tenancy is a joint tenancy, that each of the joint tenants is an individual and at least one of them occupies the dwelling house as his only or principal home (s81).

If the tenant ceases to occupy the dwelling house as his principal home the tenancy will cease to be secure. It will become an ordinary contractual tenancy, determinable by notice to quit etc (see Chapters 2 and 3). Whether the dwelling house is the tenant's 'principal home' is a question of fact for the judge to decide. The Court of Appeal is unlikely to interfere with the judge's decision (see *Crawley BC v Sawyer* (1988) 20 HLR 98: tenant went to live with his girlfriend for 14 months. Judge accepted tenant's evidence that he had not abandoned his dwelling house and that it was still his principal home).

As stated in the introduction to this chapter, the 1985 Act applies to licences (s79(3)). However, 'a licence can only create a secure tenancy if it confers exclusive possession of a dwelling house' (*Westminster City Council v Clarke* [1992] 1 All ER 695, HL *per* Lord Templeman). In that case a local authority provided homeless persons with temporary accommodation while dealing with their applications for permanent accommodation under the Housing Act 1985. The agreements under which those persons occupied, which negatived exclusive possession, were held to be genuine licences. As the occupiers did not have exclusive possession, s79(3) did not apply and their licences could not be regarded as secure tenancies.

Notwithstanding s79(3), a licensee is not treated as a secure tenant where the licence was granted as a temporary expedient to a person who entered the dwelling house or any other land as a trespasser (whether or not before the grant of another licence to occupy that or another dwelling house had been granted to him) (s79(4)). But practitioners acting for the occupiers should ensure that what was granted was not a true tenancy before they advise their clients that s79(4) prevents them from being secure tenants.

The exceptions (s79(2)(a) and Sched 1)

The exceptions are to be found in Sched 1 to the 1985 Act, the full text of which is to be found in Appendix 2. They are as follows:

(1) long leases, ie of more than 21 years (see also Chapter 13);
(2) premises occupied now or in the past three years in connection with employment by employees of certain public bodies, policemen and firemen (see Chapter 14);
(3) land acquired for development: the landlord does not have to be the person who has acquired the land for development; it only needs to be the person who is using the land pending the development as temporary housing accommodation (*Hyde Housing Association Ltd v Harrison* [1991] 1 EGLR 51, CA: land acquired for development by the Department of Transport but used pending the development by the landlord);
(4) homeless persons' accommodation occupied for less than 12 months (see *Family Housing Association v Jones* [1990] 1 All ER 385 at 393);
(5) temporary accommodation for persons taking up employment;
(6) property leased (or licensed: *Tower Hamlets LBC v Miah* [1992] 2 All ER 667, CA) to the landlord for use as temporary housing accommodation;
(7) temporary accommodation during works;
(8) agricultural holdings;
(9) licensed premises (on-licences);
(10) student lettings (see also Chapter 16);
(11) business tenancies to which Part II of the 1954 Act applies (see Chapter 14);
(12) almshouses.

Where one of the exceptions applies the tenancy is an ordinary contractual tenancy to which the common law rules relating to termination apply. For example, see *Hackney LBC v Lambourne* [1993] EGCS 151 where the local authority relying upon exception (6) (short-term arrangements) determined the tenancy by a notice to quit.

Termination and recovery of possession

The termination procedure in respect of secure tenancies is governed by ss 82 and 85 of and Sched 2 to the Housing Act 1985. Except in cases where the landlord is seeking to rely upon a forfeiture clause in a lease for a fixed term termination and recovery of possession are dealt with together. The order for possession operates to terminate the tenancy from the date upon which the order for possession takes effect (s 82(2) of the Housing Act 1985).

A fixed term comes to an end at the end of the term without the necessity of a court order but thereafter a periodic tenancy automatically arises under s 86 of the 1985 Act which will have to be terminated in court proceedings if the landlord is to recover possession. (An automatic periodic tenancy does not in fact arise under s 86 if the tenant is granted a new secure tenancy, whether for a fixed or periodic term, to begin at the end of the first tenancy.) The periods of the tenancy that arise pursuant to s86 are the same as those for which rent was last payable under the first tenancy. The terms are the same save insofar as they are incompatible with a periodic tenancy, and they do not include a forfeiture clause (s86(1), (2)).

The above provisions only relate to termination by the landlord. The tenant may terminate by giving a notice to quit of appropriate length (see *London Borough of Greenwich v McGrady* (1982) 6 HLR 36) or by surrender (*R v London Borough of Croydon, ex p Toth* (1988) 20 HLR 576).

Termination notices (s83)

Section 83 of the 1985 Act provides that the court may not entertain proceedings for termination of a secure tenancy or possession of a dwelling house let on a secure tenancy unless the landlord serves on the tenant a notice in a form prescribed by regulations. The regulations in force at the present time are the Secure Tenancies (Notices) Regulations 1987 (SI 1987 No 755). They contain two forms (Forms 23 and 24 of this book) and state that the notice must be in the form of one of those notices 'or in a form substantially to the same effect' (reg 2).

In *Dudley Metropolitan BC v Bailey* [1991] 1 EGLR 53, CA, it was held that a notice which contained the words 'The reasons for taking this action are' instead of 'Particulars of each ground are as follows' was in a form substantially to the same effect. (An argument to the effect that the regulations, in permitting 'a form substantially to the same effect' was *ultra vires* s83, was rejected.)

The notice must specify the ground upon which the court will be asked to make the order and must give particulars of that ground (s83(2)(c); compare the position in respect of assured tenancies, p110). The particulars must be sufficiently informative to tell the tenant what he has to do to put matters right before proceedings are commenced (*Torridge DC v Jones* [1985] 2 EGLR 54, CA). In that case the landlord served a notice which gave the following particulars: 'The reasons for taking this action are non-payment of rent' but failed to give any particulars of the rent alleged. It was held that the notice did not comply with the statutory requirement to give particulars and the landlord's claim was struck out. Compare *Dudley Metropolitan BC v Bailey* where the figure stated as arrears of rent in fact included amounts for rates and water rates. It was held that the notice was not invalidated by this error although it might affect the action which the judge should take on the merits of the case:

> The question is whether, at the date of the notice, the landlord has in good faith stated the ground and given particulars of that ground. The requirement of particulars is satisfied, in my judgment, if the landlord has stated in summary form the facts which he then intends to prove in support of the stated ground for possession. Error in the particulars does not, in my

judgment, invalidate the notice although it may well affect the decision of the court on the merits (*per* Ralph Gibson LJ at 55J).

Note also the ability, with the leave of the court given under s84(3), to alter or add to the grounds specified in the notice (see further p169).

There are two types of notice: one appropriate to periodic tenancies and the other appropriate to cases where the landlord is seeking to rely upon a forfeiture clause in a fixed term.

Periodic tenancies (see Form 23) Where the tenancy is a periodic tenancy the notice must specify a date after which proceedings for possession of the dwelling house may be begun. The date specified must not be earlier than the date on which the tenancy could have been brought to an end by a notice to quit given on the same day as the notice which is to be given under s83 of the 1985 Act (s83(3)). Therefore, if the tenancy is a weekly tenancy 28 days' notice is required and if it is a monthly tenancy one calendar month's notice is required (see further p63).

The termination notice served in respect of a fixed term also operates in respect of the subsequent periodic tenancy that arises by virtue of s82(3) and s86 and no further notice is required (s83(5)). Where a notice has not been served during the currency of the fixed term it will be necessary to serve a notice appropriate to periodic tenancies.

(The periodic term that follows a fixed term by virtue of s82(3) is secure: it would not be necessary to excuse service of a notice under s83(3) if the periodic tenancy was not secure as one would not be needed in any event. Section 83(5) also clearly implies that a s86 periodic tenancy is secure. See also *Hill and Redman's Law of Landlord and Tenant*, note to s82(3) on 2080.)

Fixed terms forfeiture cases (see Form 24) Where the landlord is seeking to rely upon a forfeiture clause in a fixed term the position is slightly different from the usual case. The court may not make an order for possession in pursuance of that clause, but it may make an order terminating the fixed term on a date specified in the order (s82(3) of the Housing Act 1985). Thus, the tenant may find himself without the benefit of a fixed term but still in possession under a s86 periodic tenancy. The court may, however, go on to make an order for possession if one of the grounds for possession (see *below*) applies.

Although the court may not make an order for possession in pursuance of the forfeiture clause, s146 of the Law of Property Act 1925 and any other enactments or rules of law that apply to forfeiture cases apply to the proceedings to terminate the tenancy as if they were proceedings to forfeit a lease (s82(4) of the Housing Act 1985). Thus, the provisions as to s146 notices and to relief against forfeiture apply. However, s146(4) which gives underlessees the right to claim relief does not apply.

Form 23: Section 83 notice—possession

This Notice is the first step towards requiring you to give up possession of your dwelling. You should read it very carefully.

HOUSING ACT 1985

Section 83

Notice of Seeking Possession

(1) Name(s) of
Secure Tenant(s)

1. To (¹)

If you need advice about this Notice, and what you should do about it, take it as quickly as possible to a Citizens' Advice Bureau, a Housing Aid Centre, or a Law Centre, or to a solicitor. You may be able to receive Legal Aid but this will depend on your personal circumstances.

(2) Insert name

2. The Landlord (²)   intends to apply to the Court for an Order requiring you to give up possession of:

(3) Address of
property

(³)

If you are a secure tenant under the Housing Act 1985, you can only be required to leave your dwelling if your landlord obtains an order for possession from the Court. The order must be based on one of the Grounds which are set out in the 1985 Act (see paragraphs 3 and 4 below).

If you are willing to give up possession without a Court order, you should notify the person who signed this Notice as soon as possible and say when you would leave.

(4) Give the text
in full of each
Ground which is
being relied on

3. Possession will be sought on Ground(s)
of Schedule 2 to the Housing Act 1985 which read(s) (⁴):

Whatever Grounds for possession are set out in paragraph 3 of this Notice, the Court may allow any of the other Grounds to be added at a later stage. If this is done, you will be told about it so you can argue at the hearing in Court about the new Ground, as well as the Grounds set out in paragraph 3, if you want to.

(5) Give a full
explanation of why
each Ground is
being relied upon.
**Before completing
the answer to this
question please
read the notes
overleaf.**

4. Particulars of each ground are as follows (^{5}):

Before the Court will grant an order on any of the Grounds 1 to 8 or 12 to 16, it must be satisfied that it is reasonable to require you to leave. This means that, if one of these Grounds is set out in paragraph 3 of this Notice, you will be able to argue at the hearing in Court that it is not reasonable that you should have to leave, even if you accept that the Ground applies.

Before the Court grants an order on any of the Grounds 9 to 16, it must be satisfied that there will be suitable alternative accommodation for you when you have to leave. This means that the Court will have to decide that, in its opinion, there will be other accommodation which is reasonably suitable for the needs of you and your family taking into particular account various factors such as the nearness of your place of work, and the sort of housing that other people with similar needs are offered. Your

contd

contd	new home will have to be let to you on another secure tenancy or a private tenancy under the Rent Act of a kind that will give you similar security. **There is no requirement for suitable alternative accommodation where Grounds 1 to 8 apply.**
	If your landlord is not a local authority, and the local authority gives a certificate that it will provide you with suitable accommodation, the Court has to accept the certificate.
	One of the requirements of Ground 10A is that the landlord must have approval for the redevelopment scheme from the Secretary of State (or, in the case of a housing association landlord, the Housing Corporation). The landlord must have consulted all
(6) Give the date after which Court proceedings can be brought.	secure tenants affected by the proposed redevelopment scheme.
	5. The Court proceedings will not be begun until after(6)
	Court proceedings cannot be begun until after this date, which cannot be earlier than the date when your tenancy or licence could have been brought to an end. This means that if you have a weekly or fortnightly tenancy, there should be at least 4 weeks between the date this Notice is given and the date in this paragraph.
	After this date, court proceedings may be begun at once or at any time during the following twelve months. Once the twelve months are up this Notice will lapse and a new Notice must be served before possession can be sought.

Signed

On behalf of

Address

Tel No.

Date

Commencing proceedings

Where the tenancy is a periodic tenancy, the landlord must commence proceedings after the date specified in the notice, but before 12 months from the date specified have elapsed. If he does not do so, the court may not entertain proceedings for possession and the landlord will have to serve a fresh notice (s83(4) of the Housing Act 1985). Where the tenancy is a fixed term tenancy the proceedings may not be commenced until after the expiration of the term unless the landlord is seeking to rely upon a forfeiture clause and is bringing proceedings under s82(3).

The grounds for possession

The court is not allowed to make an order for possession of a dwelling house let under a secure tenancy except on one or more of the 17 grounds for possession set out in Sched 2 to the 1985 Act. (See Appendix 2 for the full text of the Schedule.) The ground relied upon must be specified in the termination notice. If it is not, the court may not make an order for possession on that ground (see also reference to s83 on p166).

Housing Act 1985, s84(3)
   (3) The court shall not make such an order on any of those grounds unless the ground is specified in the notice in pursuance of which proceedings for

Form 24: Section 83 notice—termination of tenancy and recovery of possession

Secure Tenancies (Notices) Regulations 1987.
Schedule, Part II as amended.

**This Notice may lead to your being required to leave your dwelling.
You should read it very carefully.**

HOUSING ACT 1985
Section 83

Notice of Seeking Termination of Tenancy and Recovery of Possession

(1) Name(s) of
Secure Tenant(s)

1. To (^{1})

If you need advice about this Notice, and what you should do about it, take it as quickly as possible to a Citizens' Advice Bureau, a Housing Aid Centre, or a Law Centre, or to a Solicitor. You may be able to receive Legal Aid but this will depend on your personal circumstances.

(2) Insert name

2. The Landlord (^{2})   intends
to apply to the Court for an Order terminating your tenancy and requiring you to give up possession of:

(3) Address of
property

(^{3})

This Notice applies to you if you are a secure tenant under the Housing Act 1985 and if your tenancy is for a fixed term, containing a provision which allows your landlord to bring to and before the fixed term expires. This may be because you have got into arrears with your rent or have broken some other condition of the tenancy. This is known as a provision for re-entry or forfeiture. The Act does not remove the need for your landlord to bring an action under such a provision, nor does it affect your right to seek relief against re-entry or forfeiture, in other words to ask the Court not to bring the tenancy to an end. The Act gives additional rights to tenants, as described below.

If you are a secure tenant and have a fixed term tenancy, it can only be terminated and you can only be evicted if your landlord obtains an order for possession from the Court. The order must be based on one of the Grounds which are set out in the 1985 Act (see paragraphs 3 and 4 below).

If you are willing to give up possession without a Court order, you should notify the person who signed this Notice as soon as possible and say when you would leave.

(4) Give the Text
in full of each
Ground which is
being relied on.

3.   Termination of your tenancy and possession will be sought on Ground(s) of Schedule 2 to the Housing Act 1985 which read(s) (^{4}):

Whatever Grounds for possession are set out in paragraph 3 of this Notice, the Court may allow any of the other Grounds to be added at a later stage. If this is done, you will be told about it so you can argue at the hearing in Court about the new Ground, as well as the Grounds set out in paragraph 3, if you want to.

(5) Give a full
explanation of why
each Ground is
being relied upon.

4.   Particulars of each Ground are as follows (^{5}):

contd

contd

Before the Court will grant an order on any of the Grounds 1 to 8 or 12 to 16, it must be satisfied that it is reasonable to require you to leave. This means that, if one of these Grounds is set out in paragraph 3 of this Notice, you will be able to argue at the hearing in Court that it is not reasonable that you should have to leave, even if you accept that the Ground applies.

Before the Court grants an order on any of the Grounds 9 to 16, it must be satisfied that there will be suitable alternative accommodation for you when you have to leave. This means that the Court will have to decide that, in its opinion, there will be other accommodation which is reasonably suitable for the needs of you and your family, taking into particular account various factors such as the nearness of your place of work, and the sort of housing that other people with similar needs are offered. Your new home will have to be let to you on another secure tenancy or a private tenancy under the Rent Act of a kind that will give you similar security. **There is no requirement for suitable alternative accommodation where Grounds 1 to 8 apply.**

If your landlord is not a local authority, and the local authority gives a certificate that it will provide you with suitable accommodation, the Court has to accept the certificate.

One of the requirements of Ground 10A is that the landlord must have approval for the redevelopment scheme from the Secretary of State (or, in the case of a housing association landlord, the Housing Corporation). The landlord must have consulted all secure tenants affected by the proposed redevelopment scheme.

Signed

On behalf of

Address

Tel No.

Date

Reproduced by kind permission of The Solicitors' Law Stationery Society Ltd

possession are begun; but the grounds so specified may be altered or added to with the leave of the court.

Although the grounds in the notice may be altered or added to with the leave of the court, it is unlikely that extensive amendments to the notice will be permitted (see eg *South Buckinghamshire County Council v Francis* [1985] CLY 1900 where the notice was invalid because it did not specify the breaches of covenant said to be broken—the county court judge refused to allow the landlord leave to amend the notice to include a schedule of dilapidations and particulars of nuisance; cf the position in relation to assured tenancies on p 113).

In addition to proving that one of the grounds has been made out, the landlord must satisfy the court that the condition(s) appropriate to that ground is (are) satisfied. The grounds and the appropriate conditions are as follows (see s 84):

Grounds 1–8: the court must consider it reasonable to make the order for possession
(1) Rent arrears and breach of obligation (see Chapter 23).
(2) Nuisance and illegal purposes (see Chapter 24).
(3) Deterioration of the premises (see Chapter 24).
(4) Deterioration to furniture (see Chapter 24).
(5) Obtaining the tenancy by false statement.
(6) Premium paid on an exchange.

(7) Tenant or person residing with him guilty of conduct such that it would not be right for him to continue occupation—tenancy resulting from employment by landlord.

(8) Dwelling house occupied while improvement works being carried out to previous home which are now completed.

Grounds 9–11: the court must be satisfied that suitable alternative accommodation is available

(9) Overcrowding within the meaning of Part X of the Housing Act 1985 (see Chapter 18).

(10) Demolition or reconstruction (see *Wansbeck DC v Marley* [1988] 20 HLR 247).

(10A) Dwelling house in redevelopment area.

(11) Charity cases.

Grounds 12–16: the court must be satisfied that suitable alternative accommodation will be available and that it is reasonable to make the order for possession

(12) Dwelling house required for employee.

(13) Dwelling house designed for the physically handicapped (see *Freeman v Wansbeck DC* [1984] 2 All ER 746).

(14) Landlord a housing association or housing trust and dwelling house let to a person with special needs.

(15) Social service or special facility in close proximity.

(16) Under occupation following death of the tenant and s83 notice served more than six months but less than 12 months after the date of the previous tenant's death (see further p177).

Suitable alternative accommodation   Part IV of Sched 2 to the 1985 Act provides that accommodation is suitable if it consists of premises which are to be let under:

(a) a secure tenancy; or

(b) a protected tenancy (other than one under which the landlord would be able to recover possession by relying on one of the mandatory grounds in Sched 15 to the Rent Act 1977); or

(c) an assured tenancy (which is neither an assured shorthold tenancy nor a tenancy under which the landlord might recover possession under any of Grounds 1 to 5 in Sched 2 to that Act);

and, in the opinion of the court, the accommodation is reasonably suitable for the needs of the tenant and his family (Sched 2, Part IV, para 1 as amended by Sched 17, para 65 of the Housing Act 1988).

In determining whether it is reasonably suitable for those needs, the court must have regard to the factors set out in para 2 of Part IV (see Appendix 2). The needs of the tenant's family should not be overlooked even where husband and wife have separated (*Wandsworth London Borough Council v Fadayomi* [1987] 3 All ER 474). Sometimes the landlord may rely upon a certificate of suitability which will be conclusive evidence that the alternative accommodation is suitable (see para 4 of Part IV).

When considering cases under Part IV of Sched 2, care should be taken in comparing Rent Act cases because of the exclusion of the words 'and character' that appear in para 5(*b*) of Part IV of Sched 15 to the Rent Act 1977 and because of the inclusion in Sched 2 to the 1985 Act of a reference to 'the nature of the accommodation which it is the practice of the landlord to allocate to persons with similar needs' which permits the court to take into account the needs of other homeless persons in the borough (para 2(*a*)): see *Enfield London Borough Council v French* (1984) 49 P&CR 223.

The list in para 2 of Part IV is not exhaustive and the court may take into account needs not specified therein such as the need of the tenant for a garden or to carry on a particular hobby or other activity, but such needs can be outweighed by the fact that all other needs are satisfied by the alternative accommodation (*Enfield v French*).

The order for possession

Where the landlord is relying upon any of the Grounds 1 to 8 or 12 to 16 of Sched 2 to the Housing Act 1985 the court may stay or suspend the execution of the order, or postpone the date for possession (s85 of the Housing Act 1985). If any such stay, suspension or postponement is ordered the court must, unless it considers that to do so would cause exceptional hardship or would otherwise be unreasonable, impose conditions with regard to payment by the tenant of arrears of rent (if any) and rent or payments in respect of occupation after termination of the tenancy (mesne profits) and may impose such other conditions as it thinks fit. If any of these conditions are imposed, and then complied with the court may, if it thinks fit, discharge or rescind the order for possession.

The court has no discretion under s85 where the ground for possession is one of Grounds 9 (overcrowding), 10 (demolition or reconstruction), 10A (dwelling house in development area) or 11 (charity cases). In these cases the court may not suspend the order for possession for more than 14 days (six weeks in cases of exceptional hardship): s89 of the Housing Act 1980 (p75).

Assignment, subletting and death

Assignment

Some secure tenancies may not be assigned. Others may be, but in certain circumstances they cease to be secure. Certain tenancies which are not secure, but would be if the tenant condition were satisfied, lose the opportunity of becoming secure if they are assigned.

It is not possible to assign a secure tenancy (or a tenancy which would be secure if the tenant condition were satisfied) which is a periodic tenancy or is for a fixed term that was created on or after 5 November 1982, unless:

(a) the assignment is by way of an exchange with another secure tenant or with an assured tenant who satisfies certain conditions pursuant to the provisions of s92 of the Housing Act 1985 (as amended by s163 of the Local Government and Housing Act 1989) (see s91(1), (3)); or

(b) the assignment is made in pursuance of an order under s24 of the Matrimonial Causes Act 1973 (see also Sched 1 to the Matrimonial Homes Act 1983); or

(c) the assignment is to a person who could be a successor on death (see p176).

A secure tenancy which is for a fixed term and was granted before 5 November 1982 may be assigned but it ceases to be secure, unless one of the circumstances in (a), (b) or (c) above applies (s91(2) of the Housing Act 1985). Where such a tenancy ceases to be secure it cannot become a secure tenancy again.

A tenancy that remains secure despite an assignment does not lose its status as a secure tenancy by reason of the fact that it was an unlawful assignment, ie in breach of a covenant in the tenancy agreement (Governors of the Peabody Donation Fund v Higgins [1983] 1 WLR 1091); but it does give the landlord a ground upon which it can claim possession (Ground 1).

A tenancy that loses its security by reason of an assignment does not cease to exist, even if the assignment was unlawful. It continues to exist as a common law tenancy in the hands of the assignee (Governors of the Peabody Donation Fund v Higgins). If the landlord wishes to recover possession by reason of the assignment it must therefore determine the tenancy according to common law principles. Where there is a covenant against assigning and a forfeiture clause in the agreement the landlord should serve a notice under s146 of the Law of Property Act 1925 and then commence forfeiture proceedings. Or, if it is able to do so, the landlord may serve a notice to quit. (As to assignments generally see Chapter 4, p80.)

(Note that s91 of the Housing Act 1985 does not apply if the landlord is a co-operative housing association: s109.)

Subletting, parting with possession and lodgers

Section 93(1)–(4) of the Housing Act 1985 provides that it is a term of every secure tenancy that the tenant will not, without the written consent of the landlord, sublet or part with possession of *part* of the dwelling house. If he does so and there is a forfeiture clause in the lease the landlord may terminate under s82(3): see p167. Alternatively, if the tenancy is a periodic tenancy he may terminate the tenancy by serving a notice equivalent to at least the period of the tenancy. In each instance the landlord will have to commence proceedings for possession, in which he will be able to rely upon Ground 1. If the tenant seeks the landlord's consent, that consent must not be unreasonably withheld (s94(2)). Section 94(3) which governs the question of whether the landlord is being unreasonable in withholding his consent provides that the burden is on the landlord to show that its refusal is reasonable. Section 94(3) sets out two matters that are among those that may be taken into account when deciding whether the landlord's refusal is unreasonable. These are (*a*) that the consent would lead to overcrowding as defined by Part X of the Housing Act 1985 (see Chapter 18) and (*b*) that the landlord proposes to carry out building works and that these works will affect the accommodation likely to be used by the proposed sub-tenant. If the landlord does withhold his consent unreasonably the consent is treated as having been given (s94(2)) and it will obviously not be possible for it to recover possession under Ground 1.

The situation is rather different where the tenant parts with possession or sublets *the whole* of the dwelling house (or sublets first part of it and then the remainder). In these circumstances the tenancy ceases to be secure and can never again become secure (s93(2)). The tenancy will, however, continue as a common law tenancy and if the landlord wishes to recover possession it will have to determine it first according to common law principles, ie forfeiture or notice to quit. If a tenancy ceases to be secure because the tenant ceases to reside in the dwelling house (see s81) the restrictions on parting with possession or subletting the whole contained in s93(2) continue to apply to the tenancy (s95).

There is no equivalent in the Housing Act 1985 to s137 of the Rent Act 1977 which gives some sub-tenants security of tenure when the landlord obtains possession as against the tenant. The position of sub-tenants at common law is dealt with in Chapter 4.

The relationship between the tenant and the sub-tenant is governed by the rules that apply in the private sector. This is because the sub-tenant's immediate landlord, ie the tenant, does not fulfil the landlord condition set out in s80 of the Housing Act 1985. Where the tenant has sublet part of the dwelling house he will be a resident or sharing landlord in relation to the sub-tenant who will not therefore be an assured or a protected tenant under s1 of the Housing Act 1988 or the Rent Act 1977; but (where the tenancy was entered into before 15 January 1989) he will almost certainly hold under a restricted contract (see Chapters 9 and 11).

Section 93 of the Housing Act 1985 provides that it is a term of every secure tenancy that the tenant may allow any persons to reside as lodgers in the dwelling house. Taking in lodgers will not therefore provide a basis upon which the landlord may obtain possession but if it is entitled to possession as against the tenant on some other ground it will also be entitled to possession as against the lodger. A lodger is a licensee but if he pays rent he will (if he entered into occupation prior to 15 January 1989) almost certainly be entitled to some degree of protection as against the tenant by reason of the provisions relating to restricted contracts (see Chapter 9). As to whether a person is a licensee or sub-tenant see Chapter 5.

(Note that ss93, 94 and 95 of the Housing Act 1985 do not apply to a tenancy when the interest of the landlord belongs to a co-operative housing association: s109.)

Death (ss87–90)

Periodic tenancies (s89)   Where there are two or more tenants and one dies the remaining tenant or tenants become the sole tenant or remaining joint tenants under the laws relating to the right of survivorship. He (or they) continue to be secure in his (or their) own right. Where a secure tenant is a sole tenant and there is a person qualified under the rules set out in the Housing Act 1985 to succeed him the tenancy vests in that person. If there is more than one such person who is entitled to succeed him the tenancy vests in the person who is to be preferred according to the criteria set out in the Act (see s89).

A person is qualified to succeed to the tenancy if he occupied the dwelling house as his only or principal home at the time of the tenant's death and either:

(*a*) he is the tenant's spouse (s87(*a*)); or

(*b*) he is another member of the tenant's family and has resided with the tenant throughout the period of 12 months ending with the tenant's death (s87(*b*)). The family member is not required to have lived with the tenant at the property in question throughout that period. It is sufficient if they resided somewhere together for a 12-month period and in that property together at the date of the tenant's death (*Waltham Forest London Borough Council v Thomas* [1992] 3 All ER 245, HL).

Where there is more than one person qualified to succeed the tenant, the tenant's spouse is to be preferred to any other member of the tenant's family. Where there is no spouse who is qualified to succeed but there are two other members of the tenant's family who are qualified they may agree between them who is to succeed, but if they cannot agree the landlord may select a successor (s89(2)(*b*)).

A person is a member of another's family if he is his spouse, parent, grandparent, child, grandchild, brother, sister, uncle, aunt, nephew or niece. Relationships by marriage are treated as relationships by blood, half blood as whole blood, and a stepchild is treated as a child of the stepparent. An illegitimate child is treated as the legitimate child of his mother and reputed father. A person is also a member of another's family if they live together as man and wife (see s113). A homosexual relationship is not equated as living as man and wife and so each partner will not be treated as a member of the other's family (*Harrogate Borough Council v Simpson* (1984) 17 HLR 205).

A secure periodic tenancy may only be transferred once (ss87, 88(1)(*a*)). Furthermore, a secure tenancy may not be transferred on the tenant's death in any of the following circumstances:

(*a*) where the tenant was originally a joint tenant and at some stage before his death he became a sole tenant (s88(1)(*b*)) under the original tenancy (*Bassetlaw District Council v Renshaw* [1992] 1 All ER 925, CA: tenant originally a joint tenant under a tenancy with her husband who served a notice on the landlord terminating the tenancy and left. The tenant then entered into a new tenancy of the property as a sole tenant. Held: she was not a person who had been a joint tenant under the original tenancy and who had become a sole tenant. Her son was not, therefore, precluded from succeeding to the second tenancy); or

(*b*) where a fixed term was granted to another person or jointly with the deceased tenant and another person and the tenancy has (by virtue of s86) become a periodic tenancy at the end of the fixed term or by virtue of an order of the court under s82(3); or

(*c*) where the deceased tenant became the tenant on the tenancy being assigned to him (except in divorce proceedings pursuant to s24 of the Matrimonial Causes Act 1973 or where the assignment was by virtue of s97 of the Housing Act 1985); or

(*d*) where the tenancy became vested in him on the death of the previous tenant (ss87, 88(1)).

A situation can occur whereby a person ('the new tenant') remains in occupation after the death of the original tenant in circumstances which give rise to a new tenancy as between the landlord and the new tenant (by estoppel) so that on the death of the new tenant the person then in occupation will be treated as the first successor to the *new tenant's* tenancy, even though the original tenant's tenancy was never determined (*Epping Forest District Council v Pomphrett* [1990] 2 EGLR 46, CA).

Where there is no person qualified to become a secure tenant by succession the tenancy does not cease to exist. Instead it will devolve according to the common law rules set out in Chapter 4. If the landlord wishes to recover possession on the death of the tenant where there is no person entitled to succeed as a secure tenant the landlord should determine the tenancy in the usual way, ie by notice to quit.

Where there is a person qualified to succeed as a secure tenant the landlord may nevertheless be able to regain possession by relying upon Ground 16 if the accommodation afforded by the dwelling house is more extensive than is reasonably required by the successor. The ground does not apply if the successor was the tenant's spouse. In deciding whether it is reasonable to make an order on Ground 16 the court must take into account the age of the successor, the period during which he occupied the dwelling house as his only or principal home and any financial or other support that he gave to the previous tenant.

Fixed terms (s90) Where a secure tenancy is for a fixed term it will devolve according to the rules set out in Chapter 4. Thus, if there are joint tenants the remaining tenants continue as secure tenants. In all other cases the tenancy will remain secure until either (*a*) the tenancy is vested or otherwise disposed of in the course of the administration of the deceased's estate; or (*b*) it is known that when the tenancy has been so vested or disposed of it will not be a secure tenancy (s90(2) of the Housing Act 1985). Once the tenancy has been vested or otherwise disposed of it will only continue to be secure if (*a*) the vesting or other disposal is in pursuance of an order made under s24 of the Matrimonial Causes Act 1973, or (*b*) the person in whom the tenancy vests would have been entitled to be a secure tenant of the dwelling house by virtue of s87 had the tenancy been a periodic tenancy (s90(3)). If the tenancy ceases to be secure it cannot become a secure tenancy (s90(4)) and thus the landlord will be able to regain possession of the premises at the end of the term without having to rely upon one of the grounds set out in Sched 2.

Chapter 11

Shared Accommodation and Resident Landlords

Shared accommodation

The tenant may share all or part of his accommodation with his landlord, with other tenants or with his own tenants or lodgers. The effect of the sharing on the relationship between the different parties and their respective rights to terminate and claim possession are dealt with in this chapter.

Introduction: sharing 'essential living accommodation'

As seen in Chapters 6, 8 and 10 it is a requirement of assured, protected and secure tenancies that the dwelling house is let as a *separate* dwelling. This does not mean that the rooms that are subject to the tenancy must be physically partitioned off from the other accommodation, but that there must be a distinct unit which the tenant is not obliged, by the agreement, to share with any other person. Thus, part of a house may be a separate dwelling without being self-contained and even though the rooms which the tenant is entitled to occupy are spread throughout the house, provided that all the facilities that make it possible for a person to live there are present (*Wimbush v Cibulia* [1949] 2 KB 564).

Sometimes, however, a tenant may be obliged by the tenancy agreement to share part of his accommodation with others. If so the dwelling house is not being let as a separate dwelling and *prima facie* the tenancy is not assured, protected or secure. However, in order to prevent the accommodation from being assured, protected or secure the tenant must be obliged to share 'essential living accommodation'. Sharing the use of a toilet or bathroom is not regarded as the sharing of essential living accommodation for these purposes. Furthermore, the courts have tended to ignore minor amounts of sharing, for example where there is only a very small amount of use of the tenant's kitchen by persons other than the tenant. (See *Goodrich v Paisner* [1957] AC 65; *Marsh v Cooper* [1969] 1 WLR 803.)

179

'Tenant' sharing with the 'landlord' (see Form 25)

Where a person shares accommodation with the person who has permitted him to enter into occupation he will often be a lodger in occupation under a licence (see *Street v Mountford* [1985] 2 WLR 877 discussed in Chapter 5). And if he does not have exclusive occupation of any part of the premises he will not even be afforded the protection available to occupiers under restricted contracts (s19(6) of the Rent Act 1977), ie the right to ask for an order for possession to be suspended for a period of up to three months (see Chapter 9). Once the licence has been determined the licensor will be entitled to an order for possession which may not be suspended for more than 14 days (six weeks in cases of exceptional hardship): s89 of the Housing Act 1980 (p75).

If the occupier is a tenant, he will nonetheless not be an assured or, as the case may be, a protected tenant if he shares 'essential living accommodation' with the landlord (see *above*). However, in any case where the Rent Act 1977 continues to apply (see p156), if the rent includes payment for the use of furniture or services, which will usually be the case, the tenant will be an occupier under a restricted contract and the rules as to termination and postponement of orders for possession that apply to restricted contracts (see Chapter 9) will apply (s21 of the Rent Act 1977).

Tenant sharing part with other persons given the right to occupy by the landlord

Where a 'tenant' is required to share with other 'tenants' it is possible that they will be regarded as licensees (see p89). However, where the 'tenant' is truly a tenant his right to remain in occupation is regulated by statutory provisions.

Where a tenant, whose status is governed by the Housing Act 1988, shares *part* of his 'essential living accommodation' with any person other than his landlord the part that he does not share is deemed to be a dwelling house let on an assured tenancy (Housing Act 1988, s3(1)). The landlord cannot therefore obtain possession of that part without proving a Housing Act ground for possession. There are also provisions to protect him in his use of the shared accommodation while he is in occupation of the part that he does not share. If the landlord wishes to terminate or vary the tenant's right to use the shared accommodation he must make an application to the county court (Housing Act 1988, s10(3)).

Similar rules apply to tenancies governed by the Rent Act 1977 (see s22).

Housing Act 1988, ss3 and 10

      3.—(1) Where a tenant has the exclusive occupation of any accommodation (in this section referred to as 'the separate accommodation') and—

Form 25: Particulars of claim—shared accommodation with landlord

---

IN THE   COUNTY COURT   Case No

BETWEEN

                                           Plaintiff

—AND—

                                        Defendant

PARTICULARS OF CLAIM

1. The Plaintiff is the [*freehold/leasehold owner*] and entitled to possession of the dwelling house known as [*state address*].

2. By an oral agreement made on or about the [*insert date*] the Plaintiff agreed to allow the Defendant to share occupation of the dwelling house with the Plaintiff for the sum of £ [*state amount*] per week payable in [*advance/arrears*] each [*state which day of the week*] day. Under the terms of the said agreement the Defendant had the use of one bedroom and the shared use of the bathroom and kitchen facilities.

3. In the premises, the Defendant was a licensee of the Plaintiff in the dwelling house. In the alternative, the Defendant was a tenant of the Plaintiff but by reason of the said sharing with the Plaintiff the said tenancy is not an assured tenancy.

4. The said licence (or, in the alternative) tenancy was determined by a notice to quit served on the Defendant on or about [*insert date*], which said notice expired on the day on which a complete period of the said tenancy expired next after the end of four weeks from service of the said notice.

5. Despite the said revocation and despite service of the said notice the Defendant remains in occupation of the dwelling house, without the licence or consent of the Plaintiff.

6. The Defendant has failed to make any payments to the Plaintiff since the [*insert date*].

AND the Plaintiff claims:

(1) Possession of the said dwelling house; and

(2) Mesne profits at the rate of [*state amount*] per week (£ [*state amount*] per day) from [*insert date*]
    19   until possession be delivered up.

DATED

(*a*) the terms as between the tenant and his landlord on which he holds the separate accommodation include the use of other accommodation (in this section referred to as 'the shared accommodation') in common with another person or other persons, not being or including the landlord, and

(*b*) by reason only of the circumstances mentioned in paragraph (*a*) above, the separate accommodation would not, apart from this section, be a dwelling house let on an assured tenancy,

the separate accommodation shall be deemed to be a dwelling house let on an assured tenancy and the following provisions of this section shall have effect.

(2) For the avoidance of doubt it is hereby declared that where, for the purpose of determining the rateable value of the separate accommodation, it is necessary to make an apportionment under Part II of Schedule 1 to his Act, regard is to be had to the circumstances mentioned in subsection (1)(a) above.

(3) While the tenant is in possession of the separate accommodation, any term of the tenancy terminating or modifying, or providing for the termination or modification of, his right to the use of any of the shared accommodation which is living accommodation shall be of no effect.

(4) Where the terms of the tenancy are such that, at any time during the tenancy, the persons in common with whom the tenant is entitled to the use of the shared accommodation could be varied or their number could be increased, nothing in subsection (3) above shall prevent those terms from having effect so far as they relate to any such variation or increase.

(5) In this section 'living accommodation' means accommodation of such a nature that the fact that it constitutes or is included in the shared accommodation is sufficient, apart from this section, to prevent the tenancy from constituting an assured tenancy of a dwelling house.

. . .

10.—(1) This section applies in a case falling within subsection (1) of section 3 above and expressions used in this section have the same meaning as in that section.

(2) Without prejudice to the enforcement of any order made under subsection (3) below, while the tenant is in possession of the separate accommodation, no order shall be made for possession of any of the shared accommodation, whether on the application of the immediate landlord of the tenant or on the application of any person under whom that landlord derives title, unless a like order has been made, or is made at the same time, in respect of the separate accommodation; and the provisions of section 6 above shall have effect accordingly.

(3) On the application of the landlord, the court may make such order as it thinks just either—

> (a) terminating the right of the tenant to use the whole or any part of the shared accommodation other than living accommodation; or
>
> (b) modifying his right to use the whole or any part of the shared accommodation, whether by varying the person or increasing the number of persons entitled to the use of that accommodation or otherwise.

(4) No order shall be made under subsection (3) above so as to effect any termination or modification of the rights of the tenant which, apart from section 3(3) above, could not be effected by or under the terms of the tenancy.

Joint tenants

Where the tenant shares the *whole* of the dwelling house with a joint tenant neither may evict the other save in matrimonial and quasi-matrimonial proceedings pursuant to the provisions of the Matrimonial Homes Act 1983 or the Domestic Violence and Matrimonial Proceedings Act 1976 or pursuant to the court's inherent jurisdiction to make orders for the protection of children (see further p241).

Tenant sharing with sub-tenants or licensees

Where an assured tenant or a protected or statutory tenant sublets *part* of the accommodation he does not lose his protection under the Housing Act or Rent Act even if the sub-tenant shares with another person (s4 of the Housing Act 1988; s23 of the Rent Act 1977; see also *Baker v Turner* [1950] AC 401). However, the landlord may be able to obtain possession under Ground 12 of Sched 2 to the Housing Act 1988 or, as the case may be, Case 1 of Sched 15 to the Rent Act 1977 if the tenancy agreement contains a covenant against subletting of part of the premises.

For the position of secure tenants who sublet, part with possession or take in lodgers, see p174.

Where a tenant (of any type) has taken in a lodger or has sublet part of the premises he will either be a licensor or sharing landlord (see *above*) or a resident landlord (see *below*) as against the lodger or sub-tenant. If he has done so prior to the commencement of the 1988 Act (ie 15 January 1989) or pursuant to a contract entered into before commencement of the Act the lodger or sub-tenant will be in occupation under a restricted contract whether or not the rent includes payment for use of furniture or for services (ss20 and 21 of the Rent Act 1977) but only so long as the tenant is in 'exclusive occupation' of some part of the property (s19(6)). However, except in the limited case where the person has entered into occupation pursuant to an agreement made before the commencement of the 1988 Act no right of occupation thereafter can be a restricted contract (s36 of the Housing Act 1988).

Resident landlords

Where the landlord of a dwelling house is a 'resident landlord' the tenant is not an assured tenant under the Housing Act 1988 or, as the case may be, a protected tenant as defined in s1 of the Rent Act 1977. The situation discussed here is one step removed from the situation discussed under the heading: 'Tenant' sharing with the 'Landlord', on p180. The landlord and the tenant live in the same building but they each have their own 'separate dwelling'. In some cases they may live in the same flat, in a purpose-built block of flats, which is big enough to be divided into two separate dwelling houses. In these circumstances the resident landlord rules will also apply.

Insofar as the Housing Act 1988 is concerned the provisions for determining whether the tenancy is precluded from being assured on the resident landlord ground are found in para 10 and Part III of Sched 1 to the 1988 Act. In Rent Act cases the position is governed by s12 and Sched 1 of the Rent Act 1977.

This chapter deals with the resident landlord exception by reference to the position under the Rent Act 1977, ie in relation to tenancies granted before 15 January 1989 (see p130). The Housing Act 1988 provisions are very similar (see Appendix 2 to this book). The main difference to note is that in a Rent Act case a tenant who is not protected by reason of this exception will be a person occupying under a restricted contract (s20 of the Rent Act 1977); in a Housing Act case it is not possible for there to be a restricted contract (s36 of the Housing Act 1988; see p156). In a Housing Act case, note also that the landlord is required to occupy the residence as his 'only or principal home' (para 10(1)(*b*)).

Definition of resident landlord

The landlord will only be a resident landlord and the tenant will only thereby be excluded from protection under s1 of the Rent Act 1977 if the following three conditions are satisfied:

(1) *Date of grant (s12(1) of the Rent Act 1977)* The tenancy must have been granted on or after 14 August 1974. Where the tenancy was granted prior to that date and it was already protected under the law existing at that time (ie because the premises were *un*furnished) it remained protected even though the landlord was resident at the date of the grant and has been ever since. If the tenancy was furnished and therefore unprotected prior to 14 August 1974 it remained unprotected thereafter if the landlord was resident but became protected if the landlord was not. (See Sched 24, paras 6, 7 of the Rent Act 1977.) As to whether the tenancy was furnished or not see *Woodward v Docherty* [1974] 1 WLR 966.

(2) *Dwelling house only part of a building (s12(1)(a) and Sched 2, para 4)* The dwelling house must form part only of a building and that building must not (subject to the situation dealt with below) be a purpose-built block of flats. A building is a purpose-built block of flats if, as constructed, it contained, and it still contains, two or more flats; 'flat' means a dwelling house which (*a*) forms part only of a building and (*b*) is separated horizontally from another dwelling house which forms part of the same building. A 'conversion' is not a purpose-built block of flats (*Barnes v Gorsuch* (1981) 43 P&CR 294). Where the tenancy was granted on or after 28 November 1980 and the landlord and the tenant both live in the same flat which is divided into two or more separate dwelling houses, with the landlord living in one dwelling house and the tenant living in another, the landlord will be a 'resident landlord' even if the building in which the flat is situated is a purpose-built block of flats.

(3) *Landlord resident in another dwelling in the building* The tenancy must have been granted by a person who, at the time that he granted it *and* at all times since, has occupied, as his residence, another dwelling house which also forms part of the same building (or flat). Where the landlord's interest is owned by trustees under a trust for sale the case is deemed to be a resident landlord case if

the proceeds of sale are held on trust for any person who occupies another dwelling house in the building (or flat): Sched 2, para 2. Where the tenancy was granted by joint owners, only one of whom was residing on the premises, s 12 applies and the tenant is not protected (*Cooper v Tait* (1984) 48 P&CR 460).

Whether or not the landlord's dwelling house and the tenant's dwelling house form part of the same building is a question of fact, but in deciding this question the court will pay regard to the intention of s 12 which is to allow the landlord to remove a tenant who lives in close proximity to him.

> The English word 'building' covers an immense range of all sorts of structures. It is an ordinary English word, and its meaning must therefore be a question of fact, always assuming that the court directs itself correctly as to the intention and meaning of the statute which uses it. As a matter of law, to give a defined or precise meaning to the word 'building' is an impossibility. It is beyond the capacity of even the most consummate master of the English language to do so. This itself is, in my judgment, an indication that Parliament is leaving the question of fact to the judge. . .
>
> I have no doubt that the intention of Parliament in enacting [s 12] was to relieve landlords where it was reasonable to do so . . . [T]he mischief at which the section was aimed was the mischief of that sort of social embarrassment arising out of close proximity—close proximity which the landlord had accepted in the belief that he could bring it to an end at any time allowed by the contract of tenancy (*per* Scarman LJ, *Bardrick v Haycock* (1976) 31 P&CR 420 at 424).

Thus, in a case where the landlord lived in a self-contained unit attached to the end of a building with no interconnecting door it was held that the exception did not apply (*Bardrick v Haycock* (1976) 31 P&CR 420). Compare *Griffiths v English* (1982) 261 EG 257 where the landlord was the owner of a house with an extension built on each side. The landlord lived in one extension and the tenant in the other. It was held that s 12 applied.

In *Lewis-Graham v Conacher* [1992] 1 EGLR 112, CA an extension which was originally a granny flat and garage had been added to a semi-detached house. It had interconnecting doors between the house and the extension which were locked. There was a common gas supply, electricity supply and water supply. At that stage there was clearly one building. The landlord started carrying out works, to separate the two dwellings into two separate 'buildings', after service of the notice to quit but had not completed them by the time the notice to quit had expired. The Court of Appeal refused to interfere with the judge's finding of fact that at that date there was still one building, and in any event may not have constituted two buildings after the works had been finished:

> For my part I am not entirely convinced that, even when the building work was finished, this would have amounted to two buildings rather than one. Where something has been built as an extension to an existing house, where the other walls are continuous and the roofs are contiguous, it may be that it still remains as one building, notwithstanding that it was intended to be two

separate dwellings. Be that as it may, for my part I would not interfere with the learned judge's finding of fact (*per* Stuart-Smith LJ at 112K).

Paragraph 5 of Sched 2 provides that a person is to be treated as occupying a dwelling house as his residence for the purposes of s 12 if, so far as the nature of the case allows, he fulfils the same conditions as are required to be fulfilled by a person who claims to be a statutory tenant. A resident landlord may therefore have two homes or he may remain a resident landlord despite temporary absences; but the dwelling house must be a home for him to be able to rely upon the resident landlord exception. This subject is discussed in detail in relation to statutory tenants in Chapter 8, see p 137.

For a recent case in which the principles were applied to a resident landlord see *Palmer v McNamara* [1991] 1 EGLR 121, CA: room retained by landlord did not contain a cooker. He either bought food he did not need to cook, or take-away meals. He spent his days in the room and kept all his belongings there. He slept elsewhere because for health reasons he needed help dressing and undressing. The Court of Appeal refused to interfere with the judge's finding of fact that the landlord occupied the premises as a home.

Exclusions

Section 12 of the Rent Act 1977 does not apply where the tenancy was granted to a person who, immediately before it was granted, was a protected or a statutory tenant of that dwelling house or of any other dwelling house in the same building (or flat). The tenant will continue to be a protected or statutory tenant even if the landlord becomes resident. This prevents landlords avoiding the effect of the Rent Act 1977 by entering into occupation of a dwelling house in the building (or flat) and then granting to the tenant a new tenancy of his dwelling house or of another dwelling house in the building (or flat). (See s 12(2) as amended by s 69(4) of the Housing Act 1980.)

Prior to 28 November 1980 (when s 12 was amended by the Housing Act 1980) a landlord who granted a fixed term tenancy in succession to another fixed term of the same dwelling house or of any other dwelling house in the same building could not take advantage of the resident landlord exception. This rule has now been repealed but any tenancy that was protected by reason of it prior to 28 November 1980 continues to be protected (s 69(4) and Sched 25, para 67 of the Housing Act 1980).

Termination and recovery (see Form 26)

The tenancy is brought to an end in one of the normal ways, ie by notice to quit, forfeiture, effluxion of time or surrender. Thereafter the tenant's right to remain in possession is very limited. He was not a protected tenant and so no statutory tenancy arises. At the hearing of the possession action the landlord need only prove that he is a resident landlord and that the tenancy has been determined. Section 20 of the Rent Act 1977 does, however, provide that if and so long as a tenancy is, by virtue of the resident landlord exception, precluded from being a protected tenancy it is to be treated as a restricted contract notwithstanding that the rent may not include payments for the use of furniture or for services. Thus, where the tenancy was created after 28 November 1980 the court will be able to stay or suspend execution of the order or postpone the date of possession for up to three months. As with other restricted contracts the court will have to impose conditions as to the payment of rent etc unless to do so would cause exceptional hardship or would otherwise be unreasonable (s 106A of the Rent Act 1977). Where the tenancy was created before 28 November 1980 the tenant will be able to apply to the rent tribunal pursuant to ss 103–6 of the Rent Act 1977 for a suspension of operation of the notice to quit. If the notice to quit has expired it is not possible to make an application to the rent tribunal (*R v City of London Rent Tribunal, ex p Honig* [1951] 1 KB 641) and the court will only be able to postpone the order for possession for up to 14 days, or six weeks in cases of exceptional hardship (s 89 of the Housing Act 1980; see p 75).

Assignment, bankruptcy and death

There are no special rules that apply if the tenant assigns, sublets, goes bankrupt or dies. The law set out in Chapter 4 will generally apply although if the landlord terminates the tenancy following one of these events, perhaps by forfeiting, the court will, because the tenancy is a restricted contract, be able to suspend the order for possession for up to three months. The statutory provisions that do apply in resident landlord cases are concerned with the tenant's position on the assignment of the landlord's interest following a voluntary transfer, his bankruptcy or his death. The tenant's position is not adversely affected by these events. Indeed it may be improved, for in certain circumstances he can become a fully protected tenant.

Assignment Where the landlord assigns his successor in title must also live in the dwelling house throughout his period of ownership; so must any further assignee. If they do not the tenant will become a protected tenant (s 12(1)(c)). There are, however, periods where the failure to occupy another dwelling house in the same building is disregarded for the purpose of deciding whether the landlord is to be regarded as resident within s 12(1)(c). These periods are set out in Sched 2 to the Rent Act 1977. First, any period of not more than 28 days beginning with the date on which the interest of the landlord became vested in law and equity in the successor is disregarded. Secondly, if during that 28-day period the assignee notifies the tenant in writing of his intention to occupy another

Form 26: Particulars of claim—resident landlord

IN THE   COUNTY COURT   Case No

BETWEEN

                                           Plaintiff

—AND—

                                           Defendant

PARTICULARS OF CLAIM

1. The Plaintiff is the [*freehold/leasehold*] owner and is entitled to possession of premises comprising a dwelling house known as

2. By an oral agreement made on or about the [. . .] the Plaintiff agreed to let to the Defendant, on a weekly tenancy, the . . . floor flat at the said premises, at a rent of £. . . per week payable in advance each . . .

3. The said premises are not a purpose-built block of flats.

4. At the time of and at all times since the date of the said agreement the Plaintiff has occupied as his residence the flat on the . . . floor of the said premises.

5. The said tenancy was determined by a notice to quit served on the . . . which said notice expired on the . . .

6. By reason of the matters set out in paragraphs 3 and 4 above the premises are, by virtue of section 12 of the Rent Act 1977 [paragraph 10 of the Housing Act 1988], not premises to which the said Act applies.

AND the Plaintiff claims:

(1) Possession of the said . . . floor flat.
(2) Mesne profits at the rate of £. . . per week (£. . . per day) from . . . until possession be delivered up.

DATED

---

dwelling house in the building (or flat) the period beginning with the date upon which the assignee became the legal and equitable owner until the earlier of any of the following three periods: (*a*) the expiry of six months from that date, or (*b*) the date upon which the assignee ceases to be the owner, or (*c*) the date upon which the assignee occupies a dwelling house in the building (or flat), is disregarded. (See Sched 2, para 1(*a*),(*b*).)

The court is not allowed throughout any of these periods of disregard to make an order for possession unless it could make an order if the tenancy were a protected or statutory tenancy (Sched 2, para 3). Where the tenancy is not determined in the period of disregard the tenant will become a protected tenant unless the assignee brings that period to an end by moving into one of the dwelling houses in the building (or flat) before six months have elapsed since he became the owner. But if the absent landlord does bring the tenancy to an end during the period of disregard he will be able to obtain an order for possession at the end of that period without proving a Rent Act ground even if he never moves in. The reason for this is that because the tenancy was determined during the period of disregard it never became a protected tenancy and thus upon determination it was not capable of becoming a statutory tenancy (see *Landau v Sloane* [1981] 2 WLR 349). But if the notice to quit expired after the period of disregard came to an end the tenant will have become fully protected (*Williams v Mate* (1982) 263 EG 883).

Bankruptcy In determining whether the condition set out in s12(1)(c) has been complied with (ie that at all material times since the tenancy was granted the interest of the landlord has belonged to a person who at the time that he owned the interest occupied as his residence another dwelling house in the building (or flat) any period of not more than two years during which the tenancy is vested in trustees as trustees is to be disregarded. A trustee in bankruptcy of the landlord therefore has two years in which to determine the tenancy or sell the property to an intending resident landlord before the tenant will become a protected tenant. No order for possession may be made during that period unless one of the Rent Act grounds applies (Sched 2, para 3); but if the trustee determines the tenancy within the period of disregard the person to whom he has sold the property (or the trustee, if he has kept it and two years have expired) will be able to obtain possession without relying upon one of those grounds (*Landau v Sloane* [1981] 2 WLR 349). The trustee must make sure that the notice to quit expires before the period of disregard (*Williams v Mate* (1982) 263 EG 883).

Death Paragraph 2A of Sched 2 to the Rent Act 1977 (as added by s65 of the Housing Act 1980) provides that where the landlord died on or after 28 November 1980 the condition that the landlord must be resident throughout the tenancy is *deemed to be fulfilled* for any period beginning with the date on which the landlord's interest becomes vested in his personal representatives and ending when it ceases to be so vested or when two years have expired, whichever is the earlier. The personal representatives may therefore obtain possession pursuant to the resident landlord provisions and sell the property to a non-resident landlord during the administration of the estate. Personal representatives, like assignees and trustees in bankruptcy, must make sure that the tenancy actually comes to an end before the period of two years has expired if they are to ensure that the tenant is not to become fully protected (*Williams v Mate* (1982) 263 EG 883).

Where the landlord dies intestate and the tenancy vests in the President of the Family Division by virtue of s9 of the Administration of Estates Act 1925 there is, in determining whether there is a landlord who is resident, disregarded a period of up to two years during which it is so vested (Sched 2, para 1(c)). Once it becomes vested in personal representatives para 2A will apply.

Chapter 12

Protected Shortholds

Protected shorthold tenancies were created by the Housing Act 1980 with the purpose of enabling a landlord to let his property with the knowledge that he would be able to recover possession at the end of the contractual term or thereafter without having to rely upon the usual Rent Act grounds. A shorthold tenancy is a protected tenancy and so the rules relating to protected tenancies explained in Chapter 8 apply to shorthold tenancies unless they conflict with the shorthold provisions explained in this chapter.

Effect of the Housing Act 1988

The concept of the 'protected shorthold tenancy' has now been replaced by that of an 'assured shorthold tenancy' which was introduced by the Housing Act 1988 (see Chapter 6). The regime set out in this chapter will continue to apply to protected shorthold tenancies created prior to the commencement of the 1988 Act. However, since 15 January 1989 it has not (except in one limited circumstance) been possible to create a protected shorthold tenancy; and ex-shorthold tenants who are granted new tenancies receive assured shortholds (see details at p122).

Definition of shorthold

A tenancy will only be a shorthold if it is a protected tenancy within the meaning of s1 of the Rent Act 1977 (s52(1) of the 1980 Act), and if the conditions set out in s52 of the 1980 Act are satisfied. The conditions are:
   (1) That the tenancy was granted after 28 November 1980.
   (2) That the tenancy was granted for a fixed term of not less than one year and not more than five years. If the tenancy contains an option clause allowing the tenant to renew, or provides that at the end of the fixed term the tenancy shall continue as a periodic tenancy, it is nevertheless a shorthold (s52(5)).
   (3) That there must be no clause in the tenancy agreement allowing the landlord to determine prior to the end of the fixed term except in pursuance of a provision for reentry or forfeiture for non-

190

payment of rent or breach of any other obligation of the tenancy. (A proviso for reentry on the bankruptcy of the tenant does not prevent the tenancy from being a shorthold: *Paterson v Aggio* [1987] 2 EGLR 127).

(4) That the tenancy of the dwelling house was granted to a new tenant of the landlord, ie not an existing protected or statutory tenant of that dwelling house (but see *Dibbs v Campbell* [1988] 2 EGLR 122: was this case correctly decided?) However, if an existing protected or statutory tenant enters into a shorthold tenancy of other accommodation he may be a shorthold tenant (s52(2)).

(5) That the landlord gave the tenant a notice in the prescribed form *before* the tenancy was granted (s52(1)(*b*) and s52(3)); Protected Shorthold Tenancies (Notice to Tenant) Regulations 1987 (SI 1987 No 267); see Form 27 for a specimen form of notice). The wise landlord will have served the notice on the tenant on a date prior to the date of the commencement of the tenancy and have required him to sign, date and return a copy of the notice before the agreement was actually entered into.

(6) That if the property is in Greater London and the shorthold commenced before 4 May 1987 or if the property is outside Greater London and the shorthold tenancy commenced before 1 December 1981:

   (*a*) a rent was registered in respect of the dwelling house at the time the tenancy was granted, or

   (*b*) the landlord obtained a certificate of fair rent from the rent officer pursuant to s69 of the Rent Act 1977, and the rent payable under the tenancy for any period before the rent was registered did not exceed the rent specified in the certificate, and an application for the registration of a fair rent was made to the rent officer within 28 days of the commencement (Protected Shorthold Tenancies (Rent Registration) Order 1987, SI 1987 No 265).

Generally if the above conditions have not been complied with the tenancy will not be a shorthold tenancy but a fully protected Rent Act tenancy. However, in proceedings for possession the court may overlook requirements (5) and (6) if it considers it just and equitable to make the order for possession (s55(2)). For a similar provision in relation to Case 11 of Sched 15 to the Rent Act 1977, see p352.

Termination

At the end of the fixed term the tenancy is no longer called a shorthold tenancy. If the tenant remains in occupation he will do so either as a tenant under a new fixed term granted pursuant to an option clause, or under a periodic protected tenancy pursuant to a term of the shorthold

Form 27: Notice of a protected shorthold tenancy

NOTICE OF A PROTECTED SHORTHOLD TENANCY—SECOND REVISION

(The landlord must give this to the tenant *before* a protected shorthold tenancy is granted. It does not commit the tenant to take the tenancy.)

To ....
(Name of proposed tenant)

> IMPORTANT—PLEASE READ THIS NOTICE CAREFULLY, IF THERE IS ANYTHING YOU DO NOT UNDERSTAND YOU SHOULD GET ADVICE (FOR EXAMPLE, FROM A SOLICITOR OR A CITIZENS' ADVICE BUREAU) BEFORE YOU AGREE TO TAKE A SHORTHOLD TENANCY.
>
> N.B. This document is important; keep it in a safe place.

1. You are proposing to take a tenancy of the dwelling known as ....

   from.. 19.............. to .... 19.....
         (day)   (month)   (year)   (day) (month) (year)

2. This notice is to tell you that your tenancy is to be a *protected shorthold tenancy*. Under shorthold, provided you keep the terms of the tenancy, you are entitled to remain in the dwelling for the fixed period agreed at the start of the tenancy. At the end of this period the landlord has the right to repossession if he wants. Full details about shorthold are given in the Department of the Environment and Welsh Office booklet "Shorthold Tenancies. Second Revision" obtainable free from Rent Officers, council offices and housing aid centres. You are advised to read this booklet before you agree to take a shorthold tenancy.

> * The landlord must cross out the version of paragraph 3 below which does not apply.

*3. A fair rent of   per   is already registered for the dwelling under the Rent Act 1977.

This is the most you can be required to pay as rent until such time as a higher rent is registered. If I apply for a higher rent to be registered you will be told about my application and you will have the opportunity of a consultation with the Rent Officer.

*3 The rent for this tenancy is the rent that we have agreed, and has not been registered by the Rent Officer. But this does not affect your right as tenant or my right as landlord to apply at any time to the Rent Officer for the registration of a fair rent. This is fully explained in the booklet "Shorthold Tenancies. Second Revision."

4. This notice is given to you on .... 19 ....

Signed ....

(on behalf of)..

....

(Name and address of landlord)

> *SPECIAL NOTE FOR EXISTING TENANTS*
>
> IF YOU ARE ALREADY A PROTECTED OR STATUTORY TENANT UNDER THE RENT ACT 1977 YOUR PRESENT TENANCY CANNOT LAWFULLY BE CONVERTED INTO A SHORTHOLD. BUT SHOULD YOU GIVE IT UP AND TAKE A SHORTHOLD TENANCY IN SOME OTHER ACCOMMODATION, INCLUDING ANOTHER FLAT IN THE SAME BUILDING, YOU WILL ALMOST CERTAINLY HAVE LESS SECURITY UNDER SHORTHOLD THAN UNDER YOUR EXISTING TENANCY

Reproduced by kind permission of The Solicitors' Law Stationery Society Ltd

(s52(5)), or if there is no such term as a statutory tenant (s52(1)). However, if there has been no further grant of a fixed term, Case 19 will be available to the landlord if the notice procedure set out *below* is followed (eg see *Gent v de la Mare* [1988] 1 EGLR 104). It may also be possible for the landlord to terminate the tenancy before or after the expiry of the fixed term if the tenant is in breach of covenant. These matters are dealt with below. The tenant's rights to terminate are also dealt with in this section.

Before the fixed term has expired

The *landlord* can only seek an order for possession before the end of the fixed term in pursuance of a provision for reentry on forfeiture for non-payment of rent or breach of any other obligation of the tenancy (s52(1) of the Housing Act 1980).

The *tenant* may bring the shorthold tenancy to an end before the final term has expired by giving written notice to the landlord. The length of notice is one month for shortholds with a fixed term of two years or less, and for shortholds of over two years notice of not less than three months must be given. The right to terminate before the expiry of the fixed term cannot be excluded by any agreement to the contrary (s53 of the Housing Act 1980). If, having given notice to the landlord, the tenant refuses to leave and the landlord has contracted to sell or let the dwelling house or has otherwise been seriously prejudiced the landlord should commence proceedings for possession based upon Case 5 of Sched 15 to the Rent Act 1977.

After the fixed term has expired

Case 19 notice   If the landlord wishes the tenant to leave at the end of the term he must *during the last three months* thereof give the tenant *at least three months'* written notice of his intention to apply to the court for possession after expiry of the notice pursuant to Case 19 of Sched 15 to the Rent Act 1977; see Form 28 on p194.

If the landlord omits to serve the notice within the last three months of the term, the tenant can stay for a further year either as a statutory tenant or if the terms of the shorthold so provide as a protected periodic tenant and the landlord cannot serve another notice until the last three months of the further year.

It is not possible to serve a notice within the period of three months following the expiry of an earlier notice (Case 19(iv)).

If the landlord does not serve a notice so as to obtain possession at the end of the fixed term and the tenancy continues as a periodic tenancy pursuant to a term in the agreement the landlord must ensure that the length of notice given is at least the same as would be required for a notice to quit. The landlord must also serve a notice to quit in prescribed form (see Form 13 on p66) so as to terminate the periodic tenancy.

Form 28: Case 19 notice

Re:

To: A Tenant of [*state address*]

We, [*Landlord Estates Limited*] hereby give you notice that if you do not leave the above premises on the [date that your tenancy of the same expires, namely]   19   proceedings for possession may be commenced under Case 19 of Schedule 15 to the Rent Act 1977 after the expiry of this notice.

This notice expires on   19   .

[*Landlord Estates Limited*]

....

DATED

*Do not include words in brackets where tenant held over at end of fixed term as a statutory tenant.
*Note that it may also be necessary to serve a notice to quit in addition to the notice; see text below.

There would appear to be a potential trap for landlords where the shorthold contains a provision for the tenancy to be continued on a periodic basis, even where the landlord serves his Case 19 notice on the very first day of the three-month period. This is because if the tenant remains in occupation for a period after the end of the term certain, he presumably does so as a periodic tenant, ie as a protected contractual tenant whose contractual tenancy must be determined before proceedings can be commenced (see p139). It is, therefore, suggested that a notice to quit is served together with the Case 19 notice in all cases where the shorthold is one that contains a clause continuing the tenancy as a periodic tenancy.

Tenant's notice   If after expiry of the shorthold the tenancy continues as a periodic tenancy under a term in the agreement and the tenant wishes to leave, he must give such notice as is required by the agreement. If there is no such term, the tenant will become a statutory tenant and he must give notice in accordance with s3 of the Rent Act 1977, which will be the same period as was required when the shorthold was in existence (p137).

After fixed term has expired: forfeiture

If after the end of the fixed term the tenancy continues as a periodic contractual tenancy the forfeiture clause will continue to be a term of the

Form 29: Originating application for possession under Case 19

Title as in Form 35

1.   *I*, [*state name*] of [*state address and occupation of applicant*] apply to the Court for an order for recovery of possession of [*here describe the premises*] under Case 19 of Schedule 15 to the Rent Act 1977.

2.   On [*insert the date of the grant*] the respondent was granted a protected shorthold tenancy of the premises for a fixed term beginning on [*insert the date when the tenancy began*]; and ending on [*insert the expiry date*]; the respondent did not at the time have a protected or statutory tenancy of the premises.

3.   The respondent was given notice in writing, before the tenancy was granted, that it was to be a protected shorthold tenancy.

4.   [*Where necessary*] Before the grant, a rent for the premises was registered on [*insert the date*] or Before the grant, a certificate of fair rent for the premises was issued on [*insert the date*] and the rent payable under the tenancy did not exceed the rent specified in the certificate for any period before the registration of a rent; and an application for the registration of a rent was made on [*insert the date*] and not subsequently withdrawn.

5.   The respondent's protected shorthold tenancy has ended and there is no subsisting protected tenancy in its place; but the respondent remains in occupation.

6.   Notice in writing was given to the respondent on [*state the date when notice was served*] that proceedings for possession under Case 19 might be brought after the expiry of the notice on [*insert the date*].

7.   There are rent arrears in the sum of £ [*state amount*] calculated at the rate of [*here give the weekly or other rent*] and I apply to the Court for an order for payment.

The names and addresses of the persons on whom it is intended to serve this application are [*state names and addresses of persons intended to be served*].

My address for service is [*state applicants address for service*].

DATED

[*signed*]
Applicant

tenancy and if appropriate the landlord may seek to forfeit the lease for breach of a covenant.

Proceedings for possession

Pursuant to a Case 19 notice (see Form 28)

If the notice requirements have been complied with the landlord may recover possession pursuant to Case 19 of Sched 15 to the Rent Act 1977 which was added by s55 of the Housing Act 1980. Proceedings must not be commenced before expiry of the notice, nor more than three months after expiry. The requirement is not merely procedural but is a condition in Case 19 going to jurisdiction and cannot be waived (*Ridehalgh v Horsefield* [1992] EGCS 45, CA).

The proceedings may be commenced by originating application under the Rent Act (County Court Proceedings for Possession) Rules 1981 (SI 1981 No 139) or by action (see Chapter 20). The former procedure should not be used where the landlord intends to ask the court to waive requirements (5) and (6) set out at p191 *above*. The court must make an order for possession and has no power to postpone the effect of the order for more than 14 days or, if exceptional hardship would be caused by such a short order, six weeks (s89 of the Housing Act 1980; p75).

Forfeiture

If the landlord is seeking to rely upon a right to forfeit the tenancy either during the fixed term or during any subsequent periodic tenancy he may do so by bringing an action for possession. The usual rules as to relief against forfeiture apply (see p43) and possession should be claimed pursuant to Case 1 of Sched 15 to the Rent Act 1977. The landlord will have to show that it is reasonable to make the order (s98(1) of the Rent Act 1977).The court will have the usual powers under s100 of the Rent Act 1977 to stay or suspend execution of the order or postpone the date for possession (see p142).

Assignments, sublettings and death

Assignments

Section 54(2) of the Housing Act 1980 provides that a shorthold tenancy (and any subsequent protected or statutory tenancy held by the original shorthold tenant of a dwelling house) cannot be assigned except in divorce proceedings pursuant to a court order for a transfer of property under s24 of the Matrimonial Causes Act 1973. A purported assignee will thus have no tenancy but this section alone will not assist the landlord to obtain possession during the currency of the shorthold term. If during the fixed term the tenant does purport to assign, the landlord should, if there is a clause in the lease prohibiting the tenant from parting with possession, forfeit the lease by serving a notice under s146 of the Law of Property Act 1925 and then commencing proceedings for possession based upon forfeiture and Case 1 of Sched 15 to the Rent Act 1977 for breach of an obligation.

Sub-tenancies

A sub-tenant of a shorthold tenant (or ex-shorthold tenant who has now become a protected or statutory tenant) has no protection against the head landlord, whether or not he is a lawful sub-tenant. Thus if a landlord is entitled to possession of the premises he is entitled to possession as against the tenant and the sub-tenant (s54(1) of the Housing Act 1980).

Form 30: Protected Shorthold—periodic tenancy after fixed term Particulars of claim

---

IN THE   COUNTY COURT   **Case No**

BETWEEN

                                                                    Plaintiff

—AND—

                                                                    Defendant

PARTICULARS OF CLAIM

1.   The Plaintiff is the freehold owner and is entitled to possession of the premises known as [*state address*].

2.   By a agreement in writing dated the [*5th April*] 19[*87*] the Plaintiff let said premises to the Defendant for a term of one year commencing on the [*5th April*] 19[*87*] and expiring on the [*4th April* 19[*88*] at a rent of £ [*state amount*] per month payable in advance on the [*5th*] day of every month. The Defendant did not, at the time of the said grant, have a protected or statutory tenancy of the said premises.

4.   Prior to granting the said tenancy the Plaintiff gave notice in writing to the Defendant that the said tenancy was to be a protected shorthold tenancy within the meaning of the Housing Act 1980.

5.   At the time of the said agreement a rent was registered in respect of the said premises.

   [*not necessary outside Greater London if tenancy commenced on or after 1.12.80 or inside London if tenancy commenced on or after 4 May 1987*]

6.   The said tenancy expired by effluxion of time on the [*4th April*] 19[*88*] and thereafter the Defendant remained in occupation of the said premises as a monthly tenant pursuant to the terms of the said agreement.

7.   The said periodic tenancy was determined by a notice to quit served on the [*4th January*] 19[*94*] which said notice expired on the [*4th April*] 19[*94*].

8.   By a notice in writing served on the Defendant on the [*4th January*] 19[*94*] and expiring on [*4th April*] 19[*94*] the Plaintiff informed the Defendant that proceedings under Case 19 of Schedule 15 to the Rent Act 1977 might be brought after expiry of the said notice.

9.   The said premises are premises to which the Rent Act 1977 applies and possession is claimed pursuant to the provisions of Case 19 of Schedule 15 to the Rent Act 1977.

AND the Plaintiff Claims:

(1)   Possession of the said premises.
(2)   Rent and/or mesne profits at the rate of £ [*state amount*] per month from the date hereof until possession be delivered up.

Death

As the shorthold tenancy is a protected tenancy the Rent Act statutory succession rules apply (see Chapter 8) save that the tenancy to which the successor becomes entitled is an assured shorthold tenancy (s39(7) of the Housing Act 1988).

Chapter 13

Long Tenancies at Low Rent

A tenancy granted for a term of 21 years or more at a rent of less than two-thirds of the rateable value on the appropriate day (usually 23 March 1965) cannot be protected under s1 of the Rent Act 1977 (see s5 of the Rent Act 1977) but that does not mean that the landlord will automatically be able to regain possession at the end of the fixed term. The tenant will be entitled to the protection afforded by Part I of the Landlord and Tenant Act 1954 if the tenant would have been entitled to retain possession of the dwelling house by virtue of the Rent Act, had it not been for the fact that it was let at a low rent. In these circumstances the tenancy is said to satisfy the qualifying condition (s2(1)).

On termination of the fixed term the tenancy will, if the 1954 Act applies, continue as a contractual tenancy at the same rent and on the same terms as before until it is determined by a 1954 Act notice (s3 of the Landlord and Tenant Act 1954). A landlord seeking to recover the property will have to serve 'a notice to resume possession' and then commence proceedings for possession. As appears below the proceedings are brought after service of the notice but before it expires. If in the proceedings the landlord is unable to show that one of a number of specified grounds has been established he will not be entitled to possession and the tenant will continue as a contractual tenant unless the landlord chooses to convert it to a statutory tenancy (see further *below*).

Instead of seeking possession the landlord may accept that the tenant will continue in possession at the end of the fixed term either under a contractual tenancy or as a statutory tenant. To convert it to a statutory tenancy the landlord serves a 'notice proposing a statutory tenancy'. The advantage to the landlord is that the rent can be increased and repairs can be dealt with. If the terms of the statutory tenancy cannot be agreed the landlord may apply to the court for it to determine them (s7 of the Landlord and Tenant Act 1954).

The parties may not exclude the provisions of the 1954 Act (s17), but where it appears that the qualifying condition is not satisfied (eg because the tenant is not in occupation) and is not likely to be satisfied at the end of the lease the landlord may apply to the court, within 12 months of the end of the fixed term, for a declaration that the 1954 Act does not apply (s2(2)). The application is commenced by originating application (CCR Ord 43, r2).

Where the tenancy was entered into on or after 1 April 1990, Sched 10 of the Local Government and Housing Act 1989 applies instead of Part I of the 1954 Act (s186 and s195(2) of the 1989 Act). In short, a long leaseholder becomes an assured tenant at the end of the fixed term. Further, leases entered into before that date will become subject to Sched 10 of the 1989 Act rather than Part I of the 1954 Act if they are still in existence at 15 January 1999 (s186(3) of the 1989 Act).

Termination

By landlord: notice to resume possession

The landlord is defined by s21 of the Landlord and Tenant Act 1954 (as amended) as being that person who has an interest in the reversion expectant on the termination of the tenancy and is either the freehold owner, or has a tenancy which is at least five years longer than the tenancy in question ('the competent landlord'). If the immediate landlord does not satisfy these conditions, the next one up the chain who falls within this definition will qualify as landlord for the purpose of the Act.

In order to terminate the tenancy the landlord must serve a notice in Form 2 of the Landlord and Tenant (Notices) Regulations 1957 (SI 1957 No 1157) (as substituted by the Landlord and Tenant (Notices) Regulations 1967 (SI 1967 No 1831) termed in the Act 'a landlord's notice to resume possession' (s4 of the Landlord and Tenant Act 1954; Form 31, p202. A notice may be given at any time within the 12 months prior to the end of the fixed term or at any time thereafter (s4(1)(2)). A notice given by the competent landlord binds the interests of any other landlord (Sched 2, para 5 of the Landlord and Tenant Act 1954). The notice must specify:

(1) the termination date which will be more than six but less than 12 months after the date of service of the notice and will be the termination date of the fixed term or later (s4(1)(2));

(2) the premises (s4(3));

(3) that if the tenant does not vacate the premises on the termination date the landlord will apply to the county court for possession on one of the following grounds specified by s12 and Sched 3 of the Landlord and Tenant Act 1954 (as amended):

    (a) that suitable alternative accommodation will be available for the tenant at the date of termination of the tenancy;

    (b) that the tenant has failed to comply with any term of the tenancy as to payment of rent, rates or insurance;

    (c) that the tenant (or his sub-tenant or lodger) has been guilty of conduct which is a nuisance or annoyance to adjoining occupiers or has been convicted of using the premises or allowing the premises to be used for illegal or immoral purposes and, if the guilty person is a sub-tenant or lodger, has failed to take reasonable steps to remove him;

(d) that the premises are reasonably required by the landlord for occupation as his residence, or for any son or daughter aged over 18 years, or his father or mother, or his father-in-law or mother-in-law. This ground is only available to an immediate landlord not being a landlord by purchase after 18 February 1966 and taking into account whether greater hardship would be caused by granting possession than by refusing it;

(e) if the landlord is a local authority or other public body specified in s28(5) of the Leasehold Reform Act 1967, that the landlord intends to demolish or reconstruct a substantial part of the premises (s12(1)(a) of the 1954 Act and s38 of the 1967 Act);

(4) that the tenant must notify the landlord in writing, within two months of service of the landlord's notice, whether the tenant is willing to vacate the premises on the termination date.

(5) if a tenant has a right to acquire the freehold or extend the lease pursuant to the Leasehold Reform Act 1967 the notice must state that the tenant must notify the landlord of his desire to exercise this right within two months after service of the notice and contain consequences which follow if he does so (Sched 3, para 10(2) to the Leasehold Reform Act 1967);

(6) the names and addresses of any other persons known or believed by the landlord to have an interest superior to the tenancy (Sched 3, para 10(3)).

By landlord: notice proposing a statutory tenancy

If the landlord does not require possession (or accepts that he is not entitled to possession) but wishes to bring the continuation tenancy to an end and to replace it with a statutory tenancy he may serve a landlord's notice proposing a statutory tenancy (s4(3)(a), s4(5)). The notice must be in Form 1 of the Landlord and Tenant (Notices) Regulations. The notice must include details of various matters including the landlord's proposals in relation to rent and repairs which he requires the tenant to carry out (s7). If the landlord and tenant do not agree terms the landlord must apply to the court for the terms to be determined not later than two months prior to the date of termination specified in the notice. If he fails to do so the landlord's notice will generally cease to have effect. It will not do so if at the end of the period of two months after service of the notice the qualifying condition is not fulfilled unless the tenant has elected to retain possession (s7(2)). If the qualifying condition is not satisfied and the tenant has not elected to retain possession the Rent Act will not apply and the landlord will be entitled to possession (s6(2)).

Termination by tenant

The tenant must give not less than one month's written notice to the immediate landlord to terminate the tenancy on the termination date or later (s5 of the Landlord and Tenant Act 1954).

Possession proceedings following service of a notice to resume possession

Where the tenant fails to notify the landlord within two months of the landlord's notice to resume possession that he is unwilling to give up possession and at the end of two months from service of the landlord's notice the qualifying condition is not fulfilled (for example because the tenant is not in occupation) the tenancy comes to an end on the date specified in the notice and the landlord is entitled to possession (s13(1)).

Where the tenant has notified the landlord that he wishes to retain possession or if, at the end of the period of two months after service of the landlord's notice the qualifying condition is fulfilled, the landlord may apply to the county court for an order for possession under the Act (s13(1) of the Landlord and Tenant Act 1954). The application must be made not later than two months after the tenant elects to retain possession. If he has not made such an election, the application must be made not later than four months after service of the landlord's notice (s13(1)). The application is made by action (CCR Ord 43, r5; see Chapter 20). The particulars of claim must contain details of the land concerned, the rent, the date and term of the original lease, the date of service of the landlord's notice and the termination date specified in the notice, the date of any notice served by the tenant specifying that he does not wish to vacate, and, where the landlord is not both the freeholder and the immediate landlord, details of his qualification as competent landlord and the ground on which possession is claimed (CCR Ord 43, r5(2)).

At the time that he serves the proceedings, or soon thereafter, the landlord should serve the tenant with a notice to produce the notice to resume possession (see Chapter 22, p309).

At the hearing the landlord will have to prove the ground upon which he relies. Except in redevelopment cases the court must be satisfied that it is reasonable to make the order for possession. If an order is made the court has no power to suspend or postpone the date for possession (except in redevelopment cases) but the order will only take effect on termination of the tenancy, ie on the date specified in the landlord's notice as the termination date (s13(3)). Where the landlord's application for possession fails he may offer the tenant a statutory tenancy within one month of the end of the court proceedings to take effect three months from service of the notice (s14(3)). The terms of the statutory tenancy may be agreed between the parties or determined by the court (s7(1)). An application to the court is made by originating application (CCR Ord 43, r2; County Court Form N396). If the landlord does not serve a notice

Form 31: Notice to resume possession—long tenancy at low rent

LANDLORD AND TENANT ACT 1954: LANDLORD'S NOTICE TO RESUME POSSESSION

To   , tenant of premises known as

1.   I,   of   , landlord of the above-mentioned premises, hereby give you notice terminating your tenancy of the said premises on the   day of   , 19   . (*See Notes 4 and 10.*)

2.   You are requested within 2 months after the giving of this Notice to notify me in writing whether you are willing to give up possession of the premises on the said date (*See Notes 5 and 6.*)

Consequences of this Notice if tenant claims the freehold or an extended lease

3.   If you have a right under Part I of the Leasehold Reform Act 1967 to acquire the freehold or an extended lease of property comprised in the tenancy, you must give me notice of your desire to have the freehold or an extended lease not later than 2 months after the service of this Notice; in that event, this Notice will not operate, and I will [*or will not, as the case may be*] be entitled to apply to the county court for possession of the premises under section 17 [*or 18, as the case may be*] of that Act and propose [*or do not propose, as the case may be*] to do so. (*See Note 3.*)

4.   The following are the names and addresses of other persons known or believed by me to have an interest superior to your tenancy or to be the agent concerned with the premises on behalf of a person having such an interest—[*The names and addresses of any such persons should be stated here*] .

Consequences of this Notice if tenant does not claim the freehold or an extended lease

5.   I believe that you are entitled to the protection of Part I of the Landlord and Tenant Act 1954 in respect of the whole of the premises [*or, if part only of the premises qualifies for protection,* in respect of the following part of the premises, namely   ]. (*See Note 2.*)

6.   If you are not willing to give up possession of the premises on the   day of   , 19   , I propose to apply to the county court for possession of the premises on the ground that [*here state ground or grounds*]. (*See Notes 7 and 8.*)

7.   This Notice is given under the provision of section 4 of the Landlord and Tenant Act 1954.

Your attention is called to the Notes below.

Dated this   day of   , 19   .

       Signed   .... (Landlord)
             ....(Address)
             ....

FORM 2

NOTES

1.   Part I of the Landlord and Tenant Act 1954, as amended by the Leasehold Reform Act 1967 provides that a tenant of residential premises under a tenancy granted for more than 21 years at a rent which is less than two-thirds of the rateable value of the premises shall, at the end of the period of the original tenancy, be entitled to continue as a tenant on the same terms as before unless he terminates the tenancy himself or it is terminated by the landlord in accordance with the provisions of the Act. For purposes of the Act the rateable value is normally that shown in the valuation list on 23 March 1965; the rateable value of the premises must not, however, have exceeded £400 in Greater London or £200 elsewhere.

2.   The tenant's right to remain in occupation is confined to parts of the premises which he occupies at the end of the original tenancy.

contc

contd

3. Your rights under Part I of the Landlord and Tenant Act 1954 are in addition to, and distinct from, any right you may have under the Leasehold Reform Act 1967 to acquire the freehold or an extended lease of the premises. Any such right must, however, be exercised by service of the appropriate notice (in the form prescribed by the Leasehold Reform (Notices) Regulations 1967) within two months of the giving of this Notice. As a general rule, a person has such a right if:

    (a) he has his only or main residence in a house which he occupies under a tenancy granted for more than 21 years at a rent which is less than two-thirds of its rateable value;
    (b) he has so occupied the house for at least the previous 5 years or a total of 5 out of the previous 10 years; and
    (c) the house has a rateable value not exceeding £400 in Greater London, or £200 elsewhere.

4. The landlord may terminate the tenancy by notice given not more than 12 nor less than 6 months before the date of termination specified in the notice. The date must not normally be earlier than the date on which the original tenancy expires.

5. If you are willing to give up possession of the premises comprised in the tenancy, you should notify the landlord to that effect within 2 months of the giving of this Notice and vacate the premises on the date of termination specified in it. Failure to notify the landlord may lead to an unnecessary application to the county court and consequent expense, which you may have to bear.

6. If you are not willing to give up possession of the premises comprised in the tenancy you should within 2 months after the giving of this Notice notify the landlord to that effect. This will ensure that you do not lose the right conferred by the Landlord and Tenant Act 1954 to remain in possession unless the landlord obtains an order for possession of the premises from the county court. If you fail to notify the landlord and are not in occupation of the premises 2 months after the giving of this notice, you may lose the protection of the Act. If you fail to notify the landlord but are in occupation 2 months after the giving of this notice, you will not lose that protection.

7. The grounds on which a landlord may apply for possession are—

(i)   that suitable alternative accommodation will be available for the tenant at the date of termination of the tenancy;
(ii)   that the tenant has failed to comply with any term of the tenancy as to payment of rent or rates or as to insuring or keeping insured any premises;
(iii)   that the tenant or a person residing or lodging with him or being his sub-tenant has been guilty of conduct which is a nuisance or annoyance to adjoining occupiers, or has been convicted of using any premises comprised in the tenancy or allowing such premises to be used for an immoral or illegal purpose and, where the person in question is a lodger or sub-tenant, that the tenant has not taken such steps as he ought reasonably to have taken for the removal of the lodger or sub-tenant;
(iv)   that the premises, or any part of them which is entitled to protection under the Act, are reasonably required by the landlord for occupation as a residence for himself or any son or daughter of his over 18 years of age or his father, mother, father-in-law or mother-in-law. But the court is precluded from making an order for possession on this ground where the landlord's interest was purchased or created after 18 February 1966, or where it is satisfied that having regard to all the circumstances of the case, including the question whether other accommodation is available for the landlord or the tenant, greater hardship would be caused by making the order than by refusing to make it;
(v)   in certain cases where the landlord is a public body, that for the purposes of redevelopment relevant to its functions the landlord proposes after the termination of the tenancy to demolish or reconstruct the whole or a substantial part of the premises.

The landlord must state in this Notice on which of these grounds he proposes to apply for possession .

contd

---

contd

8.   The landlord may apply to the county court for an order for possession on any of the grounds listed above which he has stated in this Notice. In order to succeed in his application he must establish that ground and also, except where he is applying on ground (v) above, satisfy the court that it is reasonable that he should be granted possession. You will be given the opportunity to state your case before the court if you wish to resist the landlord's application.

9.   Should the landlord fail in his application for possession this Notice will lapse, but he will then be at liberty to serve a fresh notice on you proposing the new terms on which your tenancy is to continue, and it will be open to you and the landlord either to agree the terms or to have them determined by the court or the rent officer, as appropriate.

10.   The term 'landlord' for the purposes of this Notice does not necessarily mean the landlord to whom you pay the rent; it means the person who is your landlord for the purposes of Part I of the Act.

Reproduced by kind permission of The Solicitors' Law Stationery Society Ltd

proposing a statutory tenancy the original notice to resume possession ceases to operate and the original contractual tenancy continues.

Forfeiture proceedings

In addition to his usual right to claim relief against forfeiture the tenant may also rely upon s16 of the Landlord and Tenant Act 1954. Where the tenant has made an application in the forfeiture proceedings for relief and the court makes an order for possession at any time up to seven months before the end of the fixed term the order is automatically suspended for 14 days. Within that period the tenant may give the landlord and the court a notice in writing that he desires that the order for possession should have no effect except if and in so far as it provides for the payment of costs and that he desires the tenancy thereafter to have effect as if it had been granted for a fixed term expiring at the end of seven months from the making of the order. The effect of serving the notice is that at the end of the seven months the tenant will no longer have a fixed term but will continue in possession under a s3 continuation tenancy. If the landlord wishes to obtain possession he will have to serve a notice to resume possession and show that one of the 1954 Act grounds applies (s16(1), (2)). These provisions will not apply where the landlord is forfeiting on the basis that the tenant is in breach of any term of the lease relating to the payment of rent or rates, insurance of the premises, or use of the premises for immoral or illegal purposes (s16(4)).

   If the tenant has applied for relief, the court may not make any order for possession in the last seven months of the fixed term unless the landlord is forfeiting for breach of one of the terms referred to in s16(4) (s16(3)).

   Special provisions apply where proceedings are brought by a superior landlord (Sched 5, para 9 to the Landlord and Tenant Act 1954).

Possession proceedings in respect of statutory tenancies

Where a landlord wishes to claim possession of any long tenancy at a low rent that has been converted to a statutory tenancy he may do so by relying on any of the grounds for possession in the Rent Act 1977 save that the landlord cannot proceed on the basis of non-payment of rent, breach of any obligation of the tenancy and nuisance or user for illegal or immoral purposes which occurred prior to the termination of the contractual tenancy (s10(2) of the Landlord and Tenant Act 1954). However, two additional grounds are available, namely the failure of the tenant to pay any sums due to the landlord for repairs carried out by the landlord necessitated by the tenant's previous failure to comply with his repairing obligations (Sched 1, para 17 to the Landlord and Tenant Act 1954) and failure by the tenant to carry out repairs which he has agreed or the court has ordered him to do (Sched 2, para 4 to the Landlord and Tenant Act 1954).

Chapter 14

Employees, Premises with a Business Use and Company Lets

Employees

Where an employer allows an employee to occupy residential premises it will usually be very inconvenient for the employer's business if at the end of the period of employment he is unable to recover possession of the dwelling house. The consequence is that many such employees are licensees who have no interest in the property. Even where the employee is a tenant the tenancy will often not be assured under the Housing Act 1988 or, as the case may be, regulated under the Rent Act 1977 because no rent is payable or because the rent payable is too low. Certain employees of local authorities and other public sector bodies are not secure tenants. Where the premises are licensed the employee who lives on the premises will not be a protected, assured or secure tenant. Even where the employee is an assured or regulated tenant there is a special ground for regaining possession. All these situations are discussed in this chapter.

The position of workers in the agricultural sector is discussed in Chapter 15.

Licensees

In Chapter 5 we saw how the House of Lords in *Street v Mountford* [1985] 2 All ER 289 reaffirmed the traditional view that, save for certain limited exceptions, an occupier of residential premises for a term at a rent is to be regarded as a tenant if he has been granted exclusive possession of the accommodation. One of the exceptions occurs where the occupier is a 'service occupier'. It was said in *Street v Mountford* at 294b:

> A service occupier is a servant who occupies his master's premises in order to perform his duties as a servant. In those circumstances the possession and occupation of the servant is treated as the possession and occupation of the master and the relationship of landlord and tenant is not created . . . The test is whether the servant requires the premises he occupies in order to better perform his duties as a servant.

For example, in *Thompson (Funeral Furnishers) Ltd v Phillips* [1945] 2 All ER 49 the plaintiffs employed the defendant as a chauffeur. It was a term of the contract of employment that the defendant would live on the premises owned by the plaintiffs. The contract contained the following clause: 'Either I or someone else will be on the premises at all times to take orders, answer messages, or answer enquiries for you. I will vacate the premises immediately I cease to be in your employment'. Fifteen shillings was deducted from the defendant's wages in respect of his use and occupation of the premises. It was held that 'the substance of the agreement with the [plaintiffs] was that he was to occupy those premises as their servant or agent, *in order to perform his services in part of those premises*, and that it was, therefore, a service occupancy and not a service tenancy' (*per* Lawrence LJ).

Where there is no express term requiring the employee to occupy the premises for the better performance of his duties the court will not imply such a term unless there are compelling reasons for so doing (*Hughes v Greenwich London BC* [1993] 4 All ER 577, HL; no such term implied in the contract of a headmaster living on premises in the school grounds because it was not essential that he should live in the house in order to do his job).

> In my opinion, the only way in which the term which the appellant council need to imply here could be implied into the contract would be to show that, unless he lived in the Cedars, Mr Hughes could not perform his duties as headmaster . . . In order that a term may be implied, there has to be a compelling reason for deeming that term to form part of the contract, and that compelling reason is missing in this case, unless it was essential that Mr Hughes should live in the house in order to do his job, but the facts found contradict that proposition. Once the principle . . . is accepted, it becomes pointless for the appellant council to argue that a requirement must be implied in a contract just because in fact for Mr Hughes to live in Cedars may have promoted (or even did promote) the better performance of his duties . . . (*Hughes v Greenwich LBC*, *per* Lord Lowry at 583e and 584a).

If the employee is not required to live on the premises for the better performance of his duties he will be a tenant and if the agreement as properly construed is a tenancy it will be held to be such, whatever the label the parties put on it (see *Facchini v Bryson* [1952] 1 TLR 1386; a case where the employee was 'permitted' to occupy the premises rather than required to do so for the purpose of the employment; and *Street v Mountford* at 296d).

See Chapter 5 for the termination of licences and Chapter 9 for the protection afforded to the licensee if the licence is a restricted contract.

Relationship with the contract of employment   A right of occupation expressed to be granted for a period of employment creates a contractual licence which is ancillary to the contract of employment and, being ancillary, comes to an end when the contract of employment is terminated even if the employee is wrongfully dismissed, ie in breach of contract (*Ivory v Palmer* [1975] ICR 340). It is not, therefore, necessary to serve a notice to quit in accordance with s5 (1A) of the Protection from Eviction Act 1977 which only applies to *periodic* licences (*Norris v Checksfield* [1991] 4 All ER 327; see p95 *above*).

An employee may, however, have a right to claim re-instatement under the Employment Protection (Consolidation) Act 1978 where the dismissal was unfair. The court may adjourn the possession action where the employee has made a claim for unfair dismissal to an industrial tribunal in order to see the outcome of that application but not if substantial delay would result (*Elias v King* [1981] CAT 541).

However, in *Whitbread West Pennines Ltd v Reedy* (1988) 20 HLR 642 the employer stated that it would not re-instate the employee even if he were to succeed in his claim for unfair dismissal and that it would rather pay an additional amount of compensation under the Employment Protection (Consolidation) Act 1978. The Court of Appeal held that the action for possession should not be adjourned and that the employer was entitled to an order for possession.

Tenancies where the employee pays no rent or a low rent: see Appendix 1

Quite often employees who are provided with accommodation by their employers either pay a low rent or even no rent at all. If no rent is payable or the rent payable is less than two-thirds of the rateable value of the premises *on 'the appropriate day'* the employee although he may be a tenant will not be protected under the Rent Act 1977 (see s5). To constitute rent the payments made by the employee to the employer must be monetary. Money's worth is usually insufficient (*Barnes v Barratt* [1970] 2 QB 657; *Heslop v Burns* [1974] 1 WLR 1241). Where, however, the rent is paid by the provision of a service the value of which is quantified in terms of money by agreement between the parties the sum so quantified is the 'rent' and if that sum is greater than two-thirds of the rateable value of the premises the tenancy will be protected. (See *Montagu v Browning* [1954] 1 WLR 1039; the wages of the tenant, who was a caretaker, were deducted from the rent payable. It was held that the amount deducted was rent.) Note that even if the tenancy was at a low rent it may nevertheless be a restricted contract (see Chapter 9)

Where the tenancy was granted between 15 January and 31 March 1990 (or pursuant to a contract made between those dates) the tenancy will not be *assured* if under the tenancy 'either no rent is payable or the rent payable is less than two-thirds of the rateable value *for the time being*' (Sched 1, para 3, para 14 to the 1988 Act). Where the tenancy was granted on or after 1 April 1990 (otherwise than pursuant to a contract made before that date) the tenancy is not assured if the property is in

Greater London and the rent is £1,000 or less per year or the property is elsewhere and the rent is £250 or less per year (para 3A).

Local authority and other public sector employees

The fact that an employee of a local authority was a licensee would not of itself prevent him from being a secure tenant of a dwelling house provided by his employer (s79(3) of the Housing Act 1985; see p161). However, a tenancy is not a secure tenancy if the tenant is an employee of the landlord or, if not such an employee, is an employee of a local authority, a new town corporation, an urban development corporation, a development corporation, the Development Board for Rural Wales or the governors of an aided school and his contract of employment requires him to occupy the dwelling house for the better performance of his duties (Sched 1, para 2 to the Housing Act 1985; see p457). See also para 2 in relation to policemen and firemen.

Where an employee who has a secure tenancy (because his contract of employment does not require him to occupy the dwelling for the better performance of his duties) agrees new terms under which he is required to occupy the dwelling for the better performance of his duties his tenancy will cease to be secure (*Elvidge v Coventry City Council* [1993] 4 All ER 903, CA; water bailiff promoted to assistant ranger with additional duties requiring him to live in the park at the accommodation already provided).

Licensed premises

A tenancy of a dwelling house which consists of or comprises premises licensed for the sale of intoxicating liquor for consumption on the premises cannot be protected or statutory (s11 of the Rent Act 1977) or assured (Sched 1, para 5 to the Housing Act 1988).

The landlord, therefore, need only determine the tenancy by the common law rules (see Chapters 2 and 3) and he will then be able to obtain an order for possession. It will usually be employees who will be affected by this exception but it will obviously also apply to any tenant of a dwelling house on licensed premises who is not an employee of the landlord. Note that the exception applies to all 'on-licences' and therefore will include restaurants and wine bars but not 'off-licences'.

If the landlord is a local authority or other public sector body within s80 of the Housing Act 1985 (see p102) the tenancy will not be a secure tenancy (Sched 1, para 9 to the Housing Act 1985).

Regulated tenancies: premises required for a new employee (Case 8)

Where a tenant protected under the Rent Act 1977 was in the employment of the landlord (or a former landlord) *and* the dwelling house was let to him in consequence of that employment *and* he has ceased to be in that employment the landlord may obtain possession of the dwelling house after the tenancy has been determined if he can show that the dwelling house is reasonably required at the date of the hearing either:

    (1) for occupation as a residence for some person engaged in the landlord's whole time employment or in the whole time employment of one of the landlord's tenants; or

    (2) as a residence for some person with whom, conditional on housing being provided, a contract for employment as a whole time employee has been entered into.

The landlord must also satisfy the court that it is reasonable to make the order for possession (s98(1) of the Rent Act 1977).

The following points should be noted:

    (1) it does not matter that the tenant did not know that the premises were being let to him in consequence of his employment. It is the landlord's intention at the date of the letting which is relevant;

    (2) the landlord and the employer must be the same person at the grant of the tenancy but if the landlord changes and the tenant remains in the employment of the original landlord the present landlord may nevertheless rely upon Case 8 of Sched 15 to the Rent Act 1977 (*Duncan v Hay* [1956] 1 WLR 1329);

    (3) Case 8 will not apply where the tenant was employed by the landlord and one or more other persons jointly and severally. Thus if the tenant is employed by two partners, but only one of the partners is the landlord, Case 8 will not apply; or where the landlord is a director of the company employing the tenant (see *Evans v Engelson* (1979) 253 EG 577);

    (4) if the tenant remains in possession after he ceases to be an employee the landlord does not lose his right to claim under Case 8. The landlord may not, for example, immediately require the premises for another employee and the continued acceptance of rent does not prejudice his position; nor necessarily does an increase in rent (*Lever Bros v Caton* (1921) 37 TLR 664). Even if the employee dies the landlord may rely upon this Case against any person who has succeeded him as a statutory tenant (*Bolsover Colliery Co v Abbott* [1946] KB 8; *Railway Executive v Botley* (1950) 155 EG 110). If, however, the landlord and tenant either expressly or by implication enter into a new tenancy agreement the landlord will not be able to rely upon Case 8 because the new tenancy will not have been entered into 'in consequence' of the earlier employment (*J & F Stone Lighting & Radio Ltd v Levitt* [1945] 2 All ER 268);

    (5) it is not necessary for the new employee to have actually commenced work at the date of the hearing. It is sufficient that the date for commencement contained in his contract of employment

has arrived (*Fuggle (RF) Ltd v Gadsden* [1948] 2 KB 236). Thus if the new employee has not been able to start on time because he has been ill or because he has been on holiday the landlord will still be able to obtain an order evicting the old tenant if all the other requirements are satisfied.

Case 8 does not apply to agricultural workers (s99 of the Rent Act 1977).

Assured tenancies: dwelling let in consequence of employment

Where the tenancy is an assured tenancy under the Housing Act 1988 and the dwelling house was let to the tenant in consequence of his employment by the landlord seeking possession or by a previous landlord under the tenancy and the tenant has ceased to be in that employment the landlord may rely upon Ground 16 of Sched 2 to the 1988 Act as a ground for possession. This is a discretionary ground and so the court must be satisfied that it is reasonable to make the order (s7(4)). The procedure for determining assured tenancies is dealt with in Chapter 6.

Note that it is not necessary for the landlord to show that he requires the dwelling house for a new employee before the ground for possession applies. However, the court may decide not to exercise its discretion in favour of making an order if the dwelling is not so required.

Premises with a business use

This part of the chapter is concerned with the position of the tenant of a dwelling house which is used partly for residential and partly for business purposes. A number of different situations may arise. A shop with a flat above may be let together, a doctor may use his front room as a surgery, or a businessman may run his business from home. In each case the tenant may either be a 'business tenant' in which case his security of tenure will be governed by the Landlord and Tenant Act 1954, Part II, or, depending upon the date the tenancy was granted, a regulated tenant under the Rent Act 1977 or an assured tenant under the Housing Act 1988 (or in the public sector a secure tenant protected under the Housing Act 1985).

The private sector—is the tenant an assured/regulated tenant?

Subject to a few transitional cases, a tenancy of a dwelling house let prior to the commencement of the Housing Act 1988 (15 January 1989) is capable of being a regulated tenancy under the Rent Act 1977 and a tenancy of a dwelling house created on or after that date is capable of being an assured tenancy under the 1988 Act (see pp106 and 132). The rules for governing whether or not the tenancy is a 'residential' tenancy (ie regulated or assured) or a 'business' tenancy are the same whether the tenancy was granted before or after that date. There are two stages in deciding whether the tenant is a residential tenant or a business tenant. First, it is necessary to look at the purpose of the letting and, secondly, it is necessary to look at the purpose of the tenant's occupation.

The purpose of the letting   Unless the dwelling house was let as a separate dwelling it cannot be the subject of regulated (assured) tenancy as it will not fall within the definition of a protected tenancy set out in s 1 of the Rent Act 1977 and thus will be incapable of becoming a statutory tenancy on termination (or of an assured tenancy within s 1 of the Housing Act 1988). Hence, a dwelling house which is let so that the tenant may carry on a business from the premises is not 'let as a dwelling' even if the tenant in fact lives there. It is the purpose of the letting that is paramount. The relevant time for ascertaining the purpose is the date of the letting unless there is a subsequent agreement (*Russell v Booker* (1982) 263 EG 513).

In the leading case of *Wolfe v Hogan* [1949] 2 KB 194 at 204 Denning LJ explained how one goes about ascertaining the purpose of the letting.

> In determining whether a house or part of a house is 'let as a dwelling' within the meaning of the Rent Restriction Acts, it is necessary to look at the purpose of the letting. If the lease contains an express provision as to the purpose of the letting, it is not necessary to look further. But if there is no express provision, it is open to the court to look at the circumstances of the letting. If the house is constructed for use as a dwelling house, it is reasonable to infer that the purpose was to let it as a dwelling, but if, on the other hand, it is constructed for use as a lock-up shop, the reasonable inference is that it was let for business purposes. If the position were neutral, then it would be proper to look at the actual user. It is not a question of implied terms. It is a question of the purpose for which the premises were let.

Note that if the lease contains covenants against use as a dwelling house it could not have been let as a dwelling, but the fact that there are covenants that simply preclude use of the premises for any trade other than those specified in the lease does not necessarily mean that the premises are solely let for the purpose of a business.

If the premises are let for a mixed business/residential purpose they will be treated as having been let for the business purpose unless the business purpose is merely incidental to the residential purpose so that s 23(1) of the 1954 Act would not apply (see *below*) *Cheryl Investments Ltd v Saldanha* [1978] 1 WLR 1329; *Webb and Barrett v London Borough of Barnet* (1989) 21 HLR 228.

Where the premises are let for a business purpose but the tenant subsequently gives up the business use and merely lives there the letting does not become regulated/assured. This is because the premises were not originally 'let as a dwelling' (*Pulleng v Curran* (1982) 44 P&CR 58; *Trustees of Henry Smith's Charity v Wagle* (1989) 21 HLR 177).

The purpose of the tenant's occupation   Once it has been established that the purpose of the letting was residential and that any business purpose was merely incidental, it is then necessary to look at the purpose of the actual occupation. This is because s24 of the Rent Act 1977 provides that the tenancy is not a regulated tenancy where Part II of the Landlord and Tenant Act 1954 applies. Similarly, para 4 of Sched 1 to the 1988 Act provides that a tenancy cannot be assured if Part II of the 1954 Act applies. Section 23(1) of the 1954 Act provides that Part II applies:

> to any tenancy where the property comprised in the tenancy is or includes premises which are occupied by the tenant and are so occupied for the purpose of a business carried on by him or for those and other purposes.

Thus, even if the premises were let wholly for residential purposes the tenancy will not be regulated/assured if the purpose of the tenant's occupation is a business one. In *Cheryl Investments Ltd v Saldanha* [1978] 1 WLR 1329, however, it was held that it is only where the business purpose is a *significant* purpose that the 1954 Act will apply. If the business purpose is merely *incidental* to the residential purpose (eg if a person works at home in the evenings: see *Saldanha*, Lord Denning's first example at 1333) the Rent Act 1977 or the Housing Act 1988 will continue to be applicable. The purpose of the tenant's occupation is a question of fact to be decided by the judge on the evidence. The term 'business' includes 'a trade profession or employment' (s23(2) of the Landlord and Tenant Act 1954) and whether any particular activity is a business is also a question of fact to be decided in the light of all the circumstances (see *Lewis v Weldcrest* [1978] 1 WLR 1107 where it was held that a tenant who took in five lodgers at very low rents that provided very little profit was not carrying on a trade).

A tenancy is not within the 1954 Act if it is a fixed term of six months or less unless there is a clause in the lease providing for an extension or renewal or unless the tenant (or any predecessor in the business) has been in occupation for more than 12 months (s43(3)). Periodic tenancies where the period is less than six months are, however, within the 1954 Act. There are also other exceptions (see s43).

The time for deciding whether the premises are being occupied for a business purpose is the date that the contractual tenancy would have come to an end. Furthermore, it would appear that if the dwelling house was let as a separate dwelling but ceased to be regulated at some stage because it was used for a business purpose the tenancy will once again become regulated if the business occupation ceases unless in the meantime a new tenancy has been granted under the 1954 Act (see *Pulleng v Curren* (1982) 44 P&CR 58; *Webb and Barrett v London Borough of Barnet* (1989) 21 HLR 228).

It should also be noted that if the tenancy is not within the 1954 Act (perhaps because it was originally granted for a term of less than six months) the tenancy nonetheless cannot be a statutory tenancy within the meaning of s2 of the Rent Act 1977 after the protected tenancy has been determined if the tenant occupies the premises wholly for the purpose of a business (see p 134). (See s64(2) of the Housing Act 1980 for any tenancy that was a controlled tenancy on 22 November 1980.) Nor can such a tenancy be assured because the tenant will not be occupying the property as his only or principal home (s1(1)(*b*) of the Housing Act 1988).

The public sector—is the tenant a secure tenant?

As with the private sector it is necessary to go through a two-stage process. This is because s97 of the Housing Act 1985 provides that a tenancy is not capable of being a secure tenancy unless the dwelling house was let as a dwelling. Secondly, para 11 of Sched 1 to the 1985 Act provides that a tenancy is not a secure tenancy if it is one to which Part II of the 1954 Act applies. For an example in the public sector, see *Webb and Barrett v London Borough of Barnet* (1989) 21 HLR 228.

Business premises within the 1954 Act

If the tenancy does fall within the 1954 Act rather than the Rent Act 1977, Housing Act 1988, or the Housing Act 1985 the tenant may be entitled to a new tenancy under Part II of the 1954 Act (see *Possession of Business Premises*, Practitioner Series; by the author).

Business premises outside the 1954 Act

Where the premises are not protected by the Rent Act 1977, the Housing Act 1988, the Housing Act 1985 or the 1954 Act the ordinary common law rules will apply (see Chapters 2 and 3).

Company lets

General

A tenancy of a dwelling house let to a company (prior to the commencement of the Housing Act 1988) will be a *protected* tenancy provided that the conditions of s1 of the Rent Act 1977 are fulfilled. Upon the termination of the protected tenancy, however, the company tenant will not become a *statutory* tenant entitled to security of tenure as there can be no personal occupation of the premises by a company as required by s2 of the Rent Act 1977 (*Firstcross Ltd v East West (Export/Import) Ltd* (1980) 255 EG 355). A director or manager of the company tenant who was occupying the premises as his residence does not become a statutory tenant because he was not the protected tenant immediately prior to the termination of the protected tenancy (*Hiller v United Dairies (London) Ltd* [1934] 1 KB 57).

Section 1(1)(*a*) of the Housing Act 1988 provides that a tenancy will not be an *assured* tenancy unless the tenant, or where there are joint tenants each of them, is an individual. A tenancy granted to a company may not therefore be an assured tenancy.

Where a company permits its employees to occupy the premises, Part II of the Landlord and Tenant Act 1954 will not apply to the company's tenancy unless it is necessary for the employees to live there in order to carry out their duties properly (see *Chapman v Freeman* [1978] 3 All ER 878).

If a company tenant sublets to an individual, the sub-tenant may be able to remain in possession pursuant to s137(2) of the Rent Act 1977 at the end of the company's tenancy (see p145) or, as the case may be, pursuant to s18(1) of the Housing Act 1988 (p117).

'Sham' company lets

In many cases tenancies have been granted to companies for the sole purpose of avoiding the Rent Acts. In *Hilton v Plustitle Ltd* [1988] 3 All ER 1051 the landlord's advertisement for a tenant made it clear that the letting was to be a company let. At the landlord's suggestion the intending occupier, a Miss Rose, purchased a company 'off the shelf' for the specific purpose of taking the tenancy. The tenancy was then granted to the company. The judge found as a fact 'that it was both parties' clear intention with all knowledge of what this involved that the flat should be let to a company and not to Miss Rose personally'. The Court of Appeal held that the tenancy was not a 'sham' and that the company was truly the tenant. (For a similar case see *Estavest Investments v Commercial Express Travel Ltd* (1989) 21 HLR 106.)

However, *Hilton v Plustitle* was decided before the decision of the House of Lords in *Antoniades v Villiers* [1988] 3 All ER 1058 in which 'shams' in relation to licences were discussed (see p91). In *Antoniades v Villiers* (see Lord Templeman at 1067j) and in *Aslan v Murphy (Nos 1 and 2)* [1989] 3 All ER 130 it was held that it is not necessary for the court to come to the conclusion that an agreement is a 'sham' before disregarding its terms. Even where the agreement is not a 'sham' the court will consider whether in the light of the factual situation its provisions were part of the true bargain between the parties or were a pretence intended to evade the Rent Acts.

Subsequently, in *Kaye v Massbetter Ltd* [1991] 2 EGLR 97, CA Lord Donaldson said that there was nothing to stop the parties agreeing a company let provided it was a genuine one and that '[t]he test is: was the letting genuine? If you look at the facts and find that there are indicia that the company was never intended to be the tenant, then you may conclude that it was not genuine. But the issue is simply one of genuineness' (p98K). He emphasised that it 'is in the end entirely a question of fact'.

In his judgment Nicholls LJ said:

> [Counsel for the defendant] submitted that, if the only purpose for which a company was introduced onto the scene and into a residential letting

arrangement such as that involved here was to avoid the Rent Acts, the resultant tenancy agreement is not a genuine letting to the company.

I cannot accept that proposition as an accurate statement of the law. The issue in every case involves seeing what, in law, was the agreement between the parties. This involves identifying who in law were the parties to the agreement. In this regard the terms of a document signed by the parties or the form of words used by them in an oral agreement are, of course, not conclusive. Parties cannot contract out of the Rent Acts and the court wi l be astute in detecting and frustrating shams or pretences, namely, agreements expressed in a form which do not truly reflect the parties' intention. Thus, the purpose for which and the circumstances in which the company is introduced onto the scene are very important background facts. But it by no means follows that, a company having been introduced, the parties did not intend in law that the company should be the tenant and liable as such to the landlord.

The conclusion to be drawn from the cases would therefore seem to be that it is not necessary for the defendant to show that the agreement, in naming the company as a tenant, is a sham (whatever precisely that means). It will be sufficient for the defendant to show that it is a pretence. However, if the court is satisfied that the company is genuinely the tenant the 'company let' will stand even though the intention was to avoid letting to an individual who would have had statutory protection.

Chapter 15

Agricultural Accommodation

There are six different situations that may arise when one is dealing with what might be called 'agricultural accommodation'. These are as follows:
  (1) premises on agricultural land leased to a farmer—Agricultural Holdings Act 1986;
  (2) premises occupied by farmworkers who are not protected tenants but who are protected under the Rent (Agriculture) Act 1976;
  (3) assured agricultural occupancies under the Housing Act 1988;
  (4) premises occupied by farmworkers under protected tenancies—s 99 and Sched 16 of the Rent Act 1977;
  (5) a residual category of farmworkers who have protection under s 4 of the Protection from Eviction Act 1977;
  (6) premises occupied by ordinary protected tenants that were once occupied by farmworkers—Sched 15, Cases 16, 17 and 18 of the Rent Act 1977.

Agricultural holdings

A tenancy is not a protected, assured or secure tenancy if the dwelling house is *comprised* in an agricultural holding (within the meaning of the Agricultural Holdings Act 1986) and is occupied by the person responsible for the control (whether as tenant or as servant or agent of the tenant) of the farming of the holding (s 10 of the Rent Act 1977; Sched 1, para 7 of the Housing Act 1988; Sched 1, para 8 of the Housing Act 1985).

The expression 'agricultural holding' is defined in s 1 of the Agricultural Holdings Act 1986. It means the aggregate of the land (whether agricultural land or not) comprised in a contract of tenancy (as defined in s 1(5)) which is a contract for an agricultural tenancy. A contract of tenancy relating to land is 'a contract for an agricultural tenancy' if having regard to:
  (1) the terms of the tenancy;
  (2) the actual or contemplated use of the land at the time of the conclusion of the contract and subsequently; and
  (3) any other relevant circumstances;

217

the whole of the land comprised in the contract, subject to such exceptions only as do not substantially affect the character of the tenancy, is let for use as agricultural land (s 1 of the Agricultural Holdings Act 1986). 'Agricultural land' means:

(1) land used for agriculture which is so used for the purposes of a trade or business, and

(2) any other land which, by virtue of a designation under s 109(1) of the Agriculture Act 1947, is agricultural land within the meaning of that Act.

'Agriculture' is defined as including horticulture, fruit growing, seed growing, dairy farming and livestock breeding and keeping, the use of the land as grazing land, meadow land, osier land, market gardens and nursery grounds, and the use of land for woodlands where that use is ancillary to the farming of land for other agricultural purposes; and 'livestock' includes any creature kept for the production of food, wool, skins or fur or for the purpose of its use in the farming of land or the carrying on in relation to land of any agricultural activity (s 96(1) of the Agricultural Holdings Act 1986).

Where the dwelling house is comprised in an agricultural holding the tenant of the holding will enjoy the security of tenure provided by the Agricultural Holdings Act 1986. A discussion of the protection that is afforded to tenants who farm agricultural holdings is beyond the scope of this book. Putting it very briefly the landlord will usually only be ab e to regain possession of the land, in the face of the tenant's objection, f he can prove one of a number of grounds set out in the Agricultural Holdings Act 1986. Most of these grounds relate to agricultural issues.

If the tenant of the holding has himself let a dwelling house comprised in the holding to a farmer who is responsible for the control of the farming the farmer will not be a protected, assured or secure tenant either. He may, however, be protected under the Rent (Agriculture) Act 1976, Chapter III of the Housing Act 1988 or the Protection from Eviction Act 1977 (see *below*).

Rent (Agriculture) Act 1976

Application of the Act: protected occupiers

The purpose of the Rent (Agriculture) Act 1976 is to provide protection to farmworkers living in tied accommodation who are not protected under the Rent Act 1977.

The provisions governing whether a person is protected are s 2 and Scheds 2 and 3 to the 1976 Act. They are detailed and complicated and should be referred to in every case. The following is an attempt to g ve a simplified definition which should cover the situation in most cases. The 1976 Act applies where a person occupies a dwelling house and the following three conditions are satisfied:

(1) the agreement under which he occupies is a 'relevant licence or tenancy'. A 'relevant licence' is one which, if it were a tenancy, would be a protected tenancy under the Rent Act 1977 if it were not for the fact that it would be a tenancy at a low rent or a tenancy comprised in an agricultural holding. A 'relevant tenancy' is a tenancy which would be protected under the Rent Act 1977 if it were not for one of those facts. (See also Sched 2, para 3(3) for cases where board or attendance is provided);

(2) the landlord is the occupier's employer (or ex-employer) or someone with whom his employer (or ex-employer) has made arrangements for the dwelling house to be used by persons employed in agriculture;

(3) the occupier is or has been employed whole time in agriculture for a period of 91 weeks out of any period of 104 weeks during the subsistence of his licence or tenancy.

Where the above conditions are satisfied the occupier is termed a 'protected occupier in his own right' (s2(4)).

The above conditions cannot generally be satisfied where the tenancy was created on or after 15 January 1989 (commencement of the Housing Act 1988). Since that date it has not been possible (except in a few limited transitional cases: see s34 of the 1988 Act, p132) to create protected tenancies. See p221 'Assured agricultural occupancies'.

Statutory tenants

On determination of the protected occupancy, by whatever means, the protected occupier becomes a 'statutory tenant in his own right', and remains so as long as he occupies the dwelling house as his residence (s4(1) of the Rent (Agriculture) Act 1976). A statutory tenancy may arise by the payment and acceptance of rent following upon the determination of a rent for the tenancy by the rent officer (*Durman v Bell* (1988) 20 HLR 340). Use by the tenant of the property for significant business use (in addition to residential use) does not result in an automatic termination of the statutory tenancy, although it may give rise to a ground for possession if the tenant is acting in breach of a term of the tenancy (*Durman v Bell*). For the terms of the statutory tenancy see s10 and Sched 5. Where the protected occupancy was a licence the statutory tenancy will be a weekly tenancy (Sched 5, para 3).

Where a person is a licensee because he was required to occupy the dwelling for the better performance of his duties he becomes a statutory tenant on the termination of his employment if thereafter he remains in possession paying rent (*Burgoyne v Griffiths* [1991] 1 EGLR 14, CA).

A person cannot, however, be a statutory tenant at any time when his landlord is the Crown (unless the dwelling house is under the management of the Crown Estate Commissioners), one of a number of public bodies referred to in s5(2),(3) or a housing association registered under the Housing Associations Act 1985 or is a housing co-operative association within the meaning of that Act (s5).

Termination and recovery of possession

The procedure for termination and recovery of possession of the dwelling house is very similar to the procedure that applies where the tenancy is a protected or statutory tenancy under the Rent Act 1977. If the agreement under which the protected occupier occupies is a licence it is determined in accordance with the terms of the agreement by a notice in prescribed form. If it is a tenancy it is determined by notice to quit, forfeiture etc. It may also be converted to a statutory tenancy by service of a notice of increase in rent under s16 of the Rent (Agriculture) Act 1976. As with 1977 Act statutory tenancies it is not necessary to serve a notice to quit to determine a statutory tenancy that arises under the 1976 Act after termination of a protected occupancy (s6(2)). Hence, once the protected occupancy has been brought to an end the landlord should simply commence proceedings for possession. The court will not make an order for possession except in the cases mentioned in Sched 4 to the 1976 Act. There are 13 cases. Cases I–X are discretionary grounds for possession and the court may not make an order for possession unless it considers it reasonable to do so (s7(1), (2)). Cases XI, XII and XIII are mandatory grounds for possession and if the landlord proves that one of these cases applies the court must make an order for possession (s6(6)).

The discretionary grounds—Cases I–X
    I Alternative accommodation provided by a person or body other than the local authority.
    II Alternative accommodation provided or arranged by local authority (Note the local authority's duty to rehouse under s27.)
    III Arrears of rent or breach of other obligation of the tenant.
    IV Nuisance, annoyance, immoral or illegal user.
    V Deterioration of the dwelling house.
    VI Deterioration of the furniture.
    VII Tenant's notice to quit.
    VIII Assigning, subletting or parting with possession without consent.
    IX Dwelling house reasonably required by landlord.
    X Overcharging sub-tenants.

The mandatory grounds
    XI Owner-occupiers.
    XII Retirement homes.
    XIII Overcrowded dwelling houses.

Proceedings are commenced by county court summons (see Chapter 20). The originating application procedure set out in the Rent Act (County Court Proceedings for Possession) Rules 1981 (SI 1981 No 139) which may be used where the landlord is relying on one of the mandatory grounds set out in Sched 15 to the Rent Act 1977 (see p264) is not available to landlords relying on one of the mandatory grounds set out in Sched 4 to the 1976 Act.

Where the court makes an order for possession under one of the discretionary grounds the court may stay or suspend execution of the order, or postpone the date for possession for such period or periods as the court thinks fit (s7(3)). On any such stay, suspension or postponement the court must, unless it considers that to do so would cause exceptional hardship to the tenant or would otherwise be unreasonable, impose conditions with regard to the payment of arrears of rent (if any) and rent or payments in respect of occupation after termination of the tenancy (mesne profits) and may impose such other conditions as it thinks fit (s7(4)). If the conditions imposed are complied with, the court may if it thinks fit discharge or rescind the order for possession (s7(5)).

Where the order for possession is made under one of the mandatory grounds the court may only postpone the date for possession for a maximum of 14 days unless exceptional hardship would be caused by such a short order in which case the court may postpone the effect of the order for up to six weeks (s89 of the Housing Act 1980; p75).

Subletting, bankruptcy and death

See s9 of the 1976 Act and section 137 of the Rent Act 1977 for the effect upon a sub-tenant of an order for possession against the tenant and for the position on the determination of a head tenancy either as a result of such an order or otherwise. (Compare the position of protected or statutory sub-tenants: p145.)

For the position on the bankruptcy of the tenant see s283(3A) and s308A of the Insolvency Act 1986 (as introduced by s117 of the Housing Act 1988) (see generally p83).

Section 3 and s4(3), (4) relate to succession on death of the protected occupier or statutory tenant but note that these provisions have been amended by s39 and Sched 4 of Part II of the Housing Act 1988. In particular, the tenancy becomes an assured agricultural occupancy on succession (s39(8) of the Housing Act 1988).

Assured agricultural occupancies: Housing Act 1988

We are here concerned with tenancies and licences created on or after 15 January 1989 (the date of the commencement of the Housing Act 1988). Since that date it has not been possible (except in some limited cases—see p132) to create protected tenancies and therefore it has not been possible to become a protected occupier under the 1976 Act (see *above*). Instead persons who would have been protected occupiers under the 1976 Act now become 'assured agricultural occupiers' under the 1988 Act.

Assured agricultural occupancies are treated as if they are assured tenancies for the purposes of applying Chapter I of the Housing Act 1988. The provisions relating to notices and recovery of possession that apply to assured tenancies (see Chapter 6) therefore apply (subject to some modification) in relation to an assured agricultural occupancy whether the occupant is a tenant or licensee and if he is a tenant whether or not he is an assured tenant (s24(3) of the 1988 Act).

Definition of assured agricultural occupancies

In order for a tenancy or licence to be an assured agricultural occupancy two conditions must be fulfilled: (1) the tenancy/licence condition; and (2) the agricultural worker condition (s24(1)). Where a statutory periodic tenancy arises on the coming to an end of an assured agricultural occupancy it remains an assured agricultural occupancy as long as the agricultural worker condition continues to be satisfied (s25(1)(a)), and, if no rent was payable under the fixed term, as a monthly occupancy (s25(1)(b)).

(1) *The tenancy/licence condition: s24(2)* This condition is fulfilled if the tenancy or licence is:

(a) an assured tenancy (see p103) which is not an assured shorthold tenancy (p121);

(b) a tenancy which would be an assured tenancy (other than a shorthold) but is not an assured tenancy by reason only of para 3, 3A or 3B (tenancies at a low rent) and/or para 7 (tenancy of agricultural holding) of Sched 1 to the 1988 Act (ie the list of exceptions: see p104 and Appendix 1); or

(c) a licence under which a person has exclusive possession of a dwelling house as a separate dwelling and which if it were a tenancy would be a tenancy falling within (a) or (b) above.

(2) *The agricultural worker condition: s24(1) and Sched 3 to the 1988 Act* The 'agricultural worker condition' is fulfilled with respect to a relevant tenancy or licence if:

(a) the dwelling house is or has been in 'qualifying ownership' at any time during the subsistence of the tenancy or licence (whether or not it was at that time a relevant tenancy or licence); and

(b) the occupier or, where there are joint occupiers, at least one of them:

(i) is a qualifying worker or has been a qualifying worker at any time during the subsistence of the tenancy or licence (whether or not it was at that time a relevant tenancy or licence); or

(ii) is incapable of 'whole time work' in agriculture or work in agriculture as a permit worker in consequence of a qualifying injury or disease (Sched 3, para 2).

(The various terms used here have the same meanings that they have in Sched 3 to the Rent (Agriculture) Act 1976, and para 1 of Sched 3 to the 1988 Act.)

Where a tenancy/licence is granted to a person in consideration of his giving up possession of a dwelling house in respect of which the agricultural worker condition was fulfilled the agricultural worker condition is deemed to be fulfilled in respect of the second property (Sched 3, para 4).

Termination and recovery of possession: s25

As stated in the introduction to this section the provisions relating to assured tenancies for termination and recovery of possession (see Chapter 6) apply (subject to modification) to assured agricultural occupancies. The modifications are as follows:

(1) Ground 16 (dwelling house let in consequence of employment) is omitted from Sched 2 (the grounds for possession).

(2) Part III of Sched 2 (suitable alternative accommodation) is amended so that the reference in para 2 of that Part to an assured tenancy includes a reference to an assured agricultural occupancy.

Note that a notice by a *tenant* under an assured agricultural occupancy to terminate his *employment* cannot constitute a notice to quit as respects the occupancy. Only an actual notice to quit in proper form (see p69) will be sufficient (s25(4), (5)).

The provisions of s27 of the Rent (Agriculture) Act 1976 relating to rehousing by local authorities apply to assured occupants (s26 of the 1988 Act).

Bankruptcy and death

Bankruptcy   As with assured tenancies s283(3A) of the Insolvency Act 1986 (as introduced by s117 of the Housing Act 1988) applies; see further p83.

Death   Schedule 3 to the 1988 Act contains provisions providing for the 'agricultural worker condition' (see *above*) to be satisfied on the death of the original occupier thus providing for succession of the agricultural occupancy. The persons who may be entitled to succeed are the occupier's widow, widower or a member of his family. There can only be one succession (Sched 3, para 3).

Farmworkers who are protected or statutory tenants

Section 99 and Sched 16 of the Rent Act 1977 ensure that farmworkers who are protected or statutory tenants have the same protection as protected occupants or statutory tenants as defined by the Rent (Agriculture) Act 1976. If it were not for these provisions the alternative accommodation grounds would not apply.

For s99 to apply the following conditions must be satisfied:

(a) the tenancy must be a protected or statutory tenancy within the meaning of ss1 and 2 of the Rent Act 1977; and

(b) the tenancy must be such that, if it were a tenancy at a low rent and if (where relevant) any earlier tenancy granted to the tenant or to a member of his family had been a tenancy at a low rent, it would be a protected occupancy or statutory tenancy as defined in the Rent (Agriculture) Act 1976.

If the tenancy does fall within the s99 jurisdiction the court may not make an order for possession unless the court considers it reasonable to make such an order, and the circumstances are as specified in Cases 1–6, 9 and 10 of Sched 15 to the Rent Act 1977 (ie all the discretionary grounds except Case 8), or either of the two cases in Sched 16 (see below). In these circumstances the court may stay or suspend execution of the order or postpone the date for possession for such period or periods as the court thinks fit (s100 of the Rent Act 1977). Proceedings are commenced by action. The landlord can also apply for possession if the circumstances are as specified in Cases 11–15, 19 and 20 of Sched 15 (ie all the mandatory grounds except 16, 17 and 18). In these circumstances the court must make an order for possession which can only be suspended for 14 days (or six weeks in cases of exceptional hardship) s89 of the Housing Act 1980 pp75–76. Proceedings for possession may be commenced by action or, in certain cases, application. (See Chapter 20.)

Schedule 16 is concerned with the circumstances in which suitable alternative accommodation is available. Case 1 is where the accommodation is *not* to be provided or arranged by a housing authority and Case 2 is where it is. Schedule 16 is in the same form as Cases I and II of Sched 4 to the Rent (Agriculture) Act 1976 which is dealt with above.

Protection from Eviction Act 1977, s4

Where a farmworker is not a regulated tenant under s1 of the Rent Act 1977 nor an assured agricultural occupant under Chapter III of the Housing Act 1988 nor a protected occupant or statutory tenant under the Rent (Agriculture) Act 1976 he will probably be entitled to the fairly limited protection of s4 of the Protection from Eviction Act 1977 To qualify for this protection the farmworker must show that he occupied the premises under the terms of his employment as a person employed in agriculture as defined in s1 of the Rent (Agriculture) Act 1976 (s4 of the Protection from Eviction Act 1977). Both tenants and licensees fall within this definition (s38(2) of the Rent (Agriculture) Act 1976; and see s4(2A) of the 1977 Act). The farmworker's widow (or widower) is also entitled to rely upon s4 if that person was residing with him at his death.

If the farmworker leaves no widow or widower any member of his family residing with him at his death may rely upon s1 (s4(2)).

Section 4(3) gives the courts a discretionary power to suspend the execution of an order for possession, if it is made within the period of six months beginning with the date when the former tenancy or licence came to an end, for the remainder of the six months unless:

(1) the court is satisfied either:

(a) that suitable accommodation is or will be made available within that period;

(b) the efficient management of any agricultural land or the efficient carrying on of any agricultural operations will be seriously prejudiced unless the premises are available for another person employed or to be employed by the owner;

(c) that greater hardship would be caused by the suspension of the order than by its execution;

(d) that the occupier or any person residing with him has caused damage to the premises or has been a nuisance or annoyance to persons occupying other premises; and

(2) the court considers that it would be reasonable not to suspend the execution of the order.

Where the court suspends the order for possession it must do so on such terms and conditions including conditions as to payment of arrears of rent, mesne profits and otherwise as the court thinks reasonable (s4(5)).

In considering whether or how to exercise its powers to suspend execution of the order the court must have regard to all the circumstances of the case and in particular whether the efficient management of any agricultural land or the efficient carrying on of any agricultural operations would be seriously prejudiced unless the premises were available for someone employed by the owner, whether suitable alternative accommodation is available, and whether greater hardship would be caused by a suspension than an immediate order (s4(8)). An order for costs should not be made where the order for possession is suspended unless, having regard to the conduct of the parties, there are special reasons for making such an order (s4(8)).

Agricultural accommodation presently occupied by non-agricultural protected tenants (Sched 15, Cases 16, 17 and 18 of the Rent Act 1977)

This part of the chapter is concerned with the situation where the tenant is an ordinary protected or statutory tenant who would not be a protected occupant or statutory tenant under the Rent (Agriculture) Act 1976 even if the tenancy were a tenancy at low rent (ie a tenant who is not a farmworker). The landlord may, of course, rely upon any of the discretionary or mandatory grounds set out in Sched 15 to the Rent Act

1977, but Part II of that Schedule includes three grounds for possession that are of particular relevance in the agriculture sector (Cases 16, 17 and 18).

These three cases apply where the dwelling house has in the past been occupied by a person engaged in agriculture and where the landlord wishes to regain possession from the present tenant so that it can once again be occupied by a person engaged in agriculture. None of these three cases will apply unless the landlord gave the tenant notice in writing stating that possession might be recovered under the relevant case not later than the 'relevant date' (usually the date the tenancy commenced; see Sched 15, Part III, para 2). The notice does not have to be in any particular form (*Springfield Investments Ltd v Bell* [1991] 1 EGLR 115, CA; a certificate of fair rent which stated that it was proposed to let the dwelling 'on a regulated tenancy basis subject to the provisions of Case 16 . . . (whereby repossession could be obtained to house an agricultural worker, employed or to be employed by the Landlord)' was held to be sufficient). There is no power to dispense with the notice even if it is just and equitable to do so. Each ground is a mandatory ground and so if a notice was given and the case applies the court must make an order for possession which may not be suspended for more than 14 days (or six weeks in case of exceptional hardship) (s89 of the Housing Act 1980; see p75). The landlord may commence proceedings by originating application or summons (see Chapter 20).

Chapter 16

Student Accommodation, Holiday Accommodation, Board and Attendance

Student accommodation

Lettings to students

A student may, like anyone else, occupy premises under an assured or regulated tenancy, a secure tenancy, a restricted contract or a completely unprotected tenancy or licence. If he does so he will usually have the same protection, or lack of it, as all other tenants or licensees in a similar position.

Where, however, a tenancy is granted to a person who is pursuing, or intends to pursue, a course of study provided by a 'specified educational institution' and it is granted either by that institution or by another specified institution or body of persons the tenancy cannot be assured or protected even though it would normally fall within the definition of an assured or a protected tenancy (Sched 1, para 8 to the Housing Act 1988; s8 of the Rent Act 1977). The institutions and bodies specified are the universities and their colleges, and the colleges of further education. A number of other institutions and bodies are also specified. (See Assured and Protected Tenancies (Lettings to Students) Regulations 1988 (SI 1988 No 2236) as amended.)

Thus, once the tenancy has come to an end the educational institution will be able to regain possession without having to show one of the usual Rent Act/Housing Act 1988 grounds.

It is not usually necessary for the educational institution to own the freehold of the premises in question for the exception to apply. It may take a lease of private premises and then sublet those premises to the student. The student's landlord will thus be a specified educational institution and the tenancy will not be assured/protected. Once the lease has been determined the college will be able to obtain an order for possession but the owner will not be able to do so without first determining the college's lease (see *St Catherine's College v Dorling* [1980] 1 WLR 66).

Vacation lettings of student accommodation

If a college or other specified educational institution wishes to let a dwelling house which is usually let to students to someone else on an assured tenancy during the vacation period, without losing its right to recover possession at the end of the tenancy, it may do so by complying with Ground 4 of Sched 2 to the Housing Act 1988. In order to comply with the requirements of this case the dwelling house must be let for a fixed term of 12 months or less, and:

(1) not later than the date the tenancy is entered into the landlord must give notice in writing to the tenant that possession might be recovered under Ground 4 (see Part IV of Sched 2 in relation to notices); and

(2) at some time within the period of 12 months ending with the beginning of the tenancy (see s45(2)) the dwelling house must have been the subject of a tenancy falling within para 8 of Sched 1 to the 1988 Act, ie granted to a student by a specified educational institution.

Although the tenancy must be for a fixed term it may contain a forfeiture clause and a clause allowing the tenant to serve a notice to quit.

If the dwelling house is in fact privately owned but let to the college during the term time (pursuant to an agreement between the owner and the college) the owner will be able to rely on this ground himself, and thus will be able to let out the premises during the vacation without the fear of becoming saddled with an assured tenant. This follows from the wording of Ground 4 which requires that 'the landlord' give the appropriate notice which may therefore be either a college or a private owner.

If the landlord, whether it be a college or private owner, satisfies the court that the conditions in Ground 4 have been complied with, the court must make an order for possession as this ground is one of the mandatory possession grounds (s7(3) of the Housing Act 1988). The court may only suspend the order for possession for up to 14 days, or in the case of exceptional hardship, six weeks (s89 of the Housing Act 1980). The accelerated possession procedure is available (p75).

Lettings to students by local authorities, housing associations and other public sector bodies (Sched 1, para 10 to the Housing Act 1985)

If the landlord is a local authority, or other public sector body mentioned in s80 of the Housing Act 1985 and s35(4) of the Housing Act 1988 the tenant will usually be a secure tenant like any other tenant of that body (see Chapter 10). A tenancy of a dwelling house is not a secure tenancy, however, if:

(1) the tenancy was granted for the purpose of enabling the tenant to attend a 'designated course' (see Secure Tenancies (Designated

Courses) Regulations 1980 (SI 1980 No 1407) at a university or other establishment for further education; and
(2) before the grant of the tenancy the landlord notified the student in writing about this exception and the fact that it would apply. The notice must specify the relevant educational establishment.

The tenancy continues to be 'unsecure' from the date of its grant until six months after the end of the course; but if the tenant fails to take *a* designated course at *the* educational establishment specified in the notice the exception only applies for six months. If the tenancy is not brought to an end within either of these periods the tenant will become a secure tenant. The tenancy will also become secure before the expiry of either six-month period if the landlord notifies the tenant that it is to be regarded as a secure tenancy.

Holiday accommodation

The Housing Act 1988 contains two sets of provisions dealing with the question of holiday accommodation. First, it provides that a dwelling house let for the purpose of a holiday will not be subject to an assured tenancy. Secondly, it contains a provision permitting the landlord of a dwelling house used for the purpose of a holiday during the holiday season to let it out on an assured tenancy in between holiday periods and yet recover possession at the end of the term.

Holiday lets

A tenancy will not be an assured tenancy if the purpose of the tenancy is to confer on the tenant the right to occupy the dwelling house for a holiday (Sched 1, para 9 to the Housing Act 1988). Whether that is the purpose is a question of fact which, in the absence of anything in the tenancy agreement regarding the purpose of the tenancy, is determined according to the evidence given in court. Where there is a written agreement containing a term expressly stating that the dwelling house was let for the purpose of a holiday that term is evidence of the parties' intention, and unless *the tenant* can show that the statement is in the nature of a sham or a pretence the court will hold that the tenancy is not an assured tenancy (*Buchmann v May* [1978] 2 All ER 993; cf licence cases: see p91). On the other hand, a landlord who grants successive 'holiday lets' to tenants who he knows are clearly not going to use the premises for the purpose of a holiday is likely to find that the tenants will be assured tenants.

Once the holiday let has come to an end the landlord will be entitled to an order for possession the effect of which the court will not be able to postpone for more than 14 days, or six weeks in cases of exceptional hardship (s89 of the Housing Act 1980; see p75). As the tenancy is an 'excluded tenancy' he need not even take proceedings for possession and may resort to self-help so long as he does not use any violence (see pp 255–259).

Out of season lettings

Ground 3 of Sched 2 to the Housing Act 1988 is the provision that gives the owner of holiday accommodation the opportunity to let the dwelling house on an assured tenancy out of season without the danger of the tenant being able to remain in possession at the end of the term. Ground 3 provides that at the end of the tenancy the landlord will be entitled to possession of the dwelling house if:

(1) the dwelling house was let for a fixed term of eight months or less; and

(2) not later than the day on which the tenancy is entered into the landlord gave the tenant notice in writing that possession might be recovered on this ground (see Sched 2, Part IV for rules relating to notices, in particular para 2); and

(3) the dwelling house was at some time within the period of 12 months ending with the 'beginning of the tenancy' (see s45(2)) occupied under a right to occupy it for a holiday.

The tenancy is for a fixed term notwithstanding that it contains a right of reentry or a term allowing it to be determined upon the happening of any event (for example, service of a notice to quit by the tenant) other than the giving of notice by the landlord to determine the term.

If Ground 3 applies the court must make an order for possession (s7(3) of the 1988 Act). The effect of the order may not be postponed for more than 14 days, or six weeks in cases of exceptional hardship (s89 of the Housing Act 1980; see p75). The accelerated possession procedure may be used.

Board or attendance

Where the landlord provides attendance or services which require him or his servants to exercise unrestricted access to and use of the premises the occupier will be a lodger, ie a licensee, and not a tenant (see *Street v Mountford* [1985] 2 All ER 289, discussed at p00). However, even if the occupier is a tenant his tenancy cannot be protected under s1 of the Rent Act 1977 if under the tenancy the dwelling house is *bona fide* let at a rent which includes payments in respect of board or attendance (s7(1) of the Rent Act 1977). There is no equivalent provision in the Housing Act 1988 relating to tenancies granted on or after the commencement date of that Act (15 January 1989).

Board

'Board' is not defined but it is commonly understood to mean the provision of meals. The board provided must be more than minimal if the

Form 32: Particulars of claim—holiday let

IN THE   COUNTY COURT   Case No

BETWEEN

                                         Plaintiff

                     — AND —

                                         Defendant

PARTICULARS OF CLAIM

1. The Plaintiff is the [*freehold/leasehold*] owner and is entitled to possession of a dwelling house known as [*state address*].

2. By a agreement in writing dated . . . the Plaintiff let said dwelling house to the Defendant for a term of . . . months commencing on the . . . at a rent of [£] per month.

3. The said tenancy expired on the . . . but the Defendant has failed to give up possession of the said dwelling house to the Plaintiff and continues in occupation without the licence or consent.

4. The purpose of the said tenancy was to confer on the Defendant the right to occupy the said dwelling house for a holiday. In the premises the Defendant is not entitled to the protection afforded by the Housing Act 1988.

AND the Plaintiff claims:

(1) Possession of the said premises.
(2) Mesne profits at the rate of [£] per month ([£] per day) from the date hereof until possession be delivered up.

DATED

---

tenancy is to escape protection but it need be no more than that (*Otter v Norman* [1988] 2 All ER 897, HL; a 'continental breakfast' consisting of two bread rolls with butter, jam and marmalade, and unlimited tea or coffee with sugar and milk, held to constitute 'board'). Where the board is more than minimal the tenancy will be a restricted contract unless one of the exceptions set out in s 19(5) of the Rent Act 1977 applies. One of those exceptions is that the value of the board to the tenant forms a substantial proportion of the whole rent (s 19(5)(*c*) of the Rent Act 1977; see p 159).

Attendance

Where the rent includes payments in respect of attendance the tenancy will only be excluded from protection if 'the amount of rent which is fairly attributable to attendance, having regard to the value of the attendance to the tenant, forms a substantial part of the whole rent' (s 7(2) of the Rent Act 1977). 'Attendance' is a service personal to the tenant performed by an attendant provided by the landlord in accordance with his covenant for the benefit or convenience of the individual tenant in his use or enjoyment of the dwelling house. Any service that is common to the other tenants in a building, such as the heating of a communal water supply or the provision of a porter, is not personal to the tenant and so, although it is a service, it is not 'attendance' (*Palser v Grinling* [1948] AC 291).

The provision of clean bed linen and towels is attendance (*Nelson Developments Ltd v Taboada* [1992] 2 EGLR 107 at 108G).

To be 'substantial' the attendance provided must be more than that which is just sufficient to avoid the *de minimis* principle, but whether the amount of the rent that is attributable to attendance is substantial is a question of fact to be decided by the judge according to the circumstances of each case (*Palser v Grinling*; see also *Marchant v Charters* [1977] 1 WLR 1181). The date at which one assesses the situation is the date of the commencement of the tenancy (*Nelson Developments Ltd*; rent subsequently reduced by rent officer, but the issue was determined on the basis of the rent paid at the commencement of the tenancy).

If, because of the attendance provided, the tenancy is not a protected tenancy it will be a restricted contract unless one of the exceptions set out in s 19(5) of the Rent Act 1977 applies (see Chapter 9).

Chapter 17

Mobile Homes

Security of tenure for the owner of a mobile home situated on land belonging to another person is governed by the Mobile Homes Act 1983 and the Caravan Sites Act 1968. The Mobile Homes Act 1983 governs the terms of the agreement whereby the mobile home owner is allowed to station his home on that land. If it were not for this Act the mobile home owner would normally only be a licensee of the part of the site upon which the home is situated (see *Taylor v Calvert* [1978] 1 WLR 899). The Caravan Sites Act 1968 protects the owner of the mobile home from eviction without a court order, and from harassment. It also provides for suspension of court orders.

The term 'mobile home' means 'any structure designed or adapted for human habitation which is capable of being moved from one place to another (whether by being towed, or by being transported on a motor vehicle or trailer) and any motor vehicle so designed or adapted but does not include (a) any railway rolling stock which is for the time being on rails forming part of a railway system, or (b) any tent' (s5(1) of the 1983 Act and s29(1) of the Caravan Sites and Control of Development Act 1960). A houseboat on a river moored to a verge of a caravan site does not fall within the definition (*Roy Crimble Ltd v Edgecombe* (1981) 131 NLJ 928). A chalet which is capable of being moved from one place to another does fall within the definition (*Wyre Forest District Council v Secretary of State for Environment* [1990] 1 All ER 780).

The Mobile Homes Act 1983 applies to those entitled by agreement to station mobile homes which they intend to be their only or main residence on land forming part of a 'protected site' (s1 of the 1983 Act). Land forms part of a protected site when it is licensed for the purpose (or it is land which would be licensed if it were not owned by a local authority) under Part I of the Caravan Sites and Control of Development Act 1960 (see s5(1) of the 1983 Act, s1 of the Caravan Sites Act 1968 and *Balthasar v Mullane* (1985) 17 HLR 561).

In some circumstances land cannot be a protected site. Those circumstances are as follows (s5(1) of the 1983 Act and s1(2) of the 1968 Act):

(1) land occupied by the local authority as a caravan site providing accommodation for gypsies (see *London Borough of Greenwich v Powell* (1989) 21 HLR 218; the character of the site is determined by the purpose of the council in occupying it and not the character of those in occupation);

(2) land for which planning permission or a site licence is granted for holiday use only; and

(3) land for which permission or a licence is granted subject to conditions that there are times of the year when no caravan may be stationed there for human habitation (eg *Weeks v Bradshaw* [1993] EGCS 65; residential occupation forbidden in February of each year).

The residents of the mobile home are referred to in the 1983 Act as 'occupiers' and the mobile home site owner as 'the owner' (s1(1)). The Act applies regardless of when the agreement to occupy was made (s1(3)), whether it is a lease or licence, and whether or not it is for a fixed or a periodic term (see the words 'any agreement' in s1(1)); but the Act probably does not apply to agreements entered into otherwise than for valuable consideration (*Balthasar v Mullane* (1985) 17 HLR 561).

The Mobile Homes Act 1983 and CCR Ord 49, r13, which applies to applications made under the Act, are to be found together in Part II of the *Green Book*, 1994).

The agreement

The Mobile Homes Act 1983 affords the occupier some security by implying into the agreement a number of important terms, for example terms relating to termination, and by requiring the owner to provide the occupier with a written statement of the agreement. The implied terms have effect notwithstanding any express term of the agreement and whether or not a written statement has been given as required (s2(1) and Part I of the Schedule to the Act; *Barton v Care* [1992] 2 EGLR 174 at 175G, CA).

The owner is required to give the occupier the written statement within three months of the making of the agreement to occupy the site (s1(2) of the 1983 Act). The statement must set out various items, including the implied terms, and must be in prescribed form (s1(2); Mobile Homes (Written Statement) Regulations 1983 (SI 1983 No 749). If the owner fails to comply with this requirement the occupier may apply to the court for an order requiring the owner to provide the statement (s1(5)).

In addition to the terms which are statutorily implied, the court may, on application by either party within six months of the giving of the statement, order certain other terms to be implied; that is, terms relating to quiet enjoyment, rent, services provided, maintenance and repair of the mobile home and site, preservation of amenity of the site and access by the owner to the land on which the mobile home is sited (s2(2) and

Part II of the Schedule). Either party may also apply within the period of six months from the giving of the written statement for any express term to be varied or deleted (s2(3)). On any application to imply terms or to vary express terms the court will make such provision as it considers 'just and equitable in the circumstances' (s1(4)). The six-month time limit for making an application for the implication, or variation of terms, under s2 where a written statement was given by the owner outside the three-month time limit, either by virtue of a court order under s1(5) or voluntarily, begins to run from the date upon which the written statement was given (*Barton v Care*).

The agreement may specify that an arbitrator be appointed to act rather than the court. An arbitrator's decision is not appealable on findings of fact. Review of any decision must be made by the High Court. If there is no agreement regarding arbitration, the court will be the county court for the district in which the site is situated (s5(1) of the Mobile Homes Act 1983).

Duration of the agreement

The right to station a mobile home on land forming part of a protected site subsists until the agreement is determined in accordance with the rules for termination set out below (Sched 1, para 1). However, where the owner's estate or interest is insufficient to enable him to grant the right for an indefinite period the period for which the right subsists cannot extend beyond the date when the owner's estate or interest determines (para 2(1)). If planning permission for the use of the site for mobile homes expires at the end of a specified period the period for which the right subsists cannot extend beyond the date when the planning permission expires (para 2(2)). Where in either case there is a change in circumstances which allows a longer period account is taken of that change (para 2(3)).

Termination

Termination by owner

The owner must apply to the county court (or arbitrator) for an order terminating the agreement on one or more of the three grounds specified by paras 4, 5 and 6 of Sched 1, Part I to the Mobile Homes Act 1983:

(1) Breach of a term of the agreement—the owner must satisfy the court that the occupier has breached a term of the agreement and that after service of a notice to remedy the breach the occupier has failed to comply with the notice within a reasonable time. The court must also consider it reasonable for the agreement to be terminated.

(2) The court is satisfied that the occupier is not occupying the mobile home as his only or main residence. The relevant date for

determining whether the occupier is or is not occupying the mobile home as his only or main residence is the date on which the application to terminate is heard and not the date when the site owner applies to the court for the termination of the agreement (*Omar Parks Ltd v Elkington* [1993] 1 All ER 282, CA).

(3) The court is satisfied that the mobile home is having a detrimental effect on the amenity of the site or is likely to do so due to its age and condition within the next five-year period. The owner must apply at the end of each five-year period to the court for authority to terminate the agreement under this ground.

If an agreement is terminated under one of these three grounds the occupier may recover any rent paid for the period after termination. If the owner applies for termination to the county court, he must apply to the court which has jurisdiction for the area in which the mobile home is situated (s5(1)); but if he applies in the wrong court the proceedings are not regarded as a nullity and CCR Ord 16, r2 will apply (see p263) so that the court may either transfer the proceedings, leave them where they are or strike them out (*Faulkner v Love* [1977] QB 937). Application is made by originating application (CCR Ord 49, r13(1); Ord 3, r4; see Form 33), and the respondent is required to file an answer (CCR Ord 49, r13(1)). The District Judge may hear and determine the proceedings and they can be dealt with in chambers (CCR Ord 13, r13(2)). Where approved by the court an order may be made for termination of the agreement forthwith.

Termination by occupier

The occupier is entitled to terminate the agreement by giving at least four weeks' notice in writing (Sched 1, Part 1, para 3 of the Mobile Homes Act 1983).

Proceedings for possession

If the occupier refuses to remove his mobile home after the agreement has come to an end an order excluding the occupier from the land upon which it is situated is still required and the court has power to suspend the order for up to 12 months (ss3(1)(*b*) and (4) of the Caravan Sites Act 1968). The application to exclude may be made with the application to terminate (CCR Ord 49, r13(3)).

Where the order for possession is suspended, the court may impose such terms and conditions as it thinks reasonable (s4(2) of the Caravan Sites Act 1968). The court may on the application of either party extend, reduce or terminate the suspension (s4(3) of the Caravan Sites Act 1968) and in deciding whether to do so will have regard to all the circumstances and in particular will consider whether the occupier has failed to observe any terms or conditions of the agreement, whether the occupier has unreasonably refused an offer by the owner to renew the agreement or to make another agreement for a reasonable period and on reasonable terms, and also whether the occupier has failed to make reasonable efforts to obtain elsewhere other suitable accommodation (s4(4) of the Caravan Sites Act 1968). If the court suspends any order excluding the occupier from the site there will be no order for costs unless the court considers that there are special reasons having regard to the conduct of either party (s4(5) of the Caravan Sites Act 1968).

Assignment and death

The occupier may sell his mobile home and assign his agreement to a person approved by the owner and the owner must not unreasonably withhold his approval (Sched 1, Part 1, para 8 of the Mobile Homes Act 1983). He may also give the mobile home, and assign the agreement, to a member of his family approved by the owner, whose approval shall not be unreasonably withheld (para 9).

Consent should be requested before assignment and the occupier should wait a reasonable time for approval to be given. If the approval is refused or simply not given within a reasonable time the occupier can make an application to the court for a declaration that the refusal is unreasonable or the purchaser can take a risk and accept the assignment without consent. If an assignment takes place without the owner's consent it will be effective unless the court subsequently finds that the owner's refusal was reasonable or, in the case of the assignment taking place before the owner's response to the request, that the owner was not given a reasonable period of time to respond to the request for consent (s3(2); *Ron Grundy (Melbourne) Ltd v Boneheyo* [1993] 1 All ER 282 at 287h). A transfer fee not exceeding 10 per cent of the sale price is payable to the owner: the Mobile Homes (Commission) Order 1983 (SI 1983 No 748).

If the owner dies the agreement is binding on any successor in title (s3(1) of the Mobile Homes Act 1983).

On the death of the occupier, if the occupier's widow or widower is residing with the occupier at the time of death, the benefit and burden of the agreement will pass to him or her. If there is no widow or widower, the agreement will pass to any member of the deceased's family who was so resident. The successor need not occupy the mobile home and may assign but the owner must approve any assignee, such approval not to be unreasonably withheld. The owner may charge a transfer fee which cannot exceed 10 per cent of the sale price. If there is no member of the family the agreement will pass to the person entitled to the mobile home under the deceased's will or intestacy but the beneficiary will not be able to live in the mobile home unless the owner is willing to enter into a new agreement. He may, however, assign on the same terms as above (s3(4) of the Mobile Homes Act 1983).

Form 33: Originating application for termination of mobile homes agreement

IN THE   COUNTY COURT   Case No

BETWEEN

                                                        Applicant

—AND—

                                                        Respondent

ORIGINATING APPLICATION

1. [*state name of applicant*] of [*state address and occupation of Applicant*] applies to the Court for an order in the following terms:

(1) That the agreement dated [*insert the date*] and made between the Applicant and the Respondent be terminated forthwith; and

(2) That the Respondent be excluded from the site mentioned hereunder.

The grounds upon which the Applicant claims to be entitled to the order are:

1. The Applicant is the owner of [*state name and address of site*] ('the site').

2. The Respondent is the occupier of the mobile home situated on   of the site. The Respondent commenced his residence at the site on [*insert date*] under a written agreement dated [*insert date*].

3. It was an express term of the said agreement that a rent of [*state rent*] per week be paid in advance on Monday of each week, and that the mobile home be kept in good repair.

4. In breach of the said express terms the rent is now £ [   ] in arrear and the Respondent has failed to keep the mobile home in good repair in that

(a) the windows are broken

(b) the door is covered with graffiti

(c) . . .

5. By a notice served on [*insert date*] the Applicant required the Respondent to remedy the said breaches within 21 days but the Respondent has failed to comply with the notice.

7. Furthermore, the Respondent is not occupying the mobile home as his only or main residence, in that he resides permanently at [*state address*].

The names and address of the persons on whom it is intended to serve this application are [*state names and addresses*] of Respondent.

My address for service is [*state address of Applicant*].

DATED

Illegal eviction

If a person unlawfully deprives the occupier or the occupier's successor on death of his occupation or after termination enforces otherwise than by proceedings any right to exclude the occupier from the site, that person commits an offence (s3 of the Caravan Sites Act 1968).

Mobile homes owned by site owner

The Mobile Homes Act 1983 and its provisions relating to agreements and their determination do not apply where the mobile home is owned by the site owner, but the Caravan Sites Act 1968 does. The owner of the caravan will have to give at least four weeks' notice to terminate (s2 of the 1968 Act; more if the agreement so provides) and will have to obtain a court order before obtaining possession of the home (s3) and that order may be suspended (s4). For the possibility that the occupier of the caravan may be a protected tenant within the meaning of s1 of the Rent Act 1977 where there is a sufficient degree of permanence, see p131.

Chapter 18

Miscellaneous

The matrimonial home

Where one spouse occupies a dwelling house by virtue of a tenancy or licence or by virtue of any enactment giving him or her the right to remain in occupation, and the other spouse is not so entitled, s1(1) of the Matrimonial Homes Act 1983 provides that the spouse not so entitled has certain 'rights of occupation', ie a right not to be evicted or excluded from the dwelling house by the other spouse and if not in occupation a right, with the leave of the court, to enter and occupy the dwelling house. (Throughout the rest of this part of this chapter the spouse with rights of occupation under the Act is, for the sake of convenience, referred to as the wife and the other spouse is referred to as the husband.)

Landlord v spouse

A wife with rights of occupation under the Matrimonial Homes Act 1983 also has certain rights as against the 'landlord'. Any payment or tender of rent or licence fees that she makes is as good as if it were made by the husband (s1(5)). The 'landlord' may not therefore use non-payment of rent or licence fees by the husband as an excuse for obtaining possession where a wife, who has rights of occupation under the Act, is prepared to pay them.

Furthermore, by virtue of s1(6), the wife's occupation is treated as possession or occupation by the husband for the following purposes, namely:

(1) the Rent Act 1977, in relation to protected and statutory tenancies, and restricted contracts created after 28 November 1980;

(2) the Housing Act 1985, in relation to secure tenancies;

(3) the Rent (Agriculture) Act 1976, in relation to protected occupancies and statutory tenancies; and

(4) Part I of the Housing Act 1988 in relation to assured tenancies and assured agricultural occupancies.

Thus, so long as a wife with rights of occupation under the Act remains in occupation the landlord may not obtain possession by reason of her husband's absence (eg see *Griffiths v Renfree* [1989] 2 EGLR 46; tenant/ husband served a notice to quit; wife remained in occupation; tenancy continued and therefore husband continued to be liable for the rent). It also means that in any possession action against the husband the wife should be joined as a defendant.

Where in any such proceedings the tenancy or contract, under which the husband is entitled to occupy the dwelling house, is determined the wife's rights of occupation as such also come to an end (s1(10) of the Matrimonial Homes Act 1983); but if the court adjourns the hearing or makes an order staying or suspending execution of the order for possession or postpones the date for possession the wife is entitled to the benefit of that adjournment, stay, suspension or postponement. She will continue to be so entitled as long as she remains in occupation of the dwelling house and may make the application for any such adjournment, stay, suspension or postponement herself. (See s100(4A), (4B) of the Rent Act 1977; s9(5) of the Housing Act 1988; s85(5), (6) of the Housing Act 1985; s7(5A), (5B) of the Rent (Agriculture) Act 1976.)

It is important to note that the wife's rights of occupation under the Matrimonial Homes Act 1983 only last as long as the marriage is in existence (s1(10)). If she wishes to remain in occupation after decree absolute she must make an application for the tenancy to be transferred into her name in proceedings under s24 of the Matrimonial Causes Act 1973, Sched 1 to the Matrimonial Homes Act 1983 or the Children Act 1989 (see *below*). For a case where the wife failed to make such an application and thus lost her right to remain in occupation see *Metropolitan Properties Co Ltd v Cronan* (1982) 44 P&CR 1.

The above rules do not apply to a dwelling house which has at no time been a matrimonial home of the spouses in question (s1(10) of the Matrimonial Homes Act 1983). For example, see *Hall v King* [1987] 2 EGLR 121, where the husband took the tenancy for the wife. He never resided there himself and so it was never a matrimonial home.

Spouse v spouse

While the marriage exists it does not matter which spouse is the tenant. Neither one of them may be excluded from the matrimonial home by the other save by order of the court made pursuant to the provisions of the Matrimonial Homes Act 1983 or the Domestic Violence and Matrimonial Proceedings Act 1976, or pursuant to the court's inherent jurisdiction to make orders for the protection of minor children. (See further Duckworth, *Matrimonial Property and Finance*, 4th ed, chapter 3.)

After divorce the parties' relationship to each other in respect of the property is governed by the general law. They are treated as independent adults. Thus, where the former husband is the tenant the former wife remains in occupation as the husband's licensee under a licence which may be revoked at any time (*O'Malley v O'Malley* [1982] 1 WLR 244);

although the former wife must be given a reasonable amount of time to leave (*Vaughan v Vaughan* [1953] 1 QB 762; see also p95). Her rights of occupation under the Matrimonial Homes Act 1983 will have come to an end when the decree was made absolute (except where, during the subsistence of the marriage, the court directed otherwise by an order made under s1; see s1(10) and s2(4)).

Transfer of tenancy   The non-tenant spouse may, however, apply for a transfer of a contractual tenancy in proceedings for ancillary relief under s24 of the Matrimonial Causes Act 1973 (*Hale v Hale* [1975] 1 WLR 931; *Thompson v Thompson* [1976] Fam 25). A Rent Act statutory tenancy may not be transferred under s24 of the Matrimonial Causes Act 1973 because it is not 'property' within the meaning of the section. The non-tenant spouse may, however, also apply on decree *nisi* or at any time thereafter for a transfer of the tenancy into his or her sole name under Sched 1 to the Matrimonial Homes Act 1983 where the tenancy is a protected or statutory tenancy within the meaning of the Rent Act 1977, a secure tenancy within the meaning of the Housing Act 1985, a statutory tenancy within the meaning of the Rent (Agriculture) Act 1976 or an assured tenancy or assured agricultural occupancy under the Housing Act 1988.

The court can only transfer a statutory tenancy if it was in existence at the date of the application for the transfer (*Lewis v Lewis* [1985] 2 WLR 962). It will not be in existence if a decree absolute of divorce has been made and the tenant has ceased to occupy because the presence of the ex-wife will no longer be deemed to be on behalf of the tenant (s1(10); see *above*). The same rule applies in relation to secure tenancies (*Thompson v Elmbridge Borough Council* (1989) 19 HLR 526; suspended order for possession; tenancy came to an end when condition of the suspension was broken). Further, no order may be made for the transfer of a tenancy if the spouse applying has remarried unless she applied prior to the remarriage (s28(3) of the 1973 Act; Sched 1, para 7 to the 1983 Act; *Jackson v Jackson* [1973] 2 All ER 395). An application made in the petition for a property transfer order would appear to be sufficient (*Jenkins v Hargood* [1978] 3 All ER 1001).

Any application for the transfer of a tenancy under the 1983 Act must be served on the landlord who is entitled to be heard on the application (Rule 3.8(8) of the Family Proceedings Rules 1991). It has been suggested that it would not be proper to transfer the tenancy (in the face of opposition from the landlord) where there is a covenant against assignment because the landlord would have the right to forfeit (*Hale v Hale* [1975] 2 All ER 1090 at 1094).

Where an order is made for the transfer of a tenancy under the Matrimonial Causes Act 1973 the tenancy should be assigned by deed in order to ensure that it is effective against the landlord (*Crago v Julian*

[1992] 1 All ER 744; see p80). However, under the 1983 Act the order itself transfers the tenancy (para 2(1) and para 3(1)).

An order requiring either or both parents of a child to transfer to the applicant, *for the benefit of the child* 'property' (which presumably does not therefore include a statutory tenancy) to which the parent is, or the parents are, entitled may also be made pursuant to paragraph 1(2)(*e*)(i) of Sched 1 to the Children Act 1989 (and see *K v K* [1992] 1 WLR 530). The power may be exercised at any time (para 1(3)).

Once the tenancy has been transferred the spouse who is then the tenant may commence proceedings to evict the other spouse if he or she refuses to leave.

Vendor and purchaser

Where the vendor of land permits the purchaser to go into occupation prior to completion of the contract, he normally permits him to do so as licensee, notwithstanding that the purchaser enjoys exclusive possession. The circumstances are such that the *prima facie* intention to create a tenancy, normally construed from the granting of the right to exclusive possession, is negatived (see *Street v Mountford* [1985] 2 All ER 289 at 295j). The situation is dealt with in the Standard Conditions of Sale (1st edition). Condition 5 is, so far as is relevant, in the following terms:

> 5.2.1 If the buyer is not already lawfully in the property, and the seller agrees to let him into occupation, the buyer occupies on the following terms.
> 5.2.2 The buyer is a licensee and not a tenant. The terms of the licence are that the buyer:
> (a) cannot transfer it
> (b) may permit members of his household to occupy the property
> (c) is to pay all outgoings including any premium the seller pays to insure the property
> (d) is to pay the seller a fee calculated at the contract rate on the purchase price (less any deposit paid) for the period of the licence
> (e) is entitled to any rents and profits from any part of the property which he does not occupy
> (f) is to keep the property in as good a state of repair as it was when he went into occupation (except for fair wear and tear) and is not to alter it
> (g) is to quit the property when the licence ends.
> 5.2.3 The buyer's licence ends on the earliest of: completion date, rescission of the contract or when five working days' notice given by one party to the other takes effect.

However, agreements between vendor and purchaser sometimes provide that the Conditions are incorporated into the agreement 'so far as the same are not inconsistent herewith'. This was the situation in *Joel v Montgomery and Taylor Ltd* [1966] 3 All ER 763 where the plaintiff agreed to grant an underlease to the defendant at a premium. The defendant paid the deposit and went into possession prior to completion, paying rent in accordance with the terms of the agreement and the underlease. It was held that the relationship between the parties was not that of vendor and purchaser but of landlord and tenant. The relevant condition was inconsistent with the agreement and thus did not make the defendant a licensee.

Where the Standard Conditions have not been incorporated and the purchaser is let into occupation as a tenant at will, in consideration for payment of sums for use and occupation of the premises, he becomes a tenant protected by the Rent Acts (*Francis Jackson Developments Ltd v Stemp* [1943] 2 All ER 601). Compare *Dunthorne and Shore v Wiggins* [1943] 2 All ER 678 where, on the facts, it was held that the payments were not rent but payment of the outgoings and towards the purchase price. The occupant was not therefore a tenant.

Where a person is granted exclusive possession of premises for a term at a rent and no contract has actually been entered into, he will be held to be a tenant even though he entered into possession with the intention of purchasing the premises and even though neither party intended that a tenancy should be created (*Bretherton v Paton* [1986] 1 EGLR 172).

Where a person enters into possession of a property during negotiations for the grant of a lease he will usually be held to be a tenant at will (*Javad v Aqil* [1991] 1 All ER 243) but the Rent Acts apply to tenancies at will where a sufficient rent is paid (*Chamberlain v Farr* [1942] 2 All ER 567; *Francis Jackson*).

Purchasing property with 'sitting tenant'

For the dangers inherent in purchasing a property subject to a tenancy see *Appleton v Aspin and Plane* [1988] 1 EGLR 95. The vendor's tenant was a party to the contract of sale which contained a term whereby the tenant agreed that on completion she would not enforce her right to possession. The court held that the agreement infringed s98 of the Rent Act 1977 and the purchaser was unable to recover possession from the tenant.

Overcrowding and closing orders

Section 101 of the Rent Act 1977 provides that at any time when a dwelling house to which that section applies is overcrowded within the meaning of Part X of the Housing Act 1985, in such circumstances as to render the occupier guilty of an offence, nothing in Part VII of the Rent Act (ie the part relating to security of tenure) shall prevent the immediate landlord of the occupier from obtaining possession of the dwelling house. Regulated tenants and occupiers under restricted contracts will not therefore be able to rely upon ss98–106A as a means of preventing orders for possession or as a means of obtaining postponements and suspensions of such orders in circumstances where s101 applies. But note that the tenancy/licence must first be determined in the normal way before proceedings for possession can be commenced (cf *Aslan v Murphy (Nos 1 and 2)* [1989] 3 All ER 130; a case in fact relating to closing orders).

The section applies to a dwelling house which consists of premises used as a separate dwelling 'by members of the working classes or of a type suitable for such use' (s 101(2) of the Rent Act 1977). The working classes are people in the lower income groups (*Guinness Trust v Green* [1955] 1 WLR 872; *Chorley Borough Council v Barratt Developments* [1979] 3 All ER 634). For the landlord to be able to rely upon s 101 the circumstances that amount to the offence must exist at the date of the hearing (*Zbytniewski v Broughton* [1956] 2 QB 673).

Where the premises are subject to a secure tenancy within the meaning of s 79 of the Housing Act 1985 the landlord may seek to obtain possession under Ground 9 of Sched 2 to the Act if the dwelling house is overcrowded within the meaning of Part X of the Act, in such circumstances as to render the occupier guilty of an offence. The court may only make an order for possession if suitable alternative accommodation is available.

Where the premises are subject to the provisions of the Rent (Agriculture) Act 1976 the landlord may seek to obtain possession under Case XIII of Sched 4 to the said Act if the dwelling house is overcrowded within the meaning of Part X of the 1985 Act, in such circumstances as to render the occupier guilty of an offence. Case XIII is a mandatory ground.

Section 276 of the Housing Act 1985 (as amended) also provides that nothing in the Rent Act 1977 or the Rent (Agriculture) Act 1976 or Part I of the Housing Act 1988 shall prevent possession being obtained by the owner (ie the freehold owner or leasehold owner with more than three years of the lease to run: s 322) of premises in respect of which a *closing order* is in force. A closing order is in force when it is 'operative', ie when the time limit after service has expired (*Beaney v Brachett* (1987) 19 HLR 471). Closing orders are made when premises are unfit for human habitation (see s 265 of the 1985 Act). The fact that the dwelling house is in such a condition that a closing order is made by reason of some breach by the landlord of his contractual or statutory duties does not prevent him from being able to rely upon s 27(6) of the Housing Act 1985 in his claim for possession (*Buswell v Goodwin* [1971] 1 WLR 92). See also s 264(5): Rent Acts not to apply where undertaking given not to use the property for human habitation. See s 270 and *Beaney above* for 'demolition orders'.

The local authority may be able to obtain possession under s 338 of the 1985 Act where a dwelling is overcrowded. Note that evicted occupiers may have a right to compensation under ss 29–39 of the Land Compensation Act 1973.

The provisions of the Housing Act 1985 that are relevant to overcrowding are as follows:

Definition of overcrowding

324.—A dwelling is overcrowded for the purposes of this Part wher the number of persons sleeping in the dwelling is such as to contravene—

    (*a*) the standard specified in section 325 (the room standard), o
    (*b*) the standard specified in section 326 (the space standard).

325.—(1) The room standard is contravened when the number of persons sleeping in a dwelling and the number of rooms available as sleeping accommodation is such that two persons of opposite sexes who are not living together as husband and wife must sleep in the same room.

    (2) For this purpose—

    (*a*) children under the age of ten shall be left out of account, and
    (*b*) a room is available as sleeping accommodation if it is of a type normally used in the locality either as a bedroom or as a living room.

326.—(1) The space standard is contravened when the number of persons sleeping in a dwelling is in excess of the permitted number, having regard to the number and floor area of the rooms of the dwelling available as sleeping accommodation.

    (2) For this purpose—

    (*a*) no account shall be taken of a child under the age of one and a child aged one or over but under ten shall be reckoned as one-half of a unit, and
    (*b*) a room is available as sleeping accommodation if it is of a type normally used in the locality either as a living room or as a bedroom.

    (3) The permitted number of persons in relation to a dwelling is whichever is the less of—

    (*a*) the number specified in Table I in relation to the number of rooms in the dwelling available as sleeping accommodation, and
    (*b*) the aggregate for all such rooms in the dwelling of the numbers specified in column 2 of Table II in relation to each room of the floor area specified in column 1.

No account shall be taken for the purposes of either Table of a room having a floor area of less than 50 square feet.

Table 1

Number of rooms	*Number of persons*
1	2
2	3
3	5
4	$7\frac{1}{2}$
5 or more	2 for each room

Table II

Floor area of room	*Number of persons*
110 sq ft or more	2
90 sq ft or more but less than 110 sq ft	$1\frac{1}{2}$
70 sq ft or more but less than 90 sq ft	1
50 sq ft or more but less than 70 sq ft	$\frac{1}{2}$

    (4) The Secretary of State may by regulations prescribe the manner in which the floor area of a room is to be ascertained for the purposes of this

section; and the regulations may provide for the exclusion from computation, or the bringing into computation at a reduced figure, of floor space in a part of the room which is of less than a specified height not exceeding eight feet.

(5) Regulations under subsection (4) shall be made by statutory instrument which shall be subject to annulment in pursuance of a resolution of either House of Parliament.

(6) A certificate of the local housing authority stating the number and floor areas of the rooms in a dwelling, and that the floor areas have been ascertained in the prescribed manner, is prima facie evidence for the purposes of legal proceedings of the facts stated in it.

Responsibility of occupier

327.—(1) The occupier of a dwelling who causes or permits it to be overcrowded commits a summary offence, subject to subsection (2).

(2) The occupier is not guilty of an offence—

    (*a*) if the overcrowding is within the exceptions specified in section 328 or 329 (children attaining the age of 10 or visiting relatives), or

    (*b*) by reason of anything done under the authority of, and in accordance with any conditions specified in, a licence granted by the local housing authority under section 330.

328.—(1) Where a dwelling which would not otherwise be overcrowded becomes overcrowded by reason of a child attaining the age of one or ten, then if the occupier—

    (*a*) applies to the local housing authority for suitable alternative accommodation, or

    (*b*) has so applied before the date when the child attained the age in question,

he does not commit an offence under section 327 (occupier causing or permitting overcrowding), so long as the condition in subsection (2) is met and the occupier does not fail to take action in the circumstances specified in subsection (3).

(2) The condition is that all the persons sleeping in the dwelling are persons who were living there when the child attained that age and thereafter continuously live there, or children born after that date of any of those persons.

(3) The exception provided by this section ceases to apply if—

    (*a*) suitable alternative accommodation is offered to the occupier on or after the date on which the child attains that age, or, if he has applied before that date, is offered at any time after the application, and he fails to accept it, or

    (*b*) the removal from the dwelling of some person not a member of the occupier's family is on that date or thereafter becomes reasonably practicable having regard to all the circumstances (including the availability of suitable alternative accommodation for that person), and the occupier fails to require his removal.

329.—Where the persons sleeping in an overcrowded dwelling include a member of the occupier's family who does not live there but is sleeping there temporarily, the occupier is not guilty of an offence under section 327 (occupier causing or permitting overcrowding) unless the circumstances are such that he would be so guilty if that member of his family were not sleeping there.

330.—(1) The occupier or intending occupier of a dwelling may apply to the local housing authority for a licence authorising him to permit a number of persons in excess of the permitted number to sleep in the dwelling.

(2) The authority may grant such a licence if it appears to them that there are exceptional circumstances (which may include a seasonal increase of population) and that it is expedient to do so; and they shall specify in the licence the number of persons authorised in excess of the permitted number.

(3) The licence shall be in the prescribed form and may be granted either unconditionally or subject to conditions specified in it.

(4) The local housing authority may revoke the licence at their discretion by notice in writing served on the occupier and specifying a period (at least one month from the date of service) at the end of which the licence will cease to be in force.

(5) Unless previously revoked, the licence continues in force for such period not exceeding twelve months as may be specified in it.

(6) A copy of the licence and of any notice of revocation shall, within seven days of the issue of the licence or the service of the notice on the occupier, be served by the local housing authority on the landlord (if any) of the dwelling.

. . .

338.—(1) Where a dwelling is overcrowded in circumstances such as to render the occupier guilty of an offence, the local housing authority may serve on the occupier notice in writing requiring him to abate the overcrowding within 14 days from the date of service of the notice.

(2) If at any time within three months from the end of that period—

    (a) the dwelling is in the occupation of the person on whom the notice was served or of a member of his family, and

    (b) it is overcrowded in circumstances such as to render the occupier guilty of an offence,

the local housing authority may apply to the county court which shall order vacant possession of the dwelling to be given to the landlord within such period, not less than 14 or more than 28 days, as the court may determine.

(3) Expenses incurred by the local housing authority under this section in securing the giving of possession of a dwelling to the landlord may be recovered by them from him by action.

Ministers of religion

The protection that is afforded to ministers of the Church of England who have Church livings is governed by the Pluralities Act 1838 (see *Bishop of Gloucester v Cunnington* [1943] KB 101; *Worcester Diocesan Trust v Taylor* (1947) 177 LT 581).

Other ministers of religion, like anyone else, may be assured, regulated or secure tenants but where the dwelling house is let on an assured or regulated tenancy a special ground for possession exists. Where the tenancy is an assured tenancy the ground is Ground 5 (of Sched 2 to the Housing Act 1988). Where the tenancy is a regulated tenancy the ground for possession is Case 15 (of Sched 15 to the Rent Act 1977).

The landlord is entitled to possession in either case where the dwelling house is held for the purpose of being available for occupation by a minister of religion as a residence from which to perform the duties of his office *and*:

(1) not later than 'the beginning of the tenancy' (ie not later than the day on which the tenancy is entered into) if the tenancy is *assured*, or 'the relevant date' (usually the date the tenancy commenced) if the tenancy is *regulated*, the landlord gave notice in writing to the tenant that possession might be recovered on Ground 5 or, as the case may be, Case 15 (for rules governing notices in assured tenancy cases see Part IV of Sched 2 to the 1988 Act); *and*

(2) the court is satisfied that the dwelling house is required for occupation by a minister of religion as such a residence.

Ground 5 or Case 15 may be relied upon whatever the religion involved (*Re Watson* [1973] 1 WLR 1472).

The notice requirement may not be dispensed with but if the ground is made out the court must make an order for possession without considering whether or not it is reasonable to make such order (s7(3) of the 1988 Act; s98(2) of the 1977 Act). For the procedure to be used when terminating assured tenancies, see Chapter 6. The originating application procedure under the Rent Act etc Rules is available to the landlord in Rent Act cases (see Chapter 20) and the accelerated possession procedure is available in Housing Act cases (p272).

The court may not postpone or suspend the order for possession for more than 14 days or six weeks in cases of exceptional hardship (s89 of the Housing Act 1980; see p75).

Rental purchase

A 'rental purchase agreement' is an agreement for the purchase of a dwelling house under which the whole or part of the purchase price is paid in three or more instalments and completion of the purchase is deferred until the whole or a specified part of the purchase price has been paid (s88(4) of the Housing Act 1980). This definition thus excludes the normal house purchase whereby the purchase price is paid in two instalments—the deposit on exchange of contracts and the balance of the purchase price on completion. The normal purchaser who enters into possession of the property before completion is a licensee and as such has no security of tenure (see p243). However, the Housing Act 1980 extends the benefit of the Protection from Eviction Act 1977 to a rental purchaser as if the premises had been let to him under a tenancy which is not statutorily protected and his tenancy had come to an end with the termination of his agreement or with his right to possession under it (Sched 25, para 61 to the Housing Act 1980). Thus a court order is required for a 'vendor' under a rental purchase agreement to gain possession. Further protection is given to a rental purchaser by s88 of the

Housing Act 1980 whereby if possession proceedings are taken, the court has the power to adjourn the proceedings or stay or suspend execution of the order or postpone the date for possession for such period or periods as the court thinks fit (s88(1)). The usual restrictions on the court's discretion to postpone the date for possession imposed by s89 of the Housing Act 1980 do not apply (s89(2)(e)). The court may impose any conditions (in particular as to payments in respect of his continued occupation) as it thinks fit (s88(2)) and these conditions may be revoked or varied (s88(3)).

Those advising the rental purchaser should carefully examine the circumstances surrounding the creation of the agreement so as to see whether it truly reflects the intention of the parties at that time. If the agreement does not reflect their true intentions the court may hold that it is a 'sham' or a 'pretence' and that the rental purchaser is a regulated or assured tenant (cf licence agreements (p91), and holiday lets (p229) and company lets (p215)). See also *Martin v Davies* (1952) 159 EG 191.

Part 3

The Proceedings for Possession

Chapter 19

Court Proceedings

The necessity for possession proceedings

The circumstances in which a landlord or licensor is required to bring proceedings for possession are dealt with in part by the statutory provisions relating to security of tenure and in part by the Protection from Eviction Act 1977.

Statutorily protected tenants

Where the tenancy of premises let as a dwelling house comes to an end and the ex-tenant continues to reside in the premises, the landlord in most cases may only recover possession by bringing proceedings for possession. In the cases listed below this is because the relevant statutory provisions give the tenant a right to remain in occupation until the court orders otherwise. Any attempt to evict him without a court order would therefore be unlawful. The cases referred to are as follows:

(1) an assured tenant (including an assured shorthold tenant) under the Housing Act 1988;
(2) a regulated tenant under the Rent Act 1977;
(3) a secure tenant under the Housing Act 1985;
(4) a tenant of a long lease at a low rent under Part I of the Landlord and Tenant Act 1954 or under Sched 10 to the Local Government and Housing Act 1989;
(5) an assured agricultural occupant under the Housing Act 1988;
(6) a protected occupant or statutory tenant as defined in the Rent (Agriculture) Act 1976; and
(7) a tenant of an agricultural holding within the meaning of the Agricultural Holdings Act 1986.

Occupiers who are not statutorily protected tenants

Where there is no statutory protection under one of the above Acts it is nevertheless unlawful to evict the tenant (or any other person who was a lawful resident at the termination of the tenancy) without obtaining a court order after the tenancy has come to an end unless the tenancy was an 'excluded tenancy' (ss3 and 8 of the Protection from Eviction Act 1977). (There is an overlap in protection in relation to statutory tenants in that they are treated as not being statutorily protected for the purposes of s3 so that s3 also makes it unlawful to evict a statutory tenant without a court order (s8(1)(*a*))); cf *Haniff v Robinson* [1993] 1 All ER 185.)

Occupiers (*a*) under licences entered into after 28 November 1980 that are restricted contracts within the meaning of the Rent Act 1977 (s3(2A)) and (*b*) where the landlord is entitled to recover possession following the death of the tenant under a statutory tenancy within the meaning of the Rent Act 1977 or the Rent (Agriculture) Act 1976 are entitled to the same protection (s3(3)). Section 3 also applies in relation to all other premises occupied as a dwelling under a licence (whenever entered into), other than an 'excluded licence' (see *below*); s3(2B).

Protection from Eviction Act 1977, ss3 and 8
Prohibition of eviction without the process of law
    3.—(1) Where any premises have been let as a dwelling under a tenancy which is neither a statutorily protected tenancy nor an excluded tenancy and—
        (*a*) the tenancy (in this section referred to as the former tenancy) has come to an end, but
        (*b*) the occupier continues to reside in the premises or part of them,
    it shall not be lawful for the owner to enforce against the occupier, otherwise than by proceedings in the court, his right to recover possession of the premises.
    (2) In this section 'the occupier', in relation to any premises, means any person lawfully residing in the premises or part of them at the termination of the former tenancy.
    (2A) Subsections (1) and (2) above apply in relation to any restricted contract (within the meaning of the Rent Act 1977) which—
        (*a*) creates a licence; and
        (*b*) is entered into after the commencement of section 69 of the Housing Act 1980;
    as they apply in relation to a restricted contract which creates a tenancy.
    (2B) Subsections (1) and (2) above apply in relation to any premises occupied as a dwelling under a licence, other than an excluded licence as they apply in relation to premises let as a dwelling under a tenancy, and in those subsections the expressions 'let' and 'tenancy' shall be construed accordingly.
    (2C) References in the preceding provisions of this section and section 4(2A) below to an excluded tenancy do not apply to—
        (*a*) a tenancy entered into before the date on which the Housing Act 1988 came into force, or
        (*b*) a tenancy entered into on or after that date but pursuant to a contract made before that date,
    but, subject to that, 'excluded tenancy' and 'excluded licence' shall be construed in accordance with section 3A below.
    (3) This section shall, with the necessary modifications, apply where the owner's right to recover possession arises on the death of the tenant under a

statutory tenancy within the meaning of the Rent Act 1977 or the Rent
(Agriculture) Act 1976.

. . .

Interpretation

8.—(1) In this Act 'statutorily protected tenancy' means—

    (a) a protected tenancy within the meaning of the Rent Act 1977 or a
tenancy to which Part I of the Landlord and Tenant Act 1954
applies;

    (b) a protected occupancy or statutory tenancy as defined in the Rent
(Agriculture) Act 1976;

    (c) a tenancy to which Part II of the Landlord and Tenant Act 1954
applies;

    (d) a tenancy of an agricultural holding within the meaning of the
Agricultural Holdings Act 1986;

    (e) an assured tenancy or assured agricultural occupancy under Part I
of the Housing Act 1988;

    (f) a tenancy to which Schedule 10 to the Local Government and
Housing Act 1989 applies.

(2) For the purposes of Part I of this Act a person who, under the terms of
his employment, had exclusive possession of any premises other than as a
tenant shall be deemed to have been a tenant and the expressions 'let' and
'tenancy' shall be construed accordingly.

Forfeiture

Section 2 of the Protection from Eviction Act 1977 provides that it is not
lawful to enforce a right of reentry or forfeiture in *any* lease where the
premises are let as a dwelling otherwise than by proceedings in court
while any person is lawfully residing in the premises or part of them (see
p38). This section is not affected by the provisions relating to 'excluded
tenancies'. Thus, even where the tenancy is an 'excluded tenancy' the
landlord must take proceedings if he wishes to recover possession by
relying upon a right of reentry or forfeiture.

Enforcement of possession orders

Where the landlord has an order for possession he may not (if s2 or s3 of
the 1977 Act applies) 'enforce' that order otherwise than by the issue and
execution of a writ or, as the case may be, warrant for possession. If he
does so he will be liable to pay the tenant damages for unlawful eviction
(*Borzak v Ahmed* [1965] 2 QB 320; *Haniff v Robinson* [1993] 1 All ER
15; see also p296).

Excluded tenancies and licences: s3A of the Protection from Eviction Act 1977 (as introduced by s31 of the Housing Act 1988)

There are six categories of excluded tenancy and licence. They are as
follows:

(1) occupier sharing accommodation with the landlord or licensor which the latter occupied immediately before and at the end of the licence or tenancy;

(2) sharing accommodation with a member of the family of the landlord or licensor;

(3) tenancy or licence granted as a temporary expedient to a trespasser;

(4) holiday accommodation;

(5) tenancy or licence granted otherwise than for money or money's worth;

(6) accommodation in a hostel within the meaning of the Housing Act 1985 provided by local authorities and other specified public bodies.

In all of these cases the landlord or licensor may obtain possession without taking proceedings at the end of the tenancy or licence (although he must not use or threaten to use force: see *below* 'Offences'). Full details of these excluded categories are set out in s3A of the Protection from Eviction Act 1977; see below. (These provisions do not affect s2 of the 1977 Act which provides that it is not lawful to enforce a right of reentry otherwise than by proceedings; see *above*.)

Note that s3A of the 1977 Act does not apply to a *tenancy* entered into before the date on which the Housing Act 1988 came into force (15 January 1989) or to a tenancy entered into on or after that date but pursuant to a contract made before that date (s3(2C)). Any such tenancy cannot be an 'excluded tenancy' and it will be necessary to take proceedings in order to obtain possession of premises subject to such a tenancy. See further s8, subss(5), (6) of the 1977 Act where the terms of a tenancy or licence are varied on or after the date on which the Housing Act 1988 came into force.

Protection from Eviction Act 1977, s3A

Excluded tenancies and licences

3A.—(1) Any reference in this Act to an excluded tenancy or an excluded licence is a reference to a tenancy or licence which is excluded by virtue of any of the following provisions of this section.

(2) A tenancy or licence is excluded if—

(*a*) under its terms the occupier shares any accommodation with the landlord or licensor; and

(*b*) immediately before the tenancy or licence was granted and also at the time it comes to an end, the landlord or licensor occupied as his only or principal home premises of which the whole or part of the shared accommodation formed part.

(3) A tenancy or licence is also excluded if—

(*a*) under its terms the occupier shares any accommodation with a member of the family of the landlord or licensor;

(*b*) immediately before the tenancy or licence was granted and also at the time it comes to an end, the member of the family of the landlord or licensor occupied as his only or principal home premises of which the whole or part of the shared accommodation formed part; and

(c) immediately before the tenancy or licence was granted and also at the time it comes to an end, the landlord or licensor occupied as his only or principal home premises in the same building as the shared accommodation and that building is not a purpose-built block of flats.

(4) For the purposes of subsections (2) and (3) above, an occupier shares accommodation with another person if he has the use of it in common with that person (whether or not also in common with others) and any reference in those subsections to shared accommodation shall be construed accordingly, and if, in relation to any tenancy or licence, there is at any time more than one person who is the landlord or licensor, any reference in those subsections to the landlord or licensor shall be construed as a reference to any one of those persons.

(5) In subsections (2) to (4) above—

(a) 'accommodation' includes neither an area used for storage nor a staircase, passage, corridor or other means of access;

(b) 'occupier' means, in relation to a tenancy, the tenant and, in relation to a licence, the licensee; and

(c) 'purpose-built block of flats' has the same meaning as in Part III of Schedule 1 to the Housing Act 1988,

and section 113 of the Housing Act 1985 shall apply to determine whether a person is for the purpose of subsection (3) above a member of another's family as it applies for the purposes of Part IV of that Act.

(6) A tenancy or licence is excluded if it was granted as a temporary expedient to a person who entered the premises in question or any other premises as a trespasser (whether or not, before the beginning of that tenancy or licence, another tenancy or licence to occupy the premises or any other premises had been granted to him).

(7) A tenancy or licence is excluded if—

(a) it confers on the tenant or licensee the right to occupy the premises for a holiday only; or

(b) it is granted otherwise than for money or money's worth.

(8) A licence is excluded if it confers rights of occupation in a hostel, within the meaning of the Housing Act 1985, which is provided by—

(a) the council of a county, district or London Borough, the Common Council of the City of London, the Council of the Isles of Scilly, the Inner London Education Authority, a joint authority within the meaning of the Local Government Act 1985 or a residuary body within the meaning of that Act;

(b) a development corporation within the meaning of the New Towns Act 1981;

(c) the Commission for the New Towns;

(d) an urban development corporation established by an order under section 135 of the Local Government, Planning and Land Act 1980;

(e) a housing action trust established under Part III of the Housing Act 1988;

(f) the Development Board for Rural Wales;

(g) the Housing Corporation or Housing for Wales;

(*h*) a housing trust which is a charity or a registered hous ng association, within the meaning of the Housing Associations Act 1985; or

(*i*) any other person who is, or who belongs to a class of person wh ch is, specified in an order made by the Secretary of State.

(9) The power to make an order under subsection (8)(*i*) above shall be exercisable by statutory instrument which shall be subject to annulment in pursuance of a resolution of either House of Parliament.

Offences

Where a person unlawfully deprives or attempts to deprive a 'residential occupier' (ie a person occupying premises as a residence under a contr act or by virtue of any enactment or rule of law giving him the right to remain in occupation or restricting the right of any other person to recover possession of the premises) of his occupation he commits an offence unless he can prove that he believed, and had reasonable cause to believe, that the residential occupier had ceased to reside in the premises (s 1(2) of the Protection from Eviction Act 1977).

It is also an offence for any person to do any act likely to interfere with the peace or comfort of the residential occupier or members of his household or to withdraw persistently or withhold services reasonably required for occupation of the premises (eg by turning off gas, electricity or water supplies) if such acts are carried out with the *intent* to cause the residential occupier to give up occupation of the premises or to refrain from exercising any right or pursuing any remedy in respect of the premises (s 1(3) of the Protection from Eviction Act 1977). Furthermore, the landlord (see wide definition in subs 3(C)) of a residential occupier or an agent of the landlord is guilty of an offence if he engages in such conduct if he knows or has reasonable cause to believe that that conduct is *likely* to cause the residential occupier to give up occupation of the whole or part of the premises or to refrain from exercising any right or remedy in respect of the whole or part of the premises (s 1(3A)) unless the landlord or agent proves that he had reasonable grounds for doing the acts or withdrawing or withholding the services in question (s 1(3B)).

It is only an offence to withhold or withdraw services that the landlord is required to provide by the terms of the tenancy agreement, the licence or the statute under which the tenant occupies (*McCall v Abelesz* [1976] QB 585).

Finally, it is an offence for any person to use or threaten to use violence (to persons or property) to gain entry into premises where there is someone present on the premises who is opposed to the entry and the person using or threatening to use violence knows this (s 6 of the Criminal Law Act 1977). A property owner wishing to evict trespassers should therefore seek possession in proceedings brought under CCR Ord 24 or RSC Ord 113 (see Chapter 20) unless reentry can be effected peaceably.

The civil remedy of a person unlawfully evicted by his landlord is to seek an injunction and/or damages (see Chapter 27).

There is a defence to the offence under s6 to any person who is a 'displaced residential occupier' such as a person who returns home from a holiday to find squatters in occupation (s6(3), (7) and s12). See also s7 for the offence committed by the trespasser who fails to leave if required to do so by or on behalf of a displaced residential occupier.

Criminal Law Act 1977, s6
Violence for securing entry
  6.—(1) Subject to the following provisions of this section, any person who, without lawful authority, uses or threatens violence for the purpose of securing entry into any premises for himself or for any other person is guilty of an offence, provided that—
    (*a*) there is someone present on those premises at the time who is opposed to the entry which the violence is intended to secure; and
    (*b*) the person using or threatening the violence knows that that is the case.
  (2) The fact that a person has any interest in or right to possession or occupation of any premises shall not for the purposes of subsection (1) above constitute lawful authority for the use or threat of violence by him or anyone else for the purpose of securing his entry into those premises
  . . .
  (4) It is immaterial for the purposes of this section—
    (*a*) whether the violence in question is directed against the person or against property; and
    (*b*) whether the entry which the violence is intended to secure is for the purpose of acquiring possession of the premises in question or for any other purpose.

High Court or county court?

The county court has jurisdiction to hear and determine any action for the recovery of land (s21(1) of the County Courts Act 1984).

County Courts Act 1984, s21(1)
  21.—(1) A county court shall have jurisdiction to hear and determine any action for the recovery of land.

Where the owner is prevented from obtaining possession by virtue of s3 of the Protection from Eviction Act 1977 (see *above*) the proceedings must be commenced in the county court (s9(1)(*a*) of the 1977 Act) unless the claim is for forfeiture in which case proceedings may be brought in the High Court (s9(3) of the 1977 Act). However, it is more appropriate to bring them in the county court (*Peachey Property Corporation Ltd v Robinson* [1966] 2 All ER 981).

In addition to its general jurisdiction the county court has jurisdiction to hear any claim for possession arising under the following statutes by virtue of provisions within those statutes:

(1) the Housing Act 1988 (s40 of that Act);
(2) the Rent Act 1977, except where the landlord is relying upon one of the mandatory grounds referred to in s98(2), or s101 in respect of an overcrowded dwelling house (s141 of the Rent Act 1977);
(3) the Housing Act 1985 (s110 of the Housing Act 1985); and
(4) the Rent (Agriculture) Act 1976, except where the landlord is relying upon one of the mandatory grounds in Part II of Sched 4 to the said Act (s26 of the Rent (Agriculture Act) 1976).

If the county court has jurisdiction to hear the claim by virtue of any one of these additional provisions but the proceedings are commenced in the High Court the landlord will not be entitled to recover any costs (except in Housing Act 1988 cases where the landlord will be able to recover county court costs unless the purpose of taking the proceedings in the High Court was to enable them to be joined with proceedings already taken in that court in which case the landlord will be entitled to seek High Court costs (s40(4), (5)).

Applications for possession under Part I of the Landlord and Tenant Act 1954 (long tenancies at low rents) may only be commenced in the county court (s63(1) of the Landlord and Tenant Act 1954).

Parties

The plaintiff/applicant

The plaintiff is not necessarily the absolute owner of the premises. The plaintiff need only show that he has a better right to possession than the defendant. Whenever the plaintiff has let the defendant into possession as a tenant or licensee the tenant/licensee will be estopped from denying the plaintiff's title (see pp7 and 98). He is also estopped from denying his title where the plaintiff is an assignee of the original landlord (see *Cuthbertson v Irving* (1859) 4 H & N 742). One of two or more persons who are joint owners of the landlord's interest in the property may sue for possession alone, but if the other joint owner refuses to be a co-plaintiff he should be joined as a defendant (see *Robson-Paul v Farragia* (1969) 20 P&CR 820 and *Leckhampton Dairies Ltd v Artus Whitfield Ltd* (1986) 83 LS Gaz 875). The position of particular landlords is now considered before turning to the question of who should be made a defendant to the action.

Companies, partners and sole traders   In the county court a limited liability company may commence proceedings by any duly authorised agent (note to CCR Ord 3, r1) but an officer of the company who is not a solicitor will only be able to address the court with leave (s60(1) of the County Courts Act 1984). In the High Court a limited company may only operate through a solicitor (RSC Ord 5, r6). Partners may sue in the name of their firm but the defendant may compel the plaintiff to disclose the names of the partners (CCR Ord 5, r9; RSC Ord 81). Sole traders may only sue in their own name and not in their trading name.

Executors and administrators If the landlord dies leaving a will the property vests in his executors from the date of his death. The executors may therefore commence proceedings for possession prior to the grant of probate. Their title, however, is proved by the grant and so if their title is in dispute the executors will not be able to proceed with the possession action until the grant of probate. The position of an administrator, however, is rather different. He derives title entirely from the grant of letters of administration and the deceased's estate does not vest in him until that time. An administrator may thus only *commence* and continue proceedings for possession once he has obtained the grant. (See generally 17 Halsbury (4th edn) paras 729–39.) As to the right of the personal representative to costs out of estate where they are not fully recovered from the Defendant, see RSC Ord 62, r6; CCR Ord 1, r6.

LPA receivers A receiver appointed under the powers conferred by the Law of Property Act 1925 is deemed to be the agent of the mortgagor (s 109(2)). A receiver wishing to obtain possession should therefore do so in the name of the mortgagor. However, in some cases it may be more advantageous for the mortgagor to take mortgage possession proceedings, for example where the tenancy was created after the mortgage and is not binding on the mortgagee (see p399), unless the mortgagee does not wish to be a mortgagee in possession with all the responsibilities that that entails (see generally Fisher & Lightwood, *Law of Mortgages*, p368).

Change of landlord by reason of assignment, bankruptcy or death
    Where the landlord assigns, goes bankrupt or dies during the course of the proceedings the action does not cease. The assignee etc may apply *ex parte* for an order to carry on the proceedings (CCR Ord 5, r11; RSC Ord 15, r7). If the landlord dies and there are no personal representatives the court may proceed in his absence or appoint someone to represent the estate (CCR Ord 5, r7; RSC Ord 15, r15). If one of two or more plaintiffs who are suing jointly in respect of a joint cause of action dies the other(s) continue the action without appointing a personal representative.

The defendant/respondent

The defendant will be the person in possession against whom the landlord has an immediate right to possession, ie the plaintiff's immediate tenant or licensee whose contractual tenancy or licence has been determined. The order for possession operates against any person on the land so it is not necessary to join any of the tenant's licensees, such as his children or lodgers (*R v Wandsworth County Court, ex p Wandsworth London Borough Council* [1975] 1 WLR 1314). However, sub-tenants should be joined where their names are known (see the application of s 137 of the Rent Act 1977 and s 7 of the Rent (Agriculture) Act 1976 and note that these sections may also apply even where the tenant is not protected under one of those Acts; see also s 18 of the Housing Act 1988. The tenant's spouse should also be joined as he or she is entitled to some protection by virtue of his or her rights of occupation under the Matrimonial Homes Act 1983 (see Chapter 18). All adult members of the tenant's family in occupation should be joined in a 'suitable alternative accommodation' case (*Wandsworth LBC v Fadayomi* [1987] 3 All ER 474). The phrase 'in possession' includes persons who are in receipt of rents. A tenant who has sublet the whole of the premises should therefore be made a defendant even though he may not be in actual occupation.

It is not generally necessary to join the assignor of the tenancy, but if the basis of the claim for possession is the fact of the assignment both the assignor and the assignee should be joined in case the assignment is denied. All the relevant parties will then be before the court and able to give evidence.

If any person in possession has not been joined as a defendant he may apply, *ex parte*, in writing, to be joined in the proceedings. The application may be made at any stage, even after judgment. If anyone is so joined in county court proceedings the court will notify the other parties (CCR Ord 15, r3; RSC Ord 15, r10).

If the plaintiff is unsure whether any particular person claims a right to be in possession of the premises as against him the safest course is to serve a copy of the proceedings on that person together with a letter informing him of his right to be joined in proceedings. For safe measure a further copy can be put through the letter box or affixed to the front door in an envelope addressed to 'the occupiers'.

A foreign state is not immune from proceedings for possession of a dwelling house in respect of which it has a tenancy unless the premises are used for the purposes of a diplomatic mission (ss6(1)(*a*) and 16(1)(*b*) of the State Immunity Act 1978; *Intro Properties (UK) Ltd v Sauvel* [1983] QB 1019).

Chapter 20

County Court Procedure

Introduction

Which county court?

Proceedings for the recovery of land must be commenced in the court for the district in which the land is situated (CCR Ord 4, r3(a)).

CCR Ord 4, r3(a)
>   **3.**— Proceedings—
>   (*a*) for the recovery of land, . . .
>   may be commenced only in the court for the district in which the land or any part thereof is situated.

If the case is commenced in the wrong court the proceedings are valid (*Sharma v Knight* [1986] 1 WLR 757) but the judge may:
    (1) transfer the proceedings to the proper county court; or
    (2) order the proceedings to continue where they are; or
    (3) order the proceedings to be struck out (CCR Ord 16, r2).

CCR Ord 16, r2
>   **2.**—Where proceedings are commenced in the wrong court, the judge or district judge may, . . .
>   (*a*) transfer the proceedings to the court in which they ought to have been commenced, or
>   (*b*) order the proceedings to continue in the court in which they have been commenced, or
>   (*c*) order the proceedings to be struck out.

Which procedure?

There are four different possession procedures available in the county court. These are:
    (1) the fixed date action—commenced by summons;
    (2) the accelerated possession procedure—commenced by an application in prescribed form;
    (3) the procedure under the Rent Act (County Court Proceedings for Possession Rules) 1981—commenced by originating application; and

(4) the summary procedure available under CCR Ord 24—commenced by originating application.

Fixed date action This is the standard procedure which is available in all possession actions. Unless the claim for possession includes a demand for some relief other than payment of arrears of rent or mesne profits, or the court otherwise directs, the 'return day' stated on the summons will be the day listed for the hearing of the claim (see p269). If the landlord does make some other claim the 'return day' will be a day fixed for a pre-trial review at which directions will invariably be given. In proceedings commenced by summons it is necessary to give at least 21 days' notice of the hearing date. In practice, the day fixed for the hearing is invariably much more than 21 days after the proceedings are issued (see further p316).

Accelerated possession procedure This procedure is only available where the landlord is seeking to regain possession of a property let on an assured tenancy and the landlord wishes to obtain possession on Ground 1, 3, 4 or 5 or where the property is let on an assured shorthold tenancy.

The advantage of the accelerated possession procedure is that, as its name suggests, it provides a fast method of obtaining an order for possession. However, its most striking feature is that if the court is satisfied that the landlord is entitled to possession it makes an order without a court hearing. The disadvantage is that the landlord may not obtain any money judgment using the procedure. Arrears of rent, etc have to be claimed by separate action (see further p272).

Rent Act rules procedure This procedure is only available where the tenant is a regulated tenant under the Rent Act 1977 and the landlord wishes to rely upon one of the mandatory grounds for possession set out in Part II of Sched 15 to that Act, ie Cases 11–20. It is possible to claim arrears of rent in addition to possession. Evidence is given by affidavit.

In theory at least, this procedure is quicker than the fixed date action. Where the Rent Act Rules apply it is only necessary to give seven days' notice (or in some cases 14 days' notice) prior to the hearing (see further p283).

Order 24 This procedure is only available where possession is sought from licensees who have had their licences revoked or from trespassers. As with the Rent Act procedure a claim brought under Ord 24 is, in theory, heard more quickly than a claim brought by fixed date action. It is only necessary to give five days' notice of the hearing, and even this short period can be abridged. The procedure is a summary one and the evidence is given by affidavit. Although oral evidence may be given, if the court considers that there is some sort of defence, directions are usually given and the action proceeds as if it were commenced by summons.

Proceedings under Ord 24 are (as with the accelerated possession procedure) confined to the question of possession. If the plaintiff is owed arrears of licence fees or wishes to claim damages for trespass he will have to seek them in another action at a later date (see further Chapter 23).

The fixed date action

Particulars of claim

Before issuing the proceedings it is necessary to prepare the particulars of claim. As in all cases the particulars of claim must specify the plaintiff's cause of action and the relief or remedy which the plaintiff seeks and must state briefly the material facts on which he relies (CCR Ord 6, r1(1)). More particularly, in all actions for recovery of land CCR Ord 6, r3 requires four particular matters to be stated in the particulars of claim:

3.—(1) In an action for recovery of land the particulars of claim shall—
    (a) identify the land sought to be recovered;
    (b) state whether the land consists of or includes a dwelling house;
    (c) give details about the agreement or tenancy, if any, under which the land is held, stating when it commenced and the amount of money payable by way of rent or licence fee;
    (d) . . .
    (e) state the ground on which possession is claimed, whether statutory or otherwise.

In forfeiture actions and in all cases where possession is claimed because of non-payment of rent further specific provisions apply (CCR Ord 6, rr3(1)(d), 3(2), (3); see p40 in relation to forfeiture actions and p319 in relation to rent actions—prescribed form to be used). Other particular points to note are:

(1) Where the plaintiff claims interest under s69 of the County Courts Act 1984 or otherwise the particulars of claim must contain a statement to that effect (Ord 6, r1A; see further p331).

(2) Each copy of the particulars must bear the plaintiff's signature if he is suing in person, or that of his solicitor in the solicitor's own name or the firm's name where the plaintiff is suing by a solicitor. The plaintiff's address for service should be on each copy (CCR Ord 6, r8).

(3) Where the particulars of claim have been drafted by counsel they should be signed by him and his name should appear on each copy (CCR Ord 50, r6).

Further details which should sensibly be stated in a particulars of claim are to be found in the various precedents set out in this book.

Issue of proceedings

As from 1 November 1993 the position has been as follows. The plaintiff must prepare the summons (see Form 34, p266) and file sufficient copies

Form 34: Summons for possession of property

Summons for Possession of Property

Case Number	Always quote this number	

In the

County Court

The court office is open from 10 am to 4 pm Monday to Friday

Telephone:

Plaintiff's full name address.

Name and address for service and payment.
(if different from above)
Ref/Tel. no.

Seal

Defendant's full name
(including title e.g. Mr, Mrs or Miss)
and address.

The Plaintiff (your Landlord or Mortgage Lender) is **claiming possession**

of

for the reasons given in the attached particulars of claim.

The Plaintiff is also making a claim for money.
(details are given in the particulars of claim)

Court fee	
Solicitor's costs	
Total amount	
Summons issued on	

What this means
● On the date set out below, the court will decide whether or not you have to leave, and if you have to leave, when.

What you should do
● **Get help and advice immediately** from a solicitor or any of the advice agencies on the attached list.
● Make sure the court knows as much about your circumstances as possible by:
  ● **filling in the reply form** attached to this summons, and
  ● coming to the hearing.
    (The notes on the back of this form give you more information about what you should do.)

The court will make its decision

on _____ at _____ am/pm

at _____

N5 Possession Summons (Order 3, rule 3(1))

[P.T.O.]

Important notes to help you

No one can evict you from your home unless the court lets them. The court will not make a decision before the date shown on the front of the form. In certain cases the court can:

- allow you a reasonable time to pay rent arrears or the amount borrowed and let you stay in the property;
- decide not to make a possession order;
- give you time to find somewhere else to live, or
- (for mortgage cases regulated by the Consumer Credit Act only) look at the original loan agreement and decide if it is fair.

But, the court cannot decide any of these things unless it knows about your circumstances. To make sure of this, fill in the reply form **and come to the hearing, even if you have reached agreement about repayment with your landlord or mortgage lender since the summons was issued.**

Filling in the reply form

- You must fill in the reply and make sure it reaches the court **within 14 days after the date of service.** The date of service will be 7 days after the court posted the summons to you. The postmark will tell you when this was.
- Fill in the reply form and take or send it to the court even if you cannot come to the hearing.
- If you need help to fill it in you can get it from:
  - any county court;
  - any of the advice agencies on the attached list;
  - a solicitor
- Keep the summons and a copy of your reply form. The court will send a copy of your completed reply to the Plaintiff.

Disagreeing with the claim

- If you disagree with the claim it is even more important that you get help, fill in the reply form and come to the hearing. You may be able to get help with your legal costs. Ask about the legal aid scheme at any firm of solicitors showing the legal aid sign or at any advice agency. A leaflet about legal aid is available from any county court.

Registration of judgments

- If the court orders you to pay money to the Plaintiff (a money judgment) and you do not pay, your name and address may be entered in the Register of County Court Judgments. **This may make it difficult for you to get credit.**

- If the money is paid in full within the time stated on the order, the order **will not be registered.**
- If you do not pay within the time stated on any order, **the order will be registered** when the Plaintiff takes steps to enforce payment.

Interest on judgments

- If the money judgment entered against you is for more than £5,000, the Plaintiff may be entitled to interest on the total amount.

How to pay

- **PAYMENT(S) MUST BE MADE to the person named at the address for payment quoting their reference and the court case number.**
- **DO NOT bring or send payments to the court. THEY WILL NOT BE ACCEPTED.**
- You should allow **at least 4** days for your payments to reach the Plaintiff or his representative. **Ask for a receipt.**
- Make sure that you keep records and can account for all payments made. Proof may be required if there is any disagreement. It is not safe to send cash unless you use registered post.
- A leaflet giving further advice about payment can be obtained from the court.
- If you need more information you should contact the Plaintiff or his representative.

Certificate of Service

I certify that the summons of which this is a true copy was served by me on:
by posting it to the Defendant on   at the address stated on the summons.

                    Officer of the Court

OR I certify that the summons has not been served for the following reasons:

                    Officer of the Court

OYEZ The Solicitors' Law Stationery Society Ltd, Oyez House, 7 Spa Road, London SE16 3QQ   11 93 126029

County Court N5   5039016

Reproduced by kind permission of The Solicitors' Law Stationery Society Ltd

for each defendant. Where the plaintiff wishes the court to effect service he must file a request for issue (County Court Form N204). Where service is to be effected otherwise than by the court a further copy of the summons must also be filed for the court instead of a request for the issue of the summons.

The plaintiff must also file one copy of the particulars of claim for every defendant plus one for the court (CCR Ord 3, r3(1); Ord 6, r1(4)).

County Court Rules, Ord 3, r3

Commencement of action

> **3.**—(1) Subject to paragraphs (1A) and (1B), a plaintiff desiring to commence a default or fixed date action shall file a request for the issue of a summons, together with particulars of claim and copies required by Order 6.
>
> (1A) If the plaintiff so desires and the proper officer so allows, the summons may be prepared by the plaintiff and in that event the summons with a copy for each defendant shall be filed by the plaintiff with the documents mentioned in paragraph (1) and, where service is to be effected otherwise than by an officer of the court, a copy of the summons shall be filed for the court instead of a request.
>
> (1B) Without prejudice to paragraph (1A), the summons in an action for recovery of land, including one in which the mortgagee under a mortgage of land claims possession of the mortgaged land, shall be prepared by the plaintiff and in that event the summons with a copy for each defendant shall be filed by the plaintiff with the documents mentioned in paragraph (1) and, where service is to be effected otherwise than by an officer of the court, a copy of the summons shall be filed for the court instead of a request.

Issue fee and fixed costs

Issue fee   The issue fee at the date of publication in actions for recovery of land is £40 (the County Court Fees Order 1982 as amended; *Green Book*, Part 3). However, if the action includes a claim for a sum of money the fee is ascertained according to the following scale with a minimum fee of £40 (see Col 3 of the Fees Order: Method of Charging Fee):

£500 or less	10p for every £1 or part thereof
Exceeds £500 but does not exceed £1,000	£60
Exceeds £1,000 but does not exceed £5,000	£65
Exceeds £5,000	£70

Where the amount claimed is unspecified or includes a claim for an increasing and unlimited sum, for example where continuing mesne profits are claimed, a fee of £70 is payable. As a matter of practice it is better to send the maximum fee if uncertain of the amount payable. If the fee sent is too low the court will return all the papers without issuing. If the fee is too high the court will issue and send a refund.

Solicitor's fixed costs The solicitor's fixed costs to be entered on the request are the following: £56 where service is not by a solicitor and £62 where service is by a solicitor (CCR Ord 38, r18; CCR Appendix B, r3(*b*)). The summons will be served by post in the first instance unless the landlord requests otherwise. If he wishes to serve the summons personally he should ask the court to return it to him for that purpose. (See further *below* as to service.)

Receipt of the summons by the tenant

On receipt of the summons the defendant may and in most cases should complete and file the reply form supplied by the court or, if more appropriate, a defence and counterclaim. He may do so at any time until the return day (CCR Ord 9, r9(1)), but if the document is not filed within 14 days of receipt of the summons the defendant may be penalised in costs (CCR Ord 9, r9(3)). If the tenant files an admission the landlord cannot apply for judgment but he need not thereafter call any evidence to prove any fact that the admission makes it unnecessary to prove. Furthermore, he will not be able to recover the costs of proving any such fact (CCR Ord 9, r16). A Rent Act tenant is not, however, bound by an admission that the landlord is entitled to possession. The court must consider whether it is reasonable to make the order (*Smith v McGoldrick* (1977) 242 EG 1047: see further p290 for 'consent orders'). The defendant may appear on the return day and dispute the claim even though he has not delivered a defence (CCR Ord 9, r9(2)). For advice to be given to tenants see p319.

Joinder by non-parties

Any person not named as a defendant in the summons may at any stage in the proceedings apply to the court to be added as a defendant. The application is made *ex parte* in a letter stating the grounds of the application and showing that the applicant is in possession of the land, and if by a tenant naming him (CCR Ord 15, r3). The application may even be made after judgment and execution of the order for possession (*Minet v Johnson* (1890) 63 LT 507; see further 'Setting aside ', p219).

The hearing date; directions; no summary judgment

The automatic directions set out in CCR Ord 17, r11 do not apply to actions for recovery of land (Ord 17, r11(*i*)) and, as stated in the introduction to this Chapter, generally speaking, the 'return day' will be the day fixed for the hearing of the claim (CCR Ord 3, r3(3), (4)).

CCR Ord 3, r3
> (3) In the case of a fixed date action to which Order 17, rule 11 [*automatic directions*] does not apply, the return day shall, unless the court otherwise directs or paragraph (4) applies, be a day fixed for the pre-trial review.

(4) Paragraph (3) shall not apply to an action for recovery of land unless a claim is joined for some relief other than the payment of mesne profits or arrears of rent or for moneys secured by a mortgage or charge [*as to which see p384*].

However, the parties may apply for procedural directions (CCR Ord 13, r2) and the District Judge may of his own motion give directions or fix a date for a pre-trial review (Ord 13, r2; Ord 17, r10). If directions are given they will include an order for the exchange of witness statements (CCR Ord 20, r12A). If expert evidence is to be called a separate order is required (Ord 20, r27).

The initial hearing is listed for only a short period (five or ten minutes). If the plaintiff can persuade the court within that time that he is entitled to possession the matter will be dealt with. If it is likely to take longer and/or will involve further pleadings and discovery the case will usually be adjourned and directions given. Although that is the usual position, the court's list of cases often finishes earlier than originally expected. In those circumstances the court will usually be prepared to hear any case which it has time to hear so long as no further directions are required. It is therefore often worthwhile, from the plaintiff's point of view, being prepared to wait. From the defendant's point of view it should not be assumed that a case will be adjourned merely because it is going to last for more than a short period. Unless the plaintiff has agreed to an adjournment in advance the defendant should be prepared for the case to go ahead.

It is not possible to claim summary judgment in a possession action (CCR Ord 9, r14(1)(*b*)) but the fact that the return date in a fixed date action is the date upon which the claim is due to be heard in effect means that the first hearing in all claims for possession takes place soon after issue and without having to wait for lengthy procedural steps to be completed. (Distinguish the summary procedure available under CCR Ord 24 where the defendant is a licensee who has had his licence revoked or is a trespasser; see Chapter 25.)

Further and better particulars, discovery, interim payments

As in any other county court proceedings the parties may seek orders in respect of further and better particulars of the pleadings (CCR Ord 6, r7), interrogatories (CCR Ord 14, r11) and discovery (CCR Ord 14, rr1, 2). The county court has power to make an order for interim payments of rent or mesne profits for use and occupation (CCR Ord 13, r12).

Amendment

Before service of the summons it is possible to amend the summons so as to add or delete a party without leave (CCR Ord 7, r17); but after service it is necessary to make an application to the court (CCR Ord 15, r1). Any other amendment of the pleadings may be made without leave at any time prior to the pre-trial review (CCR Ord 15, r2(1)). If there is no pre-trial review, as is the case in most possession actions, the pleading may be amended at any time before the hearing date by filing the amended pleading with the court and serving a copy on the other party (CCR Ord 15, r2(1)). The court may of its own motion or on the application of the other party disallow any amendment made after service of the summons in respect of the pleading, or even before service of the summons in respect of an amendment adding or deleting a party. The court will disallow the amendment where it is satisfied that, if an application for leave had been made, it would have been refused (CCR Ord 15, r2(3)). An amendment will always be allowed if it can be made without injustice to the other side, and there is no injustice if the other side can be compensated by costs (see note to CCR Ord 15, r1).

Adjournment

The court may at any time adjourn any proceedings upon application by either party or of its own motion (CCR Ord 13, r3). The court's power to adjourn is discretionary but must be exercised judicially. The parties cannot themselves adjourn the trial without the sanction of the District Judge or the judge (see note to CCR Ord 13, r3). If a party is too ill to attend he should not be refused an application to adjourn unless there is evidence to show that the application is not genuine (see note). If a hearing has been adjourned generally any party may apply for a new hearing date (CCR Ord 13, r3(3)). If no application is made for a new hearing within 12 months of the adjournment the court will serve notice on the parties in Form N250 and unless any party applies within 14 days of receipt of the notice to have a date fixed for the hearing of the action or for a further adjournment the action will be struck out (CCR Ord 13, r3(4)).

The court has an additional power (except in respect of proceedings under Cases 11–20 of Part II of Sched 15 to the Rent Act 1977) to adjourn proceedings for such period or periods as it thinks fit where the property is a dwelling house let on a protected tenancy or subject to statutory tenancy (s100(1) of the Rent Act 1977, as amended by s75 of the Housing Act 1980). If the court decides to adjourn the proceedings under s100 it must impose conditions with regard to the payment of rent, or payments for use and occupation (mesne profits), or such other conditions as it thinks fit although the court need not do so if it would cause hardship to the tenant or would otherwise be unreasonable. Similar provisions apply to the adjournment of hearings in respect of secure tenancies where possession is claimed under Grounds 1–8 or 12–16 of Sched 2 to the Housing Act 1985 (see s85); agricultural tenancies where possession is claimed under Cases I–X of Sched 4 to the Rent (Agriculture) Act 1976 (see s7); and assured tenancies except where the landlord is entitled to possession on one of the mandatory grounds in Part I of Sched 2 to the

Housing Act 1988 or by virtue of s21(1) or (4) of the 1988 Act (assured shorthold cases).

Discontinuance (CCR Ord 18)

The plaintiff may discontinue the proceedings at any time before judgment or final order by filing a notice of discontinuance (Form N279) with the court office. He will have to pay the defendant's taxed costs unless the court, on the application of the plaintiff, otherwise directs (r2(1)). Discontinuance of a claim is no bar to further proceedings based upon the same or a similar cause of action (r2(3)).

Jurisdiction of the District Judge

The District Judge has power to hear and determine (*a*) any claim for possession in which the defendant fails to appear at the hearing or admits the claim; and (*b*) by leave of the judge *and* with the consent of the parties, any other action or matter (CCR Ord 21, r5). Further, any powers of a county court in proceedings for the recovery of possession of any premises in the circumstances mentioned in s3(1) of the Protection from Eviction Act 1977 (see p254) may be exercised with the leave of the judge by any District Judge of the court, except in so far as the rules of the court otherwise provide (s9(2) of the 1977 Act). With regard to applications under the Rent Act, originating application procedure may also be heard by the District Judge (p283).

In any other case the claim must be heard by the Circuit Judge.

Accelerated possession procedure

Rules 6 and 6A of Ord 49 of the County Court Rules (as introduced by the County Court (Amendment No 3) Rules 1993) provide for an accelerated possession procedure in certain assured and assured shorthold tenancy cases. Where various conditions are satisfied this procedure may be used by the landlord instead of the fixed date action. The main features of the procedure are that:

(1) the application is made by prescribed form and the defendant's reply is given on a form provided by the court.

(2) if the court is satisfied that the landlord is entitled to an order for possession no hearing takes place.

Rule 6 relates to assured tenancies and rule 6A relates to assured shortholds. The full text of these rules is set out on p276. It will be noted that some features are common to both situations and that others apply to the specific type of tenancy in question.

The conditions

There are two conditions that apply in all cases. The accelerated possession procedure may only be used:

(1) where the tenancy and any agreement for the tenancy were entered into on or after 15 January 1989 (r6(3)(*a*); r6A(3)(*a*), (9)(*a*)). It would, therefore, seem that the procedure may not be used where the tenancy is an assured tenancy by succession following a tenancy which was regulated under the 1977 Act (cf s39(6); and see p155).

(2) where the only purpose of the proceedings is to recover possession of the dwelling house and no other claim is made in the proceedings, such as for arrears of rent (r6(3)(*c*), r6A(3)(*b*), (9)(*b*)).

There are further conditions that apply only to assured or to assured shorthold cases.

Assured tenancies   Where the landlord is seeking to recover a dwelling house let on an assured tenancy the procedure may only be used where the proceedings are brought:

(*a*) on Ground 1 (landlord occupation);
(*b*) on Ground 3 (former holiday occupation);
(*c*) on Ground 4 (former student letting); or
(*d*) on Ground 5 (occupation by a minister of religion);

and the proceedings are brought against the tenant to whom the requisite notice was given (r6(3)(*b*), (*e*)). The tenant must have been given the requisite notice not later than the relevant date, that is, the beginning of the tenancy (r6(3)(*f*)). The 'requisite' notice means such notice as is mentioned in any of the Grounds for possession (r6(1); see p113).

For the other conditions that apply to assured tenancies see r6(3)(*d*), (*g*).

Assured shortholds   Where the landlord is seeking to recover possession under s21 of the Act, that is, of a dwelling house let on an assured tenancy which is an assured shorthold, the specific conditions for the use of the procedure vary depending upon whether a notice has been served in accordance with s21(1)(*b*) (notice served before or on the expiry date of a fixed term; see p127) or a notice was served in accordance with s21(4) (notice served after expiry date of a fixed term; see p129).

Where the landlord is relying upon a notice served pursuant to s21(1)(*b*) of the 1988 Act the specific conditions that must be satisfied are set out in subparagraphs (*c*)–(*e*) of r6A(3).

Where the landlord is relying upon a notice served pursuant to s21(4) of the 1988 Act the specific conditions that must be satisfied are set out in subparagraphs (*c*)–(*e*) of r6A(9).

Making the application; the prescribed form

The application must be made in the prescribed form (County Court Form N5A; see p283) and a copy of the application, with a copy for each defendant, must be filed in the court for the district in which the house is situated (Ord 49, r6(5), r6A(5)). The fixed sum allowed in respect of solicitor's charges for preparing and filing the application, the documents attached to the application and the request for possession where an order for possession is made is currently £64.

The rules state that the application must:

(1) include the information and statements set out in r6(6) if Grounds 1, 3, 4 or 5 are being relied upon; or the information and statements set out in r6A(6) in the case of an assured shorthold; and

(2) have attached to it copies of the documents mentioned in r6(7) or, in the case of an assured shorthold, of the documents mentioned in r6A(7).

The information required by the rules can be seen by a perusal of the prescribed form. It should be noted that para 7 of the form is pertinent where the tenancy is *not* an assured shorthold and paras 8–11 are pertinent where the tenancy *is* an assured shorthold.

The statements made in the application and any documents attached to the application must be verified by oath (r6(8), r6A(8)). As can be seen, the prescribed form is in fact in the form of an affidavit containing the details required and exhibiting the necessary documents.

Service of the application

Service of the application and of the attachments to it is effected by an officer of the court sending them by first class post to the defendant at the address stated in the application and the usual rules that relate to service (Ord 7, r10(3), (4), r15; see p293) apply (Ord 49, r6(9), r6A(11)).

Opposing the application

A defendant who wishes to oppose the plaintiff's application must, within 14 days after service of the application on him, complete and deliver at the court office the form of reply which was attached to the application (Ord 49, r6(10), r6A(12); County Court Form N11A. If the tenant wishes to oppose the order for possession it is very important that the form be completed otherwise the court will undoubtedly make the order.

If the tenant accepts that an order for possession will be made but wishes to obtain more than the usual 14-day order he should set out such matters that may assist in Box 11 of the reply. The court may only give an extension of time up to six weeks and even then only in exceptional circumstances (s89 of the Housing Act 1980; see p75) so it is important to set out full details of the matters relied upon.

Filing a request for possession; reference to the judge

Where the 14-day period referred to above has expired without the defendant filing a reply, the plaintiff may file a written request for an order for possession and 'the proper officer shall without delay refer the plaintiff's application to the judge' (r6(12), r6A(14)) or the District Judge (r6(18), r6A(20)).

If the court receives a reply from the defendant the court officer will send a copy of it to the plaintiff and refer the reply and the plaintiff's application to the judge. If the reply is received after the 14-day period referred to above but before the plaintiff files a request for judgment 'the proper officer shall without delay refer the plaintiff's application to the judge' (r6(11), r6A(13)).

The judge's decision

After considering the application and the defendant's reply (if any) the judge must either (*a*) make an order for possession or (*b*) fix a day for a hearing and give directions regarding the steps to be taken before and at the hearing (r6(13), r6A(15)). However, as will be seen below, the judge is not given a discretion in the matter. He must make the order for possession if the plaintiff is entitled to it.

Assured tenancies   A day will be fixed for the hearing of the application where the judge is not satisfied as to any of the following:
  (1) that the requisite notice was given before the relevant date;
  (2) that a notice was served in accordance with s8 of the 1988 Act and that the time limits specified in the 1988 Act have been complied with;
  (3) that service of the application was duly effected; or
  (4) that the plaintiff has established that he is entitled to recover possession under the ground relied on against the defendant (r6(14)).

Assured shorthold cases   A day will be fixed for the hearing of the application where the judge is not satisfied as to any of the following:
  (1) that a written notice was served in accordance with s20 of the 1988 Act;
  (2) that a written notice was given in accordance with s21 of the 1988 Act;
  (3) that service of the application was duly effected; or
  (4) that the plaintiff has established that he is entitled to recover possession under s21 of the 1988 Act against the defendant (r6A(16)).

Where the judge is not satisfied as to one or more of the above factors and a hearing is fixed the court must give all parties not less than 14 days' notice of the day so fixed and 'the judge may give such directions regarding the steps to be taken before and at the hearing as may appear to him to be necessary or desirable' (r6(16), r6A(18)).

However, where the judge is satisfied as to all the above matters he 'shall without delay make an order for possession without requiring the attendance of the parties' (r6(15), r6A(17)). The usual order for possession will be 14 days. However, the court may in exceptional circumstances make an order giving the defendant up to six weeks before he is required to give possession (s89 of the Housing Act 1980; see p73).

Setting aside the order for possession

In addition to the usual rule permitting a defendant to apply to set aside a court order on failure of postal service (CCR Ord 37, r3), the court may, on application made on notice *within 14 days of service of the order* or of its own motion, set aside, vary or confirm any order made under the accelerated possession procedure (r6(17), r6A(19)). The application should be made in accordance with CCR Ord 13, r1, by notice of application supported by affidavit. If more than 14 days have elapsed application for an extension of time should be made under CCR Ord 13, r4, supported by an affidavit setting out the reason for the delay.

CCR Ord 49, rr6, 6A
Housing Act 1988: assured tenancies
6.—(1) In this rule—
'the 1988 Act' means the Housing Act 1988;
'dwelling house' has the same meaning as in Part I of the 1988 Act;
a Ground referred to by number means the Ground so numbered in Schedule 2 to the 1988 Act;
'the requisite notice' means such a notice as is mentioned in any of those Grounds and
'the relevant date' means the beginning of the tenancy.
(2) This rule applies to proceedings brought by a landlord to recover possession of a dwelling house which has been let on an assured tenancy in a case where all the conditions mentioned in paragraph (3) below are satisfied.
(3) The conditions referred to in paragraph (2) are these:
(a) The tenancy and any agreement for the tenancy were entered into on or after 15th January 1989.
(b) The proceedings are brought
(i) on Ground 1 (landlord occupation),
(ii) on Ground 3 (former holiday occupation),
(iii) on Ground 4 (former student letting) or
(iv) on Ground 5 (occupation by a minister of religion).
(c) The only purpose of the proceedings is to recover possession of the dwelling house and no other claim is made in the proceedings (such as for arrears of rent).
(d) The tenancy is an assured tenancy within the meaning of the 1988 Act (and consequently is not a protected, statutory or housing association tenancy under the Rent Act 1977) and
(i) is the subject of a written agreement, or

(ii) is on the same terms (though not necessarily as to rent) as a tenancy which was the subject of a written agreement and arises by virtue of section 5 of the 1988 Act, or

(iii) relates to the same or substantially the same premises which were let to the same tenant and is on the same terms (though not necessarily as to rent or duration) as a tenancy which was the subject of a written agreement.

Where the tenancy in relation to which the proceedings are brought arises by virtue of section 5 of the 1988 Act but follows a tenancy which was the subject of an oral agreement, the condition mentioned in sub-paragraph (*d*)(ii) or (iii) above is not satisfied.

(*e*) The proceedings are brought against the tenant to whom the requisite notice was given.

(*f*) The tenant was given the requisite notice, not later than the relevant date.

(*g*) The tenant was given notice in accordance with section 8 of the 1988 Act that proceedings for possession would be brought.

(4) Where the conditions mentioned in paragraph (3) of this rule are satisfied, the landlord may bring possession proceedings under this rule instead of making a claim in accordance with Order 6, rule 3 (action for recovery of land by summons).

(5) The application must be made in the prescribed form and a copy of the application, with a copy for each defendant, must be filed in the court for the district in which the dwelling house is situated.

(6) The application shall include the following information and statements.

(*a*) A statement identifying the dwelling house which is the subject matter of the proceedings.

(*b*) A statement identifying the nature of the tenancy, namely—

(i) whether it is the subject of a written agreement, or

(ii) whether the tenancy arises by virtue of section 5 of the 1988 Act, or

(iii) where it is the subject of an oral agreement whether the tenancy is periodic or for a fixed term and, if for a fixed term, the length of the term and the date of termination.

(*c*) A statement that the dwelling house (or another dwelling house) was not let to the tenant by the landlord (or any of his predecessors) before 15th January 1989.

(*d*) The date on which and the method by which the requisite notice was given to the tenant.

(*e*) A statement identifying the Ground on which possession is claimed giving sufficient particulars to substantiate the plaintiff's claim to be entitled to possession on that Ground.

(*f*) A statement that a notice was served on the tenant in accordance with section 8 of the 1988 Act,

(i) specifying the date on which and the method by which the notice was served, and

(ii) confirming that the period of notice required by section 8 of the 1988 Act has been given.

(*g*) The amount of rent which is currently payable.

(7) Copies of the following documents shall be attached to the application—

(i) the current (or most recent) written tenancy agreement

(ii) the requisite notice (referred to in paragraph (6)(*d*) above), and

(iii) the notice served in accordance with section 8 of the 1988 Act,

together with any other documents necessary to prove the plaintiff's claim.

(8) The statements made in the application and any documents attached to the application shall be verified by the plaintiff on oath.

(9) Service of the application and of the attachments shall be effected by an officer of the court sending them by first class post to the defendant at the address stated in the application and paragraphs (3) and (4) of Order 7, rule 10 (mode of service) and Order 7, rule 15 (service of summons for recovery of land) shall apply as they apply where service is effected under those rules.

(10) A defendant who wishes to oppose the plaintiff's application must, within 14 days after the service of the application on him, complete and deliver at the court office the form of reply which was attached to the application.

(11) On receipt of the defendant's reply the proper officer shall—

(*a*) send a copy of it to the plaintiff;

(*b*) refer the reply and the plaintiff's application to the judge,

and where a reply is received after the period mentioned in paragraph (10) but before a request is filed in accordance with paragraph (12) the reply shall be referred without delay to the judge.

(12) Where the period mentioned in paragraph (10) has expired without the defendant filing a reply, the plaintiff may file a written request for an order for possession and the proper officer shall without delay refer the plaintiff's application to the judge.

(13) After considering the application and the defendant's reply (if any), the judge shall either—

(*a*) make an order for possession under paragraph (15), or

(*b*) fix a day for a hearing under paragraph (14) and give directions regarding the steps to be taken before and at the hearing.

(14) The proper officer shall fix a day for the hearing of the application where the judge is not satisfied as to any of the following—

(*a*) that the requisite notice was given before the relevant date,

(*b*) that a notice was served in accordance with section 8 of the 1988 Act and that the time limits specified in the 1988 Act have been complied with,

(*c*) that service of the application was duly effected, or

(*d*) that the plaintiff has established that he is entitled to recover possession under the Ground relied on against the defendant.

(15) Except where paragraph (14) applies, the judge shall without delay make an order for possession without requiring the attendance of the parties.

(16) Where a hearing is fixed under paragraph (14)—

(*a*) the proper officer shall give to all parties not less than 14 days' notice of the day so fixed;

(*b*) the judge may give such directions regarding the steps to be taken before and at the hearing as may appear to him to be necessary or desirable.

(17) Without prejudice to Order 37, rule 3 (setting aside on failure of postal service), the court may, on application made on notice within 14 days

of service of the order or of its own motion, set aside, vary or confirm any order made under paragraph (15).

(18) Without prejudice to Order 21, rule 5 and to Order 50, rule 3, a district judge shall have power to hear and determine an application to which this rule applies and references in this rule to the judge shall include references to the district judge.

Housing Act 1988: assured shorthold tenancies

6A.—(1) In this rule, 'the 1988 Act' means the Housing Act 1988 and 'dwelling house' has the same meaning as in Part I of the 1988 Act.

(2) This rule applies to proceedings brought by a landlord under section 21 of the 1988 Act to recover possession of a dwelling house let on an assured shorthold tenancy on the expiry or termination of that tenancy in a case where all the conditions mentioned in paragraph (3) below (or, as the case may be, paragraph (9)) are satisfied.

(3) The conditions referred to in paragraph (2) are these:
- (a) The tenancy and any agreement for the tenancy were entered into on or after 15th January 1989.
- (b) The only purpose of the proceedings is to recover possession of the dwelling house and no other claim is made in the proceedings (such as for arrears of rent).
- (c) The tenancy—
    - (i) was an assured shorthold tenancy and not a protected, statutory or housing association tenancy under the Rent Act 1977;
    - (ii) did not immediately follow an assured tenancy which was not an assured shorthold tenancy;
    - (iii) fulfilled the conditions mentioned in section 20(1)(a) to (c) of the 1988 Act; and
    - (iv) was the subject of a written agreement.
- (d) A notice in writing was served on the tenant in accordance with section 20(2) of the 1988 Act and the proceedings are brought against the tenant on whom that notice was served.
- (e) A notice in accordance with section 21(1)(b) of the 1988 Act was given to the tenant in writing.

(4) Where the conditions mentioned in paragraph (3) or paragraph (9) of this rule are satisfied, the landlord may bring possession proceedings under this rule instead of making a claim in accordance with Order 6, rule 3 (action for recovery of land by summons).

(5) The application must be made in the prescribed form and a copy of the application, with a copy for each defendant, shall be filed in the court for the district in which the dwelling house is situated.

(6) The application shall include the following information and statements:
- (a) A statement identifying the dwelling house which is the subject matter of the proceedings.
- (b) A statement that the dwelling house (or another dwelling house) was not let to the tenant by the landlord (or any of his predecessors) before 15th January 1989.
- (c) A statement that possession is claimed on the expiry of an assured shorthold tenancy under section 21 of the 1988 Act giving sufficient particulars to substantiate the plaintiff's claim to be entitled to possession.

(*d*) A statement that a written notice was served on the tenant in accordance with section 20(2) of the 1988 Act.

(*e*) A statement that a notice in writing was given to the tenant in accordance with section 21(1) of the 1988 Act specifying the date on which, and the method by which, the notice was given.

(*f*) In a case where the original fixed term tenancy has expired, a statement that no other assured tenancy is in existence other than an assured shorthold periodic tenancy (whether statutory or not).

(*g*) A statement confirming that there is no power under the tenancy agreement for the landlord to determine the tenancy (within the meaning given for the purposes of Part I of the 1988 Act by section 45(4) of the 1988 Act) at a time earlier than six months from the beginning of the tenancy.

(*h*) A statement that no notice under section 20(5) of the 1988 Act has been served.

(7) Copies of the following documents shall be attached to the application—

(i) the written tenancy agreement (or, in a case to which paragraph (9) applies, the current (or most recent) written tenancy agreement),

(ii) the written notice served in accordance with section 20(2) of the 1988 Act, and

(iii) the notice in writing given in accordance with section 21 of the 1988 Act,

together with any other documents necessary to prove the plaintiff's claim.

(8) The statements made in the application and any documents attached to the application shall be verified by the plaintiff on oath.

(9) Where on the coming to an end of an assured shorthold tenancy (including a tenancy which was an assured shorthold but ceased to be assured before it came to an end) a new assured shorthold tenancy of the same or substantially the same premises (in this paragraph referred to as the premises') comes into being under which the landlord and the tenant are the same as at the coming to an end of the earlier tenancy, then the provisions of this rule apply to that tenancy but with the following conditions instead of those in paragraph (3)—

(*a*) The tenancy and any agreement for the tenancy were entered into on or after 15th January 1989.

(*b*) The only purpose of the proceedings is to recover possession of the dwelling house and no other claim is made in the proceedings (such as for arrears of rent).

(*c*) The tenancy in relation to which the proceedings are brought—

(i) is an assured shorthold tenancy within the meaning of section 20 of the 1988 Act and consequently is not a protected, statutory or housing association tenancy under the Rent Act 1977;

(ii) did not immediately follow an assured tenancy which was not an assured shorthold tenancy, and

(*aa*) is the subject of a written agreement, or

(*ab*) is on the same terms (though not necessarily as to rent) as a tenancy which was the subject of a written agreement and arises by virtue of section 5 of the 1988 Act, or (*ac*) relates to the same or substantially the same premises which were let to the same tenant and is on the same terms (though not necessarily as to rent or duration) as a tenancy which was the subject of a written agreement.

Where the tenancy in relation to which the proceedings are brought arises by virtue of section 5 of the 1988 Act but follows a tenancy which was the subject of an oral agreement, the conditions mentioned in sub-paragraph (*c*)(ii)(*ab*) or (*ac*) above is not satisfied.

(*d*) A written notice was served in accordance with section 20(2) of the 1988 Act on the tenant in relation to the first assured shorthold tenancy of the premises and the proceedings are brought against the tenant on whom that notice was served.

(*e*) A notice in writing was given to the tenant in accordance with section 21(4) of the 1988 Act.

(10) In a case to which paragraph (9) applies, the application shall include the following information and statements:

(*a*) A statement identifying the dwelling house which is the subject matter of the proceedings.

(*b*) A statement identifying the nature of the tenancy, namely—
  (i) whether it is the subject of a written agreement;
  (ii) whether the tenancy arises by virtue of section 5 of the 1988 Act; or
  (iii) where it is the subject of an oral agreement whether the tenancy is periodic or for a fixed term and, if for a fixed term, the length of the term and the date of termination.

(*c*) A statement that the dwelling house (or another dwelling house) was not let to the tenant by the landlord (or any of his predecessors) before 15th January 1989.

(*d*) A statement that possession is claimed under section 21 of the 1988 Act giving sufficient particulars to substantiate the plaintiff's claim to be entitled to possession.

(*e*) A statement that a written notice was served in accordance with section 20(2) of the 1988 Act in relation to the first assured shorthold tenancy of the premises on the tenant against whom the proceedings are brought.

(*f*) A statement that a notice in writing was given to the tenant in accordance with section 21(4) of the 1988 Act specifying the date on which, and the method by which, the notice was given.

(*g*) In a case where the tenancy is a fixed term tenancy which has expired, a statement that no other assured tenancy is in existence other than an assured shorthold periodic tenancy (whether statutory or not).

(*h*) A statement confirming that there was no power under the tenancy agreement for the landlord to determine (within the meaning given for the purposes of Part I of the 1988 Act by section 45(4) of the 1988 Act) the first assured shorthold tenancy of the premises to the tenant against whom the proceedings are brought at a time earlier than six months from the beginning of the tenancy.

(*i*) A statement that no notice under section 20(5) of the 1988 Act has been served.

(*j*) The amount of rent which is currently payable.

(11) Service of the application and of the attachments shall be effected by an officer of the court sending them by first class post to the defendant at the address stated in the application and paragraphs (3) and (4) of Order 7, rule 10 (mode of service) and Order 7, rule 15 (service of summons for recovery of land) shall apply as they apply where service is effected under those rules.

(12) A defendant who wishes to oppose the plaintiff's application must, within 14 days after the service of the application on him, complete and deliver at the court office the form of reply which was attached to the application.

(13) On receipt of the defendant's reply the proper officer shall—

(*a*) send a copy of it to the plaintiff;

(*b*) refer the reply and the plaintiff's application to the judge

and where a reply is received after the period mentioned in paragraph (12) but before a request is filed in accordance with paragraph (14) the reply shall be referred without delay to the judge.

(14) Where the period mentioned in paragraph (12) has expired without the defendant filing a reply, the plaintiff may file a written request for an order for possession and the proper officer shall without delay refer any such request to the judge.

(15) After considering the application and the defendant's reply (if any), the judge shall either—

(*a*) make an order for possession under paragraph (17); or

(*b*) fix a day for a hearing under paragraph (16) and give directions regarding the steps to be taken before and at the hearing.

(16) The proper officer shall fix a day for the hearing of the application where the judge is not satisfied as to any of the following—

(*a*) that a written notice was served in accordance with section 20 of the 1988 Act,

(*b*) that a written notice was given in accordance with section 21 of the 1988 Act,

(*c*) that service of the application was duly effected, or

(*d*) that the plaintiff has established that he is entitled to recover possession under section 21 of the 1988 Act against the defendant.

(17) Except where paragraph (16) applies, the judge shall without delay make an order for possession without requiring the attendance of the parties.

(18) Where a hearing is fixed under paragraph (16)—

(*a*) the proper officer shall give to all parties not less than 14 days' notice of the day so fixed;

(*b*) the judge may give such directions regarding the steps to be taken before and at the hearing as may appear to him to be necessary or desirable.

(19) Without prejudice to Order 37, rule 3 (setting aside on failure of postal service), the court may, on application made on notice within 14 days of service of the order or of its own motion, set aside, vary or confirm any order made under paragraph (17).

(20) Without prejudice to Order 21, rule 5 and to Order 50, rule 3, a district judge shall have power to hear and determine an application to which this rule applies and references in this rule to the judge shall include references to the district judge.

Form 35: Application for possession (assured tenancies)

Application for Possession

(Assured Tenancies)

Case Number	Always quote this number

In the

County Court

The court office is open from 10 am to 4 pm Monday to Friday

Telephone

Seal

Plaintiff's full name and address.

Name and address for service and payment.
(if different from above)
Ref/Tel. no.

Defendant's name *(including title e.g. Mr Mrs or Miss)* and address.

The Plaintiff (your Landlord) is **claiming possession** of

Court fee	
Solicitor's costs	
Total amount	
Application issued on	

What this means

- The court will be deciding whether or not you have to leave, and if you have to leave, when.

You must act immediately — there will not normally be a court hearing.

- **Read this application**, the information leaflet enclosed and the affidavit.
- **Get advice** from an advice agency (a list of agencies is attached) or a solicitor.
- **Fill in the form of reply** and return it to the court office.

More information about assured tenancies is available in Housing Booklet 19 (Assured Tenancies). The booklet is produced by the Department of the Environment. Your local Citizens Advice Bureau will have a copy.

Affidavit to support my application for possession

Paragraph 1.
Insert full name, address and occupation of person making this affidavit. Give the address of the property and delete words in brackets to show whether property is a house or part of one.

1 I,

make this affidavit to support my application for an order for possession of

which is a [dwelling-house] [part of a dwelling-house].

Paragraph 2(a).
Give the date of the current (or latest) written tenancy agreement. A copy of the agreement must be attached (exhibited) to this affidavit. It must contain all the terms of the agreement.

2 (a) On the   day of   19   , I entered into a written tenancy agreement with the Defendant(s). A copy of that agreement, marked 'A', is exhibited to this affidavit. Both the tenancy and the agreement were made on or after 15 January 1989.

Paragraph 2(b).

Delete the words in brackets if the rent and duration of the tenancy are as set out in the written agreement. If either has changed, delete (i) or (ii) as appropriate.

(b) The current agreement relates to the same, or substantially the same, property. The terms are the same as set out in the agreement at paragraph 2(a) (except for:

(i) the amount of rent to be paid. The current rent is

£   per   ;

(ii) the duration of the tenancy.)

Paragraph 3.

Delete the words in brackets if there was no previous landlord.

3

Neither I, [nor the previous landlord] let the property mentioned above, or any other property, to the Defendant[s] before 15 January 1989.

Paragraph 4.

Delete the words in brackets, as appropriate, to show whether there is/are one or more defendant(s) and whether the tenancy is an assured tenancy i.e. you are claiming possession on one of the grounds set out in paragraph 7, or an assured shorthold tenancy. Give date when tenant(s) moved into the property.

4

The Defendant[s] [is] [are] the original tenant[s] to whom the property was let under the assured [shorthold] tenancy agreement. The tenant[s] first occupied the property on

Paragraph 5.

Delete the word in brackets to show whether the tenancy is an assured tenancy i.e. you are claiming possession on one of the grounds set out in paragraph 7, or an assured shorthold tenancy.

5

The tenancy is an assured [shorthold] tenancy and not a protected, statutory or housing association tenancy under the Rent Act.

Paragraph 6.

Delete the words in brackets to show whether the tenancy is an assured or an assured shorthold tenancy. Delete paragraphs (a)–(c) as appropriate to show how the latest tenancy agreement came about.

6

The tenancy is an assured [shorthold] tenancy:

(a) It is subject to the written agreement referred to in paragraph 2(a) above. I have served a notice on the Defendant[s] that I wish to have possession of the property.

(b) The written agreement referred to in paragraph 2(a) has expired. There is now a further assured [shorthold] tenancy for an unspecified period. The terms of this tenancy are the same as in the written tenancy except as indicated at paragraph 2(b). Since the written agreement, there has not been a tenancy which was agreed orally and which was followed by a statutory tenancy.

(c) The written agreement referred to in paragraph 2(a) has expired. There is now a further assured [shorthold] tenancy for a fixed period of months. That period ends on the   day of 19   . The terms of this tenancy are the same as in the written tenancy except as indicated at paragraph 2(b).

Paragraph 7.

Delete the whole of this paragraph if the tenancy is an **assured shorthold tenancy**. If not, delete paragraphs (a)–(e) as appropriate to show the grounds on which you are claiming possession. Evidence to support those grounds must be given in paragraph 16.

7

The tenancy is an assured tenancy and I am seeking an order for possession on the following grounds:

(a) At some time before the start of the tenancy [I] [a joint landlord] occupied the property as my main home. [The joint landlord's name is

.]

(b) [I] [a joint landlord] bought the property before the tenancy started and [I] [my husband] [my wife] [a joint landlord] or the joint landlord's [husband] [wife] intend[s] to live in it as [my] [his] [her] main home. [The joint landlord's name is

.]

(c) The tenancy was for a fixed term of eight months or less and, in the twelve months before the tenancy started, the property was let for a holiday.

(d) The tenancy was for a fixed term of twelve months or less and, in the twelve month period before the tenancy started, the property was let to students by a specified educational establishment.

(e) The property is held for use by a minister of religion as a residence from which to carry out [his] [her] duties and is now needed for this purpose.

Paragraph 8.

Delete this paragraph if the tenancy is an **assured tenancy** i.e. you are claiming possession on one of the grounds set out in paragraph 7 or the latest tenancy is an assured shorthold tenancy for a fixed period.

8

The fixed term tenancy has come to an end. No other assured tenancy exists except an assured shorthold tenancy for an unspecified period.

Paragraph 9.

Delete this paragraph if the tenancy is an **assured tenancy** i.e. you are claiming possession on one of the grounds set out in paragraph 7.

9

The assured shorthold tenancy was for a period of not less than six months. It did not follow an assured tenancy which was not an assured shorthold tenancy.

Paragraph 10.

Delete this paragraph if your tenancy is an **assured tenancy** i.e. you are claiming possession on one of the grounds in paragraph 7.

10

I could not end the tenancy earlier than six months after it began except where the tenant broke the terms of the tenancy agreement.

Paragraph 11.
Delete this paragraph if your tenancy is an **assured tenancy** i.e. you are claiming possession on one of the grounds in paragraph 7.

11 I did not serve a notice on the Defendant[s], before the current assured shorthold tenancy expired, saying that any new tenancy would not be as an assured shorthold tenancy.

Paragraph 12.
Give the date on which the notice was served. A copy of the notice must be exhibited to this affidavit. Delete the words in brackets as appropriate.

12 A notice was served on the Defendant[s] on the   day of
19   which said [I might ask for possession] [confirming that the tenancy was to be an assured shorthold tenancy]. A copy of the notice, marked 'B', is exhibited to this affidavit.

Paragraph 13.
Give details of how the notice (in paragraph 12) was served e.g. delivered personally, by post, etc. Exhibit any proof of service e.g. recorded delivery slip marking it 'B1'.

13

Paragraph 14.
Give the date on which the notice was served and the length of notice given. A copy of the notice must be exhibited to this affidavit.

14 A further notice was served on the Defendant[s] on the   day of
19   which said I intended to make an application for possession of the property. A copy of that notice, marked 'C', is exhibited to this affidavit. The notice of   month[s] has expired.

Paragraph 15.
Give details of how the notice (in paragraph 14) was served e.g. delivered personally, by post, etc. Exhibit any proof of service e.g. recorded delivery slip marking it 'C1'.

15

Paragraph 16.
Give details of further evidence you wish to use to prove your claim for possession. Exhibit any written document(s) which support that evidence marking them 'D1', 'D2' and so on.

16

Paragraph 17.
Insert address of property and the time within which you want possession. You may **not** make any claim for rent arrears.

17 I ask the court to grant me an order for possession of

within   days and for payment of my costs of making this application.

Sworn at

in the   of

this   day of   19

Before me

Officer of a court, appointed by the Circuit Judge to take affidavits.

Certificate of Service

CASE No.

I certify that the summons of which this is a true copy was served by me on (date):

Officer of the Court

OR I certify that the summons has not been served for the following reasons:

Officer of the Court

Reproduced by kind permission of The Solicitors' Law Stationery Society Ltd

Originating application procedure: certain Rent Act grounds

The Rent Act (County Court Proceedings for Possession) Rules 1981 (SI 1981 No 139) provide that in certain cases under the Rent Act 1977 the landlord may, instead of bringing an action for possession, make his claim by an originating application in the county court for the district in which the dwelling house is situated (RA(CCPP)R, r2(2)). The application may be heard by the District Judge or may be referred by him to the judge; and may be heard in private or in open court as the District Judge or judge, as the case may be, thinks fit (RA(CCPP)R, r6). Subject to the provision of the Rent Act Rules, the County Court Rules 1981 apply to originating applications commenced pursuant to those rules (RA(CCPP)R, r2(3)).

Application of the Rent Act Rules

The Rent Act (County Court Proceedings for Possession) Rules 1981 apply to proceedings:
  (1) under Cases 11, 12 or 20, *provided that* the dwelling house is required as a residence for the owner or for any member of the owner's family who resided with him at his death or, where the proceedings are brought under Case 11, for any member of the owner's family who resided with him when he last occupied the dwelling house as his residence—in each case the tenant must also have been given the requisite notice, not later than the relevant date, that possession might be recovered under the Case relied on. (Generally, the landlord may not use this procedure if he needs to ask the court to dispense with the notice requirement but in *Minay v Sentongo* (1983) 45 P&CR 190 the court allowed the landlord to use the procedure where he had sent the notice but it turned out that the tenant had not received it);
  (2) under Cases 13–18 inclusive;
  (3) under Case 19 provided that the dwelling house was let on a protected shorthold tenancy.

Procedure

Rule 3 of the Rent Act (County Court Proceedings for Possession) Rules 1981 provides that the originating application must be in one of the forms prescribed in the rules. These forms are set out in this book:
  (1) Cases 11, 12 or 20, use Form A (Form 35 of this book)
  (2) Cases 13–18 inclusive, use Form B (Form 36 of this book)
  (3) Case 19, use Form C2 (Form 29 of this book)
  Note that the prescribed forms allow for a claim for arrears of rent to be included in addition to a claim for possession. They do not specifically

refer to arrears/mesne profits which may accrue after issue but it is submitted that there is no reason why such further sums should not be claimed in the proceedings.

An affidavit in support of the application verifying the statement in the application, deposing to any other material matter and exhibiting any material documents, should be filed (RA(CCPP)R, r4). The applicant should file the originating application together with as many copies as there are respondents and a request for the issue of the originating application (CCR Ord 3, r4(3)).

Where possession is claimed under Case 11, 12 or 20, each respondent must be served at least seven clear days before the return day (RA(CCPP)R, r5(1)). Service is effected in the same way as a summons is effected (CCR Ord 3, r4(6)). In particular the special provisions set out in CCR Ord 7, r15 apply (RA(CCPP)R, r5; see p294). The respondent need serve no defence or answer.

Where either party wishes any person to attend for cross-examination he should apply to the court for an order that that person do attend (CCR Ord 20, r5).

The hearing

If the proceedings have been incorrectly commenced by originating application under the Rent Act (County Court Proceedings for Possession) Rules 1981 they will not thereby be nullified, but the court may set aside the proceedings wholly or in part or exercise its powers to allow any such amendments and to give any such directions as it thinks fit (CCR Ord 37, r5; *Minay v Sentongo* (1983) 45 P&CR 190). The power to give such directions which is contained in CCR Ord 13, r2 would also be appropriate where the respondent raises a defence at the hearing that could not properly be dealt with on that day. If the case is of any complexity and is listed before the District Judge he will usually transfer it to the judge under r6(1).

The order, costs, appeals and homelessness

Where the plaintiff succeeds in obtaining an order for possession the court's power to postpone that order depends upon the statutory provisions that apply. The position in respect of any particular type of tenancy is dealt with in the appropriate chapter (eg see p115 in assured tenancy cases). If in any particular case there is no such statutory power the court may not make any order postponing the date for possession for more than 14 days, or six weeks in cases of exceptional hardship (s89 of the Housing Act 1980; see p75). Where the defendant entered into possession unlawfully the court has no power to postpone the order for possession without the consent of the plaintiff (*McPhail v Persons Unknown* [1973] Ch 447).

Form 36: Originating application for possession under Case 11, 12 or 20

IN THE	COUNTY COURT	No of Application

IN THE MATTER OF The Rent Act 1977

BETWEEN

                                                 Applicant

—And—

                                                Respondent

1. I, [*state name*] of [*state address and occupation of the applicant*] apply to the Court for an order for recovery of possession of [*here describe the premises*] under Case [11][1], [12][2], [20][3] of Schedule 15 to the Rent Act 1977.

2. The premises were let to the respondent on [*here give the date*] on a protected tenancy having the following terms [*here set out the terms material to the proceedings*].

3. Notice in writing was given to the respondent on [*here give the date*] that possession might be recovered under Case [11][1], [12][2], [20][3] of Schedule 15 to the Rent Act 1977

4. As regards previous lettings of the premises [since they became protected by the Rent Acts][1] [since 14th August 1974][2] [since 28th November 1980][3].   *[Delete whichever two are not applicable]*

    (a)   There has been no such letting; or

    (b)   There has been such a letting, but a notice, such as mentioned in paragraph 3, was given on each occasion, namely [*state, in respect of each notice. the date when it was given and the person to whom it was given*]; or

    (c)   There has been such a letting, or lettings, for which no notice, such as is mentioned in paragraph 3, was given and I ask the Court to make an order for possession notwithstanding on the grounds set out below. [*Here identify the letting. or lettings, referred to and set out the grounds for dispensing with the requirements as to notice*].

[5.   I[4] previously occupied the premises as a residence.][1]

[5.   I[4] intended, at all material times, to occupy the premises as a residence on retirement and retired on [*state the date*].][2]

[5.   I[4] was a member of the regular armed forces of the Crown when the premises were acquired and when the tenancy was granted.][3]

6. The premises are required as a residence.   *[Delete whichever two are not applicable]*

    (a)   for myself; or

    (b)   for [*here identify the person concerned*], who is member of the family of the original owner by whom the tenancy was granted and who was residing with the original owner of his [or her] death; or

    (c)   for [*here identify the person concerned*], who was residing with me when I last occupied the premises as a residence.[5]

7. The protected tenancy has come to an end as follows:—   *[Delete whichever two are not applicable]*

    (a)   by expiring on [*here give date of expiry*], or

    (b)   by a notice to quit being served on [*here give the date*] which expired on [*here give the date*]. but the respondent remains in occupation.

contd

contd

8.   There are rent arrears in the sum of £ [*state amount*], calculated at the rate of   [*Delete if*
[*here give the weekly or other rent*] and I apply to the Court for an order for payment.   *unapplicable*]

The names and addresses of the persons on whom it is intended to serve this application are:
[*state names and addresses for persons intended to be served.*]

My address for service is [*state applicant's address for service*].

DATED

[*Signed*]
Applicant.

---

1   Include this and delete the others where the claim is under Case 11.
2   Include this and delete the others where the claim is under Case 12.
3   Include this and delete the others where the claim is under Case 20.
4   Where the original owner by whom the tenancy was granted has died substitute, for 'I', the
    words 'The original owner by whom the tenancy was granted'. and where Case 12 is relied
    on delete from paragraph 5 the words 'and retired' to the end.
5   Sub-paragraph (c) applies to claims under Case 11 only.

Form 37: Originating application for possession under Cases 13–18

[*Title: as in Form 00*]

1.   I, [*state name*] of [*state address and occupation of the applicant*] apply to the Court for order for recovery of possession of [*here describe the premises*] under Case [*here identify the Case relied on*] of Schedule 15 to the Rent Act 1977.

2.   [*As in Form 00*]

3.   [*As in Form 00 except that the Case referred to in the notice must correspond with the Case cited in paragraph 1, above.*]

4, 5 and 6.   [*Here set out the matters of substance on which the applicant relies as bringing the claim within the Case cited in paragraph 1, above, and state, where relevant, the purpose for which possession is required.*] ·

7 and 8.   [*As in Form 00*].

The names and address of the persons on whom it is intended to serve this application are: [*state name and addresses of persons intended to be serve.*]

My address for service is [*state applicant's address for service*].

DATED

[*Signed*]
Applicant.

The order will be made in one of the county court forms with such variations as the circumstances may require (County Court (Forms) Rules 1982, r2). The forms which are to be found in Appendix 3 are as follows:

N26   Possession and judgment for rent
N26A   Assured tenancy—without judgment for rent
N27   Forfeiture for non-payment of rent
N27(1)   Forfeiture—order for possession refused under Rent Acts but judgment for the rent
N27(2)   Forfeiture—order for possession suspended under the Rent Acts
N28   Suspended order for possession in rent case

The County Court Rules (unlike the High Court Rules; see p304) do not require the landlord to serve the tenant with notice of his intention to enforce the order for possession or to obtain the leave of the court (*Scott James v Chehab* [1988] 2 EGLR 59; *Leicester City Council v Aldwirkle* [1992] 24 HLR 40, CA). The tenant should therefore ask the court to make it a term of any suspended order for possession that the order should not be enforced without the leave of the court after notice to the tenant of the application for leave. (See further p296.)

'Consent' orders

Strictly speaking, a consent order cannot be made in a claim for possession of a dwelling house. The court may only make an order for possession without hearing evidence if the tenant admits that:

(1) no statutory protection applies; or
(2) the landlord is entitled to possession on a Rent Act etc ground; and where the ground is a discretionary one, that it is reasonable to make the order.

If the tenant does so concede, the judge is under no duty to investigate the facts of the case. (See *R v Bloomsbury and Marylebone County Court, ex p Blackburne* (1984) 14 HLR 56; *Syed Hussain v A M Abdullah Sahib and Co* [1985] 1 WLR 1392; *R v Newcastle-upon-Tyne County Court, ex p Thompson* [1988] 2 EGLR 119.) An admission can be implied from the terms of the draft consent order. Whether there is such an admission depends on the terms of the order construed in the light of the surrounding circumstances including the issues in the case (*Bruce v Worthing BC* (1994) 26 WLR 223).

There are many cases where the landlord appreciates that he may have difficulty in obtaining possession and is prepared to compromise the action by paying the tenant a sum to leave. This is often the case where he is seeking to rely upon Case 9 of Sched 15 to the Rent Act 1977 or where he is seeking to show that suitable alternative accommodation is available. The inability simply to present the court with an agreed order can be very inconvenient. In the first edition of this book it was suggested that the way to deal with the problem was for the parties to come to an agreement that the landlord will make the payment to the tenant if, and only if, the order for possession is made. Since then Lord Keith of Kinkel in *Syed Hussain* (a Privy Council case) has said: 'Special considerations might arise if in subsequent proceedings the defendant established by evidence that his agreement was given in pursuance of a compromise which might have involved his being paid a sum of money. Their Lordships prefer to reserve their opinion as to the legal consequences in such a situation'. It is possible, therefore, that the courts will hold that an order for possession made upon an admission by a tenant, induced by a promise of payment, can be set aside. In making any such agreement, the landlord should therefore ensure that it is a term of the agreement that delivery up of possession and payment of the money are concurrent events. It would seem a little difficult for a tenant to challenge an order for possession once he has actually been paid and left the premises even if he can challenge it before then. In these circumstances there will have been a valid surrender.

Where a compromise is reached the parties should write out the terms of the agreement and each sign the document so that there can be no misunderstanding at a later stage. When the case is called on the landlord should inform the judge that an agreement has been reached and the tenant should admit that the Rent Act etc doesn't apply (if that be the case) or that the landlord is entitled to possession under the Act. In the latter case the tenant must make admissions as to the ground for possession (*R v Newcastle-upon-Tyne County Court, ex p Thompson* [1988] 2 EGLR 119). The judge may not readily make the order where the tenant is unrepresented and in those circumstances it may be necessary for the landlord to call the evidence he has in support for his case; but if both parties are represented there will usually be no problem in obtaining the order. Where a 'consent order' is made without jurisdiction or without the necessary admissions being made the tenant may apply to quash the decision by means of judicial review (*ex p Thompson* (1988)).

Costs

Costs are taxed under such scale as the court thinks fit (CCR Ord 38, r4(7)). The court's discretion to award costs under CCR Ord 38, r4(7) is very wide and there are no hard and fast rules to be followed in exercising the discretion (*Brown v Sparrow* [1982] 1 WLR 1269).

Instead of ordering the costs to be taxed the court may assess the costs at the hearing (CCR Ord 38, r19). The amount awarded will depend upon the scale that the court regards as appropriate (see Appendix C to the County Court Rules and CCR Ord 38, r3(3)):

Lower Scale	£46 to £71.50
Scale 1	£51.50 to £130.00
Scale 2	£80.50 to £488.00

In addition to these costs the court may, where appropriate, allow the court fee and make an allowance for witnesses. The amount awarded when costs are assessed varies greatly from court to court. Sums awarded are quite unrealistic and barely seem to increase between editions of this book. An assessment between £150 and £200 is not unusual where the advocate has no other cases in court that day. Even though such a figure will not cover all the landlord's costs it is usually not worth pursuing the matter to taxation. It often helps to tell the court exactly how much the costs come to. In those circumstances a higher sum is often awarded.

Appeals

From a District Judge   The appeal should be made to the county court judge on notice *served* within 14 days after the day on which the judgment or order appealed from was given or made (CCR Ord 37, r6), or within five days in the case of an appeal against an interlocutory order (CCR Ord 13, r1(11)). Where a party has consented to a judgment or final order he may not appeal therefrom (CCR Ord 37, r6).

From a county court judge   Leave to appeal is now required against all orders which *include* the giving or refusing of possession of land (RSC Ord 59, r1B). In the first instance the application should be made to the trial judge and if he refuses to the Court of Appeal (RSC Ord 59, r14(4)). If the application to the judge is not made within the time limit for serving the notice of appeal it may be made directly to the Court of Appeal (*Warren v T Kilroe & Sons Ltd* [1988] 1 All ER 638). The appeal must be made to the Court of Appeal on notice served within four weeks of the date of the order (RSC Ord 59, r4 and r19(3).

Where a tenant wishes to appeal an order for possession he should apply for a stay of execution pending appeal immediately after the judge has made his order (see further p298).

Homelessness and the local authority

A tenant who has been evicted and as a result is homeless may be left with no alternative other than to apply to the local authority for accommodation under Part III of the Housing Act 1985 (as amended). A person is said to be homeless under that Act if he has no accommodation which can be occupied by himself together with any member of his family or any other person who normally resides with him. The housing authority is under a duty to make appropriate enquiries on receipt of an application for assistance in obtaining accommodation. If the applicant is homeless and has a priority need the local authority is obliged to find accommodation for him. Priority need cases are those where the applicant has dependent children residing with him, where the applicant is homeless or threatened with homelessness as a result of an emergency or where the applicant or a member of his household is vulnerable as a result of old age, mental illness or physical disability or some other special reason, or is a pregnant woman or a person who might reasonably be expected to live with him is pregnant. There is no duty to house a tenant who has made himself intentionally homeless (s60 of the Housing Act 1985).

A licensee who has no right to remain in possession is homeless (s58(2); *R v Kensington and Chelsea RBC, ex p Minton* (1988) 20 HLR 648) and unless the licence has been revoked as a result of misconduct on his part the fact that he leaves prior to the obtaining of a court order by the licensor does not of itself make him intentionally homeless (*R v Surrey Heath BC, ex p Li* (1984) 16 HLR 83). See also *Code of Guidance to Local Authorities on Homelessness*, 3rd edn, in particular paras 5.5).

Code of Guidance for Local Authorities
> 5.5. . . . if someone has been occupying property as a licensee and the licence has been terminated they are homeless. . . In all these circumstances authorities should not ask applicants to obtain a court order; sufficient evidence of homelessness is provided by confirmation of the termination of the applicant's licence.

Compare *R v LB Croydon ex p. Jarves* (1993) 26 HLR 194 where it was held that notwithstanding the code it is not necessarily wrong for an authority to require a person to remain in possession until an order is made.

Service of documents

Proceedings may be served by post or personally (CCR Ord 7, r 10(1)). In the first instance they are usually served by post (see *below* 'Postal service').

Personal service

All documents may be served personally and some documents such as injunctions or witness summonses must be served personally, although where there is a choice between postal and personal service it is far cheaper to effect service by post.

Documents required to be served personally may be served by the court bailiff, a party to the proceedings or that party's agent or solicitor or a person employed by the solicitor to effect service. The document may not be served by a person under 16 years of age. (See CCR Ord 7, r2.)

If a defendant refuses to accept the document it is sufficient to inform him of what it is and to throw it to the floor in his presence (*Thompson v Pheney* (1832) 1 Dowl 441). If the document is in an envelope, the defendant must be informed of the nature of the document whether or not he accepts it.

No document may be served on a Sunday, Good Friday or Christmas Day except in the case of urgency with leave of the court (CCR Ord 7, r3).

Postal service

All fixed date summonses are now in the first instance served by post by the court unless the plaintiff or his solicitor wishes to arrange personal service (CCR Ord 7, r10(2)). Service may not be effected by post unless the address to which the summons is to be sent is a place at which the defendant has some continuing presence (*Willowgreen Ltd v Smithers* [1994] 2 All ER 533. Property originally occupied by tenant, parents and subsequently by others. He never lived there).

Service by post is deemed to be effected on the seventh day after the summons was sent and the seven-day period starts to run the day after the summons is posted (r10(3)). The summons must be served at least 21 clear days before the return day but may be served at any time before the return day if the plaintiff, by affidavit, satisfies the District Judge that the defendant is about to leave the address stated in the plaintiff's request for the summons (CCR Ord 7, r10(5)). If a summons has been served in accordance with the rules but appears to have come to the defendant's knowledge less than 21 days before the hearing date, the court has a discretion to allow the matter to proceed or to adjourn it (CCR Ord 7, r16).

If postal service has been attempted and has failed at the address given, notice of non-service is given to the plaintiff who may ask the county court bailiff to serve the summons. The bailiff may effect service by inserting the summons enclosed in an envelope addressed to the defendant through the letter box, or by delivering the summons to some person apparently not less than 16 years of age at the address or by delivering the summons to the defendant personally (CCR Ord 7, r10(4)).

Service on defendant's solicitor

If the defendant is represented by a solicitor he should be asked to accept service. If the solicitor agrees to accept service on the defendant's behalf, the summons may be sent to him by post by the plaintiff's solicitor and on receipt the defendant's solicitor must certify to the court that he accepts service, stating an address for service. The date of service is the day the certificate is made (CCR Ord 7, r11).

Special rules for service in possession proceedings

The County Court Rules provide a special procedure for service in the case of a summons for the recovery of land where the court is of the opinion 'that it is impracticable to serve the summons' in accordance with the usual provisions. The procedure only applies where the summons is to be served by the court bailiff. In such a case the summons may be served on any person on the premises who is the defendant's husband or wife or 'common law spouse' or any person who has or appears to have the authority of 'the defendant to reside or carry on business in the premises or to manage them on behalf of the defendant, or to receive any rents or profits of the premises, or to pay any outgoings in respect of the premises or to safeguard or to deal with the premises or *with* the furniture or other goods on the premises' (CCR Ord 7, r15). The request for service of a summons on such a person is set out in County Court Form N220.

If the bailiff is satisfied that the defendant has vacated the premises permanently, the summons may be effectively served by affixing it to some conspicuous part of the premises (CCR Ord 7, r15(4)). If a summons which includes a monetary claim is served in this way the summons will be marked 'not served' with regard to the money claim unless the court in special circumstances thinks it just to hear both claims (CCR Ord 7, r15(5)).

In any other case where the defendant is proving difficult to serve and the plaintiff is uncertain as to the best mode of service, an application for an order for substituted service under CCR Ord 7, r8 should be made. The application must be supported by an affidavit showing the grounds for the making of such an order and the court will make the order if it is satisfied that it is impracticable for any reason to effect service by post or personally. Examples of substituted service would be affixing a copy of the summons to the premises, posting an envelope addressed to the defendant and containing the summons through the letter box of the premises, posting a copy at his last known address, sending a copy to a member of the defendant's family by post, or by advertising in a newspaper or journal.

Service of pleadings, applications and notices

All these documents may be served by post. Pleadings are usually filed with the court and the court serves copies on the other parties to the action. Applications may be served by the party making the application although the court will also effect service. The notice of application should be filed and served not less than two days before the hearing of the application (CCR Ord 13, r1(2)). Notices to admit facts or to admit or produce documents must be served not less than 14 days before the hearing (CCR Ord 20, r2(1) and Ord 20, r3(1) and (4)). If the written admission of facts is not served within seven days, the recipient of the notice must pay the costs of proving the facts unless the court otherwise orders (CCR Ord 20, r2(2)). If the recipient of a notice to admit a document does not admit the authenticity of the document he must, within seven days of service, serve on the other party a notice that he does not admit the authenticity of the document and requiring him to prove it at the trial. In such a case he will be required to pay the costs of proving it unless the court otherwise orders (CCR Ord 20, r3(2)).

Proof of service

Where the document was served by the court a certificate of service will be produced and will be before the judge at the hearing with the rest of the court file. (See County Court Forms N12 and N13.) Where a court document is served by a party an affidavit of service is required (CCR Ord 7, r6(1)). For a precedent see County Court Form N215 which is sent to the person requesting personal service.

Enforcement and setting aside

Warrant of possession: issue (CCR Ord 26, r17)

Except in the case of an 'excluded tenancy or licence' (see p255) the landlord must apply for a warrant of possession to enforce an order for possession (*Borzak v Ahmed* [1965] 2 QB 320). It has also been held that a statutory tenant continues as such until the order is lawfully executed and so any attempt by the landlord to evict without the assistance of the court gives rise to a claim for unlawful eviction (*Haniff v Robinson* [1993] 1 All ER 185).

The landlord should apply for the warrant the day after the day on which the court has ordered the tenant to give up possession.

Where the order for possession is suspended on certain terms the suspension terminates automatically if the tenant fails to comply with those terms and the landlord may then apply for a warrant of possession without further notice to the tenant (cf the High Court), *unless* the order for possession required that the landlord apply for leave to execute the order (see *Yates v Morris* [1951] 1 KB 77 at 81). However, in *R v Ilkeston County Court, ex p Kruza* (1985) *The Times*, 24 May, the court held that an order for possession which was 'suspended for seven days or for as long as the tenant paid her rent' was not to be read as an order that enabled the landlord to execute the order as soon as the rent was not paid.

In order to obtain the warrant for possession the landlord must send the court a request for it (County Court Form N325) plus a fee (currently £50). Where a money judgment was made in addition to the order for possession the landlord may also apply for execution against the tenant's goods (CCR Ord 26, r17(3)). An extra fee of 15p for every £1 or part thereof with a minimum fee of £10 and a maximum fee of £50 will be payable (County Court Fees Order 1982 (as amended)). The warrant remains in force for one year. After that time it may be renewed without fee but with the leave of the court. The application for renewal may be made by letter setting out the circumstances and the reason for the delay (CCR Ord 26, rr6 and 17(6)).

Execution of the warrant

The landlord will be given an appointment when the bailiff will call at the premises to execute the warrant which, where the court has many warrants to issue, may be more than a month from the date of the application. The landlord or his solicitor should be at the premises to meet the bailiff together with a locksmith if the landlord wishes to change the locks. The landlord or his agent will be asked to sign a receipt indorsed on the warrant to acknowledge having received possession. In order to enforce the warrant the bailiff need not remove any goods or chattels from the premises (s111(1) of the County Courts Act 1984) although it is suggested that the request for the warrant should include the removal of the tenant's furniture and possessions so as to leave the property completely vacant. If the tenant's possessions are left on the property and the landlord prevents the tenant from obtaining them after execution of the warrant by locking them away or selling them as a result of which the tenant suffers loss, the tenant may have a right of action under the Torts (Interference with Goods) Act 1977 for the return or monetary value of such goods. The bailiff is entitled to evict anyone he finds on the premises even though that person was not a party to the proceedings (*R v Wandsworth County Court, ex p Wandsworth London Borough Council* [1975] 1 WLR 1314 and the note to CCR Ord 26, r17). Where a bailiff is executing a warrant against a person who has entered into or remained in occupation of the premises without the licence or consent of the person claiming possession, and the occupier resists or intentionally obstructs the bailiff, the occupier commits an offence (s10 of the Criminal Law Act 1977). If a person found on the premises claims to have some right as against the landlord to remain there, he should apply to the court to be joined in the proceedings pursuant to CCR Ord 15, r3 and for the order for possession to be set aside (see p269). If he fails to do this after having been given a reasonable opportunity to do so the bailiff may evict him.

Warrant of restitution

Where the tenant unlawfully reenters the premises after the warrant for possession has been executed the landlord should apply for a warrant of restitution (CCR Ord 26, r17(4)). Leave to issue the warrant is required and may be applied for *ex parte*. The application should be supported by an affidavit evidencing the wrongful reentry and of such further facts as would, in the High Court, enable the judgment creditor to have a writ of restitution issued (CCR Ord 26, r17(5)).

The warrant may be issued in order to evict any persons on the land, whether they had been parties to the original possession proceedings or not, provided there was a sufficient nexus between the acts of trespass concerned. The question to ask is, 'were the acts or episodes of trespass complained of during the overall period properly to be regarded as essentially one transaction?' (*Wiltshire County Council v Frazer* [1986] 1 All ER 65).

Suspension of warrant

Where the warrant for possession is issued pursuant to an order for possession made following proof by the landlord of one of the following grounds for possession, namely Grounds 9–16 of Sched 2 to the Housing Act 1988, Cases 1–10 of Sched 15 to the Rent Act 1977; Grounds 1–8 or 12–16 of Sched 2 to the Housing Act 1985; or Cases I–X of Sched 4 to the Rent (Agriculture) Act 1976, the tenant may apply for execution of the order to be stayed or suspended, or the date for possession to be postponed, at any time before execution of the order. The court may stay or suspend execution of the order or postpone the date of possession for such period or periods as it thinks fit. On any such stay, suspension or postponement the court must, unless it considers that to do so would cause exceptional hardship to the tenant or would otherwise be unreasonable, impose conditions with regard to payment of arrears of rent (if any) and rent or mesne profits in respect of occupation after termination of the tenancy and may impose such other conditions as it thinks fit. (See s9 of the Housing Act 1988; s100 of the Rent Act 1977; s85 of the Housing Act 1985; s7 of the Rent (Agriculture) Act 1976.

The court has no power to stay execution in any other case unless the landlord consents (*Moore v Lambeth County Court Registrar* [1969] 1 WLR 141; *West Sussex County Council v Wood* [1982] CLY 1779, county court).

In *R v Ilkeston County Court, ex p Kruza* (1985) 17 HLR 539, it was held that an order for possession which was 'suspended for seven days or for as long as the tenant paid her rent' was not to be read as an order that enabled the landlord to execute the order as soon as rent was not paid. The court, therefore, had jurisdiction to entertain an application by the tenant for suspension of the warrant for possession which the landlord sought to execute for non-payment of rent.

Stay of execution pending appeal

A party wishing to appeal against an order for possession made by the District Judge may ask the court for a stay of execution pending the hearing of the appeal. The notice of application will not of itself operate as a stay but the court may order a stay pending the appeal (CCR Ord 37, r8(2)). The application, if not made at the hearing, should be in County

Court Form N244 and should be supported by an affidavit setting out the grounds of the application. Filing of the application will usually prevent execution of the order until the application is heard.

An appeal from the judge to the Court of Appeal will not operate as a stay of execution unless the judge of the county court, or the Court of Appeal, so orders (RSC Ord 59, r19(5)). Where the application for a stay is not made at the hearing it should be made on notice.

Setting aside

An application to set aside and order is made pursuant to CCR Ord 37. The application may be made after the order for possession has been executed (*Minet v Johnson* (1890) 63 LT 507). An application by someone who was not a party to the proceedings should be made together with an application to be joined in the proceedings under CCR Ord 15, r3 (p269; eg see *Wandsworth LBC v Fadayomi* [1987] 3 All ER 474). In deciding whether to accede to the applicant's request for the proceedings to be set aside the court will take into account any delay in making the application and the effect on third parties (*Rhodes Trust v Khan* (1979) SJ 719; tenant went abroad in February 1978 making no arrangements for the payment of rent whilst he was away. He returned in July 1979 after a possession order had been made in May 1979 which was executed in June. His application to set aside was refused because the absence had created a situation where the reasonable landlord would treat the premises as abandoned and because the property had been relet. The rights of the new tenant had to be weighed against the rights of the old tenant).

If a judgment or order for possession is set aside 'any execution issued on the judgment or order shall cease to have effect unless the Court otherwise orders' (CCR Ord 37, r8(3)); even if the order for possession has actually been executed (*Governors of Peabody Donation Fund v Hay* (1986) 19 HLR 145) in which case the landlord should let the occupier back into occupation.

Chapter 21

High Court Procedure

Possession proceedings are not usually commenced in the High Court either because the High Court does not have jurisdiction or because the landlord will not be entitled to recover his costs (see Chapter 19). Furthermore, a plaintiff may not enter judgment in default of appearance or defence or apply for summary judgment under Ord 14 if the defendant is entitled to the protection of the Rent Act 1977 (*White Book*, 6/2/20). Any judgment obtained in any of these ways of premises subject to a Rent Act protected tenancy will be a nullity and cannot be enforced in the High Court (*Peachey Property Corporation v Robinson* [1967] 2 QB 543). Where proceedings are taken in the High Court the normal procedure for non-possession proceedings should be followed subject to the following points.

Steps in the action

Writ of summons

Any claim for possession of land must be indorsed with a statement showing whether the claim relates to a dwelling house and if so whether the rateable value of the premises on every day specified by s4(2) of the Rent Act 1977 in relation to the premises exceeds the sum so specified or whether the rent for the time being payable in respect of the premises exceeds the sum specified in s4(4)(*b*) of the Rent Act 1977 (RSC Ord 6, r2(1)(*c*); see Appendix 1). Where the tenancy was created after 15 January 1989 (otherwise than in pursuance of a contract made before that date) it is suggested that the indorsement be adapted so as to make clear that the tenancy is not an assured tenancy and that the Housing Act 1988 does not apply (see Chapter 6). Where the claim is based on forfeiture, see p41.

Service of proceedings

Service of proceedings will usually be effected by post or personally, in the normal way (Ord 10, r1). Sometimes, however, these methods are not possible. The court may therefore order service on the defendant by affixing a copy of the writ to some conspicuous part of the property if satisfied that no one is in possession of the property (Ord 10, r4(*a*)). The application is made by affidavit showing that efforts have been made to serve the defendant in the usual way and why service cannot be effected. If service has been effected in this way before the application to the court is made, it may be ordered on such application that the service be treated as good service (Ord 10, r4(*b*)).

An application for substituted service may be made to the master *ex parte* on affidavit (Ord 65, r4). The affidavit should show why service in the normal manner is impracticable and state the method of service which the deponent believes is most likely to bring the document to the knowledge of the party to be served. See Queen's Bench Masters' Practice Form 120 for the form of affidavit and Form 121 for the order which will stipulate the method of service to be used.

Joinder of non-parties as defendants

Any person not named as a party to the action who is in possession of the property may apply to the court *ex parte* to a master by affidavit to be added as a defendant (RSC Ord 15, r10). The application should be made as soon as possible after the applicant has had notice of the writ and may be made even if judgment has been entered and execution issued (see p299). If the application is made after judgment the applicant should apply *ex parte* for leave to issue a summons to set aside the judgment and file an affidavit in support for leave to be joined as a party to the action and a stay pending the hearing of the summons. The summons should be served on all parties to the action (*White Book*, 15/10/2).

Judgment in default

If the defendant fails to give notice of intention to defend, the plaintiff may enter judgment in default after the prescribed time provided he produces to the court a certificate signed by his solicitor stating that the matter does not relate to an action under Ord 88 (mortgage possession proceedings) and that the claim does not relate to a dwelling house or if it does relate to a dwelling house stating that the rateable value on the appropriate days was in excess of the specified limits (Ord 13, r4(2)). If the plaintiff is acting in person he must swear an affidavit stating these matters. In default of a solicitor's certificate or affidavit, judgment may only be entered with leave of the court. The application for leave should be made by summons stating the grounds of the application which will be either that the Rent Act 1977/Housing Act 1988 does not apply to the dwelling house or that the defendant is not entitled to the protection of the relevant Act, stating the grounds on which either contention is based. The summons must be served on the defendant against whom the plaintiff wishes to enter judgment (Ord 13, r4(3)). On the hearing of the summons the plaintiff must satisfy the master that the Rent Act 1977/ Housing Act 1988 is inapplicable or that the defendant is not protected by the relevant Act by affidavit evidence or otherwise (*White Book*, 13/4/ 2). The court may give leave to enter judgment or, if the master refuses leave, he may proceed to give directions as if the hearing had been an application for summary judgment under Ord 14 (RSC Ord 13, r4(4)). Normally the action will be transferred to the county court. The master has no power to consider whether it is reasonable to give judgment for possession (*White Book*, 13/4/2).

If there is more than one defendant, judgment must be entered against all the defendants before the judgment may be enforced (Ord 13, r4(5)). The form of judgment in default will be found in Queen's Bench Masters' Practice Form 42.

Similar rules apply in relation to judgment in default of service of a defence (RSC Ord 19, r5(5)).

The defence

The defendant in his defence must plead every ground on which he relies and must give full particulars to support these grounds. It is not sufficient for him to merely plead that he is in possession by himself or his tenant (Ord 18, r8(2)).

Proceedings for summary judgment

Order 14 proceedings may be used for the recovery of land but not for the recovery of a dwelling house to which the provisions of the Rent Act etc apply. The court will only make an order for possession of a dwelling house if it is satisfied that the occupier is not entitled to the protection of the Rent Act/Housing Act (*White Book*, 14/3–4/29). In forfeiture proceedings the tenant may request the master at the hearing of the summons to grant relief, but failure to apply at the hearing does not prevent the tenant from applying at a later stage (Ord 14, r10). Relief against forfeiture is an equitable defence which is inextricably linked with a claim for forfeiture. It is, therefore, a counterclaim which ought to result in unconditional leave to defend being given if it is a genuine counterclaim which might succeed (see p42 *above*).

An appeal to set aside an order under Ord 14 must be made to the judge in chambers within five days of the hearing (seven days in district registries). Service of the notice of appeal does not constitute a stay of execution and this must be separately applied for to the master or the judge (RSC Ord 58, r1(4); *White Book*, 14/3–4/35).

Interim payments

An application for an order that the defendant make an interim payment may be made at any time after the writ has been issued and the time for filing an acknowledgement of service has expired (Ord 29, r10). The rules provide a means by which a plaintiff landlord may recover monies for the continued use and occupation of a property from a defendant at an early stage in the proceedings so that he will not be made to wait until the trial of the action before receiving the money that he is entitled to recover from the defendant in any event (Ord 29, r12(*b*)). However, the claim for an interim payment will be dismissed if the defendant raises a *bona fide* claim for damages for a sum in excess of that claimed by the plaintiff (*Old Grovebury Manor Farm Ltd v W Seymour Plant Sales and Hire Ltd* [1979] 1 WLR 263).

The application is made by summons to the master but may be included in a summons for summary judgment under Ord 14 (Ord 29, r10(2)). The summons must be supported by an affidavit (Ord 29, r10(3)).

The summons and copy affidavit must be served on the defendant not less than ten clear days before the return day (Ord 29, r10(4)).

Any order should expressly state that it is made 'by way of interim payment' which will have the effect that the payment will be without prejudice to any contentions of the parties as to the nature of the sums to be paid by the defendant. Directions as to the future conduct of the action may be given at the hearing of the application (RSC Ord 29, r14).

Interrogatories

The parties have the right to request interrogatories as in any other action (*White Book*, 26/1/16) and both the parties can be ordered to produce evidence of their title to the property.

Power to postpone orders for possession

The High Court's general jurisdiction to postpone orders for possession is (probably) not fettered by s89 of the Housing Act 1980 which only applies to county courts (*Bain & Co v Church Commissioners* [1989] 1 WLR 24).

Costs

In certain cases if proceedings are taken in the High Court which could have been taken in the county court the landlord will not be entitled to his costs (s141(4) of the Rent Act 1977; s110(3) of the Housing Act 1985; s26 of the Rent (Agriculture) Act 1976; and s40 of the Housing Act 1988; see p260).

Appeals

From a master   The appeal is to a judge in chambers and no leave is required. The notice of appeal in London must be issued within five days of the master's decision and must be served two clear days before the appeal hearing date (Ord 58). In district registries the notice must be filed seven days after the decision appealed from and served three clear days before the hearing (Ord 58, r3). The matter will be considered anew by the judge.

From a High Court judge   The appeal is made to the Court of Appea . Leave to appeal is required against all orders which *include* the giving cr refusing of possession of land (RSC Ord 59, r18). The appeal must be filed within four weeks of the judgment or order (Ord 59, r4(1)).

Enforcement

Prior to enforcement of a judgment or order in the High Court the defendant should be served with a copy of the judgment or order under which possession is claimed and be asked to give up possession on a specified date. If there are other parties in possession of the property who were not party to the proceedings they should also be served with a copy of the order together with such written notice as will give them a reasonable opportunity to apply to the court for relief (RSC Ord 45, r3(3)(*a*); *White Book*, 45/3/5).

If the defendants fail to give possession on the specified date and the property is a dwelling house, the plaintiff cannot (except in the case of an 'excluded licence or tenancy'; see p255) enter into possession himself, and must apply for a writ of possession so to do (s3 of the Protection from Eviction Act 1977; *Borzak v Ahmed* [1965] 2 QB 320; *Haniff v Robinson* [1993] 1 All ER 185).

Except in the case of mortgage possession proceedings (Ord 88) and summary possession actions (Ord 113), leave of the court is required before a writ of possession may be issued (Ord 45, r3(2)).

Application for leave to issue the writ of possession

The application for leave is made *ex parte* to the Practice Master and must be supported by an affidavit (Ord 46, r4), which should, amongst other things give such information as is necessary to satisfy the Master that the Rent Act 1977/Housing Act 1988 does not apply.

The court will only grant leave if it is satisfied that every person in possession of the premises has received a notice of the proceedings to enable him to apply to the court for any relief to which he may be entitled (Ord 45, r3). The court has power to order that any issue or question a decision on which is necessary to determine the right of the parties, be tried in any manner in which any question of fact or law arising in an action may be tried and, in either case, may impose such terms as to costs or otherwise as it thinks just (Ord 46, r4(3)).

Leave will only be given to issue a writ for the breach of a suspended order for possession if the defendant has been given the chance of being heard (*Fleet Mortgage and Investment Co Ltd v Lower Maisonette 46 Eaton Place Ltd* [1972] 1 WLR 765). Application for leave in such cases must be by summons supported by affidavit (Ord 46, r4(1)) and the procedure to be followed is set out in the note 46/4/2 in the *White Book*.

Issue of a writ of possession

A *praecipe* (Queen's Bench Masters' Practice Form 91) signed by the landlord's solicitor must be filed with the court and at the same time there must be produced to the court the judgment or order on which the writ is to issue and an order granting leave if required (Ord 46, r6). The writ must contain a description of the property of which possession is to be given (*White Book*, 45/3/2). The writ is valid for 12 months from the date of issue (Ord 46, r 8) although if it is not executed the period may be extended on application *ex parte* to the Practice Master supported by affidavit stating why the writ has not been executed although normally it will only be extended in cases where priority of date is important. Otherwise a new writ may be issued on the certificate of a solicitor stating that nothing has been levied under the first writ (*White Book*, 46/8/2).

Execution of the writ

The landlord or his solicitor should meet the sheriff at the premises with a locksmith. A notice of the appointment will have been sent to the premises so that anyone on the premises has a chance to apply for the judgment to be set aside but they cannot sue the sheriff or landlord for damages for eviction (*White Book*, 45/3/6). The sheriff is required to deliver up possession as soon as is reasonably practicable (*Six Arlington Street Investments Ltd v Persons unknown* [1987] 1 All ER 474. If the sheriff is prevented by the tenant from executing the writ an order of committal for contempt can be applied for (*Alliance Building Society v Austen* [1951] 2 All ER 1068).

It is the view of the author that the sheriff executing a writ of possession is required by the writ to clear the premises of all persons and goods so as to give vacant possession to the plaintiff (relying upon *Norwich Union Life Insurance Society v Preston* [1957] 2 All ER 428 and a Canadian case *Rogerson v Wilkinson* [1973] 2 WWR 350 at 356; see also *Green Book* note to CCR Ord 26, r17 and 17 Halsbury para 501; compare the position of a bailiff executing a county court warrant for possession; p297). However, the Under-Sheriffs Association is of the view that the law does not require the sheriff to remove goods from the premises when delivering up possession to the plaintiff (see *City of London Law Society Newsletter*, April 1990, article by the then Under-Sheriff of Greater London). Practitioners should therefore be aware that the sheriff executing the writ is unlikely to remove such goods as may be found on the premises unless the plaintiff obtains a specific order requiring him to do so. This leaves the plaintiff with the problem of knowing what to do with any articles found on the premises. The plaintiff is usually best advised to act cautiously in relation to any such goods as remain before disposing of them if he wishes to avoid a claim under the Torts (Interference with Goods) Act 1977 from the former tenant. If practicable the best solution is to store them safely until they have been collected.

After execution the sheriff must send a copy of the writ to the plaintiff indorsed with a statement of the name in which he has executed it (*White Book*, 45/3/2). If the sheriff is unsuccessful, the plaintiff cannot have a second writ issued unless the first writ has been indorsed by the sheriff stating that possession has not been given (*White Book*, 45/3/2).

Writ of restitution

If after the sheriff has completed execution the tenant unlawfully re-enters the property, the landlord should apply for a writ of restitution to be issued. The application should be made *ex parte* to the Master in chambers on an affidavit of facts (*White Book*, 46/3/3).

The warrant may be issued in order to evict any persons on the land whether they were parties to the original possession proceedings or not, provided there was a sufficient nexus between the acts of trespass concerned. The question to ask is whether the acts or episodes of trespass complained of during the overall period are properly to be regarded as essentially one transaction? (*Wiltshire County Council v Frazer* [1985] 1 All ER 65).

A tenant may apply by summons for a writ of restitution to the Master where the tenant has lost possession to a landlord and the tenant later sets aside the judgment but the landlord fails to restore possession to the tenant, or a landlord has obtained possession under an irregular writ (*White Book*, 46/3/3).

Chapter 22

Evidence

Documentary evidence in possession actions

Proof of title

It will rarely be necessary for a landlord or licensor to prove actual title to the land as the tenant or licensee will be estopped from denying his title (see p7 and p98). Where the occupiers of the land are alleged to be trespassers the plaintiff will have to prove his title. Section 68 of the Land Registration Act 1925 provides that 'a land certificate or charge certificate shall be admissible as evidence of the several matters therein contained'. If it is not possible to prove title by means of such a certificate evidence of prior possession is evidence of a right to possession (17 Halsbury (4th edn) para 36).

Production of originals: the lease

The general rule is that a party seeking to rely upon the contents of a document such as a lease must produce the original. Although the relationship of landlord and tenant may be proved by evidence other than a lease (eg by evidence of the payment of rent), it is not possible to give evidence of the terms of the lease without producing the actual document (*Augestien v Challis* (1847) 1 Exch 279). If the landlord wishes to rely upon its terms it is the counterpart signed by the lessee which is regarded as the original (even where the lease has been assigned) and which the landlord must produce. If the tenant wishes to rely upon the terms of the lease he must produce the part signed by the landlord (*Roe d West v Davis* (1806) 7 East 363).

It is rare for the authenticity of a document to be in dispute and so the rules provide for the production of documents without the necessity of proving execution. In the county court a document which would, if duly proved, be admissible in evidence is admitted without further evidence if it is produced to the court from 'proper custody' and if in the opinion of the court it appears genuine and if no objection is taken to its admission (CCR Ord 20, r11). The person to have proper custody is the person who might reasonably be expected to have possession of the document. If therefore a landlord produces a tenancy agreement which appears to be signed by the tenant it will be admitted in evidence unless the tenant objects. Where there is an objection to any document produced from proper custody the court may adjourn the hearing for proof of the document. If it is proved the party objecting must pay the costs occasioned by the objection unless the court otherwise orders (CCR Ord 20, r11(2)). If the party producing the document wishes to ensure that there will be no dispute over its authenticity at the hearing he may serve the other party with a notice to admit that it is authentic not later than 14 days beforehand. If the other party decides to challenge the document's authenticity he must, within seven days of service upon him of the notice to admit, serve on the party seeking to rely upon the document a notice of non-admission. If the document is subsequently proved he will have to pay the costs of proving the document unless the court otherwise orders. A party who fails to give notice of non-admission is deemed to have admitted the authenticity of the document unless the court otherwise orders (CCR Ord 20, r3). In the High Court a party on whom a list or affidavit of documents is served is deemed to admit the authenticity of the documents listed unless he has already denied their authenticity in the pleadings or he serves a notice of non-admission within 21 days after inspection (RSC Ord 27, r4). The High Court rules also provide for a specific notice to admit authenticity which should be served within 21 days of setting down. Any notice of non-admission should be served within the next 21 days and as with the county court failure to serve such a notice amounts to an admission of the document's authenticity unless the court otherwise orders (RSC Ord 27, r5).

If the other party does deny the authenticity of a document it may be proved by evidence of someone who saw the document being signed. If no one saw it being signed the signature may be proved by someone who is familiar with the alleged signatory's writing. A signature may also be proved by comparison in which case an expert will have to be called to give evidence.

A lease is not admissible in evidence if it is not properly stamped (s 14 of the Stamp Act 1891). However, the duty and penalty may be paid to an officer of the court. The document will also be admitted in evidence upon a solicitor's undertaking to have the document stamped and to pay the penalty (see note in *Green Book* to Ord 20, r11).

Notices to quit and other documents in the hands of another party to the action

In order to be able to rely upon a notice to quit (or other notice served on the tenant) it is not sufficient merely to produce a copy. The landlord must also prove actual service of the original notice at the proper time. The person who effected service should give evidence to that effect, either orally, or if possible by affidavit or in the form of a statement pursuant to the provisions of the Civil Evidence Act 1968 (see below 'Evidence by statement: Civil Evidence Act 1968' p312). The person proving service should produce his copy of the notice. If it bears a memorandum of service signed and dated by the tenant service will have been proved to have taken place on that date. If not, the person proving service must state where, when and how the notice was served upon the tenant. Where the notice was served by post the person who put the notice in the envelope, addressed it to the tenant and put it in the letter box must state as much. It is not sufficient simply to produce a recorded delivery slip. Who knows what was in the envelope? Evidence that the notice was sent by post in a properly stamped addressed envelope will be sufficient evidence of service unless the contrary is shown. (See also s196 of the Law of Property Act 1925, p68.)

As explained above a party seeking to rely upon the contents of a document must, as a general rule, produce the original. This will not be possible when the original is in the hands of the other party to the action and so the procedural rules provide that secondary evidence may be adduced if the other party is first served with a *notice to produce* the original at the hearing (CCR Ord 20, r3(4)). It is not in fact necessary to serve a notice to produce where the document to be relied upon is a notice to quit (*Doe d Fleming v Somerton* (1875) 7 QB 58; *Practice Note* [1950] 1 All ER 37). It is also probably not necessary to serve a notice to produce any other type of notice that the landlord has served on the tenant in connection with the proceedings for possession (see generally 17 Halsbury (4th edn) 143); but it is wise to do so. Where either party wishes to rely upon correspondence sent to the other party it will be necessary to serve a notice to produce the relevant letters at the hearing before copies of them can be adduced in evidence.

There is no time limit in respect of service of a notice to produce but if it is served an unreasonably short time before the hearing the other party may be able to obtain an adjournment in order that the notice may be complied with and the party serving the notice will probably have to pay any costs thrown away. If the document is in court the notice to produce may be served during the course of the hearing (*Dwyer v Collins* (1852) 7 Exch 639). Service of the notice to produce may be proved by oral evidence, affidavit or statement under the Civil Evidence Act 1968 in the same way as any other fact is proved. It is not necessary to serve a notice to produce the notice to produce (*R v Turner* [1910] 1 KB 346 at 359; *Practice Note* [1950] 1 All ER 37)!

Where the tenant denies receiving the relevant document the landlord may, if he can prove service of the original, adduce a copy in evidence even if he has failed to serve a notice to produce the original (*Minay v Sentongo* (1983) 45 P&CR 190 at 195).

In the High Court it is not necessary to serve a notice to produce if discovery has taken place, as a party who has provided a list of

Form 38: Notice to produce documents

IN THE　　**COUNTY COURT**　　　　　　　　　　　　　　　　**Case No**

BETWEEN

　　　　　　　　　　　　　　　　　　　　　　　　　　　　　Plaintiff

—AND—

　　　　　　　　　　　　　　　　　　　　　　　　　　　　Defendant

NOTICE TO PRODUCE DOCUMENTS

　　TAKE NOTICE that you are hereby required to produce and show to the Court at the hearing of this action the following documents, namely:

1. Notice dated [*insert date of Notice*] stating that possession might be recovered under Case 11 after termination of your tenancy.

2. Notice to quit dated [*insert date of Notice to quit*] and served on you by the Plaintiff.

3. Letter dated [*insert date of letter*] from the Plaintiff to you.

DATED

---

documents is deemed to have been served with a notice to produce the documents that he has specified in his list as being in his possession.

At the hearing the party seeking to rely upon the contents of the document should call for its production at the point in the hearing when the document becomes of relevance. If the other party fails to produce the document the party seeking to rely upon it will be able to adduce the secondary evidence once he has proved service of the notice to produce and that the original is in the possession of the other party.

If secondary evidence is allowed it may be in the form of a copy or of oral evidence from someone who saw the original and can speak of its contents. It is clearly better, however, to produce a copy, if one is available. As with original documents, the production of a copy from proper custody will, in county court proceedings, be presumed to be a true copy if it appears to be genuine and if no objection is taken (CCR Ord 20, r11), and in the High Court if discovery has taken place.

If the party seeking to rely upon the document does have to call secondary evidence of its contents, because the recipient of the notice to produce has failed to produce the document, the recipient may not rely upon the original to contradict the secondary evidence (*Doe d Thompson v Hodgson* (1840) 12 Ad & El 135).

If the party wishing to rely upon the document is not in a position to adduce any secondary evidence of its contents he should not serve the other party with a notice to produce (which need not be complied with) but with a witness summons in the county court (CCR Ord 20, r12) or a *subpoena duces tecum* in the High Court (court orders which must be complied with).

Documents in the hands of a stranger

If the relevant document is in the hands of a stranger the party seeking production of it should serve the stranger with a *subpoena duces tecum* (High Court) or a witness summons in the county court (CCR Ord 20, r12). It is necessary to file a request for the issue of the summons and if the summons is to be served by the court to deposit in the court office 'conduct money' (£6.00 for a police officer and £8.50 for any other person plus a sum reasonably sufficient to cover the witnesses' expenses in travelling to and from the court (CCR Ord 20, r12(2)). The summons must be issued not less than seven days before the date upon which the attendance is required unless the judge or District Judge otherwise directs. The summons must be served on the witness not less than four days beforehand unless the judge or District Judge otherwise directs (CCR Ord 20, r12(4)(*a*)). If the witness fails to produce the document secondary evidence does not become admissible. The witness summons should be enforced. Secondary evidence is, however, admissible where the stranger establishes a claim to privilege (*Mills v Oddy* (1934) 6 C&P 728); where the other party has already managed to obtain possession of the document from the person served with the summons; or where the stranger has lost the document.

Documents lost or destroyed

The party seeking to rely upon the contents of a document may rely upon secondary evidence of the document, either a copy or oral evidence, if the original has been lost or destroyed. Before being allowed to call secondary evidence it will first be necessary to call direct evidence of its existence at an earlier stage and of its destruction. If it has been lost it is necessary to give evidence of where the document was last seen; that a thorough search has been made at the place; and that the search was unsuccessful. If the court allows secondary evidence to be called production of a copy from proper custody will be allowed if the copy appears to be genuine and there is no objection, or in the High Court if discovery has taken place (CCR Ord 20, r11; RSC Ord 27, r4).

Evidence of facts

The general rule is that any fact required to be proved at the hearing of a claim must be proved by the oral evidence of witnesses given in open court (CCR Ord 20, r4; RSC Ord 38, r1). In certain circumstances, however, facts may be proved by affidavit or by a statement made under the Civil Evidence Act 1968.

Evidence by affidavit

Where proceedings take place in chambers, as will usually be the case where the landlord is relying on one of the mandatory grounds contained in Part II of Sched 15 to the Rent Act 1977, the evidence given will be by affidavit unless the court directs otherwise. If either side wishes any person to attend for cross-examination he must apply to the court for an order that that person do attend. If after any such order is made the person concerned does not attend his affidavit may not be used without the leave of the court (CCR Ord 20, r5; see RSC Ord 38, r2(3)). In all other cases the court may order that the affidavit of any witness may be read at the hearing if in the circumstances of the case it thinks it reasonable to do so (CCR Ord 20, r6; RSC Ord 38, r2(1) and (2)).

Where county court proceedings are not in chambers and the court has not made an order that evidence may be given by affidavit under CCR Ord 20, r5 but one of the parties desires to adduce affidavit evidence he may do so if, not less than 14 days before the hearing, he gives notice of his desire accompanied by a copy of the affidavit to the party against whom it is to be used. If the recipient of the notice does not give notice that he objects to the use of the affidavit within seven days of receipt of the notice the affidavit may be used at the hearing (CCR Ord 20, r7(1) and Ord 1, r9(3)). Where it is the plaintiff who wishes to use an affidavit he need not give notice of his desire to do so to the defendant if the defendant has not delivered a defence within 14 days after service of the summons on him, or if he does not appear on the pre-trial review (if there is one), unless the court otherwise orders (CCR Ord 20, r7(2)).

Nothing in the above rules affects the weight to be attached to any statement contained in any such affidavit or the power of the court to refuse to admit the statement in evidence if in the interest of justice the court thinks fit to do so (CCR Ord 20, r9). Unless the court otherwise orders, an affidavit may be used notwithstanding that it contains statements of information or belief (CCR Ord 20, r10(4)). The sources and grounds of the information or belief must be stated (r10(5)).

Evidence by statement: Civil Evidence Act 1968

Another way the plaintiff or the defendant may adduce evidence other than by calling the person who can give direct evidence of the relevant facts is in accordance with the provisions of the Civil Evidence Act 1968. Section 2(1) of that Act provides that:

> In any civil proceedings a statement made, whether orally or in a document or otherwise, by any person, whether called as a witness in those proceedings or not, shall, subject to this section and to rules of court, be admissible as evidence of any fact stated therein of which direct oral evidence by him would be admissible.

The rules referred to are CCR Ord 20, rr 14–26 in the county court and RSC Ord 38, rr 20–34 in the High Court. The procedural rules dealt with below are those that apply in the county court. The procedure is slightly different in the High Court. (See in particular RSC Ord 38, rr 21, 26.)

Form 39: Notice of intention to use affidavit

IN THE   **COUNTY COURT**   **Case No**

BETWEEN

                                                     Plaintiff

                     —AND—

                                                   Defendant

NOTICE OF INTENTION TO USE AFFIDAVIT

TAKE NOTICE that the Plaintiff intends to use at the hearing of this Action an Affidavit of [*state name*] sworn on [*insert date*] a copy of which accompanies this Notice.

AND FURTHER TAKE NOTICE that unless you give notice to the Plaintiff within 7 days of receipt of this Notice, that you object to the use of the said Affidavit you will be taken to have consented to the use thereof and the same may be used at the hearing unless the Judge otherwise orders.

This notice is given pursuant to Order 20, r7 of the County Court Rules 1981.

DATED

Where the statement upon which it is intended to rely is contained in a document, that document is produced. Where, however, the statement was not made in a document direct oral evidence of the matters contained in the statement may be given by 'any person who heard or otherwise perceived it being made' (s2(3) of the Civil Evidence Act 1968). Thus, a friend of a landlord who is presently abroad and who is seeking to rely upon Case 11 of Sched 15 to the Rent Act 1977 may give evidence of what the landlord said about his intention to return to his dwelling house but if that friend gives the information to the landlord's solicitor the solicitor cannot give evidence of the landlord's statement. Even though oral evidence of a statement may therefore be given it is clearly preferable to obtain a written statement from the landlord in all cases.

A party who wishes to adduce hearsay evidence under the Civil Evidence Act is required to serve a notice of his intention to do so upon the District Judge and every other party not less than 14 days before the hearing (CCR Ord 20, r15(1)). In the county court it is not necessary to give such a notice in any action or matter in which no defence has been filed unless in any particular case the court otherwise directs. Where a defence is filed less than 14 days before the hearing the plaintiff 'shall apply to the court for an adjournment of the trial or hearing or for such other directions as may be appropriate' (CCR Ord 20, r15(2)).

If the statement is contained in a document a copy or transcript of the document, or of the relevant part thereof, must be annexed to the notice and the notice must contain particulars of:

Form 40: Notice of intention to adduce hearsay evidence

IN THE   **COUNTY COURT**   **Case No**

BETWEEN

                                                                    Plaintiff
                              —AND—

                                                                    Defendant

NOTICE OF INTENTION TO ADDUCE HEARSAY EVIDENCE

We hereby give you Notice of our intention to adduce evidence to be used at the Hearing of this matter on [*insert date of Hearing*] at [*state time of hearing*] in the form of a Statement a copy of which is attached hereto. The Statement was made in a letter signed by the Plaintiff and sent to Messrs   , the Managing Agents of [*hers/his*] property at [*state address of property*].

The letter was written in [*state where and when the letter was written*].

The reason why the Plaintiff cannot attend the hearing is that he is beyond the seas.

This notice is given pursuant to Order 20, r15 of the County Court Rules 1981.

DATED

---

(1) the time, place and circumstances at or in which the statement was made; and

(2) the person by whom, and the person to whom, the statement was made, if they are not apparent on the face of the document or part thereof (CCR Ord 20, r16; RSC Ord 38, r22(2)).

If the statement was made otherwise than in a document the notice must contain the particulars in (1) and (2) *above* and also 'the substance of the statement or, if material, the words used' (CCR Ord 20, r16; RSC Ord 38, r22(1)).

If the party giving notice alleges that the maker of the statement cannot or should not be called as a witness at the hearing for any of the reasons specified in CCR Ord 20, r17(5), the notice must contain a statement to that effect specifying the reason relied on. The reasons that may be relied on are that the witness:

(1) is dead; or

(2) is beyond the seas; or

(3) is unfit, by reason of his bodily or mental condition, to attend as a witness; or

(4) cannot with reasonable diligence be identified or found; or

(5) cannot reasonably be expected (having regard to the time which has elapsed since he was connected or concerned as aforesaid and to all the circumstances) to have any recollection of matters relevant to the accuracy or otherwise of the statement.

Any party receiving a notice may, within seven days after service of the notice on him, give to the proper officer of the court and to the party who gave the notice a counter-notice requiring that party to call as a witness at the trial or hearing any person (naming him) particulars of whom are contained in the notice (CCR Ord 20, r17). Where the notice contains a statement that the witness cannot be called for one of the five reasons set out above the recipient of the notice cannot send a counter-notice unless he contends that that person can or, as the case may be, should be called, and in that case he must include in his counter-notice a statement to that effect (CCR Ord 20, r17(2)). (For the rules as to the computation of time see CCR Ord 1, r9.)

Where a counter-notice is served the party serving the notice cannot rely upon the statement unless one of the five exceptions applies or the court uses its discretion under CCR Ord 20, r20. Where a question arises as to whether one of the exceptions applies the issue can be determined prior to the trial (see CCR Ord 20, r18).

The court may, if it thinks it just to do so, allow the statement of an absent person to be given in evidence at the trial or hearing of an action or matter notwithstanding that the rules as to notice have not been complied with or that another party has been served a counter-notice requiring the witness to attend (CCR Ord 20, r20). But the court will not allow the statement to be adduced in evidence if the reason for failing to give proper notice was a tactical one (*Ford v Lewis* [1971] 1 WLR 623).

These rules do not apply where the statement is contained in an affidavit (CCR Ord 20, r15(5)).

As to the admissibility of certain records and statements produced by computers, see p326.

Chapter 23

Rent Cases

The most common ground for possession is that the tenant is in arrears with his rent. It is a ground under the Housing Act 1988 (Grounds 8, 10 and 11), the Rent Act 1977 (Case 1), the Housing Act 1985 (Ground 1) and the Rent (Agriculture) Act 1976 (Case III).

Some preliminary considerations

It should be borne in mind that it can take several months between the time a notice is served and the time that possession is finally obtained. In London it takes about five months which are made up as follows:

Notice of proceedings for possession—minimum period	14 days
Average time between filing proceedings at court and hearing date	2 months
Possession order (if granted as an absolute order) usually	28 days
Average time between the issue of a warrant for possession and execution	28 days
Total	5 months

The delay will be even greater if a pre-trial review is necessary. The tenant may request a pre-trial review where he seeks discovery of the landlord's books or where he is pursuing a counterclaim, eg where the tenant is claiming that the landlord is in breach of his repairing obligations under s 11 of the Landlord and Tenant Act 1985, in which case directions as to expert evidence may be necessary (see CCR Ord 20, rr 27, 28). Even where an order for possession is made it will (unless Ground 8 of the Housing Act 1988 is relied upon) usually be suspended upon terms that the arrears are paid off by instalments which will often be small. Accordingly, at the first hint that the rent is not being paid regularly the landlord should take steps to serve the appropriate notice and commence proceedings for possession. This will minimise the delay and ensure that the arrears are no greater than necessary by the date of the hearing.

It is, of course, better to avoid proceedings altogether. Where the tenant is having difficulty paying the rent, perhaps because he has

316

become unemployed, the landlord could suggest that the tenant apply for housing benefit and that it be paid directly to the landlord (see *below*). He could also try to reach a compromise:

(a) the landlord could agree to waive any arrears of rent if the tenant leaves by a specified date;

(b) the landlord could offer the tenant a sum of money to leave. The tenant will not be bound by any such agreement (see p290) and so the landlord should ensure that any such payment is made concurrently with the giving up of possession. Where this course is adopted the landlord should attend the premises with a 'respectable' witness on the date that the tenant has agreed to give up possession. He should ensure that the tenant clears out all his possessions and that the keys are handed over, at which point the tenant should be paid. It is also suggested that the locks should then be changed. (See also 'Surrender', Chapter 3.)

If proceedings need to be taken it is best at an early stage to consider how any money judgment may be enforced. If rent has been paid by cheque details of the tenant's bank account should be noted for potential garnishee proceedings. Details of the tenant's employers would enable attachment of earnings proceedings to be taken. This information could be ascertained before the commencement of the tenancy by requiring references.

Landlord and Tenant Act 1987, ss47 and 48

The landlord must be careful to ensure that ss47 and 48 of the Landlord and Tenant Act 1987 have been complied with. (These sections do not apply where a receiver or manager has been appointed by the court to collect the rent/service charges: s47(3) and s48(2)). They apply to premises which consist of or include a dwelling and which are not held under a tenancy to which Part II of the Landlord and Tenant Act 1954 applies. The word 'premises' refers to the subject matter of the letting, so that an agricultural holding which includes a dwelling comes within the ambit of the Act (*Dallhold Estates (UK) Property Ltd v Lindsey Trading Properties Ltd* [1993] EGCS 195, CA). These sections apply to tenancies created prior to the date upon which they came into force (*Hussain v Singh* [1993] 2 EGLR 700A).

Section 47 requires the landlord to state his name and address on any *written demand* given to the tenant. If that address is not in England and Wales an address in England and Wales at which notices (including notices in proceedings) may be served on the landlord by the tenant must also be stated. 'Demand' means 'a demand for rent or other sums payable to the landlord under the terms of the tenancy'. If the written demand does not contain the required information any part of the amount demanded which consists of a *service charge* is 'treated for all purposes as not being due from the tenant to the landlord *at any time before that information is furnished by the landlord by notice given to the tenant'*. The landlord should ensure that the information is given *before* proceedings are commenced. If he does not do so he will have no cause of action in respect of the service charge at that date and will not be able to recover them in the proceedings.

Section 48 of the 1987 Act requires the landlord 'by notice' to furnish the tenant with an address in England and Wales at which notices (including notices in proceedings) may be served on him by the tenant. Where a landlord fails to comply with this provision 'any *rent* or *service charge* otherwise due from the tenant to the landlord shall . . . be treated for all purposes as not being due from the tenant to the landlord at any time before the landlord does not comply' with this requirement. Once again therefore the landlord must ensure that the address is given to the tenant *before* proceedings are commenced in order to ensure that at that date the landlord has a cause of action. The wording of the notice should follow precisely the wording of the section if the landlord wishes to avoid any challenges to the validity of the notice. However, an error in completing the notice which could not reasonably have misled the tenart might be held in appropriate cases not to invalidate the notice (compare *Official Solicitor v Thomas* [1986] 2 EGLR 1 at 6H-H).

Another consequence of a failure to comply with ss 47 and 48 is that interest will not begin to accrue upon the arrears until the sections have been complied with. Until they have been complied with there are no arrears.

Landlord and Tenant Act 1987, ss 46, 47 and 48

46.—(1) This Part applies to premises which consist of or include a dwelling and are not held under a tenancy to which Part II of the Landlord and Tenant Act 1954 apply.

(2) In this Part 'service charge' has the meaning given by section 18(1) of the 1985 Act.

47.—(1) Where any written demand is given to a tenant of premises to which this Part applies, the demand must contain the following information, namely—

        (*a*) the name and address of the landlord, and

        (*b*) if that address is not in England and Wales, an address in England and Wales at which notices (including notices in proceedings) may be served on the landlord by the tenant.

(2) Where—

        (*a*) a tenant of any such premises is given such a demand, but

        (*b*) it does not contain any information required to be contained in it by virtue of subsection (1),

then (subject to subsection (3)) any part of the amount demanded which consists of a service charge ('the relevant amount') shall be treated for all purposes as not being due from the tenant to the landlord at any time before that information is furnished by the landlord by notice given to the tenant.

. . .

(4) In this section 'demand' means a demand for rent or other sums payable to the landlord under the terms of the tenancy.

. . .

48.—(1) A landlord to which this Part applies shall by notice furnish the tenant with an address in England and Wales at which notices (including notices in proceedings) may be served on him by the tenant.

(2) Where a landlord of any such premises fails to comply with subsection (1), any rent or service charge otherwise due from the tenant to the landlord shall (subject to subsection (3)) be treated for all purposes as not being due from the tenant to the landlord at any time before the landlord shall comply with that subsection.

. . .

54.—(1) Any notice required or authorised to be served under this Act (*a*) shall be in writing; and (*b*) may be sent by post.

. . .

60.—(1) In this Act—

'landlord' . . . means the immediate landlord or, in relation to a statutory tenant, the person who, apart from the statutory tenancy, would be entitled to possession of the premises subject to the tenancy.

'notices in proceedings' means notices or other documents served in, or in connection with, any legal proceedings.

Terminating the tenancy and commencing proceedings

The methods of determining tenancies and the stage at which proceedings for possession should be commenced are dealt with in Parts 1 and 2 of this book. In a Rent Act case where there is a choice between forfeiture and service of a notice to quit it is usually preferable to serve a notice to quit. This avoids the awkward relief provisions in s138(1) of the County Courts Act 1984. Where the landlord does not really want possession but simply requires the rent to be paid forfeiture is, however, preferable because it avoids having to wait until a notice to quit has expired before proceedings for possession can be commenced.

Proceedings should be commenced by summons in the county court for the area in which the property is situated (see Chapter 20). (Proceedings should only be commenced in the High Court where the tenancy is not statutorily protected and the High Court has jurisdiction; see p259.)

The particulars of claim; prescribed form

A form prescribed by the County Court Rules *must* now be used in all rent cases (CCR Ord 6, r3(3); on p320). Note in particular the requirement to give details of the tenant's financial and other circumstances, so far as known (para 6). Where there are grounds relied upon other than non-payment of rent, these may be included (para 3(*b*)).

The tenant's actions on receipt of the summons

Advice to tenants

The first thing that an adviser to a tenant should do is to check that the landlord has complied with the provisions of ss47 and 48 of the Landlord

Form 41: Particulars of claim for possession (rented property)

Particulars of Claim for Possession (Rented Property)

In the

County Court

Case Number

Notes to help you complete this form.

This form should only be used to recover possession of residential premises where one of the grounds is non-payment of rent. If you need more space, please continue on a separate sheet. Mark the sheet clearly with the names of the parties and the paragraph number(s) to which the information relates.

Plaintiff

Defendant[s]

Paragraph 1(a).
Give the address of the property the Plaintiff wishes the Defendant to leave.

Paragraph 1(b).
Delete the appropriate words in brackets to show whether the property is a dwelling-house or part of one.

1

About the tenancy

(a) The Plaintiff has a right to possession of the property at

(b) The property is a [dwelling-house] [part of a dwelling-house.]

Paragraph 2(a).
Give the type of tenancy e.g. assured, protected, etc (or licence), the date of the agreement, amount of current rent and when it is payable e.g. weekly, fortnightly.

Paragraph 2(b).
If the claim for possession is not based on forfeiture for non-payment of rent, delete this paragraph. If it is, give the daily rate at which unpaid rent should be calculated.

2

(a) The property is let to the Defendant[s] under a[n]

tenancy agreement [or licence]

which began on

The rent is £   per

(b) The daily rate at which any unpaid rent should be calculated is £   per day.

Paragraph 3(a).
Say how much rent is outstanding up to the time the summons is issued, giving details of payments missed. If a schedule of payments missed or not made on time is attached, say so. Say whether payments generally have been made regularly and on time giving sufficient detail to support your claim for possession.

3

The reason the Plaintiff is asking for possession is:

(a) because the rent has not been paid as it should have under the terms of the tenancy agreement. Details are set out below.

Paragraph 3(b).
Delete this paragraph if the claim for possession is because of rent arrears only or you are claiming possession on statutory grounds. If not, give details of any other failure to comply with the tenancy agreement (or licence).

(b) because the Defendant[s] has failed to comply with the terms of the tenancy agreement in the following way:

Paragraph 3(c).
Delete this paragraph if you are not claiming possession on statutory grounds. If you are, say what the statutory grounds are.

(c) because:

Paragraph 4.
Give details of any steps taken to recover the arrears. If there have been previous court proceedings, give the date they were started and concluded, and the terms of any order(s) made.

4 The following steps have already been taken to recover the arrears:

Paragraph 5.
Give the date notice to quit (of breach of lease) (or seeking possession) was given to the Defendant[s]. Delete the words in brackets to show which type of notice was served.

5 The appropriate notice to quit [notice of breach of lease] [or notice seeking possession] was served on the Defendant[s] on

Paragraph 6.
Give what details you know of the Defendant's[s'] financial and other circumstances. Say in particular, whether Housing Benefit or arrears are paid direct to the Plaintiff by DSS and if so, how much.

6 About the Defendant[s]

The following information is known about the Defendant's[s'] circumstances:

Paragraph 7.
Delete this paragraph if you do not wish to give details of the Plaintiff's financial and other circumstances to support the claim for possession.

7 About the Plaintiff

The Plaintiff is asking the court to take the following information into account when making its decision whether or not to grant an order for possession:

Paragraph 8.
Delete this paragraph if the claim for possession is not based on forfeiture for non-payment of rent. If it is, delete (a) or (b) as appropriate. If (a) is deleted give the name and address of the person entitled to make a claim.

8 (a) There is no underlessee [or mortgagee] entitled to claim relief against forfeiture.

(b)

> of

is entitled to claim relief against forfeiture as underlessee [or mortgagee].

What the court is being asked to do

Paragraph 9.
Delete paragraphs (a) – (c) as appropriate.

9 The Plaintiff is asking the court to make an order that the Defendant[s]:

(a) give the Plaintiff possession of the property [land] mentioned in paragraph 1:

(b) pay the unpaid rent due from

to the date of issue of this summons, and from the date of issue of the summons

to the date an order is made, at the rate of £ per

(c) pay the costs of making this application for possession.

Paragraph 10.
Delete if not applicable

10 The Plaintiff is also asking that judgment is entered against the Defendant[s] for the total amount of the arrears outstanding up to the time an order is made [and costs].

> Signed
>
> *(Solicitors for) Plaintiff*
>
> *Date*

> Give an address where notices about this case can be sent to you
>
> Postcode

Reproduced by kind permission of The Solicitors' Law Stationery Society Ltd

and Tenant Act 1987 (see *above*). If he has not done so the tenant will have a complete defence (at least until those provisions have been complied with) to an action for rent and/or service charges.

Where it would appear that the tenant has fallen into arrears because of financial difficulties advise him to make an immediate application for housing benefit unless he has already done so (see p324). Apply for emergency legal aid which should be granted, particularly where the tenant wishes to raise some sort of defence or counterclaim.

If necessary write a letter to the landlord's solicitors asking for an adjournment. Send a copy of the letter to the court. The landlord is unlikely to agree to the adjournment but if he does refuse and the hearing is eventually adjourned by the judge on the return date the tenant should not have to pay the costs thrown away. But note that the case may go ahead even though only listed for a short period (see further p270). The court will have sent the tenant a standard form of reply (Form N11R) and this should be completed.

Where the tenant may have some sort of defence or counterclaim his representative should consider whether it is an appropriate case for directions, requests for further and better particulars etc. Although the rules permit the defendant to turn up at the hearing and defend the action without serving a defence (see p269) a proper defence and/or counterclaim should be drafted and served. Some possible counterclaims are as follows:

(1) that the landlord is in breach of his obligations to repair (see s 11 of the Landlord and Tenant Act 1985 for the statutorily implied obligations where the lease is for a term of less than seven years and *Barrett v Lounova* [1989] 1 All ER 351, CA for common law implied terms. For the general principles governing assessment of damages see *Calabar Properties v Stitcher* [1983] 3 All ER 759, CA; see further under 'Set-off', p339);

(2) that the landlord has been harassing the tenant and is therefore liable to pay the tenant damages for breach of covenant for quiet enjoyment (see Chapter 27).

(3) recovery of overpaid rent (see s57(3) of the Rent Act 1977);

(4) recovery of unlawful premiums (see s 125 of the Rent Act 1977);

(As to a counterclaim operating as a set-off see p337.)

As the time allocated for the hearing is only 15 minutes, if the tenant either files a very long defence and/or counterclaim and/or notifies the court that he has a large number of witnesses he wishes to call to give evidence it is likely that the matter will be adjourned to a day when the court has sufficient time to hear it and that directions will be given.

If the tenant alleges that rent has been paid which the landlord claims has not been paid he should bring evidence to the court to show this, eg cheque stubs, bank statements and rent book. Those acting for the tenant should also check that any requisite notice is in the correct form and that proceedings have not been issued before the proper date.

The tenant should enquire as to the availability of alternative accommodation. If this is scarce, the judge may not find it reasonable to make the order (where the ground relied on is a discretionary one) despite the arrears.

Where the landlord suggests that agreement be reached upon the lines set out in the first part of this chapter the tenant should bear in mind that any voluntary departure from the dwelling house will make him 'intentionally homeless' and thus ineligible for rehousing by the local authority under Part III of the Housing Act 1985. If he is a person with a 'priority need' and so eligible for housing he should only agree to such a course of action if he already has other secure accommodation. (See further p292.)

Housing benefit

The housing benefit scheme enables those entitled to receive such benefits to have their rent, licence fees or mesne profits, etc paid by the local authority. The rules governing housing benefit are contained in the Housing Benefit (General) Regulations 1987 (SI 1987 No 1971). A useful book dealing with the subject is *National Welfare Benefits Handbook*, CPAG (published annually).

Licensees as well as tenants may apply for housing benefit. Housing benefit is intended to pay for current rent but in exceptional cases the local authority has a discretion to backdate the benefit payments for up to 12 months (reg 72(15)). For example, it may agree to do so where the tenant is in substantial arrears due to illness and/or where the tenant was unaware of his eligibility to receive benefits. A tenant who thinks that he may be entitled to housing benefit must apply directly to the local authority, which is responsible for paying the benefit. Where the tenant is entitled to both income support and housing benefit a claim for both may be made at the same time by completing the necessary forms and sending them to the local DSS office; although he may make the application for housing benefit direct to the local authority if he wishes to do so.

Where the landlord is a local council the benefit takes the form of a rent rebate. In all other cases a payment (known as a rent allowance) is made. Housing benefit is usually paid to the tenant (reg 92(1)). However, it *must* be paid directly to the landlord:

(1) where the tenant is eight weeks or more in arrears with his rent (except where it is in the overriding interest of the tenant not to make direct payments to the landlord); or

(2) where the DSS is paying deductions from income support to the landlord in respect of arrears (see *below*) (reg 93).

If neither (1) or (2) *above* apply the payments *may* nevertheless be made direct to the landlord if:

(3) the tenant has requested or consented to such a payment;

(4) payment to the landlord is in the interest of the claimant and his family; or

(5) the tenant has abandoned the property owing rent arrears (reg 94).

A local authority may also withhold payment where it is satisfied that the tenant is not paying the rent regularly. It will hold the rent until satisfied that the tenant has paid or will pay the landlord (reg 95). Further, where the tenant is in receipt of housing benefit but is not paying it to the landlord, the court may, in order to protect the landlord and to prevent abuse of the housing benefit system, grant an *ex parte* injunction requiring the tenant to pay the benefit which he is receiving into court pending determination of the landlord's claim for possession (*Berg v Markhill* (1985) *The Times*, 10 May).

Income support

Where a tenant is in arrears for at least eight weeks and the arrears equal or exceed four times the weekly rent, the landlord may ask the DSS to deduct a sum from the tenant's entitlement to income support to be paid directly to the landlord. Deductions may also be made if the arrears are for less than eight weeks if the DSS adjudication officer considers that it is in the overriding interests of the tenant or his family for payments to be made directly to the landlord. (See para 5(1) of Sched 9 to the Social Security (Claims and Payments) Regulations 1987 (SI 1987 No 1968.) If, in a claim for possession on the basis of non-payment of rent where the tenant is in receipt of income support, the court makes a suspended order for possession the amount which the tenant is usually ordered to pay towards the arrears of rent is the amount deducted by the DSS and paid to the landlord. This sum is very small. In the year ending April 1995 it is £2.30.

The hearing

The tenant is usually unrepresented in rent actions. In most cases he will not be disputing the fact of the arrears or their amount but will simply be seeking an opportunity to pay them off by instalments and to avoid eviction. The fact that the tenant is unrepresented should not prevent the landlord's representative from talking to him and asking him what his proposals for payment are. If the tenant makes an offer to pay off the arrears at a reasonable rate plus the current rent this should be accepted as it is likely that the judge will find such an offer to be reasonable and make a suspended order in any event. Once in court indicate to the judge that the offer has been made and accepted and ask him to make an order for possession suspended upon condition that the payments are made. The agreement will not be binding on the court but the order sought will usually be made after some brief enquiry as to the facts of the case.

However, the judge will often require the landlord formally to prove his case even where agreement has been reached particularly if the tenant is unrepresented. (See further p290, 'Consent orders'.)

Title

The landlord will not have to prove his title to the land as the tenant will be estopped from denying it (see p7).

The tenancy and its terms

Where the tenancy is in the form of a written agreement signed by the parties the landlord should produce the part signed by the tenant (see p307). Draw the judge's attention to the terms affecting rent and if appropriate, the forfeiture clause. Where the tenancy is an oral one the landlord or his managing agent should state the day upon which the rent is payable, the amount payable and whether it is payable in arrears or in advance (see p332). If the rent is registered produce a copy of the certificate of rent registration and where the rent has been increased since the arrears began to accrue produce a copy of the notice of increase. Actual service of the notice of increase should be proved by the person who served it. (See further p308.)

Notices; proof of service

See p308.

Proving the arrears

Two issues may arise. First, the tenant may deny that the rent is as claimed by the landlord and, secondly, he may deny the failure to pay. The landlord must satisfy the court on both matters. The basis upon which the *amount* of rent due is calculated is dealt with in 'Calculating the exact amount of rent due' below (p332). Here we are concerned with proof of non-payment. (Note that the landlord must also comply with the provisions of ss47 and 48 of the Landlord and Tenant Act 1987 (see p317).)

The landlord's books   The landlord will often seek to rely upon a record that he has kept in order to prove non-payment. Where the landlord has personally compiled the record himself, as the rent was paid, he may rely upon it when giving evidence to refresh his memory. The tenant will be entitled to see the document and to cross-examine upon it. Where the record was made up by some person who is not called to give evidence it may be adduced in evidence under s2 of the Civil Evidence Act 1968 where the appropriate notice has either been served or dispensed with (see p312).

Where the compiler of the record made up the book from information given to him the record will be admissible under s4 of the 1968 Act if it was compiled by a person acting under a duty from information supplied by a person who had or may reasonably be supposed to have had personal knowledge of the matters dealt with in that information, and even if supplied through intermediaries. Thus if the property is managed by managing agents and it is the duty of one person in the firm to go out and collect the rents and then come back and tell the bookkeeper how much has been collected so that he can make a record of it the record will be admissible under s4 (see Form 42 for the requisite notice to be given; p328). Where the supplier of the information is to be called, ie the rent collector, the record cannot be given in evidence without the leave of the court, and in any event not before the examination-in-chief of the rent collector (s4(2) of the Civil Evidence Act 1968).

Computer records are admissible under s5 of the Civil Evidence Act 1968 provided that the conditions set out in subs (2) are satisfied. That the conditions have been satisfied is proved by a certificate under s5(4). As to the notice required to be given by a party wishing to rely upon a computer record see CCR Ord 20, r15 and RSC Ord 38, r24 and Form 43, p329.

Where the landlord alleges that any person, particulars of whom are contained in the notice, cannot or should not be called as a witness, for any of the reasons specified in CCR Ord 20, r17(5) (see p314) the notice must contain a statement to that effect specifying the reason relied on (CCR Ord 20, r16; RSC Ord 38, rr23(2), 24(3)). A counternotice requiring the maker of the statement to be called as a witness should be served within seven days (CCR Ord 20, r17).

Rent books   The signature of the landlord or his agent in the rent book is evidence of payment by the tenant, but lack of a signature is not of itself evidence of the tenant's failure to pay. The landlord may have refused to sign.

The order

If the tenant pays or tenders the arrears after the proceedings are commenced but before the hearing the court is unlikely to make an order for possession unless the tenant's past payment record is particularly bad in which case an order for possession suspended on condition that the rent is paid is likely to be made (see in particular Ground 11 in an assured tenancy case). However, see *Lee-Steere v Jennings* (1988) 20 HLR 1 where there was a bad history of arrears and the order for possession was not suspended.

Where the arrears remain unpaid at the date of the hearing in a case where the landlord is relying upon a discretionary ground the court usually makes an order for possession to take effect within 28 days but

Form 42: Notice of intention to give in evidence a statement from a compiled record of collected rents

---

IN THE   **COUNTY COURT**   **Case No**

BETWEEN

                                               Plaintiff

—AND—

                                              Defendant

NOTICE OF INTENTION TO GIVE IN EVIDENCE A STATEMENT FROM A COMPILED RECORD OF COLLECTED RENTS

TAKE NOTICE that the Plaintiff intends to give in evidence at the hearing of this action pursuant to section 4 of the Civil Evidence Act 1968 a statement contained in a 'rent collection book' compiled at [*state address of Managing Agent*] by [*state name of Managing Agent*] acting in the course of his duty as Managing Agent of the premises known as [*state address of premises*] from information supplied to him by his rent collector [*state name of rent collector*] who visited the premises at [*state address of premises*] on Monday in each week and thereafter returned to the premises of [*state name of Managing Agent*] at [*state address of Managing Agent*] where the information as to the rent paid by the Defendant was recorded by the said [*state name of Managing Agent*] in the said 'rent collection book' a copy of which is annexed hereto.

DATED

---

suspended upon the condition that the tenant pays off a certain amount of the arrears each week plus the current rent. When the arrears and any costs that have been ordered are paid the order ceases to be enforceable (see County Court Form N27(2), N28; Appendix 3). The amount that the tenant will be ordered to pay off the arrears depends upon the circumstances of each case but where the tenant is on income support the court will usually order that only the amount that is deductible from that benefit in respect of arrears be paid (see p325). The tenant may apply for a variation of the instalments or for more time to pay (CCR Ord 22, r10).

Where the arrears are substantial in a discretionary ground case the court will sometimes make an absolute order for possession (County Court Form N26), although the tenant should usually be given an opportunity to pay off any arrears due (*Lal v Nakum* [1981] CLY 1557). It is submitted that where the only reasons for the arrears are problems caused by the local authority in making payments of housing benefit it will not usually be reasonable to make any order for possession.

Forfeiture cases

In forfeiture actions where the Rent Act 1977 applies the court has to consider both s138 of the County Courts Act 1984 and s98 of the 1977 Act (*Wolmer Securities v Come* [1966] 2 QB 243; *Peachey Property*

Form 43: Notice of intention to give in evidence a statement produced by computer

IN THE   COUNTY COURT   Case No

BETWEEN

                                                                                    Plaintiff
                                —AND—

                                                                                    Defendant

NOTICE OF INTENTION TO GIVE IN EVIDENCE A STATEMENT PRODUCED BY COMPUTER

TAKE NOTICE that the Plaintiff intends to give in evidence at the hearing of this action pursuant to section 5 of the Civil Evidence Act 1968 a statement contained in a document produced in compliance with the condition, prescribed by section 5(2) of the said Act, by a computer on [*insert date*] from information supplied to the said computer between [*insert late*] and [*insert date*], a copy of which is annexed hereto.

AND FURTHER TAKE NOTICE that [*state name of Managing Agent*] was during the material period and still is the Managing Agent responsible for collecting the rent from the Defendant in respect of the Defendant's occupation of the premises known as [*state address of premises*] and was responsible for the supply of information to the computer and in particular of the information reproduced in the said statement and that throughout the material period the said [*state name*] was the chief operator of the said computer.

AND FURTHER TAKE NOTICE that throughout the material period the said computer was operating properly.

DATED

Corporation Ltd v Robinson [1967] 2 QB 243). Where the court considers that the landlord is entitled to possession it must make an order under both Acts. Special forms have therefore been devised to cope with this situation. Form N27(1) applies where the court does not wish to exercise its jurisdiction to make an order for possession under s98 and N27(2) applies where the court wishes to make an order for possession upon terms as to payment of arrears and current rent. (For the situation in relation to secure tenants see p167 and assured tenants see p108.)

Rent and mesne profits (damages for use and occupation)

Where the landlord proves that the tenant is in arrears with his rent the court will give judgment for the amount of arrears even where no order for possession is made. It will also make an order for mesne profits, ie for the sum due to the landlord for the period after the tenancy has come to an end until possession is delivered up. The standard form county court orders referred to above contain provisions relating to the 'money judgment' and sums for use and occupation. Strictly speaking a statutory tenant under the Rent Act 1977 is liable to pay the landlord rent rather than mesne profits as he is not a trespasser but continues in occupation by right under the statutory tenancy (see p136). It is fairly common, however, to talk of 'mesne profits' in Rent Act cases for the period after the *contractual* tenancy has come to an end. The difference is not of any great importance.

In the High Court the order may provide for payment of more profits until 'possession be delivered up'. It is not necessary to bring a second action for the amount due after the writ (*Southport Tramways Co v Gundy* [1897] 2 QB 66). The county court forms do not make express provision for such an order (see Appendix 3) but it is submitted that the county court also has the power to make such an order and in practice often does so.

Calculation of mesne profits

In order to claim mesne profits it is not necessary to show that the property would have been let to another person had the defendant vacated. The amount awarded is usually the same as the amount of rent (*Swordheath Properties Ltd v Tabet* [1979] 1 All ER 240):

> . . . the plaintiff, when he has established that the defendant has remained on as a trespasser in residential property, is entitled, without bringing evidence that he could or would have let the property to someone else in the absence of the trespassing defendant, to have as damages for the trespass the value of the property as it would fairly be calculated; and, in the absence of anything special in the particular case it would be the ordinary letting value of the property that would determine the amount of damages (*Swordheath Properties Ltd v Tabet* [1979] 1 All ER 240 at 242g).

However, the landlord is entitled to the true value of the property. He may therefore claim such sum as he is able to prove is equivalent to a market rent for the property even if this is higher than the rent originally payable (*Clifton Securities v Huntley* [1948] 2 All ER 283). And if the tenant wishes to argue that the market value was less than the rent he previously paid he is probably entitled to do so but the burden will be upon him to prove it; 27(1) Halsbury (Reissue) (4th edn), para 258; cited with approval by Lloyd LJ in *Ministry of Defence v Ashman* [1993] 2 EGLR 102 AC.

But it seems that a landlord has a choice between (*a*) a restitutionary remedy and (*b*) a claim for damages, and that where he chooses to pursue his restitutionary remedy the sum awarded is equivalent to the amount of the benefit to the *defendant*, which may not necessarily be the same as the rent he was paying particularly where that rent was a concessionary one. In such a case the amount of rent that he would have been paying for local authority accommodation suitable to his needs may, for example, be equivalent of the value to him. (See *Ministry of Defence v Ashman* [1993] 2 EGLR 102 CA and *Ministry of Defence v Thompson* [1993] 2

EGLR 107 CA; servicemen paying concessionary rent required to pay greater sums in respect of mesne profits):

> The principles in *Ashman* may, in my judgment, be summarised as follows: first, an owner of land which is occupied without his consent may elect whether to claim damages for the loss which he has been caused or restitution of the value of the benefit which the defendant has received.
>
> Second, the fact that the owner, if he had obtained possession, would have let the premises at a concessionary rent, or even would not have let them at all, is irrelevant to the calculation of the benefit for the purposes of *a restitutionary claim*. What matters is the benefit which the defendant has received.
>
> Third, a benefit may be worth less to an involuntary recipient than to one who has a free choice as to whether to remain in occupation or move elsewhere.
>
> Fourth, the value of the right of occupation to a former licensee who has occupied at a concessionary rent and who has remained in possession only because she could not be rehoused by the local authority until a possession order has been made would ordinarily be whichever is the higher of the former concessionary rent and what she would have paid for local authority housing suitable for her needs, if she had been rehoused at the time when the notice expired (*per* Hoffman LJ in *Ministry of Defence v Thompson*; but compare the approach adopted by Kennedy LJ and Lloyd LJ in *Ashman*).

Interest

By virtue of s69 of the County Courts Act 1984 the landlord is entitled to claim interest on the rent and (it is submitted) mesne profits outstanding. He may also have a right to claim such interest by reason of the tenancy agreement. However, any claim for interest, whether under the Act or the agreement, must be pleaded (CCR Ord 6, r1A).

The particulars of claim should show the amount of interest claimed at the rate at which it is claimed (see cases referred to in *Green Book*, note to s69). The amount of interest awarded is usually the sum payable on judgment debts in the High Court, currently 8 per cent.

Where the claim for interest is made under s69 of the 1984 Act the court's power to award interest is discretionary but the burden is upon the tenant to show why interest should not be awarded (*Allied London Investments Ltd v Hambro Life Assurance Ltd* (1985) 50 P&CR 207 at p210, CA). It is submitted that the absence of a clause in a written tenancy agreement entitling the landlord to interest is not a good reason for depriving him of interest under s69 (there was no such clause in the *Allied London* case, see p209).

County Courts Act 1984, s69

> **69.**—(1) Subject to County Court Rules, in proceedings (whenever instituted) before a county court for the recovery of a debt or damages there may be included in any sum for which judgment is given simple interest, at such rate as the court thinks fit or as may be prescribed, on all or any part of the debt or damages in respect of which judgment is given, or payment is

made before judgment for all or any part of the period between the date
when the cause of action arose and—

(*a*) in the case of any sum paid before judgment, the date of the
payment; and

(*b*) in the case of the sum for which the judgment is given, the date of
the judgment.

(2) . . .

(3) Subject to county court rules, where—

(*a*) there are proceedings (whenever instituted) before a county court
for the recovery of a debt; and

(*b*) the defendant pays the whole debt to the plaintiff (otherwise than
in pursuance of a judgment in the proceedings),

the defendant shall be liable to pay the plaintiff simple interest, at such rate
as the court thinks fit or as may be prescribed, on all or any part of the debt
for all or any part of the period between the date when the cause of action
arose and the date of the payment.

(4) Interest in respect of a debt shall not be awarded under this section for
a period during which, for whatever reason, interest on the debt already
runs.

(5) Interest under this section may be calculated at different rates in
respect of different periods.

(6) In this section 'plaintiff' means the person seeking the debt or
damages and 'defendant' means the person from whom the plaintiff seeks
the debt or damages . . .

(8) In determining whether the amount of any debt or damages exceeds
that prescribed by or under any enactment, no account shall be taken of any
interest payable by virtue of this section except where express provision to
the contrary is made by or under that or any other enactment.

CCR Ord 6, r1A

Where the plaintiff claims interest under section 69 of the Act or otherwise
his particulars of claim shall contain a statement to that effect.

Interest on judgment debts   Although as a general rule a plaintiff in the
county court may recover interest on a judgment debt for a sum of not
less than £5,000 such interest is not payable where the relevant judgment
grants the landlord of a dwelling house a suspended order for possession
(s74 of the County Courts Act 1984 and the County Court (Interest on
Judgment Debts) Order 1991).

Calculating the exact amount of rent due

Payable in arrears or in advance

Rent is payable in arrears unless there is an express agreement that it
should be payable in advance. Where the rent is payable in *arrears* the
landlord is only entitled to rent up until the date the tenancy is
determined. If therefore it is determined in the middle of a rent period it
is necessary to calculate, on a daily basis, the proportion of the rent due
from the last rent day until the date of determination. Where the rent is

payable in *advance* the landlord is entitled to the whole of the rent that was due on the last rent day before termination even though the tenancy has come to an end in the middle of the rent period (*Ellis v Rowbotham* [1900] 1 QB 740).

Where the landlord forfeits, the date of termination is the date the proceedings are served. Therefore, if the rent was payable in arrears rent is calculated up to the date of service. The landlord is entitled to mesne profits for the period thereafter (*Canas Property Co Ltd v KL Television Services Ltd* [1970] 2 QB 433).

It is important therefore to ascertain the rent day and to see whether the termination occurred before or after that date. If the rent was payable quarterly the quarters are calculated from the date of the agreement unless the lease states that the rent is to be paid on the usual quarter days, which are:

Lady Day—25 March
Midsummer—24 June
Michaelmas—29 September
Christmas Day—25 December

If the rent is payable in advance the tenant is not liable for the rent unless the tenancy has continued up until the end of the rent day (*Re Aspinall* [1961] Ch 526).

Local authority rents are usually payable weekly, in advance, each Monday.

Amount of rent: fair rent

The amount of rent that is due depends upon the terms of the tenancy. Certain tenancies, however, are subject to a limit. Where the tenancy is a protected or statutory tenancy, or a 'housing association tenancy' (ie a tenancy, other than a co-ownership tenancy, where the landlord is a registered housing association, housing trust or the Housing Corporation; see s86) the rent will probably be registered (see Parts IV and VI of the 1977 Act). A registered rent is the maximum rent that can be charged for the premises. It is registered in respect of the property and not the tenancy; so if a tenant goes into possession of premises subject to a registered rent only the amount that is registered is recoverable, whatever the terms of the tenancy (s44(1), (2) and s88(1), (2) of the 1977 Act). The rent limit in respect of a 'housing association tenancy' where the rent is not registered is determined by s88(4) of the 1977 Act. Except in limited circumstances, a tenancy entered into on or after 15 January 1989 cannot be a 'housing association tenancy' and this cannot be subject to the rent control discussed above (see s35(2) of the Housing Act 1988).

Rents in respect of restricted contracts may also be registered (see Part V of the 1977 Act). (See also s13 of the Rent (Agriculture) Act 1976 in relation to statutory tenancies under that Act.)

Local housing authority rents should be 'reasonable' (see s24(1) of the Housing Act 1985; and *Belcher v Reading Corporation* [1950] Ch 380).

Variation of rents   An application can be made to increase the registered rent in respect of a protected or statutory tenancy every two years (s67(3) of the Rent Act 1977). Phasing of rent increases was abolished in respect of rents for regulated tenancies that were registered on or after 4 May 1987 (Rent (Relief from Phasing) Order 1987 (SI 1987 No 264)). Once the rent has been registered, the landlord must serve a notice of increase in rent if he wishes to recover the higher rent (s49 of the Rent Act 1977; Rent Act 1977 (Forms etc) Regulations 1980 (SI 1980 No 1697)). If the tenancy is protected it will also be necessary to determine the contractual tenancy before the rent can be increased. In order to deal with this situation without the necessity of also having to serve a notice to quit, s49(4) of the 1977 Act provides that where a notice of increase is served during a contractual period and the protected tenancy could, by a notice to quit served by the landlord at the same time, be brought to an end before the date specified in the notice of increase, the notice operates to convert the protected tenancy into a statutory tenancy from that date. At the hearing the landlord should prove service of the notice of increase (see p326).

An application for an interim increase in rent on account of council tax may be made under s67A of the Rent Act 1977 or s13 of the Rent (Agriculture) Act 1976, pending the next full rent registration.

See s93 of the 1977 Act in relation to periodical 'housing association tenancies'. See ss102 and 103 of the Housing Act 1985 in respect of other secure tenancies (other than where the interest of the landlord belongs to a co-operative housing association: s109 of the 1985 Act). See s25 of the 1985 Act where the landlord is a local housing authority but the tenancy is not secure.

Assured tenancies; market rents

There is no provision for variation of rents agreed by landlords and tenants in respect of assured tenancies (unless the tenancy is an assured shorthold: s22 of the 1988 Act). However, the landlord may apply for an increase in rent where (*a*) the tenant has remained in occupation at the end of a fixed term tenancy as a statutory periodic tenant, or (*b*) in the case of any other periodic tenancy which is an assured tenancy without a rent review clause (s13(1)). The rent may be increased at the end of the fixed term and in all other cases annually (s13(2)). The increase is brought into operation by a notice served by the landlord under s13 unless the tenant applies to the rent assessment committee within the time limit prescribed or the parties come to some other agreement (s13(4)). The rent assessment committee determines the rent in accordance with s14. The obligation in s14(2)(*c*) of the 1988 Act to disregard 'any reduction in the value of the dwelling house attributable to a failure by the tenant to comply with any terms of the tenancy' refers to the present tenant (*N&D (London) Ltd v Gadson* [1992] 1 EGLR 112; son who succeeded to father's tenancy not affected by father's failure to keep the property in good repair—rent therefore assessed on basis that the property was in bad repair.

Period of the tenant's liability

The tenant is liable to pay rent from the commencement of the tenancy until its end. An ordinary contractual tenancy comes to an end when the landlord serves forfeiture proceedings upon the tenant, when a notice to quit served upon the tenant has expired, or when a fixed term has expired. Where the tenant remains in possession after termination of the tenancy he is liable to pay the landlord mesne profits. Statutory tenants are not trespassers and so they remain liable to pay rent until the statutory tenancy is brought to an end by order of the court and pay mesne profits thereafter (see also p329). For the position where the tenant abandons/surrenders see 'Rent'. In *Griffiths v Renfree* (1989) 21 HLR 338 the tenant husband served a notice to quit on his landlord and left but his wife remained in occupation. Held: the tenant continued to be liable for the rent after expiry of the notice to quit until possession was given up. (See also p241.)

Although a tenant is estopped from disputing his landlord's title he is under no obligation to pay the rent after the landlord's title has been determined, even where there is no third party claiming title. The tenant will only be estopped if he continued to pay rent after having knowledge that the landlord's title had come to an end (*National Westminster Bank Ltd v Hart* [1983] QB 773).

Failure by tenant to remove sub-tenant etc.

Where a tenancy comes to an end the tenant must give up complete possession. If a sub-tenant (or, presumably, other person who originally entered into occupation under the tenant) remains in occupation the tenant remains liable to pay the rent until possession is delivered up, unless the landlord accepts that person as a new tenant (*Harding v Crethorn* (1793) 1 Esp 57); even if the occupier remains in occupation against the wishes of the tenant (*Ibbs v Richardson* (1839) 9 A&E 849).

> When a lease is expired, the tenant's responsibility is not at an end; for if the premises are in possession of an under-tenant, the landlord may refuse to accept the possession, and hold the original lessee liable; for the lessor is entitled to receive the absolute possession at the end of the term. But it may be proved, that the lessor had accepted the under-tenant as his tenant, as by his having accepted the key from the original lessee, while the under-tenant was in possession, by his acceptance of rent from him, or by some act tantamount to it. (*Harding v Crethorn*, per Lord Kenyon).

Assignment by landlord

Where the landlord has assigned his interest in the property only the new landlord may recover rent from the date of the assignment (s141 of the Law of Property Act 1925; *Re King, Robinson v Gray* [1963] Ch 459). Where the assignment takes place in the middle of the rent period the new landlord is entitled to the rent for the whole of the period on the next rent day (*Rickett v Green* [1910] 1 KB 253). He is also entitled to recover any arrears of rent that accrued before the assignment in place of the original landlord (*London and County Securities Ltd v Wilfred Sportsman Ltd* [1971] Ch 764; *Arlesford Trading Co Ltd v Servansingh* [1971] 1 WLR 1080). However, the tenant is not to be considered to be in breach of covenant to pay rent by failure to pay rent to the new landlord before notice of the assignment has been given to him; and payment to the old landlord before that time is a sufficient discharge of the obligation to pay rent (s151 of the Law of Property Act 1925).

If the tenant pays the rent before it is due and before that date the landlord assigns his interest the tenant remains liable to the new landlord for the rent (*De Nicholls v Saunders* (1870) LR 5 CP 589 at 594).

As for the tenant's inability to sue, or counterclaim against, the new landlord in respect of breaches committed by the previous landlord, see p78.

Irrecoverable rent and reductions in rent

The landlord may not recover rent that is more than six years in arrears (s22 of the Limitation Act 1980).

The landlord is not entitled to recover any rent paid by the tenant to a managing agent whose instructions have been withdrawn, unless he has already informed the tenant of the same.

A landlord's agreement to allow a reduction in rent must be supported by consideration if the tenant is to be able to rely upon it. A threat by the tenant to terminate and leave unless the landlord agrees to a reduction together with the promise to stay if the landlord agrees to a reduction is sufficient consideration. The courts construe the circumstances as a surrender and the grant of a new lease at a lower rent (*Parker v Briggs* (1893) 37 SJ 452). No consideration for the landlord's promise to accept a lower rent is required if the tenant acts in reliance upon that promise. The landlord will be estopped from recovering the full rent unless he gives the tenant reasonable notice to pay it (*Central London Property Trust Ltd v High Trees House Ltd* [1947] KB 130; see also *Brikom Investments Ltd v Carr* [1979] QB 467).

Lost rent

Where the tenant sends the rent by post he takes the risk and if it is lost will continue to be liable for that amount of the rent unless the parties have expressly or impliedly agreed that payment should be made by posting (*Beevers v Mason* (1979) 37 P&CR 452).

Payment of rent to the landlord by a third party does not discharge the tenant unless the payer was the tenant's agent (*Smith v Cox* [1940] 2 KB 558). If the payer had no authority at the time of the payment the tenant can later ratify.

Rent books

Where a tenant has a right to occupy premises as a residence in consideration of a rent payable weekly the landlord must provide the tenant with a rent book or other similar document for use in respect of the premises which contains information specified by statutory instrument (s4(1) of the Landlord and Tenant Act 1985; Rent Book (Forms of Notice) Regulations 1982 (SI 1982 No 1474)). Failure to provide such a rent book is an offence but the rent does not thereby become irrecoverable (*Shaw v Groom* [1970] 2 QB 504).

Service charges

The amount of service charges recoverable from the tenant in respect of a flat is limited by ss18–30 of the Landlord and Tenant Act 1985 (as amended by Sched 2 of the Landlord and Tenant Act 1987). Note also the provisions of ss47 and 48 of the 1987 Act (see p317).

Set-off

Where the landlord is in breach of his covenant to repair the dwelling house and the tenant has carried out the repairs himself, the tenant may have a right at common law to set off the cost of repairs. If he has not actually carried out the repairs the set-off will not arise at common law but equity may allow him to set off any claim for damages that he might have had against the rent. Although most of the cases are concerned with a landlord's failure to repair equity will permit the tenant to set off any other claims for damages that he has against the rent due. If the set-off is equal to or greater than the amount of rent claimed, the landlord will have lost the ground upon which he claims possession (for a recent example, see *Televantos v McCulloch* [1991] 1 EGLR 123, CA; tenant successfully resisted a claim for possession based upon non-payment of rent by setting off a counterclaim for damages for failure to repair).

The common law and equitable principles are discussed in *Lee-Parker v Izzet* [1971] 1 WLR 1688 and *British Anzani v International Marine* [1979] 2 All ER 1063.

Common law

There are at least two sets of circumstances in which at common law there can be a set-off against rent, one where the tenant expends money on repairs to the demised premises which the landlord has covenanted to carry out, but in breach has failed to do so (at any rate where the breach significantly affects the use of the premises), and the other where the tenant has paid the money at the request of the landlord in respect of some obligation of the landlord connected with the land demised. To this proposition must be added *two riders*. First, that as the landlord's obligation to repair premises demised does not arise until the tenant has notified him of want of repair, such notification must be given before the set-off can arise; and secondly that the set-off must be for a sum which has actually been paid and in addition its quantum has either been acknowledged by the landlord or in some other way can no longer be disputed by him, as, for instance, if it is the subject of an award on a submission to arbitration. (*British Anzani per* Forbes LJ at 1070).

In *Lee-Parker v Izzet* Goff LJ had said that he considered that the full amount of expenditure *properly* incurred could be set off against the rent and that it was a question of fact in each case whether and to what extent the expenditure was proper. Forbes J takes a slightly narrower view:

My view is that the right is slightly more restricted, namely that it can only be exercised when the sum is certain and its amount cannot really be disputed by the landlord . . . It seems the quantum of the sum must have been either unchallenged or unchallengeable before it could be regarded as deductible (see at 1070f).

Tenants should, therefore, be careful before rushing out and spending large sums of money on repairs, with a view to then withholding rent. They must try to make sure that the amount 'cannot really be disputed by the landlord'. It will usually be better to seek an order under s 17 of the Landlord and Tenant Act 1985 for specific performance of the repairing covenant.

If the tenant is permitted to deduct the sums expended he may do so from future rent (*Lee Parker v Izzet*) or from arrears of rent (*Asco Developments Ltd v Garden* (1978) 248 EG 683).

Equity

Where the tenant does not actually expend sums on having the repairs carried out he cannot set off the sum which it would have cost against the rent and, contrary to popular belief, he cannot simply stop paying rent until the repairs are carried out (*Taylor v Webb* [1937] 2 KB 283). He may, however, set off a sum equal to the amount of damages to which he is entitled for breach of the landlord's covenant to repair (*British Anzani v International Marine* [1979] 2 All ER 1063 at 1074c) and, if there is a reasonable prospect of the tenant's counterclaim matching or exceeding the landlord's claim, the tenant may be granted a stay of the claim for possession until the hearing of the counterclaim (*Haringey LBC v Stewart* [1991] 2 EGLR 252 at 253B). As the tenant is not spending the money on repairs the sum awarded will not be the cost of repair. The basis upon which damages for breach of a landlord's repairing covenant are assessed has been explained in *Calabar Properties v Stitcher* [1983] 3 All ER 759, CA:

> The object of awarding damages against a landlord is not to punish the landlord but, so far as money can, to restore the tenant to the position he would have been in had there been no breach. This object will not be achieved by applying one set of rules to all cases regardless of the particular circumstances of the case. The facts of each case must be looked at carefully to see what damage the tenant has suffered and how he may be fairly compensated by a monetary award (*per* Griffiths LJ at 768f).

Where repairs are eventually carried out the tenant is entitled to damages under three heads: (*a*) the cost of alternative accommodation while the works are being carried out; (*b*) the cost of redecorating; and (*c*) 'some award for all the unpleasantness of living in the [dwelling] as it deteriorated until it became uninhabitable', (*per* Griffiths LJ at 768j). If the tenant has rented the property to let it out and the landlord is aware of this the tenant may be entitled to his loss of rent if he cannot let it because of the breach (*per* Griffiths LJ at 770a).

As stated above the right of set-off in equity is not limited to repair cases but may arise whenever the tenant has a claim for damages against the landlord, but only so long as the counterclaim arises out of the tenancy (*British Anzani*).

Notice of want of repair

The landlord's obligation to start carrying out works of repair to the demised premises does not arise until he has notice of the work of repair (*O'Brien v Robinson* [1973] 1 All ER 583 HL). It is therefore imperative that the tenant give the landlord such notice. However, it is sufficient notice if the landlord actually receives the relevant information from a person other than the tenant (*Dinefwr Borough Council v Jones* [1987] 2 EGLR 58 CA).

It is not necessary to give notice of repairs required to parts retained by the landlord (*Duke of Westminster v Guild* [1984] 3 All ER 144 at 152 h; *Long v Hammer* [1989] 2 EGLR 249 at 258L).

Excluding the tenant's right to set off

Many leases seek to prevent the tenant from deducting sums from the rent by stating that it must be paid 'without deductions'. However, these words will not normally be sufficient to exclude the equitable right to set off. Clear words are required. (*Connaught Restaurants Ltd v Indoor Leisure Ltd* [1993] EGCS 143, CA). However, if the words are sufficiently clear the Unfair Contracts Term Act 1977 does not apply (*Electricity Supply Nominees v IAH Group* [1993] 3 All ER 372).

Failure of tenant's counterclaim

In ordinary circumstances it will not be reasonable to make a possession order if the tenant has made arrangements in the event of failure of his counterclaim to clear the arrears by an anticipatory payment into court (to give one example), or by setting aside funds which can be devoted for that purpose (to give another example) or, at the very least, to put forward proposals for an early discharge of the arrears.

If he is able to take those steps towards satisfying the proper demands of the lessor for payment of rent it will, in general, be unreasonable for an order to be made against him. In exceptional cases, however, as for example where the tenant has already a very poor record for persistent late payment of rent, the ordinary benevolent course will not be followed, and the making of an order would be regarded as reasonable upon the ground that the tenant has disqualified himself from the court's sympathy by the persistency of his past defaults . . . (*Haringey LBC v Stewart* [1991] 2 EGLR 252, CA, *per* Waite LJ at 253B).

Chapter 24

Other Common Grounds for Possession

'Bad' tenants

There are three grounds for possession contained in Sched 15 to the Rent Act 1977 that are available to the landlord where the tenant is a 'bad tenant' once he has determined the contractual tenancy. Case 2 is appropriate where the tenant is causing a nuisance or annoyance to adjoining occupiers or where the tenant has been convicted of using or allowing the dwelling house to be used for immoral or illegal purposes. Case 2 is also available where any person residing or lodging with the tenant or where any sub-tenant is carrying out such activities. Cases 3 and 4 are available where there has been a deterioration to the dwelling house or furniture therein. Case 1 may also be relied upon where the tenant is in breach of any obligation of the tenancy.

Similar provisions are contained in the Housing Act 1988 (Grounds 12, 13, 14 and 15); the Housing Act 1985 (Grounds 1, 2, 3 and 4) and the Rent (Agriculture) Act 1977 (Cases III, IV, V and VI).

Case 2: nuisance, annoyance etc

'Nuisance' is an interference with the ordinary comfort of adjoining occupiers. 'Annoyance' is wider and covers anything which an ordinary sensible person would deem to be a disturbance. What would annoy an over-sensitive occupier is not an annoyance for the purposes of Case 2 (see *Tod-Heatly v Benham* (1989) 40 ChD 80).

Nuisance caused by a third party will not allow the landlord to use this case unless the tenant should be, but is not, taking reasonable steps to prevent it (*Commercial General Administration Ltd v Thomsett* (1979) 250 EG 547). Nuisance or annoyance suffered by the landlord is not sufficient unless he is an adjoining occupier. The term 'adjoining occupiers' is not narrowly construed so as to mean only persons occupying properties physically adjoining the tenant's property. All that is required is that the premises of the adjoining occupier should be near enough to be affected by the tenant's conduct at the demised premises (*Cobstone Investments Ltd v Maxim* [1984] 2 All ER 635).

In order to prove nuisance or annoyance the adjoining occupiers who have complained of the nuisance or annoyance should be brought to court to give evidence. If they will not attend court, perhaps because they are frightened of the tenant, any letters of complaint that they have written may be produced to the court if the requirements of the Civil Evidence Act 1968 are complied with (see Chapter 22). Evidence on oath, however, will obviously be of much greater weight. Where there is a history of allegations between the tenant and the adjoining occupier with each side accusing the other of causing the nuisance or annoyance, for example by continually making loud and unwarranted noise, it may be worthwhile the landlord employing an investigator to make an assessment of the situation and then using his evidence at the hearing. It may be possible to prove nuisance or annoyance without calling the adjoining occupiers. For example, where it is proved that the premises are used for prostitution it will be assumed that a nuisance has been caused (*Frederick Platts Co Ltd v Grigor* [1950] 1 All ER 941).

Any conviction relied upon must be for a crime committed on the premises. The premises must also have something to do with the crime. It is not sufficient if they are merely the scene of the crime (*Abrahams v Wilson* [1971] 2 QB 88; possession of drugs).

Although the court always continues to have a discretion an order for possession will usually be made where the landlord has proved illegal or immoral user (*Yates v Morris* [1951] 1 KB 77).

Conviction of an offence tried on indictment is proved by production of a certified extract of the court record signed by the clerk or other officer of the Crown Court (s 13 of the Evidence Act 1851). Conviction of an offence tried in a magistrates' court is proved by the record of conviction signed by a magistrate or properly authorised officer (s 18 of the Prevention of Crimes Act 1871).

Cases 3 and 4: deterioration of the dwelling house or furniture

Where the landlord seeks to rely upon Cases 3 and 4 he will have to prove two matters: (*a*) that there has been a deterioration in the condition of the dwelling house or the furniture and (*b*) that the deterioration has been caused by the neglect or default of the tenant or one of the persons referred to in the cases. The landlord must therefore call evidence to prove the state of the premises or the furniture at some earlier stage and make a comparison to their present state. It will usually be possible to infer that the tenant is responsible for any deterioration that has taken place from the fact that the dwelling house and the furniture are under his control. In more difficult cases it may be necessary to call the evidence of a surveyor to prove the cause of the deterioration.

Any person seeking to rely upon such expert evidence may not simply call the expert at the trial. He must first seek directions from the District

Judge as to the preparation and disclosure of reports so that the other side is not taken by surprise (see CCR Ord 20, rr27, 28).

The landlord may rely upon a deterioration in the state of the tenant's garden (*Holloway v Povey* (1984) 271 EG 195).

The order for possession

Cases 2, 3 and 4 are, of course, discretionary grounds for possession and the court may not make the order unless it considers it reasonable to do so (s98(1) of the Rent Act 1977). The court may also suspend the order for possession (s100 of the Rent Act 1977); and this may well be the appropriate solution where the basis of the landlord's complaint is founded on the tenant's behaviour or his treatment of the premises or furniture. If the court makes an order for possession suspended on condition that (for example) the tenant does not play music past 11 pm the tenant should make sure that the terms of the order contain a provision to the effect that the order should not be enforced without leave of the court. Thus, if the landlord alleges that there has been a breach of the condition he will not be able to obtain a warrant for possession until he has proved the breach to the court (see p296).

Recovering possession of a home

Where the landlord of a dwelling house let on a protected tenancy wishes to recover possession of the premises so that he may live there himself he may rely upon any of the normal grounds for possession that may be available to him. He may, for example, be in a position to offer the tenant suitable alternative accommodation or if the tenant has neglected the premises he may be able to rely upon Case 3. There are, however, four grounds for possession that are particularly appropriate to the situation where the landlord wishes to live in the dwelling house himself. The two most important are Cases 9 and 11. Case 9, which is a discretionary ground, may be used where the landlord *reasonably* requires possession for himself (or for certain other members of his family). Generally speaking Case 11 is available where the landlord occupied the premises prior to the letting and not later than the commencement of the tenancy served upon the tenant a notice informing him that the landlord would require possession at the end of the term pursuant to Case 11. The landlord will also have to show that he requires possession for himself (or a member of his family) but he will not have to show that his requirement is a reasonable one.

The two other cases are Cases 12 and 20 which relate to premises purchased as a retirement home and premises let by members of the armed services.

Where the tenancy is an assured tenancy see Ground 1 of Sched 2 to the Housing Act 1988 (see p437).

Form 44: Particulars of claim—Cases 2, 3 and 4

IN THE   COUNTY COURT   Case No

BETWEEN

Plaintiff

—AND—

Defendant

PARTICULARS OF CLAIM

1. The Plaintiff is and was at all material times the [*freehold/leasehold*] owner and entitled to possession of the premises known as [*state address of premises*]. The said premises are divided into [*state number*] separate dwelling houses.

2. By an oral agreement made on or about the [*state date of agreement*] the Plaintiff agreed to let one of the said dwelling houses, namely Flat [*state number*], on a weekly tenancy from the said date at a rent of £ [*state rent*] per week payable in advance each [*state day of week*].

3. The Defendant has been guilty of conduct which is a nuisance or annoyance to adjoining occupiers.

PARTICULARS

The Defendant [plays loud music late at night which causes a nuisance and/or annoyance to other tenants upon the said premises, in particular to Mr and Mrs Fragile who occupy Flat ⸏ which is directly below the dwelling house let to the Defendant.]

4. [The condition of the dwelling house let to the Defendant has deteriorated owing to acts of waste committed by, or the neglect or default of, the Defendant.]

PARTICULARS

(1) [Wall paper has been torn from the walls in the lounge and in the bedroom.]
(2) [A window in the bathroom and the toilet window have been broken.]
(3) [There are numerous stains on the carpets throughout the said dwelling house.]
(4) [The said dwelling house is generally filthy and smells.]

5. [The condition of certain items of furniture provided by the Plaintiff to the Defendant under the terms of the tenancy has deteriorated owning to ill-treatment by the Defendant.]

PARTICULARS

The Defendant has broken the following items of furniture, namely [*state items*]

6. The said tenancy was duly determined by a notice to quit served on the Defendant on the [*insert date notice to quit was served*] which said notice expired on the [*state date of expiry*].

7. The said dwelling house is a dwelling house to which the Rent Act 1977 applies and possession is claimed pursuant to Cases 2, 3 and 4 of Schedule 15 to the said Act.

contd

> *contd*
>
> 8.   By reason of the matters set out in paragraphs 4 and 5 above the Plaintiff has suffered loss and damage.
>
> PARTICULARS
>
> AND the Plaintiff claims:
> (1)   Possession of the said dwelling house.
>
> (2)   Damages under paragraph 8.
>
> (2)   Rent and/or mesne profits at the rate of £. . . from the date hereof until possession be delivered up.
>
> DATED

Case 9: premises reasonably required

A landlord wishing to rely upon Case 9 must, once he has determined the contractual tenancy, commence proceedings by summons in the county court for the area in which the property is situated (Chapter 20). There will be four matters that the court will have to consider at the hearing of the action:
  (1) the landlord's requirement;
  (2) whether the landlord is a landlord by purchase;
  (3) the greater hardship test;
  (4) overall reasonableness.

The landlord's requirement   In order to recover possession of the dwelling house the landlord will have to show that he reasonably requires possession of the dwelling house for occupation as a residence for:
  (1) himself; or
  (2) any son or daughter of his over 18 years of age; or
  (3) his father or mother; or
  (4) the father or mother of his spouse.
  The burden of proving that he reasonably requires possession rests upon the landlord and so he must produce evidence to that effect. Where he is seeking possession so that one of the listed members of his family can live there that person should, if at all possible, be called to give evidence. The landlord must show that he has a genuine need for possession. He need not show an absolute necessity but he must show something more than a desire. The landlord should adduce evidence to show that he requires possession at the date of the hearing (*Alexander v Mohamadzadeh* (1986) 51 P&CR 41) or at some time in the not too distant future (*Kidder v Birch* (1983) 265 EG 773). Whether the landlord requires possession is a question of fact to be decided on the evidence available to the court at the date of the hearing. When drafting the particulars of claim on behalf of the landlord it is better to give some

detail as to the reasons for requiring possession rather than simply stating that possession is claimed under Case 9. The judge will then have some idea of the landlord's case before he hears the evidence.

In deciding whether the landlord requires possession for 'himself' the court will take into account the requirements of his wife and children who are under 18, even where the landlord is not actually going to live on the premises himself (*Smith v Penny* [1947] KB 230; a father separated from his wife and living in a public house where he was the manager wanted possession of the dwelling house so that his two children and a housekeeper could live there. Held: he required possession for 'himself' and was entitled to possession). In all other cases where the landlord is requiring possession for 'himself' he must be part of the household which is to occupy the dwelling house (see *Richter v Wilson* [1963] 2 QB 426; partially blind 83-year-old landlord living on the ground floor of the building which he owned required the upper floor for friends who were to look after him. Held that he did not require the upper floor for 'himself').

Joint owners may claim possession under Case 9 for occupation by themselves but only if the dwelling house is required for all of them (*McIntyre v Hardcastle* [1948] 2 KB 82). If only one of the joint owners requires possession the others should transfer their interest to him. A husband and wife who are joint landlords of a house are entitled to claim possession pursuant to Case 9 if it is required as a residence for a child who is the natural son of the wife but neither the natural nor the adopted son of the husband (*Potsos v Theodotou* [1991] 2 EGLR 93, CA).

A person who in his capacity as a personal representative or trustee is a landlord of a dwelling house cannot claim possession for a beneficiary unless the beneficiary is also one of the relatives listed in Case 9. Nor can such a person usually claim possession for himself as to do so would be in breach of trust and therefore unreasonable. In *Patel v Patel* [1981] 1 WLR 1342, however, personal representatives claimed possession so that they could live in the dwelling house with the children of the deceased, whom they had adopted. The children were beneficiaries of their parents' estate. In these circumstances there was no breach of trust and the personal representatives were entitled to possession.

The landlord may rely upon Case 9 where he needs only part of the premises but in such circumstances it may not be reasonable to make the order (*Kelley v Goodwin* [1947] 1 All ER 810).

Landlord by purchase   The court may not make an order for possession where the landlord purchased the dwelling house after one of the dates set out in Case 9 (usually 23 March 1965) and in so doing became the tenant's landlord. The intention of this provision is to prevent landlords from buying houses over the heads of sitting tenants and then having them evicted. The tenant will usually know whether the present landlord was the landlord at the commencement of the tenancy but where he is not sure, which is sometimes the case where the property is managed by managing agents, his solicitors should use the power to seek further and better particulars and discovery of documents to ascertain the true position. The relevant date to discover is the date that contracts were exchanged on the purchase and not the date of completion (*Emberson v Robinson* [1953] 1 WLR 1129).

Where the landlord has become the landlord after the commencement of the tenancy in some way other than by purchase he is not precluded from relying on Case 9 by reason of the landlord by purchase provision: 'the acquisition of the reversion, whether it be a freehold or leasehold, for money or money's worth . . . is plainly a purchase, but the acquisition of it under a will is not a purchase' (see *Thomas v Fryer* [1970] 2 All ER 1).

In *Mansukhani v Sharkey* [1992] 2 EGLR 107, CA a transfer by parents to a son of a property 'in consideration of mutual love and affection' which was subject to a mortgage and in which the son covenanted to pay money due under the mortgage was held to be a gift rather than a purchase.

Where the landlord claims that he has become the landlord otherwise than by way of purchase the ability to seek discovery should once again be used. The tenant's representative should demand to see any relevant testamentary documents or trust deeds, etc which should be carefully scrutinised so as to ensure that the landlord really has not given anything by way of money or money's worth in return for his present interest in the property.

The greater hardship test   Before making an order for possession of the dwelling house the court must be satisfied that having regard to all the circumstances of the case, including the question of whether other accommodation is available to the landlord or the tenant, greater hardship would be caused by granting the order than by refusing to grant it. This is a question of fact and the judge's decision on the question is final. The burden of proving greater hardship is on the tenant who must therefore adduce evidence to show the hardship that an order for possession would cause him (*Sims v Wilson* [1946] 2 All ER 261; *Baker v McIver* [1990] 2 EGLR 105).

Each party should make investigations as to alternative accommodation that may be available to him, in particular by making enquiries of the local authority. If the tenant is able to give evidence that he sought other accommodation and that none is available he will be in a better position to show that greater hardship would be caused by making the order than refusing it; but if he is not able to give such evidence the court may come to the conclusion that he has not satisfied the burden placed on him (see eg *Alexander v Mohamadzadeh* (1986) 51 P&CR 41 at 49). The effect of a local authority's duty to give priority to certain persons under Part III of the Housing Act 1985 should also be borne in mind (see p292). Paradoxically it may mean that a single person who does not have a

Form 45: Particulars of claim—Case 9

IN THE   COUNTY COURT   Case No

BETWEEN

                                     Plaintiff

—AND—

                                    Defendant

PARTICULARS OF CLAIM

1. The Plaintiff is the [*freehold/leasehold*] owner and is entitled to possession of the dwelling house known as [*state address*].

2. By an oral agreement commencing [*insert date*] the Plaintiff let the said premises to the Defendant at a rent of £[*State rent*] per week payable in advance.

3. The said tenancy was duly determined by a Notice to quit served on the Defendant on [*insert date of Notice to quit*] and which expired on [*insert date of expiry*].

4. The ground on which possession is claimed is that the said premises are reasonably required [by the Plaintiff for occupation as a residence for his mother, Mrs [*insert name*].

PARTICULARS

On the [*insert date*] the said [*insert name*] [lost her home when it was completely destroyed by fire. She is presently living in overcrowded accommodation with her daughter at [*insert address*]].

5. The said premises are premises to which the Rent Acts apply and possession is claimed pursuant to the provisions of Case 9 of Schedule 15 to the Rent Act 1977.

AND the Plaintiff claims:

(1) Possession of the said premises.
(2) Rent and/or mesne profits at the rate of £ [*state amount*] per week from the date hereof until possession be delivered up.

DATED

---

priority need is better able to show greater hardship than a person with young children who will have a priority need; although it should be borne in mind that the housing shortage is such that in many areas families spend long periods in bed and breakfast accommodation before be ng housed permanently.

The representative for each party should also cross-examine the other party on his income and capital position as this will obviously be relevant to the ability of either of them to find other accommodation. The tenant may not be able to find anything as cheap as his present accommodation but such a factor is not likely to have much weight if he can afford a higher rent.

Hardship to persons other than the landlord or the tenant may be taken into account (eg members of the landlord's or the tenant's family or lodgers who are residing with the tenant) but regard must be had to the proximity of third parties to the landlord or the tenant and the extent to which hardship to the former would constitute hardship to the latter (*Harte v Frampton* [1948] 1 KB 73).

Where the court is considering making a possession order to take effect at some time in the future the judge should consider whether greater hardship will be caused at the end of the period of postponement (*Wheeler v Evans* [1948] 1 KB 459).

Overall reasonableness The tenant, in particular, should remember that the court must finally consider the question of overall reasonableness before making the order for possession (s98 of the Rent Act 1977). Where the judge finds that greater hardship would be caused by refusing the order than by granting it he will nearly always consider it reasonable to make the order but there may be other factors that the tenant is able to draw to the court's attention in an attempt to persuade it that it would not be reasonable to do so. For example, the court may not consider it reasonable to make the order if the tenant has recently redecorated the premises or turned down other accommodation in reliance upon a representation from the landlord that he would not be seeking possession in the near future. Where the court does make an order for possession under Case 9 it may stay or suspend execution of the order or postpone the date for possession for such period or periods as it thinks fit on the usual conditions (s100 of the Rent Act 1977; see Chapter 8, p142). It is usual to postpone possession for a period of longer than the 28 days that is normally granted in rent cases. Three months is not uncommon but obviously every case will turn upon its own facts and if the landlord's requirement for possession is particularly urgent a much shorter order may be made. The fact that the landlord will already have had to wait for some time by the date of the hearing may be drawn to the judge's attention, particularly where the landlord has disclosed full details of his case prior to commencing proceedings.

Unless the case is clear cut, which is not likely, the unsuccessful tenant should try to persuade the judge to use his discretion to make no order as to costs.

Case 11: premises let by a previous occupier

Case 11 (as amended by the Rent (Amendment) Act 1985) is available where a person (referred to in the Case as 'the owner-occupier') who let the dwelling house on a regulated tenancy had, at any time before the letting, occupied it as his residence. The owner-occupier need not be the freehold owner. He may be a leasehold owner or a person who occupied under a more informal tenancy agreement. What is important is that the person who granted the tenancy is a person who occupied the dwelling house as his residence at some time prior to the letting. (He need not have occupied it immediately prior to the letting but he must not, since certain dates set out in the Case, have let the premises on a protected tenancy without first having given a Case 11 notice; see *below*.) However, the landlord does not need to show that he occupied the residence 'as a home' prior to the letting (cf the position of statutory tenants; p137). Temporary or intermittent occupation as a residence will be sufficient (*Mistry v Isidore* [1990] 2 EGLR 97, CA).

Where the landlord seeks to rely upon Case 11 he should determine the contractual tenancy if it has not already been determined (see p139) and then commence proceedings based upon this Case. He may commence proceedings by summons or he may use the summary procedure available under the Rent Act (County Court Proceedings for Possession) Rules 1981 (see Chapter 20). Where the landlord foresees problems with proving service of the Case 11 notice it is wise to commence proceedings based upon Case 11 and Case 9 in the alternative in which case it will be necessary to commence proceedings by summons.

The landlord's requirements for possession The owner-occupier may rely upon Case 11 where he requires possession of the dwelling house as a residence for himself or for any member of his family who resided with him when he last occupied the dwelling house as a residence (Case 11(*e*); Part V, para 2(*a*)).

Where there were joint owner-occupiers who let the premises any one of them may seek to obtain possession alone (*Tilling v Whiteman* [1980] AC 1). Note that it is not necessary for the owner-occupier to show that the dwelling house is *reasonably* required for himself as he would have to if he were relying upon Case 9. It is sufficient for him to show that he genuinely intends to occupy the premises at once or within a reasonable time (*Kennealy v Dunne* [1977] QB 837). There is nothing in Case 11 which imports a requirement for permanent residence as a 'home', or rules out temporary or intermittent occupation. The landlord will, therefore, be entitled to possession even if he only intends to reside in it at times when he is able to take advantage of it by reason of his presence in England (see *Naish v Curzon* (1985) 273 EG 1221; *Davies v Peterson* (1988) 21 HLR 63). (If the landlord is abroad and not in a position to return until possession has been obtained it may be possible to give his evidence of intention to return and live in the house by affidavit or statement under the Civil Evidence Act 1968 (see Chapter 22, p311).) An intention to live in the house until it is sold is sufficient (*Whitworth v Lipton* [1993] EGCS 172.)

The owner-occupier may also recover possession of the dwelling house if it is not reasonably suitable to his needs, having regard to his place of work, and he requires it for the purpose of disposing of it with vacant possession so that he can use the proceeds to acquire, as his residence, a

Form 46: Originating application for recovery of possession under Case 11 (see also Form 36)

IN THE   COUNTY COURT   No of Application

IN MATTER OF the Rent Act 1977

BETWEEN

                                                                          Applicant

—AND—

                                                                          Respondent

1.   I, [*state name and address of Applicant*], retired restaurateur, apply to the Court for an order for recovery of possession of [*state address of property*] under Case 11 of Schedule 15 to the Rent Act 1977.

2.   The premises were let to the respondent on [*insert date*] on a protected tenancy having the following terms:—

A weekly tenancy at a rent of £ [*insert amount*] per week payable in advance.

3.   Notice in writing was given to the respondent on [*insert date of Notice*] that possession might be recovered under Case 11 of Schedule 15 to the Rent Act 1977.

4.   As regards previous lettings of the premises since they became protected by the Rent Act there has been no such letting.

5.   I previously occupied the premises as a residence.

6.   The premises are required as a residence for myself.

7.   The protected tenancy has come to an end as follows:—

By a Notice to quit being served on [insert date of service of Notice to quit] which expired on [insert date of expiry], but the respondent remains in occupation.

The name and address of the person on whom it is intended to serve the application is:—
[*insert name and address of Respondent*]

My address for service is [*insert address for service*].

DATED

---

dwelling house which is more suitable to those needs (Sched 15, Part V, para 2(*f*)). See *Bissessar v Ghosn* (1986) 18 HLR 486.

Case 11 requirements   In order to recover possession under Case 11 the landlord must show:

(1) that not later than the 'relevant date', which is usually the date the tenancy commenced (see Sched 15, Part III), the landlord gave the tenant a notice in writing that possession might be recovered under Case 11; and

(2) that the dwelling house has not since the prescribed date (in most cases 8 December 1965; see the text of Case 11(*b*)) been let by him on a protected tenancy in regard to which a Case 11 notice has not been served upon the tenant in accordance with the above paragraph.

Thus, if the owner-occupier has let the dwelling house on a protected tenancy at any time since the prescribed date without first having served a Case 11 notice the owner-occupier will never (subject to the power to dispense with the requirements) be able to rely on Case 11.

Dispensing with the requirements   The court may dispense with either or both of the above requirements if it is just and equitable to make the order for possession. The question of when it will be just and equitable to dispense with the above requirements was considered in *Bradshaw v Baldwin-Wiseman* (1985) 49 P&CR 382 where Griffiths LJ expressed the following view:

> I would regard the use of those words (just and equitable) as directing the court to look at all the circumstances of the case. Those would embrace the circumstances affecting the landlord, or his successors-in-title, the circumstances of the tenant and, of course, the circumstances in which the failure to give written notice arose. It is only if, having considered all those circumstances, the court considers that it would be just and equitable to give possession that it should do so, because it must be borne in mind that, by failing to give the written notice, the tenant may well have been led into a wholly false position. As I say, in the circumstances of this case, where it is apparent that there never was any intention to create what I might call 'a Case 11 tenancy' it cannot be just and equitable to dispense with written notice (at 388).

In *Fernandes v Pavardin* (1982) 264 EG 49 an oral notice was given but not a written one. It was held that as the oral notice was clearly made and understood no injustice or inequity had flowed from failing to put the notice in writing, and the requirements were waived. See also *Mincy v Sentongo* (1983) 45 P&CR 190 where the notice had been sent but the tenant alleged that it had never been received. The court dispensed with the notice requirements because the landlord honestly believed that the tenant had been given proper notice.

The order   Where Case 11 is applicable the court must make an order for possession. The landlord does not have to show that it would be reasonable to make the order (s98(2) of the Rent Act 1977). The order for possession may be postponed for no more than 14 days, or six weeks in cases of exceptional hardship (s89 of the Housing Act 1980; p75).

Recovering possession of a home: Housing Act 1988

Where a landlord of an assured tenant wishes to recover possession of a home the appropriate ground of Sched 2 to the Housing Act 1988 is Ground 1. This ground is similar to but much wider in its scope than Case 11 of Sched 15 to the Rent Act 1977. If the landlord wishes to recover possession under Ground 1 he should serve a notice of intention to bring proceedings for possession, pursuant to s8 of the 1988 Act, and after

Form 47: Affidavit in support of originating application for possession under Case 11

IN THE   COUNTY COURT   No of Applicationo

BETWEEN

—AND—

Applicant

Respondent

AFFIDAVIT IN SUPPORT OF ORIGINATING APPLICATION

I [state name] of [state address], Managing Agent, MAKE OATH and say as follows:

1. I am the Managing Agent appointed by the Applicant to manage her property at [state address of property]. I am authorised to make this affidavit on her behalf and do so from the information obtained by me in my capacity as managing agent.

2. I have read the Originating Application in this action dated [insert date] and say that the same is true and accurate in all respects at the date hereof.

3. The Applicant is [at present in Bora Bora on an extended holiday but wishes to return to this country to live. Her only residence in this country is at 3 Posh Place, Notown and she requires possession of this property so that she has somewhere to live on her return. She hopes to return to this country in . . . There is now produced and shown to me marked 'BL 1' a letter written by the Applicant to myself wherein she expresses her wish to return to this country and reside at the said property].

4. There is now produced and shown to me marked 'BL 2' a true copy of the notice dated [insert date] given to the Respondent on [insert date] stating that possession might be recovered under Case 11 after termination of the Respondent's tenancy.

5. There is now produced and shown to me marked 'BL 3' a true copy of the notice to quit dated [insert date of Notice to quit] and served on the Respondent by myself on [insert date of service].

6. There is now produced and shown to me marked 'BL 4' a true copy of the Notice of Intention to Adduce Hearsay Evidence dated [insert date] which I sent to the Respondent by first class post on the said date, notifying the Respondent that I intended to use the letter 'BL 1' at the hearing of this action [See Form 39; p313].

SWORN

expiry of the date specified in the notice commence proceedings by summons. (For Particulars of Claim see Form 17, p114.)

Notice requirement   The landlord may only recover possession if not later than the beginning of the tenancy the landlord who granted the tenancy gave notice in writing to the tenant that possession might be recovered on Ground 1 or the court is of the opinion that it is just and equitable to dispense with the requirement of notice (cf Rent Act cases, p352).

Facts to prove   The landlord must also establish one or other of the two following facts:

(1) Previous occupation: he may show that at some time before the beginning of the tenancy, he or, in the case of joint landlords seeking possession at least one of them, occupied the dwelling house as his only or principal home.

(2) Required now for occupation: he may show that he or, in the case of joint landlords seeking possession at least one of them, requires the dwelling house as his or his spouse's only or principal home.

However, this ground is not available if the landlord seeking possession (or, in the case of joint landlords, any one of them) or any other person who, as landlord, derived title under the landlord who gave the Ground 1 notice acquired the reversion on the tenancy for money or money's worth.

Suitable alternative accommodation

If it considers it reasonable to do so the court may make an order for possession of a dwelling house which has been let on a *protected or statutory* tenancy if it is satisfied that suitable alternative accommodation is available for the tenant or will be available for him when the order takes effect (see s98(1)(*a*), (4) and Sched 15, Part IV of the Rent Act 1977 as amended). The burden is on the landlord to show that the alternative accommodation is suitable (*Nevile v Hardy* [1921 1 Ch 404). He need not provide the accommodation himself. He may persuade either the local housing authority for the district in which the dwelling house is situated or some other person or body to do so.

(Where the tenancy is an assured tenancy see Sched 2, Part II, para 9 and Part III of the Housing Act 1988.)

Local authority certificates

If the accommodation is to be provided by the local housing authority a certificate from that body certifying that it will provide suitable alternative accommodation by a date specified in the certificate is conclusive evidence that suitable alternative accommodation will be available for him by that date (Sched 15, Part IV, para 3 of the Rent Act 1977). Any document purporting to be signed by a proper officer of the local housing authority may be adduced in evidence, and unless the contrary is shown, is deemed to be such a certificate without further proof (Sched 15, Part IV, para 7 of the Rent Act 1977).

Other accommodation

Where the landlord is unable to rely upon a local housing authority certificate under para 3 the alternative accommodation is deemed to be suitable if it is to be let to the tenant on a protected tenancy (other than one under which the landlord might recover possession under Cases 11–20 of Sched 15, ie the mandatory grounds) or on terms which will, in the opinion of the court, afford to the tenant security of tenure reasonably equivalent to that afforded by the Rent Act 1977 to such a protected tenancy. For the status of a person granted a protected tenancy after the commencement of the Housing Act 1988 (15 January 1989) see s34(1)(c) of that Act (p134). It would seem that since the passing of the Housing Act 1980 a secure tenancy of a dwelling house provided by a local housing authority or housing association would suffice. So would a tenancy for a reasonably lengthy fixed term (*Fulford v Turpin* [1955] JPL 365).

Paragraphs 4 and 5 of Part IV of Sched 15 to the Rent Act 1977 provide that where there is no local authority certificate under para 3 the court must also be satisfied that:

(1) the accommodation is reasonably suitable to the needs of the tenant and his family as regards proximity to place of *work*; and

(2) either:

    (*a*) similar as regards rental and extent to the accommodation afforded by dwelling houses *provided by* the local authority to tenants with similar needs to the tenant in the case (see further paras 5(2) and 7; and *Jones v Cook* [1990] 2 EGLR 109; the actual extent of accommodation provided by the local housing authority is proved by a certificate of that authority but the judge must still determine whether or not the alternative accommodation proposed is similar to it); or

    (*b*) reasonably suitable to the *means* of the tenant and to the needs of the tenant and his family as regards *extent and character*; and

(3) if any *furniture* is provided in his present home, the alternative accommodation contains furniture which is either similar to the furniture in the present home or is reasonably suitable to the needs of the tenant and his family.

In considering whether the alternative accommodation is reasonably suitable to the needs of the tenant's family regard is only had to those members of the family who reside with the tenant on a permanent basis (see *Standingford v Probert* [1950] 1 KB 377; *Scrace v Windust* [1955] 1 WLR 475). As to the meaning of 'family' see p154. Each member of the family has a right to be heard and should be joined in the proceedings (see *Wandsworth LBC v Fadayomi* [1987] 3 All ER 474; husband and wife wanting different things). The place of work to which regard must be had is not necessarily an office or factory. It may be an area (*Yewbright Properties Ltd v Stone* (1980) 40 P&CR 402).

Comparison with the tenant's present accommodation

A common objection that is raised by the tenant to the proposed alternative accommodation is that it is not suitable as regards character because it does not come up to the same standard as his present home. In *Redspring v Francis* [1973] 1 WLR 134 Buckley LJ stated that 'what [the tenant] needs is somewhere where he can live in reasonably comfortable conditions suitable to the style of life to which he leads, and environmental matters must inevitably affect the suitability of offered accommodation to provide him with the sort of conditions in which it is reasonable that he should live'. The standard to be applied, however, is that of the ordinary tenant and not one which will completely satisfy 'all the fads and fancies and preferences of the tenant' (*Christie v Macfarlane* (1930) SLT (Sh Ct) 5 at 10). Difference in character will normally only make the accommodation unsuitable if it relates to a difference in kind rather than degree. (See *Redspring v Francis* (1973), *per* Sachs LJ at 140.)

A good (but not typical) example of the problems that arise is to be found in the case of *Hill v Rochard* [1983] 1 WLR 478. The dwelling house was set in one and a half acres of land, consisted of many rooms and had attached to it a stable and a paddock. The landlord offered the tenants a modern detached house in the country on the outskirts of a village. It had a large garden and four bedrooms but no stable and paddock. The judge held that although the alternative accommodation would not enable them to have the same lifestyle as before it would permit them to live in a reasonably comfortable condition in a reasonably similar way, and that therefore the accommodation was suitable. The Court of Appeal refused to interfere with the decision and commented that the Rent Act 1977 was not concerned with incidental advantages but with the provision of housing.

Having failed to persuade the court that the alternative accommodation is unsuitable, the tenant will sometimes argue that it is not reasonable to make the order for possession on the basis that the alternative is far below the standard of his present accommodation (see further *below*). However, such arguments do not tend to find a great deal of favour in the more extreme cases as can be seen from the following comment of Nourse LJ in *Dame Margaret Hungerford Charity Trustees v Beazley* [1993] 2 EGLR 143 at 146H, CA, a case in which the tenant was being required to move from a 17-bedroom 'Warden's House' to a three-bedroom council house:

> The tragedy of this case from the defendant's point of view, and I well understand that that may not be too strong a word, is that the eccentricities of the Rent Act have accustomed her and her family to accommodation of a quality and character far in excess of anything to which they can be compelled to move as an alternative. It is no great comfort for them now to be told that they have been very fortunate to be there for nearly ten years since the contractual term expired, nor that there are many other families

who, for economic reasons, find themselves facing a similar prospect, when they themselves have to face it for quite different reasons.

(Compare *Dawncar Investments Ltd v Plews*; see p359)

It is the character of the property that is relevant and so it is not possible to take into account the fact that the tenant will be moved far from friends or his present cultural and religious activities if he has to move to the alternative accommodation (*Siddiqui v Rashid* [1980] 1 WLR 1018; which concerned a Muslim tenant who would not be able to attend his mosque if he moved to the new accommodation).

In deciding whether the alternative accommodation is suitable the judge may visit either dwelling house (CCR Ord 21, r6). Solicitors acting for tenants should always visit the premises and consider whether counsel should make a visit and whether an application should be made to the judge for a view to take place. The decision to inspect is a matter of judicial discretion and neither party may compel the judge to hold a view or prevent him from doing so (*Salsbury v Woodland* [1970] 1 QB 324). He invariably does do so. Both sides should be present at the view which is part of the evidence. Photographs of both dwelling houses and the immediate area are always useful.

Other matters

A part of the accommodation presently occupied by the tenant may be held to be a suitable alternative (*Mykolyshyn v Noah* [1970] 1 WLR 1271), but it may nevertheless still not be reasonable to make the order for possession (*Yoland v Reddington* (1982) 263 EG 157; offer of part held to be suitable but not reasonable to make the order as the tenant would lose his small but crucial income from subletting). If the court does also consider it reasonable to order possession it should do so upon the condition that the landlord grant a tenancy of the relevant part (*Parmee v Mitchell* [1950] 2 KB 199). In deciding whether the accommodation is suitable the court may take into account the provision or otherwise of a garden (*Redspring v Francis* [1973] 1 WLR 134), or of a garage (*McDonnell v Daly* [1969] 1 WLR 1482). The alternative accommodation will not be unsuitable merely because the tenant will not be able to get all his furniture into it (*McIntyre v Hardcastle* [1948] 2 KB 82; see *Selwyn v Hamill* [1948] 1 All ER 70 at 72).

Accommodation is not deemed to be suitable to the needs of the tenant and his family if the result of their occupation would be that it would be an overcrowded dwelling house for the purpose of Part X of the Housing Act 1985; see Chapter 18 (Sched 15, Part IV, para 6 of the Rent Act 1977).

The landlord may himself be a tenant of the accommodation that he is offering as an alternative. If there is a covenant against subletting the tenant may then find himself being evicted by the head landlord from the

Form 48: Particulars of claim—suitable alternative accommodation

IN THE   COUNTY COURT   Plaint No

BETWEEN

                                                     Plaintiff

—AND—

                                                 Defendant

PARTICULARS OF CLAIM

1. The Plaintiffs are the [*freehold/leasehold*] owners and are entitled to possession of premises comprising a dwelling house known as [*state address*].

2. The said premises were held by the Defendant under a monthly tenancy, which commenced on [*insert date*], at a rent of £ [*insert amount*] per month payable in advance on the [*insert date*] day of each month.

3. The said tenancy was duly determined by a notice to quit dated the [*insert day*] day of [*state month and year*] and served on the Defendant on the [*state day*] day of [*state month and year*], and which expired on the [*state day*] day of [*state month and year*].

4. The said premises are premises to which the Rent Act 1977 applies and possession is claimed pursuant to Section 98 of the said Act.

5. The ground upon which possession is claimed is that suitable alternative accommodation is available at [*address of accommodation*] for the Defendant and will be available for her if and when an order for possession takes effect. The said suitable alternative accommodation consists of:

(a) [2 rooms. One is 11 feet 3 inches by 9 feet 6 inches and the other is 14 feet 3 inches by 9 feet 6 inches;]

(b) [a kitchenette measuring 4 feet 3 inches by 6 feet 6 inches;]

(c) [a bathroom measuring 5 feet by 8 feet 6 inches;]

(d) [a hall measuring 4 feet by 6 feet 3 inches.]

[Hot water is provided by an immersion heater and the said alternative accommodation is only some few hundred yards from the said premises.]

AND the Plaintiff claims:

(1) Possession of the said premises.

(2) Rent or alternatively mesne profits at the rate of £ [*state amount*] per month from the date hereof until possession be delivered up.

DATED

---

alternative accommodation. It has been suggested therefore that the tenant should insist upon the landlord disclosing his title documents on discovery. If there is a covenant against subletting without the landlord's consent the tenant should insist upon the consent being obtained. If it is not the tenant should argue that it is not reasonable to make the order for possession. (See the article by Nic Madge [1983] LAG Bulletin 140.)

The alternative accommodation may be a property owned by the *tenant* but the landlord is not entitled to seek an injunction preventing the tenant from disposing of that property prior to the hearing (*Fennbend Ltd v Millar* (1988) 20 HLR 19).

Reasonableness

It is important to remember that the court must also consider the question of reasonableness. Many of the factors that may not be taken into account when deciding whether the alternative accommodation is suitable may be relied upon by the *tenant* when it comes to arguing that it is not reasonable to make the order. In *Battlespring Ltd v Gates* (1983) 268 EG 355 the tenant was an elderly lady who had been in occupation for 35 years. The landlord was interested in the property for financial reasons. Although the court considered that the alternative accommodation was suitable it did not consider that it was reasonable to make the order. See also *Dawncar Investments Ltd v Plews* [1993] EGCS 117 where the court considered that it was not reasonable to expect the tenant, a woman with a young child, to live in the alternative accommodation. The flat the landlord sought to recover was in a pleasant part of Hampstead. The alternative was on a busy commercial road with heavy lorries going by, a railway to the front and back and two public houses nearby.

The landlord must also remember to put forward those facts and matters upon which he relies in support of his contention that it would be reasonable to make the order (*Wint v Monk* (1981) 259 EG 45; where the landlord failed to do so and no order was made). The question is not whether it is reasonable for the landlord to make the claim but whether it is reasonable for the court to make the order.

Costs

The question of costs at the end of the hearing should be fully considered and will not necessarily follow the event.

Chapter 25

Summary Possession Proceedings

In both the High Court and the county court there is a summary procedure available whereby possession of property can be obtained from persons who have entered into, or remained in, possession without the consent of the owner. The proceedings are commenced by originating application in the county court under CCR Ord 24 and by originating summons in the High Court under RSC Ord 113. In the county court the parties are known as applicant and respondent, and in the High Court as plaintiff and defendant. In this chapter they are referred to as applicant and respondent. The scope of the procedure is set out in r 1 of each order which is in the following terms:

> Where a person claims possession of land which he alleges is occupied solely by a person or persons (not being a tenant or tenants holding over after the termination of the tenancy) who entered into or remained in occupation without his licence or consent or that of any predecessor in title of his, the proceedings may be brought by originating application [summons] in accordance with the provisions of this Order.

The procedure is most commonly associated with 'squatters' but it is clear from the wording of r 1 that it may also be used where bare or contractual licensees have had their licences revoked (see *Greater London Council v Jenkins* [1975] 1 WLR 155). It is sometimes used by parents against children who have overstayed their welcome, and so that the children can obtain a court order to show to the local authority which then may provide accommodation; but *quaere* whether the word 'solely' means that the procedure can only be used where the applicant is not in occupation himself.

In *Moore Properties (Ilford) Ltd v McKeon* [1976] 1 WLR 1278 it was held that the words 'not being a tenant or tenants holding over after the termination of the tenancy' referred to a tenancy granted *by the applicant to the respondent*. Thus, the applicant was allowed to use the procedure against sub-tenants who had remained in possession after the tenant's tenancy had come to an end. As they were unlawful sub-tenants they did not become the landlord's direct tenants pursuant to s 137 of the Rent Act 1977 (see p 145). It is submitted that this procedure is also available to the

360

landlord who wishes to remove sub-tenants who are not entitled to rely upon s137 for any other reason. In these circumstances the sub-tenants will, as against the landlord, be mere trespassers or at best licensees who have not held over after termination of a tenancy granted by the applicant to the respondent.

The procedure may also be used by a tenant whose landlord, in breach of the tenancy, has gone into possession himself or has put someone else into possession (see *Borg v Rogers, below*).

The application may not be made in the High Court in the case of a licence that has been revoked unless the licence is an excluded licence (see p259, referring to s9(1) of the Protection from Eviction Act 1977).

Procedure

The Application

The originating application should be in County Court Form N312 (originating summons; High Court Form No 11A, Appendix A); see Form 49, p363 of this book). It should state the names known to the applicant of the persons to be served, or that no person is intended to be served (CCR Ord 3, r4(2)(*b*)). It should also be indorsed with, or contain, a statement showing that possession is claimed in respect of residential premises (RSC Ord 113, r2(2)).

The Affidavit

The originating application (summons) must be supported by an affidavit (CCR Ord 24, r2; RSC Ord 113, r3) stating:
  (1) the applicant's interest in the land (if the respondent is a licensee he will be estopped from denying the applicant's title but if he is a trespasser the applicant will have to prove his title—the best method is by production of the land certificate, a copy of which should be exhibited to the affidavit, or simply by evidence of prior possession) (see p307);
  (2) the circumstances in which the land has been occupied without licence or consent and in which the claim to possession arises; and
  (3) that the applicant does not know the name of any person occupying the land who is not named in the originating application (summons).
(See Form 50, p364 for a specimen affidavit.)

Unless the court otherwise orders, the affidavit may contain statements of information or belief (CCR Ord 20, r10(4); RSC Ord 113, r3). The sources and grounds of the information or belief must be stated (r10(5)).

Service

Where any person in occupation of the land is named in the originating application (ie in county court proceedings) that document must be served on him (CCR Ord 24, r3):

(1) by delivering it to him personally together with a notice of the return day (which the court office in the case of the county court will have attached to the application when it was filed) and a copy of the affidavit in support; or

(2) by an officer of the court leaving the documents mentioned in (1), or sending them to him, at the premises; or

(3) where the respondent's solicitor has given a certificate that he accepts service on behalf of the person named and states an address for service, the application is deemed to have been duly served on the applicant on the date on which the certificate was made; or

(4) in such other manner as the court may direct.

Where any person not named as a respondent is in occupation of the land application must also be served, unless the court otherwise directs, by (*a*) affixing a copy of the application, notice of return day, and affidavit to the main door or other conspicuous part of the premises and, if practicable, inserting through the letter box at the premises a copy of those documents enclosed in a sealed envelope addressed to 'the occupiers' or (*b*) (where there are no premises) placing stakes in the ground at conspicuous parts of the occupied *land* and affixing a sealed transparent envelope addressed to 'the occupiers' containing a copy of those documents. In the latter case where the proceedings are brought in the county court the applicant must provide the court with sufficient stakes and sealable transparent envelopes for service (CCR Ord 24, r2(2)). (The methods of service in High Court proceedings are the same, save that the plaintiff must arrange service himself: RSC Ord 113, r4.)

It is important to get service right. If it is not correct the proceedings are not automatically nullified (CCR Ord 37, r5; RSC Ord 2, r1) and where all the occupants have knowledge of the proceedings and turn up at the hearing the case may sometimes go ahead without any adjournment (*Westminster City Council v Chapman* [1975] 1 WLR 1112). Usually, however, the proceedings will be adjourned for proper service.

Except in an urgent case and where the court gives leave service must be effected in the case of residential premises not less than five days before the hearing and in the case of other land not less than two days before the hearing (CCR Ord 24, r5(1); Ord 1, r9; RSC Ord 113, r6(2)). Any day on which the court office is closed is not included in the period of five/two days (CCR Ord 1, r9(4), Ord 2, r2; RSC Ord 3, r2(5)). Where service is short because the case is an urgent one the application to abridge time should be made at the hearing. If that application is refused the proceedings will not be dismissed (unless the applicant clearly has no

Form 49: Originating application under Order 24

IN THE   COUNTY COURT   **Case No**

IN THE MATTER OF [*state address of property*]

BETWEEN

Applicant

—AND—

Respondent *

ORIGINATING APPLICATION UNDER ORDER 24

I, [*state name address and occupation of Applicant*] apply to the Court for an order for recovery of possession of the residential premises known as [...] on the ground that I am entitled to possession and that the person in occupation of the premises is in occupation without licence or consent.

The person who is in occupation and who is intended to be served individually with this application is [*state name of Respondent*]. [There are other persons in occupation whose names I do not know.] [*or* It is not intended to serve any person individually with notice of this application.]

My address for service is [*state address for service*].

DATED

* *if any whose name is known to the Applicant*

---

case). Instead the court will adjourn the matter until five/two days have elapsed (*Westminster City Council v Monahan* [1981] 1 WLR 698).

Unless service has been by the court an affidavit of service must be prepared for use at the hearing.

Any person not named as a respondent who is in occupation of the land and who wishes to be heard on the question of whether an order for possession should be made may apply at any stage in the proceedings to be joined as a respondent (CCR Ord 24, r4; RSC Ord 113, r5).

The hearing

In the county court the matter may be heard by the judge, or where the judge gives his leave by the District Judge (CCR Ord 24, r5(2)). In the High Court the case is normally heard by a master or district District Judge unless he refers it to the judge (RSC Ord 113, r1A). The applicant should make sure that the court has the affidavit of service and the affidavit in support of the application. Once the court is satisfied that the applicant has proved his title the burden is then on the tenant to prove that he has a right to remain in possession (*Portland Managements Ltd v Harte* [1976] 2 WLR 174).

Where the case is a simple one with no defence raised the judge can decide the matter on the affidavit evidence. In many cases the respondent will only be refusing to leave because the local authority will not house him until a court order is made. The procedure is not, however,

Form 50: Affidavit in support of originating application under Order 24

IN THE   COUNTY COURT   Case No

IN THE MATTER OF [*state address of property*]

BETWEEN

                                                       Applicant

—AND—

                                                     Respondent

AFFIDAVIT IN SUPPORT OF ORIGINATING APPLICATION UNDER ORDER 24

I, [*state name, address and occupation of Applicant*] MAKE OATH AND SAY as follows:—

1. I have been the leasehold owner of the residential premises situate and known as [*state address of property*] since [*insert date*]. There is now produced and shown to me marked 'SS 1' a copy of the property and proprietorship Register relating to the said premises.

2. [In March 1994 my daughter married the Respondent and in April 1994 I allowed them to take up occupation of the said premises. I told them that they would be able to stay there for a short period whilst they looked for their own property to live in. I have never demanded or accepted any rent from either of them.]

3. [On or about the 24th May 1994 my daughter left the Respondent and came to live with me. Since that date I have asked the Respondent to leave the said premises on numerous occasions but he has consistently refused to do so.]

4. [I have been informed by several sources that there may be someone living with the Respondent at the said premises.]

5. [I consulted my solicitors, Best Lawyer & Co, on or about the 1st June 1994 and I am informed and believe that on 2nd June 1994 my solicitors, acting upon my instructions, sent a letter by recorded delivery to the Respondent demanding that the Respondent vacate the said premises within 14 days of receipt of the said letter. A copy of that letter together with the recorded delivery slip is now shown to me and marked 'SS 2'. The Respondent has still not however vacated the premises and thus remains in occupation without my licence or consent.]

6. I do not know the name of any person occupying the land who is not named in the originating application.

SWORN

---

confined to cases where the occupants of the premises are unable to raise an arguable defence. If a defence is raised the court may still hear oral evidence and legal argument and decide the issue (*Shah v Givert* (1980) *The Times*, 9 July; *Borg v Rogers* (1981), 30 November; these cases are not properly reported anywhere but a useful article containing passages from the judgments is to be found in [1983] LAG Bulletin 53). In each case 'the judge must exercise his discretion and decide whether it is wiser to continue the summary hearing, or to adjourn it for a further hearing after the parties have had a chance to reconsider the position, or possibly to dismiss the application and leave the applicant to have the issue determined in a subsequent action' (*per* Griffiths LJ, *Henderson v Law* (1984) 17 HLR 237 at 241). Very often the respondents in these proceedings are unrepresented and if matters are raised which indicate that the respondent may have a defence the court will be reluctant to hear the case without first giving the respondent an opportunity to obtain advice and file evidence. If so the following order, or something similar, might be suggested to the judge:

(1) respondent to file an affidavit within 14 days setting out all the facts and matters relied upon in support of his defence;

(2) if an affidavit is not filed as aforesaid the respondent to be debarred from defending;

(3) originating application adjourned generally with liberty to restore to the first open day after 21 days;

(4) applicants may apply *ex parte* by letter to restore earlier if respondent debarred from defending;

(5) costs reserved.

If it is clear, either at the first hearing or after the respondent has filed his affidavit, that the case is particularly complicated and that justice requires pleadings and/or discovery then the court should give the appropriate directions (*Shah v Givert*, Lawton LJ; and see *Islamic Republic of Pakistan v Ghani* [1983] LAG Bulletin 53 where the Court of Appeal set aside an order made under RSC Ord 113 because there were complicated issues involved that required full and proper directions as to the conduct of the case to be given). The authorities cited above make it quite clear, however, that the court will not allow a respondent to use a request for directions as a delaying tactic. The court's power to give such directions as it thinks proper is derived from CCR Ord 13, r2 and RSC Ord 28, r4. In the High Court the master may also order that the proceedings continue as if begun by writ (RSC Ord 28, r8).

Where a local authority has commenced summary possession proceedings against gypsies who claim that the authority is in breach of its duty under s6 of the Caravan Sites Act 1968 to provide caravans for them the gypsies should apply for an adjournment of the proceedings to enable judicial review proceedings to be taken. The court will only grant the adjournment if there is a real chance of the application for leave for judicial review being granted. (*Avon County Council v Buscott* [1988] 1 All ER 841). For a case in which an adjournment was granted see *South Hams District Council v Slough* [1992] EGCS 153.

The order

The order for possession is to the effect that 'The Plaintiff do recover possession of the land mentioned in the originating application' (CCR Ord 24, r5(3)). In the High Court the order is in Form 42A (RSC Ord 113, r6(2)). Where the respondent entered into the land unlawfully the court has no power to postpone the order for possession unless the applicant consents to such a postponement (*McPhail v Persons Unknown* [1973] Ch 447; *Swordheath Properties Ltd v Floydd* [1978] 1 WLR 550).

The mere fact that the proceedings have been brought under CCR Ord 24 or RSC Ord 113 does not, however, mean that the court is deprived of any discretion it would have to suspend or postpone, etc if the claim for possession had been brought in any other proceedings (CCR Ord 24, r5; RSC Ord 113, r6(3)). Where a contractual licensee occupied under a restricted contract the court can suspend the order for possession for up to three months (see Chapter 9). In most other cases the court's discretion would be limited to two weeks or in exceptional cases, six weeks (s89 of the Housing Act 1980, p75).

The court has no power, in summary possession proceedings, to make an order for arrears of licence fees that may be due to the applicant These will have to be sought later in other proceedings.

Successful applicants usually ask for their costs to be assessed (CCR Ord 38, r19, Appendix C; RSC Ord 62, r7(4)(*b*)).

After the hearing

A warrant or writ of possession to enforce the order for possession may be issued at any time after the making of the order but not before the date on which possession is ordered to be given (CCR Ord 24, r6; RSC Ord 113, r7). No warrant or writ of possession will be issued after the expiry of three months from the date of the order without the leave of the court. The application for leave may be made *ex parte* unless the court otherwise directs. In the county court the warrant is in Form N52 and in the High Court in Form 66A.

The bailiff enforcing the warrant may evict any person he finds on the premises even though that person was not a party to the proceedings (*R v Wandsworth County Court, ex p Wandsworth London Borough Council* [1975] 1 WLR 1314). Where a person who has been evicted returns the applicant may apply *ex parte* for leave to issue a warrant/writ of restitution (CCR Ord 26, r17(4) and (5); *White Book*, 46/3/3; see pp297 and 304). An affidavit sworn in support is required.

The court may, on such terms as it thinks just, set aside or vary any order made in the proceedings (CCR Ord 24, r7; RSC Ord 113, r8). An order may be *set aside* even after it has been executed (see p299). Thus, a person improperly evicted should apply to set aside the order and to be joined under CCR Ord 24, r4 or RSC Ord 113, r5. *Quaere* whether an order may be *varied* after execution (perhaps, for example, where the respondent originally was in occupation under a restricted contract so as to extend a suspension of the order for possession). Any application made should be supported by affidavit evidence.

As to appeals see Chapter 20, p292.

Chapter 26

Mortgage Possession Proceedings

Introduction: the mortgagee's right to possession

A mortgage operates by way of legal demise (ss85, 86 and 87 of the Law of Property Act 1925) and so in the absence of any contractual or statutory right the mortgagee (the lender) is entitled to possession the moment the mortgage has been executed.

> [T]he right of the mortgagee to possession in the absence of some specific contract has nothing to do with default on the part of the mortgagor. The mortgagee may go into possession before the ink is dry on the mortgage unless by a term expressed or necessarily implied in the contract he has contracted himself out of that right. He has the right because he has a legal term of years in the property (*Fourmaids Ltd v Dudley Marshall (Properties) Ltd* [1957] 2 All ER 35 at 36).

In practice the lender leaves the borrower in possession of the property, the mortgage being security for repayment of the debt. Furthermore, in many cases there is an express term stating that the lender may only seek an order for possession where the borrower is, say, two months in arrears with repayments, or in breach of some other term of the mortgage. This is typical of building society mortgages. A mortgage entered into to secure a consumer credit debt only becomes enforceable after a default notice has been served in respect of the debt (see further p368). A bank mortgage taken out to secure an overdraft usually becomes enforceable once the bank has made a demand for the sums owed. A mortgage entered into to secure the debts of another or the obligations of another, such as a tenant's covenants under a lease, usually becomes enforceable as soon as the principal debtor is in default.

Adjourning the order for possession   At common law the court's power to adjourn an order for possession in a mortgage case is limited to a short period enabling the borrower to redeem the mortgage by paying the loan in full (*Birmingham Citizens Permanent Building Society v Caunt* [1962] 1 All ER 163 at 182; *Western Bank Ltd v Schindler* [1976] 2 All ER 393). Parliament has, however, given the court extensive discretionary powers to adjourn proceedings, stay or suspend execution of the judgment or postpone the date for possession where a lender is seeking to recover possession of residential premises (see p393) and even greater powers in Consumer Credit Act cases (see p397).

Relationship with sale and leasing   The lender usually wishes to obtain possession so that it may exercise its statutory power of sale (s101 of the Law of Property Act 1925). Unless the lender has possession it will not be able to sell the property with vacant possession. However, the lender does not have to sell the property. It may instead exercise its power to grant leases (s99 of the Law of Property Act 1925). The lender may wait before selling the property but if it does so the borrower may apply to the court for an order for sale. If the borrower makes such an application the court has an unfettered discretion to deal with the property to do what is just and equitable (*Palk v Mortgage Services Funding plc* [1993] 2 All ER 481; the lender wanted to let the property on short-term lettings until the market improved but the court considered that it would be unduly prejudicial to do so because a much greater debt would accrue and ordered a sale).

Consumer credit cases: preliminary points

Where the loan was made pursuant to a consumer credit agreement that is a 'regulated agreement' the court's powers to prevent an immediate order for possession will be governed by the Consumer Credit Act 1974 rather than the Administration of Justice Act 1970 (see ss8, 16 of the 1974 Act; the Consumer Credit (Increase of Monetary Limits) Order 1983 (SI 1983 No 1878); s38A of the Administration of Justice Act 1970). An agreement can only be a regulated agreement if the loan is for £15,000 or less and the agreement is not an exempt agreement (s8; the exemptions are dealt with in s16). It will be apparent from the documentation whether or not the agreement is a regulated agreement.

The main provisions of the Consumer Credit Act 1974 that are likely to be relevant in consumer credit cases are contained in this chapter. See the *Green Book*, Part 2, Consumer Credit, for other provisions, eg s10 in relation to bank overdrafts and ss76 and 98 where the creditor is seeking to take action notwithstanding that the borrower is not in breach.

Default notices   Where the 1974 Act does apply the lender must serve a 'default notice', in prescribed form (Consumer Credit (Enforcement, Default and Termination Notices) Regulations 1983 (SI 1983 No 1561) as amended (SI 1984 No 1109)) pursuant to ss87 and 88 of the 1974 Act. If he does not do so he will not be able to enforce his security. Nor will he be able to terminate the agreement or demand earlier payment of any sum (see further s87). If the borrower complies with the requirements of the default notice he is treated as not being in default (s89). Service of documents, such as default notices, is dealt with in s176 of the 1974 Act. (These sections, so far as is relevant, are set out *below*.)

In many agreements the lender has the right on the default of the borrower to terminate the agreement and to demand immediate repayment of all sums due. If the lender exercises those rights judgment is given for the full amount owed by the borrower without any allowance for the rebate to which he may be entitled on early settlement pursuant to ss 94 and 95 of the 1974 Act. However, when the borrower pays the judgment debt he may deduct the amount of credit for early settlement to which he may be entitled from the sum paid (*Forward Trust Ltd v Whymark* [1989] 3 All ER 915). In practice, many lenders in consumer credit cases merely claim possession based on non-payment of the arrears. This prevents the court from making a 'time order' in respect of the whole debt (see p 397).

If the borrower fails to comply with the default notice the lender *must* take court proceedings if it wishes to enforce the security (s 126 of the Consumer Credit Act 1974). As to jurisdiction of the county court see *below*. The court's powers to protect the borrower are dealt with on p 397.

Consumer Credit Act 1974, ss 87, 88, 89, 126 and 176

Need for default notices

    87.—(1) Service of a notice on the debtor or hirer in accordance with section 88 (a 'default notice') is necessary before the creditor or owner can become entitled, by reason of any breach by the debtor or hirer of a regulated agreement—

    (*a*) to terminate the agreement, or

    (*b*) to demand earlier payment of any sum, or

    (*c*) to recover possession of any goods or land, or

    (*d*) to treat any right conferred on the debtor or hirer by the agreement as terminated, restricted or deferred, or

    (*e*) to enforce any security.

Contents and effect of default notice

    88.—(1) The default notice must be in the prescribed form and specify—

    (*a*) the nature of the alleged breach;

    (*b*) if the breach is capable of remedy, what action is required to remedy it and the date before which that action is to be taken;

    (*c*) if the breach is not capable of remedy, the sum (if any) required to be paid as compensation for the breach and the date before which it is to be paid.

    (2) A date specified under subsection (1) must not be less than *seven* days after the date of *service* of the default notice, and the creditor or owner shall not take action such as is mentioned in section 87(1) before the date so specified or (if no requirement is made under subsection (1)) before those seven days have elapsed.

    (3) The default notice must not treat as a breach failure to comply with a provision of the agreement which becomes operative only on breach of some other provision, but if the breach of that other provision is not duly remedied or compensation demanded under subsection (1) is not duly paid, or (where no requirement is made under subsection (1)) if the seven days mentioned in subsection (2) have elapsed, the creditor or owner may treat the failure as a breach and section 87(1) shall not apply to it.

(4) The default notice must contain information in the prescribed terms about the consequences of failure to comply with it.

(5) A default notice making a requirement under subsection (1) may include a provision for the taking of action such as is mentioned in section 87(1) at any time after the restrictions imposed by subsection (2) will cease, together with a statement that the provision will be ineffective if the breach is duly remedied or the compensation duly paid.

Compliance with default notice

89.—If before the date specified for that purpose in the default notice the debtor or hirer takes the action specified under section 88(1)(*b*) or (*c*) the breach shall be treated as not having occurred.

. . .

126.—A land mortgage securing a regulated agreement is enforceable (so far as provided in relation to the agreement) on an order of the court only.

. . .

Service of documents

176.—(1) A document to be served under this Act by one person ('the server') on another person ('the subject') is to be treated as properly served on the subject if dealt with as mentioned in the following subsections.

(2) The document may be *delivered* or *sent* by post to the subject, or addressed to him by name and left at his proper address.

(3) For the purposes of this Act, a document sent by post to, or *left* at, the address last known to the server as the address of a person shall be treated as sent by post to, or left at, his proper address.

(4) Where the document is to be served on the subject as being the person having any interest in land, and it is not practicable after reasonable inquiry to ascertain the subject's name or address, the document may be served by—

    (*a*) addressing it to the subject by the description of the person having that interest in the land (naming it), and

    (*b*) delivering the document to some responsible person on the land or affixing it, or a copy of it, in a conspicuous position on the land.

(5) Where a document to be served on the subject as being a debtor, hirer or surety, or as having any other capacity relevant for the purposes of this Act, is served at any time on another person who—

    (*a*) is the person last known to the server as having that capacity, but

    (*b*) before that time has ceased to have it,

the document shall be treated as having been served at that time on the subject.

(6) Anything done to a document in relation to a person who (whether to the knowledge of the server or not) has died shall be treated for the purposes of subsection (5) as service of the document on that person if it would have been so treated had he not died.

(7) Neither of the following enactments (which provide for the vesting of the estate of an intestate in the Probate Judge) shall be construed as authorising service on the Probate Judge of any document which is to be served under this Act—

        section 9 of the Administration of Estates Act 1925;

        section 3 of the Administration of Estates Act (Northern Ireland) 1955.

(8) References in the preceding subsections to the serving of a document on a person include the giving of the document to that person.

Matrimonial homes

Unless the defendants are husband and wife who are joint mortgagors the plaintiff must carry out a search at the Land Registry (Land Registry Form 106) to ascertain whether any notice or caution has been registered or, in the case of unregistered land, at the Land Charges Department to ascertain whether any Class F land charge has been registered, to protect the rights of occupation under the Matrimonial Homes Act 1967 or s1 of the Matrimonial Homes Act 1983. If the search reveals any rights of occupation that fact must be alluded to in the particulars of claim (p375) and the result of the search must be exhibited to the affidavit in support (p380). It will also be necessary to serve the particulars of claim on the protected spouse (s8(3) of the Matrimonial Homes Act 1983; CCR Ord 6, r5A(3), see p376; County Court Form N438).

The non-owning spouse who is able to meet the borrowing spouse's liabilities may apply to the court to be made a party before the action is 'finally disposed of in the court'. The court can refuse to make him or her a party if it is not satisfied that the non-owning spouse can satisfy the borrower's liabilities and obligations (s8(2)). The non-owning spouse has a right to make such payments (s1(5)).

Matrimonial Homes Act 1983

1.

. . .

(5) Where a spouse is entitled under this section to occupy a dwelling house or any part thereof, any payment or tender made or other thing done by that spouse in or towards satisfaction of any liability of the other spouse in respect of rent, rates, mortgage payments or other outgoings affecting the dwelling house shall, whether or not it is made or done in pursuance of an order under this section, be as good as if made or done by the other spouse.

8.

. . .

(2) Where a mortgagee of land which consists of or includes a dwelling house brings an action in any court for the enforcement of his security, a spouse who is not a party to the action and who is enabled by section 1(5) or (8) above to meet the mortgagor's liabilities under the mortgage, on applying to the court at any time before the action is finally disposed of in that court, shall be entitled to be made a party to the action if the court—

    (*a*) does not see any special reason against it, and

    (*b*) is satisfied that the applicant may be expected to make such payments or do such things in or towards satisfaction of the mortgagor's liabilities or obligations as might affect the outcome of the proceedings or that the expectation of it should be considered under section 36 of the Administration of Justice Act 1970.

(3) Where a mortgagee of land which consists or substantially consists of a dwelling house brings an action for the enforcement of his security, and at the relevant time there is—

(*a*) in the case of unregistered land, a land charge of Class F registered against the person who is the estate owner at the relevant time or any person who, where the estate owner is a trustee, preceded him as trustee during the subsistence of the mortgage, or

(*b*) in the case of registered land, a subsisting registration of a notice under section 2(8) above or a notice or caution under section 2(7) of the Act of 1967,

notice of the action shall be served by the mortgagee on the person on whose behalf the land charge is registered or the notice or caution entered, if that person is not a party to the action.

(4) For the purpose of subsection (3) above, if there has been issued a certificate of the result of an official search made on behalf of the mortgagee which would disclose any land charge of Class F, notice or caution within subsection (3)(*a*) or (*b*) above, and the action is commenced within the priority period, the relevant time is the date of that certificate; and in any other case the relevant time is the time when the action is commenced.

(5) In subsection (4) above, 'priority period' means, for both registered and unregistered land, the period for which, in accordance with section 11(5) and (6) of the Land Charges Act 1972, a certificate on an official search operates in favour of a purchaser.

Jurisdiction; High Court or county court

The county court has jurisdiction to hear all claims for possession whatever the rateable value of the premises (s21(1) of the County Courts Act 1984 (as amended)). It has exclusive jurisdiction in mortgage possession claims where the land consists of or includes a dwelling house situated outside Greater London (s21(3)) except where the claim for possession is made in an action for foreclosure or sale (s21(4)).

County Courts Act 1984, s21
    21.—(1) A county court shall have jurisdiction to hear and determine any action for the recovery of land.
    (2) . . .
    (3) Where a mortgage of land consists of or includes a dwelling house and no part of the land is situated in Greater London then, subject to subsection (4), if a county court has jurisdiction by virtue of this section to hear and determine an action in which the mortgagee under that mortgage claims possession of the mortgaged property, no court other than a county court shall have jurisdiction to hear and determine that action.
    (4) Subsection (3) shall not apply to an action for foreclosure or sale in which a claim for possession of the mortgaged property is also made.
    . . .
    (7) In this section—
        'dwelling house' includes any building or part of a building which is used as a dwelling;
        'mortgage' includes a charge and 'mortgagor' and 'mortgagee' shall be construed accordingly;

'mortgagor' and 'mortgagee' includes any person deriving title under
the original mortgage or mortgagee.

(8) The fact that part of the premises comprised in a dwelling house is
used as a shop or office or for business, trade or professional purposes shall
not prevent the dwelling house from being a dwelling house for the purposes
of this section.

(9) This section does not apply to a mortgage securing an agreement
which is a regulated agreement within the meaning of the Consumer Credit
Act 1984.

Generally, the lender only claims possession. It does not need to make
a money claim because its intention is usually to sell the property and
then to take all sums due from the proceeds of sale. However, the lender
may wish to make a claim for sums due, in addition to possession, if the
value of the property is less than the total of the sums owed. Should it
wish to make such a claim it may do so pursuant to the court's unlimited
jurisdiction in contract (s15 of the County Courts Act 1984; paras 9 and
10 of the prescribed form; p377).

Consumer credit cases

Where the agreement secured by the mortgage is a regulated agreement
within the meaning of the Consumer Credit Act 1974 the proceedings
must be brought in the county court (ss21(9), 141 of the Consumer Credit
Act 1974). If they are commenced in the High Court the claim will not be
struck out (*Sovereign Leasing v Ali* (1991) *The Times*, 21 March, QBD)
but will be transferred to the county court (s141(1), (2) of the 1974 Act).

Consumer Credit Act, s141
(1) In England and Wales the county court shall have jurisdiction to hear
and determine—
  (*a*) any action by the creditor or owner to enforce a regulated
      agreement or any security relating to it;
  (*b*) any action to enforce any linked transaction against the debtor or
      hirer or his relative;
and such an action shall not be brought in any other court.
(2) Where an action or application is brought in the High Court which, by
virtue of this Act, ought to have been brought in the county court it shall not
be treated as improperly brought but shall be transferred to the county
court.

County court procedure

Which county court?

The proceedings must be commenced in the court which has jurisdiction
for the area in which the mortgaged property is situated (CCR Ord 4,
r3). For the position where the proceedings have been commenced in the
wrong court, see CCR Ord 16, r2 (p263).

Issuing the proceedings

When issuing the proceedings the following must be filed with the court:

(1) the summons (which the plaintiff is required to prepare; see County Court Form N5, p266) plus a copy for each defendant, plus a further copy (instead of a request) where service is to be effected otherwise than by an officer of the court (Ord 3, r3(1B));

(2) where service is to be effected by an officer of the court, a request for issue of a summons (County Court Form N204);

(3) the particulars of claim (see *below*) plus a copy for each defendant to be served with the summons (CCR Ord 6, r1(1), (4)) plus a further copy if the plaintiff's search has shown that there is a person who is required to be served in accordance with s8(3) of the Matrimonial Homes Act 1983 (see p371);

(4) the court fee (see p268).

An action in which a claim is made for possession is a 'fixed date action' and unless the claim is joined for some relief other than for moneys secured under the mortgage or charge the return date on the summons will be the date upon which the action is due to be heard (see further p384).

Proceedings taken by a second mortgagee

If proceedings are proposed to be taken by a second mortgagee, he should write to the first mortgagee asking whether he has already obtained an order for possession and whether he has any observations to make on the proposed application. A copy of the letter and any reply should be produced at the hearing. If there is more than one prior mortgagee letters on the same lines should be sent to them all (*Practice Direction* [1968] 1 WLR 422; a practice direction that relates to the Chancery Division but which the author suggests should be followed in the county court).

The particulars of claim

The rules relating to the particulars of claim have been substantially amended with effect from 1 November 1993 (CCR Ord 6, rr5, 5A; see *below*). They now specify in greater detail the information required in all mortgage possession cases and there are specific provisions relating to claims of residential premises. The main points to note are as follows:

(1) In all mortgage possession actions where the land consists of or includes a dwelling the particulars of claim must be in *prescribed form* (r5A; County Court Form N120; see p377). The form is to be used where the mortgage secures a regulated consumer credit agreement and in cases where it does not do so (para 3). The particulars of claim must state whether or not the agreement is a regulated consumer credit agreement.

(2) As will be seen the prescribed form includes boxes and notes on the side. It is therefore suggested that solicitors who put the form on their word processors include the boxes and notes so as not to risk the possibility that the claim will be dismissed on the basis that the prescribed form has not been used.

(3) Substantially more information is required than was previously the case. In particular, the plaintiff must give details of the defendant's financial *and other* circumstances so far as they are known to it and must state whether the plaintiff is paid interest or arrears direct under social security regulations and, if so, how much (r5A(2)(*d*); para 7 of the form). Relevant information might include the defendant's age, marital and family circumstances, his occupation and any physical or mental handicap.

(4) As before the plaintiff must state whether there is any person on whom notice of the action is required to be served in accordance with s8(3) of the Matrimonial Homes Act 1983 (r5A(3); see further p371).

County Court Rules, Ord 6, rr5, 5A

Mortgage action

5.—(1) Where a plaintiff claims as mortgagee payment of moneys secured by a mortgage of real or leasehold property or possession of such property, the particulars of claim shall contain the information required under this rule and, as the case may be, by rule 5A.

(2) Where there is more than one loan secured by the mortgage, the information required under the following paragraphs of this rule and under rule 5A shall be provided in respect of each loan agreement.

(3) The particulars shall state the date of the mortgage and identify the land sought to be recovered.

(4) Where possession of the property is claimed, the particulars of claim shall state whether or not the property consists of or includes a dwelling house within the meaning of s21 of the Act.

(5) The particulars shall state whether or not the loan which is secured by the mortgage is a regulated consumer credit agreement and, if so, specify the date on which any notice required by s76 or s87 of the Consumer Credit Act 1974 was given.

(6) The particulars shall show the state of account between the plaintiff and the defendant by including:

(*a*) the amount of the advance and of any periodic repayment and any payment of interest required to be made;

(*b*) the amount which would have to be paid (after taking into account any adjustment for early settlement) in order to redeem the mortgage at a stated date not more than 14 days after the commencement of proceedings specifying the amount of solicitor's costs and administrative charges which would be payable;

(*c*) where the loan which is secured by the mortgage is a regulated consumer credit agreement, the total amount outstanding under the terms of the mortgage;

(*d*) the rate of interest payable:

(i) at the commencement of the mortgage,

   (ii) immediately before any arrears referred to in subparagraph (*e*) accrued, and

   (iii) where it differs from that provided under (ii) above, at the commencement of the proceedings;

  (*e*) the amount of any interest or instalments in arrear at the commencement of the proceedings.

(7) The particulars of claim shall state any previous steps which the plaintiff has taken to recover the moneys secured by the mortgage or the mortgaged property and, in the case of court proceedings, state:

   (i) the dates when proceedings were commenced and concluded, and

   (ii) the dates and terms of any orders made.

(8) In this rule 'mortgage' includes a legal or equitable mortgage and a legal or equitable charge, and references to the mortgaged property and mortgagee shall be construed accordingly.

Mortgage action—dwelling house

   5A.—(1) This rule applies where a plaintiff claims as mortgagee possession of land which consists of or includes a dwelling house and in such a case the particulars of claim shall be in prescribed form.

(2) Where the plaintiff's claim is brought because of failure to make the periodic payments due, the particulars of claim shall:

  (*a*) give details (whether by means of a schedule or otherwise) of all payments which have been missed altogether;

  (*b*) where a history of late or under-payments is relied upon, provide sufficient details to establish the plaintiff's case;

  (*c*) give details of any other payments required to be made as a term of the mortgage (such as for insurance premiums, legal costs, default interest, penalties, administrative or other charges) together with any other sums claimed stating the nature and amount of each such charge, whether any payment is in arrear and whether or not it is included in the amount of any periodic payment;

  (*d*) give such relevant information as is known by the plaintiff about the defendant's circumstances and, in particular, whether (and, if so, what) payments on his behalf are made direct to the plaintiff by or under the Social Security Contributions and Benefits Act 1992.

(3) In an action to which this rule applies, the plaintiff shall state in his particulars of claim whether there is any person on whom notice of the action is required to be served in accordance with s8(3) of the Matrimonial Homes Act 1983 and, if so, he shall state the name and address of that person and shall file a copy of the particulars of claim for service on that person.

(4) In this rule 'mortgage' has the same meaning as in rule 5(8).

Affidavit in support

As will be seen below, any action by a lender for possession to which s36 of the Administration of Justice Act 1970 applies (ie a non-consumer credit case) is dealt with in chambers unless the court otherwise directs.

Form 51: Particulars of claim of possession (mortgaged property)

**Particulars of Claim
for Possession
(Mortgaged Property)**

In the

County Court

Case Number

**Notes to help you
complete this form**

This form should only be
used to recover possession of
residential premises where
the grounds include
non-payment of agreed
repayments. If you need
more space, please continue
on a separate sheet. Mark
the sheet clearly with the
names of the parties and the
paragraph number to which
the information relates.

Plaintiff

Defendant[s]

About the mortgage [legal charge]

Paragraph 1.

Insert date of legal charge or
mortgage. Give the address of
the property charged. If there
is more than one loan
agreement, the details
required in paragraphs 1–5
should be given for each of
them (see note above).

1 A mortgage [legal charge] was agreed between the Plaintiff[s] and

the Defendant[s] on

The property charged was

Paragraph 2.

Delete the words in brackets to
show whether the property is a
dwelling house or part of one.

2 The property is a [dwelling-house] [part of a dwelling-house].

Paragraph 3.

Delete paragraph (a) if the loan
is not secured by a regulated
consumer credit agreement. If it
is, give date notice of default
was given to defendant and
delete paragraph (b).

3 (a) The loan secured by the mortgage is a regulated consumer credit agreement.

Notice of default was given to the Defendant[s] on

(b) The loan secured by the mortgage is not a regulated consumer credit
agreement.

Paragraph 4(a).

Say what the amount of arrears
outstanding is up to the date of
issue of the summons. Give
details of all payments missed.
If a schedule of payments
missed or not made on time is
attached, say so. Say whether
payments generally have been
made regularly and on time
giving sufficient detail to
support your claim for
possession.

4 The reason[s] the Plaintiff is asking for possession is that the Defendant[s]
has [have] not complied with the conditions which apply to the mortgage
[legal charge] because:

(a) the agreed repayments of the loan and interest have not been made.
Details are set out below:

Paragraph 4(b).

Delete this paragraph if the
claim for possession is for
arrears of repayments only. If
not, give details of any other
failure to comply with the
agreed terms of the loan.

(b)

Paragraph 5(a).

Give the amount loaned. But
see note to paragraph 1 if more
than one loan agreement.

5 (a) The amount loaned was £

Paragraph 5(b).
Give the current terms of repayment. Where appropriate, give the amounts of any regular instalments and (separately) any interest which has to be paid.

(b) The current terms of repayment are:

Paragraph 5(c).
Give the amount required to pay the mortgage in full. The date of the calculation must not be more than 14 days after the issue of the summons. Also, give details of the costs which the Plaintiff would incur if the mortgage were to be paid in full.

(c) The amount required to pay the mortgage in full as at [   ]

would be £ [   ] taking into account any

adjustment for early settlement. The solicitors and administrative costs

which would be involved if there were full settlement would

amount to £ [   ]

Paragraph 5(d).
Delete this paragraph if there are not additional payments due under the terms of the mortgage, e.g. default interest, penalties, insurance, costs of previous court proceedings, etc. If there are payments due, say how much and what it is for. Indicate whether or not they are included in the amounts at paragraph 5(b).

(d) The following additional payments are also due under the terms of the mortgage [legal charge]:

		Included in paragraph 5(b)
		Yes	No
£	for		
£	for		
£	for		

Paragraph 5(e).
Delete this paragraph if there are no additional payments listed at paragraph 5(d). If there are payments, give details of any payments which are in arrear and say by how much.

(e) Of the payments in paragraph 5(d), the following are in arrear:

arrears of £

arrears of £

arrears of £

Paragraph 5(f).
Delete this paragraph if the loan is not secured by a regulated consumer credit agreement. If it is, give the total amount of the loan outstanding.

(f) The total amount outstanding under the loan agreement secured by

the mortgage is £ [   ]

Paragraph 5(g).
Give the rates of interest which applied when the agreement was first made, the rate which applied immediately before the arrears now claimed occurred and the current rate, if different.

(g) Interest rates which have applied to the mortgage (legal charge) are as follows:

Date	%	Date	%

Paragraph 6.
Give details of any steps already taken to recover arrears or repayment of money. If there have been previous court proceedings, give the date they were started and concluded and the terms of any order(s) made.

6

The following steps have already been taken to recover the money secured by the mortgage:

About the Defendant(s)

Paragraph 7.
Give what details you know of the Defendant's financial and other circumstances. Say in particular whether the Plaintiff is paid interest or arrears direct under Social Security regulations and if so, how much.

7

The following information is known about the Defendant's circumstances:

Paragraph 8.
Delete this paragraph if the property (land) being claimed does not include a dwelling-house. If it does, delete (a) or (b) as appropriate. Give the name of the person to be given notice under section 8(3) of the Matrimonial Homes Act 1983.

8

(a) There is no one who should be given notice of these proceedings because of a registered interest in the property.

(b) Notice of these proceedings will be given to

who has a registered interest in the property.

What the court is being asked to do.

Paragraph 9.
Delete paragraph(s) (a) to (c) as appropriate.

9

The Plaintiff is asking the court to make an order that the Defendant[s]:

(a) give the Plaintiff possession of the property mentioned in paragraph 1;

(b) pay the outstanding arrears;

(c) pay the costs of making this application.

Paragraph 10.
Delete if not applicable.

10

The Plaintiff is also asking that judgment is entered against the Defendant[s] for the total amount outstanding under the mortgage [legal charge].

Signed

(Solicitors for) Plaintiff

Date

Give an address where notices about this case can be sent to you

Postcode

Reproduced by kind permission of The Solicitors' Law Stationery Society Ltd

Where a hearing is in chambers evidence is given by affidavit (Ord 20, r5; p381). It is therefore necessary to prepare an affidavit for use at the hearing.

The affidavit should be sworn by the person having the conduct of the matter (eg in the case of a building society a manager or assistant manager). Unless the court otherwise orders the affidavit may contain statements of information or belief but the affidavit should state which of the facts deposed to are within the deponent's knowledge and which are based on information or belief and it must, in the former case, give the means of knowledge and in the latter case give the sources and grounds of the information or belief (CCR Ord 20, r10(4), (5); compare the position in the High Court; RSC Ord 41, r5).

It is not necessary for the affidavit to repeat all the matters in the particulars of claim. It may simply confirm that those matters were true at the date of the particulars and bring matters up to date (see Form 52, p382). The affidavit should (if known) state whether the defendant is still in physical occupation of the property and the names of any other occupiers of the property.

The following documents should be exhibited to the affidavit:

(1) A copy of the charge certificate. (The original must be produced at the hearing.)

(2) If the mortgage incorporates standard mortgage conditions, those conditions.

(3) The 'offer letter' if that document rather than the mortgage contains particulars of the advance, the term of the loan, the rate of interest or the amount of instalments, etc.

(4) A computer printout or other schedule showing how the arrears have accrued.

(5) Unless the defendants are husband and wife who are joint mortgagors, an up-to-date certificate of search from the Land Registry or in the case of unregistered land from the Land Charges Department (see p371).

(6) Unless a certificate has been filed stating that a notice of the proceedings has been sent to the property addressed to the occupiers in accordance with Ord 7, r15A, a copy of that notice (see p381).

Although the rules do not specifically require it the lender should send a copy of his affidavit to the borrower prior to the hearing. The borrower may apply to the court for an order that the maker of the affidavit attend for cross-examination (CCR Ord 20, r5).

In a consumer credit case the rules do not specifically provide for the hearing to be heard in chambers and for the use of affidavit evidence. However, this is the practice adopted in many courts. Affidavit evidence is admissible under CCR Ord 20, r7(2)(a) without notice if the defendant does not enter a defence but in order to ensure that it will be admitted it is worth serving a notice of intention to use the affidavit (r7(1)).

CCR Ord 20, rr5, 7

5.—In any proceedings in chambers evidence may be given by affidavit unless by any provision of these rules it is otherwise provided or the court otherwise directs, but the court may, on the application of any party, order the attendance for cross-examination of the person making any such affidavit, and where, after such an order has been made, the person in question does not attend, his affidavit shall not be used in evidence without the leave of the court.

. . .

7.—(1) Where a party desires to use at the hearing of an action or matter an affidavit which is not rendered admissible by rule 5 and in respect of which no order has been made under rule 6 [*for the giving of evidence by affidavit*], he may, not less than 14 days before the hearing, give notice of his desire, accompanied by a copy of the affidavit, to the party against whom it is to be used, and unless that party, within 7 days after receipt of the notice, gives notice to the other party that he objects to the use of the affidavit, he shall be taken to have consented to its use and accordingly the affidavit may be used at the hearing.

(2) Where—

    (*a*) the defendant in a fixed date action has not delivered a defence within the time limited by Order 9, rule 2, or

    (*b*) the defendant in a default or fixed date action does not appear on a pre-trial review of the action,

evidence by affidavit shall be admissible in support of the plaintiff's claim without notice being given under paragraph (1), unless the court otherwise directs.

Payment by the borrower after commencement

Where the borrower pays the arrears after commencement of the action the lender should not withdraw the proceedings but adjourn the claim generally (Ord 13, r3). If arrears accrue again the claim can be restored without the necessity of commencing fresh proceedings (see *Green Book*, note to s21 of the County Courts Act 1984 citing *Greyhound Guaranty Ltd v Caulfield* [1981] CLY 1808), presuming, of course, that the proceedings have not been struck out pursuant to CCR Ord 13, r3(4) (striking out claims that have been adjourned for more than 12 months).

Service of the proceedings; notice to occupiers

Service of the proceedings may be effected in the same way as for proceedings against a tenant (see p293). It has been held that service effected on one of two joint borrowers where one borrower was not resident at the mortgaged property and whose whereabouts were unknown was good service to which an order for possession could be obtained (*Alliance Building Society v Yap* [1962] 1 WLR 857).

In addition to the ordinary service of the proceedings on the defendants, notice of the proceedings containing certain details of them is required to be sent to the property addressed to the occupiers not less than 14 days before the hearing. The plaintiff must file a certificate

Form 52: Affidavit of the plaintiff—building society mortgage

---

IN THE   COUNTY COURT   Case No

BETWEEN

                                             Plaintiff

—AND—

                                          Defendant

AFFIDAVIT OF THE PLAINTIFF

I, [JOHN BROWN, manager of the Notown Branch of the Notown Building Society] situated at [*state address*] MAKE OATH AND SAY as follows:

1. I am the person having the conduct of this matter on behalf of the Plaintiff and am authorised to make this affidavit on its behalf. I make this affidavit from facts within my own knowledge as manager of the Notown branch of the Plaintiff and from investigation of the documents and papers of the Plaintiff.

2. I have read the particulars of claim in this action dated [*state date*] and say that the same were true and accurate in all respects at the date thereof.

3. A true copy of the Mortgage is now produced and shown to me and marked 'JB 1'.

4. The amount of the arrears under the mortgage is now [£1,025.00] and the balance outstanding is [£15,153.46]. The basis upon which these figures and the figures stated in the Particulars of Claim have been calculated is set out in a schedule which is now produced and shown to me and marked 'JB 2'.

5. No previous proceedings of any kind in connection with the mortgaged property or the monies secured by mortgage have been taken against the defendant.

6. There is now produced and shown to me marked 'JB 3' a true copy of a certificate of search at H. M. Land Registry showing that no Notice or Caution has been registered against the said title.

7. To the best of my knowledge and belief the defendant is still in physical occupation of the said property.

SWORN

---

stating that the rule has been complied with or exhibit the notice to his affidavit to be used at the hearing (CCR Ord 7, r15A; see *below*). Occupiers may apply to be joined in the proceedings pursuant to CCR Ord 15, r3 (see p269). The rights of tenants are dealt with on p399.

County Court Rules, Ord 7, r15A

Mortgage possession actions

15A.—(1) After the issue of the summons in a mortgage possession action, the plaintiff shall not less than 14 days before the hearing send to the address of the property sought to be recovered a notice addressed to the occupiers which:

(*a*) states that possession proceedings have been commenced in respect of the property;

(*b*) shows the name and address of the plaintiff, of the defendant and of the court which issued the summons; and

(*c*) gives details of the case number and of the hearing date.

(2) The plaintiff shall either:

(*a*) not less than 14 days before the hearing, file a certificate stating that a notice has been sent in accordance with paragraph (1), or

(*b*) exhibit the notice to any affidavit used at the hearing.

(3) In this rule 'mortgage possession action' means an action in which the plaintiff claims as mortgagee possession of land which consists of or includes a dwelling house and 'mortgage' has the same meaning as in Ord 6, rule 5(8) [see *above*].

Defendant's action on receipt of proceedings

When the defendant receives the particulars of claim he will find that the court has also sent him a form entitled 'Reply to possession summons (mortgaged property)' (County Court Form N11M). It is very important that this form be completed by the defendant. It contains a large number of questions designed to assist the court in determining whether or not to make an order for possession and whether or not to exercise its discretionary powers to suspend orders, etc.

The reply form contains one somewhat unusual question: Do you want the court to consider whether or not the terms of your original loan agreement are fair? (Question 10). This presumably relates to the court's powers to re-open 'extortionate credit bargains' under ss137–140 of the Consumer Credit Act 1974. A credit bargain is extortionate if it requires the debtor or a relative of his to make payments which are grossly extortionate or if it otherwise grossly contravenes ordinary principles of fair dealing (s138(1)). If the defendant does wish to re-open the agreement it is suggested that an originating application also be issued and served making it clear that this is what he wishes to do and setting out the grounds upon which the defendant wishes to re-open the agreement; but note that the burden of proof is on the creditor to show that the agreement is not extortionate (s171(7) of the Consumer Credit Act 1974; see also Ord 49, r4, paras (14), (15)).

If the defendant wishes to raise any other substantive defence to the claim he should file a full defence in addition to or, if appropriate, instead of the reply. Strictly speaking any defence should be filed within 14 days after service of the summons (CCR Ord 9, r6). The defendant may appear on the date fixed for the hearing and dispute the claim notwithstanding that no defence has been served but he will usually place himself in a better position if he serves a defence early and may risk an order for costs being made against him if he does not do so (r9(2), (3)). As to defences that may be raised see p387.

County Court Rules, Ord 9, r9(2), (3)

(2) Notwithstanding that he has failed to deliver a defence the defendant in a fixed date action may appear on the return day and dispute the plaintiff's claim.

(3) In any case to which paragraph (1) or (2) applies, the court may order the defendant to pay any costs properly incurred in consequence of his delay or failure.

The hearing

Mortgage possession claims are invariably heard by the District Judge (pursuant to CCR Ord 21, r5(1)(c) and if the case is one in which the court has discretionary powers under the Administration of Justice Act 1970 (see p393), the rules expressly state that the hearing should take place in chambers unless the court otherwise orders (CCR Ord 49, r1A).

County Court Rules, Ord 49, r1A

(1A) Any action by a mortgagee for possession of a dwelling house, being an action to which section 36 of the Administration of Justice Act 1970 applies, shall be dealt with in chambers unless the court otherwise directs.

There is no similar rule in relation to consumer credit cases but in practice they are also often heard in chambers before the District Judge.

An action in which a claim is made for possession is a fixed date action and unless the claim is joined for some relief other than for moneys secured under the mortgage or charge the return date on the summons will be the date upon which the action is due to be heard (CCR Ord 3, r2(1) and r3(4); p270). The lender should therefore be prepared to deal with the case and should attend court with the original charge certificate. If the defendant raises no substantive defence but merely wishes the court to exercise its powers to suspend orders, etc (see p393) or in a consumer credit case to make a time order (see p397) the District Judge will determine the issue. The borrower should give *evidence* as to his means and his proposals for repayment, whether by way of oral evidence or affidavit. Where the defendant has completed the court's reply form he should confirm its contents on oath or by affirmation and supplement it with any up-to-date information that he wishes to draw to the court's attention. But see further note (4), p394.

If a defence is raised the District Judge will usually order a defence to be filed, give other directions and refer the matter to the circuit judge (CCR Ord 13, r2; Ord 17, r10).

High Court procedure

Introduction

Proceedings in the High Court are assigned to the Chancery Division (RSC Ord 88, r2) and are governed by RSC Ord 88. The action may be begun by writ or originating summons. This section assumes that the proceedings are to be commenced by summons.

The summons

The summons is in High Court Form 8 of Appendix A.

In order to ensure that the proceedings have been properly commenced in the High Court (see p372) the rules require the summons to be indorsed with a statement showing where the mortgaged property is situated and if the property is situated outside Greater London that the property consists of or includes a dwelling house. It should be remembered that the High Court has no jurisdiction where the dwelling is outside Greater London. The summons must also be indorsed with a certificate that the action is not one to which s141 of the Consumer Credit Act 1974 applies (RSC Ord 88, r3(3)).

If the lender wishes to claim a money judgment for the principal sum and/or interest in addition to possession the summons should contain a claim to this effect (see also p377).

The summons may only be issued in a Chancery district registry if the property to which the action relates is situated in the district of that registry (Ord 88, r3(2)).

Service

In addition to serving the defendant, copies of the proceedings should be served upon any person on whose behalf a land charge is registered or a notice or caution is entered, any person who the lender believes may have an interest in the property and any tenants or licensees that the lender knows or believes to be in occupation of the property. It is suggested that each such person should be informed of their right to apply to be joined in the proceedings pursuant to RSC Ord 15, r10. (See also p301).

For notice of proceedings to prior mortgagees, see p374.

Where the borrower has acknowledged service the affidavit in support (see *below*) must be filed with the court and served upon the borrower before the expiration of 14 days after the borrower has acknowledged service (RSC Ord 28, r1A) and notice of the appointment should be served at least four clear days before the hearing. Notice should also be given to all other persons who have acknowledged service (RSC Ord 28, r3(1)).

Where the defendant fails to acknowledge service of the summons the procedure set out in RSC Ord 88, r4 should be followed; see also *White Book*, notes at 88/2–7/11.

The affidavit: RSC Ord 88, r5

The affidavit in support of the summons must exhibit a true copy of the mortgage. It must:

(1) show the circumstances under which the right to possession arises and the state of the account between the lender and the borrower with particulars of—

    (*a*) the amount of the advance,

    (*b*) the amount of the periodic payments required to be made

    (*c*) the amount of any interest or instalments in arrear at the date of issue of the originating summons *and* at the date of the affidavit,

    (*d*) and the amount remaining due under the mortgage;

(2) give particulars of every person who to the best of the plaintiff's knowledge is in possession of the mortgaged property;

(3) state whether a land charge of Class F has been registered, or a notice or caution pursuant to s2(7) of the Matrimonial Homes Act 1967 or notice registered under s2(8) of the Matrimonial Homes Act 1983 has been entered and, if so, on whose behalf (a copy of the result of the Land Registry/Land Charges Department search should be exhibited);

(4) state whether the plaintiff has served notice of proceedings on the person on whose behalf the land charge is registered or the notice or caution entered;

(5) show how and when, if the mortgage creates a tenancy other than a tenancy at will between the lender and the borrower, the tenancy was determined and if by service of a notice when the notice was duly served;

(6) state the amount of a day's interest where the lender's claim includes a claim for interest to judgment.

A recent practice direction in the Chancery Division emphasises the need to exhibit the offer letter where the charge incorporates the primary terms of the mortgage by reference to that letter.

Chancery Division Practice Direction (14), (White Book, Part 2, p211)

    (1) RSC Ord 88, r5(2) requires that in mortgage actions a copy of the mortgage must be exhibited to the affidavit in support of the originating summons, and the original mortgage or charge certificate must be produced at the hearing.

    (2) Most building society mortgages now incorporate standard mortgage conditions, and in such cases a copy of the relevant conditions must also be exhibited.

    (3) Some standard forms of building society mortgage are now so abbreviated that they give no particulars of the amount of the advance, the term of the loan, the rate of interest or the amount of the instalments, but all these matters are defined in the mortgage conditions by reference to the offer letter. Where the offer letter is thus in effect incorporated into the mortgage by reference, that also should be exhibited to the affidavit.

    (4) Many bank mortgages, although expressed in the usual bank 'all moneys' form, are also qualified by an offer letter or other side letter, providing for repayment of the advance by instalments. In *Bank of Scotland v Grimes* [1985] 2 All ER 254 it was held that in such cases the mortgage may

be treated as an instalment mortgage for the purposes of s36 of the Administration of Justice Act 1970 and s8 of the Administration of Justice Act 1973. In these cases also the relevant letter should be exhibited to the affidavit in support.

The hearing

The hearing will be in chambers before the master. The master may adjourn the case to the judge (RSC Ord 32, rr12, 14(2)) but is only likely to do so in exceptional circumstances.

The original mortgage or, in the case of a registered charge, the charge certificate must be produced at the hearing (RSC Ord 88, r5(2)).

The provisions of the Administration of Justice Acts referred to *below* (see p393) apply in respect of the orders which the court can make.

If a party is dissatisfied with the master's order he may appeal to the judge. The notice must be lodged within five days of the order appealed against. The appeal does not operate as a stay of execution which must be applied for separately (see RSC Ord 58, r1; *Practice Direction (Chancery Orders)* [1982] 3 All ER 124, para 10; *White Book*, Part II 213). However, where the order for possession has been suspended upon conditions the lender will need leave to enforce the order (see p403).

Defences: setting aside the mortgage

Non-borrowing spouse in occupation not asked for consent

In *Williams and Glynn's Bank Ltd v Boland* [1980] 2 All ER 408 it was held that a spouse with a beneficial interest in the matrimonial home registered at the Land Registry who is in actual occupation has an 'overriding interest' within the meaning of s70(1)(g) of the Land Registration Act 1925 (see p401) and that if the other spouse enters into a mortgage the lender's interest is subject to the non-borrowing spouse's rights of occupation. It is, therefore incumbent on the lender to obtain the non-borrowing spouse's consent to the mortgage even though he/she is not the legal owner. If the lender does not do so it will not be able to enforce the mortgage against the spouse.

The relevant date for determining whether or not the non-borrowing spouse has an overriding interest is the date the mortgage was executed, not the date of registration (*Abbey National Building Society v Cann* [1990] 1 All ER 1085, HL).

If the non-borrowing spouse's consent is obtained the mortgage will be binding upon him or her. In *Bristol and West Building Society v Henning* [1985] 2 All ER 606 the husband was the legal owner of the property which had been mortgaged to the building society to raise the money for the purchase with the knowledge and consent of the wife who was not a party to the mortgage. The marriage between the parties broke down and the husband left and stopped paying the mortgage. The wife claimed to have an equitable interest in the property, or alternatively an irrevocable licence, which she argued prevented the lender from obtaining possession. There was no declaration of trust in writing or any express agreement as to her having a beneficial interest or the lesser right of an irrevocable licence. It was, therefore, necessary to determine from the parties' actions what their express or imputed intentions as to her beneficial interest or irrevocable licence were. It was held that as the wife knew of and supported the proposal to raise the purchase money for the house by the mortgage the common intention of the parties must have been that any interest the wife had was subject to the lender's charge which the lender was therefore entitled to enforce by obtaining possession.

As to whether or not a spouse or other person has an equitable interest based upon a constructive trust see *Grant v Edwards* [1986] 2 All ER 426 and *Lloyds Bank plc v Rosset* [1990] 1 All ER 1111. See also *Sprigette v Defoe* (1992) *The Independent* 10 March, referred to on p95.

In *Boland* the money was advanced by the lender to a sole proprietor who held the land as sole trustee. The position is very different where the legal ownership is in the names of two or more persons and the money is advanced to two or more of those persons. In these circumstances the interest of a beneficiary of the trust for sale will be 'overreached' and he will not be able to obtain the benefit of s70 of the Land Registration Act 1925 notwithstanding that he may be in actual occupation. The lender will be entitled to possession. (See *City of London Building Society v Flegg* [1987] 3 All ER 435.)

In *Equity and Law Home Loans Ltd v Prestridge* [1992] 1 All ER 909, CA, the court considered the effect on the equitable interest of a wife who had consented to a first mortgage where her husband had subsequently re-mortgaged the property without her consent. The court held that it was to be imputed that the wife consented to the second mortgage to the extent to which she consented to the first.

Misrepresentation or undue influence of a third party

It is very common for one person (the surety) to charge his property to the lender to secure the debts of the borrower. A company director charges his home to secure the company's debts, a wife agrees to the matrimonial home in which she has an equal share being charged to secure her husband's business debts. In the usual case if the borrower defaults the lender is entitled to possession of the property.

In some cases the surety contends that he (or, more commonly, she) was induced to enter into the mortgage by undue influence or that it is vitiated for some other reason. In the husband and wife context the wife will commonly assert that the husband presented her with the documents and misrepresented their meaning or that he somehow forced her to sign them against her will. The question then arises as to whether or not the mortgage is invalidated by that misconduct: Is the lender to be affected by the borrower's misconduct?

In *Barclays Bank plc v O'Brien* [1993] 4 All ER 417 the House of Lords considered this issue. The judgment was given by Lord Browne-Wilkinson. Having considered the earlier authorities he summarised the position as follows:

> Where one cohabitee has entered into an obligation to stand surety for the debts of the other cohabitee and the creditor is aware that they are cohabitees: (1) the surety obligation will be valid and enforceable by the creditor unless the suretyship was procured by the undue influence, misrepresentation or other legal wrong of the principal debtor; (2) if there has been undue influence, misrepresentation or other legal wrong by the principal debtor, unless the creditor has taken reasonable steps to satisfy himself that the surety entered into the obligation freely and in knowledge of the true facts, the creditor will be unable to enforce the surety obligation because he will be fixed with the constructive notice of the surety's right to set aside the transaction; (3) unless there are special exceptional circumstances, a creditor will have taken such reasonable steps to avoid being fixed with constructive notice if the creditor warns the surety (at a meeting not attended by the principal debtor) of the amount of her potential liability and of the risks involved and advises the surety to take independent legal advice.
>
> I should make it clear that in referring to the husband's debts I include the debts of a company in which the husband (but not the wife) has a direct financial interest.

Particular points to note are as follows:

(1) The principle enunciated in *O'Brien* is not only applicable to wives. It applies in all cases 'where there is an emotional relationship between cohabitees', including homosexual ones (at 431d), if the lender is aware of the relationship (at 431g).

(2) The principle applies where one cohabitee has entered into an obligation to stand as surety for the debts of another. It does not apply where a loan was advanced to cohabitees jointly and there was nothing to indicate to the lender that the loan was anything other than a normal advance to the cohabitees for their joint benefit. In those circumstances the lender will not be affected by the undue influence, misrepresentation or other wrong of one of the cohabitees which has led the other to execute the mortgage (*CIBC Mortgages plc v Pitt* [1993] 4 All ER 433, HL; loan to husband and wife made on their joint application, but as a result of pressure on the wife, ostensibly to purchase a holiday home but which the husband in fact used to purchase shares).

(3) The cohabitee seeking to set aside the charge must show that the other cohabitee has procured the suretyship by misrepresentation, undue influence or other legal wrong (see further *below*). It is not enough to show only that the 'surety lacked an adequate understanding' (*per* Scott LJ in the Court of Appeal) or that she was not properly advised as to the effect of the mortgage.

(4) The basis upon which the lender is affected by the borrower's misconduct is notice whether actual or constructive.

(5) Where the cohabitee seeking to set aside the mortgage is a wife the lender is put on inquiry by the combination of two factors: (c) the fact that the transaction is on its face not to the financial advantage of the wife; and (b) there is a substantial risk in transactions of that kind that, in procuring the wife to act as surety, the husband has committed a legal or equitable wrong that entitles the wife to set the transaction aside (429f).

(6) Although each case will turn upon its own facts a personal interview with the wife signing as surety will usually be required before the lender can escape the consequences of the husband's behaviour. Lord Browne-Wilkinson regarded it as 'essential because a number of the decided cases show that written warnings are often not read and are sometimes intercepted by the husband' (431c). The author's view is that the lender would also be wise to follow up the interview with a letter to the cohabitee confirming the advice given.

(7) In *Barclays Bank v O'Brien* the wife believed that the security was limited to £60,000. In fact it secured a much greater debt. In the Court of Appeal the charge was held to be unenforceable against her save to the extent of £60,000. It seems that the House of Lords considered that it should not be enforceable at all (432f) but the position is not entirely clear.

The husband's misconduct   As stated, the first step in any attempt to set aside the transaction is to show misconduct on the husband's part sufficient to entitle the wife to have it set aside. The conduct relied upon is either misrepresentation or undue influence (as to forgery, see *below*). Undue influence falls into two categories: presumed or actual. Undue influence will be presumed where there is a relationship of trust and confidence between the complainant and the wrongdoer. In all other cases it is necessary for the claimant to prove affirmatively that the wrongdoer exerted undue influence on the complainant to enter into the particular transaction which is impugned (ie it is necessary to prove actual undue influence).

The relationship of husband and wife does not of itself raise a presumption of undue influence. A wife must therefore prove that such trust and confidence as is necessary for presumed undue influence did in fact exist or that there was actual undue influence (see *O'Brien* at 423).

A person who relies upon *presumed* undue influence must also show that the transaction was to his manifest disadvantage (*National West-minster Bank v Morgan* [1985] 1 All ER 821, HL). A claimant who proves *actual* undue influence, *or misrepresentation*, is not under a further burden of proving that the transaction induced by the undue influence or misrepresentation was manifestly disadvantageous. He is entitled as of right to have it set aside as against the person exercising undue influence (*CIBC Mortgages plc v Pitt* [1993] 4 All ER 433):

> Actual undue influence is a species of fraud. Like any other victim of fraud, a person who has been induced to carry out a transaction which he did not freely and knowingly enter into is entitled to have that transaction set aside as of right . . . A man guilty of fraud is no more entitled to argue that the transaction was beneficial to the person defrauded than is a man who has procured a transaction by misrepresentation. The effect of the wrongdoer's conduct is to prevent the wronged party from bringing a free will and properly informed mind to bear on the proposed transaction which accordingly must be set aside in equity as a matter of justice.
>
> I therefore hold that a claimant who proves actual undue influence is not under the further burden of proving that the transaction induced by undue influence was manifestly disadvantageous: he is entitled as of right to have it set aside.

Signature to mortgage a forgery

There are now many cases where one spouse, let us say the husband, who is the joint owner of the property with his wife, forges his wife's signature on the mortgage deed. In these circumstances the mortgage is ineffective as a legal charge but the husband's conduct does have the effect of creating a valid equitable charge in the lender's favour on the husband's share in the proceeds of sale in the house (*Ahmed v Kendrick and Ahmed* [1988] 2 FLR 22, CA).

The lender could apply to the court for an order for sale *of that beneficial interest* but would be unlikely to be able to sell it. Hence, lenders who cannot enforce the mortgage because of the forgery tend to bring proceedings for the money loaned and interest and costs. Once a judgment has been obtained a charging order is applied for in respect of the husband's share in the proceeds of sale with the intention of subsequently applying for an order for sale of the house pursuant to s30 of the Law of Property Act 1925. In *Midland Bank plc v Pike* [1988] 2 All ER 434, QBD it was held that a person entitled to a charging order on the share of a co-owner in the proceeds of sale of land has a proprietary interest in that share and is a 'person interested' for the purposes of s30 as much as the co-owner himself. He may therefore apply for an order for sale.

At the hearing of the application for the charging order *nisi* to be made absolute the wife, who is not unnaturally seeking to divorce her husband, requests the court to adjourn the matter to be heard at the same time as her application for ancillary relief in which she is seeking a property transfer order. If the application for ancillary relief was made after the charging order *nisi* the court will almost certainly refuse the wife's application and make the charging order absolute. The competing equities between the lender and the wife will be determined on the application for sale made by the lender pursuant to s30 of the Law of Property Act 1925 (*First National Securities v Hegerty* [1984] 3 All ER 641, CA; *Abbey National plc v Moss* (1994) 26 HLR 249). Where however the wife's application for ancillary relief is made before the charging order *nisi*, the court is more likely to order the application to be adjourned to be heard with the application for financial relief (*Harman v Glencross* [1986] 1 All ER 513, CA; *Austin-Fell v Austin-Fell* [1990] 2 All ER 455

(*Quaere*: whether it is necessary for the lender to apply for a charging order at all. Is the equitable charge created by the husband's behaviour not sufficient to permit the lender to apply for an order for sale of the house; see *First National Securities* at 644h–645a; *Abbey National plc v Moss* (1993) 26 HLR 249.)

Lender misrepresenting the mortgage

> The relationship between banker and customer is not one which ordinari y gives rise to a presumption of undue influence; and . . . in the ordinary course of banking business a banker can explain the nature of the proposed transaction without laying himself open to a charge of undue influence (*National Westminster Bank v Morgan* [1985] 1 All ER 821, HL per Lord Scarman at 892j).

A bank is of course under a duty to ensure that it does not negligent y misstate the effect of the mortgage. In particular, where the mortgage covers further advances this should be explained to the customer. If the bank is negligent the customer will be entitled to damages for any loss suffered but the mortgage will not be set aside unless the customer can show that the bank has taken unfair advantage of him (*Cornish v Midland Bank plc* [1985] 3 All ER 513).

Counterclaims

The existence of a counterclaim for a sum of money, however valid, and even if it exceeds the amount of the debt to the lender, will not by itself defeat the lender's claim to possession (*National Westminster Bank plc v Skelton* [1993] 1 All ER 242, CA at 249c). This principle rests on the rule that a lender is entitled to possession at any time after the mortgage is executed (see 'Introduction', p367). The principle is applicable both where the counterclaim is a mere counterclaim *and* where it is a counterclaim for *unliquidated* damages which if established would give rise to a right by way of equitable set-off (*Skelton* at 249f; whether or not a claim to a liquidated sum discharges the debt is undecided).

The principle is not confined to principal debtors but applies where the mortgage has been executed by a person guaranteeing the debts of a third party (*Ashley Guarantee plc v Zacaria* [1993] 1 All ER 254):

> I can see no distinction in principle between a case where the mortgagor is the principal debtor of the mortgagee and one where he is only a guarantor. In each case the mortgagee has, as an incident of his estate in the land, a right to possession of the mortgaged property. In each case the cross-claims

cannot be unilaterally appropriated in discharge of the mortgage debt. The fact that in the latter case the mortgagor is not primarily liable for payment of the debt is immaterial. When he comes to be made liable his position vis-a-vis the appropriation of the cross-claims is at best no different from, and certainly cannot be better than, that of a mortgagor who is the primary debtor.

Further, it is highly unlikely that the existence of a counterclaim will entitle the court to exercise its powers under the Administration of Justice Act 1970 to adjourn, suspend, etc (p395, note (7)).

Discretionary powers: Administration of Justice Act 1970

If the court is satisfied that the lender is entitled to possession under the terms of the mortgage it must (unless the agreement under which the money was lent is a 'regulated agreement' within the meaning of the Consumer Credit Act 1974 (see p368)) go on to consider s36(1)–(4) of the Administration of Justice Act 1970 which is in the following terms:

> **36.**—(1) Where the mortgagee under a mortgage of land which consists of or includes a dwelling house brings an action in which he claims possession of the mortgaged property . . . the court may exercise any of the powers conferred on it by subsection (2) below *if it appears to the court that in the event of its exercising the power the mortgagor is likely to be able within a reasonable period to pay any sums due under the mortgage or to remedy a default* consisting of a breach of any other obligation arising under or by virtue of the mortgage.
>
> (2) The court—
>   (a) may adjourn the proceedings, or
>   (b) on giving judgment, or making an order, for delivery of posses-sion of the mortgaged property, *or at any time before the execution* of such judgment or order, may—
>   (i) stay or suspend execution of the judgment or order, or
>   (ii) postpone the date for delivery of possession, for such period or periods as the court thinks reasonable.
>
> (3) Any such adjournment, stay, suspension or postponement as is referred to in subsection (2) above may be made subject to such conditions with regard to payment by the mortgagor of any sum secured by the mortgage or the remedying of any default as the court thinks fit.
>
> (4) The court may from time to time vary or revoke any condition imposed by virtue of this section.

Section 39 of the Administration of Justice Act 1970 provides as follows:

> **39.**—(1) In this Part of this Act [*ie Part IV, which includes section 36*]—
> 'dwelling house' includes any building or part thereof which is used as a dwelling;
> 'mortgage' includes a charge and 'mortgagor' or 'mortgagee' shall be construed accordingly;

'mortgagor' and 'mortgagee' includes any person deriving title under the original mortgagor or mortgagee.

(2) The fact that part of the premises comprised in a dwelling house is used as a shop or office or for business, trade or professional purposes shall not prevent the dwelling house from being a dwelling house for the purposes of this Part of this Act.

Notes:

(1) The court may not exercise its powers under s36 of the Administration of Justice Act 1970 by ordering an indefinite postponement of the case. The period for which the order is to be stayed or suspended must be defined or rendered ascertainable; for example for so long as the borrower pays off the arrears at so much per month plus the current mortgage repayments. See *Royal Trust Co of Canada v Markham* [1975] 1 WLR 1416.

(2) The borrower may apply for a stay etc under s36 of the Administration of Justice Act 1970 even where the lender is entitled to possession under the mortgage without showing any default on the part of the borrower: *Western Bank v Schindler* [1977] Ch 1. In that case, however, the court refused to exercise its discretion under s36 to stay or suspend the order because, although the borrower had not broken any term of the mortgage he had allowed a collateral insurance policy to lapse and thereby prejudiced the lender's interest.

(3) It is important to remember that the court may only exercise the powers conferred on it by s36(2) of the 1970 Act 'if it appears to the court that in the event of its exercising the power the mortgagor is likely to be able within a reasonable period to pay any sums due under the mortgage or to remedy a default' (eg see *Citibank Trust Ltd v Ayivor* [1987] 3 All ER 241 at 245). It is not proper, with a view ostensibly to clearing the arrears within a reasonable period, to make an order for payments which the defendant cannot afford and has no reasonable prospect of being able to afford within a reasonable time. It is also improper to make an order for payments which the defendant can afford but which will not be enough to pay off the arrears within a reasonable period and which will not also cover the current instalments (*First National Bank plc v Syed* [1991] 2 All ER 250, CA). The practice of some District Judges, particularly at times of rising house prices, to adjourn proceedings when there is no evidence of ability to pay within a reasonable period merely because there seems to be sufficient equity in the property to protect the lender (or because the principal sum is secured by an endowment policy: see *Citibank Ltd v Ayivor* at 246) is therefore wrong.

(4) The borrower should adduce evidence, either orally on oath or by way of affidavit, as to his means with the intention of showing that

he will be able to pay off the arrears within a reasonable period but the court may act without evidence on the basis of informal material (*Cheltenham & Gloucester BS v Grant* (1994) *The Independent* 23 May, CA). Any relevant documents should be produced at the hearing or exhibited to the affidavit. The borrower should always complete the Court Reply form (see also p83). Confirmation of the answers given together with any up-to-date information will provide the court with the necessary evidence to assist the borrower.

(5) Practice varies widely from court to court but a period of two years is usually the maximum period considered to be reasonable. The normal order made is for possession to be given within 28 days suspended upon condition that the arrears are paid off at the rate of £x per month plus the current payments as they fall due. See County Court Forms N29 (for a final order) and N31 (for a suspended order).

(6) In *Royal Trust Co of Canada v Markham* at 439 it was held that where there is clear evidence that a sale of the property is going to take place in the near future and that the price will cover all the sums due to the lender the court has jurisdiction to suspend etc an order for possession to allow the sale to take place. In *Target Home Loans Ltd v Clothier* [1994] 1 All ER 439 the court was more generous to the borrower. There was no evidence of an actual sale due to take place but the only way the borrower could pay off the arrears was by selling the property. The Court of Appeal appears to have considered that the prospect of achieving an early sale was greater if effected by the borrower while in occupation than by the lender if it had vacant possession. The order for possession was suspended for four months by the court at first instance and for a further three months by the Court of Appeal.

(7) The existence of a counterclaim does not affect the lender's legal right to possession. It is unlikely that this rule can be circumvented by the provisions of s36 of the 1970 Act but even if it can do so the borrower will only be able to forestall the order for possession where he can show that the counterclaim means that he is 'likely within a reasonable period' to pay off the arrears (an unlikely event in most cases) (see *Citibank Trust Ltd v Ayivor* at 246g).

In certain cases s8(1), (2) and (4) of the Administration of Justice Act 1973 must also be borne in mind:

8.—(1) Where by a mortgage of land which consists of or includes a dwelling house, or by any agreement between the mortgagee under such a mortgage and the mortgagor, the mortgagor is entitled or is to be permitted to pay the principal sum secured *by instalments or otherwise to defer payment* of it in whole or in part, but provision is also made for *earlier payment in the event of any default by the mortgagor or of a demand by the mortgagee or otherwise*, then for purposes of section 36 of the Administration of Justice

Act 1970 (under which a court has power to delay giving a mortgagee possession of the mortgaged property so as to allow the mortgagor a reasonable time to pay any sums due under the mortgage) a court may treat as due under the mortgage on account of the principal sum secured and of interest on it only such amounts as the mortgagor would have expected to be required to pay if there had been no such provision for earlier payment.

(2) A court shall not exercise by virtue of subsection (1) above the powers conferred by section 36 of the Administration of Justice Act 1970 unless it appears to the court not only that the mortgagor is likely to be able within a reasonable period to pay any amounts regarded (in accordance with subsection (1) above) as due on account of the principal sum secured, together with the interest on those amounts, but also that he is likely to be able by the end of that period to pay any further amounts that he would have expected to be required to pay by then on account of that sum and of interest on it if there had been no such provision as is referred to in subsection (1) above for earlier payment.

. . .

(4) For purposes of this section the expressions 'dwelling house', 'mortgage', 'mortgagee' and 'mortgagor' shall be construed in the same way as for the purposes of Part IV of the Administration of Justice Act 1970.

Notes:
(1) *Example*: A borrower borrows £20,000 from a building society which he repays at the rate of £200 per month but is two months in arrears. Under the terms of the mortgage the borrower must now repay the whole of the outstanding principal sum because he has defaulted. However, by virtue of s8 of the Administration of Justice Act 1973 the court may treat the sum due under the mortgage as being only £400.
(2) Section 8 of the 1973 Act has been held to apply where the interest payable under the mortgage was to be paid regularly but the principal was to be paid as a lump sum at an unspecified date after it had become formally due; ie a loan secured by a mortgage to be paid by the proceeds of a collateral insurance policy which will mature after a number of years (*Centrax Trusts Ltd v Ross* [1979] 2 All ER 952 and *Bank of Scotland v Grimes* [1985] 2 All ER 254).
(3) Section 8 of the 1973 Act does not however apply to a bank overdraft on a borrower's current account secured by a charge on the borrower's house because there is no express term deferring payment of the principal sum after it has become due. Usually the sum simply does not become due until the bank makes a written demand for it and up until that time there is no due date from which any deferment of payment can be made. If s8 were to apply in these circumstances the result would be 'to deprive banks who use the usual charge for security for an overdraft of any right of enforcement, as long as the debtor continued to pay interest on the capital lent' (*Habib Bank Ltd v Tailor* [1982] 1 WLR 1218, *per* Cumming-Bruce LJ).

Discretionary powers: Consumer Credit Act cases

Section 36 of the Administration of Justice Act 1970 (see *above*) does not apply to a mortgage securing an agreement which is a regulated agreement within the meaning of the Consumer Credit Act 1974 (s38A of the 1970 Act). The court's powers in consumer credit cases are contained in the 1974 Act and are twofold. First, it may make a 'time order' in relation to any sum owed, or any other breach of the agreement providing for payment of the arrears by instalments or for the remedying of the breach within a specified period. Secondly, it may suspend orders for possession and impose conditions in relation to any such order. In addition, the court has power to amend any agreement or security in consequence of a term of any order made. The relevant provisions are ss129, 130, 135 and 136 of the 1974 Act (see p398).

The test to be applied under these provisions is different to that which applies under the Administration of Justice Acts. The court does not have to be satisfied that the borrower 'is likely to be able within a reasonable period' to pay the sums due under the agreement. The court may make a time order under s129 or suspend an order under s135(1) if it appears to the court 'just to do so'.

However, consideration of what is 'just' includes consideration of the creditor's position as well as that of the debtor. Further, where as a result of the default the principal sum has become due the court will take into account that the section is directed at rescheduling the whole of the indebtedness under the regulated agreement, as well as the arrears and the current interest and if there is no prospect of the debtor being able to pay any part of the principal the court is unlikely to exercise its discretion in his favour (*First National Bank plc v Syed* [1991] 2 All ER 250, CA). The circumstances of the case were that there had been a fairly long history of default and sporadic payments on the defendants' part. There was no realistic, as opposed to merely speculative, prospect of improvement in the defendants' finances and the instalments that the defendants could afford were too little even to keep down the accruing interest on their account. There was no prospect whatsoever of being able to repay the principal without a sale of the house. The court therefore considered that it would not be just to require the plaintiff to accept the instalments offered by the defendants and upheld the order for possession.

The new reply form sent to defendants when a claim is made for possession (see p383), if completed, should give the District Judge the information he requires to come to a decision. However, that information should if necessary be updated at the hearing.

The creditor does not always claim the principal in addition to the arrears. He will only do so if he exercises a power in the agreement making the whole sum due in the event of default. It has been held (in the county court) that s129(2)(*a*) when taken with s136 gives the court the power to alter the contractual terms so as to reduce the monthly payments and interest payable under the agreement (*Cedar Holdings Ltd v Jenkins* (1987) Legal Action, October 19; *Green Book*, note to s129). However, it is difficult to see how these powers can apply in relation to future payments due under the agreement as they are only exercisable in relation to 'sums owed' (see s129(2)(*a*) and s130(2)). The decision has been criticised (see *Consumer Credit Legislation*, Professor Goode, Vo: I, para 280 and Vol III, para 137 (note to s136)) and has been rejected in other county court cases (see *Green Book*, note to section 129 or *Ashbroom Facilities v Bodley*, unreported). Note also that the debtor may seek to challenge the terms of the agreement by arguing that it is an 'extortionate credit bargain' (see p383).

The borrower may make an application for a time order pursuant to s129(1)(*b*) without waiting for the lender to commence proceedings. The application is made by originating application (CCR Ord 49, r4(5); *Green Book*, p 827; see that rule for the contents of the application and County Court Form N440).

On the application of 'any person affected' by a time order or by a provision included under s135(1) the court may vary or revoke the order (s130(6); s135(4)).

Consumer Credit Act 1974

Time orders

129.—(1) If it appears to the court just to do so—

    (*a*) . . .

    (*b*) on an application *made by a debtor or hirer* under this paragraph after service on him of—

        (i) a default notice, or

        (ii) a notice under section 76(1) or section 98(1); or

    (*c*) in an action brought *by a creditor or owner* to enforce a regulated agreement or any security, or recover possession of any goods or land to which a regulated agreement relates, the court may make an order under this section (a 'time order').

(2) A time order shall provide for one or both of the following, as the court considers just—

    (*a*) the payment by the debtor or hirer or any surety of *any sum owed* under a regulated agreement or a security by such instalments, payable at such times, as the court, having regard to the means of the debtor or hirer and any surety, considers reasonable;

    (*b*) the remedying by the debtor or hirer of any breach of a regulated agreement (other than non-payment of money) within such period as the court may specify.

Supplemental provisions about time orders

130.—(1) Where in accordance with rules of court an offer to pay any sum by instalments is made by the debtor or hirer and accepted by the creditor or owner, the court may in accordance with rules of court make a time order under section 129(2)(*a*) giving effect to the offer without hearing evidence of means.

(2) In the case of a hire-purchase or conditional sale agreement *only*, a time order under section 129(2)(*a*) may deal with sums which, although not payable by the debtor at the time the order is made, would if the agreement continued in force become payable under it subsequently.

. . .

(5) Without prejudice to anything done by the creditor or owner before the commencement of the period specified in a time order made under section 129(2)(*b*) ('the relevant period')—

    (*a*) he shall not while the relevant period subsists take in relation to the agreement any action such as is mentioned in section 87(1):

    (*b*) where—

        (i) a provision of the agreement ('the secondary provision') becomes operative only on breach of another provision of the agreement ('the primary provision'), and

        (ii) the time order provides for the remedying of such a breach of the primary provision within the relevant period;

    (*c*) if while the relevant period subsists the breach to which the order relates is remedied it shall be treated as not having occurred.

(6) On the application of any person affected by a time order, the court may vary or revoke the order.

Power to impose conditions, or suspend operation of order

    135.—(1) If it considers it just to do so, the court may in an order made by it in relation to a regulated agreement include provisions—

    (*a*) making the operation of any term of the order conditional on the doing of specified acts by *any party* to the proceedings;

    (*b*) *suspending* the operation of any term of the order either—

        (i) until such time as the court subsequently directs or,

        (ii) until the occurrence of a specified act or omission.

. . .

(4) On the application of any person affected by a provision included under subsection (1), the court may vary the provision.

Power to vary agreements and securities

    136.—The court may in an order made by it under this Act include such provision as it considers just for amending any agreement or security in consequence of a term of the order.

Relationship between lender and borrower's tenant

As has been noted (p381) it is now a requirement of the County Court Rules that the plaintiff send a notice to the property not less than 14 days before the hearing notifying the occupiers of the hearing. This should help to prevent cases arising where the occupiers are not aware of the case until bailiffs seek to enforce the order for possession. Any occupier so notified of the hearing who wishes to oppose the claim should apply to be joined as a party pursuant to CCR Ord 15, r3 (see p269).

The rights of tenants in occupation are considered below.

Where tenancy granted after the mortgage

By statute a borrower in possession has the power to grant certain leases so as to bind the lender (s99 of the Law of Property Act 1925). However, building society and most other mortgages exclude this statutory power. A lease made outside the provisions of s99 of the 1925 Act or contrary to the provisions of the mortgage deed will be binding on both the borrower and his tenant by estoppel but as between the tenant and the lender the lease is of no effect. Even a protected or statutory tenant under the Rent Act 1977 has no rights as against a lender where the tenancy has been granted without the consent of the lender (*Britannia Building Society v Earl* [1990] 2 All ER 469, CA). In any such case the tenant will not be able to resist proceedings for possession brought by the lender once it is entitled to possession against the borrower. Nor is the tenant entitled to ask the court to exercise its powers to suspend, etc the order for possession under s36 of the Administration of Justice Act 1970 (*Britannia Building Society v Earl*).

Where the lender's consent in writing is required the onus of proving that consent was given is upon the tenant. Mere inaction on the part of the lender after it has become aware of the unlawful tenancy does not amount to consent (*Taylor v Ellis* [1960] 1 All ER 549).

A discharge of a mortgage and its replacement with an almost identical charge does not make the tenancy lawful (*Walthamstow Building Society v Davies* (1991) *The Times*, November 11).

However, it is open to the lender to accept the tenant as its own tenant and acceptance of rent by the lender raises an implication of a new tenancy, particularly where the payment is made pursuant to a notice from the lender to pay rent (*Chatsworth Properties Ltd v Effiom* [1971] 1 WLR 144). A new tenancy with the lender destroys the old tenancy (*Taylor v Ellis*).

Lenders should not take summary proceedings pursuant to CCR Ord 24 or RSC Ord 113 to evict tenants of mortgagors. The claim for possession should either be made in the claim against the borrower or by separate fixed date action (*London Goldhawk Building Society v Eminer* (1977) 242 EG 462).

Where tenancy granted before the mortgage

If the borrower creates a tenancy before the mortgage, the tenancy will, in most cases, be binding on the lender. If the land is registered, the lender is deemed to have notice of the tenancy, by virtue of s70(1)(*k*) of the Land Registration Act 1925 in the case of a lease granted for a term of 21 years (ie validly granted) or by s70(1)(*g*) in other cases if the tenant is in occupation unless enquiry has been made of the tenant and the right not disclosed. The relevant date for determining whether or not the tenancy is protected by actual occupation and so has priority over the mortgage pursuant to s70(1)(*g*) is the date when the mortgage is created and not the date when it is registered (*Abbey National Building Society v Cann* [1990] 1 All ER 1085).

Where the property is unregistered the tenant will have a similar prior right to the lender (*Universal Permanent Building Society v Cooke* [1951] 2 All ER 893, CA).

Land Registration Act 1925, s 70(1)

70.—(1) All registered land shall, unless under the provisions of this Act the contrary is expressed on the register, be deemed to be subject to such of the following overriding interests as may be for the time being subsisting to reference thereto, and such interests shall not be treated as incumbrances within the meaning of this Act, (that is to say):

. . .

> (g) The rights of every person in actual occupation of the land or in receipt of rents and profits thereof, save where enquiry is made of such person and the rights are not disclosed;

. . .

> (k) Leases granted for a term not exceeding 21 years.

The fact that the tenancy is binding upon the lender does not mean that the lender cannot in any circumstances obtain possession from the tenant. The strict legal position is that the mortgage operates as a concurrent lease. The lender is therefore entitled to possession as against the borrower the moment the mortgage deed is signed (or, where there is a clause in the deed to that effect, when the mortgagor defaults) and is the owner of the reversion immediately expectant on the termination of the tenant's tenancy (ss 85, 86 and 87 of the Law of Property Act 1925). The tenant in practice pays his rent to the person who granted him the tenancy (the borrower) but this is only because the lender permits it.

If the lender seeks possession he therefore takes the same steps that the original landlord/borrower would take in order to recover possession. If the tenancy is a protected tenancy he serves a notice to quit (if possible; p 139) and if the tenancy is an assured tenancy or an assured shorthold he serves an appropriate notice under the Housing Act 1988 (see Chapters 6 and 7).

Section 45 of the 1988 Act states that except where the context otherwise requires 'landlord' includes any person from time to time deriving title under the original landlord and also includes, in relation to a dwelling house, any person other than a tenant who is, or but for the existence of an assured tenancy would be, entitled to possession of the dwelling house. There is a similar provision in s 152 of the Rent Act 1977. The lender is therefore treated as 'the landlord' for the purpose of either Act and may rely upon any ground that is available to 'the landlord'. In each Act there are also particular provisions that apply to mortgagors:

Rent Act 1977 A lender under a mortgage created by deed before the commencement of the tenancy, who is entitled to exercise a power of sale under the mortgage or s 101 of the Law of Property Act 1925, may (if the Rent Act 1977 applies to the tenancy) rely upon Cases 11, 12 or 20 of Sched 15 to the 1977 Act if possession of the dwelling house is required for the purpose of disposing of it with vacant possession in exercise of that power (see Sched 15, Part V, para 2(*f*)). The lender must obviously show that the requirements of the Case relied upon have been satisfied.

Housing Act 1988   Where the tenancy is an assured tenancy under the Housing Act 1988 the lender, seeking to obtain possession for the purpose of disposing of it with vacant possession in exercise of the power of sale, may rely upon Ground 2 of Sched 2 to the 1988 Act if either:

(1) a Ground 1 notice was given not later than the beginning of the tenancy (see p352);

(2) or the court is satisfied that it is just and equitable to dispense with the requirement of notice.

Where the assured tenancy is for a fixed term the lender may recover possession under this ground during the fixed term if the terms of the tenancy make provision for it to be brought to an end under Ground 2 (whether that provision takes the form of a provision for re-entry, for forfeiture, for determination by notice or otherwise) (s7(6) of the 1988 Act; see p115).

Costs

A lender who successfully takes possession proceedings is almost invariably entitled to add the costs of the action to his security under the terms of the mortgage. When making the order the District Judge or master will often say words such as 'costs to be added to the security'. But where the lender is under-secured an order for costs should be asked for. Where an order for costs is made they are subject to taxation in the normal way but in exercising its discretion the court has to give effect to the contractual right to add costs to the security (*Gomba Holdings (UK) Ltd v Minories Finance Ltd (No 2)* [1992] 4 All ER 588, CA). The borrower may therefore challenge items of costs but as the lender is contractually entitled to costs on an indemnity basis it is for the borrower to show that any particular item was unreasonably incurred or unreasonable in amount.

For costs in claims involving third parties, see *Parker-Tweedale v Dunbar Bank plc (No 2)* [1990] 2 All ER 588.

Interest on judgment debts

Although as a general rule a plaintiff in the county court may recover interest on a judgment debt for a sum of not less than £5,000 such interest is not payable where the relevant judgment:

(1) is given in proceedings to recover money due under an agreement regulated by the Consumer Credit Act 1974; or

(2) grants the mortgagee under a mortgage of land which consists of or includes a dwelling house a suspended order for possession.

(See s74 of the County Courts Act 1984 and r2 of the County Court (Interest on Judgment Debts) Order 1991). The lender will of course retain its contractual right to interest.

Execution

Enforcement of the order may be effected in the same way as possession orders against a tenant. However, in the High Court, if the possession order has been suspended on conditions leave to issue execution is required (RSC Ord 46, r2(1)(*d*)). The application must be supported by an affidavit (for contents see Ord 46, r4(2)). The borrower must be given the opportunity of being heard (*Fleet Mortgage and Investment Co Ltd v Lower Maisonette, 46 Eaton Place Ltd* [1972] 2 All ER 737). Special rules as to service of the application apply where the acknowledgment of service was filed (see *White Book*, notes 46/4/2 and 88/2–7/19).

Chapter 27

Unlawful Eviction and Harassment: The Occupier's Remedies

A person who unlawfully evicts or harasses an occupier of residential premises commits an offence under s1 of the Protection from Eviction Act 1977 (see p258). That provision does not give the occupier a civil remedy in respect of any such unlawful action, but neither does it take away any such remedy that he might have (s1(5); *McCall v Abelesz* [1976] 1 All ER 727, CA).

The principle civil remedy of a tenant, or other occupier, who has been unlawfully evicted or who is being harassed is an injunction requiring the landlord to permit the tenant to return to live in the premises and to discontinue the harassment. Where the landlord actually goes into possession or puts someone else into possession the tenant may obtain an order for possession in summary proceedings (*Borg v Rogers* [1981] LAG *Bulletin* 53; see p361).

An occupier of residential premises who has been unlawfully evicted or harassed may also claim damages. These may be claimed in contract or tort or under ss27 and 28 of the Housing Act 1988. As will be seen *below*, damages awarded under the 1988 Act are based upon the profit that the landlord obtains by evicting the tenant and can, depending on the expert evidence, be substantial. They are only awarded where the tenant is not restored to the property before a certain point in time (see notes(5) and (7), p416). As a result there has been an increasing tendency, since the introduction of the 1988 Act, for tenants only to claim damages and not to seek injunctions.

Basis of the claim   A tenant's claim for an injunction or damages is based upon the covenant for quiet enjoyment or the covenant not to derogate from the tenant's grant. If not expressed in a tenancy agreement these covenants will be implied as a matter of law. An unlawful eviction also constitutes a trespass giving rise to a claim in tort. Where the tenant is a statutory tenant the covenants in the tenancy are carried over from the protected tenancy into the statutory tenancy by s3 of the Rent Act 1977.

A licensee may also seek an injunction to prevent the licensor from excluding him from the premises in breach of contract (*Millennium*

Productions Ltd v Winter Garden Theatre (London) Ltd [1946] 1 All ER 678 *per* Lord Greene MR; *Hounslow London Borough Council v Twickenham Garden Development Ltd* [1971] Ch 233). Where the eviction is unlawful by virtue of s3 of the Protection from Eviction Act 1977 (see p253), an actionable tort is committed which gives the occupier a right to claim an injunction (*Warder v Cooper* [1970] 1 Ch 495; *Love v Herrity* [1991] 2 EGLR 44).

An occupier of residential premises who has been unlawfully evicted or harassed may also claim damages.

Examples of harassment   The following are examples where the landlord has not actually evicted the tenant but where he has been found in breach of the covenant for quiet enjoyment: where the landlord removed doors and windows from the premises (*Lavender v Betts* [1942] 2 All ER 72); where the gas and electricity were cut off causing the tenant to leave (*Perera v Vandiyar* [1953] 1 WLR 672); where the landlord failed to pay the electricity bill so that it was cut off (*McCall v Abelesz* [1976] QB 585); where the landlord knocked on the tenant's door, shouted threats of physical eviction and wrote letters threatening immediate eviction (*Kenny v Preen* [1963] 1 QB 499); and where there were extensive building works (*Mira v Aylmer Square Investment Ltd* [1990] EGLR 45).

Where the harassment reaches such a level that the occupier is forced to leave he will be treated as having been evicted and will be entitled to claim damages accordingly (*Sampson v Floyd* [1989] 2 EGLR 49; *Dowkes v Athelston* (1993); see *below*, p421).

Injunctions in the county court

County court jurisdiction

An application for an injunction seeking to restrain the landlord from keeping the tenant out or from harassing the tenant may be made in the county court, whatever the rateable value of the premises and notwithstanding there is no other claim (ss15 and 38 of the County Courts Act 1984). However, if the occupier is relying upon an agreement for a lease so that he needs to seek specific performance (see p8) he may only bring proceedings in the county court if the value of the land (ie the value of the freehold interest) does not exceed the county court limit, currently £30,000 (s23(*d*) of the County Courts Act 1984; and see note in the *Green Book* to that section).

Which county court and which judge?

The application should be made in the court for the district in which the land is situated (CCR Ord 4, r3). If the application is made in the wrong court the judge may transfer the proceedings to the proper court, order the proceedings to continue where they are, or order the proceedings to be struck out (CCR Ord 16, r2).

The application should be made to the circuit judge, not the district judge (r6(2)).

Ex parte applications

An *ex parte* application is one that is made by one party in the absence of the other and may be made prior to the commencement of proceedings. Such an application should only be made in urgent cases (CCR Ord 13, r6(4)). However, applications in unlawful eviction cases (although not necessarily in harassment cases) are invariably urgent, for two reasons:

(1) the plaintiff has been evicted from his home and needs somewhere to live; and

(2) the defendant may relet the property to someone else unless the plaintiff takes quick action.

The difficulties that can arise are demonstrated by the case of *Love v Herrity* [1991] 2 EGLR 44. Between the eviction and the application to the court for an injunction, the landlord relet the property to someone else. An order requiring the landlord to remove the new tenant would have been unenforceable because the landlord had no right to possession against the new tenant and so was not made. The court, therefore, made a declaration that the original tenant was entitled to possession as against the landlord and gave liberty to apply to join the new tenant for the purpose of obtaining possession. In similar circumstances, the displaced tenant is probably best advised to seek an order for possession in summary possession proceedings under Order 24, with both the landlord and new tenant joined as defendants (see reference to *Borg v Rogers above*, p404).

> *Application for injunction; CCR Ord 13, r6*
>
> **6.**—(1) An application for the grant of an injunction may be made by any party to an action or matter before or after the trial or hearing, whether or not a claim for the injunction was included in that party's particulars of claim, originating application, petition, counterclaim or third party notice, as the case may be.
>
> (2) Except where the district judge has power under Ord 21, rule 5 or otherwise to hear and determine the proceedings in which the application is made, the application shall be made to the judge and rule 1(6) shall not apply.
>
> (3) The application shall be made in the appropriate prescribed form and shall—
>
> > (*a*) state the terms of the injunction applied for; and
> >
> > (*b*) be supported by an affidavit in which the grounds for making the application are set out,
>
> and a copy of the affidavit and a copy of the application shall be served on the party against whom the injunction is sought not less than 2 days before the hearing of the application.

Form 53: Application for injunction

Order 13, rule 6(3), Order 47, rule 8(2)

[Title – Form N.16]

(Seal)

Notes on completion
Tick whichever box applies

(1) Enter the full name of the person making the application

(2) Enter the full name of the person the injunction is to be directed to

(3) Set out here the proposed restraining orders (If the defendant is a limited company delete the wording in brackets and insert "Whether by its servants, agents, officers or otherwise"

(4) Set out here any proposed mandatory orders requiring acts to be done

(5) Set out here any further terms asked for including provision for costs

(6) Enter the names of all persons who have sworn affidavits in support of this application

(7) Enter the names and addresses of all persons upon whom it is intended to serve this application

(8) Enter the full name and address for service and delete as required

☐ By application in pending proceedings
☐ In the matter of the Domestic Violence and Matrimonial Proceedings Act 1976
The Plaintiff (Applicant/Petitioner)[1]
applies to the court for an injunction order in the following terms:
That the Defendant (Respondent)[2]
be forbidden (whether by himself or by instructing or encouraging any other person)[3] *[from excluding the plaintiff from the premises at [state address of the property] and from interfering with her quiet enjoyment of the said premises]*

And that the Defendant (Respondent)[4] *[shall forthwith permit the plaintiff to return to the said premises]*
And that[5]

The grounds of this application are set out as in the sworn statement(s) of[6]
This (these) sworn statement(s) is (are) served with this application.

This application is to be served upon[7]

This application is filed by[8]
(the Solicitors for) the Plaintiff (Applicant/Petitioner) whose address for service is

Signed   **Dated**

This section to be completed by the court

*Name and address of the person application is directed to

To*
of

This application will be heard by the (District) Judge
at
on   the   day   of   199   at   o'clock
If you do not attend at the time shown the court may make an injunction order in your absence
If you do not fully understand this application you should go to a Solicitor, Legal Advice Centre or a Citizens' Advice Bureau

The Court Office at
is open from 10am to 4pm. When corresponding with the court, address all forms and letters to the Chief Clerk and quote the case number

[Text in large italics supplied by the author]

Injunction Order—Record of Hearing   **Case No ... .**

On................. the ....day of.......................................199....
Before H   Honour (District) Judge ....
The court was sitting at ....
....

The ☐ **Plaintiff** ☐ **Applicant** ☐ **Petitioner**   **(Name)** ....
was ☐ represented by Counsel
☐ represented by a Solicitor
☐ in person

The ☐ **Defendant** ☐ **Respondent**   **(Name)** ....
was ☐ represented by Counsel
☐ represented by a Solicitor
☐ in person
☐ did not appear having been given notice of this hearing
☐ not given notice of this hearing

The court read the affidavit(s) of
☐ the Plaintiff/Applicant/Petitioner   sworn on ....
☐ the Defendant/Respondent   sworn on ....
And of ....sworn on ....
....

The court heard spoken evidence on oath from
....
....

The Plaintiff (Applicant Petitioner) gave an undertaking (through his counsel or solicitor) promising to pay any damages ordered by the court if it later decides that the Defendant/Respondent has suffered loss or damage as a result of this order.*

Delete this paragraph if the court does not require this undertaking

Signed   **Dated**

(Judge's Clerk)

Reproduced by kind permission of The Solicitors' Law Stationery Society Ltd

(3A) Where an order is sought *ex parte* before a copy of the application has been served on the other party, the affidavit shall explain why the application is so made and a copy of any order made *ex parte* shall be served with the application and affidavit in accordance with paragraph (3).

(4) An application may not be made before the issue of the summons, originating application or petition by which the action or matter is to be commenced except where the case is one of urgency, and in that case—

(a) the affidavit in support of the application shall show that the action or matter is one which the court to which the application is made has jurisdiction to hear and determine, and (*b*) the injunction applied for shall, if granted, be on terms providing for the issue of the summons, originating application or petition in the court granting the application and on such other terms, if any, as the court thinks fit.

(4A) Paragraph 4(*a*) and (*b*) shall apply, with the necessary modifications, where an application for an injunction is made by a defendant in a case of urgency before issuing a counterclaim or cross-application.

(5) Unless otherwise directed, every application not made *ex parte* shall be heard in open court.

(6) Except where the case is one of urgency, a draft of the injunction shall be prepared beforehand by the party making an application to the judge under paragraph (1) and, if the application is granted, the draft shall be submitted to the judge by whom the application was heard and shall be settled by him.

(7) The injunction, when settled, shall be forwarded to the proper officer for filing.

The application should be made in the appropriate prescribed form (County Court Form N16A; Form 53 of this book, p407–8) and should state the terms of the injunction applied for (r6(3)(*a*)). It should be supported by an affidavit (r6(3)(*b*): Form 55, p412) which should:

(1) show that the court has jurisdiction to hear the application (r6(4)(*a*));
(2) state the grounds upon which the application is made; and
(3) explain why the application is made *ex parte* (r6(3A)).

As stated *above*, the application may be made before commencement of proceedings (r6(4)). It is possible to obtain an *ex parte* injunction without first preparing a draft of the order (r6(6)). However, drafting an order is no more difficult than drafting an application and it will be a rare case where the case is so urgent that a draft order could not first be prepared, even if only by hand. A draft injunction is to be found on p411 (Form 54; on County Court Form N16).

The rules state that an application should be filed within a reasonable time before it is heard 'unless the court otherwise directs' (CCR Ord 13, r1(3)), but in these cases a reasonable time will often be just before the hearing. It is, therefore, possible to obtain an *ex parte* injunction by turning up at court with an application, short affidavit and draft order, although the court should be telephoned in advance to notify the staff of the intention to make the application.

In ignorance of the rules, county court staff sometimes require the applicant to issue proceedings and to pay the necessary fee before the papers will be put before the judge. In order to avoid any difficulty it is therefore worth drafting particulars of claim (Form 56, p413) and issuing the proceedings if time will allow. If there really has been no opportunity to do so, the legal representative should point out the above rules and politely insist upon the matter being put before the judge. If necessary, ask to speak to the Chief Clerk.

The application is heard in chambers 'unless allowed or authorised to be made otherwise' (CCR Ord 13, r1(4); r6(5)).

If the application is granted, it will be on terms providing for the issue of the summons in the court granting the application (if it has not already been issued) and on such other terms as the court thinks fit (r6(4)(b). The tenant will always be required to give an undertaking as to damages, the effect of which should be explained to the tenant in advance. As part of his order, the judge will usually fix a return date for an *inter partes* hearing. If not, he will give liberty to the defendant to apply for a discharge of the injunction on short notice. Even where he makes ro such provision, the defendant is always at liberty to apply, *ex parte* if necessary, although it will be a rare case where an order discharging an injunction will be made without notice to the tenant.

Injunctions on notice

Where the matter is not so urgent the plaintiff should issue proceedings by filing with the court a request for a summons together with:
   (1) the particulars of claim;
   (2) an application for an interim injunction;
   (3) an affidavit in support; and
   (4) a draft order.

An extra copy of each of the above four documents should be prepared in respect of each defendant (CCR Ord 6, r1(4)). Service should take place not less than two days before the hearing (Ord 13, r1(2)).

When drafting the Particulars of Claim at this stage, the plaintiff will be unlikely to be able to give full particulars of the damages claimed. It is, therefore, suggested that a general claim be made and that the particulars be amended subsequently to provide all the details required (see Form 56, p413; and further the section *below* on damages).

The application for the interim injunction (whether as an original injunction or the return date following upon an *ex parte* injunction) will be heard by the judge in open court unless otherwise directed (CCR Ord 13, r6(2) and (5)). The general principles governing the granting of interim injunctions will apply, ie can the plaintiff demonstrate that there is a serious issue to be tried, would damages be an adequate compensation for any loss that he may suffer and where does the balance of convenience lie (*American Cyanamid Co v Ethicon Ltd* [1975] AC 396)? In practice, this means that if the plaintiff can show that he is an occupier of residential premises who has been put out otherwise than by proceedings in court he will almost invariably be granted an order compelling the landlord to allow him to return (*Warder v Cooper* [1970] 1 Ch 495). But compare the position when the landlord has re-let the property (p406—reference to *Love v Herrity*).

Form 54: Injunction

Order 13, rule 6

Injunction Order	In the
	County Court

Plaintiff	**Case Number**	*Always quote this*
Between . . . . **Applicant**		
Petitioner	**Plaintiff's Ref**	
Defendant		
and . . . . **Respondent**	**Defendant's ref**	

To[*The name of the person the order is directed to*]

of [*The address of the person the order is directed to*]

For completion by the court
Issued on   **199**

Seal

If you do not obey this order you will be guilty of contempt of court and you may be sent to prison

On the   of   199   the court considered an application for an injunction

The Court ordered that [*The name of the person the order is directed to*]

is forbidden (Whether by himself or by instructing or encouraging any other person)
[*The terms of the restraining order. If the defendant is a limited company, delete the words in brackets and insert "whether by its servants, agents, officers or otherwise"*]

[*from excluding the Plaintiff from the premises at* [*state address of the property*] *and from interfering with her quiet enjoyment of the said premises*]

This order shall remain in force until (the   of
199   at   o'clock
unless before then it is revoked by a) further order of the court

And it is ordered that [*The name of the person the order is directed to*]

shall [*The terms of any orders requiring acts to be done*]
on or before [*Enter time (and place) as ordered*]

[*forthwith permit the Plaintiff to return to the said premises*]

It is further ordered that [*The terms of any other orders costs etc*]

Notices of further hearing [*Use when the order is temporary or ex parte otherwise delete*]

The court will re-consider the application and whether the order should continue at a further hearing at

on   the   day of   199   at   o'clock
If you do not attend at the time shown the court may make an injunction order in your absence
Your are entitle to apply to the court to re-consider the order before that day [*Delete if order made on notice*]

If you do not understand anything in this order you should go to a Solicitor, Legal Advice Centre or a Citizens' Advice Bureau

The Court Office at
is open from 10am to 4pm. Mon–Fri. When corresponding with the court, address all forms and letters to the Chief Clerk and quote the case number

Reproduced by kind permission of The Solicitors' Law Stationery Society Ltd

Form 55: Affidavit in support of application for interim injunction

IN THE   COUNTY COURT   Case No

BETWEEN

                                        Plaintiff

—AND—

                                        Defendant

I, [*state name and address of Plaintiff*] MAKE OATH and say as follows:

1. I make this affidavit in support of my application for an injunction compelling the Defendant to allow me to return to [*state address of premises*] and for an injunction preventing him from excluding me from the said property.

2. [In about February 1992 I became the Defendant's tenant at 2, Scone Street, Bakewell, Derbyshire ('the premises'). It was agreed orally between us that I would pay him a rent of £40 per week, payable on Mondays in advance. The Defendant does not live at the premises.

3. From the time I moved in I paid the rent every Monday. However, in early 1994 I lost my job and it has taken some time to sort out payment of housing benefit. I have not therefore been able to pay all the rent due. On 24 May 1994 I went away to Dundee for a long weekend to see my parents who live there. I returned to Bakewell on 29th May 1994 and on arriving at the premises found that the locks on the front door had been changed. I went around to the back of the property and noticed through a window that there was no sign of my clothes or possessions on the premises. It was too late to go to the Defendant's office but I immediately went to his house. Nobody was there. I had very little money on me and no family in Bakewell with whom I could stay. In the end a friend said I could sleep the night on her sofa.]

4. [I telephoned the Defendant's office this morning, 30 May, and was told by him that as I had not paid the rent he would not let me live at the premises. He told me that I could collect my belongings from his office. As stated above I have no family in Bakewell I can stay with and only a friend's sofa to sleep on.]

5. I therefore require an injunction as a matter of urgency and apply to the court for an order in the following terms:

(1) that the Defendant do forthwith permit me to return to the premises; and.

(2) that the Defendant whether by himself his servants or agents or otherwise howsoever be forbidden from excluding me from the premises or interfering with my quiet enjoyment of the premises.

SWORN

The procedure after the hearing is that the case is listed for a pre-trial review in the normal way. The plaintiff may then continue his claim for a permanent injunction and, if he so wishes, damages.

Service of the order; breach of the order

The order for an injunction is indorsed with a penal notice indicating that disobedience of the order amounts to contempt punishable by imprison-

Form 56: Particulars of claim—changing the locks

IN THE   COUNTY COURT   Case No

BETWEEN

                                                                    Plaintiff

—AND—

                                                                    Defendant

PARTICULARS OF CLAIM

1. The Defendant is the freehold or leasehold owner of a dwelling-house situate at and known as [*insert address of premises*] ('the premises').

2. By an oral agreement made on or about [*state date*] the Defendant agreed to let the premises to the Plaintiff on a weekly tenancy at a rent of £[*State amount of rent*] per week payable in advance each and every [*state day of week*].

3. It was an implied term of the said agreement that the Defendant would not interfere with the Plaintiff's quiet enjoyment of the premises.

4. On or about the [*insert date*] the Defendant, in breach of the said agreement and of the said implied term, changed the locks on the front door of the premises and thereby excluded the Plaintiff from the same. The Defendant refuses to allow the Plaintiff to re-enter the premises.

5. By reason of the matters aforesaid the Plaintiff has suffered loss and damage, inconvenience, frustration, vexation and distress.

AND the Plaintiff claims:

(1) An order that the Defendant do forthwith permit the Plaintiff to return to the premises;
(2) An order that the Defendant, whether by himself his servants or agents or otherwise howsoever be restrained from excluding the Plaintiff from the said premises or interfering with her quiet enjoyment of the said premises; and
(3) Damages including aggravated and exemplary damages and damages pursuant to sections 27 and 28 of the Housing Act 1988. [*Note that it will be necessary to amend the particulars after the injunction has been granted in order to fully particularise the claim, see p410*].

DATED

---

ment (see Form 54, p411). The order must be served personally on the party against whom the order has been made. Failure to obey the order can result in that person having to show the court why a committal order should not be made (CCR Ord 29). In order to save time the applicant can arrange for a process server to attend court to collect the injunction for service. Alternatively the applicant may serve the injunction but if violence is feared he should ask for a police officer to be present. An affidavit of service should be filed with the court (CCR Ord 7, r6(1)(*b*), County Court Form N215).

Injunctions in the High Court

High Court proceedings for injunctions are similar to county court practice. A plaintiff may apply *ex parte* for an injunction in cases of urgency by affidavit and if the application is made prior to the issue of a writ, the injunction will be granted on terms providing for the issue of the writ (RSC Ord 29, r1; *White Book*, 29/1/8). The injunction indorsed with the prescribed penal notice must be served personally. If the injunction is applied for on notice, the other party must be given at least two clear days' notice of the application (Ord 32, r3), unless leave is given for short notice.

Damages

The Housing Act 1988 substantially amended the law relating to damages that may be awarded to a residential occupier who has been unlawfully evicted or who has been so harassed by the landlord that he has been forced to leave. Damages are awarded 'in respect of his loss of the right to occupy' the dwelling as his residence (s27(3)). Section 27 sets out the circumstances in which damages are payable. Section 28 explains/directs how the damages are to be assessed.

Where the occupier has remained or returned to the property ss27 and 28 will not apply (see notes *below*), but he will be able to claim damages in contract or tort.

> *Housing Act 1988: entitlements to damages*
> 27.—(1) This section applies if, at any time after 9th June 1988, a landlord (in this section referred to as 'the landlord in default') or any person acting on behalf of the landlord in default unlawfully deprives the residential occupier of any premises of his occupation of the whole or part of the premises.
> (2) This section also applies if, at any time after 9th June 1988, a landlord in this section referred to as ('the landlord in default') or any person acting on behalf of the landlord in default—
> > (a) attempts unlawfully to deprive the residential occupier of any premises of his occupation of the whole or part of the premises, or
> > (b) knowing or having reasonable cause to believe that the conduct is likely to cause the residential occupier of any premises—
> > > (i) to give up his occupation of the premises or any part thereof, or
> > > (ii) to refrain from exercising any right or pursuing any remedy in respect of the premises or any part thereof, does acts like y to interfere with the peace or comfort of the residential occupier or members of his household, or persistently withdraws or withholds services reasonably required for the occupation of the premises as a residence and, as a result, the residential occupier gives up his occupation of the premises as a residence.
> (3) Subject to the following provisions of this section, where this section applies, the landlord in default shall, by virtue of this section, be liable to pay

to the former residential occupier, in respect of his loss of the right to occupy the premises in question as his residence, damages assessed on the basis set out in section 28 below.

(4) Any liability arising by virtue of subsection (3) above—

    (a) shall be in the nature of a liability in tort; and

    (b) subject to subsection (5) below, shall be in addition to any liability arising apart from this section (whether in tort, contract or otherwise).

(5) Nothing in this section affects the right of a residential occupier to enforce any liability which arises apart from this section in respect of his loss of the right to occupy premises as his residence; but damages shall not be awarded both in respect of such a liability and in respect of a liability arising by virtue of this section on account of the same loss.

(6) No liability shall arise by virtue of subsection (3) above if—

    (a) before the date on which proceedings to enforce the liability are finally disposed of, the former residential occupier is reinstated in the premises in question in such circumstances that he becomes again the residential occupier of them; or

    (b) at the request of the former residential occupier, a court makes an order (whether in the nature of an injunction or otherwise) as a result of which he is reinstated as mentioned in paragraph (a) above;

and, for the purposes of paragraph (a) above, proceedings to enforce a liability are finally disposed of on the earliest date by which the proceedings (including any proceedings on or in consequence of an appeal) have been determined and any time for appealing or further appealing has expired, except that if any appeal is abandoned, the proceedings shall be taken to be disposed of on the date of the abandonment.

(7) If, in proceedings to enforce a liability arising by virtue of subsection (3) above, it appears to the court—

    (a) that, prior to the event which gave rise to the liability, the conduct of the former residential occupier or any person living with him in the premises concerned was such that it is reasonable to mitigate the damages for which the landlord in default would otherwise be liable, or

    (b) that, before the proceedings were begun, the landlord in default offered to reinstate the former residential occupier in the premises in question and either it was unreasonable of the former residential occupier to refuse that offer or, if he had obtained alternative accommodation before the offer was made, it would have been unreasonable of him to refuse that offer if he had not obtained that accommodation, the court may reduce the amount of damages which would otherwise be payable to such amount as it thinks appropriate.

(8) In proceedings to enforce a liability arising by virtue of subsection (3) above, it shall be a defence for the defendant to prove that he believed, and had reasonable cause to believe—

    (a) that the residential occupier had ceased to reside in the premises in question at the time when he was deprived of occupation as mentioned in subsection (1) above or as the case may be, when the attempt was made or the acts were done as a result of which he gave up his occupation of those premises; or (*b*) that, where the liability would otherwise arise by virtue only cf the doing of acts or the withdrawal or withholding of service, he had reasonable grounds for doing the acts or withdrawing cr withholding the services in question.

(9) In this section—

    (*a*) 'residential occupier', in relation to any premises, has the same meaning as in section 1 of the 1977 Act;

    (*b*) 'the right to occupy', in relation to a residential occupier, includes any restriction on the right of another person to recover possession of the premises in question;

    (*c*) 'landlord', in relation to a residential occupier, means the persc n who, but for the occupier's right to occupy, would be entitled ˙o occupation of the premises and any superior landlord und∍r whom that person derives title;

    (*d*) 'former residential occupier', in relation to any premises, mea⅂s the person who was the residential occupier until he was deprived of or gave up his occupation as mentioned in subsection (1) ɔr subsection (2) above (and, in relation to a former resident⸀al occupier, 'the right to occupy' and 'landlord' shall be constru∍d accordingly).

Notes:

(1) A purchaser of a house who is let into occupation as licens∍e under the terms of the contract to purchase prior to completion (see p243) is a 'landlord' for the purposes of s27(1). He may ɔe ordered to pay damages under that section if he unlawfully evicts any residential occupier during that period (s27(9)(*c*); *Jones v Miah* [1992] 2 EGLR 50).

(2) A 'residential occupier' is defined in s1 of the Protection from Eviction Act 1977 as 'a person occupying the premises as a residence, whether under a contract or by virtue of any enactment or rule of law giving him the right to remain in occupation or restricting the right of any other person to recover possession of the premises' (see s27(9)).

(3) In a harassment case it is not necessary to prove that the landlord intended to deprive the residential occupier of the property (subs(2)(*b*)).

(4) The right to damages given by the section is in addition to any other right the residential occupier may have (whether in tort, contract or otherwise; see *below*, p418), but damages may not be awarded twice in respect of the same loss (subss(4), (5)). The plaintiff does not have to elect formally under which tranche to seek damages, but whatever is awarded, the smaller amount must be deducted in reaching the net amount (*Mason v Nwokerie* [1993] EGCS 161, CA—see *below* p420).

(5) No liability arises under the section if the residential occupier is reinstated to the property before the proceedings are finally disposed of (subs(6)) but the occupier is not obliged to accept reinstatement under this subsection. He may choose between

reinstatement and damages under the Act (*Tagro v Cafane* [1991] 2 All ER 235, CA). Damages awarded under ss27 and 28 can be substantially greater than those awarded in contract and tort. There will, therefore, be many cases where the displaced occupier will prefer not to accept an offer of reinstatement.

(6) The presentation by the landlord to the tenant of a key to a broken door and an invitation to resume occupation in a wrecked room was held not to constitute proper reinstatement (*Tagro v Carfane*).

(7) However, where an offer of reinstatement is made *before proceedings are begun*, damages may be reduced under s27(7)(*b*). The word 'proceedings' in that subsection refers to the claim for damages rather than an initial claim for an injunction. Thus, damages awarded will be reduced under s27(7)(*b*) if an offer of reinstatement is made at any time before proceedings for damages are commenced, notwithstanding that proceedings to obtain an injunction to force reinstatement have already been commenced (*Tagro v Carfane (obiter)*).

(8) Subs(7)(*a*) contains a further basis upon which damages may be reduced and subs(8) provides a defence in certain circumstances.

Housing Act 1988: measure of damages

28.—(1) The basis for the assessment of damages referred to in section 27(3) above is the difference in value, determined as at the time immediately before the residential occupier ceased to occupy the premises in question as his residence, between—

(*a*) the value of the interest of the landlord in default determined on the assumption that the residential occupier continues to have the same right to occupy the premises as before that time; and

(*b*) the value of that interest determined on the assumption that the residential occupier has ceased to have the right.

(2) In relation to any premises, any reference to his interest in the interest of the landlord in default is a reference to his interest in the building in which the premises in question are comprised (whether or not that building contains any other premises) together with its curtilage.

(3) For the purposes of the valuations referred to in subsection (1) above, it shall be assumed—

(*a*) that the landlord in default is selling his interest on the open market to a willing buyer; and

(*b*) that neither the residential occupier nor any member of his family wishes to buy; and

(*c*) that it is unlawful to carry out any substantial development of any of the land in which the landlord's interest subsists or to demolish the whole or part of any building on that land.

(4) In this section 'the landlord in default' has the same meaning as in section 27 above and subsection (9) of that section applies in relation to this section as it applies in relation to that.

(5) Section 113 of the Housing Act 1985 (meaning of 'members of a person's family') applies for the purposes of subsection (3)(*b*) above.

(6) The reference in subsection (3)(c) above to substantial development of any of the land in which the landlord's interest subsists is a reference to any development other than—

  (a) development for which planning permission is granted by a general development order for the time being in force and which is carried out so as to comply with any condition or limitation subject to which planning permission is so granted; and

  (b) a change of use resulting in the building referred to in subsection (2) above or any part of it being used as, or as part of, one or more dwelling-houses;

and in this subsection 'general development order' has the same meaning as in section 43(3) of the Town and Country Planning Act 1971 and other expressions have the same meaning as in that Act.

Notes:

(1) The effect of the section is to deprive the landlord of the profit that he will make by forcing the tenant out. The measure of damages is the difference between (i) the value of the landlord's interest (in the building containing the premises) with the occupier enjoying a right to occupy and (ii) the value of the landlord's interest without the occupier having a right to occupy. Each side should call expert evidence.

(2) The time of the assessment is at the time immediately before the residential occupier ceased to occupy the premises.

(3) For s 113 of the Housing Act 1985 (members of a person's family); see p 176.

Damages for breach of contract/tort

As stated above ss 28 and 29 of the Housing Act 1988 do not apply where the residential occupier has been reinstated to the property. However, the residential occupier will still be entitled to damages in respect of any tort or breach of contract which occurred prior to the reinstatement. Since the object of a covenant for quiet enjoyment in a lease or tenancy agreement cannot be described as being to provide peace of mind or freedom from distress, damages for injured feelings and mental distress are not recoverable for breach of a covenant for quiet enjoyment. However, such damages may be recoverable in tort as damages for trespass (*Branchett v Bearney* [1992] 3 All ER 910 at 914, CA).

  Some examples are given under heading 'Quantum; recent cases', p 420.

Aggravated and exemplary damages

Aggravated damages and exemplary damages are not only different in themselves, they are awarded for two different purposes. Aggravated damages are awarded to compensate the plaintiff for injury to his proper feelings of dignity and pride and for aggravation generally, whereas exemplary damages are awarded in order to punish the defendant (*Ramdath v Oswald Daley* [1993] 1 EGLR 82 *per* Nourse LJ at 84D).

Exemplary damages may be awarded where 'the defendant's conduct has been *calculated by him to make a profit* for himself which may exceed the compensation payable to the plaintiff', that is:

> Where a defendant with a cynical disregard for a plaintiff's rights has calculated that the money to be made out of his wrongdoing will probably exceed the damages at risk, it is necessary for the law to show that it cannot be broken with impunity. This category is not confined to money making in the strict sense. It extends to cases in which the defendant is seeking to gain at the expense of the plaintiff some object—perhaps some property which he covets—which he either could not obtain at all or not obtain except at a price greater than he wants to put down. Exemplary damages can properly be awarded whenever it is necessary to teach a wrongdoer that tort does not pay (*Rookes v Barnard* [1964] AC 1129, *per* Lord Devlin at 1226–7).

In *Drane v Evangelou* [1978] 1 WLR 455, CA, it was held that this principle applies to cases of unlawful eviction of a tenant ('more accurately an action for trespass to land and goods', Nourse LJ in *Ramdath v Oswald Daley*):

> To my mind this category includes cases of unlawful eviction of a tenant. The landlord seeks to gain possession at the expense of the tenant—so as to keep or get a rent higher than that awarded by the rent tribunal—or to get possession from a tenant who is protected by the Rent Acts. So he resorts to harassing tactics. Such conduct can be punished now by the criminal law. But it also can be punished by the civil law by an award of exemplary damages (*per* Lord Denning, *Drane v Evangelou* at 459F).

However, it must be shown that the defendant has a sufficient interest in the property to bring him within the category (*Ramdath v Oswald Daley* [1993] 1 EGLR 82, CA—an award for exemplary damages could not be made against the landlord's managing agent who actually carried out the eviction because he had no interest in the property).

Exemplary damages have also been awarded in cases where the tenant has been forced to leave by harassment (*Guppy's (Bridport) Ltd v Brookling* (1984) 269 EG 846—disconnection of electricity, interference with water supply, washing and toilet facilities and demolition of rooms).

In assessing the amount of the exemplary damages awarded the court should have regard to the means of the parties (*Cassell & Cox v Broome* [1972] AC 1027). The fact that a person has been fined for an offence under the Protection from Eviction Act 1977 should be taken into account, but does not preclude the court from making an award of exemplary damages (*Ashgar v Ahmed* (1984) 17 HLR 25).

A claim for aggravated or exemplary damages must be properly pleaded:

CCR Ord 6, r1B
> Where a plaintiff claims aggravated, exemplary or provisional damages, his particulars of claim shall contain a statement to that effect and shall state the facts on which he relies in support of his claim for such damages.

Quantum; recent cases

Care needs to be taken when reading reports of 'comparables' in unlawful eviction cases. The details given are always brief yet each case very much turns upon its own facts. In particular, the factual basis upon which an award for exemplary damages has been given is not always clear and it often seems that the principles set out above in relation to exemplary damages are not strictly followed. It is also important to note that in many cases now the major element of the award is the item of damages given under ss 27 and 28 of the 1988 Act. As the amount of such damages depends on the expert evidence as to the value of the property in the particular case the award in one case under this head will be of no assistance in any other case.

Cases are regularly reported in *Legal Action* and *Current Law*. A thorough review of the law on damages for unlawful eviction, which includes many recent cases, appears in an article by Nic Madge in the *New Law Journal*, 11 and 18 June 1993.

The following are some recent examples (note in particular the relationship between the 1988 Act and the award of general damages that appears in some of them):

Cadman v Wood (1992) *Current Law*, December (HH Judge Morrison, Nottingham County Court, 18 June 1992): two tenants were granted a tenancy of a flat in August 1989. In September the male lost his job and the female, who was pregnant, was a student. Delays in payment of benefits led to rent arrears. The landlord embarked on a course of harassment that was 'high-handed, oppressive and outrageous' which was designed to force them out, which included cutting off gas and electricity, taking away keys, intimidation and threats of violence by large men, on one occasion by a man with a Rotweiller. The tenants left through fear on 21 November 1989. They were awarded £3,000 in damages under the 1988 Act and £1,500 aggravated damages for injury to feelings.

Jenkins v Deen (1993) *Legal Action*, March (Cardiff County Court, District Judge Hendicott, 18 January 1993): the landlord evicted the tenant, after threatening him and pushing him across the room. The tenant obtained an injunction but had difficulties in serving it which meant that he was out of occupation for 13 days. During this time he slept on his parents' floor. The tenant was awarded £1,500 for general damages, exemplary damages of £1,500 and aggravated damages of £1,000.

Mason v Nworkie [1993] ECGS 161: the plaintiff occupied a bed-sitting room without security of tenure, but he was entitled to 28-days notice. The defendant gave 14-days notice to quit and enforced it without taking proceedings. Plaintiff was awarded £500 general damages, £1,000 exemplary and aggravated damages and £4,500 Housing Act damages. The Court of Appeal held that exemplary damages were not appropriate (see *above*), but considered that the conduct of the defendant in evicting the plaintiff was calculated to cause humiliation and shame and that on the evidence an award of £1,000 for aggravated damages was appropriate. However, the award for general and aggravated damages was set off against the sum of £4,500 which was awarded under the Housing Act.

Sullman v Little (1993) *Halsbury's Monthly Review*, October, 93/2511, (Canterbury County Court, 23 July 1993): the occupier was evicted from the annexe of the owner's property. In breach of agreement the occupier had kept cats indoors causing the premises to become filthy and refused to vacate at the end of the informally agreed period, despite indicating that he would do so when he took up occupation. His belongings were removed from the premises and the door was bolted against him. Damages of £3,000 were awarded under the 1988 Act, but these were reduced by four-fifths to take account of the occupier's conduct in keeping the cats in the premises and reneging on his agreement to leave, although it may be doubted whether the second reason is a good one.

Dowkes v Athelston (1993) *Current Law*, May (HH Judge Crowther QC, 20 November 1992): the tenant, who was six months pregnant, moved into occupation on 2 January 1991. From 5 January, the landlord harassed the tenant by frequently showing prospective purchasers round the property without notice, aggressively telling her to leave and disconnecting the gas and electricity, which were restored within two or three hours after the police were called. She was forced out by 1 February 1991. She slept on her sister's floor for about a fortnight and spent the following 18 months in temporary accommodation. She was awarded £12,000 damages under the 1988 Act, £1,000 for breach of covenant and quiet enjoyment and trespass (not including any award for loss of occupation), and £1,000 exemplary damages because the landlord had sought to profit from his own actions.

Two Rent/Housing Act Exceptions

Dwelling houses above certain rateable values/high rents

Tenancies where no rent or a low rent is payable

Two Rent/Housing Act Exceptions

Dwelling houses above certain rateable values/high rents

In order to ascertain whether the tenancy is precluded from being protected under the Rent Act 1977 by reason of this exception it is first necessary to discover the 'rateable value' of the dwelling house on the 'appropriate day' (ss4 and 25 of the 1977 Act). The appropriate day is 23 March 1965 unless the property first appeared in the Valuation List on a later day, in which case the appropriate day is the day on which the dwelling's rateable value first appeared in the Valuation List. If the appropriate day fell on or after the 22 March 1973 but before 1 April 1973 it will also be necessary to discover the rateable value of the property on 1 April 1973. If the appropriate day fell before 22 March 1973 it will be necessary to know the rateable value on (a) the appropriate day (b) 22 March 1973 and (c) 1 April 1973. The rates department of the local council will be able to provide this information.(Note that the rateable value of the premises on the appropriate day is not the same as the 'net annual value for rating' which needs to be ascertained in order to discover whether the county court has jurisdiction.)

Sometimes the dwelling house forms part of a larger property in respect of which there is a rateable value in the Valuation List for the whole but not for the part. In these circumstances, an apportionment should be made. If the dwelling house consists of more than one property, each of which is separately rated, an aggregation is made. If there is any dispute as to the proper apportionment or aggregation to be made the issue is determined by the county court, the decision of which cannot be appealed against. Events which take place after the appropriate day are disregarded in determining the rateable value on the appropriate day (*Dixon v Allgood* [1987] 3 All ER 1082), except where the rateable value is varied after the appropriate day so that the variation takes effect not later than the appropriate day in which case it is the figure as varied which is taken for the purposes of the Rent Act 1977 and not the original figure (s25(4)).

Once the rateable value on the appropriate day, and if necessary, the rateable values on 22 March 1973 and 1 April 1973, have been discovered it is next necessary to see whether the dwelling house falls within one of the classes set out below.

If the premises are in Greater London the tenancy is not protected if:
  (1) The appropriate day in relation to the dwelling house falls or fell on or after 1 April 1973 and the dwelling house on the appropriate day has or had a rateable value exceeding £1,500.
  (2) The appropriate day in relation to the dwelling house fell on or after 22 March 1973, but before 1 April 1973 and the dwelling house (a) on the

425

appropriate day had a rateable value exceeding £600 and (*b*) on 1 April 1973 has a rateable value exceeding £1,500.

(3) The appropriate day in relation to the dwelling house fell before 22 March 1973 and the dwelling house (*a*) on the appropriate day had a rateable value exceeding £400 (*b*) on 22 March 1973 had a rateable value exceeding £600, and (*c*) on 1 April 1973 had a rateable value exceeding £1,500.

If the premises are outside Greater London the figure set out below should be substituted for the above figures as follows:

(1) £750 for £1,500;
(2) £300 for £600 and £750 for £1,500;
(3) £200 for £400, £300 for £600, and £750 for £1,500.

If in any proceedings there is a dispute as to whether the dwelling house falls within one of these three categories the court will presume that it does *not* unless the contrary is shown (Rent Act 1977, s4(3)).

Where the tenancy was entered into on or after 1 April 1990 see s4(1) of the 1977 act as amended and s4(4)–(7) as introduced by para 15 and 16 of The References to Rating (Housing) Regulations 1990 (SI No 434). Generally, the tenancy will not be protected if the rent payable exceeds £25,000.

For the position in relation to assured tenancies see Housing Act 1988, Sched 1, paras 2, 2A and 14–16.

Tenancies where no rent or a low rent is payable

A tenancy which was entered into before 1 April 1990 or (where the dwelling house under the tenancy had a rateable value on 31 March 1990) is entered into on or after 1 April in pursuance of a contract made before that date is not a protected tenancy if under the tenancy either no rent is payable or, the rent payable is less than two-thirds of the rateable value which is or was the rateable value of the dwelling house on the appropriate day (s5 of the Rent Act 1977).

As to 'the rateable value on the appropriate day' see the previous exception relating to high rateable values. But note that where premises are in Greater London and the appropriate day fell before 22 March 1973 and on the appropriate day the rateable value exceeded £400 the appropriate day for the purposes of this section is deemed to be 22 March 1973. If the premises are outside Greater London read £200 for £400 (Rent Act 1977 s5(2)).

Where the tenancy is entered into on or after 1 April 1990 (otherwise than where the dwelling house had a rateable value on 31 March 1990 in pursuance of a contract made before that date) the tenancy is not protected if the rent payable is £1,000 or less (Greater London) or £250 or less (elsewhere) (The Reference to Rating (housing) Regulations 1990, reg 7).

To constitute rent within the meaning of the section the payments made by the tenant may be payable in kind, for example by the provision of goods or services, but only if these payments have by agreement been quantified in terms of money. Otherwise the payments must be monetary (see *Montague v Browning* [1954] 1 WLR 1039; *Barnes v Barratt* [1970] 2 QB 657). 'Rent' usually includes the amount of any rates and other taxes payable to the landlord (*Sidney Trading Co Ltd v Finsbury Corporation* [1952] 1 All ER 460). But, if the tenancy was originally granted for a term exceeding twenty-one years and it may not be determined before the end of that term by notice given to the tenant, any sums expressed to payable 'in respect of rates, services, repairs, maintenance, or insurance' paid by the tenant to the landlord should be disregarded in calculating the rent for the purposes of this section of the Act (Rent Act 1977, s 5(4) and (5)). For the protection afforded to tenants with long leases at low rents by the Landlord and Tenant Act 1954, see Chapter 13). The burden is on the tenant to show that the rent he pays is sufficient (*Ford v Langford* [1949] 1 All ER 483).

Where this exception does not apply because the rent is more than two-thirds of the rateable value it does not apply after the protected tenancy is determined if after that date the rent in respect of the statutory tenancy is reduced to less than two-thirds (*McGhee v London Borough of Hackney* (1969) 210 EG 1431).

Section 5 of the Rent Act 1977 does not apply to any tennacy which, immediately before the repeal of controlled tenancies on 28 November 1980, was a controlled tenancy. Thus, the tenancy will remain protected even if the rent is less than two-thirds of the rateable value on the appropriate day (s 125 and Sched 25, para 75 of the Housing Act 1980).

For the position in relation to assured tenancies, see Housing Act 1988, Sched I, paras 3, 3A, 3B, 3C and 14 to 16.

Appendix 2

Statutory Extracts

HOUSING ACT 1988

SCHEDULE 1

TENANCIES WHICH CANNOT BE ASSURED TENANCIES

PART I

THE TENANCIES

Tenancies entered into before commencement

(1) A tenancy which is entered into before, or pursuant to a contract made before, the commencement of this Act.

Tenancies of dwelling houses with high rateable values

2.—(1) A tenancy—
  (a) which is entered into on or after 1 April 1990 (otherwise than, where the dwelling house had a rateable value on 31 March 1990, in pursuance of a contract made before 1 April 1990), and
  (b) under which the rent payable for the time being is payable at a rate exceeding £25,000 a year.

(2) In sub-paragraph (1) 'rent' does not include any sum payable by the tenant as is expressed (in whatever terms) to be payable in respect of rates (council tax), services, management, repairs, maintenance or insurance, unless it could not have been regarded by the parties to the tenancy as a sum so payable.

2A. A tenancy—
  (a) which was entered into before 1 April 1990, or on or after that date in pursuance of a contract made before that date, and
  (b) under which the dwelling house had a rateable value on 31 March 1990 which, if it is in Greater London, exceeded £1,500 and, if it is elsewhere, exceeded £750.

Tenancies at a low rent

3. A tenancy under which for the time being no rent is payable.

3A. A tenancy—
  (a) which is entered into on or after 1 April 1990 (otherwise than, where the dwelling house had a rateable value on 31 March 1990, in pursuance of a contract made before 1 April 1990), and
  (b) under which rent payable for the time being is payable at a rate of, if the dwelling house is in Greater London, £1,000 or less a year and, if it is elsewhere, £250 or less a year.

3B. A tenancy—
  2(a) which was entered into before 1 April 1990 or, where the dwelling house had a rateable value on 31 March 1990, on or after 1 April 1990 in pursuance of a contract made before that date, and
  (b) under which the rent for the time payable is less than two-thirds of the rateable value of the dwelling house on 31 March 1990.

3C. Paragraph 2(2) above applies for the purposes of paragraphs 3, 3A and 3B as it applies for the purposes of paragraph 2(1).

Business tenancies

4. A tenancy to which Part II of the Landlord and Tenant Act 1954 applies (business tenancies).

Licensed premises

5. A tenancy under which the dwelling house consists of or comprises premises licensed for the sale of intoxication liquors for consumption on the premises.

Tenancies of agricultural land

6.—(1) A tenancy under which agricultural land, exceeding two acres, is let together with the dwelling house.

(2) In this paragraph 'agricultural land' has the meaning set out in section 26(3)(a) of the General Rate Act 1967 (exclusion of agricultural land and premises from liability for rating).

Tenancies of agricultural holdings

7. A tenancy under which the dwelling house—
- (a) is comprised in an agricultural holding (within the meaning of the Agricultural Holdings Act 1986); and
- (b) is occupied by the person responsible for the control (whether as tenant or as servant or agent of the tenant) of the farming of the holding.

Lettings to students

8.—(1) A tenancy which is granted to a person who is pursuing, or intends to pursue, a course of study provided by a specified educational institution and is so granted either by that institution or by another specified institution or body of persons.

(2) In sub-paragraph (1) above 'specified' means specified, or of a class specified, for the purposes of this paragraph by regulations made by the Secretary of State by statutory instrument.

(3) A statutory instrument made in the exercise of the power conferred by sub-paragraph (2) above shall be subject to annulment in pursuance of a resolution of either House of Parliament.

Holiday lettings

9. A tenancy the purpose of which is to confer on the tenant the right to occupy the dwelling house for a holiday

Resident landlords

10.—(1) A tenancy in respect of which the following conditions are fulfilled—
- (a) that the dwelling house forms part only of a building and, except in a case where the dwelling house also forms part of a flat, the building is not a purpose-built block of flats; and
- (b) that, subject to Part III of this Schedule, the tenancy was granted by an individual who, at the time when the tenancy was granted, occupied as his only or principal home another dwelling house which,—

(i) in the case mentioned in paragraph (*a*) above, also forms part of the flat;
        or
(ii) in any other case, also forms part of the building; and
(*c*) that, subject to Part III of this Schedule, at all times since the tenancy was granted the interest of the landlord under the tenancy has belonged to an individual who, at the time he owned that interest, occupied as his only or principle home another dwelling house which—
        (i) in the case mentioned in paragraph (*a*) above, also formed part of the flat;
        or
        (ii) in any other case, also formed part of the building; and
(*d*) that the tenancy is not one which is excluded from this sub-paragraph by sub-paragraph (3) below.

(2) If a tenancy was granted by two or more persons jointly, the reference in sub-paragraph (1)(*b*) above to an individual is a reference to any one of those persons and if the interest of the landlord is for the time being held by two or more persons jointly, the reference in sub-paragraph (1)(*c*) above to an individual is a reference to any one of those persons.

(3) A tenancy (in this sub-paragraph referred to as 'the new tenancy') is excluded from sub-paragraph (1) above if—
(*a*) it is granted to a person (alone, or jointly with others) who, immediately before it was granted, was a tenant under an assured tenancy (in this sub-paragraph referred to as 'the former tenancy') of the same dwelling house or of another dwelling house which forms part of the building in question; and
(*b*) the landlord under the new tenancy and under the former tenancy is the same person or, if either of those tenancies is or was granted by two or more persons jointly, the same person is the landlord or one of the landlords under each tenancy.

Crown tenancies

11.—(1) a tenancy under which the interest of the landlord belongs to Her Majesty in right of the Crown or to a government department or is held in trust for Her Majesty for the purposes of a government department.

(2) The reference in sub-paragraph (1) *above* to the case where the interest of the landlord belongs to Her Majesty in right of the Crown does not include the case where that interest is under the management of the Crown Estate Commissioners.

Local authority tenancies etc

12.—(1) A tenancy under which the interest of the landlord belongs to—
(*a*) a local authority, as defined in sub-paragraph (2) below;
(*b*) the Commission for New Towns
(*c*) the Development Board for Rural Wales;
(*d*) an urban development corporation established by an order under section 135 of the Local Government, Planning and Land Act 1980;
(*e*) a development corporation, within the meaning of the New Towns Act 1981;

(f) an authority established under section 10 of the Local Government Act 1985 (waste disposal authorities);

(g) a residuary body, within the meaning of the Local Government Act 1985;

(h) a fully mutual housing association; or

(i) a housing action trust established under Part III of this Act.

(2) The following are local authorities for the purposes of sub-paragraph (1)(a) above—

(a) the council of a county, district or London borough.

(b) the Common Council of the City of London;

(c) the Council of the Isles of Scilly;

(d) the Broads Authority;

(e) the Inner London Education Authority; and

(f) a joint authority, within the meaning of the Local Government Act 1985.

Transitional cases

13.—(1) A protected tenancy, within the meaning of the Rent Act 1977.

(2) A housing association tenancy, within the meaning of Part VI of that Act.

(3) A secure tenancy.

(4) Where a person is a protected occupier of a dwelling house, within the meaning of the Rent (Agriculture) Act 1976, the relevant tenancy, within the meaning of that Act, by virtue of which he occupies the dwelling house.

PART II

RATEABLE VALUES

14.—(1) The rateable value of a dwelling house at any time shall be ascertained for the purposes of Part I of this Schedule as follows—

(a) if the dwelling house is a hereditament for which a rateable value is then shown in the valuation list, it shall be that rateable value;

(b) if the dwelling house forms part only of such a hereditament or consists of or forms part of more than one such hereditament, its rateable value shall be taken to be such value as is found by a proper apportionment or aggregation of the rateable value or values so shown.

(2) Any question arising under this Part of this Schedule as to the proper apportionment or aggregation of any value or values shall be determined by the county court and the decision of that court shall be final.

15. Where, after the time at which the rateable value of a dwelling house is material for the purposes of any provision of Part I of this Schedule, the valuation list is altered so as to vary the rateable value of the hereditament of which the dwelling house consists (in whole or in part) or forms part and the alteration has effect from that time or from an earlier time, the rateable value of the dwelling house at the material time shall be ascertained as if the value shown in the valuation list at the material time had been the value shown in the list as altered.

16. Paragraphs 14 and 15 above apply in relation to any other land which, under section 2 of this Act, is treated as part of a dwelling house as they apply in relation to the dwelling house itself.

PART III

PROVISIONS FOR DETERMINING APPLICATION OF PARAGRAPH 10
(RESIDENT LANDLORDS)

17.—(1) In determining whether the condition in paragraph 10 (1) (c) above is at any time fulfilled with respect to a tenancy, there shall be disregarded—

(a) any period of not more than twenty-eight days, beginning with the date on which the interest of the landlord under the tenancy becomes vested at law and in equity in an individual who, during that period, does not occupy as his only or principal home another dwelling house which forms part of the building, or as the case may be, flat concerned;

(b) if within a period falling within paragraph (a) above, the individual concerned notifies the tenant in writing of his intention to occupy as his only or principal home another dwelling house in the building, or as the case may be, flat concerned, the period beginning with the date on which the interest of the landlord under the tenancy becomes vested in that individual as mentioned in that paragraph and ending—

(i) at the expiry of the period of six months beginning on that date, or

(ii) on the date on which that interest ceases to be so vested, or

(iii) on the date on which that interest becomes again vested in such an individual as is mentioned in paragraph 10(1)(c) or the condition in that paragraph becomes deemed to be fulfilled by virtue of paragraph 18(1) or paragraph 20 below.

whichever is the earlier; and

(c) any period of not more than two years beginning with the date on which the interest of the landlord under the tenancy becomes, and during which it remains vested—

(i) in trustees as such; or

(ii) by virtue of section 9 of the Administration of Estates Act 1925, in the Probate Judge, within the meaning of that Act.

(2) Where the interest of the landlord under a tenancy becomes vested at law and in equity in two or more persons jointly, of whom at least one was an individual, sub-paragraph (1) above shall have effect subject to the following modifications—

(a) in paragraph (a) for the words from 'an individual' to 'occupy' there shall be substituted 'the joint landlords if, during that period none of them occupies';
and

(b) in paragraph (b) for the words 'the individual concerned' there shall be substituted 'any of the joint landlords who is an individual' and for the words 'that individual' there shall be substituted 'the joint landlords'.

18.—(1) During any period when—

(a) the interest of the landlord under the tenancy referred to in paragraph 10 above is vested in trustees as such, and

(b) the interest is or, if it is held on trust for sale, the proceeds of its sale are held on trust for any person who or for two or more persons of whom at least one occupies as his only or principal home a dwelling house which forms part of the building or, as the case may be, flat referred to in paragraph 10(1)(a), the condition in paragraph 10(1)(c) shall be deemed to be fulfilled and accordingly, no part of that period shall be disregarded by virtue of paragraph 17 above.

(2) If a period during which the condition in paragraph 10(1)(c) is deemed to be fulfilled by virtue of sub-paragraph (1) above comes to an end on the death of a person who was in occupation of a dwelling house as mentioned in paragraph (b) of that sub-paragraph, then, in determining whether that condition is at any time thereafter fulfilled, there shall be disregarded any period—

(a) which begins on the date of the death;

(b) during which the interest of the landlord remains vested as mentioned in sub-paragraph (1) (a) above; and

(c) which ends at the expiry of the period of two years beginning on the date of the death or on any earlier date on which the condition in paragraph 10(1)(c) becomes again deemed to be fulfilled by virtue of sub-paragraph (1) above.

19. In any case where—

(a) immediately before a tenancy comes to an end the condition in paragraph 10(1)(c) is deemed to be fulfilled by virtue of paragraph 18(1) above, and

(b) on the coming to an end of that tenancy the trustees in whom the interest of the landlord is vested grant a new tenancy of the same or substantially the same dwelling house to a person (alone or jointly with others) who was the tenant or one of the tenants under the previous tenancy, the condition in paragraph 10(1)(b) above shall be deemed to be fulfilled with respect to the new tenancy.

20.—(1) The tenancy referred to in paragraph 10 above falls within this paragraph if the interest of the landlord under the tenancy becomes vested in the personal representatives of a deceased person acting in that capacity.

(2) If the tenancy falls within this paragraph, the condition in paragraph 10(1)(c) shall be deemed to be fulfilled for any period, beginning with the date on which the interest becomes vested in the personal representatives and not exceeding two years, during which the interest of the landlord remains so vested.

21. Throughout any period which, by virtue of paragraph 17 or paragraph 18(2) above, falls to be disregarded for the purpose of determining whether the condition in paragraph 10(1)(c) is fulfilled with respect to a tenancy, no order shall be made for possession of the dwelling house subject to that tenancy, other than an order which might be made if that tenancy were or, as the case may be, had been an assured tenancy.

22. For the purposes of paragraph 10 above, a building is a purpose-built block of flats if as constructed it contained, and it contains, two or more flats; and for this purpose 'flat' means a dwelling house which—

(a) forms part only of a building; and

(b) is separated horizontally from another dwelling house which forms part of the same building.

SCHEDULE 2

GROUNDS FOR POSSESSION OF DWELLING HOUSE LET ON ASSURED TENANCIES

PART I

GROUNDS ON WHICH COURT MUST ORDER POSSESSION

Ground 1

Not later than the beginning of the tenancy the landlord gave notice in writing
to the tenant that possession might be recovered on this ground or the court is of
the opinion that it is just and equitable to dispense with the requirement of notice
and (in either case)—

(*a*) at some before the beginning of the tenancy, the landlord who is
seeking possession or, in the case of joint landlords seeking possession, at lease one of them occupied the dwelling house as his only or
principal home; or

b) the landlord who is seeking possession or, in the case of joint landlords
seeking possession, at least one of them requires the dwelling house as
his or his spouse's only or principal home and neither the landlord (or,
in the case of joint landlords, any one of them) nor any other person
who, as landlord, derived title under the landlord who gave the notice
mentioned *above* acquired the reversion on the tenancy for money or
money's worth.

Ground 2

The dwelling house is subject to a mortgage granted before the beginning of
the tenancy and—

(*a*) the mortgagee is entitled to exercise a power of sale conferred on him
by the mortgage or by section 101 of the Law of Property Act 1925; and

(*b*) the mortgagee requires possession of the dwelling house for the
purpose of disposing of it with vacant possession in exercise of that
power; and

(*c*) either notice was given as mentioned in Ground 1 above or the court is
satisfied that it is just and equitable to dispense with the requirement of
notice;

and for the purposes of this ground 'mortgage' includes a charge and 'mortgagee'
shall be construed accordingly.

Ground 3

The tenancy is a fixed term tenancy for a term not exceeding eight months
and—

(*a*) not later than the beginning of the tenancy the landlord gave notice in
writing to the tenant that possession might be recovered on this
ground; and

(*b*) at some time within the period of twelve months ending with the
begining of the tenancy, the dwelling house was occupied under a right
to occupy it for a holiday.

Ground 4

The tenancy is a fixed term tenancy for a term not exceeding twelve months
and—

(*a*) not later than the beginning of the tenancy the landlord gave notice in writing to the tenant that possession might be recovered on this ground; and

(*b*) at some time within the period of twelve months ending with the beginning of the tenancy, the dwelling house was let on a tenancy falling within paragraph 8 of Schedule 1 to this Act.

Ground 5

The dwelling house is held for the purpose of being available for occupation by a minister of religion as a residence from which to perform the duties of his office and—

(*a*) not later than the begining of the tenancy the landlord gave notice in writing to the tenant that possession might be recovered on this ground; and

(*b*) the court is satisfied that the dwelling house is required for occupation by a minister of religion as such a residence.

Ground 6

The landlord who is seeking possession or, if that landlord is a registered housing association or charitable housing trust, a superior landlord intends to demolish or reconstruct the whole or a substantial part of the dwelling house or to carry out substantial works on the dwelling house or any part thereof or any building of which it forms part and the following conditions are fulfilled—

(*a*) the intended work cannot reasonably be carried out without the tenant giving up possession of the dwelling house because—

(i) the tenant is not willing to agree to such a variation of the terms of the tenancy as would give such access and other facilities as would permit the intended work to be carried out, or

(ii) the nature of the intended work is such that no such variation is practicable, or

(iii) the tenant is not willing to accept an assured tenancy of such part only of the dwelling house (in this sub-paragraph referred to as 'the reduced part') as would leave in the possession of his landlord so much of the dwelling house as would be reasonable to enable the intended work to be carried out and, where appropriate, as would give such access and other facilities over the reduced part as would permit the intended work to be carried out, or

(iv) the nature of the intended work is such that such a tenancy is not practicable;

and

(*b*) either the landlord seeking possession acquired his interest in the dwelling house before the grant of the tenancy or that interest was in existence at the time of that grant and neither that landlord (or, in the case of joint landlords, any of them) nor any other person who, alone or jointly with others, has acquired that interest since that time acquired it for money or money's worth;

and

(*c*) the assured tenancy on which the dwelling house is let did not come into being by virtue of any provision of Schedule 1 to the Rent Act 1977, as amended by Part I of Schedule 4 to this Act or, the case may be, section 4 of the Rent (Agriculture) Act 1976, as amended by Part II of that Schedule.

For the purpose of this ground, if, immediately before the grant of the tenancy, the tenant to whom it was granted or, if it was granted to joint tenants, any of them was the tenant or one of the joint tenants under an earlier assured tenancy of the dwelling house concerned, any reference in paragraph (*b*) above to the grant of the tenancy is a reference to the grant of that earlier assured tenancy.

For the purposes of this ground 'registered housing association' has the same meaning as in the Housing Associations Act 1985 and 'charitable housing trust' means a housing trust, within the meaning of that Act, which is a charity, within the meaning of the Charities Act 1960.

Ground 7

The tenancy is a periodic tenancy (including a statutory periodic tenancy) which has devolved under the will or intestacy of the former tenant and the proceedings for the recovery of possession are begun not later than twelve months after the death of the former tenant or, if the court so directs, after the date on which, in the opinion of the court, the landlord or, in the case of joint landlords, any one of them became aware of the former tenant's death.

For the purposes of this ground, the acceptance by the landlord of rent from a new tenant after the death of the former tenant shall not be regarded as creating a new periodic tenancy, unless the landlord agrees in writing to a change (as compared with the tenancy before the death) in the amount of the rent, the period of the tenancy, the premises which are let or any other term of the tenancy.

Ground 8

Both at the date of the service of the notice under section 8 of this Act relating to the proceedings for possession and at the date of the hearing—

(*a*) if the rent is payable weekly or fortnightly, at least thirteen weeks' rent is unpaid;

(*b*) if rent is payable monthly, at least three months' rent is unpaid;

(*c*) if rent is payable quarterly, at least one quarter's rent is more than three months in arrears;

(*d*) if rent is payable yearly, at least three months' rent is more than three months in arrears;

and for the purpose of this ground 'rent' means rent lawfully due from the tenant.

Part II

Grounds on which Court may order Possession

Ground 9

Suitable alternative accommodation is available for the tenant or will be available for him when the order for possession takes effect.

Ground 10

Some rent lawfully due from the tenant—

(*a*) is unpaid on the date on which the proceedings for possession are begun; and

(b) except where subsection (1) (b) of section 8 of this Act applies, was in arrears at the date of the service of the notice under that section relation to those proceedings.

Ground 11

Whether or not any rent is in arrears on the date on which proceedings for possession are begun, the tenant has persistently delayed paying rent which has become lawfully due.

Ground 12

. Any obligation of the tenancy (other than one related to the payment of rent) has been broken or not performed.

Ground 13

The condition of the dwelling house or any of the common parts has deteriorated owing to acts of waste by, or the neglect or default of, the tenant or any other person residing in the dwelling house and, in the case of an act of waste by, or the neglect or default of, a person lodging with the tenant or a sub-tenant of his, the tenant has not taken such steps as he ought reasonably to have taken for the removal of the lodger or sub-tenant.

For the purposes of this ground 'common parts' means any part of a building comprising the dwelling house and any other premises which the tenant is entitled under the terms of the tenancy to use in common with the occupiers of other dwelling houses in which the landlord has an estate or interest.

Ground 14

The tenant or any other person residing in the dwelling house has been guilty of conduct which is a nuisance or annoyance to adjoining occupiers, or has been convicted of using the dwelling house or allowing the dwelling house to be used for immoral or illegal purposes.

Ground 15

The condition of any furniture provided for use under the tenancy has, in the opinion of the court, deteriorated owing to ill-treatment by the tenant or any other person residing in the dwelling house and, in the case of ill-treatment by a person lodging with the tenant or by a sub-tenant of his, the tenant has not taken such steps as he ought reasonably to have taken for the removal of the lodger or sub-tenant.

Ground 16

The dwelling house was let to the tenant in consequence of his employment by the landlord seeking possession or a previous landlord under the tenancy and the tenant has ceased to be in that employment.

PART III

SUITABLE ALTERNATIVE ACCOMMODATION

1. For the purposes of Ground 9 above, a certificate of the local housing authority for the district in which the dwelling house in question is situated, certifying that the authority will provide suitable alternative accommodation for the tenant by a date specified in the certificate, shall be conclusive evidence that suitable alternative accommodation will be available for him by that date.

2. Where no such certificate as is mentioned in paragraph 1 above is produced to the court, accommodation shall be deemed to be suitable for the purposes of Ground 9 above if it consists of either—

(*a*) premises which are to be let as a separate dwelling such that they will then be let on an assured tenancy, other than—

(i) a tenancy in respect of which notice is given not later than the beginning of the tenancy that possession might be recovered on any of Grounds 1 to 5 above, or

(ii) an assured shorthold tenancy, within the meaning of Chapter II of Part I of this Act, or

(*b*) premises to be let as a separate dwelling on terms which will, in the opinion of the court, afford to the tenant security of tenure reasonably equivalent to the security afforded by Chapter I of Part I of this Act in the case of an assured tenancy of a kind mentioned in sub-paragraph (*a*) above,

and, in the opinion of the court, the accommodation fulfils the relevant conditions as defined in paragraph 3 below.

3.—(1) For the purposes of paragraph 2 above, the relevant conditions are that the accomodation is reasonably suitable to the needs of the tenant and his family as regards proximity to place of work, and either—

(*a*) similar as regards rental and extent to the accommodation afforded by dwelling houses provided in the neighbourhood by any local housing authority for persons whose needs as regards extent are, in the opinion of the court, similar to those of the tenant and of his family; or

(*b*) reasonably suitable to the means of the tenant and to the needs of the tenant and his family as regards extent and character; and

that if any furniture was provided for use under the assured tenancy in question, furniture is provided for use in the accomodation which is either similar to that so provided or is reasonably suitable to the needs of the tenant and his family.

(2) For the purposes of sub-paragraph (1)(*a*) above, a certificate of a local housing authority stating—

(*a*) the extent of the accomodation afforded by dwelling houses provided by the authority to meet the needs of tenants with families of such number as may be specified in the certificate, and

(*b*) the amount of the rent charged by the authority for dwelling houses affording accommodation of that extent,

shall be conclusive evidence of the facts so stated.

4. Accommodation shall not be deemed to be suitable to the needs of the tenant and his family if the result of their occupation of the accommodation would be that it would be an overcrowded dwelling house for the purposes of Part X of the Housing Act 1985.

5. Any document purporting to be a certificate of a local housing authority named therein issued for the purposes of this Part of this Schedule and to be signed by the proper officer of that authority shall be received in evidence and, unless the contrary is shown, shall be deemed to be such a certificate without further proof.

6. In this Part of this Schedule 'local housing authority' and 'district', in relation to such an authority, have the same meaning as in the Housing Act 1985.

Part IV

Notices Relating to Recovery of Possession

7. Any reference in Grounds 1 to 5 in Part I of this Schedule or in the following provisions of this Part to the landlord giving notice in writing to the tenant is, in the case of joint landlords, a reference to at least one of the joint landlords giving such a notice.

8.—(1) If, not later than the beginning of a tenancy (in this paragraph referred to as 'the earlier tenancy'), the landlord gives such a notice in writing to the tenant as is mentioned in any of Grounds 1 to 5 in Part I of this Schedule, then, for the purposes of the ground in question and any further application of this paragraph, that notice shall also have effect as if it had been given immediately before the beginning of any later tenancy falling within sub-paragraph (2) below.

(2) Subject to sub-paragraph (3) below, sub-paragraph (1) above applies to a later tenancy—

    (a) which takes effect immediately on the coming to an end of the earlier tenancy; and

    (b) which is granted (or deemed to be granted) to the person who was the tenant under the earlier tenancy immediately before it came to an end; and

    (c) which is of substantially the same dwelling house as the earlier tenancy.

(3) Sub-paragraph (1) above does not apply in relation to a later tenancy if, not later than the beginning of the tenancy, the landlord gave notice in writing to the tenant that the tenancy is not one in respect of which possession can be recovered on the ground in question.

9. Where paragraph 8(1) above has effect in relation to a notice given as mentioned in Ground 1 in Part I of this Schedule, the reference in paragraph (b) of that ground to the reversion on the tenancy is a reference to the reversion on the earlier tenancy and on any later tenancy falling within paragraph 8(2) above.

10. Where paragraph 8(1) above has effect in relation to a notice given as mentioned, in Ground 3 or Ground 4 in Part I of this Schedule, any second or subsequent tenancy in relation to which the notice has effect shall be treated for the purpose of that ground as beginning at the beginning of the tenancy in respect of which the notice was actually given.

11. Any reference in Grounds 1 to 5 in Part I of this Schedule to a notice being given not later than the beginning of the tenancy is a reference to its being given not later than the day on which the tenancy is entered into and, accordingly, section 45(2) of this Act shall not apply to any such reference.

SCHEDULE 3

AGRICULTURAL WORKER CONDITIONS

Interpretation

1.—(1) In this Schedule—
'the 1976 Act' means the Rent(Agriculture) Act 1976;
'agriculture' has the same meaning as in the 1976 Act; and
'relevant tenancy or licence' means a tenancy or licence of a description specified in section 24(2) of this Act.
    (2) In relation to a relevant tenancy or licence—
(*a*) 'the occupier' means the tenant or licensee;and
(*b*) 'the dwelling house' means the dwelling house which is let under the tenancy or as the case may be, is occupied under licence.
(3) Schedule 3 to the 1976 Act applies for the purposes of this Schedule as it applies for the purposes of that Act and, accordingly, shall have effect to determine—
(*a*) whether a person is a qualifying worker;
(*b*) whether a person is incapable of whole-time work in agriculture, or work in agriculture as a permit worker, in consequence of a qualifying injury or disease; and
(*c*) whether a dwelling house is in qualifying ownership.

The conditions

2. The agricultural worker condition is fulfilled with respect to a dwelling house subject to a relevant tenancy or licence if—
(*a*) the dwelling house is or has been in qualifying ownership at any time during the subsistency of the tenancy or licence (whether or not it was at that time a relevant tenancy or licence); and
(*b*) the occupier or, where there are joint occupiers, at least one of them—
    (i) is a qualifying worker or has been a qualifying worker at any time during the subsistence of the tenancy or licence (whether or not it was at that time a relevant tenancy or licence); or
    (ii) is incapable of whole-time work in agriculture or work in agriculture as a permit worker in consequence of a qualifying injury or disease.
3.—(1) The agricultural worker condition is also fulfilled with respect to a dwelling house subject to a relevant tenancy or licence if—
(*a*) that condition was previously fulfilled with respect to the dwelling house but the person who was then the occupier or, as the case may be, a person who was one of the joint occupiers (whether or not under the same relevant tenancy or licence) has died; and
(*b*) that condition ceased to be fulfilled on the death of the occupier referred to in paragraph (*a*) above (hereinafter referred to as 'the previous qualifying occupier');
    and
(*c*) the occupier is either—
    (i) the qualifying widow or widower of the previous qualifying occupier; or

(ii) the qualifying member of the previous qualifying occupier's family.

(2) For the purposes of sub-paragraph (1)(c) (i) above and sub-paragraph (3) below a widow or widower of the previous qualifying occupier of the dwelling house is a qualifying widow or widower if she or he was residing in the dwelling house immediately before the previous qualifying occupier's death.

(3) Subject to sub-paragraph (4) below, for the purposes of sub-paragraph (1)(c) (ii) above, a member of the family of the previous qualifying occupier of the dwelling house is the qualifying member of the family if—

(a) on the death of the previous qualifying occupier there was no qualifying widow or widower; and

(b) the member of the family was residing in the dwelling house with the previous qualifying occupier at the time of, and for the period of two years before, his death.

(4) Not more than one member of the previous qualifying occupier's family may be taken into account in determining whether the agricultural worker condition is fulfilled by virtue of this paragraph and, accordingly, if there is more than one member of the family—

(a) who is the occupier in relation to the relevant tenancy or licence, and

(b) who, apart form this sub-paragraph, would be the qualifying member of the family by virtue of sub-paragraph (3) above,

only that one of those members of the family who may be decided by agreement or, in default of agreement by the county court, shall be the qualifying member.

(5) For the purposes of the preceding provisions of this paragraph a person who, immediately before the previous qualifying occupier's death, was living with the previous occupier as his or her wife or husband shall be treated as the widow or widower of the previous occupier.

(6) If, immediately before the death of the previous qualifying occupier, there is, by virtue of sub-paragraph (5) above, more than one person who falls within sub-paragraph (1) (c)(i) above such one of them as may be decided by agreement or, in default of agreement, by the county court shall be treated as the qualifying widow or widower for the purposes of this paragraph.

4. The agricultural worker condition is also fulfilled with respect to a dwelling house subject to a relevant tenancy or licence if—

(a) the tenancy or licence was granted to the occupier or, where there are joint occupiers, at least one of them in consideration of his giving up possession of another dwelling house of which he was then occupier (or one of joint occupiers) under another relevant tenancy or licence; and

(b) immediately before he gave up possession of that dwelling house, as a result of his occupation the agricultural worker condition was fulfilled with respect to it (whether by virtue of paragraph 2 or paragraph 3 above or this paragraph);

and the reference in paragraph (a) above to a tenancy or licence granted to the occupier or at least one of joint occupiers includes a reference to the case where the grant is to him together with one or more other persons.

5.—(1) This paragraph applies where—

(a) by virtue of any of paragraphs 2 to 4 above, the agricultural worker condition is fulfilled with respect to a dwelling house subject to a relevant tenancy or licence (in this paragraph referred to as 'the earlier tenancy or licence'); and

(b) another relevant tenancy or licence of the same dwelling house (in this paragraph referred to as 'the later tenancy or licence') is granted to the person who, immediately before the grant, was the occupier or one of the joint occupiers under the earlier tenancy or licence and as a result of whose occupation the agricultural worker condition was fulfilled as mentioned in paragraph (a) above;

and the reference in paragraph (b) above to the grant of the later tenancy or licence to the person mentioned in that paragraph includes a reference to the case where the grant is to that person together with one or more other persons.

(2) So long as a person as a result of whose occupation of the dwelling house the agricultural worker condition was fulfilled with respect to the earlier tenancy or licence continues to be the occupier, or one of the joint occupiers, under the later tenancy or licence, the agricultural worker condition shall be fulfilled with respect to the dwelling house.

(3) For the purposes of paragraphs 3 and 4 above and any further application of this paragraph, where sub-paragraph (2) above has effect, the agricultural worker condition shall be treated as fulfilled so far as concerns the later tenancy or licence by virtue of the same paragraph of this Schedule as was applicable (or, as the case may be, last applicable) in the case of the earlier tenancy or licence.

RENT ACT 1977

SCHEDULE 15

GROUNDS FOR POSSESSION OF DWELLING HOUSES LET ON OR SUBJECT TO
PROTECTED OR STATUTORY TENANCIES

PART I

CASES IN WHICH COURT MAY ORDER POSSESSION

Case 1

Where any rent lawfully due from the tenant has not been paid, or any
obligation of the protected or statutory tenancy which arises under this Act, or—

(a) In the case of a protected tenancy, any other obligation of the tenancy,
in so far as is consistent with the provisions of Part VII of this Act, or

(b) in the case of a statutory tenancy, and other obligation of the previous
protected tenancy which is applicable to the statutory tenancy,
has been broken or not performed.

Case 2

Where the tenant or any person residing or lodging with him or any sub-tenant
of his has been guilty of conduct which is a nuisance or annoyance to adjoining
occupiers, or has been convicted of using the dwelling house or allowing the
dwelling house to be used for immoral or illegal purposes.

Case 3

Where the condition of the dwelling house has, in the opinion of the court,
deteriorated owing to acts of waste by, or the neglect or default of, the tenant or
any person residing or lodging with him or any sub-tenant of his and, in the case
of any act of waste by, or the neglect or default of, a person lodging with the
tenant or a sub-tenant of his, where the court is satisfied that the tenant has not,
before the making of the order in question, taken such steps as he ought
reasonably to have taken for the removal of the lodger or sub-tenant, as the case
may be.

Case 4

Where the condition of any furniture provided for use under the tenancy has,
in the opinion of the court, deteriorated owing to ill-treatment by the tenant or

any person residing or lodging with him or any sub-tenant of his and, in the case of any ill treatment by a person lodging with the tenant or a sub-tenant of his, where the court is satisfied that the tenant has not, before the making of the order in question, taken such steps as he ought reasonably to have taken for the removal of the lodger or sub-tenant as the case may be.

Case 5

Where the tenant has given notice to quit and, in consequence of that notice, the landlord has contracted to sell or let the dwelling house or has taken any other steps as the result of which he would, in the opinion of the court, be serious y prejudiced if he could not obtain possession.

Case 6

Where without the consent of the landlord, the tenant has, at any time after—
>   (b) 22 March 1973 in the case of a tenancy which became a regulated tenancy by virtue of section 14 of the Counter-Inflation Act 1973;
>   (bb) the commencement of section 73 of the Housing Act 1980, in the case of a tenancy which became a regulated tenancy by virtue of that section;
>   (c) 14 August 1974 in the case of a regulated furnished tenancy; or
>   (d) 8 December 1965, in the case of any tenancy;

assigned or sublet the whole of the dwelling house or sublet part of the dwelling house, the remainder being already sublet.

Case 8

Where the dwelling house is reasonably required by the landlord for occupation as a residence for some person engaged in his whole-time employ-ment, or in the whole-time employment of some tenant from him, or with whom, conditional on housing being provided, a contract for such employment has been entered into, and the tenant was in the employment of the landlord or a former landlord, and the dwelling house was let to him in consequence of that employment and he has ceased to be in that employment.

Case 9

Where the dwelling house is reasonably required by the landlord for occupation as a residence for—
>   (a) himself, or
>   (b) any son or daughter of his over 18 years of age, or
>   (c) his father or mother, or
>   (d) if the dwelling house is let on or subject to a regulated tenancy, the father or mother of his wife or husband,

and the landlord did not become landlord by purchasing the dwelling house or any interest therein after—
>   (i) 7 November 1956, in the case of a tenancy which was then a controlled tenancy;
>   (ii) 8 March 1973, in the case of a tenancy which became a regulated tenancy by virtue of section 14 of the Counter-Inflation Act 1973;
>   (iii) 24 May 1974, in the case of a regulated furnished tenancy, or

(iv) 23 March 1965, in the case of any other tenancy.

Case 10

Where the court is satisfied that the rent charged by the tenant—
- (a) for any sublet part of the dwelling house which is a dwelling house let on a protected tenancy or subject to a statutory tenancy is or was in excess of the maximum rent for the time being recoverable for that part, having regard to Part III of this Act, or
- (b) for any sublet part of the dwelling house which is subject to a restricted contract is or was in excess of the maximum (if any) which it is lawful for the lessor, within the meaning of Part V of this Act to require or receive having regard to the provisions of that Part.

PART II

Cases in Which Court Must Order Possession Where Dwelling House Subject to Regulated Tenancy

Case 11

Where a person (in this case referred to as 'the owner-occupier') who let the dwelling house on a regulated tenancy, had at any time before the letting, occupied it as his residence and—
- (a) not later than the relevant date the landlord gave notice in writing to the tenant that possession might be recovered under this Case, and
- (b) the dwelling house has not since—
    - (i) 22 March 1973, in the case of a tenancy which became a regulated tenancy by virtue of section 14 of the Counter-Inflation Act 1973;
    - (ii) 14 August 1974, in the case of a regulated furnished tenancy; or
    - (iii) 8 December 1965, in the case of any other tenancy, been let by the owner-occupier on a protected tenancy with respect to which the condition mentioned in paragraph (a) above was not satisfied, and
- (c) the court is of the opinion that of the conditions set out in Part V of this Schedule one of those in paragraphs (a) and (c) to (f) is satisfied.

If the court if of the opinion that, notwithstanding that the condition in paragraph (a) or (b) above is not complied with, it is just and equitable to make an order for possession of the dwelling house, the court may dispense with the requirements of either or both of those paragraphs, as the case may require.

The giving of a notice before 14 August 1974 under section 79 of the Rent Act 1968 shall be treated, in the case of a regulated furnished tenancy, as compliance with paragraph (a) of this Case.

Where the dwelling house has been let by the owner-occupier on a protected tenancy (in this paragraph referred to as 'the earlier tenancy') granted on or after 16 November 1984 but not later than the end of the period of two months beginning with the commencement of the Rent (Amendment) Act 1985 and either—
- (i) the earlier tenancy was granted for a term certain (whether or not to be followed by a further term or to continue thereafter from year to year of some other period) and was during that term a

protected shorthold tenancy as defined in section 52 of the Housing Act 1980, or

(ii) the conditions mentioned in paragraphs (a) to (c) of Case 20 were satisfied with respect to the dwelling house and the earlier tenancy.

then for the purposes of paragraph (b) above the condition in paragraph (c) above is to be treated as having been satisfied with respect to the earlier tenancy.

Case 12

Where the landlord (in this Case referred to as 'the owner') intends to occupy the dwelling house as his residence at such time as he might retire from regular employment and has let it on a regulated tenancy before he has so retired and—

(a) not later than the relevant date the landlord gave notice in writing to the tenant that possession might be recovered under this Case; and

(b) the dwelling house has not, since 14 August 1974, been let by the owner on a protected tenancy with respect to which the condition mentioned in paragraph (a) above was not satisfied; and

(c) the court is of the opinion that, of the conditions set out in Part V of this Schedule one of those in paragraphs (b) to (e) is satisfied.

If the court is of the opinion that, notwithstanding that the condition in paragraph (a) or (b) *above* is not complied with, it is just and equitable to make an order for possession of the dwelling house, the court may dispense with the requirements of either or both of those paragraphs, as the case may require.

Case 13

Where the dwelling house is let under a tenancy for a term or years certain not exceeding 8 months and—

(a) not later than the relevant date the landlord gave notice in writing to the tenant that possession might be recovered under this Case; and

(b) that dwelling house was, at some time within the period of 12 months ending on the relevant date, occupied under a right to occupy it for a holiday.

For the purposes of this Case a tenancy shall be treated as being for a term of years certain notwithstanding that it is liable to determination by re-entry or on the happening of any event other rather than the giving of notice by the landlord to determine the term.

Case 14

Where the dwelling house is let under a tenancy for a term of years certain not exceeding 12 months and—

(a) not later than the relevant date the landlord gave notice in writing to the tenant that possession might be recovered under this Case; and

(b) at some time within the period 12 months ending on the relevant date, the dwelling house was subject to such a tenancy as is referred to in section 8(1) of this Act.

For the purposes of this Case a tenancy shall be treated as being for a term of years certain notwithstanding that it is liable to determination by re-entry or on the happening of any event other than the giving of notice by the landlord to determine the term.

Case 15

Where the dwelling house is held for the purpose of being available for occupation by a minister of religion as a residence from which to perform the duties of his office and—

(a) not later than the relevant date the tenant was given notice in writing that possession might be recovered under this Case, and

(b) the court is satisfied that the dwelling house is required for occupation by a minister of religion as such a residence.

Case 16

Where the dwelling house was at any time occupied by a person under the terms of his employment as a person employed in agriculture, and

(a) the tenant neither is nor at any time was so employed by the landlord and is not the widow of a person who was so employed, and

(b) not later than the relevant date, the tenant was given notice in writing that possession might be recovered under this Case, and

(c) the court is satisfied that the dwelling house is required for occupation by a person employed, or to be employed, by the landlord in agriculture.

For the purpose of this Case 'employed', 'employment' and 'agriculture' have the same meanings as in the Agricultural Wages Act 1948.

Case 17

Where proposals for amalgamation, approved for the purpose of a scheme under section 26 of the Agriculture Act 1967, have been carried out and, at the time when the proposals were submitted, the dwelling house was occupied by a person responsible (whether as owner, tenant, or servant or agent of another) for the control of the farming of any part of the land comprised in the amalgamation and—

(a) after the carrying out of the proposals, the dwelling house was let on a regulated tenancy otherwise than to, or to the widow of, either a person ceasing to be so responsible as part of the amalgamation or a person who is, or at any time was, employed by the landlord in agriculture, and

(b) not later than the relevant date the tenant was given notice in writing that possession might be recovered under this Case, and

(c) the court is satisfied that the dwelling house is required for occupation by a person employed, or to be employed, by the landlord in agriculture, and

(d) the proceedings for possession are commenced by the landlord at any time during the period of 5 years beginning with the date on which the proposals for the amalgamation were approved or, if occupation of the dwelling house after the amalgamation continued in, or was first taken by, a person ceasing to be responsible as mentioned in paragraph (a) above or his widow, during a period expiring 3 years after the date on which the dwelling house next became unoccupied.

For the purposes of this Case 'employed' and 'agriculture' have the same meanings as in the Agricultural Wages Act 1948 and 'amalgamation' has the same meaning as in Part II of the Agriculture Act 1967.

Case 18

Where—

(a) the last occupier of the dwelling house before the relevant date was a person, or the widow of a person, who was at some time during his occupation responsible (whether as owner, tenant, or servant or agent of another) for the control of the farming of land which formed, together with the dwelling house, an agricultural unit within the meaning of the Agriculture Act 1947, and

(b) the tenant is neither—

    (i) a person, or the widow of a person, who is or at any time has been responsible for the control of the farming of any part of the said land, nor

    (ii) a person, or the widow of a person, who is or at any time was employed by the landlord in agriculture, and

(c) the creation of the tenancy was not preceded by the carrying out in connection with any of the said land of an amalgamation approved for the purposes of a scheme under section 26 of the Agriculture Act 1967, and

(d) not later than the relevant date the tenant was given notice in writing that possession might be recovered under this Case, and

(e) the court is satisfied that the dwelling house is required for occupation either by a person responsible (whether as owner, tenant, or servant or agent of another) for the control of the farming of any part of the said land or by a person employed or to be employed by the landlord in agriculture, and

(f) in a case where the relevant date was before 9 August 1972, the proceedings for possession are commenced by the landlord before the expiry of five years from the date on which the occupier referred to in paragraph (a) above went out of occupation.

For the purposes of this Case 'employed' and 'agriculture' have the same meanings as in the Agricultural Wages Act 1948 and 'amalgamation' has the same meaning as in Part II of the Agricultural Act 1967.

Case 19

Where the dwelling house was let under a protected shorthold tenancy (or is treated under section 55 of the Housing Act 1980 as having been so let) and—

(a) there either has been no grant of a further tenancy of the dwelling house since the end of the protected shorthold tenancy or, if there was such a grant, it was to a person who immediately before the grant was in possession of the dwelling house as a protected or statutory tenant and

(b) the proceedings for possession were commenced after appropriate notice by the landlord to the tenant and not later than 3 months after the expiry of the notice.

A notice is appropriate for this Case if—

    (i) it is in writing and states that proceedings for possession under this Case may be brought after its expiry and

    (ii) it expires not earlier than 3 months after it is served nor, if, when it is served, the tenancy is a periodic tenancy, before that periodic tenancy could be brought to an end by a notice to quit served by the landlord on the same day;

(iii) it is served—

    (a) in the period of 3 months immediately preceding the date on which the protected shorthold tenancy comes to an end; or

    (b) if that date has passed, in the period of 3 months immediately preceding any anniversary of that date and

(iv) in a case where a previous notice has been served by the landlord on the tenant in respect of the dwelling house, and that notice was an appropriate notice, it is served not earlier than 3 months after the expiry of the previous notice.

Case 20

Where the dwelling house was let by a person (in this Case referred to as 'the owner') at any time after the commencement of section 67 of the Housing Act 1980 and—

    (a) at the time when the owner acquired the dwelling house he was a member of the regular armed forces of the Crown;

    (b) at the relevant date the owner was a member of the regular armed forces of the Crown;

    (c) not later than the relevant date the owner gave notice in writing to the tenant that possession might be recovered under this Case;

    (d) the dwelling house has not, since the commencement of section 67 of the Act of 1980 been let by the owner on a protected tenancy with respect to which the condition mentioned in paragraph (c) above was not satisfied; and

    (e) the court is of the opinion that—

        (i) the dwelling house is required as a residence for the owner; or

        (ii) of the conditions set out in Part V of this Schedule one of those in paragraphs (c) to (f) is satisfied.

If the court is of the opinion that, notwithstanding that the condition in paragraph (c) or (d) *above* is not complied with, it is just and equitable to make an order for possession of the dwelling house, the court may dispense with the requirements of either or both of these paragraphs as the case may require.

For the purposes of this Case 'regular armed forces of the Crown' has the same meaning as in Section 1 of the House of Commons Disqualification Act 1975.

Part III

Provisions Applicable to Case 9 and Part II of this Schedule

Provision for Case 9

1. A court shall not make an order for possession of a dwelling house by reason only that the circumstances of the case fall within Case 9 in Part I of this Schedule if the court is satisfied that, having regard to all the circumstances of the case, including the question whether other accommodation is available for the landlord or the tenant, greater hardship would be caused by granting the order than by refusing to grant it.

Provision for Part II

2. Any reference in Part II of this Schedule to the relevant date shall be construed as follows—

    (*a*) except in a case falling within paragraph (*b*) or (*c*) below, if the protected tenancy, or in the case of a statutory tenancy, the previous contractual tenancy, was created before 8 December 1965, the relevant date means 7 June 1966; and

    (*b*) except in a case falling within paragraph (*c*) below, if the tenancy became a regulated tenancy by virtue of section 14 of the Counter-Inflation Act 1973 and the tenancy or, in the case of a statutory tenancy, the previous contractual tenancy, was created before 22 March 1973, the relevant date means 22 September 1973; and

    (*c*) in the case of a regulated furnished tenancy, if the tenancy, or, in the case of a statutory furnished tenancy, the previous contractual tenancy was created before 14 August 1974, the relevant date means 13 February 1975; and

    (*d*) in any case, the relevant date means the date of the commencement of the regulated tenancy in question.

Part IV

Suitable Alternative Accommodation

3. For the purposes of section 98(1)(*a*) of this Act, a certificate of the local housing authority for the district in which the dwelling house in question is situated, certifying that the authority will provide suitable alternative accommodation for the tenant by a date specified in the certificate, shall be conclusive evidence that suitable alternative accommodation will be available for him by that date.

4.(1) Where no such certificate as is mentioned in paragraph 3 above is produced to the court, accommodation shall be deemed to be suitable for the purposes of section 98(1)(*a*) of this Act if it consists of either—

    (*a*) premises which are to be let as a separate dwelling such that they will then be let on a protected tenancy, (other than one under which the landlord might recover possession of the dwelling house under one of the Cases in Part II of this Schedule), or

    (*b*) premises to be let as a separate dwelling on terms which will, in the opinion of the court, afford to the tenant security of tenure reasonably equivalent to the security afforded by Part VII of this Act in the case of a protected tenancy of a kind mentioned in paragraph (*a*) above,

and, in the opinion of the court, the accommodation fulfils the relevant conditions as defined in paragraph 5 below.

(2.) For the purposes of sub-paragraph (1)(*b*) the terms of a tenancy shall not be treated as affording the required security by reason only of the fact that the tenancy is an assured tenancy within the meaning of section 56 of the Housing Act 1980.

5.(1) For the purposes of paragraph 4 above, the relevant conditions are that the accommodation is reasonably suitable to the needs of the tenant and his family as regards proximity to place of work, and either—

(*a*) similar as regards rental and extent to the accommodation afforded by dwelling houses provided in the neighbourhood by any local housing authority for persons whose needs as regards extent are, in the opinion of the court, similar to those of the tenant and of his family; or

(*b*) reasonably suitable to the means of the tenant and to the needs of the tenant and his family as regards extent and character; and

that if any furniture was provided for use under the protected or statutory tenancy in question, furniture is provided for use in the accommodation which is either similar to that so provided or is reasonably suitable to the needs of the tenant and his family.

(2) For the purposes of sub-paragraph(1)(*a*) above, a certificate of a local housing authority stating—

(*a*) the extent of the accommodation afforded by dwelling houses provided by the authority to meet the needs of tenant with families of such number as may be specified in certificate, and

(*b*) the amount of rent charged by the authority for dwelling houses affording accommodation of that extent, shall be conclusive evidence of the facts so stated.

6. Accommodation shall not be deemed to be suitable to the needs of the tenant and his family if the result of their occupation of the accommodation would be that it would be an overcrowded dwelling house for the purposes of Part X of the Housing Act 1985.

7. Any document purporting to be a certificate of a local housing authority named therein issued for the purposes of this Schedule and to be signed by the proper officer of that authority shall be received in evidence and, unless the contrary is shown, shall be deemed to be such a certificate without further proof.

8. In this Part 'local housing authority' and 'district' in relation to such an authority have the same meaning as in the Housing Act 1985.

PART V

PROVISIONS APPLYING TO CASES 11, 12 *AND* 20

1. In this part of this Schedule—

'mortgage' includes a charge and 'mortgagee' shall be construed accordingly; 'owner' means, in relation to Case 11, the owner-occupier; and 'successor in title' means any person deriving title from the owner, other than a purchaser for value or a person deriving title from a purchaser for value.

2. The conditions referred to in paragraph (*c*) in each Cases 11 and 12 and in paragraph (*e*)(ii) of Case 20 are that—

(*a*) the dwelling house is required as a residence for the owner or any member of his family who resided with the owner when he last occupied the dwelling house as a residence;

(*b*) the owner has retired from regular employment and requires the dwelling house as a residence;

(*c*) the owner has died and the dwelling house is required as a residence for a member of his family who was residing with him at the time of his death;

(*d*) the owner has died and the dwelling house is required by a successor in title as his residence or for the purpose of disposing of it with vacant possession;

(*e*) the dwelling house is subject to a mortgage, made by deed and granted before the tenancy, and the mortgagee—

    (i) is entitled to exercise a power of sale conferred on him by the mortgage or by section 101 of the Law of Property Act 1925; and

    (ii) requires the dwelling house for the purpose of disposing of it with vacant possession in exercise of that power; and

(*f*) the dwelling house is not reasonably suitable to the needs of the owner, having regard to his place of work, and he requires it for the purpose of disposing of it with vacant possession and of using the proceeds of that disposal in acquiring, as his residence, a dwelling house which is more suitable to those needs.

HOUSING ACT 1985

SCHEDULE 1

TENANCIES WHICE ARE NOT SECURE TENANCIES

Long Leases

1. A tenancy is not a secure tenancy if it is a long tenancy.

Premises occupied in connection with employment

2.—(1) A tenancy is not a secure tenancy if the tenant is an employee of the landlord or of—
  a local authority,
  a housing action trust new town corporation,
  an urban development corporation,
  the Development Board for Rural Wales,
  or the governors of an aided school,
and his contract of employment requires him to occupy the dwelling house for the better performance of his duties.

(2) A tenancy is not a secure tenancy if the tenant is a member of a police force and the dwelling house is provided for him free of rent and rates in pursuance of regulations made under section 33 of the Police Act 1964 (general regulations as to government administration and conditions of service of police forces).

(3) A tenancy is not a secure tenancy if the tenant is an employee of a fire authority (within the meaning of the Fire Services Acts 1947 to 1959) and—
  (*a*) his contract of employment requires him to live in close proximity to a particular fire station, and
  (*b*) the dwelling house was let to him by the authority in consequence of that requirement.

(4) A tenancy is not a secure tenancy if—
  (*a*) within the period of three years immediately preceding the grant the conditions mentioned in sub-paragraph (1),(2) or (3) have been satisfied with respect to a tenancy of the dwelling house, and
  (*b*) before the grant the landlord notified the tenant in writing of the circumstances in which this exception applies and that in its opinion the proposed tenancy would fall within this exception,
until the periods during which those conditions are not satisfied with respect to the tenancy amount in aggregate to more than three years.

(5) In this paragraph 'contract of employment' means a contract of service or apprenticeship, whether express or implied and (if express) whether oral or in writing.

Land acquired for developement

3.—(1) A tenancy is not a secure tenancy if the dwelling house is on land which has been acquired for development and the dwelling house is used by the landlord, pending development of the land, as temporary housing accommodation.

(2) In this paragraph 'development' has the meaning given by section 22 of the Town and County Planning Act 1971 (general 1971 definition of development for purposes of that Act).

Accommodation for homeless persons

4.—(1) A tenancy granted in pursuance of—
   (a) section 63 (duty to house pending inquiries in case of apparent priority need),
   (b) section 65(3) (duty to house temporarily person found to have priority need but to have become homeless intentionally), or
   (c) section 68(1) (duty to house pending determination whether conditions for referral of application are satisfied),
is not a secure tenancy before the expiry of the period of twelve months beginning with the date specified in sub-paragraph (2), unless before the expiry of that period the tenant is notified by the landlord that the tenancy is to be regarded as a secure tenancy.

(2) The date referred to in sub-paragraph (1) is the date on which the tenant received the notification required by section 64(1) (notification of decision on question of homelessness or threatened homelessness) or, if he received a notification under section 68(3) (notification of which authority has duty to house), the date on which he received that notification.

Temporary accommodation for persons taking up employment

5.—(1) A tenancy is not a secure tenancy before the expiry of one year from the grant if—
   (a) the person to whom the tenancy was granted was not, immediately before the grant, resident in the district in which the dwelling house is situated,
   (b) before the grant of the tenancy, he obtained employment, or an offer of employment, in the district or its surrounding area,
   (c) the tenancy was granted to him for the purpose of meeting his need for temporary accommodation in the district or its surrounding area in order to work there, and of enabling him to find permanent accommodation there, and
   (d) the landlord notified him in writing of the circumstances in which this exception applies and that in its opinion the proposed tenancy would fall within this exception;
unless before the expiry of that year the tenant has been notified by the landlord that the tenancy is to be regarded as a secure tenancy.

(2) In this paragraph—
'district' means district of a local housing authority; and
'surrounding area', in relation to a district means the area consisting of each district that adjoins it.

Short-term arrangements

6. A tenancy is not a secure tenancy if—
   (*a*) the dwelling house has been leased to the landlord with vacant possession for use as temporary housing accommodation,
   (*b*) the terms on which it has been leased include provision for the lessor to obtain vacant possession from the landlord on the expiry of a specified period or when required by the lessor.
   (*c*) the lessor is not a body which is capable of granting secure tenancies, and
   (*d*) the landlord has no interest in the dwelling house other than under the lease in question or as a mortgagee.

Temporary accommodation during works

7. A tenancy is not a secure tenancy if—
   (*a*) the dwelling house has been made available for occupation by the tenant (or a predecessor in title of his) while works are carried out on the dwelling house which he previously occupied as his home, and
   (*b*) the tenant or predecessor was not a secure tenant of that other dwelling house at the time when he ceased to occupy it as his home.

Agricultural holdings

8. A tenancy is not a secure tenancy if the dwelling house is comprised in an agricultural holding (within the meaning of the Agricultural Holdings Act 1948) and is occupied by the person responsible for the control (whether as tenant or as servant or agent of the tenant) of the farming of the holding.

Licensed premises

9. A tenancy is not a secure tenancy if the dwelling house consists of or includes premises licensed for the sale of intoxicating liquor for consumption on the premises.

Student Lettings

10.—(1) A tenancy of a dwelling house is not a secure tenancy before the expiry of the period specified in sub-paragraph (3) if—
   (*a*) it is granted for the purpose of enabling the tenant to attend a designated course at an educational establishment, and
   (*b*) before the grant of the tenancy the landlord notified him in writing of the circumstances in which this exception applies and that in its opinion the proposed tenancy would fall within this exception;
unless the tenant has before the expiry of that period been notified by the landlord that the tenancy is to be regarded as a secure tenancy.

(2) A landlord's notice under sub-paragraph (1)(*b*) shall specify the educational establishment which the person concerned proposes to attend.

(3) The period referred to in sub-paragraph (1) is—
   (*a*) in a case where the tenant attends a designated course at the educational establishment specified in the landlord's notice, the period ending six months after the tenant ceases to attend that (or any other) designated course at that establishment;

(*b*) in any other case, the period ending six months after the grant of the tenancy.

(4) In this paragraph—

'designated course' means a course of any kind designated by regulations made by the Secretary of State for the purposes of this paragraph;

'educational establishment' means a university or establishment of further education.

(5) Regulations under sub-paragraph (4) shall be made by statutory instrument and may make different provision with respect to different cases or descriptions of case, including different provision for different areas.

1954 Act tenancies

11. A tenancy is not a secure tenancy if it is one to which Part II of the Landlord and Tenant Act 1954 applies (tenancies of premises occupied for business purposes).

Almshouses

12.—(1) a licence to occupy a dwelling house is not a secure tenancy if—

(*a*) the licence was granted by an almshouse charity, and

(*b*) any sum payable by the licensee under the licence does not exceed the maximum contribution that the Charity Commissioners have from time to time authorised or approved for the almshouse charity as a contribution towards the cost of maintaining its almshouses and essential services in them.

(2) In this paragraph 'almshouse charity' means a corporation or body of persons which is a charity and is prevented by its rules or constituent instrument from granting a tenancy of the dwelling house.

SCHEDULE 2

GROUNDS FOR POSSESSION OF DWELLING HOUSES LET UNDER SECURE TENANCIES

PART I

GROUNDS ON WHICH COURT MAY ORDER POSSESSION IF IT CONSIDERS IT REASONABLE

Ground 1

Rent lawfully due from the tenant has not been paid or an obligation of the tenancy has been broken or not performed.

Ground 2

The tenant or person residing in the dwelling house has been guilty of conduct which is a nuisance or annoyance to neighbours, or has been convicted of using the dwelling house or allowing it to be used for immoral or illegal purposes.

Ground 3

The condition of the dwelling house or of any of the common parts has deteriorated owing to acts of waste by, or the neglect or default of, the tenant or a person residing in the dwelling house and, in the case of an act of waste by, or the neglect or default of, a person lodging with the tenant or a sub-tenant of his, the tenant has not taken such steps as he ought reasonably to have taken for the removal of the lodger or sub-tenant.

Ground 4

The condition of furniture provided by the landlord for use under the tenancy, or for use in common parts, has deteriorated owing to ill-treatment by the tenant or a person residing in the dwelling house and, in the case of ill-treatment by a person lodging with the tenant or a sub-tenant of his, the tenant has not taken such steps as he ought reasonably to have taken for the removal of the lodger or sub-tenant.

Ground 5

The tenant is the person, or one of the persons, to whom the tenancy was granted and the landlord was induced to grant the tenancy by a false statement made knowingly or recklessly by the tenant.

Ground 6

The tenancy was assigned to the tenant, or to a predecessor in title of his who is a member of his family and is residing in the dwelling house, by an assignment made by virtue of section 92 (assignments by way of exchange) and a premium was paid either in connection with that assignment or the assignment which the tenant or predecessor himself made by virtue of that section.

In this paragraph 'premium' means any fine or other like sum and any other pecuniary consideration in addition to rent.

Ground 7

The dwelling house forms part of, or is within the curtilage of, a building which, or so much of it as is held by the landlord, is held mainly for purposes other than housing purposes and consists mainly of accomodation other than housing accomodation, and—

(a) the dwelling house was let to the tenant or a predecessor in title of his in consequence of the tenant or predecessor being in the employment of the landlord, or of—

a local authority,

a new town corporation,

a housing action trust,

an urban development corporation,

the Development Board for Rural Wales, or

the governors of an aided school,

and

(b) the tenant or a person residing in the dwelling house has been guilty of conduct such that, having regard to the purpose for which the building is used, it would not be right for him to continue in occupation of the dwelling house.

Ground 8

The dwelling house was made available for occupation by the tenant (or a predecessor in title of his) while works were carried out on the dwelling house which he previously occupied as his only or principal home and—

    (a) the tenant (or predecessor) was a secure tenant of the other dwelling house at the time when he ceased to occupy it as his home.

    (b) the tenant (or predecessor) accepted the tenancy of the dwelling house of which possession is sought on the understanding that he would give up occupation when, on completion of the works, the other dwelling house was again available for occupation by him under a secure tenancy, and

    (c) the works have been completed and the other dwelling house is so available.

Part II

Grounds on which the Court may Order Possession if Suitable Alternative Accommodation is Available

Ground 9

The dwelling house is overcrowded, within the meaning of Part X, in such circumstances as to render the occupier guilty of an offence.

Ground 10

The landlord intends, within a reasonable time of obtaining possession of the dwelling house—

    (a) to demolish or reconstruct the building or part of the building comprising the dwelling house, or

    (b) to carry out work on that building or on land let together with, and thus treated as part of, the dwelling house,

and cannot reasonably do so without obtaining possession of the dwelling house.

Ground 10A

The dwelling house is in an area which is the subject of a redevelopment scheme approved by the Secretary of State or the Corporation in accordance with Part V of this Schedule and the landlord intends within a reasonable time of obtaining possession to dispose of the dwelling house in accordance with the scheme.

    or

Part of the dwelling house is in such an area and the landlord intends within a reasonable time of obtaining possession to dispose of that part in accordance with the scheme and for that purpose reasonably requires possession of the dwelling house.

Ground 11

The landlord is a charity and the tenant's continued occupation of the dwelling house would conflict with the objects of the charity.

PART III

GROUNDS ON WHICH THE COURT MAY ORDER POSSESSION IF IT CONSIDERS IT
REASONABLE AND SUITABLE ALTERNATIVE ACCOMMODATION IS AVAILABLE

Ground 12

The dwelling house forms part of, or is within the curtilage of, a building which, or so much of it as is held by the landlord, is held mainly for purposes other than housing purposes and consists mainly of accommodation other than housing accommodation, or is situated in a cemetery, and—

(a) the dwelling house was let to the tenant or a predecessor in title of his in consequence of the tenant or predecessor being in the employment of the landlord or of—

a local authority,
a new town corporation,
a housing action trust,
an urban development corporation,
the development Board for Rural Wales, or
the governors of an aided school,

and that the employment has ceased, and

(b) the landlord reasonably requires the dwelling house for occupation as a residence for some person either engaged in the employment of the landlord, or of such a body, or with whom a contract for such employment has been entered into conditional on housing being provided.

Ground 13

The dwelling house has features which are substantially different from those of ordinary dwelling houses and which are designed to make it suitable for occupation by a physically disabled person who requires accommodation of a kind provided by the dwelling house and—

(a) there is no longer such a person residing in the dwelling house, and

(b) the landlord requires it for occupation (whether alone or with members of his family) by such a person.

Ground 14

The landlord is a housing association or housing trust which lets dwelling houses only for occupation (whether alone or with others) by persons whose circumstances (other than merely financial circumstances) make it especially difficult for them to satisfy their need for housing, and—

(a) either there is no longer such a person residing in the dwelling house or the tenant has received from a local housing authority an offer of accommodation in premises which are to be let as a separate dwelling under a secure tenancy, and

(b) the landlord requires the dwelling house for occupation (whether alone or with members of his family) by such a person.

Ground 15

The dwelling house is one of a group of dwelling houses which it is the practice of the landlord to let for occupation by persons with special needs and—

(a) a social service or special facility is provided in close proximity to the group of dwelling houses in order to assist persons with those special needs,

(b) there is no longer a person with those special needs residing in the dwelling house, and

(c) the landlord requires the dwelling house for occupation (whether alone or with members of his family) by a person with those special needs.

Ground 16

The accommodation afforded by the dwelling house is more extensive than is reasonably required by the tenant and—

(a) the tenancy vested in the tenant by virtue of section 89 (succession to periodic tenancy), the tenant being qualified to succeed by virtue of section 87(b) (members of family other than spouse), and

(b) notice of the proceedings for possession was served under section 83 more than six months but less than twelve months after the date of the previous tenant's death.

The matters to be taken into account by the court in determining whether it is reasonable to make an order on this ground include—

(a) the age of the tenant.

(b) the period during which the tenant has occupied the dwelling house as his only or principal home, and

(c) any financial or other support given by the tenant to the previous tenant.

Part IV

Suitability of Accommodation

1. For the purposes of section 84(2)(b) and (c) (case in which court is not to make an order for possession unless satisfied that suitable accommodation will be available) accommodation is suitable if it consists of premises—

(a) which are to be let as a separate dwelling under a secure tenancy, or

(b) which are to be let as a separate dwelling under a protected tenancy, not being a tenancy under which the landlord might recover possession under one of the Cases in Part II of Schedule 15 to the Rent Act 1977 (cases where court must order possession), or

(c) which are to be let as a separate dwelling under an assured tenancy which is neither an assured shorthold tenancy, within the meaning of Part I of the Housing Act 1988, nor a tenancy under which the landlord might recover possession under any of Grounds 1 to 5 in Schedule 2 to that Act.

and, in the opinion of the court, the accommodation is reasonably suitable to the needs of the tenant and his family.

2. In determining whether the accommodation is reasonably suitable to the needs of the tenant and his family, regard shall be had to—

(a) the nature of the accommodation which it is the practice of the landlord to allocate to persons with similar needs;

(b) the distance of the accommodation available from the place of work or education of the tenant and of any members of his family;

(c) its distance from the home of any member of the tenant's family if proximity to it is essential to that member's or the tenant's well-being;

(d) the needs (as regards extent of accommodation) and means of the tenant and his family;

(e) the terms on which the accommodation is available and the terms of the secure tenancy;

(f) if furniture was provided by the landlord for use under the secure tenancy, whether furniture is to be provided for use in the other accommodation, and if so the nature of the furniture to be provided.

3. Where possession of a dwelling house is sought on ground 9 (overcrowding such as to render occupier guilty of offence), other accommodation may be reasonably suitable to the needs of the tenant and his family notwithstanding that the permitted number of persons for that accommodation, as defined in section 326(3) (overcrowding: the space standard), is less than the number of persons living in the dwelling house of which possession is sought.

4.—(1) A certificate of the appropriate local housing authority that they will provide suitable accommodation for the tenant by a date specified in the certificate is conclusive evidence that suitable accommodation will be available for him by that date.

(2) The appropriate local housing authority is the authority for the district in which the dwelling house of which possession is sought is situated.

(3) This paragraph does not apply where the landlord is a local housing authority.

RENT (AGRICULTURE) ACT 1976

SCHEDULE 4

GROUNDS FOR POSSESSION OF DWELLING HOUSES SUBJECT TO PROTECTED OCCUPANCY OR STATUTORY TENANCY

PART I

CASES WHERE COURT HAS A DISCRETION

Case 1

Alternative accommodation not provided or arranged by housing authority

1. The court is satisfied that suitable alternative accommodation is available for the tenant, or will be available for him when the order for possession takes effect.

2.—(1) Accommodation shall be deemed suitable in this Case if it consists of
   (*a*) premises which are to be let as a separate dwelling such that they will then be let on a protected tenancy within the meaning of the Rent Act 1977, or
   (*b*) premises which are to be let as a separate dwelling on terms which will, in the opinion of the court, afford to the tenant security of tenure reasonably equivalent to the security afforded by Part VII of the Rent Act 1977 in the case of a protected tenancy,

and in the opinion of the court, the accommodation fulfils the conditions in paragraph 3 below.

3.(1) The accommodation must be reasonably suitable to the needs of the tenant and his family as regards proximity to place of work and either—
   (*a*) similar as regards rental and extent to the accommodation afforded by dwelling houses provided in the neighbourhood by the housing authority concerned for persons whose needs as regards extent are similar to those of the tenant and his family, or
   (*b*) reasonably suitable to the means of the tenant, and to the needs of the tenant and his family as regards extent and character.

(2) For the purposes of sub-paragraph (1)(*a*) above, a certificate of the housing authority concerned stating—
   (*a*) the extent of the accommodation afforded by dwelling houses provided by the authority to meet the needs of tenants with families of such number as may be specified in the certificate, and
   (*b*) the amount of the rent charged by the housing authority concerned for dwelling houses affording accommodation of that extent,

shall be conclusive evidence of the facts so stated.

(3) If any furniture was provided by the landlord for use under the tenancy, furniture must be provided for use in the alternative accommodation which is either similar, or is reasonably suitable to the needs of the tenant and his family.

4. Accommodation shall not be deemed to be suitable to the needs of the tenant and his family if the result of their occupation of the accommodation would be that it would be an overcrowded dwelling house for the purposes of Part X of the Housing Act 1985.

5. Any document purporting to be a certificate of the housing authority concerned issued for the purposes of this Case and to be signed by the proper officer of the authority shall be received in evidence and, unless the contrary is shown, shall be deemed to be such a certificate without further proof.

6. In this Case no account shall be taken of accommodation as respects which an offer has been made, or notice has been given, as mentioned in paragraph 1 of Case II below.

Case 11

Alternative accommodation provided or arranged by housing authority

1. The housing authority concerned have made an offer in writing to the tenant of alternative accommodation which appears to them to be suitable, specifying the date when the accommodation will be available and the date (not being less than 14 days from the date of offer) by which the offer must be accepted.

OR

The housing authority concerned have given notice in writing to the tenant that they have received from a person specified in the notice an offer in writing to rehouse the tenant in alternative accommodation which appears to the housing authority concerned to be suitable, and the notice specifies both the date when the accommodation will be available and the date (not being less than 14 days from the date when the notice was given to the tenant) by which the offer must be accepted.

2. The landlord shows that the tenant accepted the offer (by the housing authority or other person) within the time duly specified in the offer.

OR

The landlord shows that the tenant did not so accept the offer, and the tenant does not satisfy the court that he acted reasonably in failing to accept the offer.

3.(1) The accommodation offered must in the opinion of the court fulfil the conditions in this paragraph.

(2) The accommodation must be reasonably suitable to the needs of the tenant and his family as regards proximity to place of work.

(3) The accommodation must be reasonably suitable to the means of the tenant, and to the needs of the tenant and his family as regards extent.

4. If the accommodation offered is available for a limited period only, the housing authority's offer or notice under paragraph 1 *above* must contain an assurance that other accommodation—

    (a) the availability of which is not so limited,

    (b) which appears to them to be suitable, and

(*c*) which fulfils the conditions in paragraph 3 above.
will be offered to the tenant as soon as practicable.

Case III

Rent lawfully due from the tenant has not been paid,

OR

Any other lawful obligation of the tenancy, whether or not it is an obligation created by this Act, has been broken or not performed.

Case IV

The tenant, or any person residing or lodging with him or sub-tenant of his, has been guilty of conduct which is a nuisance or annoyance to adjoining occupiers, or has been convicted of using the dwelling house, or allowing the dwelling house to be used, for immoral or illegal purposes.

Case V

1. The condition of the dwelling house has, in the opinion of the court, deteriorated owing to acts of waste by, or the neglect or default of, the tenant or any person residing or lodging with him, or any sub-tenant of his.
2. If the person at fault is not the tenant, the court must be satisfied that the tenant has not, before the making of the order for possession, taken such steps as he ought reasonably to have taken for the removal of the person at fault.

Case VI

1. The condition of any furniture provided by the landlord for use under the tenancy has, in the opinion of the court, deteriorated owing to ill-treatment by the tenant or any person residing or lodging with him, or any sub-tenant of his.
2. If the person at fault is not the tenant, the court must be satisfied that the tenant has not, before the making of the order for possession, taken such steps as he ought reasonably to have taken for the removal of the person at fault.

Case VII

1. The tenant has given notice to quit and in consequence of that notice the landlord has contracted to sell or let the dwelling house, or has taken any other steps as a result of which he would, in the opinion of the court, be seriously prejudiced if he could not obtain possession.
2. This Case does not apply where the tenant has given notice to terminate his employment and that notice has operated to terminate the tenancy.

Case VIII

1. The tenant has, without the consent of the landlord, assigned, sub-let or parted with possession of the dwelling house or any part of it.
2. This Case does not apply if the assignment, subletting or parting with possession was effected before the operative date.

Case IX

1. The dwelling house is reasonably required by the landlord for occupation as a residence for—

    (*a*) himself, or

    (*b*) any son or daughter of his over 18 years of age, or

    (*c*) his father or mother, or the father or mother of his wife, or husband, or

    (*d*) his grandfather, or grandmother, or the grandfather or grandmother of his wife, or husband

and the landlord did not become landlord by purchasing the dwelling house, or any interest in it, after 12 April 1976.

2. The court, having regard to all the circumstances of the case, including the question whether other accommodation is available for the landlord or tenant, is satisfied that no greater hardship would be caused by granting the order than by refusing to grant it.

Case X

1. Any part of the dwelling house is sublet.

2. The court is satisfied that the rent charged by the tenant is or was in excess of the maximum rent recoverable for that part, having regard to the provisions of Part III or Part V of the Rent Act 1977 or Part II of this Act, as the case may require.

3. Paragraph 2 does not apply to a rental period beginning before the operative date.

PART II

CASES IN WHICH COURT MUST ORDER POSSESSION

Case XI

1. The person who granted the tenancy or, as the case may be, the original tenancy ('the original occupier') was, prior to granting it, occupying the dwelling house as his residence.

2. The court is satisfied that the dwelling house is required as a residence for the original occupier or any member of his family who resided with the original occupier when he last occupied the dwelling house as his residence.

3. Not later than the relevant date the original occupier gave notice in writing to the tenant that possession might be recovered under this Case.

4. The dwelling house has not since the operative date been let by the original occupier to a tenant as respects whom the condition mentioned in paragraph 3 *above* was not satisfied.

5. The court may dispense with the requirements of either or both of paragraphs 3 and 4 if of opinion that it is just and equitable so to do.

6. In this case and in Case XII below—

'original tenancy', in relation to a statutory tenancy, means the tenancy on the termination of which the statutory tenancy arose;

'the relevant date' means the date of the commencement of the tenancy or, as the case may be, the original tenancy, or the expiration of the period of six months beginning with the operative date, whichever is the later.

Case XII

1. The person who granted the tenancy or, as the case may be, the original tenancy ('the owner') acquired the dwelling house, or any interest in it, with a view to occupying it as his residence at such time as he should retire from regular employment.

2. The court is satisfied—

   (a) that the owner has retired from regular employment and requires the dwelling house as his residence, or

   (b) that the owner has died and the dwelling house is required as a residence for a member of his family who was residing with him at the time of his death.

3. Not later than the relevant date the owner gave notice in writing to the tenant that possession might be recovered under this Case.

4. The dwelling house has not since the operative date been let by the owner to a tenant as respects whom the condition mentioned in paragraph 3 above was not satisfied.

5. The court may dispense with the requirements of either or both of paragraphs 3 and 4 if of opinion that it is just and equitable so to do.

Case XIII

The dwelling house is overcrowded, within the meaning of Part X of the Housing Act 1985, in such circumstances as to render the occupier guilty of an offence.

Appendix 3

County Court Orders For Possession

Order for possession (rented property)

Order that plaintiff have possession (assured tenancies)

Judgment for plaintiff (non-payment of rent)

Judgment for plaintiff (order refused under Rent Acts)

Judgment for plaintiff (suspended under Rent Acts)

Order for possession (possession suspended)

Order for possession (mortgaged property)

Order for possession (possession suspended)

The forms overleaf are Crown copyright and are reproduced with the permission of the Controller of Her Majesty's Stationery Office

Order for possession (rented property)

Order for possession
(rented property)

Plaintiff

Defendant(s)

In the

                                          County Court

Case No.	*Always quote this*	
Plaintiff's Ref.		
Defendant's Ref.		

Seal

To the defendant(s)

1. The court has decided that you should give the plaintiff possession of

   This means you must leave the property on

2. You must also pay to the plaintiff £   for unpaid rent, use and occupation of the property and

   (i) *delete if not applicable*

   (a)(i) £   for the plaintiff's costs of making the application for possession.

   (b)(i) the plaintiff's costs to be taxed* on scale

   * *If the plaintiff's costs are to be taxed, that is looked at by a judge to decide if they are reasonable you will have to pay those costs within 14 days of taxation. You will be sent a copy of the plaintiff's bill and will be able to object to any amounts in it. The judge will decide if your objections are valid.*

3. You must pay:

   (a)(i) the total amount of £   to the plaintiff on or before

   (b)(i) the total amount of £   to the plaintiff by instalments of £
        per   the first instalment to be paid to the plaintiff on or before

4. **If you do not leave the property and pay the money owed by the dates given, the plaintiff can ask the court bailiff to evict you and remove your goods to obtain payment.** This is called 'enforcing the order and money judgment'.

5. Payments should be made to the plaintiff at the place where you would normally pay your rent. If you need more information about making payments you should contact the plaintiff. The court cannot accept any payments.

                              Date

Plaintiff's / Defendant's address

──────── **Note** ────────

If you do not pay the money when it is due and the plaintiff takes steps to enforce payment, the order will be registered in the Register of County Court Judgments. **This may make it difficult for you to get credit.** Further information about registration is available in a leaflet which you can get from any county court office.

The court office at
is open between 10 am and 4 pm. Monday to Friday. When writing to the court, please address forms or letters to the Chief Clerk and quote the case number

N26 Order for possession (rented property)(Order 22, rule1(1))

Order that plaintiff have possession (assured tenancies)

Order that plaintiff have possession
(Assured tenancies)

Plaintiff

Defendant

In the

County Court

Case No. *Always quote this*	
Plaintiff's Ref.	
Defendant's Ref.	

Seal

To the defendant(s)

1. The court has decided that you should give the plaintiff possession of

   This means you must leave the property on

2. You must also pay the plaintiff's costs of making the application for possession. You must pay

   (a) £   to the plaintiff on or before

   (b) £   to the plaintiff by instalments of £   per

   The first instalment to be paid on or before

3. Payments should be made to the plaintiff at the address given on the front of the application for possession.

4. If you **do not leave** the property and **pay the costs** by the dates given, the plaintiff can ask the **court bailiff to evict you and remove sufficient of your goods to pay the costs.** This is called 'enforcing the order and money judgment'.

   Date

Plaintiff's / Defendant's address

Note

If you do not pay the money owed when it is due and the plaintiff takes steps to enforce payment, the order will be registered in the Register of County Court Judgments. **This may make it difficult for you to get credit.** Further information about registration is available in a leaflet which you can get from any county court office.

The court office at

is open between 10 am and 4 pm. When writing to the court, please address forms or letters to the Chief Clerk and quote the case number.

N26A Order that plaintiff have possession (Assured tenancies) (Order 49 rule1(1))

Judgment for plaintiff (non-payment of rent)

Judgment for plaintiff (forfeiture)
(non payment of rent)

Plaintiff

Defendant(s)

In the	
	County Court
Case No. *Always quote this*	
Plaintiff's Ref.	
Defendant's Ref.	

Seal

To the defendant(s)

1 The court has decided that you should give the plaintiff possession of

because you have not paid the rent due under the terms of your lease.

2 You must also pay to the plaintiff £   for unpaid rent, £   for use and occupation of the property and

(i) delete if not applicable

(a) (i) £   for the plaintiff's costs of making the application for possession.

(b) (i) the plaintiff's costs to be taxed* on scale
     * *If the plaintiff's costs are to be taxed, that is looked at by a judge to decide if they are reasonable you will have to pay those costs within 14 days of taxation. You will be sent a copy of the plaintiff's bill and will be able to object to any amounts in it. The judge will decide if your objections are valid.*

3 You must pay :
(a) the total sum of £   to the plaintiff on or before
(b) the total sum of £   to the plaintiff by instalments of £   , the first instalment to be paid to the plaintiff on or before

4 **If you pay** the unpaid rent and costs as set out in paragraph 3, **the existing lease will continue** and the plaintiff will no longer be entitled to possession of the property under this order. **If you do not pay** the amounts owing, the plaintiff **can take steps to evict you and your goods may be sold** or other enforcement proceedings taken to obtain payment. This is called 'enforcing the order and money judgment'.

5 Payments should be made to the plaintiff at the place where you would normally pay your rent. If you need more information about making payments you should contact the plaintiff. The court cannot accept any payments.

Date

Plaintiff's / Defendant's address

─── Note ───

If you do not pay the money owed when it is due and the plaintiff takes steps to enforce payment, the order will be registered in the Register of County Court Judgments. This **may make it difficult for you to get credit.** Further information about registration is available in a leaflet which you can get from any county court office.

The court office at

is open between 10 am and 4 pm Monday to Friday. When writing to the court, please address forms or letters to the Chief Clerk and quote the case number.

N27 Judgment for plaintiff (forfeiture)(non payment of rent)(Order 22, rule 1(1))

Judgment for plaintiff (order refused under Rent Acts)

**Judgment for plaintiff
(forfeiture)**
(order refused under Rent Acts)

Plaintiff

Defendant(s)

In the	
	County Court
Case No. *Always quote this*	
Plaintiff's Ref.	
Defendant's Ref.	

Seal

To the defendant(s)

1 The court has decided that you should give the plaintiff possession of

because you have not paid the rent due under the terms of your lease, but that no steps should be taken to evict you under this order.

2 You must also pay to the plaintiff £   for unpaid rent, £   for use and occupation of the property and

(¹) delete if not applicable

(a) (¹) £   for the plaintiff's costs of making the application for possession.

(b) (¹) the plaintiff's costs to be taxed* on scale
  * *If the plaintiff's costs are to be taxed, that is looked at by a judge to decide if they are reasonable you will have to pay those costs within 14 days of taxation. You will be sent a copy of the plaintiff's bill and will be able to object to any amounts in it. The judge will decide if your objections are valid.*

3 You must pay :
(a) the total sum of £   to the plaintiff on or before
(b) the total sum of £   to the plaintiff by instalments of £   , the first instalment to be paid to the plaintiff on or before

4 **If you pay** the total amount as set out in paragraph 3, **your existing lease will continue. If you do not pay** the amounts owing, the plaintiff **can issue further proceedings to evict you.**

5 Payments should be made to the plaintiff at the place where you would normally pay your rent. If you need more information about making payments you should contact the plaintiff. The court cannot accept any payments.

Date

Plaintiff's / Defendant's address

── Note ──

If you do not pay the money owed when it is due and the plaintiff takes steps to enforce payment, the order will be registered in the Register of County Court Judgments. This may make it difficult for you to get credit. Further information about registration is available in a leaflet which you can get from any county court office.

The court office at

is open between 10 am and 4 pm Monday to Friday. When writing to the court, please address forms or letters to the Chief Clerk and quote the case number.

N27(1) Judgment for plaintiff (forfeiture)(order refused under Rent Acts) (Order 22, rule 1(1))

Judgment for plaintiff (suspended under Rent Acts)

Judgment for plaintiff (forfeiture)
(suspended under Rent Acts)

Plaintiff

Defendant(s)

In the

County Court

Case No. *Always quote this*

Plaintiff's Ref.

Defendant's Ref.

Seal

To the defendant(s)

1   The court has decided that you should give the plaintiff possession of

because you have not paid the rent due under the terms of your lease.

2   You must also pay to the plaintiff £   for unpaid rent, £   for use and occupation of the property and

(i) delete if not applicable

   (a) (i) £   for the plaintiff's costs of making the application for possession.

   (b) (i) the plaintiff's costs to be taxed* on scale   .

   *   *If the plaintiff's costs are to be taxed, that is looked at by a judge to decide if they are reasonable you will have to pay those costs within 14 days of taxation. You will be sent a copy of the plaintiff's bill and will be able to object to any amounts in it. The judge will decide if your objections are valid.*

3   You must pay the total sum of £   to the plaintiff on or before
   If you do pay, the existing lease will continue and the plaintiff will no longer be entitled to possession of the property under this order.

4   If you cannot pay the total amount owing within the time mentioned in paragraph 3, you can still stay in the property. To be able to do this, you must pay the total sum by instalments of £   per   in addition to the current rent. **Once the arrears and costs have been paid, the plaintiff will not be entitled to possession of the property under this order.**

5   Payments should be made to the plaintiff at the place where you would normally pay your rent. If you need more information about making payments you should contact the plaintiff. The court cannot accept any payments.

Date

Plaintiff's / Defendant's address

Note

If you do not pay the money owed when it is due and the plaintiff takes steps to enforce payment, the order will be registered in the Register of County Court Judgments. This may make it difficult for you to get credit. Further information about registration is available in a leaflet which you can get from any county court office.

The court office at

is open between 10 am and 4 pm Monday to Friday. When writing to the court, please address forms or letters to the Chief Clerk and quote the case number.

N27(2) Judgment for plaintiff (forfeiture)(suspended under Rent Acts)(Order 22, rule 1(1))

Order for possession (possession suspended)

Order for possession (possession suspended)
(rented property)

In the _____ **County Court**

Case No.	*Always quote this*	
Plaintiff's Ref.		
Defendant's Ref.		

Plaintiff

Defendant(s)

Seal

To the defendant(s)

1 The court has decided that **unless** you make the payments as set out in paragraph 3 you must give the plaintiff possession of

on

2 You must also pay to the plaintiff £   for unpaid rent , use and occupation of the property and

(1) delete if not applicable

  (a) (1) £   for the plaintiff's costs of making the application for possession.

  (b) (1) the plaintiff's costs to be taxed* on scale

     * *If the plaintiff's costs are to be taxed, that is looked at by a judge to decide if they are reasonable you will have to pay those costs within 14 days of taxation. You will be sent a copy of the plaintiff's bill and will be able to object to any amounts in it. The judge will decide if your objections are valid.*

3 You must pay the plaintiff the total amount of £   by instalments of £   per   **in addition to the current rent.** The current rent is £   per   . The first payment of **both** these amount: must be made on or before   . When you have paid the total amount mentioned, the plaintiff will not be able to take any steps to evict you as a result of this order.

4 If you **do not pay** the money owed and costs by the dates given **and the current rent**, the plaintiff can ask the court bailiff to evict you and remove your goods to obtain payment. This is called 'enforcing the order and money judgment'.

5 Payments should be made to the plaintiff at the place where you would normally pay your rent. If you need more information about making payments you should contact the plaintiff. The court cannot accept any payments.

Date

Plaintiff's / Defendant's address

Note

If you do not pay the money owed when it is due and the plaintiff takes steps to enforce payment, the order will be registered in the Register of County Court Judgments. This may make it difficult for you to get credit. Further information about registration is available in a leaflet which you can get from any county court office.

The court office at

is open between 10 am and 4 pm Monday to Friday. When writing to the court, please address forms or letters to the Chief Clerk and quote the case number.

N28 Order for possession (possession suspended) (rented property) (Order 22, rule1(1))

Order for possession (mortgaged property)

Order for possession (mortgaged property)	**In the** **County Court**

Plaintiff	**Case No.** *Always quote this*	
	Plaintiff's Ref.	
Defendant(s)	**Defendant's Ref.**	

(Seal)

To the defendant(s)

1   The court has decided that you should give the plaintiff possession of

This means you must leave the property on

2   You must also pay to the plaintiff

(1) delete if not applicable

(a)⁽¹⁾ £   which is the amount outstanding under the mortgage

and

(b)⁽¹⁾ the plaintiff's costs of making the application for possession which will be added to the amount outstanding under the mortgage.

(c)⁽¹⁾ £   for the plaintiff's costs of making the application for possession.

(d)⁽¹⁾ the plaintiff's costs to be taxed* on scale

*If the plaintiff's costs are to be taxed, that is looked at by a judge to decide if they are reasonable, you will have to pay those costs within 14 days of taxation. You will be sent a copy of the plaintiff's bill and will be able to object to any amounts in it. The judge will decide if your objections are valid.

3   You must pay the costs of £   to the plaintiff:

(a)⁽¹⁾ on or before

(b)⁽¹⁾ by instalments of £   per   , the first instalment to be paid to the plaintiff on or before

4   If you **do not leave the property** and pay any costs set out in paragraph 3, any amount mentioned in paragraph 2(a) (less any payments you have made) **will immediately become payable.** The plaintiff will also be able to ask the court bailiff to evict you and ask the court to take steps to obtain payment. This is called 'enforcing the order and money judgment'

5   Payments should be made to the plaintiff at the place where you would normally pay your monthly repayments. If you need more information about making payments you should contact the plaintiff. The court cannot accept any payments.

Date

Plaintiff's / Defendant's address

Note

If you do not pay the money owed when it is due and the plaintiff takes steps to enforce payment, the order will be registered in the Register of County Court Judgments. This may make it difficult for you to get credit. Further information about registration is available in a leaflet which you can get from any county court office.

The court office at

is open between 10 am and 4 pm, Monday to Friday. When writing to the court, please address forms or letters to the Chief Clerk and quote the case number

N29 Order for possession (mortgaged property) (Order22, rule1(1))

Order for possession (possession suspended)

Order for possession
(possession suspended)
(mortgaged property)

Plaintiff

Defendant(s)

In the	
	County Court
Case No. *Always quote this*	
Plaintiff's Ref.	
Defendant's Ref.	

(Seal)

To the defendant(s)

1 The court has decided that **unless** you make the payments as set out in paragraph 3 you must give the plaintiff possession of

on

2 You must also pay to the plaintiff

(1) delete if not applicable

(a)⁽¹⁾ £   for arrears due under the mortgage

(b)⁽¹⁾ £   which is the amount outstanding under the mortgage

(c)⁽¹⁾ the plaintiff's costs of making the application for possession which will be added to the amount outstanding under the mortgage.

(d)⁽¹⁾ £   for the plaintiff's costs of making the application for possession.

(e)⁽¹⁾ the plaintiff's costs to be taxed* on scale
* If the plaintiff's costs are to be taxed, that is looked at by a judge to decide if they are reasonable you will have to pay those costs within 14 days of taxation. You will be sent a copy of the plaintiff's bill and will be able to object to any amounts in it. The judge will decide if your objections are valid.

3 You must pay the plaintiff the arrears (and costs) by instalments of £   per
in addition to the current repayments. The first payment of **both** these amounts should be made on or before   . When you have paid the total amount of arrears (and costs) mentioned, the plaintiff will not be able to take any steps to evict you as a result of this order.

4 If you **do not make the payments** as set out in paragraph 3, any amount mentioned in paragraph 2(a) (less any payments you have made) **will immediately become payable.** The plaintiff will also be able to ask the court bailiff to evict you and ask the court to take steps to obtain payment. This is called 'enforcing the order and money judgment'.

5 Payments should be made to the plaintiff at the place where you would normally pay your monthly repayments. If you need more information about making payments you should contact the plaintiff. The court cannot accept any payments.

Date

Plaintiff's / Defendant's address

Note

If you do not pay the money owed when it is due and the plaintiff takes steps to enforce payment, the order will be registered in the Register of County Court Judgments. This may make it difficult for you to get credit. Further information about registration is available in a leaflet which you can get from any county court office.

The court office at

is open between 10 am and 4 pm, Monday to Friday. When writing to the court, please address forms or letters to the Chief Clerk and quote the case number

N31 Order for possession (possession suspended mortgaged property) (Order 22, rule 1(1))

Index